The Clinical EFT Handbook:
A Definitive Resource for Practitioners, Scholars, Clinicians, and Researchers

VOLUME 1

Edited by
Dawson Church and Stephanie Marohn

Energy Psychology Press
3340 Fulton Rd., #442, Fulton, CA 95439
www.EFTUniverse.com

Library of Congress Cataloging-in-Publication Data

The clinical EFT handbook / edited by Dawson Church and Stephanie Marohn. — First edition.
   pages cm
      multiple volumes
ISBN 978-1-60415-210-4
1. Emotional Freedom Techniques. 2. Emotion-focused therapy. I. Church, Dawson, 1956- editor of compilation. II. Marohn, Stephanie, editor of compilation.
RC489.F62C55 2013
616.89'142—dc23
                    2013038885

© 2013 Dawson Church

This book demonstrates an impressive personal improvement tool. It is not a substitute for training in psychology or psychotherapy. Nothing contained herein is meant to replace qualified medical advice. The author urges the reader to use these techniques under the supervision of qualified therapist or physician. The author and publisher do not assume responsibility for how the reader chooses to apply the techniques herein.

All rights reserved. No part of this publication may be reproduced, stored in a retrieval system, or transmitted in any form or by any means, electronic, mechanical, photocopy, recording, or otherwise, without prior written permission from Energy Psychology Press, with the exception of short excerpts used with acknowledgement of publisher and author. "Clinical EFT" is a registered trademark belonging to Energy Psychology Press.

Cover design by Victoria Valentine
Editing by Dawson Church and Stephanie Marohn
Typeset by Medlar Publishing Solutions Pvt Ltd, INDIA
Printed in USA by Bang Printing
First Edition

10 9 8 7 6 5 4 3 2 1

Chapter 2, "An Anatomical, Biochemical, Biophysical, and Quantum Basis for the Unconscious Mind," by James L. Oschman and Maurie D. Pressman, reprinted with permission by *Energy Psychology: Theory, Research, & Treatment*.

Chapter 6, "Energy Healing at the Frontier of Genomics," by Garret Yount, reprinted with permission by *Energy Psychology: Theory, Research, & Treatment*.

Chapter 8, "Energy for Healing Trauma: Energy Psychology and the Efficient Treatment of Trauma and PTSD," by Fred P. Gallo, reprinted with permission by *Energy Psychology: Theory, Research, & Treatment*.

Chapter 15, "EFT for Stress-Related Symptoms after Motor Vehicle Accidents," by Larry Burk, reprinted with permission by *Energy Psychology: Theory, Research, & Treatment*.

Important Disclaimer

While EFT (Emotional Freedom Techniques) has produced remarkable clinical results, it must still be considered to be in the experimental stage and thus practitioners and the public must take complete responsibility for their use of it. Further, the authors offer the information in this book solely as their opinions. Readers are strongly cautioned and advised to consult with a physician, psychologist, psychiatrist, or other licensed health care professional before utilizing any of the information in this book. The information is from sources believed to be accurate and reliable and every reasonable effort has been made to make the information as complete and accurate as possible, but such completeness and accuracy cannot be guaranteed and is not guaranteed. The authors, publisher, and contributors to this book, and their successors, assigns, licensees, employees, officers, directors, attorneys, agents, and other parties related to them (a) do not make any representations, warranties, or guarantees that any of the information will produce any particular medical, psychological, physical, or emotional result; (b) are not engaged in the rendering of medical, psychological, or other advice or services; (c) do not provide diagnosis, care, treatment, or rehabilitation of any individual; and (d) do not necessarily share the views and opinions expressed herein. The information in this book has not undergone evaluation and testing by the United States Food and Drug Administration or similar agency of any other country and is not intended to diagnose, treat, prevent, mitigate, or cure any disease. Risks that might be determined by such testing are unknown. The information is provided on an "as is" basis without any warranties of any kind, express or implied, whether warranties as to use, merchantability, fitness for a particular purpose, or otherwise. The authors, publisher, and contributors to this book, and their successors, assigns, licensees, employees, officers, directors, attorneys, agents, and other parties related to them (a) expressly disclaim any liability for and shall not be liable for any loss or damage including but not limited to use of the information; (b) shall not be liable for any direct or indirect compensatory, special, incidental, or consequential damages or costs of any kind or character; (c) shall not be responsible for any acts or omissions by any party including but not limited to any party mentioned or included in the information or otherwise; (d) do not endorse or support any material or information from any party mentioned or included in the information or otherwise; and (e) will not be liable for damages or costs resulting from any claim whatsoever. If the reader or user does not agree with any of the terms of the foregoing, the reader or user should not use the information in this book or read it. A reader who continues reading this book will be deemed to have accepted the provisions of this disclaimer.

Contents

Volume 1

INTRODUCTION
Clinical EFT as an Evidence-Based Practice for the Treatment of Psychological
and Physiological Conditions 1
Dawson Church

Biomedical and Physics Principles

CHAPTER 1
The Wisdom of Your Cells 17
Bruce H. Lipton

CHAPTER 2
An Anatomical, Biochemical, Biophysical, and Quantum Basis for the Unconscious Mind 25
James L. Oschman and Maurie D. Pressman

CHAPTER 3
PTSD, Neurodynamics, and Memory 41
John Arden

CHAPTER 4
The Roots of EFT in Medicine and Psychology 53
Dawson Church

CHAPTER 5
What Does *Energy* Have to Do with Energy Psychology? 65
David Feinstein

CHAPTER 6
Energy Healing at the Frontier of Genomics 87
Garret Yount

CHAPTER 7
The Curious Phenomenon of Surrogate Tapping 93
David Feinstein

Psychological Trauma

CHAPTER 8
Energy for Healing Trauma: Energy Psychology and the Efficient
Treatment of Trauma and PTSD 107
Fred P. Gallo

CHAPTER 9
The Physiology of Trauma: The "Freeze" Response and the Trauma Capsule 121
Rob Nelson

CHAPTER 10
Integrating EFT and Traditional Trauma Treatment: A Four-Staged Model for Safely Treating Trauma 127
Mary T. Sise

CHAPTER 11
The Affect Bridge in EFT: A Reliable Method for Finding Core Issues 133
Brigitte Hansoul and Yves Wauthier

CHAPTER 12
How Childhood Experiences Shape Adult Attachment 139
Alina Frank

CHAPTER 13
Resolving the Frozen Forms of Parents and Children: Energy Treatment Focused on Archaic States and Their Triggers 145
Willem Lammers

CHAPTER 14
Important Aspects of the Healing Relationship in EFT: Bringing the Unconscious into Consciousness 155
Judith H. Frost

CHAPTER 15
EFT for Stress-Related Symptoms after Motor Vehicle Accidents.. 163
Larry Burk

CHAPTER 16
Energy Psychology with Rwandan Orphans... 171
Barbara Stone, Lori Leyden, and Bert Fellows

CHAPTER 17
EFT-Centered Humanitarian Work: Opportunities and Challenges for Nonprofit Organizations 187
Carrie McCabe

Fundamental Techniques of Clinical EFT

CHAPTER 18
Finding Core Issues... 201
Peter Donn

CHAPTER 19
Aspects... 209
Karin Davidson and Kathryn B. Sherrod

CHAPTER 20
"Tell the Story" and "Watch the Movie" Techniques 219
Rue Anne Hass

CHAPTER 21
Being Specific 229
Ann Adams

CHAPTER 22
Testing Your Results and Why 237
Charles B. Crenshaw, Jr.

CHAPTER 23
Why EFT Focuses on Negative Cognitions First... 243
Valerie Lis

CHAPTER 24
Treating Psychological Reversal and Secondary Gain to Ensure Lasting Client Results 247
Betsy Bartter Muller

CHAPTER 25
The Generalization Effect 255
Suzanne D. Alfandari

CHAPTER 26
Tabletops and Table Legs... 263
Annie O'Grady

CHAPTER 27
Tail-enders... 271
Jenny Johnston

CHAPTER 28
The Gentle Techniques.. 275
Jan L. Watkins

CHAPTER 29
The 9 Gamut Procedure: Procedure, Evidence, Case Histories,
Indications, and Clinical Refinements 285
Dawson Church

CHAPTER 30
Reframing the Problem.. 291
Ann Adams

CHAPTER 31
Daisy Chaining... 297
Valerie Lis

CHAPTER 32
When Physical Symptoms Persist (Persistence) 301
Alina Frank

CHAPTER 33
EFT Through Phone, Videoconferencing, and Other Online Modalities........ 305
Carol Crenshaw

CHAPTER 34
The Constricted Breathing Technique 311
Claudia Schecter

CHAPTER 35
Dissociation 315
Valerie J. Burke

CHAPTER 36
Borrowing Benefits 323
Karin Davidson

CHAPTER 37
The Floor to Ceiling Eye Roll 329
Claudia Schecter

CHAPTER 38
Personal Peace Procedure 331
Angela Amias

Introduction
Clinical EFT as an Evidence-Based Practice for the Treatment of Psychological and Physiological Conditions

Dawson Church

Abstract

Emotional Freedom Techniques (EFT) has moved in the past two decades from a fringe therapy to widespread professional acceptance. This paper defines Clinical EFT, the method validated in many research studies, and shows it to be an "evidence-based" practice. It describes standards by which therapies may be evaluated, such as those of the American Psychological Association (APA) Division 12 Task Force, and reviews the studies showing that Clinical EFT meets these criteria. Several research domains are discussed, summarizing studies of: (a) psychological conditions such as anxiety, depression, phobias, and posttraumatic stress disorder (PTSD); (b) physiological problems such as pain and autoimmune conditions; (c) professional and sports performance; and (d) the physiological mechanisms of action of Clinical EFT. The paper lists the conclusions that may be drawn from this body of evidence, which includes 23 randomized controlled trials and 17 within-subjects studies. The three essential ingredients of Clinical EFT are described: exposure, cognitive shift, and acupressure. The latter is shown to be an essential ingredient in EFT's efficacy, and not merely a placebo. New evidence from emerging fields such as epigenetics, neural plasticity, psychoneuroimmunology, and evolutionary biology confirms the central link between emotion and physiology, and points to somatic stimulation as the element common to emerging psychotherapeutic methods. The paper outlines the next steps in EFT research, such as smartphone-based data gathering, large-scale group therapy, and the use of biomarkers. It concludes that Clinical EFT is a stable and mature method with an extensive evidence base. These characteristics have led to growing acceptance in primary care settings as a safe, rapid, reliable, and effective treatment for both psychological and medical diagnoses.

Keywords: research, evidence-based, Emotional Freedom Techniques, EFT, exposure, cognitive therapy, acupressure, placebo

Dawson Church is a health writer and researcher in the field of energy medicine. He is author of the award-winning best-seller *The Genie in Your Genes*, editor of the peer-reviewed professional journal *Energy Psychology*, executive director of the National Institute for Integrative Healthcare (niih.org), and CEO of Energy Psychology Group (EFTuniverse.com). Send correspondence to Dawson Church, 334 Fulton Road, #442, Fulton, CA 95439, or dawsonchurch@gmail.com. This chapter appeared earlier in a different form in the journal *Psychology* (see Church, 2013a). The author receives income from books and speaking engagements on the approach described in this chapter.

Emotional Freedom Techniques (EFT; Craig, 2010) has moved in the past two decades from a novel intervention derived from Thought Field Therapy (TFT; Callahan, 2001) to an "evidence-based" practice in its own right. Evidence-based practices are methods that meet formally established criteria for efficacy (Melnyk & Fineout-Overholt, 2005; Beautler, Norcross, & Beutler, 2005). There are several organizations that define and publish such standards. One of these is the U.S. government's Food and Drug Administration (FDA; Food and Drug Administration, 1998). Another is the U.K. government's National Institute for Clinical Excellence (NICE; National Institute for Clinical Excellence, 2009). The most influential set of standards in the field of psychology is the one published by the Task Force on Empirically Validated Treatments set up by Division 12 (Clinical Psychology) of the American Psychological Association (APA; Chambless et al., 1996, 1998; Chambless & Hollon, 1998). For convenience these are referred to as "APA" standards.

The Need for a Definition of Clinical EFT

Several million people worldwide have been exposed to or practice EFT (Feinstein, 2009). As of 2013 over 1.5 million individuals had downloaded from the Internet *The EFT Manual* (Craig & Fowlie, 1995) or *The EFT Mini-Manual* (Church, 2009/2013). Thousands of videos made by hundreds of different individuals appear on YouTube, social networking sites, and individual websites, attesting to the popularity of the method as well as practitioners' conviction of its efficacy.

This proliferation of sources offering EFT presents both challenges and opportunities. Many of these sources offer variants of EFT. A few sources present the original EFT method as detailed in the manual (Craig, 2008/2010; Church, 2013b). Others present methods that share only a name with EFT while being devoid of an accurate description of any of its methods. The remainder are found somewhere on a spectrum between the two extremes. Tangentially, many variants of EFT have been developed by others, and there are even variants on the variants (Feinstein, 2009).

This crowded field of candidates has led to the question of what, exactly, is EFT? This and the other volumes in *The Clinical EFT Handbook* series answer that question. A brief definition is as follows: "Clinical EFT is the 'evidence-based' method that has been validated in research studies that meet APA standards." These studies typically use a manual, *The EFT Manual* (Craig, 2008/2010; Church, 2013b), which ensures that the method as tested in one study is the same method being tested in another study. The studies typically apply EFT with fidelity to the method described in the manual, and many studies describe methods of testing therapist fidelity to the method. Training of practitioners is expected to adhere to the method as described in the manual, and as demonstrated in research. Clinical EFT identifies 48 distinct techniques described in the manual and supplementary materials (www.ClinicalEFT.com).

APA Standards, Fidelity, and Implementation

The APA standards were developed in a series of papers (Chambless et al., 1996; Chambless et al., 1998; Chambless & Hollon, 1998). Methods demonstrating efficacy according to certain criteria, such as two high-quality studies performed by independent investigators finding the method statistically superior to a placebo or another method, are said to be "efficacious." Methods that meet lesser standards are classified as "probably efficacious."

The APA standards may be summarized as comprising seven essential criteria (Energy Psychology Journal, 2012). Studies cannot be measured in order to determine if the method under investigation is "empirically validated" unless they meet all seven. Chambless & Hollon (1998) also list additional criteria that may be divided into two further gradations: "highly desirable" and "desirable" (Energy Psychology Journal, 2012). The seven essential criteria are:

1. **Randomized controlled trials** (RCTs)—subjects were randomly assigned to the treatment of interest condition or to one or more comparison conditions.
2. **Adequate sample size** to detect statistically significant ($p < .05$ or better) differences between the treatment of interest and the comparison condition(s) were used.
3. **The population for which the treatment was designed and tested must be clearly defined** through the use of diagnosis by qualified clinicians, through cutoff scores

on questionnaires that are reliable and valid, through interviews identifying the focus of the study's interest, or through some combination of these.
4. Assessment tools must have demonstrated **reliability and validity** in previous research.
5. Any interview assessments were made by interviewers who were **blind to group assignment**.
6. **Treatment manuals** that make clear the nature of the treatment being tested were used. If the treatment was relatively simple, it could be described in the procedure section of the journal article presenting the experiment, in lieu of a treatment manual.
7. The paper reporting the study **provided enough data** that the study's conclusions can be reviewed for appropriateness, including sample sizes, use of instruments that detect changes targeted by the study's design, and **magnitude of statistical significance**.

Studies of efficacious or probably efficacious therapies are required to demonstrate "statistically significant" results, meaning that there is less than 1 possibility in 20 that the results are due to chance (Criterion #2). This meaning of the word "significance" as in "demonstrating statistically significant results" is expressed in research statistics as $p < .05$, or a probability of 5% (i.e., .05) that the results are due to chance. The term "highly significant" is often used to refer to studies with outcomes showing that there is less than 1 possibility in 100 that the results are due to chance, or $p < .001$.

These APA criteria then are a stable, defined, published set of standards by which the efficacy of a therapeutic technique may be judged. When that technique is then translated into training, certification, and clinical practice, these criteria provide reasonable assurance that the method as practiced in the field is the method that has been validated in research.

EFT as an Empirically Validated Treatment

Having defined Clinical EFT and identified the set of standards upon which measurement of efficacy is based, we can now examine the evidence base that supports the efficacy of EFT. The first group of EFT studies performed were outcome studies. Outcome studies use experimental designs that highlight participant outcomes, asking the question "Are participants better off after treatment?" We will examine studies demonstrating the efficacy of Clinical EFT for:

- Psychological conditions such as PTSD, phobias, depression, and anxiety;
- Physiological problems such as pain and autoimmune conditions;
- Performance in sports, business, and academic pursuits.

We will also summarize the key research on the physiological mechanisms of action of Clinical EFT, showing how EFT works in the body to effect change. These studies, rather than measuring whether treatment benefits patients, ask the questions characteristic of basic science, such as "How does this treatment work?" and "What is going on in the body as a result of this treatment?" The final group of studies reviewed investigate EFT's application to performance issues such as public speaking anxiety as well as sports performance. We will also investigate whether EFT's somatic component, tapping with the fingertips on acupressure points, is an inert placebo or an active ingredient in the results obtained. Finally, we will derive the meaning of this whole body of work and extend it to show the next steps in EFT research, such as data gathering via smartphone apps, patient tolerance trials, large group studies, and its application in primary care settings.

Psychological Health Outcome Studies

Clinical EFT has met APA standards as an "efficacious" or "probably efficacious" treatment for a number of conditions, including anxiety, depression, phobias, and PTSD (Feinstein, 2012). Since RCTs are regarded as the Gold Standard of research, and are the type of experimental design usually used to evaluate a therapy against APA standards, only RCTs are listed in this section on mental health outcomes. There have been many other studies of EFT for these mental health conditions that were not RCTs, and some of these are referenced outside of this section on psychological health.

Anxiety. EFT has shown efficacy in several RCTs of anxiety. In one study, students with fear of public speaking received a 45-minute EFT session and improved significantly (Jones, Thornton, & Andrews, 2011). In another, high school students with test anxiety were evaluated before their university entrance exams (Sezgin & Özcan, 2009). Those who learned EFT improved significantly. A control group was taught progressive muscular relaxation. The improvement in the EFT group was significantly greater than that of the control group.

Other studies have also shown statistically significant reductions in anxiety in a variety of populations. A study of fibromyalgia sufferers found significant improvements in anxiety (Brattberg, 2008), as have studies of veterans and hospital patients with PTSD (Church, 2013c; Karatzias et al., 2011). An RCT of university students with test anxiety found significant improvements after both EFT and diaphragmatic breathing (DB) following EFT treatments (Jain & Rubino, 2012). EFT was compared to cognitive behavioral therapy (CBT) in an RCT with female trauma survivors in the Congo (Nemiro, 2013). EFT was found to be as efficacious as CBT in reducing symptoms of anxiety, depression, and PTSD.

Three studies of anxiety fail to meet one or more APA standards. An RCT of psychological conditions in participants in a weight loss program found reductions in anxiety that closely approached significance ($p < .053$) but did not meet the required $p < .05$ threshold (APA criterion #2; Stapleton, Church, Sheldon, Porter, & Carlopio, 2013). Benor, Ledger, Toussaint, Hett, and Zaccaro (2010) found significant reductions in anxiety in university students, but class scheduling conflicts among participants prevented true randomization (APA criterion #1). Waite and Holder (2003) compared EFT to two sham tapping interventions and a non-tapping control group. However, the RCT failed to use valid and reliable assessments (APA Criterion #4), failed to apply EFT with fidelity to the manual (APA criterion #6), and failed to recognize that the "sham" points chosen were in fact actual acupressure points (APA criterion #6). These errors resulted in all three tapping groups improving relative to the non-tapping group.

Depression. RCTs in which depression was measured before and after EFT have demonstrated large drops in depressive symptoms. A study examining college students with high levels of depression ("clinical" depression as measured by the Beck Depression Inventory) found that they were in the "normal" range after EFT (Church, De Asis, & Brooks, 2012). The fibromyalgia study also found significant improvements in depression (Brattberg, 2008), as did the studies of hospital patients and veterans with PTSD (Karatzias et al., 2011; Church, 2013c). An RCT of weight loss program participants also found significant reductions in depressive symptoms (Stapleton, Church, Sheldon, Porter, & Carlopio, 2013). The study of Congolese female trauma survivors also found EFT to be efficacious for depression when compared to CBT (Nemiro, 2013).

Phobias. Three RCTs have examined the effects of EFT on phobias and found that a single session is usually enough to resolve a phobia (Wells, Polglase, Andrews, & Carrington, 2003; Baker & Siegel, 2010; Salas, Brooks, & Rowe, 2011). All three studies included a follow-up period and found that the phobic responses of participants remained significantly lower than before treatment.

PTSD. EFT has been studied as a treatment for clinical PTSD in three RCTs. One, in a population of 59 war veterans, found that PTSD symptoms dropped into the "normal" range after six sessions of EFT and remained that way on follow-up (Church et al., 2013). A hospital in Britain's National Health Service (NHS) compared EFT to another efficacious treatment, Eye Movement Desensitization and Reprocessing (EMDR), and found that both treatments normalized PTSD in an average of four sessions (Karatzias et al., 2011). An RCT of abused male teenagers found, on follow-up, that their PTSD symptoms had been resolved in a single EFT session (Church, Piña, Reategui, & Brooks, 2011). When EFT was taught to groups of Congolese women with PTSD, EFT's efficacy was found to be comparable to that of CBT (Nemiro, 2013). As with most PTSD studies, Nemiro (2013) used the PTSD Checklist or PCL to evaluate symptoms (Ruggiero, Del Ben, Scotti, & Rabalais, 2003). Studies with veterans usually use the military version of the same instrument, the PCL-M (Weathers, Huska, & Keane, 1991).

Data from Church et al., (2013) were analyzed to determine if telephone sessions produced the same symptom reductions as office visits (Hartung & Stein, 2012). While 67% of veterans were subclinical after phone sessions, a significantly larger percentage of the sample recovered after office sessions. A further substudy based on

Church et al., (2013) examined the performance of live coaches compared to licensed mental health professionals (Stein & Brooks, 2011). It found larger reductions in symptoms in veterans treated by licensed practitioners, though the difference did not rise to the level of statistical significance. These analyses indicate the utility of EFT when delivered over the telephone, and by practitioners with very basic levels of training.

Physiological Issues: Pain, Weight Loss, Cravings, and Physical Symptoms

The studies of EFT for physical symptoms include a range of experimental designs, with both RCTs and studies without a control group ("uncontrolled" studies). The latter "within-subjects" studies use subjects as their own controls, comparing their symptom levels before and after EFT.

Pain and physical symptoms. Veterans were found to experience significant drops in physical pain after EFT (Church, 2013c), as were fibromyalgia sufferers (Brattberg, 2008). When PTSD symptoms were remediated in veterans, symptoms of traumatic brain injury (TBI) were reduced by 41% ($p < .0021$; Church & Palmer-Hoffman, 2013). An RCT of patients with tension headaches performed at the Red Cross Hospital in Athens found that the frequency and intensity of their headaches dropped by more than half after EFT, and other physical symptoms improved ($p < .001$; Bougea et al., 2013). Uncontrolled studies and case reports showed improvement in a variety of conditions.

One study examined symptoms in 216 health care workers such as doctors, nurses, chiropractors, psychotherapists, and alternative medicine practitioners who attended a one-day EFT workshop at one of five professional conferences (Church & Brooks, 2010). They experienced a 68% drop in physical pain ($p < .001$). Though this was an uncontrolled study, it examined the five different groups separately, making it, in effect, five small studies. In addition, EFT was delivered by two different practitioners. Despite these disparities, all five groups showed similar results.

EFT was adopted by a clinic in Britain's NHS, which performed a "service evaluation" in order to determine the acceptance of EFT by patients and its success in reducing symptoms. This study found a significant improvement in anxiety, with a mean treatment time frame of eight sessions. It also found a significant improvement in overall psychological health and physical functioning (Stewart et al., 2013).

A pilot study of psoriasis symptoms also showed improvement in skin problems (Hodge & Jurgens, 2011). Other authors report success with victims of motor accidents (Burk, 2010), dyslexia (McCallion, 2012), seizure disorders (Swingle, 2010), and TBI (Craig, Bach, Groesbeck, & Benor, 2009).

Three studies have examined the effect on insomnia after EFT. The veterans PTSD study referenced above (Church et al., 2013) found a significant improvement in insomnia scores, with mean values dropping from the clinical range to the subclinical range ($p < .001$). A pilot study of 10 geriatric patients with insomnia noted a similar reduction in insomnia, along with decreases in anxiety and depression, and an increase in life satisfaction (Lee, Suh, Chung, & Kim, 2011). This led to an RCT conducted with 20 participants that compared EFT to an active control, Sleep Hygiene Education (Lee & Kim, 2013). It demonstrated significant reductions in depression and insomnia. Insomnia is related to stress and to the regulation of the autonomic nervous system; the improvements found in these studies demonstrate the association between a reduction in stress symptoms and decreases in insomnia.

Weight loss and cravings. Studies have examined the use of EFT for weight loss and food cravings. An RCT found that EFT improved restraint (Stapleton, Sheldon, Porter, & Whitty, 2011) and that, in the year following an EFT weight loss program, participants lost an average of 11.1 pounds (Stapleton, Sheldon, & Porter, 2012). An uncontrolled study of clients in a 6-week online weight loss program found a 12-pound weight reduction during the 6 weeks of the program, followed by a further 3-pound drop in the ensuing 6 months ($p < .001$; Church & Wilde, 2013). In the health care workers study (Church & Brooks, 2010) summarized previously, cravings for substances such as chocolate, sweets, and alcohol were reduced by 83% ($p < .001$). Group application of EFT was also found to reduce psychological symptoms such as anxiety in a group self-identified with addiction issues (Church & Brooks, 2013b). A review found that EFT could also be useful as an adjunctive therapy for weight loss (Sojcher, Perlman, & Fogerite, 2012).

Sports and Professional Performance

Mental health studies usually measure reductions in conditions such as anxiety, depression, and PTSD. They typically use reliable and valid assessments, such as the Beck Depression Inventory (BDI; Beck, Steer, & Carbin, 1988), the Beck Anxiety Inventory (BAI; Fydrich, Dowdall, & Chambless, 1992), the Fear Questionnaire (FQ; Mavissakalian, 1986), or the Hospital Anxiety and Depression Scale (HADS; Zigmond & Snaith, 1983), as called for in APA standards, to measure symptom levels before and after treatment, to determine if they decrease. The focus of performance studies is different. They take individuals who are already performing at a certain level, and seek to determine if their level of performance can be increased. Rather than a decrease in, for example, anxiety, they seek to measure an increase in, for example, confidence.

Two RCTs have examined EFT's efficacy for sports performance. One measured the difference in basketball free throw percentages between an EFT and a placebo control group and found a performance difference of 38% after a brief session (Church, 2009; Baker, 2010). Another found similar benefits for soccer free kicks (Llewellyn-Edwards & Llewellyn-Edwards, 2012). A case study of golf performance found stress-related errors decreasing after EFT (Rotherham, Maynard, Thomas, Bawden, & Francis, 2012). A 20-minute EFT session was found to increase confidence and decrease anxiety in an uncontrolled study of female college-aged athletes (Church & Downs, 2012).

Several studies summarized in the previous paragraphs examined the application of EFT to professional performance issues such as public speaking anxiety and test anxiety, and found improvements (Jones, Thornton, & Andrews, 2011; Sezgin & Özcan, 2009; Benor et al., 2009). Fox and Malinowski (2013) examined positive and negative emotions relating to academic study in a population of undergraduates, and found significant increases in enjoyment and hope, and decreases in anger and shame. The NHS service evaluation performed by Stewart et al., (2013) examined patient self-esteem using the Rosenberg Self-Esteem Scale (Rosenberg, 1989) and mental well-being using the Warwick-Edinburgh Mental Well-being Scale (University of Warwick and University of Edinburgh, 2012). It found that both mental well-being and self-esteem improved significantly ($p < .001$). A study of university students preparing for exams found that EFT reduced their anxiety, and improved their test scores (Boath, Stewart, & Carryer, 2013). Nursing students had reduced stress 4 weeks after learning EFT ($p < .005$), and also exhibited decreases in both the state of anxiety, and the character trait of anxiety ($p < .05$; Patterson, 2013). Taken as a whole, this body of research indicates EFT's robust ability to reduce anxiety, whether it is occasioned by athletic, public speaking, or academic performance stress.

Physiological Mechanisms of Action

Outcome studies, which compare patient results before and after treatment, are clearly the most clinically important type of research. However, while showing *that* a treatment works allows it to be designated as an "evidence-based" practice, showing *how and why* it works allows us to understand the physiological changes that underlie its clinical benefits.

Three studies have used electroencephalogram (EEG) to examine the brain wave frequencies of participants before and after EFT. These studies provide us with objective physiological evidence, as opposed to the type of subjective self-report characteristic of mental health studies that use pen-and-paper assessments. Swingle, Pulos, and Swingle (2004) compared the EEG readings of auto accident victims before and after they learned EEG, and found a reduction in the frequencies associated with PTSD. Lambrou, Pratt, and Chevalier (2003) used acupressure tapping with claustrophobics, comparing them with a non-claustrophobic group, and found an increase in theta EEG frequencies associated with relaxation after treatment. Using electromyography (EMG), they also found significant relaxation of the trapezius muscle. Claustrophobic subjects declined significantly in anxiety as well, with gains maintained on 2-week follow-up. Swingle (2010) found EFT to be beneficial in the treatment of seizure disorders. These three studies all reinforce the body of work in acupuncture that uses fMRI to demonstrate regulation of the fear centers of the brain (reviewed by Feinstein, 2010).

If EFT is regulating the body's stress response and the hypothalamus-pituitary-adrenal (HPA) axis, then it is also logical to look for changes in stress hormones such as norepinephrine (adrenaline) and cortisol. A triple-blind study examined the cortisol levels of 83 normal subjects before and after an hour of EFT (Church, Yount, & Brooks, 2012). A control group received talk therapy while a second control group simply rested. Comparison of the three groups revealed significant reductions in cortisol in the EFT group compared to the other two groups (p < .03). The overall severity of psychological symptoms dropped by 50.5% in the EFT group (p < .001). This study demonstrated a significant relationship between the reduction in psychological conditions such as anxiety and depression, and cortisol. Improvements in mental health after therapy can be reflected in reduced levels of cortisol and regulation of the genes that code for such hormones (Feinstein & Church, 2010). Scientists studying epigenetics emphasize the role stress and emotion plays in gene expression (Jirtle & Skinner, 2007; Church, 2010b; Fraga et al., 2005; Eley & Plomin, 1997).

Is Acupoint Tapping an Active Ingredient in EFT?

EFT's "Setup Statement" is an essential part of the "Basic Recipe." The Setup Statement has two parts. One is a statement of the client's presenting problem, and clients are instructed to focus on the problem by saying something like, "Even though I have this problem..." while tapping on a specified acupressure point. They repeat the name of the problem while tapping on the other points. This focus on the problem is reminiscent of the exposure techniques practiced in Prolonged Exposure (PE) and other exposure therapies. The second half of the Setup Statement directs the client toward acceptance of conditions as they are: "... I deeply and completely accept myself." This cognitive reframe is akin to the techniques used in cognitive therapies, which seek to modify dysfunctional client cognitions and emotional responses to events. In a review of therapies for PTSD, the U.S. government's Institute of Medicine found that therapies that use exposure and cognitive shift were efficacious (Institute of Medicine, 2007). EFT's Setup Statement draws from elements of these two established therapies.

The third ingredient used by EFT is tapping on points used in acupuncture and acupressure (acupoints). Is this component of EFT an active ingredient, or is EFT's efficacy dependent solely on the exposure and cognitive components it shares with other therapies?

Fox (2013) sought to answer the question of whether tapping is an active ingredient or an inert placebo. Their study examined mindfulness, and study-related positive and negative emotions in an RCT of 20 undergraduates using the Achievement Emotions Questionnaire (Pekrun, Goetz, Frenzel, Barchfeld, & Perry, 2011). The EFT group received the Basic Recipe as described in *The EFT Manual*. The control group received the cognitive and exposure elements of the Basic Recipe but without acupoint tapping. Instead, they received an active control of gentle breathing in its place. The intervention lasted 40 minutes, and participants were reassessed 7 days later. Significant improvement in study-related positive emotions such as enjoyment and hope was found, along with decreases in negative emotions such as anger and shame. No change in mindfulness was detected.

This indicates that EFT's acupoint stimulation is an active ingredient. This finding supports studies that use fMRI to measure the effects of acupuncture on the areas of the brain associated with fear (Hui et al., 2005; Fang et al., 2009; Napadow et al., 2007). These studies uniformly report acupuncture to produce rapid regulation of these brain regions. They are also consistent with the studies that use EEG (electroencephalogram) to evaluate EFT. They find that EFT reduces the brain wave frequencies associated with stress or amplifies those associated with relaxation, as well as producing other beneficial physiological changes (Swingle, Pulos, & Swingle, 2004; Lambrou, Pratt, & Chevalier, 2003; Swingle, 2010). When the established protocols drawn from exposure and cognitive therapies are paired with acupressure, their effects appear to be enhanced. It is probable that the amygdala and other fear-processing centers of the nervous system are being regulated, as stress-laden emotions are calmed (Phelps & LeDoux, 2005).

EFT as Group Therapy

During the early development of EFT, practitioners reported lower levels of stress and burnout than they had experienced previously, while administering therapies other than EFT to clients. This led to the hypothesis that tapping on oneself while demonstrating tapping to others, or witnessing tapping on others while tapping on oneself, diminished distress. This phenomenon is known as "Borrowing Benefits" (Craig, 2010). A series of studies has measured the efficacy of Borrowing Benefits for psychological and physical symptoms.

The first such study was performed by Rowe (2005). Rowe examined the psychological symptom levels of participants in a weekend EFT workshop using a valid and reliable assessment, the Symptom Assessment 45 (SA-45). The SA-45 has two general scales for the breadth and depth of psychological distress, as well as measuring levels of nine common conditions such as anxiety and depression. Rowe found a reduction in both general and specific scales, with participant gains maintained on follow-up.

The health care workers study cited previously (Church & Brooks, 2010) also utilized the SA-45, with similar results. Most participant gains were maintained at 3-month follow-up ($p < .0001$). The physical pain of subjects was reduced by 68%, and their cravings were reduced by 83% (both $p < .0001$). At follow-up, this study also compared the relative symptom levels of participants who had used EFT frequently with those who had not. It found greater improvements in more frequent users. Another study also found that EFT was effective in groups taught by a variety of trained practitioners (Palmer-Hoffman & Brooks, 2011), suggesting that the improvements were due to the EFT method itself, rather than the unique gifts of any one practitioner. The addiction study summarized previously found similar improvements from Borrowing Benefits, with durable gains (Church & Brooks, 2013b).

PTSD symptoms were examined in a study of 218 veterans and spouses who attended 7-day group retreats (Church & Brooks, 2013a). On pretest, 82% of veterans and 29% of spouses met the criteria for clinical levels of PTSD symptoms. After the retreat, at 6-week follow-up, only 28% of veterans and 4% of spouses were PTSD-positive ($p < .001$). The study compared the results of five such retreats, reporting in effect the results of five individual substudies. Similar symptom declines were noted in all five groups. This study points to EFT's ability to reduce PTSD symptoms in large groups of people simultaneously.

Though these were uncontrolled studies, several RCTs also utilized a group therapy design. The study of college students with depression (Church, De Asis, & Brooks, 2012) offered the EFT intervention in four group counseling sessions. The study of depression in weight loss subjects also taught participants EFT in group classes (Stapleton, Church, Sheldon, Porter, & Carlopio, 2013). Two of the studies of depression (Jones, Thornton, & Andrews, 2011; Sezgin & Özcan, 2009) also provided EFT instruction to participants as a group. In two of the studies of sports performance, Church (2009) and Llewellyn-Edwards & Llewellyn-Edwards (2012), the EFT cohort received at least part of the intervention as a group. EFT was also provided in groups of 10 in the Congo RCT of traumatized females, and found to be as effective as CBT in reducing PTSD, anxiety, and depression (Nemiro, 2013). The insomnia RCT also administered both EFT and the active control in group format (Lee & Kim, 2013).

These studies are notable in that significant reductions in symptoms occurred when EFT was delivered as group therapy, as opposed to individual counseling. If EFT is able to consistently reduce psychological symptoms by 45%, as the five groups treated in Church and Brooks (2010) demonstrate, EFT may be unusually effective when delivered to groups. The number of recent Middle East war veterans with PTSD is estimated at a minimum of 500,000; according to a September 2012 report from the Department of Veterans Affairs, almost 30% of the 834,463 Iraq and Afghanistan War veterans treated at VA hospitals and clinics over the course of the previous decade have been diagnosed with PTSD (Veterans Health Administration, 2012). This is in addition to the estimated 479,000 Vietnam veterans with PTSD (Dohrenwend et al., 2006). Each veteran with PTSD is estimated to cost society $1,400,000 (Kanter, 2007), implying a social cost of about a trillion dollars to treat these two cohorts. Therapies such as Clinical EFT, which produce symptom reductions without the need for lengthy individual courses of psychotherapy or chronic use of prescription drugs, are efficient and cost effective.

Simultaneous Symptom Reduction

Most psychological research seeks to isolate a single condition and excludes multiple diagnoses (Seligman, 1995). For instance, a study of PTSD might exclude clients with comorbid major depression or generalized anxiety. EFT's client-centered approach focuses on the distress as experienced by the client, rather than the primacy of diagnosis by the therapist. EFT is often successful at treating several diagnoses simultaneously. An RCT found that EFT was efficacious for PTSD in six sessions, with 86% of veterans subclinical after six sessions

(Church et al., 2013). Data from the same study were later analyzed to reveal that EFT simultaneously reduced anxiety and depression (Church, 2013c). Furthermore, EFT's pervasive treatment effects encompass both psychological and physiological symptoms. Analysis showed that TBI symptoms diminished significantly and continued to decline throughout the follow-up period, cumulatively reducing 41% from pretest baseline ($p < .0021$; Church & Palmer-Hoffman, 2013). Physical pain was reduced by 41% ($p < .0001$; Church, 2013c). Two early pilot studies of EFT for PTSD found that not only did PTSD symptoms drop significantly, but anxiety and depression symptoms also declined in parallel (Church, 2010a; Church, Geronilla, & Dinter, 2009). EFT is thus extraordinarily efficient, addressing multiple symptom domains simultaneously. Scholars have noted that most clients present with a complex of disorders, rather than a single one (Gorman, 1998).

Safety

EFT also appears to be safe when administered by a therapist or life coach, or self-administered. Therapists treating victims of childhood sexual abuse preferred energy psychology treatments such as EFT over talk therapy because they found the risk of abreaction low with the former (Schulz, 2009). Mollon (2007) reports a general reduction of client distress during acupoint tapping, while Flint, Lammers, and Mitnick (2005) remark on the absence of abreactions during energy psychology treatments. Most studies of EFT have been performed after Institutional Review Board (IRB) review. IRB procedures require that studies be designed and conducted in a manner that protects human subjects, including a requirement that participants be monitored for adverse events. Cumulatively, over 1,000 subjects have participated in trials of EFT without a single adverse event being reported, indicating a high degree of safety.

Research Reviews

Many review articles about EFT have been written. Reviews systematically gather the evidence for a method and ask, "What does this mean?" and "What does this body of research, taken as a whole, suggest?" Notable reviews include those of Feinstein (2012) on the evidence for the efficacy of acupoint tapping, Lane (2009) on the physiological mechanism of action of energy therapies, Feinstein (2010) for energy psychology as applied to PTSD, Feinstein and Church (2010) showing how successful psychotherapy can be measured physiologically, Church and Feinstein (2012) emphasizing that EFT in clinical practice is fast and effective, and Feinstein (2008) for the effects of acupoint tapping for survivors in disaster zones. The body of primary research summarized and evaluated in these review articles, as well as the studies reviewed previously, allow us to draw several conclusions about Clinical EFT:

1. It reduces symptoms for a variety of psychological conditions including phobias, PTSD, anxiety, and depression.
2. It improves physical symptoms such as pain, and autoimmune conditions such as psoriasis and fibromyalgia.
3. It aids in reducing cravings and promoting weight loss.
4. It produces physiological regulation of the autonomic nervous system and the HPA axis.
5. It can simultaneously reduce a range of psychological conditions, e.g., diminishing anxiety and depression along with PTSD.
6. It can simultaneously reduce both psychological and physiological problems, e.g., fibromyalgia or TBI concurrent with PTSD, anxiety, and depression.
7. It is safe, both when self-administered and when administered by others.
8. It is efficient and cost effective, showing efficacy when delivered to both groups and individuals.
9. It works quickly. Treatment time frames range from one session for phobias to six sessions for PTSD.
10. Early evidence points to its efficacy when it is delivered online.
11. It can play a useful part in early intervention following human-caused and natural disasters.

Future Research Directions

Having met APA criteria as an "efficacious" or "probably efficacious" treatment for several conditions, such as phobias, PTSD, anxiety, and depression, what are the next steps for EFT research?

Larger trials. Most of the RCTs conducted have had a small number of participants. Because of EFT's robust treatment effects, studies are able to achieve statistical significance with a small number of participants. However, confirmation with trials involving 100 or more participants per group will provide strata of information not possible with smaller groups, such as whether EFT is more effective with certain demographics.

Institutional trials. Most studies have been conducted in outpatient settings by private foundations. Studies within institutions such as large hospitals will provide a framework for institution-wide implementation of EFT.

Online application. There are only two studies to date in which EFT has been delivered online (Brattberg, 2008; Church & Wilde, 2013). The results of these studies were encouraging, showing improvements in depression and anxiety in both fibromyalgia sufferers and weight loss program participants. Yet this early research only hints at the possibilities. Much more work is needed to determine how EFT can be applied effectively in online programs. Emerging technologies like smartphones allow EFT to be used portably during times of heightened stress. There are several EFT iPhone apps, but none has been subject to experimental testing. Given the low cost of delivery and ease of automated data gathering, online trials of EFT are a logical next step.

Medical applications. Only one of the trials of EFT for physiological functioning, the cortisol study, had a large number of participants (Church, Yount, & Brooks, 2012). The three EEG studies (Swingle, Pulos, & Swingle, 2004; Lambrou, Pratt, & Chevalier, 2003; Swingle, 2010) all had a small number of participants, yet all four studies taken together point to EFT's potential as a medical intervention. Cortisol is known to correlate with HPA arousal, heart rate variability (HRV), and other stress-regulation systems in the body. Depression and anxiety are associated with many diseases. Yet the existing studies of EFT only hint at EFT's potential to affect the course of such diseases. Medical trials could explicitly identify EFT's utility as a medical intervention for conditions such as hypertension, diabetes, cancer, and cardiac events, all of which are stress-related. Such studies could ask research questions like: Does EFT:

Speed wound healing?
Reduce cardiac events markers like C-reactive protein?
Increase circulatory cytokines?
Reduce hypertension?
Reduce chronic pain?
Slow aging by decreasing telomere loss?
Downregulate oncogenes?
Raise levels of cell repair hormones like dehydroepiandrosterone (DHEA)?
Promote healthy balances of neurotransmitters such as serotonin and dopamine?

If EFT is able to demonstrate any of these effects, it can be introduced into primary care as an auxiliary behavioral treatment that is safe and free of side effects.

Patient tolerance studies. Behavioral interventions such as meditation, yoga, diaphragmatic breathing, and EFT are rarely integrated into regular patient care. Research can determine how to effectively introduce patients to EFT and encourage compliance with a health-promoting stress-reduction regimen. Might outpatients benefit from using an EFT app loaded into their smartphones before an appointment? Might patients preparing for surgery benefit by being taught EFT as a stress-management tool to use before and after a procedure? These and other questions could be answered by research aimed at improving patient care.

Group scale studies. EFT is notable in its ability to improve symptoms when delivered to groups. However, the optimal group size has not yet been tested. The group evaluated by Rowe (2005) comprised 259 participants, with 102 providing complete data, while some of the groups in other studies have been as small as 10 (Church & Brooks, 2010). What is the minimum size to produce a group effect? What is the optimum size for each condition? Is there a group size at which the effects diminish? Research that answers these questions of scale will assist institutions using group therapy to optimize their use of Clinical EFT.

Pervasive symptom focus. While research has tended to isolate conditions such as chronic pain or depression, EFT's ability to reduce both psychological and physiological symptoms in tandem might push research toward measuring client-centered reports of symptom clusters, and away from reliance solely on observer-rated clinical diagnoses.

Biomarkers for psychological change. Feinstein and Church (2010) advocate salivary cortisol testing as an objective measure for the efficacy of psychotherapy. A holistic approach means that physiological markers might become a standard measure of efficacy. As cheaper and simpler gene assays become available, the effect of EFT and other therapies on gene expression might be measured by these objective biomarkers.

The Maturing Field of Clinical EFT

Clinical EFT, as validated in many RCTs and outcome studies, has established itself as an efficacious treatment for both psychological and physical conditions. Clinical EFT enjoys a large and growing body of research that has validated it as an "evidence-based" practice that is safe, fast, reliable, and cost effective. Clinical EFT is supported by professional training programs that teach practitioners to deliver the method as validated by research based on *The EFT Manual* (Craig, 2008/2010; Church, 2013b).

Volumes in *The Clinical EFT Handbook* series build upon this solid foundation. Chapters by expert practitioners describe the methods in more detail than the manual can provide, amplifying their explanations through case studies drawn from clinical practice. Other authors describe the principles of Clinical EFT that are derived from the fields of biology and physics. The application of EFT to psychological trauma is of particular interest, since research shows that Clinical EFT is able to rehabilitate even chronic conditions such as PTSD, which were previously believed intractable (Sherman, 1998). Contributors describe the application of Clinical EFT to special populations such as veterans, children, and refugees. Therapists working in institutional settings describe how EFT may be brought into an integrative medical practice. Practitioners working in sports and business settings describe how EFT can increase the performance levels of even high-achieving individuals and teams. Extensions of EFT such as Matrix Reimprinting (childhood issues) and Tapping Deep Intimacy (relationship skills) reveal a dynamic and evolving field.

The rich diversity of experience captured in *The Clinical EFT Handbook* reveals EFT to be a stable and mature method, moving rapidly from the fringes of professional acceptance to a well-deserved position in the front line of primary care.

References

Baker, A. H. (2010). A re-examination of Church's (2009) study into the effects of Emotional Freedom Techniques (EFT) on basketball free-throw performance. *Energy Psychology: Theory, Research, & Treatment, 2*(2), 39–44.

Baker, A. H. & Siegel, M. A. (2010). Emotional Freedom Techniques (EFT) reduces intense fears: A partial replication and extension of Wells et al. *Energy Psychology: Theory, Research, and Treatment, 2*(2), 13–30. doi:10.9769.EPJ.2010.2.2.AHB

Beautler, L. E., Norcross, J. C., & Beutler, L. E. (Eds.). (2005). *Evidence-based practices in mental health: Debate and dialogue on the fundamental questions*. Washington, DC: American Psychological Association.

Beck, A. T., Steer, R. A., & Carbin, M. G. (1988). Psychometric properties of the Beck Depression Inventory: Twenty-five years of evaluation. *Clinical Psychology Review, 8*(1), 77–100.

Benor, D. J., Ledger, K., Toussaint, L., Hett, G., & Zaccaro, D. (2009). Pilot study of Emotional Freedom Techniques, wholistic hybrid derived from Eye Movement Desensitization and Reprocessing and Emotional Freedom Techniques, and cognitive behavioral therapy for treatment of test anxiety in university students. *Explore: The Journal of Science and Healing, 5,* 338–340. doi:10.1016/j.explore.2009.08.001

Boath, E., Stewart, A., & Carryer, A. (2013). Tapping for success: A pilot study to explore if Emotional Freedom Techniques (EFT) can reduce anxiety and enhance academic performance in university students. *Innovative Practice in Higher Education, 1*(3).

Bougea, A. M., Spandideas, N., Alexopoulos, E. C., Thomaides, T., Chrousos, G. P., & Darviri, C. (2013). Effect of the Emotional Freedom Technique on perceived stress, quality of life, and cortisol salivary levels in tension-type headache sufferers: A randomized controlled trial. *Explore: The Journal of Science and Healing, 9*(2), 91–99. doi:10.1016/j.explore.2012.12.005

Brattberg, G. (2008). Self-administered EFT (Emotional Freedom Techniques) in individuals with fibromyalgia: A randomized trial. *Integrative Medicine: A Clinician's Journal, 7*(4), 30–35.

Burk, L. (2010, May). Single session EFT (Emotional Freedom Techniques) for stress-related symptoms after motor vehicle accidents. *Energy Psychology: Theory, Research, and Treatment, 2*(1), 65–71.

Callahan, R. J. (2001). The impact of thought field therapy on heart rate variability. *Journal of Clinical Psychology, 57*(10), 1153–1170.

Chambless, D., Baker, M. J., Baucom, D. H., Beutler, L. E., Calhoun, K. S., Crits-Christoph, P., . . . Woody, S. R. (1998). Update on empirically validated therapies, II. *Clinical Psychologist, 51,* 3–16.

Chambless, D. & Hollon, S. D. (1998). Defining empirically supported therapies. *Journal of Consulting and Clinical Psychology, 66,* 7–18.

Chambless, D. L., Sanderson, W. C., Shoham, V., Bennett Johnson, S., Pope, K. S., Crits-Christoph, P., . . . McCurry, C. (1996). An update on empirically validated therapies. *Clinical Psychologist, 49,* 5–18.

Church, D. (2009/2013). *The EFT mini-manual*. Santa Rosa, CA: Energy Psychology Press.

Church, D. (2010a). The treatment of combat trauma in veterans using EFT (Emotional Freedom Techniques): A pilot protocol. *Traumatology, 16*(1), 55–65. http://dx.doi.org/10.1177/1534765609347549

Church, D. (2010b). Your DNA is not your destiny: Behavioral epigenetics and the role of emotions in health. *Anti-Aging Therapeutics, 13,* 35–42.

Church, D. (2013a). Clinical EFT as an evidence-based practice for the treatment of psychological and physiological conditions. *Psychology, 4*(8), 645–654. doi:10.4236/psych.2013.48092

Church, D. (2013b). *The EFT manual,* (3rd ed.). Santa Rosa, CA: Energy Psychology Press.

Church, D. (2013c). Pain, depression, and anxiety after PTSD symptom remediation in veterans. *Explore: The Journal of Science and Healing,* (in press).

Church, D. & Brooks, A. J. (2010). The effect of a brief EFT (Emotional Freedom Techniques) self-intervention on anxiety, depression, pain and cravings in healthcare workers. *Integrative Medicine: A Clinician's Journal, 9*(4), 40–44.

Church, D. & Brooks, A. J. (2013a). CAM and energy psychology techniques remediate PTSD symptoms in veterans and spouses. *Explore: The Journal of Science and Healing,* (in press).

Church, D. & Brooks, A. J. (2013b). The effect of EFT (Emotional Freedom Techniques) on psychological symptoms in addiction treatment: A pilot study. *International Journal of Scientific Research and Reports, 2*(2).

Church, D., De Asis, M. A., & Brooks, A. J. (2012). Brief group intervention using EFT (Emotional Freedom Techniques) for depression in college students: A randomized controlled trial. *Depression Research and Treatment, 2012,* 1–7. doi:10.1155/2012/257172

Church, D. & Downs, D. (2012). Sports confidence and critical incident intensity after a brief application of Emotional Freedom Techniques: A pilot study. *Sport Journal, 15,* 2012.

Church, D. & Feinstein, D. (2013). Energy psychology in the treatment of PTSD: Psychobiology and clinical principles. In T. Van Leeuwen & M. Brouwer (Eds.), *Psychology of trauma* (pp. 211–224). Hauppage, NY: Nova Science Publishers.

Church, D., Geronilla, L., & Dinter, I. (2009). Psychological symptom change in veterans after six sessions of EFT (Emotional Freedom Techniques): An observational study. *International Journal of Healing and Caring, 9*(1).

Church, D., Hawk, C., Brooks, A., Toukolehto, O., Wren, M., Dinter, I., & Stein, P. (2013). Psychological trauma symptom improvement in veterans using EFT (Emotional Freedom Techniques): A randomized controlled trial. *Journal of Nervous and Mental Disease, 201,* 153–160.

Church, D. & Palmer-Hoffman, J. (2012, October). TBI symptoms improve after PTSD remediation with Emotional Freedom Techniques. Presented at the conference Veterans, Treatment, and Trauma, Omega Institute, Rhinebeck, New York. Submitted for publication.

Church, D., Piña, O., Reategui, C., & Brooks, A. (2012). Single session reduction of the intensity of traumatic memories in abused adolescents after EFT: A randomized controlled pilot study. *Traumatology, 18*(3), 73–79. doi:10.1177/1534765611426788

Church, D. & Wilde, N. (2013, May). Emotional eating and weight loss following Skinny Genes, a six week online program. Reported at the annual conference of the Association for Comprehensive Energy Psychology (ACEP), Reston, VA.

Church, D., Yount, G., & Brooks, A. J. (2012). The effect of Emotional Freedom Techniques (EFT) on stress biochemistry: A randomized controlled trial. *Journal of Nervous and Mental Disease, 200,* 891–896. doi:10.1097/NMD.0b013e31826b9fc1

Craig, G. (2008/2010). *The EFT manual.* Santa Rosa, CA: Energy Psychology Press.

Craig, G., Bach, D., Groesbeck, G., & Benor, D. J. (2009). Emotional Freedom Techniques (EFT) for traumatic brain injury. *International Journal of Healing and Caring, 9*(2).

Craig, G. & Fowlie, A. (1995). *Emotional freedom techniques: The manual.* Sea Ranch, CA: Gary Craig.

Dohrenwend, B. P., Turner, J. B., Turse, N. A., Adams, B. G., Koenen, K. C., & Marshall, R. (2006). The psychological risks of Vietnam for U.S. veterans: A revisit with new data and methods. *Science, 313*(5789), 979–982. http://dx.doi.org/10.1126/science.1128944

Eley, T. C. & Plomin, R. (1997). Genetic analyses of emotionality. *Current Opinion in Neurobiology, 7*(2), 279–284.

Energy Psychology Journal. (2012). *Research-supported psychological treatments.* Retrieved from http://energypsychologyjournal.org/div12

Fang, J., Jin, Z., Wang, Y., Li, K., Kong, J., Nixon, E. E., … Hui, K. K.-S. (2009). The salient characteristics of the central effects of acupuncture needling: Limbic-paralimbic-neocortical network modulation. *Human Brain Mapping, 30,* 1196–1206. doi:10.1002/hbm.20583

Feinstein, D. (2008). Energy psychology in disaster relief. *Traumatology, 14*(1), 124–137. http://dx.doi.org/10.1177/1534765608315636

Feinstein, D. (2009). Controversies in energy psychology. *Energy Psychology: Theory, Research, Practice, Training, 1*(1), 45–56.

Feinstein, D. (2010). Rapid treatment of PTSD: Why psychological exposure with acupoint tapping may be effective. *Psychotherapy: Theory, Research, Practice, Training, 47,* 385–402. doi:10.1037/a0021171

Feinstein, D. (2012). Acupoint stimulation in treating psychological disorders: Evidence of efficacy. *Review of General Psychology, 16,* 364–380. doi:10.1037/a0028602

Feinstein, D. & Church, D. (2010) Modulating gene expression through psychotherapy: The contribution of non-invasive somatic interventions. *Review of General Psychology, 14*(4), 283–295. doi: 10.1037/a0021252

Flint, G. A., Lammers, W., & Mitnick, D. G. (2005). Emotional Freedom Techniques: A safe treatment intervention for many trauma based issues. In J. Garrick & M. B. Williams (Eds.), *Trauma treatment techniques: Innovative trends* (p. 125–150). New York, NY: Routledge.

Food and Drug Administration. (1998). *Guidance for industry: Providing clinical evidence of effectiveness for human drug and biological products.* Rockville, MD: U.S. Department of Health and Human Services.

Fox, L. (2013). Is acupoint tapping an inert placebo or an active ingredient in Emotion Freedom Techniques (EFT)? A randomized controlled trial. *Energy Psychology: Theory, Research, and Treatment, 5*(2), 13–24.

Fraga, M. F., Ballestar, E., Paz, M. F., Ropero, S., Setien, F., Ballestar, M. L., … Esteller, M. (2005). Epigenetic differences arise during the lifetime of monozygotic twins.

Proceedings of the National Academy of Sciences USA, 102(30), 10604–10609.

Fydrich, T., Dowdall, D., & Chambless, D. L. (1992). Reliability and validity of the Beck Anxiety Inventory. *Journal of Anxiety Disorders, 6*(1), 55–61.

Gorman, J. M. (1998). Comorbid depression and anxiety spectrum disorders. *Depression and Anxiety, 4*(4), 160–168.

Hartung, J. & Stein, P. (2012). Telephone delivery of EFT (Emotional Freedom Techniques) remediates PTSD symptoms in veterans: A randomized controlled trial. *Energy Psychology: Theory, Research, & Treatment, 4*(1), 33–42.

Hodge, P. M. & Jurgens, C. Y. (2011). A pilot study of the effects of Emotional Freedom Techniques in psoriasis. *Energy Psychology: Theory, Research, & Treatment, 3*(2), 13–24.

Hui, K. K. S., Liu, J., Marina, O., Napadow, V., Haselgrove, C., Kwong, K. K., ... Makris, N. (2005). The integrated response of the human cerebro-cerebellar and limbic systems to acupuncture stimulation at ST 36 as evidenced by fMRI. *Neuro Image, 27*, 479–496.

Institute of Medicine, Committee on Treatment of Posttraumatic Stress Disorder. (2007). *Treatment of posttraumatic stress disorder: An assessment of the evidence*. Washington DC: Institute of Medicine. Retrieved from http://www.nap.edu/catalog/11955.html

Jain, S. & Rubino, A. (2012). The effectiveness of Emotional Freedom Techniques (EFT) for optimal test performance: A randomized controlled trial. *Energy Psychology: Theory, Research, and Treatment, 4*(2), 13–24. doi:10.9769.EPJ.2012.4.2.SJ

Jirtle, R. L. & Skinner, M. K. (2007). Environmental epigenomics and disease susceptibility. *Nature Reviews. Genetics, 8*, 253–262.

Jones, S., Thornton, J., & Andrews, H. (2011). Efficacy of EFT in reducing public speaking anxiety: A randomized controlled trial. *Energy Psychology: Theory, Research, and Treatment, 3*(1), 19–32. doi:10.9769.EPJ.2011.3.1.SJ

Kanter, E. (2007). *Shock and awe hits home*. Washington, DC: Physicians for Social Responsibility.

Karatzias, T., Power, K., Brown, K., McGoldrick, T., Begum, M., Young, J., ... Adams, S. (2011). A controlled comparison of the effectiveness and efficiency of two psychological therapies for posttraumatic stress disorder: Eye Movement Desensitization and Reprocessing vs. Emotional Freedom Techniques. *Journal of Nervous and Mental Disease, 199*(6), 372–378. doi:10.1097/NMD.0b013e31821cd262

Lambrou, P. T., Pratt, G. J., & Chevalier, G. (2003). Physiological and psychological effects of a mind/body therapy on claustrophobia. *Subtle Energies and Energy Medicine, 14*, 239251.

Lane, J. (2009). The neurochemistry of counterconditioning: Acupressure desensitization in psychotherapy. *Energy Psychology: Theory, Research, and Treatment, 1*(1), 31–44.

LeDoux, J. (2002). *Synaptic self: How our brains become who we are*. New York, NY: Penguin.

Lee, J-H. & Kim, J. W. (2013). Randomized controlled trial for the evaluation of the effects of EFT-Insomnia (EFT-I) for the elderly (Master's thesis). Department of Neuropsychiatry, Kyung Hee University, Korea.

Lee, J-H., Suh, H-U., Chung, S-Y., & Kim, J. W. (2011). A Preliminary study for the evaluation of the effects of EFT-I (EFT program for insomnia) for insomnia in the elderly. *Journal of Oriental Neuropsychiatry, 22*(4), 101–109.

Llewellyn-Edwards, T. & Llewellyn-Edwards, M. (2012). The effect of Emotional Freedom Techniques (EFT) on soccer performance. *Fidelity: Journal for the National Council of Psychotherapy, 47*, 14–21.

Mavissakalian, M. (1986). The Fear Questionnaire: A validity study. *Behaviour Research and Therapy, 24*(1), 83–85.

McCallion, F. (2012). Emotional Freedom Techniques for Dyslexia. *Energy Psychology: Theory, Research, and Treatment, 4*(2), 35–46.

Melnyk, B. M. & Fineout-Overholt, E. (2005). *Making the case for evidence-based practice*. Philadelphia, PA: Lippincott Williams & Wilkins.

Mollon, P. (2007). Thought Field Therapy and its derivatives: Rapid relief of mental health problems through tapping on the body. *Primary Care and Community Psychiatry, 12*(3–4), 123–127.

Napadow, V., Kettner, N., Liu, J., Li, M., Kwong, K. K., Vangel, M., ... Hui, K. K. (2007) Hypothalamus and amygdala response to acupuncture stimuli in carpal tunnel syndrome. *Pain, 130*(3), 254–266.

National Institute for Clinical Excellence. (2009). *How NICE clinical guidelines are developed: An overview for stakeholders, the public and the NHS*. Retrieved from http://www.nice.org.uk/media/62F/36/How_NICE_clinical_guidelines_are_developed_4th_edn_FIANL_LR.pdf

Nemiro, A. (2013, May). EFT vs. CBT in the treatment of sexual gender based violence in the Democratic Republic of the Congo. Presented at the conference of the Association for Comprehensive Energy Psychology (ACEP), San Diego, CA.

Ornish, D., Magbanua, M. J. M., Weidner, G., Weinberg, V., Kemp, C., Green, C., ... Carroll, P. R. (2008). Changes in prostate gene expression in men undergoing an intensive nutrition and lifestyle intervention. *Proceedings of the National Academy of Sciences USA, 105*(24), 8369–8374.

Palmer-Hoffman, J. & Brooks, A. J. (2011). Psychological symptom change after group application of Emotional Freedom Techniques (EFT). *Energy Psychology: Theory, Research, & Treatment, 3*(1), 33–38.

Patterson, S. L. (2013, May). The effect of Emotional Freedom Technique on stress and anxiety in nursing students. Presented at the conference of the Association for Comprehensive Energy Psychology (ACEP), San Diego, CA.

Pekrun, R., Goetz, T., Frenzel, A. C., Barchfeld, P., & Perry, R. P. (2011). Measuring emotions in students' learning and performance: The Achievement Emotions Questionnaire (AEQ). *Contemporary Educational Psychology, 36*, 36–48.

Phelps, E. A. & LeDoux, J. E. (2005). Contributions of the amygdala to emotion processing: From animal models to human behavior. *Neuron, 48*, 175–187.

Rosenberg, M. (1989). *Society and the adolescent self-image* (Rev. ed.). Middletown, CT: Wesleyan University Press.

Rotherham, M., Maynard, I., Thomas, O., Bawden, M., & Francis, L. (2012). Preliminary evidence for the treatment of type I 'yips': The efficacy of the Emotional Freedom Techniques. *Sports Psychologist, 26*(4), 551–570.

Rowe, J. E. (2005). The effects of EFT on long-term psychological symptoms. *Counseling and Clinical Psychology, 2*, 104–111.

Ruggiero, K. J., Del Ben, K., Scotti, J. R., & Rabalais, A. E. (2003). Psychometric properties of the PTSD Checklist-Civilian Version. *Journal of Traumatic Stress, 16*(5), 495–502. http://dx.doi.org/10.1023/A:1025714729117

Salas, M. M., Brooks, A. J., & Rowe, J. E. (2011). The immediate effect of a brief energy psychology intervention (Emotional Freedom Techniques) on specific phobias: A pilot study. *Explore: The Journal of Science and Healing, 7*(3), 255–260.

Schulz, P. (2009). Integrating energy psychology into treatment for adult survivors of childhood sexual abuse. *Energy Psychology: Theory, Research, and Treatment, 1*(1), 15–22.

Seligman, M. E. P. (1995). The effectiveness of psychotherapy: The Consumer Reports study. *American Psychologist, 50*(12), 965–974.

Sezgin, N. & Özcan, B. (2009). The effect of progressive muscular relaxation and Emotional Freedom Techniques on test anxiety in high school students: A randomized controlled trial. *Energy Psychology: Theory, Research, and Treatment, 1*(1), 23–30. doi:10.9769.EPJ.2009.1.1.NS

Sherman, J. J. (1998). Effects of psychotherapeutic treatments for PTSD: A meta-analysis of controlled clinical trials. *Journal of Traumatic Stress, 11*(3), 413–435.

Sojcher, R., Perlman, A., & Fogerite, S. (2012). Evidence and potential mechanisms for mindfulness practices and energy psychology for obesity and binge-eating disorder. *Explore: The Journal of Science and Healing, 8*(5), 271–276.

Stapleton, P., Church, D., Sheldon, T., Porter, B., & Carlopio, C. (2013). Depression symptoms improve after successful weight loss with EFT (Emotional Freedom Techniques): A randomized controlled trial. *Depression Research and Treatment*, in press.

Stapleton, P., Sheldon, T., Porter, B., & Whitty, J. (2011). A randomised clinical trial of a meridian-based intervention for food cravings with six-month follow-up. *Behaviour Change, 28*(1), 1.

Stapleton, P. B., Sheldon, T., & Porter, B. (2012). Clinical benefits of Emotional Freedom Techniques on food cravings at 12-months follow-up: A randomized controlled trial. *Energy Psychology: Theory, Research, and Treatment, 4*(1), 1–12.

Stein, P. & Brooks, A. J. (2011). Efficacy of EFT (Emotional Freedom Techniques) provided by coaches vs. licensed therapists in veterans with PTSD. *Energy Psychology: Theory, Research, & Treatment, 3*(1), 11–17.

Stewart, A., Boath, E., Carryer, A., Walton, I., Hill, L., Phillips, D., & Dawson, K. (2013). Can Matrix Reimprinting using EFT be effective in the treatment of emotional conditions? *Energy Psychology: Theory, Research, & Treatment*, in press.

Swingle, P. (2010). EFT in the neurotherapeutic treatment of seizure disorders. *Energy Psychology: Theory, Research, & Treatment, 2*(1), 27–38.

Swingle, P. G., Pulos, L., & Swingle, M. K. (2004). Neurophysiological indicators of EFT treatment of posttraumatic stress. *Subtle Energies and Energy Medicine, 15*(1), 75–86.

University of Warwick and University of Edinburgh. (2012). The Warwick-Edinburgh Mental Well-being Scale (WEMWBS). Retrieved from http://www.healthscotland.com/documents/1467.aspx

Veterans Health Administration. (2012). *Report on VA facility specific Operation Enduring Freedom (OEF), Operation Iraqi Freedom (OIF), and Operation New Dawn (OND) veterans coded with potential PTSD.* Retrieved from http://www.publichealth.va.gov/docs/epidemiology/ptsd-report-fy2012-qtr3.pdf

Waite, L. W. & Holder, M. D. (2003). Assessment of the emotional freedom technique: An alternative treatment for fear. *Scientific Review of Mental Health Practice, 2*(1), 20–26.

Weathers, F., Huska, J., & Keane, T. (1991). The PTSD checklist military version (PCL-M). Boston, MA: National Center for PTSD.

Wells, S., Polglase, K., Andrews, H. B., Carrington, P., & Baker, A. H. (2003). Evaluation of a meridian-based intervention, Emotional Freedom Techniques (EFT), for reducing specific phobias of small animals. *Journal of Clinical Psychology, 59*, 943–966. doi:10.1002/jclp.10189

Zigmond, A. S. & Snaith, R. P. (1983). The Hospital Anxiety and Depression Scale. *Acta Psychiatrica Scandinavica, 67*(6), 361–370.

Biomedical and Physics Principles

Chapter 1
The Wisdom of Your Cells
Bruce H. Lipton

Abstract

In the past decades, the theory of genetic determinism has been supplanted. Epigenetics has demonstrated that the environment outside the DNA and even outside the organism itself may control the expression of genes. Consciousness allows individuals to assess the environment, while self-consciousness allows them to modify their behavior based on expectations and beliefs. Perception can fine-tune gene expression to maximize the organism's opportunities for survival. In humans, the conscious mind is responsible for only a small fraction of cognitive capacity. The subconscious part of the mind is responsible for the rest. It can process large quantities of data at high speeds and, unobserved, it controls most of our decisions, actions, emotions, and behaviors. Its most influential programs originated between the ages of birth and 6 years old, and were modeled on our caregivers and other immediate community members. During this period the predominant brain wave frequencies were delta (0.5 Hz) and theta (4–8 Hz). These frequencies are associated with reverie, trance, hypnosis, super learning, and dreaming. Dysfunctional cognitions acquired at this early age form the basis of subconscious behavior patterns, and changing these patterns in later life is challenging. Mindfulness, hypnotherapy, and energy psychology are some of the emerging practices that are evolving to change these early life programs.

Keywords: epigenetics, genes, consciousness, brain waves, subconscious, early childhood, emotions

Bruce H. Lipton, PhD, cell biologist and author of the best-selling *The Biology of Belief,* is an internationally recognized authority in bridging science and spirit. His breakthrough studies on the cell membrane presaged the new science of epigenetics, and made him a leading voice of the new biology. Send correspondence to Bruce Lipton, ℅ Hay House, 2776 Loker Avenue West, Carlsbad, CA 92010, or sally@brucelipton.com.

Underneath your skin is a bustling metropolis of 50 trillion cells, each biologically and functionally equivalent to a miniature human. Current popular opinion holds that the fate and behavior of our internal cellular citizens are preprogrammed in their genes, a notion derived from the now dated scientific concept known as *genetic determinism*. Since Watson and Crick's discovery of the genetic code, the public has been programmed with the conventional belief that DNA "controls" the attributes passed down through a family's lineage, including dysfunctional traits such as cancer, Alzheimer's, diabetes, and depression, among scores of others. As "victims" of heredity, we naturally perceive of ourselves as being powerless in regard to the unfolding of our lives. Unfortunately, the assumption of being powerless is the road to personal irresponsibility: "Since I can't do anything about it anyway…why should I care?"

Shattering Illusions

Just as the Human Genome Project got off the ground in the late 1980s, scientists began to acquire a paradigm-shattering new view of how life works. Their revolutionary research has become the foundation for a new branch of science known as *epigenetic control*, which has shaken the foundations of biology and medicine. It reveals that we are not "victims," but rather "masters" of our genes.

The conventional version of heredity still taught in schools emphasizes *genetic control*, or "control by genes." However, newly revealed *epigenetic control* mechanisms provide a profoundly different view of how life is managed. The Greek-derived prefix *epi-* means "over or above." Consequently, the literal translation of *epigenetic control* is "control *above* the genes." Genes do NOT control life—life is controlled by something *above* the genes. This knowledge of how life works provides the most important element in our quest for self-empowerment.

The new science of epigenetics recognizes that environmental signals are the primary regulators of gene activity. As described in my book, *The Biology of Belief: Unleashing the Power of Consciousness, Matter, and Miracles*, cells read and respond to the conditions of their environment using membrane protein perception switches. Activated switches send signals to control behavior and regulate the activity of the genes—the hereditary blueprints used to make the body. Amazingly, epigenetic information can modify or edit the readout of a gene blueprint to create over 30,000 different variations of proteins—the cell's molecular building blocks—from the same gene. This editing process can provide for normal or dysfunctional protein products from the same gene. One can be born with healthy genes and through epigenetic processes express mutant behaviors, such as cancer. Similarly, one can be born with defective mutant genes and through epigenetic mechanisms create normal healthy proteins and functions.

The conventional belief that the genome represents the equivalent of a computer's "read-only" programs is now proven to be false. Epigenetic mechanisms modify the readout of genetic the code—which means that genes actually represent "read-write" programs, wherein life experiences actively redefine an individual's genetic expression. The "new" biology is based upon the fact that perception controls behavior *and* gene activity! This revised version of science emphasizes the reality that we actively control our genetic expression moment by moment throughout our lives. Rather than seeing ourselves as victims of our genes, we must come to own the responsibility that our perceptions are dynamically shaping our biology and behavior.

As organisms experience the environment, their perception mechanisms fine-tune genetic expression so as to enhance their opportunities for survival. The expression of a healthy or diseased biology is directly influenced by the accuracy of an individual's interpretation or perception of their environment. Misperceptions rewrite genetic expression just as effectively as accurate perceptions, yet with far graver, perhaps even life threatening consequences.

From the Microcosm of the Cell to the Macrocosm of the Mind

For the first 3.5 billion years of life on this planet, the biosphere consisted of a massive population of individual single-celled organisms, such as bacteria, yeast, algae, and protozoa. About 700 million years ago, individual cells started to assemble into multicellular colonies. The collective awareness afforded in a community of cells was far greater than an individual cell's awareness. Since awareness is a primary factor in organismal survival, the communal experience offered its citizens a far greater opportunity to stay alive and reproduce.

The first cellular communities, like the earliest human communities, were basic hunter-gatherer clans wherein each member of the society offered the same services to support the survival of the community. However, as the population densities of both cellular and human communities reached greater numbers, it was no longer efficient or effective for all individuals to do the same job. In both types of communities, evolution led to individuals taking on specialized functions. For example, in human communities some members focused upon hunting, others upon domestic chores or child rearing. In cellular communities specialization meant that some cells began to differentiate as digestive cells, others as heart cells, and still others as muscle cells.

Most of the trillions of cells forming bodies such as ours have no direct perception of the external environment. Liver cells "see" what's going on in the liver, but don't directly know what's going on in the world outside of the skin. The function of the brain and nervous system is to interpret environmental stimuli and send out signals to the cells that integrate and regulate the life-sustaining functions of the body's organ systems.

The successful nature of multicellular communities allowed evolving brains to dedicate vast numbers of cells to cataloguing, memorizing, and integrating complex perceptions. The ability to remember and select among the millions of experienced perceptions in life provides the brain with a powerful creative database from which it can create complex behavioral repertoires. When put into play, these behavioral programs endow the organism with the characteristic trait of *consciousness*: the state of being awake and aware of what is going on around you.

Many scientists prefer to think of consciousness in terms of a digital quality, an organism either has it or not. However, an assessment of the evolution of biological properties suggests consciousness, like any other quality, evolved over time. Consequently, the character of consciousness would likely express itself as a gradient of awareness from its simpler roots in primitive organisms to the unique character of *self-consciousness* manifest in humans and other higher vertebrates.

The expression of *self-consciousness* is specifically associated with a small evolutionary adaptation in the brain known as the *prefrontal cortex*. This is the neurological platform that enables us to realize our personal identity and experience the quality of "thinking." Monkeys and lower organisms do not express self-consciousness. When looking into a mirror, monkeys will never recognize that they are looking at them selves; they will always perceive the image to be that of another monkey. In contrast, neurologically more advanced chimps looking in the mirror perceive the mirror's reflection as an image of themselves.

An important difference between the brain's *consciousness* and the prefrontal cortex's *self-consciousness* is that consciousness enables an organism to assess and respond to the immediate conditions of its environment that are relevant at that moment. In contrast, self-consciousness enables the individual to factor in the consequences of their actions in regard to not only how they impact the present moment but also how they will influence the future.

Self-consciousness is an evolutionary adjunct to consciousness in that it provided another behavior-creating platform: the role of a "self" in the decision-making process. While conventional *consciousness* enables organisms to participate in the dynamics of life's "play," the quality of *self-consciousness* offers an opportunity to simultaneously be an observer in the "audience." From this perspective, self-consciousness provides the individual with the option for self-reflection, reviewing and editing their character's performance. The conscious and self-conscious functions of the brain may be collectively referred to as the *mind*.

In conventional parlance, the brain's conscious mechanism associated with automated stimulus-response behaviors is referred to as the *subconscious* or *unconscious mind*, for the reason that its functions require neither observation nor attention from the self-conscious mind. Subconscious mind functions evolved long before the prefrontal cortex; consequently, it is able to successfully operate a body and its behavior without any contribution from the more evolved *self-conscious mind*.

The subconscious mind is an astonishingly powerful information processor that can record and replay perceptual experiences (programs). Interestingly, many people only become aware of their subconscious mind's automated programmed behaviors when they realize they're engaged in an undesirable behavior as a result of someone "pushing their buttons."

The power of the subconscious mind lies in its ability to process massive amounts of data acquired from direct and indirect learning experiences at extraordinarily high rates of speed. It has been estimated that the disproportionately larger brain mass providing the subconscious mind's function has the ability to interpret and respond to over 40 million nerve impulses per second. In contrast, it is estimated that the diminutive self-conscious mind's prefrontal cortex can only process about 40 nerve impulses per second. As an information processor, the subconscious mind is *one million times* more powerful than the self-conscious mind.

As a tradeoff for its computational bravado, the subconscious mind expresses only a marginal creative ability—one that may be best compared to that of a precocious 5-year-old. In contrast to the freewill offered by the conscious mind, the subconscious mind primarily expresses prerecorded stimulus-response "habits," such as walking, getting dressed, or driving a car.

Although the prefrontal cortex's ability for multitasking is physically constrained, the self-conscious mind can focus upon and control *any* function in the human body. It was once thought that some bodily functions—such as the regulation of heartbeat, blood pressure, and body temperature—were beyond the control of the self-conscious mind. It is now recognized, however, that yogis and other practitioners that train their conscious minds can absolutely control functions formerly defined as involuntary behaviors.

The subconscious and self-conscious components of the mind work in tandem, with the subconscious controlling every behavior not attended to by the self-conscious mind. Most people's self-conscious minds are rarely focused upon the current moment, since their mental processing continuously flits from one thought to another. The self-conscious mind is so preoccupied with thoughts about the future, the past, or resolving some imaginary problem, that most of our lives are actually controlled by programs in the subconscious mind.

Simple Insights… Profound Consequences!

Cognitive neuroscientists conclude that the self-conscious mind contributes only about 5% of our cognitive activity. Consequently, 95% of our decisions, actions, emotions, and behaviors are derived from the unobserved processing of the subconscious mind. This data reveals that our lives are not controlled by our personal intentions and desires, as we may inherently believe. Do the math! Our fate is actually under the control of the preprogrammed experiences managed by the *subconscious mind*.

The most powerful and influential programs in the subconscious mind originated during the formative period between gestation and six years of age. Now here's the catch—these life-shaping subconscious programs are direct downloads derived from observing our primary teachers: our parents, siblings, and local community. Unfortunately, as psychiatrists, psychologists, and counselors are keenly aware, many of the perceptions acquired about ourselves in the formative period are expressed as limiting and self-sabotaging beliefs.

Unbeknownst to most parents, their words and actions are being continuously recorded by their children's minds. Since the role of the mind is to make coherence between its programs and real life, the brain generates appropriate behavioral responses to life's stimuli to assure the "truth" of the programmed perceptions.

Let's apply this understanding to real-life behavior: Consider that you were a five-year-old child throwing a tantrum over your desire to have a particular toy. In silencing your outburst, your father yelled, "*You* don't deserve things!" You are now an adult and in your self-conscious mind you are considering the idea that you have the qualities and power to assume a position of leadership at your job. While in the process of entertaining this positive thought in the self-conscious mind, all of your behaviors are automatically managed by the programs in your more powerful subconscious mind. Since your fundamental behavioral programs are those derived in your formative years, your father's admonition that "you do not deserve things" may become the subconscious mind's automated directive. So while you are entertaining wonderful thoughts of a positive future and not paying attention, your subconscious mind automatically engages self-sabotaging behavior to assure that your reality matches your program of not-deserving.

Now here's the catch: Behavior is automatically controlled by the subconscious mind's programs when the self-conscious mind is not focused on the present moment. When the reflective self-conscious mind is preoccupied in thought and not paying attention, it does not observe the automatic behaviors derived from subconscious mind. Since 95% or more of our behavior is derived from the subconscious mind...then most of our own behavior is invisible to us!

For example, consider you intimately know someone and you also know his or her parent. From your perspective you see that your friend's behavior closely resembles their parent. Then one day you casually remark to your friend something like, "You know Mary, you're just like your mom." Back away! In disbelief and perhaps shock, Mary will likely respond with, "How can you say that!" The cosmic joke is that everyone else can see that Mary's behavior resembles her mom's *except* Mary. Why? Simply because when Mary is engaging the subconscious behavioral programs she downloaded in her youth from observing her mom, it's because her self-conscious mind is not paying attention. At those moments, her automatic subconscious programs operate without observation.

Consequently, when life does not work out as planned, we rarely recognize that we were very likely contributing to our own disappointments. Since we are generally unaware of the influence of our own subconscious behaviors, we naturally perceive of ourselves as victims of outside forces. Unfortunately, assuming the role of victim means that we assume we are powerless in manifesting our intentions. Nothing is further from the truth! The primary determinant in shaping the fate of our lives is the database of perceptions and beliefs programmed in our minds.

Where Did That Behavior Come From?

There are three sources of perceptions that control our biology and behavior. The most primitive perceptions are those we acquire with our genome. Built into our genes are programs that provide fundamental reflex behaviors referred to as instincts. Pulling your hand out of an open flame is a genetically derived behavior that does not have to be learned. More complex instincts include the ability of newborn babies to swim like a dolphin or the activation of innate healing mechanisms to repair a damaged system or eliminate a cancerous growth. Genetically inherited instincts are perceptions acquired from *nature*.

The second source of life-controlling perceptions represents memories derived from life experiences downloaded into the subconscious mind. These profoundly powerful learned perceptions represent the contribution from *nurture*. Among the earliest perceptions of life to be downloaded are the emotions and sensations experienced by the mother as she responds to her world. Along with nutrition, the emotional chemistry, hormones, and stress factors controlling the mother's responses to life experiences cross the placental barrier and influence fetal physiology and development. When the mother is happy, so is the fetus. When the mother is in fear, so is the fetus. When the mother "rejects" her fetus as a potential threat to family survival, the fetal nervous system is preprogrammed with the emotion of being rejected. Sue Gearhardt's very valuable book *Why Love Matters*, reveals that the fetal nervous system records memories of the womb experiences. By the time the baby is born, emotional information downloaded from the life experiences in womb have already shaped half of that individual's personality.

However, the most influential perceptual programming of the subconscious mind occurs in the time period spanning from the birth process through the first 6 years of life. During this time the child's brain is recording all sensory experiences as well as learning complex motor programs for speech, and for learning first how to crawl, then stand, and ultimately run and jump. Simultaneously, the subconscious mind acquires perceptions in regard to parents, who are they and what they do. Then by observing behavioral patterns of people in their immediate environment, a child learns perceptions of acceptable and unacceptable social behaviors that become the subconscious programs that establish the "rules" of life.

Nature facilitates the enculturation process by developmentally enhancing the subconscious mind's ability to download massive amounts of information. EEG readings from adult brains reveal that neural electrical activity is correlated with at least five different states of awareness, each associated with a different frequency level:

Activity	Frequency	Brain State
delta	0.5–4 Hz	sleeping/unconscious
theta	4–8 Hz	imagination
alpha	8–12 Hz	calm consciousness
beta	12–35 Hz	focused consciousness
gamma	>35 Hz	peak performance

EEG vibrations continuously shift from state to state over the whole range of frequencies during normal brain processing in adults. However, EEG vibration rates and their corresponding states evolve in incremental stages over time. The predominant brain activity during the child's first 2 years of life is *delta*, the lowest EEG frequency range. In the adult brain, *delta* is associated with sleeping or unconsciousness.

Between 2 and 6 years of age, the child's brain activity state ramps up and operates primarily in the range of *theta*. In the adult, *theta* activity is associated with states of reverie or imagination. While in the *theta* state, children spend much of their time mixing the imaginary world with the real world. Calm consciousness associated with emerging *alpha* activity only becomes a predominant brain state after 6 years of age. By 12 years, the brain expresses all frequency ranges although it's primary activity is in the *beta's* state of focused consciousness. Children leave elementary education behind at this age and enter into the more intense academic programs of junior high.

A profoundly important fact in the above timeline that may have missed your attention is that children do not express the *alpha* EEG frequencies of conscious processing as a predominant brain state until *after* they are 6 years old. The predominant *delta* and *theta* activity of children under six signifies that their brains are operating at levels below consciousness. *Delta* and *theta* brain frequencies define a brain state known as a hypnogogic trance, the same neural state that hypnotherapists use to download new behaviors directly into the subconscious mind of their clients.

The first 6 years of a child's life are spent in a hypnotic trance. Its perceptions of the world are directly downloaded into the subconscious during this time, without the discrimination of the dormant self-conscious mind. Consequently, our fundamental perceptions about life are learned before we express the capacity to choose or reject those beliefs. We are simply "programmed." The Jesuits were aware of this programmable state and proudly boasted, "Give us a child until it is six or seven years old and it will belong to the Church for the rest of its life." They knew that once the dogma of the Church was implanted into the child's subconscious mind, that information would inevitably influence 95% of that individual's behavior for the rest of his or her life.

The inhibition of conscious processing (*alpha* EEG activity) and the simultaneous engagement of a hypnogogic trance during the formative stages of a child's life are a logical necessity. The thinking processes associated with the self-conscious mind cannot operate from a blank slate. Self-conscious behavior requires a working database of learned perceptions. Consequently, before self-consciousness is expressed, the brain's primary task is to acquire a working awareness of the world by directly downloading experiences and observations into the subconscious mind.

However, there is a very, *very* serious downside to acquiring awareness by this method. The consequence is so profound that it not only impacts the life of the individual, it can also alter an entire civilization. The issue concerns the fact that we download our perceptions and beliefs about life long before we acquire the ability for critical thinking. Our primary perceptions are literally written in stone as unequivocal truths in the subconscious mind, where they habitually operate for life, unless there is an active effort to reprogram them. When as young children we download limiting or sabotaging beliefs about ourselves, these perceptions become our truths and our subconscious processing will invisibly generate behaviors that are coherent with those truths.

Acquired perceptions in the subconscious mind can even override genetically endowed instincts. For example, every human can instinctually swim like a dolphin the moment they emerge from the birth canal. So, why do we have to work so hard at teaching our children how to swim? The answer lies in the fact that every time the infant encounters open water, such as a pool, a river, or a bathtub, the parents freak out in concern for the safety of their child. In the baby's mind, the parent's behavior causes the child to equate water as something to be feared. The acquired perception of water as dangerous and life threatening, overrides the instinctual ability to swim and makes the formerly proficient child susceptible to drowning.

Through our developmental experiences we acquire the perception that we are frail, vulnerable organisms subject to the ravages of contagious germs and disease. The belief of being frail actually leads to frailty since the mind's limiting perceptions inhibit the body's innate ability to heal itself. This influence of the mind on healing processes is the focus of psychoneuroimmunology, the field that describes the mechanism by which our thoughts change brain chemistry, which in turn regulates the function of the immune system. While negative beliefs can precipitate illness (nocebo effect), the resulting disease state can be alleviated through the healing effects of positive thoughts (placebo effect).

Finally, the third source of perceptions that shape our lives is derived from the self-conscious mind. Unlike the reflexive programming of subconscious mind, the self-conscious mind is a creative platform that provides for the mixing and morphing of a variety of perceptions with the infusion of imagination, a process that generates an unlimited number of beliefs and behavioral variations. The quality of the self-conscious mind endows organisms with one of the most powerful forces in the Universe, the opportunity to express free will.

Taking Personal Responsibility

We have all been shackled with emotional chains wrought by dysfunctional behaviors programmed by the stories of the past. However, the next time you are "talking to yourself" with the hope of changing sabotaging subconscious programs, it is important to realize the following information. Using reason to communicate with your subconscious in an effort to change its behavior would essentially have the same influence as trying to change a program on a cassette tape by talking to the tape player. In neither case is there an entity in the mechanism that will respond to your dialogue.

Subconscious programs are not fixed, unchangeable behaviors. We have the ability to rewrite our limiting beliefs and in the process take control of our lives. However, to change subconscious programs requires the activation of a process other than simply engaging in the usual running dialogue with the subconscious mind. There are a large variety of effective processes to reprogram limiting beliefs, which include clinical hypnotherapy, Buddhist mindfulness practice, and a number of newly developed and very powerful modalities collectively referred to as Energy Psychology.

Learning how to harness our minds to promote growth is the secret of life, which is why I refer to the new science as *The Biology of Belief.* As we become more conscious and rely less on subconscious automated programs, we become the masters of our fates rather than the "victims" of our programs. In this way we can rewrite old, limiting perceptions and actively transform the character of our lives so that they are filled with the love, health, and prosperity that are our true birthrights.

Chapter 2
An Anatomical, Biochemical, Biophysical, and Quantum Basis for the Unconscious Mind

James L. Oschman and Maurie D. Pressman

Abstract

Sigmund Freud made a major advance in the study of the unconscious mind from his work with a patient who had "converted" an emotional experience into a paralyzed arm. Through hypnosis, his patient disclosed the emotional experience that led to the paralysis, and this resolved her condition. Later in his career, Freud recognized that such "conversion disorders" and other "provisional ideas in psychology" would someday be based on organic substructures. This chapter suggests that it is now possible to develop some theoretical and experimental bases for organic substructures involved in psychological phenomena. We propose a mechanism for conversion disorders based on the concept that there are two or more interconnected systems that can sense and respond to the environment and that can also convert repressed emotions into chronic muscle contraction or other somatic issues. One connection between sensation and action is the well-established neurophysiological mechanism and another involves semiconduction through the living matrix. This is a "hardware" system and functions in parallel to the nervous system and in concert with the "wetware" or biochemical systems described by Dennis Bray. It is proposed that one aspect of the unconscious, its capacity to absorb and process vast amounts of sensory information, involves rapid signal processing through a combination of ultra-fast biological processes that are present in all cells and tissues, including but not limited to neurons. Semiconduction, wetware, and quantum coherence are examples of such processes.

Keywords: semiconduction, wetware, quantum coherence, conversion disorder, neurophysiology

> *A single-celled paramecium swims gracefully, avoids predators, finds food, mates, and has sex, all without a single synapse. "Of nerve there is no trace. But the cell framework, the cytoskeleton might serve."*
>
> —Sherrington (1951)

James L. Oschman, PhD, is the award-winning author of *Energy Medicine: The Scientific Basis* and *Energy Medicine in Therapeutics and Human Performance*. Send correspondence to James Oschman, Nature's Own Research Association, PO Box 1935, Dover, NH 03821, or joschman@aol.com.

Maurie D. Pressman, MD, is the medical director and founder of the Pressman Center for Mind/Body Wellness, with offices in Philadelphia, focusing on spiritual psychotherapy and the exploration of the human soul. Send correspondence to Maurie D. Pressman, Pressman Center for Mind/Body Wellness, 200 Locust Street, Suite 17B, Philadelphia, PA 19106, or mauriedavid@earthlink.net.

Introduction

Sigmund Freud popularized the concept of the unconscious mind, following on the pioneering work of Wilhelm Wundt, William James, William Carpenter, Charles Sanders Pierce, and Josef Jastrow, who laid the foundation for our modern scientific methodology and thinking about the subject. For example, in his classic treatise entitled *Principles of Mental Physiology*, William Carpenter (1874) suggested that our brains process information through two parallel tiers, one conscious and the other unconscious. Freud (1895) is credited with a major advance in the understanding of the unconscious mind through his work with a patient named "Dora" who had a paralyzed arm (Breuer & Freud, 2000).* To Freud's great surprise, the paralysis was relieved when Dora recalled, under hypnosis, her childhood memory of having her father sleeping on the couch with his hand in the crook of her arm. The story was that she wanted to go out and dance, but to keep from waking her father, she could not move her arm. This was distressing, and eventually she had a thought that was reprehensible to her, "Oh, I wish he would die already." She hated herself for that thought and repressed it, only to have it surface again in the form of a paralyzed arm. The paralysis was relieved after she had sufficiently remembered with abreaction (pouring forth and draining of) the memory.

This was the beginning of Freud's understanding that the mind has content that is not available to consciousness, yet can affect physical structure, function, and behavior. Such issues are now referred to as "conversion disorders," based on Freud's doctrine that anxiety can be converted into physical symptoms. While such conditions are widespread, conversion symptoms do not conform to any known anatomical or physiological pathways, and no neuropsychological model has been clearly established. Freud expressed the situation:

> I cannot, I must confess, give any hint of how a conversion of this kind is brought about. It is obviously not carried out in the same way as an intentional and voluntary action. It is a process which occurs under the pressure of the motive of defense in someone whose organization or a temporary modification of it has a proclivity in that direction. (Breuer & Freud, 2000)

Freud pointed out that much of our mental activity is unconscious. In the province of the mind, consciousness is the visible sentient tip of the iceberg (Figure 1). "Preconscious" is a term used in Freudian psychoanalysis to describe thoughts which are unconscious at a particular moment, but are not repressed and therefore are readily available for recall and easily "capable of becoming conscious," a phrase that Freud attributed to Joseph Breuer (Freud, 1991). The unconscious mind consists of dynamic mental processes that occur automatically and are not available to introspection. They include, for example, thought processes, as opposed to thoughts and intuitive insights. The vast unconscious reservoir below the surface is functioning all of the time. In essence, we see and interact with the world through the "eyes" of our unconscious assumptions, usually without really knowing it. The unconscious strongly influences the directions of our activities as well as our feelings and perceptions.

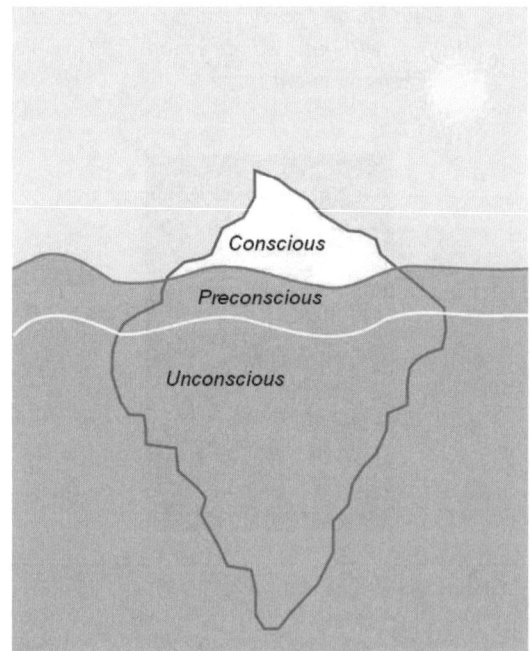

Figure 1. An iceberg is often used to represent Freud's theory that most of the human mind operates unconsciously.

---

*Dates for some of the classic references are for recent reprints or reproductions.

Freud understood that the language of the unconscious is different from the language of consciousness but did not appreciate that under many circumstances unconscious processes are vastly faster and more efficient at integrating sensory inputs and adaptive actions than conscious processes. The unconscious mind enables us to survive in a world that requires massive information intake and rapid processing. This aspect is commonly referred to as the "adaptive unconscious," to distinguish it from the unconscious, which contains repressed memories and emotions that are too disturbing to be thought about consciously—the stuff of Freudian psychotherapy. The unconscious mind can also integrate life events happening over a long or short period of time. The unconscious and conscious minds function simultaneously with psychological barriers between them. Traumatic memories and repressed feelings can become conscious when barriers, called resistances or defenses, are lifted.

The unconscious delivers to consciousness images and thoughts that integrate and interpret current as well as stored information (memories, traumatic memories, personality structure, archetypes). Neurologist Jason W. Brown documented this on the basis of his studies of aphasias, leading to his fascinating concept of microgenesis (Brown, 1977, 1988, 1989, 1991). In his early years, Freud was also an aphasiologist; he studied linguistic problems caused by brain damage. He noticed that we don't consciously pick the words and grammatical structures that we're going to use. All of that is done for us unconsciously and automatically, and we just speak. We know the gist of what we are going to say, but we do not know precisely what we are going to say until we say it. This involves astonishingly complex processing and exemplifies what the unconscious accomplishes in our everyday experience.

Freud (1914) recognized that his provisional ideas in psychology would one day be based on an organic substructure. This essay explores possible organic substructures for the unconscious mind. To our knowledge, no scientific basis has previously been suggested to explain the connections between repressed emotions and physical issues such as Dora's paralysis.

To anticipate, we are going to suggest that chronic muscle contraction in so-called conversion disorders can be triggered by several definable interacting pathways in addition to the well-established neuromuscular system.

Character of the Unconscious

The conscious mind only holds a small amount of information at any given time. (Murphy, 1982)

Each second, our consciousness reveals to us a tiny fraction of the 11 million bits* of information our senses pass on to our brains. Most of the information from our senses goes to our unconscious... Trust your hunches and intuitions—they are closer to reality than your perceived reality, as they are based on far more information. (Nørretranders, 1999).

A variety of phenomena point toward the unconscious as an aspect of consciousness that is able to sense and process large amounts of information and synthesize creative or intuitive or successful actions or behaviors or solutions to complex problems. Here we refer to such behaviors as "authentic" to distinguish them from actions based on conscious "thoughtful" analysis of a situation. Psychologists make a distinction between procedural knowledge—when your body knows how to do something—and declarative knowledge—when your conscious mind knows how to do something (Allard & Burnett, 1985). It is recognized that the conscious mind can usually only focus on a few items at a time, whereas the unconscious mind can deal with many items simultaneously.

Many refer to left-brain function as opposed to right-brain function, rather than unconscious as opposed to conscious. This is based on the recognition that functions involving logical or sequential analysis generally reside in the left hemisphere, while the right hemisphere seems to control processing of spatio-visual information and creative activities such as art and music. Hellige (2001) argues that this view may be far too simplistic.

---

*Note that Nørretranders refers to "the 11 million bits of information our senses pass on to our brains" each second. "Bits of information" refers to digital information, the word being a contraction of "binary" and "digit." In the discussion that follows we suggest that information taken in by our senses is actually analog, and that the receptors convert some but not all of that information into digital signals that are processed by the nervous system.

If you have to make a decision between two alternatives, conscious thought may give a suitable result. If you have to make a decision between many alternatives, however, the unconscious often leads to more satisfactory solutions. Such solutions may emerge as sudden flashes of insight, intuitions, in dreams, or extremely rapid adaptive actions. In *Blink: The Power of Thinking Without Thinking*, Malcolm Gladwell (2007) gives examples of individuals answering complex questions without knowing how they do it.

We begin with a description of athletic, artistic, and martial arts performances that seem to involve sensation and information processing and actions that occur too rapidly to be explainable by the well-established properties of nerves and synapses. We then consider a number of biological processes that are 10 or more times faster than nerve transmission. There is no reason in principle that these processes should not be utilized by biological systems and contribute to the information storage and processing of the unconscious mind. Processes to be explored are:

1. Semiconduction in the fabric of the body known as the living matrix or ground regulation system.
2. Biochemical processes as described by Dennis Bray in his 2009 book, *Wetware: A Computer in Every Cell*.
3. Various quantum processes including quantum coherence as described by Herbert Fröhlich, spin resonance as described by Mae Wan Ho and Emilio Del Giudice, and wavelike energy transfer that takes place in chloroplasts of green plants as documented by Fleming and colleagues.

Human Performance

The role of the unconscious in peak performance is validated by the work of one of the authors (MDP) in his experiences with Olympic ice skaters, beginning in 1972. This was the first use of hypnosis and visualization by athletes, with a focus on using the powers of the unconscious mind to prepare for a perfect program. The results were startling (Pressman, 1978, 1979, 1980a, 1980b). With appropriate preparation, the perfect athletic performance emerges as a near-meditative and open state in which, for example, the skater becomes one with the music and the audience. The performer looks completely relaxed and un-self-conscious. The brain and nervous system are essentially on automatic. With this surrender comes virtually effortless speed, coordination, and power. And it is beautiful to watch! Performers refer to this state of consciousness as "the zone." Experience has shown that conscious thought can disrupt this state and compromise the quality of the performance. Extensive research has confirmed that individuals training for athletic events, dance, theater, music, and combat and for healing work benefit significantly from mental rehearsals or internal imaging, without physically doing anything (Suinn, 1985; Warner & McNeill, 1988, Meyers, Whelan, & Murphy, 1996).

From Sensation to Action

Nerve impulses are triggered by changes in environmental energies (heat, light, sound, smell, taste, gravity and touch) interacting with sensory receptors. Receptors, in turn, initiate patterns of nerve impulses in afferent neurons that propagate to other parts of the nervous system. For example, a change in the intensity, wavelength (color), or pattern of intensities of light striking the retina sets up characteristic nerve impulses in the optic nerve, which delivers this information to the visual cortex and other parts of the brain.

Each receptor has a low threshold for some specific form of energy (Figure 2). Psychophysics investigates the quantitative relationships between the strength of physical stimuli and the sensations and perceptions they produce (Gescheider, 1997). To accomplish this, the researcher commonly applies stimuli of increasing strength to a receptor until a subject acknowledges being able to sense the stimulation. At first, the strength of the stimulation is subliminal or below the level of detection, but there comes a point where the stimulation is consciously sensed, referred to as supraliminal stimuli or above threshold for the individual. Visual and auditory stimuli may be flashed so quickly or at such low intensity that an individual is not consciously aware of them. A review of functional magnetic resonance imaging (fMRI) studies showed that such subliminal stimuli activate specific regions of the brain even though subjects are not consciously aware of them (Brooks et al., 2012). The following discusses the possible significance of the distinction between subliminal and supraliminal stimuli.

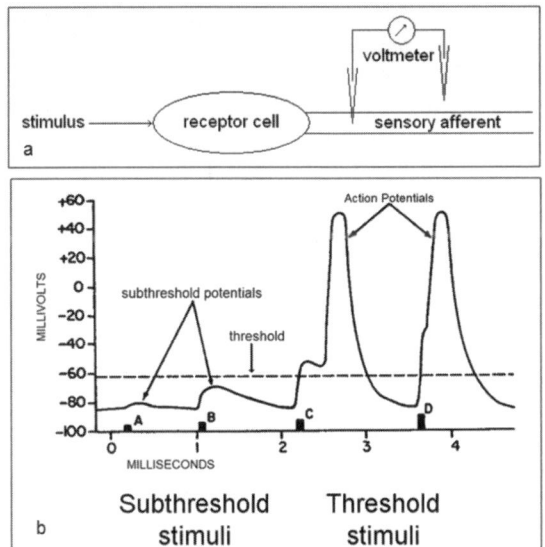

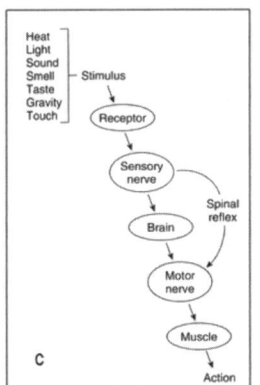
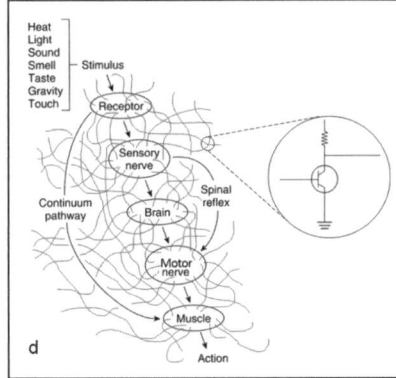

Figure 2. Hypothesis: Sensory receptors transduce the environmental signals they receive from the environment into two pathways. One is the conventional neurological pathway, and the other is the living matrix/ground regulation system. It is further suggested that these two pathways separate subliminal or sub-threshold stimuli from stimuli that are strong enough (supraluminal) to trigger an action potential in the sensory nerve. If this is correct, the matrix would be able to transfer and process very subtle information from the environment with a sensitivity and velocity far exceeding that of the nervous system. (a) Conventional method for study of receptors. In psychophysics, the intensity of a stimulus to a particular receptor is increased gradually until the subject reports a sensation. Stimuli too weak to elicit a sensation are termed subliminal; stronger signals are supraluminal. Neurophysiologists perform a similar experiment, increasing the strength of stimulus while recording the membrane potential of the afferent nerve. (b) The intensity sufficient to produce an action potential is termed threshold. Stimuli of lesser intensity, subthreshold, can cause small depolarizations of the afferent nerve, but are unsufficient to cause an action potential to develop. Supraluminal stimuli result in an action potential in the afferent nerve. (c) The well-documented sequence of events between the perception of a stimulus and an appropriate response such as a muscular activity. Information is conducted via the sensory nerve to the brain where it is combined with other information to determine if an action is appropriate. If so, various muscles will be activated. The spinal reflex can bypass the brain and produce a rapid response such as pulling the hand back from the hot stove. (d) Alternate pathway between sensation and action. The receptor is a cell with a cytoskeleton that connects across its cell surface to a continuous extracellular fiber network, the living matrix or ground regulation system. Signal transfer through this system could account for extremely fast and astonishingly coordinated responses that occur in the martial arts and peak athletic and artistic performances that require communication that is much faster than can be accomplished by nerve conduction, with its attendant synaptic delays. It is suggested that this is also the system that is compromised when emotional or traumatic memories lead to functional disorders, such as the case of "Dora" that led Freud to suggest the existence of the unconscious mind.

In contrast to psychophysics, neurophysiology studies the neural correlates of subliminal and supraliminal stimulation by using microelectrodes to record the electrical activity in a receptor nerve (afferent) while increasing the stimulation intensity until an action potential is produced (Figure 2a). Stimuli below threshold can produce a small depolarization of the nerve membrane, but no action potential is triggered until threshold is reached (Figure 2b).

The well-documented sequence of events between the perception of a stimulus and an adaptive action such as a muscular activity is illustrated in Figure 2c. Information is conducted via the sensory nerve to the brain where it is combined with other information to determine if an action is appropriate. If so, various muscles will be activated. The spinal reflex can produce a rapid response such as pulling the hand back from the hot stove before a person becomes consciously aware of the burn.

Semiconduction in the Living Matrix

Figure 2d describes one alternate pathway between the sensory system and action. This pathway is based on the fact that the receptor is a cell with a cytoskeleton that connects across the cell surface to a continuous fibrous network, the living matrix or ground regulation system that extends throughout the body. The living matrix is a term introduced by Oschman and Oschman (1993). It is also referred to as the "continuum pathway" in recognition of the continuity between the nuclear matrix, cytoskeleton, and extracellular matrix that extends throughout the body. This pathway is one candidate for the substrate involved in so-called conversion disorders. The matrix is the largest organ in the body, since it touches all of the other systems. We could refer to it as the "hardware" of the body, in contrast to the "wetware" that will be discussed in the following. The concept that the living matrix can transfer energy and information throughout the body evolved from Albert Szent-Györgyi's classic reports (1941a, 1941b) and documented in his books *Introduction to a Submolecular Biology* (1960) and *Bioelectronics* (1968) and his research papers.* Mark Bretscher (1971a, b) discovered that certain membrane proteins extend from the cell interior to the exterior, linking the cytoskeleton with the extracellular matrix. This was a key concept in the development of the living matrix concept, and added another dimension to the "ground regulation" concept developed by a group of German and Austrian researchers led by Alfred Pischinger (1975, 2007) and Hartmut Heine (2007) who pointed out that the fundamental unit of life is not the cell, but is a triad consisting of the cell, matrix and capillary.

Recall the quote about the paramecium at the beginning of this chapter. Sir Charles Sherrington (1951) recognized that the cell cytoskeleton might serve as the "nervous system" of the cell, and many modern cell biologists agree with this perspective.

Oschman (2003) hypothesized that sensory receptors transfer signals they receive from the environment to two anatomically distinct pathways. This concept arose during an attempt to understand the mechanisms involved in the effects of optometric phototherapy or Syntonics, in which a patient observes certain colors of light to relieve various disorders (Oschman, 2001). Syntonics was developed by Harry Riley Spitler (1941), who stated, "There exists a relationship which is largely predictable between light frequency, environment, and the restoration of health following departures from normal, which are still within the physiologic limits…"

Recalling the histology of the retina (Figure 3), there is a densely staining line called the outer limiting membrane (a) lying between the photoreceptor layer and the outer nuclear layer of the retina. Under the electron microscope, this "membrane" is revealed to be a precisely aligned planar array of densely spaced plaque-bearing junctions with bundles of actin filaments attached to them (b). This row of adhering junctions attaches the photoreceptor cells to Müeller cells, which are neuroglial connective tissue cells. It is suggested that subliminal or subthreshold stimuli create waves of conformational change or solitons that are conducted or semiconducted through the cytoskeletons of the photoreceptor cells, across the junctional complexes and into the Müeller cells, and thence throughout the living matrix of the body (Oschman, 2003). If the sensory stimulus is strong enough to depolarize the cell membrane of the receptor, the synapses at the base of the photoreceptor cells are activated and the signal jumps to the bipolar and other neurons, through the optic nerve, to the visual cortex and other brain areas.

---

*For a complete list of Albert Szent-Györgyi's books and articles, see *Biological Bulletin*, *174*, 234–240.

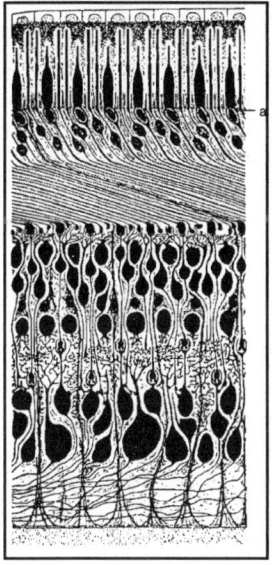 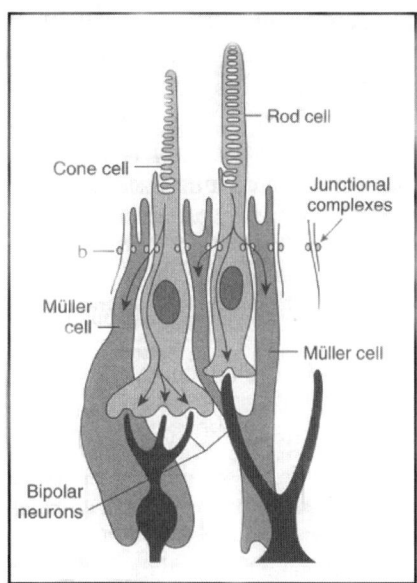

Figure 3. Histologists have identified a dense staining line called the outer limiting membrane (**a**) lying between the photoreceptor layer and the outer nuclear layer of the retina. With the electron microscope, this "membrane" is revealed to be precisely aligned planar array of densely spaced plaque-bearing junctions with bundles of actin filaments attached to them (**b**). This row of adhering junctions attaches the photoreceptor cells to the Müeller cells, which are neuroglial connective tissue cells. It is suggested that subliminal or sub-threshold stimuli create waves of conformational change that are conducted through the cytoskeletons of the photoreceptor cells, across the junctional complexes and into the Müeller cells, and thence throughout the living matrix of the body. If the sensory stimulus is strong enough to depolarize the cell membrane of the receptor, the synapses at the base of the photoreceptor cells are activated and the signal jumps to the bipolar and other neurons, through the optic nerve, and into the brain. This second pathway is the established neurological pathway that transfers nerve impulses digitally (all or none) at velocities of 100 or more meters per second (Figure 1c). The first pathway is via the living matrix/ground regulation system, which forms an analog network operating at hundreds or thousands of meters per second, as described above (Figure 1d). If this is correct, the matrix could transfer and process very subtle information from the environment at velocities far exceeding those taking place in the nervous system – characteristics often attributed to the unconscious.

This second pathway is the established neurological pathway that transfers nerve impulses digitally (all or none) at velocities of 100 or more meters per second (Figure 2c).

The living matrix/ground regulation system forms an analog network operating at hundreds or thousands of meters per second, as described previously (Figure 2d). From this perspective it can be hypothesized that there is a separation of subliminal or subthreshold stimuli from stimuli that are strong enough to trigger an action potential in the sensory nerve. If this is correct, the matrix could transfer and process very subtle information from the environment at velocities far exceeding those taking place in the nervous system—characteristics often attributed to the unconscious. This scheme recognizes a distinction between conscious awareness and thoughtful actions mediated by the nervous system and unconscious processing leading to authentic or automatic actions mediated by the living matrix or ground regulation system. While this concept is speculative, it could account for extremely fast and astonishingly coordinated responses that occur in the martial arts and peak athletic and artistic performances that require communication that is much faster than can be accomplished by nerve conduction, with its attendant synaptic delays. At the same time, the scheme also provides a means for producing and painful chronic muscle contraction (conversion disorders) because of subconscious phenomena such as repressed emotions.

Semiconductors

A semiconductor is a material with electrical conductivity that is intermediate between that of an insulator and a conductor. Importantly, the conductivity of a semiconductor can be modified in precise ways by introducing impurities in a process known in the electronics industry as doping. The ability to control conductivity in small and well-defined regions of semiconductor materials has led to the development of a broad array of miniaturized electronic devices that have become the basis for nearly all modern electronics. This is mentioned because most if not all biomolecules have semiconductor properties, and this fact is key to the development of the flourishing molecular electronics industry (e.g., Cuevas & Scheer, 2010). Moreover, the properties of organic semiconductors in living tissues can vary from place to place, allowing for the possibility that the structural fabric of cells and tissues can form a kind of biological electronic circuit with the ability to carry out processes that are directly analogous to those built into commercial transistors and integrated circuits. Specifically, the microcircuitry of the living body may be capable of conducting, storing, and processing energy and information and transforming energy from one form to another, using efficient high-speed electronic and quantum processes comparable to those found in transistors, integrated circuits, computers, and other electronic devices. Barnett (1986) described how molecules can act as string processors.

> The Primitive String Transformer (PST) is an abstract computing device to process analog or digital information algorithmically by transferring electrons from a donor to a polymer and switching a non-conjugated chain to a conjugated form, thereby delocalizing some of the electronic orbitals along the chain.

This is a profound concept! If living tissues can accurately be described in terms of microcircuitry, string processors, and integrated circuits comparable to those used in the electronics industry, a whole new understanding of the nature of life opens up.

The Mind of the Cell: "Wetware"

One of the major questions in biology is how living cells can carry out hundreds of thousands of processes per second with extremely high speed and efficiency, seemingly without errors. In his book *Wetware,* Dennis Bray (2009) proposed that all cells are built of molecular biochemical circuits that process information from the environment and perform logical operations, comparable in sophistication to those taking place in electronic devices. Bray defines *wetware* as the sum of all of the information-rich processes and "computations" taking place inside a cell, distinct from the solid *hardware,* because wetware relates to cell biochemistry—the interactions of dissolved molecules forming complex webs or circuits. He also suggested that the computational properties of cells provide the basis for the distinctive properties of living systems, including the ability to embody in their internal structures "images" of the world around them. This concept was supported by the work of Albrecht-Buehler (1992) who described a rudimentary form of cellular "vision" based on the light-sensing properties of a cytoskeletal component known as the centriole. After some 30 years of observation, Albrecht-Buehler concluded that single tissue cells have their own data- and signal-processing capacities that help control their movements and orientation (Albrecht-Buehler, 1985, 1992). These concepts, supported by the information that follows, could help explain the adaptability, responsiveness, and intelligence of cells and organisms. These cellular attributes probably extend into the extracellular or connective tissue terrain surrounding all of the cells within us.

High-Speed Processing in Cells and Tissues

Note that the "circuits" envisioned by Bray exist in "biochemical space"—they are based on enzymes, genes, and small sets of genes acting as switches, logic gates, oscillators, and other computational elements, with information conveyed through the cell in the form of small enzymatic products such as glucose or amino acids. Enzymatic products can move at very high velocities, as documented with techniques invented by Ahmed H. Zewail, who received the Nobel Prize in Physics in 1999 for the development of the world's fastest camera. Using ultrafast lasers, Zewail was able to show that reactants can move at speeds of the order of 1000 meters per second or 0.6 miles per second—about as fast as a rifle bullet. Hence, the biochemical "circuits" Bray described could allow for extremely fast flow of information and signal processing—one of the attributes of unconscious processing that has been difficult to explain in terms of neurophysiology. The fastest neurons propagate signals at 100–150 meters per second, with each synapse introducing a delay of 0.5 to 4 m sec (Katz & Miledi, 1965), greatly limiting the speed with which neural circuits can transmit and process sensory information and produce meaningful actions.

Zewail's discoveries mean that we might actually be able to use sophisticated molecular cameras to image unconscious processes taking place within individual neurons or other kinds of cells and tissues. Imagine biophysical study of psychological phenomena occurring at speeds 10 or more times faster than nerve transmission, using the "4D ultrafast diffraction and microscopy" developed by Zewail, which would make it possible to image transient subcellular and tissue correlates of unconscious processes in space and time with atomic-scale resolution! Perhaps studies of this kind will be part of the neuroscience and psychobiology research in the future.

The diameter of a typical human cell is about one-tenth of the diameter of a human hair (about 10 microns). If one takes the size of a typical cell and the velocity of chemical processes as determined by Zewail, one can see that a chemical signal could be propagated back and forth throughout a single cell literally millions of times in a second. If the unconscious mind supports extremely rapid responses, as some have proposed, Zewail's observations imply that there may be virtually no inherent limit to the speed of signaling and information processing in cells and tissues. Recent explorations of the quantum properties of such systems provide a basis for extremely fast signaling and, remarkably, simultaneous processing in multiple pathways. By going beyond the brain, one can envision unconscious mechanisms that extend throughout the body and that can operate 10 or more times faster than neural networks.

Interactions of Hardware with Wetware

Bray's focus was on "wetware" and he did not discuss the properties of the hardware—the possibilities that emerge from the study of the more solid cellular fabric with the methods of solid-state physics and soft-condensed-matter physics. Many if not all of the proteins and other molecules in the cytoskeleton, extracellular matrix, and connective tissues have semiconductor properties, with the capability of carrying out electronic, photonic, and other submolecular operations comparable in speed and subtlety to those taking place in integrated electronic or photonic circuits. In principle, such hardware systems can compete with or surpass wetware in terms of velocity of information flow and processing.

In the 1970s biochemists introduced the concept of the metabolon: a structural-functional complex formed between sequential enzymes of a metabolic pathway, held together by noncovalent interactions and structural elements of the cell such as integral membrane proteins and proteins of the cytoskeleton. The concept was first conceived by Kuzin (1970) in the USSR and adopted by Srere (1972) of the University of Texas for the enzymes of the tricarboxilic acid (Szent-Györgyi-Krebs) cycle. This hypothesis was accepted in the former USSR and further elaborated for the complex of glycolytic enzymes (Embden-Meyerhof-Parnas pathway) by Lyubarev and Kurganov (1986) and Kurganov and Lyubarev (1988a,b). The name "metabolon" was published in 1985 by Srere (1985).

Metabolons enable rapid and efficient channeling of an intermediary metabolic product from an enzyme directly as substrate into the active site of the consecutive enzyme of the metabolic pathway. In terms of the unconscious, the hardware concepts of the living matrix and the wetware of Bray converge at the cytoskeleton-associated metabolon, because changes in the tensions and charges on the matrix will influence enzymatic activities.

Quantum Coherence

Another way energy and information can move from place to place within the body involves groups of electrons, protons, atoms, and molecules vibrating in synchrony to create electromagnetic fields that operate at the speed of light. Physicists refer to free electrons as being present as a "cloud" or "gas" composed of mobile electrons in a material such as a crystal or a metal. The human body contains many structures that are best described as liquid crystals—materials that are intermediate between solids and liquids (Ho, 2010).

Quantum physical descriptions provide the most reliable and accurate pictures relevant to liquid crystals. The reason for this is that the standard chemical perspective focuses on atoms and molecules interacting with one another, dominated by atom-atom, atom-molecule, or molecule-molecule collisions. The perspectives of physics, quantum physics, quantum chemistry, and biophysics enable study of the forces and motions involved in chemical reactions at much smaller and more fundamental scales, the subatomic or electronic levels.

In the past, it was thought that the term "quantum fluid" applied only to clusters of atoms or subatomic particles that condense under extreme conditions of pressure and temperature. Much research has been done to demonstrate the existence of unusual properties such as superconduction, superfluidity, and quantum coherence that take place in other extreme conditions.

Under such conditions, electrons, atoms, and even molecules can be condensed into unusual states of matter known as Bose-Einstein condensates.* One of the leading theorists in the field of superconduction, Herbert Fröhlich, demonstrated that the Bose-Einstein condensation can take place in living tissues at body temperatures and pressures because of the high degree of order or crystallinity (identified by Ho as *liquid crystals*) in certain cellular and tissue components (Fröhlich, 1988). It had been thought that Bose-Einstein condensation could only take place at extremely low temperatures, as was demonstrated by Cornell and Wieman in 1995 using a gas of rubidium atoms cooled to 170 nanokelvin (nK). Under such conditions, a large fraction of the atoms collapsed into the lowest quantum state, at which point quantum effects become apparent on a macroscopic scale (Cornell & Wieman, 2001). Research in this field is driven, in part, by the need to reduce the size and increase the efficiency of electronic technologies. Engineers are constantly looking for applications that take advantages of the extraordinary quantum properties of materials so they can develop and manufacture efficient circuits composed of atoms or molecules.

Fröhlich (1968) concluded that giant dipolar molecules such as proteins, nucleic acids, and lipids in cellular membranes, which have enormous electrical fields of some 10^7 V/m across them, should vibrate intensely and coherently at characteristic frequencies and create a physical situation analogous to a Bose-Einstein condensation at body temperature. These molecular vibrations can build up into collective modes of both electromechanical oscillations (phonons or sound waves) and electromagnetic radiations (photons) that extend over large distances within the organism and that can also be radiated into the space surrounding the cell or tissue or the organism as a whole.

We are learning about energy transfers from the study of the energy harvesting systems in green plants (chloroplasts) and the energy utilization systems in animals (mitochondria). It is suggested that all of these processes may be part of unconscious processing. Recent research from the Fleming group at the University of California in Berkeley has revealed remarkable quantum processes taking place in the leaves of green plants:

> Wavelike electron energy transfer within the photosynthetic complex explains its extreme efficiency. It allows the excited electron to sample vast areas of phase space to find the most efficient path. (Engel et al., 2007)

Discussion

It is nearly a century since Freud suggested that his provisional ideas in psychology would one day be based on an organic substructure. This chapter begins to define such an organic substructure. Figure 4 is a summary.

Many of the hypotheses introduced here are speculative, but they are made with the confidence that emerging technologies will eventually validate or refute them. For example, Pienta & Coffee stated in 1991, "Cells and intracellular elements are capable of vibrating in a dynamic manner with complex harmonics, the frequency of which can now be measured and analyzed in a quantitative manner by Fourier analysis." In the decades since that statement was made, other technologies have been developed that can characterize activities in the molecular fabric of the living matrix/ground regulation systems and wetware. One valuable resource is a series of symposia on ultrafast phenomena in semiconductors and nanostructure materials, including living tissues. For example, the development of powerful ultra-fast laser pulsing technologies has led to the use of terahertz scanning

---

*Satyendra Nath Bose was an Indian mathematician and physicist who wrote a paper in 1924 describing a statistical theory for light. Albert Einstein showed that the same rules apply to atoms, as in a gas. Bose and Einstein collaborated to develop a mathematics called Bose-Einstein statistics, that describes the gas-like qualities of both electromagnetic radiation (light) and collections of coherent electrons or atoms. The theory describes the behavior of a group of particles in the same energetic state and accounts for the cohesive streaming of laser light and other quantum phenomena. The Bose-Einstein condensate is a dense collection of bosons, which are elementary particles or atoms with integer spin, named after Bose.

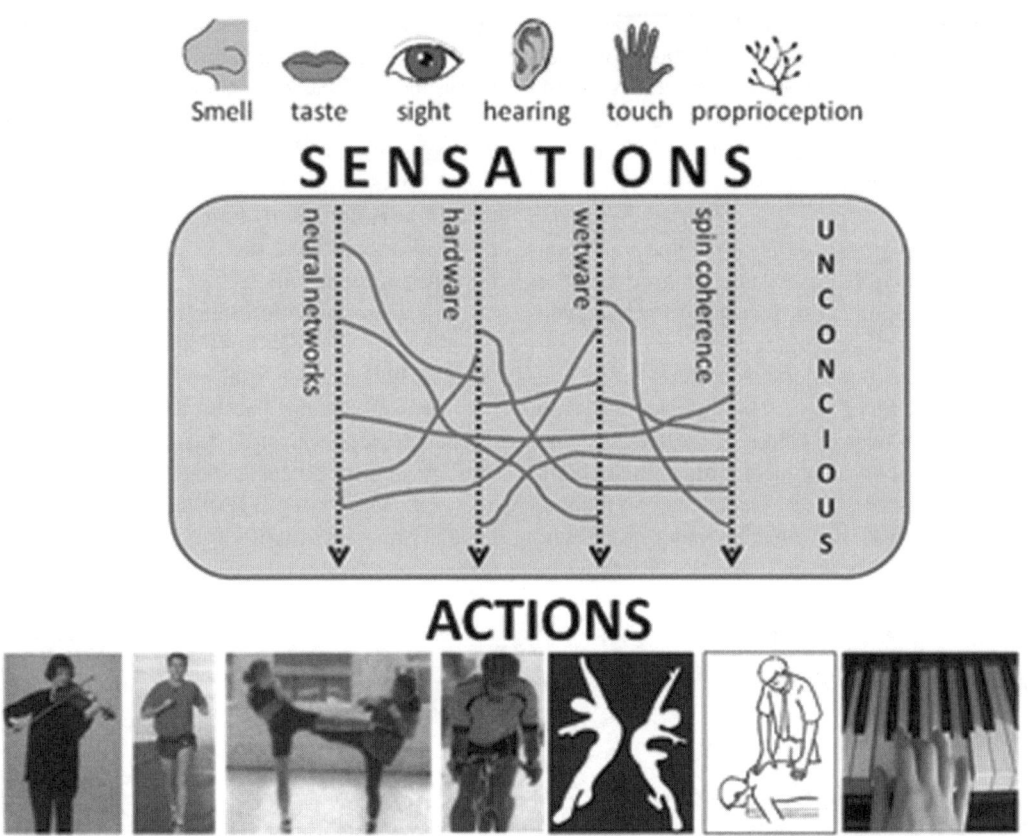

Figure 4. A summary of the concepts presented in this chapter. It is suggested that sensory information is processed by the unconscious mind in various ways that influence behavior (actions). Neural networks, hardware (the living matrix or ground regulation system), wetware (biochemical pathways) and quantum spin coherence are some of the information pathways that may be involved. These informational pathways interact with each other in various ways (red lines). The behavioral outcome is the result of both conscious and unconscious processes.

near-field infrared microscopy of biological materials (Schade, Holldack, Martin, & Fried, 2005). A second application of terahertz technologies involves spectroscopic methods for measuring the interactions between water and proteins at a very small time scales (Havenith, 2010). Atomic force microscopy can provide topographical information and measurements of mechanical stiffness, electrical conductance, resistivity, and magnetic properties at micro- and nano-scales in living material (Darling & Desai, 2012). The fascinating ideas of Bray, that is, a biochemical basis for "a computer in every cell," may be testable by the use of the methods introduced by Zewail in 1999.

One lesson from this discussion is the need for multidisciplinary and holistic approaches to the study of consciousness and the unconscious. Consider memory, for example. Neuroscientists have long been convinced that consciousness, the unconscious, and memory will eventually be found somewhere in the brain, although definitive locations for these phenomena have not been found in spite of an enormous amount of research. In this connection, it is useful to look at a statement by one of the leaders in neuroscience in the 20th Century, F. O. Schmitt (1903–1995), who founded the Neurosciences Research Program at MIT and served as its Chairman from 1962 to 1974.

Contrary to widespread belief, the problems of memory and consciousness are not likely to be resolved by further elaboration of electrophysiological techniques, however detailed. It is possible that much of the higher activity of the brain eludes detection by conventional electrophysiological methods. Only in giant macromolecular polymers is the diversity possible that is required for the specificity manifested in fundamental life phenomena. A polymer composed of 1,000 monomers of 4 monomer species (e.g., RNA) could have 4^{1000} variants; with 20 monomer species (e.g. collagen) there could be 20^{1000} variants! (Schmitt, 1961).

Giant arrays of liquid crystalline macromolecular polymers (e.g., collagen, Figure 5) occur throughout the human body as they form the connective tissues (Figure 6). They also form the perineural sheathes of the nervous system. A tiny neuron, a thousandth of an inch in diameter, has about 9 feet of cytoskeleton. Hence, there are close to a billion miles of semiconducting fibers in the brain. They form a sophisticated electronic communication network that may function independently or parallel to neural transmission. Polymers such as collagen, which are found throughout the body, are just as likely places for memory and consciousness as are neural networks! It is worthwhile to continue this exploration with the modern research tools that have been mentioned, because a thorough description of the cellular and tissue changes produced by physical or emotional trauma is a key issue for all branches of therapeutics.

An ever-widening circle of modern scholars is embracing the idea that mind, learning, memory, the unconscious, and consciousness are not confined to the brain. These are leading authorities in mathematics, physics, quantum physics, cosmology, brain science, cognitive psychology, and philosophy (e.g., Karl H. Pribram, David Bohm, Stuart Hameroff, Roger Penrose, Rupert

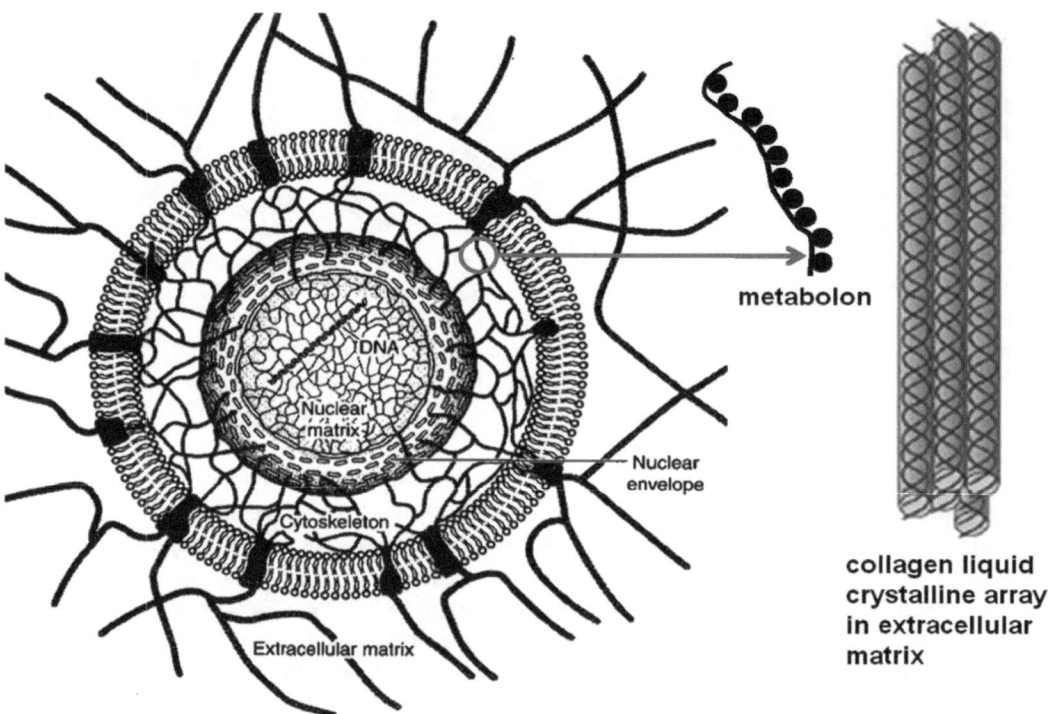

Figure 5. The living matrix consists of the various matrices within the cells, including the nuclear matrix, mitochondrial matrix (not shown here), and cytoskeleton, which connect to the extracellular matrix via the integrins that span the cell membranes. The metabolon is an assembly of enzymes for a particular metabolic pathway. Here we show 10 enzymes in sequence, as would be the case for glycolysis. Metabolons are structural-functional complexes formed between sequential enzymes of a metabolic pathway, held together by non-covalent interactions and structural elements of the cell such as integral membrane proteins and proteins of the cytoskeleton. The formation of metabolons allows rapid and efficient channeling of an intermediary metabolic product from an enzyme directly as substrate into the active site of the consecutive enzyme of the metabolic pathway. In terms of the unconscious, the hardware concepts of the living matrix and the wetware of Bray converge at the cytoskeleton-associated metabolon, because changes in the tensions and charges on the matrix will influence metabolic activities. The arrays of collagen molecules, each surrounded by a hydration shell, form the various tissues as shown in Figure 6.

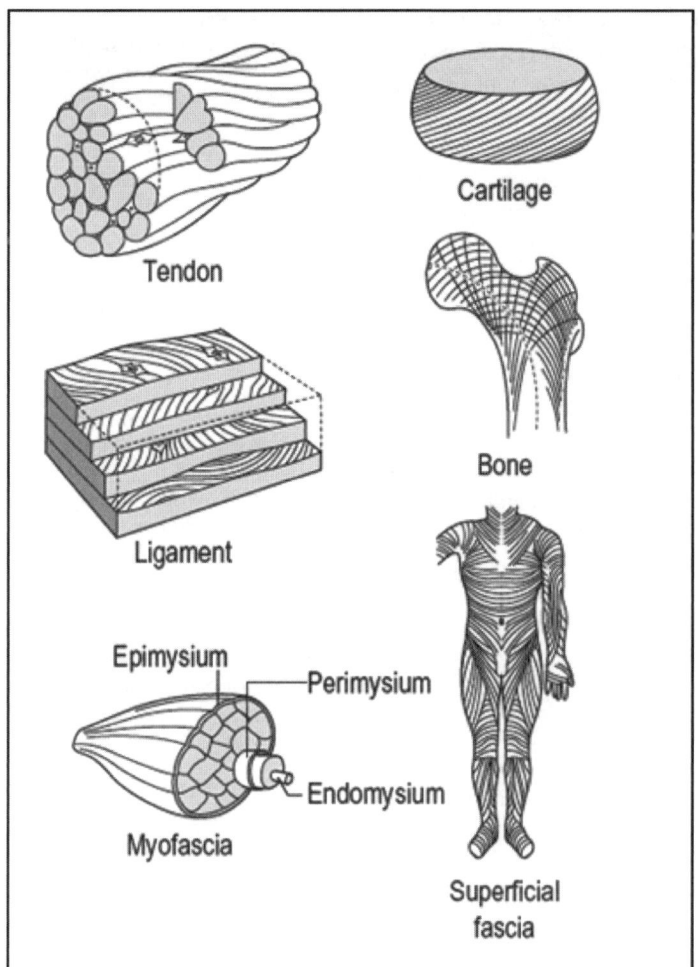

Figure 6. Connective tissues formed from arrays of collagen molecules. These tissues, along with muscles (also composed of liquid crystals) form some 75% of the body by weight.

Sheldrake, Edgar Mitchell, Hiroomi Umezawa, Deepak Chopra, Richard L. Amoroso, Ervin László, Rudolf E. Schild, and Francisco di Biase). For example, Carl Jung (1952) stated, "We must completely give up the idea of the psyche's being somehow connected with the brain, and remember instead the 'meaningful' or 'intelligent' behavior of the lower organisms, which are without a brain." Sir Charles Scott Sherrington focused on the cell cytoskeleton as a candidate for the "brain" of the cell. Neuroscientist Candace Pert (2004) stated, "Your body is your subconscious mind." Hence, while the dominant assumption in neuroscience is that consciousness is a by-product of the operations of the human brain, many established scholars with outstanding credentials are extending the inquiry beyond the brain and even beyond the body. For example, Stuart Hameroff collaborated with quantum physicist Roger Penrose to develop a model of memory and consciousness in which molecular arrays of microtubules in brain neurons are capable of storing information and regulating neuronal activities. The resulting model suggested a connection between biomolecular processes in brain microtubules and the fine-scale structure of the universe (Penrose, Hameroff, & Kak, 2011). If these phenomena are confirmed, it is probable that they apply equally to the extracellular macromolecular collagen arrays that form the bulk of structure of the human body (e.g., tendons, ligaments, fascia, bone, cartilage, superficial fascia, etc.).

The idea of a relationship between consciousness and the physical properties of space, has arisen again and again in scholarly inquiries. Some quantum physicists trace these concepts to ancient Buddhist and Vedic teachings, as summarized, for example, by Fritjof Capra in *The Tao of Physics* (1975) and in his subsequent writings. For a recent summary of these ideas, see a compilation of classic papers on *Consciousness and the Universe: Quantum Physics, Evolution, Brain, and Mind* published by the *Journal of Cosmology* (Penrose, Hameroff, & Kak, 2011). This compilation contains a series of articles by leading thinkers on the connections between the fine-scale structure of the cosmos and consciousness, including the roles of information fields in the origins of life and form. For example, in "The Quantum Hologram and the Nature of Consciousness," Apollo astronaut Edgar Mitchell, in collaboration with Robert Staretz (2011), presents a quantum holographic model to explain how all of creation learns, self-corrects, and evolves as a self-organizing, interconnected holistic system (see box). While these ideas do not appeal to some, they are resonant with the theoretical explorations and the experiences of the authors of this chapter.

> We present a new model of information processing in nature called the Quantum Hologram, which we believe is supported by strong evidence. This evidence suggests that quantum hologram is also a model that describes the basis for consciousness. It explains how living organisms know and use whatever information they know and utilize. It elevates the role of information in nature to the same fundamental status as that of matter and energy. We speculate that quantum hologram seems to be nature's built-in vast information storage and retrieval mechanism and one that has been used since the beginning of time (Mitchell & Staretz, 2011).

References

Albrecht-Buehler, G. (1985). Is cytoplasm intelligent too? In R. M. Dowben & J. W. Shay (Eds.), *Cell and muscle motility* (Vol. VI, pp. 1–21). New York, NY: Plenum Press.

———. (1992, September 1). Rudimentary form of cellular "vision." *Proceedings of the National Academy of Sciences of the United States of America, 89*(17), 8288–8292.

Allard, F., & Burnett, N. (1985). Skill in sport. *Canadian Journal of Psychology/Revue canadienne de psychologie, 39*(2), 294–312.

Barnett, M. P. (1986). Molecular systems to process analog and digital data associatively. In: F. L. Carter, R. E. Siatkowski, & H. Wohltjen (Eds.). *Molecular electronic devices: Proceedings of the 3rd International Symposium on Molecular Electronic Devices, Arlington, Virginia, 6–8 October, 1986.* Amsterdam: North-Holland Publishing.

Bray, D. (2009). *Wetware: A computer in every cell.* New Haven, CT: Yale University Press.

Bretscher, M. (1971a). A major protein which spans the human erythrocyte membrane. *Journal of Molecular Biology, 59,* 351–357.

———. (1971b). Major human erythrocyte glycoprotein spans the cell membrane. *Nature New Biology, 231,* 229–232.

Breuer, H. & Freud, S. (2000). *Studies on hysteria* (Reissue ed.) New York, NY: Basic Books Classics.

Brooks, S. J., Savov, V., Allzén, E., Benedict, C., Fredriksson, R., & Schiöth, H. B. (2012). Exposure to subliminal arousing stimuli induces robust activation in the amygdala, hippocampus, anterior cingulate, insular cortex and primary visual cortex: a systematic meta-analysis of fMRI studies. *Neuro Image, 59*(3), 2962–2973.

Brown, J. W. (1977). *Mind, brain, and consciousness: The neuropsychology of cognition.* New York, NY: Academic Press.

———. (1988). *The life of the mind: selected papers.* Hillsdale, NJ: Lawrence Erlbaum.

———. (Ed.) (1989). *Neuropsychology of visual perception.* Hillsdale, NJ: Lawrence Erlbaum.

———. (1991). *Self and process: Brain states and the conscious present.* New York, NY: Springer-Verlag.

Capra, F. (1975). *The tao of physics: An exploration of the parallels between modern physics and eastern mysticism.* Berkeley, CA: Shambhala.

Carpenter, W. (1874 [2012]). *Principles of mental physiology: With their applications to the training and discipline of the mind, and the study of its morbid conditions* (Classic reprint). Charleston, SC: Forgotten Books.

Cornell, E. A. & Wieman, C. E. (2001, December 8). Bose-Einstein condensation in a dilute gas: The first 70 years and some recent experiments. [Nobel lecture]. In T. Frangsmyr (Ed.), *Les Prix Nobel 2007.* Stockholm, Sweden: Nobel Foundation, 2002.

Cuevas, J. C. & Scheer, E. (2010). *Molecular electronics: An introduction to theory and experiment.* Hackensack, NJ: World Scientific.

Darling, E. M. & Desai, H. V. (2012, January). Force scanning for simultaneous collection of topographical and mechanical properties. *Microscopy and Analysis, 26*(1), 7–10.

Engel, G. S., Calhoun, T. R., Read, E. L., Ahn, T. K., Mancal, T., Cheng, Y. C., Blankenship, R. E., & Fleming, G. R. (2007, April 12). Evidence for wavelike energy transfer through quantum coherence in photosynthetic systems. *Nature, 446,* 782–786.

Freud, S. (1895 [1953]). *Project for a scientific psychology.* In S. Freud, *The complete psychological works of Sigmund Freud* (Standard ed., Vol. 1, pp. 283–397). London, UK: Hogarth Press.

———. (1914 [1957]). On narcissism: An introduction. In S. Freud, *The complete psychological works of Sigmund Freud* (Standard ed., Vol. 14, pp. 67–102). London, UK: Hogarth Press.

Fröhlich, H. (1968). Long range coherence and energy storage in biological systems. *International Journal of Quantum Chemistry, 2,* 641–649.

———. (Ed.) (1988). *Biological coherence and response to external stimuli.* Berlin: Springer Verlag.

Gescheider, G. (1997). *Psychophysics: The fundamentals* (3rd ed.). Hillsdale, NJ: Lawrence Erlbaum.

Gladwell, M. (2007). *Blink: The power of thinking without thinking.* New York, NY: Back Bay Books.

Havenith, M. (2010). THz spectroscopy as a new tool to probe hydration dynamics. In J-J. Song, K-T. Tsen, M. Betz, & A. Y. Elezzabia (Eds.), *Ultrafast Phenomena in Semiconductors and Nanostructure Materials XVI* (pp. 1–5). Bellingham, WA: SPIE Press.

Heine, H. (2007). *Lehrbuch der biologischen Medizin. Grundregulationkund Extrazellulare Matrix.* Stuttgart, Germany: Hippokrates Verlag.

Hellige, J. B. (2001). Hemispheric asymmetry: What's right and what's left. Cambridge, MA: Harvard University Press.

Ho, M-W. (2010). Liquid crystalline water, quantum molecular machines and the living state. ISIS Lecture at Biomaterials Symposium, YUCOMAT 2010, Plaza Hotel, Herceg Novi, Montenegro, September 6–10, 2010.

Jung, C. G. (1952 [2010]). *Synchronicity: An acausal connecting principle.* In *The Collected Works of C. G. Jung* (Vol. 8). NJ: Princeton University Press.

Katz, B. & Miledi, R. (1965, February 16). The measurement of synaptic delay, and the time course of acetylcholine release at the neuromuscular junction. *Proceedings of the Royal Society of London, Series B, Biological Sciences, 161*(985), 483–495.

Kurganov, B. I., & Lyubarev, A. E. (1988a). Hypothetical structure of the complex of glycolytic enzymes (glycolytic metabolon), formed on the membrane of erythrocytes. (In Russian). *Molekuliarnaia Biologiia, 22*(6), 1605–1613.

———. (1988b). Enzymes and multienzyme complexes as controllable systems. In V. P. Skulachev (Ed.), *Soviet Scientific Reviews: Section D, Physicochemical Biology Reviews* (Vol. 8, pp. 111–147). Glasgow, UK: Harwood Academic Publishers.

Kuzin, A. M. (1970). Structural-metabolic hypothesis in radiobiology. Moscow, Russia: Nauka Publishers.

Lyubarev, A. E. & Kurganov, B. I. (1986). Suprampolecular organisation of tricarboxilic acids cycle's enzymes (in Russian, p. 13). Proccedings of the All-Union Symposium "Molecular mechanisms and regulation of energy metabolism," Puschino, Russia.

Meyers, A. W., Whelan, J. P:, & Murphy, S. M. (1996). Cognitive behavioral strategies in athletic performance enhancement. *Progress in Behavor Modification, 30,* 137–164.

Mitchell, E. D. & Staretz, R. (2011). The quantum hologram and the nature of consciousness. In R. Penrose, S. Hameroff, & S. Kak (Eds.), Consciousness and the universe: Quantum physics, evolution, brain, and mind (pp. 933–963). Cambridge, MA: Cosmology Science Publishers.

Murphy, J. (1982). *The power of your subconscious mind.* New York, NY: Bantam.

Nørretranders, T. (1999). *The user illusion: Cutting consciousness down to size.* New York, NY: Penguin.

Oschman, J. L. (2001). Exploring the biology of phototherapy. *Journal of Optometric Phototherapy,* April 2001, 1–9.

———. (2003). Energy medicine in therapeutics and human performance. Boston, MA: Butterworth Heinemann.

Oschman, J. L. & Oschman, N. H. (1993, October). Matter, energy, and the living matrix. *Rolf Lines, 21*(3), 55–64.

Penrose, R., Hameroff, S., & Kak, S. (Eds.) (2011). *Consciousness and the universe: Quantum physics, evolution, brain, and mind.* Cambridge, MA: Cosmology Science Publishers.

Pert, C. (2004). *Your body is your subconscious mind* [Audio CD]. Louisville, CO: Sounds True.

Pienta, K. J. & Coffey, D. (1991). Cellular harmonic information transfer through a tissue tensegrity-matrix system. *Medical Hypotheses, 34,* 88–95.

Pischinger, A. (1975). *Matrix and matrix regulation. Basis for a holistic theory in medicine.* Ed. H. Heine. Heidelberg, Germany: Karl F. Haug Verlag GmbH.

———. (2007). *The extracellular matrix and ground regulation: Basis for a holistic biological medicine.* Berkeley, CA: North Atlantic Books.

Pressman, M. D. (1977, March). Mind over figures. *Skating Magazine, 54*(3).

———. (1979). Psychological techniques for the advancement of sports potential. In P. Klavora & J. Daniel (Eds.), *Coach, athlete, and the sport psychologist.* Toronto, Canada: University of Toronto.

———. (1980a). Psychological techniques for the advancement of sport potential. In R. W. Suinn (Ed.), *Psychology in sports: Methods of applications.* Minneapolis, MN: Burgess Publishing.

———. (1980b). Psychodynamic experience in an Olympic skating camp. In W. F. Straub (Ed.), *Sports psychology: An analysis of athlete behavior.* Ithaca, NY: Movement Publications.

Schade, U., Holldack, K., Martin, M. C., & Fried, D. (2005). THz near-field imaging of biological tissues employing synchrotron radiation. In K-T. Tsen, J-J. Song, & H. Jiang (Eds.), *Ultrafast Phenomena in Semiconductors and Nanostructure Materials IX* (pp. 46–52). Bellingham, WA: SPIE Press.

Schmitt, F. O. (1961). Molecule-cell, component-system reciprocal control as exemplified in psychophysical research. In *Molecular structure and biochemical reactions, Robert A. Welch Foundation conferences on chemical research* (Vol. V, Chapter III). Houston, TX: Robert A. Welch Foundation.

Sherrington, C. S. (1951). *Man on his nature.* Garden City, NJ: Doubleday Anchor.

Spitler, H. R. (1941). The syntonic principle. Eaton, OH: College of Syntonic Optometry.

Srere, P. A. (1972). Is there an organization of Krebs cycle enzymes in the mitochondrial matrix? In R. W. Hanson & W.A. Mehlman (Eds.), *Energy metabolism and the regulation of metabolic processes in mitochondria* (pp. 79–91). New York, NY: Academic Press.

———. (1985). The metabolon. *Trends in Biochemical Sciences, 10,* 109–110.

Suinn, R. M. (1985). Imagery rehearsal: Application to performance enhancement. *Behavior Therapist, 8,* 155–159.

Szent-Györgyi, A. (1941a). Towards a new biochemistry? *Science, 93,* 609–611.

———. (1941b). The study of energy levels in biochemistry. *Nature, 148,* 157–159.

———. (1960). Introduction to a submolecular biology. New York, NY: Academic Press.

———. (1968). Bioelectronics. New York, NY: Academic Press.

Warner, L. & McNeill, M. E. (1988). Mental imagery and its potential for physical therapy. *Physical Therapy, 68,* 516–521.

Zewail, A. H. (1999, December 8). Femtochemistry: Atomic-scale dynamics of the chemical bond using ultrafast lasers. [Nobel lecture]. In Ingmar Grenthe (Ed.), *Nobel Lectures, Chemistry 1996–2000.* Singapore: World Scientific Publishing, 2003.

Chapter 3
PTSD, Neurodynamics, and Memory
John Arden

Abstract

Posttraumatic stress disorder (PTSD) has gained considerable attention over the past 25 years, and important questions of interest to the mental health community have arisen over this time. What makes some people develop PTSD while others do not? What factors contribute to the vulnerability of some and the resiliency of others? How have therapeutic approaches to PTSD changed? Is there a coherent understanding of how to help people who have been traumatized that goes beyond particular theoretical schools? Can new insights be gained from neuroscience and memory research that look for common denominators? Working within a three-phase approach as best practice for the treatment of PTSD, the focus of this article is on Phase 2: Focused Work on Traumatic Memories. This phase forms the heart of the therapeutic effort and involves the integration of the dysregulated memory systems, both implicit and explicit. Prior to a consideration of the processes of memory, the chapter examines the complex neurodynamics of PTSD, including the roles of the amygdala and the hippocampus, in order to identify the most efficacious therapeutic approaches.

Keywords: PTSD, resilience, memory, hippocampus, amygdala, emotion, hormones, neurotransmitters

John Arden, PhD, author and psychologist, is the director of training in mental health for Kaiser Permanente, Northern California. Among his numerous books are *Brain-Based Therapy with Adults* and *Brain-Based Therapy with Children and Adolescents* (both with Lloyd Linford), *Conquering Post-Traumatic Stress Disorder* (with Victoria Beckner), and *Rewire Your Brain*. Send correspondence to John Arden, 900 Lakeville Highway, Petaluma, CA 94954, or john.arden@kp.org.

The effects of trauma have always interested me, in part due to the traumatic experiences of my Armenian relatives. Those who escaped the genocide perpetrated by the Turks brought with them traumatic memories of watching their relatives murdered in front of them or narrowly escaping death with one eye or having been brutally raped. Why did some of them develop posttraumatic stress disorder (PTSD) and some did not? What contributed to the vulnerability of some and the resiliency of others?

During the past few years I have taken part in the Best Practices research group for the Kaiser Permanente Medical Centers. We, like many groups, recommend a phased approach to helping people with PTSD. A three-phase approach to the treatment of PTSD has been endorsed by the International Society for the Study of Trauma and Dissociation (Brown, Scheflin, & Hammond, 1998; Chu, 1998; Herman, 1992; Van der Hart, Brown, & Van der Kolk, 1989). Although Phases 1 and 3 are not the focus of this article, it is important to note what they are.

Phase 1: Establishing Safety Stabilization and Symptom Reduction is employed immediately after a traumatic event when victims are provided with support through a crisis intervention model (Slaikeu, 1990). Therapists can provide "psychological first aid" to stabilize, calm, and orient the victim. It is important to note that Critical Incident Debriefing administered immediately after the trauma is considered countertherapeutic (Barlow, 2010). Best practice in Phase 1 is viewed as providing some initial psychoeducational support. Support for this model comes from research with trauma victims who were administered the drug propranolol immediately after the trauma. Compared to controls, this group was less prone to develop PTSD. This practice allows for less traumatic memory to be encoded because of the lowering of elevated stress hormones (Vaiva et al., 2003; Pitman et al., 2002).

Once elevated stress hormones drop to a new (albeit elevated) baseline, Phase 2 of therapy is Focused Work on Traumatic Memories (the subject of this paper), which involves the integration of the dysregulated memory systems, both implicit and explicit memory. Emotional engagement with traumatic memories is a critical part of recovery, whereas avoidance of engagement serves to maintain PTSD symptoms (Zoellner, Fitzgibbons, & Foa, 2001).

Phase 3: Integration and Rehabilitation involves the movement toward long-term recovery and the development of resilience that can contribute to what Tedeschi (1999) refers to as "posttraumatic growth." Developing a sense of meaning and direction in life is paramount. Having experienced traumatic event(s) necessitates posttraumatic growth—broadening one's sense of self, relationships, and philosophy of life. This "self" organization (borrowed from complexity theory) involves helping clients acknowledge their connection to the world and depth of meaning.

Phase 2 forms the heart of the therapeutic effort. The foundation for this phase is based on the integration of implicit and explicit memory systems. Before launching into a discussion on memory and therapeutic approaches, let us first examine the neurodynamics of PTSD. From this framework we can make better sense of what might be the most efficacious therapeutic approaches.

Neurodynamic Aspects

Over the past 15 years neuroimaging studies involving the PTSD symptom provocation have indentified some consistent findings including reduced activity in the left hemisphere, the dorsolateral prefrontal cortex (DLPFC), the hippocampus, and Broca's area. These studies also have shown increased activation in the parahippocampus gyrus, the posterior cingulate, and the amygdala (Bremner, 2002; Nutt & Malizia, 2004; Rauch, 1996).

The decreased activity in Broca's area appears to correspond to the difficulty in coherently expressing a narrative of the traumatic event (Hull, 2002). And the dysfunction of the DLPFC may be associated with problems in working memory, language, cognition, and integration of verbal expression with emotions.

Failure to regulate the activity of the amygdala has been one of the most consistent findings reported for PTSD. There appears to be a range of hyperactivity of the amygdala based on the type of trauma. For example, the general pattern of amygdala activation for PTSD lies midway between those for combat-exposed individuals and non-traumatized controls, indicating partial or less effective regulation of amygdala activation than combat-exposed controls (Britton, Phan, Taylor, Fig, & Liberzon, 2005).

Consistent with these findings it has been reported that PTSD is associated with failure to activate the anterior cingulate cortex (ACC). Meanwhile there is diminished medial prefrontal cortex (mPFC) activity in response to traumatic memories. For example, studies have utilized PET to measure patterns of neural activity associated with traumatic images and sounds have shown decreased activity in the left prefrontal cortex (L-PFC) and anterior cingulate cortex (Bremner et al., 1999).

Given that the ACC is important in monitoring emotional experience, and that there is generally greater intensity of negative emotions associated with PTSD, this neurodynamic pattern may represent a failure of this region to exert appropriate top-down inhibition of the amygdala. Also, since the L-PFC is associated with positive emotion there is a breakdown in monitoring and maintaining positive emotion. This picture, coupled with the studies showing increased amygdala and R-PFC activity (associated with negative emotion), reflects a failure to inhibit negative emotion.

Hippocampal Volume Update

Beginning in the 1990s studies related to adults with PTSD have shown reductions in hippocampal volume. Using MRI-based measurement of hippocampal volume, Bremner has shown reduced volumes for combat related PTSD (Bremner et al., 1995) and childhood physical and sexual abuse related PTSD (Bremner et al., 1997).

The initial explanatory model for hippocampal volume reductions described how high levels of cortisol have been associated with a range of separate neuroanatomical effects on the hippocampus, including the impairment of synaptic plasticity, the inhibition of neurogenesis, and ultimately neuronal death (Sapolsky, 2003). In general, the hippocampal deficits occurring as a result of excitotoxicity and the cortisol cascade, which include the retraction of dendritic processes, reduced synaptic plasticity, and the inhibition of neurogenesis, are thought to be potentially reversible (Sapolsky, 2003; Alderson & Novack, 2002).

The aversive effects of high stress are in contrast with the effects of moderate stress. This variation involves different types of receptors in the hippocampus. At low levels of stress there is a heavy occupancy of mineralocorticoid receptors in the hippocampus. The classic memory impairment appears to be associated with high levels of stress and occupancy of cortisol receptors.

The old model that PTSD is associated with hippocampal volume reductions changed with reports of traumatized children who had not suffered from hippocampal shrinkage (De Bellis et al., 1999; Karl, Malta, & Maercker, 2006). Indeed, the hippocampal size differences between adults and children with PTSD have been a topic of much discussion. This discrepancy may reflect a gradual adverse effect on the structure of the hippocampus so that it may not be evident until postpubertal development, or that it may be an inherent vulnerability for chronic PTSD that persists into adulthood (Gilbertson et al., 2002).

Though the reduction in hippocampal volume does not appear at the time of the trauma, it does appear with the passage of time. Additionally, in contrast to people without PTSD (who have hippocampal asymmetry, with the left larger than the right), adults who experienced childhood abuse have been reported to have near symmetry. Woon and Hedges (2008) found that maltreatment resulting in adult PTSD may disrupt normal hippocampal development manifested as hippocampal asymmetry. They also found evidence for bilateral hippocampal volume reductions for adults that had experienced abuse during childhood; but this reduction was not evident in children who had experienced abuse. This study supports the view that the hippocampal volume reduction occurs sometime between childhood and adulthood and those reductions are associated with symptom severity of PTSD.

The failure to find reductions in hippocampal volumes in children with PTSD, which have been found in adults with PTSD, led some researchers to wonder if smaller hippocampal volumes represent a predisposing factor instead of a result of PTSD. In an interesting counterpoint to the glucocorticoid cascade hypothesis, whereby cortisol is thought to lead to hippocampal volume reductions in PTSD patients, Gilbertson and colleagues (2002) explored a "vulnerability hypothesis," which suggests that people with premorbid smaller hippocampi are more vulnerable to PTSD. In response to trauma these people overreact to traumatic events because they have a less viable internal thermostat to shut down cortisol release.

In an effort to determine if the reduction of hippocampal volume is a cause or a risk factor for PTSD, Gilbertson and colleagues (2002) compared monozygotic twin brothers, one who had combat related PTSD and the other who never went to war. These researchers found a concordance between the twins regardless of combat status. Both had smaller hippocampal volumes. These results suggest that the vulnerability hypothesis may be viable as a possible partial explanation for increased risk. On the other hand, Bremner and colleagues reported a 9% reduction in hippocampal volume in twins with combat-related PTSD relative to their non-combat exposed twin brothers (Bremner, 1999). These studies support the notion of a combined genetic and environmental contribution to smaller hippocampal volume in PTSD.

Amygdala Activity

The general model of PTSD envisions amygdala hyperactivity not inhibited by mPFC. This includes heightened amygdala activity even in the resting state. Thus, while high levels of stress appear to be corrosive to the hippocampus, the same stress can produce enhanced dendritic arborization in the amygdala (Vyas, Mitra, Rao, & Chattarji, 2002; Vyas, Bernal, & Chattarji, 2003). Overall there is a positive relationship between the degree of amygdala activity and anxiety symptom severity.

A further illustration of heightened amygdala activity comes from researchers who have found increased blood flow in the amygdala, reflecting overactivity in patients with PTSD (Pissiota et al., 2002; Semple et al., 2000). Correspondingly, there is reduced grey matter volume in the mPFC (Carrion et al., 2001; De Bellis et al., 2002). The reduction in the mPFC represents the inability to inhibit the overactivity of the amygdala.

During the past several years there has been an accumulation of evidence that extinction does not erase or undo fear learning. Indeed, after extinction a conditional fear can return in a range of circumstances, including the simple passage of time via spontaneous recovery, exposure to the unconditioned stimulus, or exposure to the conditioned stimulus in a novel context. The recovery or reappearance of fear indicates that extinction training actually involves new learning via the mPFC, hippocampus, and amygdala to inhibit the expression of conditioned fear rather than eliminating the underlying representation of conditioned fear (Phelps, 2009).

The Role of Norepinephrine

Norepinephrine (NE) plays a major role in the pathophysiology of PTSD. Not surprisingly a hyperactive amygdala can trigger elevated levels of NE through its rich connections with the locus coeruleus (LC), which is the primary source of NE in the brain. Built into the presynaptic (releasing) membranes are alpha-2 auto receptors that provide a breaking function for NE. Thus, when NE is released by the presynaptic neuron it makes contract with both the postsynaptic and presynaptic neurons. When it makes contact with the postsynaptic neuron, it can trigger an action potential. When NE interlocks with the alpha-2 autoreceptor on the presynaptic neuron, which released the NE, it will act to slow down the release of NE.

If the alpha-2 presynaptic NE autoreceptor is agonized (blocked), however, the braking action does not occur. Yohimbine and caffeine are alpha-2 agonists. When a person with PTSD consumes excessive amounts of yohimbine or caffeine they may experience excessive NE, which may precipitate a panic attack. Alternatively, a person may have hyposensitive alpha-2 NE autoreceptors, which are insensitive to NE, and do not act to shut down NE. As a result of their insensitivity, NE is not shut down, but rather, is increased.

Several factors impair the PFC of which elevations of NE is part. These include: (1) low serotonin and the corresponding reduction of the PFC's capacity to inhibit the overactivity of the amygdala; (2) elevation of NE, through activation of the alpha-1 adrenergic receptors; and (3) increases in cortisol and its interactions with catecholines.

These factors ramp up anxiety through unleashing the amygdala and further trigger the release of NE through the LC, and dopamine via the ventral tegmental area, as well as acetylcholine via the dorsolateral tegmental nucleus. All these factors further dampen the PFC's capacity for problem solving and rational behavior. Consequently, there is a heightened tendency toward startle response, vigilance, insomnia, flashbacks, intrusive memories, and increased fear conditioning.

Though NE, when excessive, can act to take the PFC offline through the alpha-1 adrenergic receptors, moderate levels can actually act to enhance PFC activation through the alpha-2A receptors. This underscores the utility of a moderate degree of activation. It is also a moderate degree of activation that is critical for neuroplasticity through the glutamate circuits and specifically the NMDA (N-methyl-D-aspartate) receptors. These dynamics underscore the efficacy of exposure and the "safe emergency," which I will address.

Complexity in the HPA Activity

By the mid 1990s researchers were reporting that victims of trauma and chronic stress experienced wide variations in elevations in cortisol levels. Yehuda and colleagues found that some combat veterans, Holocaust survivors, and other trauma victims actually had reduced cortisol secretion as well as other factors indicating abnormal hypothalamic-pituitary-adrenal (HPA) activity (Yehuda, Boisoneau, Lowy, Giller, 1995; Yehuda, McFarlane, & Shalev, 1998). The most robust evidence comes from patients who experienced chronic and intractable PTSD. By 2000, stress-related hypocortisolism gained considerable attention (Gunnar & Vazquez, 2001; Fries, Hesse, Hellhammer, & Hellhammer, 2005).

Yehuda (2001) has suggested that, although PTSD is associated with hyperactivity in the HPA axis, it leads secondarily to reduced cortisol levels through negative feedback. In a meta-analysis of 107 studies on hypocortisolism in the morning, Miller, Chen, and Zhou (2007) found that the dysregulation in cortisol reflected greater concentrations of afternoon/evening cortisol, (especially if the person was subjected to shame), a flatter diurnal rhythm, and a higher daily volume of cortisol output. They note that collectively these findings suggest that chronic stress is accompanied by a deregulated pattern of secretion through lower than normal morning output, a higher than expected secretion across the rest of the day, and a flattened diurnal rhythm. Also, there was evidence that cerebrospinal fluid concentrations of corticotropin-releasing hormone (CRH) were significantly increased.

There seems to be a time factor operative here. The more months that had elapsed since the stress first emerged, the lower a person's morning cortisol, daily volume, and adrenocorticotropic hormone (ACTH). On the other hand, when chronic stressors were still present in the person's environment, morning, afternoon/evening, and daily cortisol outputs were significantly higher.

Miller, Chen, and Zhou (2007) also examined whether HPA activity varies based on the nature of the threat. For example, if stress involves how threatened a person is physically, there tends to be a higher and flat cortisol output. Though morning cortisol can be lower, afternoon/evening output is higher. If the stress is of a social nature (i.e., divorce), the overall cortisol output is higher, including morning, afternoon, and evening.

The issue of when cortisol levels are high or low may be correlated with vulnerability to developing PTSD. For example, some studies have shown that initially low urinary cortisol concentrations immediately after the trauma predict subsequent PTSD diagnosis in adults (Yehuda, McFarlane, & Shalev, 1998; Delahanty, Nugent, Christopher, & Walsh, 2005).

It appears that a marked elevation in cortisol in the evening is a more reliable prediction of later PTSD than measures of cortisol during other times of the day. Also, elevations of pro-inflammatory cytokines such as interleukin (IL)-6 soon after the trauma, is predictive of PTSD development 6 months later.

Elevated cytokines have shown to be not only indicators of the inflammatory response to physical and emotional stress, but also of disruption of the HPA axis (Chrousos, 1995). It also appears that an elevation in cytokines is significantly correlated with evening cortisol. Several studies have examined the immune system function of adults with PTSD and found increased levels of pro-inflammatory cytokines circulating or in the cerebral spinal fluid (Maes et al., 1999; Baker et al., 2001).

The secretion of IL-6 inflammatory cytokines can also be triggered by activating B-adrenergic receptors, with increases in NE. Inflammation can also occur through other aspects of acute stress including the CRH/P-histamine axis and by the combination of elevated cortisol and IL-6 (Elenkov, Iezzoni, Daly, Harris, & Chrousos, 2005). It has been shown that children who experienced trauma and also had elevations of IL-6 and evening cortisol were more likely to develop PTSD than children who experienced trauma and did not have those elevations (Papanicolaou, Wilder, Manolagas, & Chrousos, 1998).

Further complexity of the stress response systems occurs when there is hypersecretion of CRH released by the hypothalamus that may lead to an adaptive downregulation of CRH receptors in the anterior pituitary (Bremner et al., 1997). This downregulation may be adaptive to regulate pituitary hypertrophy because, without it, the elevated CRH would result in higher cortisol levels and damage to multiple systems including the hippocampus. This mechanism, therefore, involves a feedback system that is an attempt to put on the brakes. But it is not without adverse consequences. Pituitary volumes were found to be significantly larger in pubertal/postpubertal maltreated pediatric subjects with PTSD (Thomas & De Bellis, 2004). The duration of the abuse correlated negatively with pituitary volume.

Ramping up of this amygdala-HPA system involves the process known as "priming" or sensitization that occurs when responses to repeated stress increase in magnitude. This phenomenon reflects the chronic compensatory adaptation of the amygdala-HPA axis long after trauma exposure so that ACTH and cortisol are set at lower 24-hour leads. Other hormones such as arginine, vasopressin, and the catecholamines act synergistically with CRH. Thus, when a new emotion stressor is experienced, the amygdala-HPA axis functions are enhanced through higher ACTH and higher 24-hour urinary free cortisol concentration in response to stress. Thus, this primed system hyper-responds to stress (De Bellis, Hooper, & Sapia, 2005).

Finally, one last note about the breakdown of this system. The interaction with the noradrenergic system and CRH results in dysregulation of serotonin and increases the risk of depression. This has led theorists to note that people suffering from PTSD are at risk for developing a major depression. Indeed, Breslau and colleagues (2000) showed that onset of major depression is significantly increased for people who are exposed to trauma compared to those who are not exposed.

Based on this background of neurodynamics we can move on to a discussion of how a person suffering from PTSD may experience dysregulated memory systems. Since our memory systems form the fabric of who we are, a coherent therapeutic approach necessitates putting the memory systems in perspective.

Memory and Neurodynamics

People with PTSD typically remember that the traumatizing event happened but describe blank periods or gaps in the details of what occurred. Their recollections of these details are often vague, unclear, and disorganized (Harvey & Bryant, 1999). These symptoms are largely related to the differing effects of explicit and implicit memories corresponding to the hippocampus and the amygdala, respectfully.

The reported damage to the hippocampus among PTSD patients, via both cortisol and excitotoxicity, has shown to be associated with verbal memory deficits (Bremner, Krystal, Southwick, & Charney, 1995). Consistent with these findings, it is reported that PTSD patients also have declarative and autobiographical memory problems. For example, inpatient adolescents who had experienced trauma were reported to have reduced autobiographical memory with the degree of memory loss correlated with the number and severity of traumatic events (De Decker, Hermans, Raes, & Eelen, 2003).

Yehuda and colleagues (1995) found deficits and semantic memory related to adult veterans with PTSD compared to controls. Clark and colleagues (2003) explored working memory of people with PTSD utilizing PET technology and found significantly less activation of the left dorsolateral prefrontal cortex (DLPFC), which is associated with working memory, in patients with PTSD compared to controls.

The dynamics of memory and asymmetrical hemisphere activation has been explored with people with PTSD. Teicher (2000) found that people with a childhood history of abuse tend to use their left hemisphere when thinking about neutral memories. When they recall early upsetting memories they use their right hemisphere. Control subjects tended to have more integrated and bilateral response to recalling both neutral and traumatic memories. The abused subjects had hyperactivated right hemispheres, but their left hemispheres appeared developmentally arrested. A similar pattern was found with frontal lobe asymmetry (Van der Kolk, 2003).

Implicit and Explicit Memory Systems

The single representation theory of memory that has gained influence with many anxiety researchers oriented to cognitive behavior therapy (CBT) envisions networks involving many thousands of nodes with dense interconnections between them. A person, feature, shape, concept, or emotion is represented by a node. The representation consists of patterns of interconnections between the nodes. Building on this theory, Lang (1985) proposed that a frightening experience creates a "fear network" in memory, consisting of information about the traumatic event, meaning information, and the response information about emotional and physiological reactions. Reactivation of the fear network automatically occurs when the person with PTSD encounters a situation that matches cues or features of the original fear network, which then produces the same physiological responses and interpretation of being in danger.

Based on these ideas, Edna Foa and colleagues (1998) developed the Emotional Processing Theory. They proposed a variety of ways that memories from frightening events differ from memories from a traumatic event. For example, large numbers of stimulus danger interconnections between stress-related nodes become stronger than their connections to non–trauma related nodes. The memory networks contain large numbers of response elements associated with negative self-appraisals that include thoughts of being vulnerable and weak. Also, they argue that the severity of the traumatic event leads to disrupted cognitions and fragmented and disjointed fear structures.

Teasdale and Barnard (1993) were some of the first to point out the limits of the single-representation network model, based on the premise that it only represents one node for each emotion. A single level would not account for how an emotionally laden "hot" way of remembering trauma on one occasion, can be remembered in a more detached "cool" way on another occasion. These extra dimensions are critical to recognize and integrate in therapy. For example, a client can understand that even though she feels like she is a bad person, she can be a good person.

Owing perhaps to its adaption to the CBT perspective where language is paramount, the single network model cannot account for levels of meaning beyond that of words or sentences. Meaning and significance of memory is complex, multilayered, and beyond the reductionism that words provide (Dalgleish, 2004). Moreover, memory of a traumatic event(s) involves implicit as well as explicit memory.

Addressing some of the limitations of this single representation network theory, Brewin (2003) proposed a Dual Processing Theory that accounts for such phenomena as flashbacks and other non–verbally accessible memories. Brewin (2005) highlighted the dynamic relationship between the two memory systems—situationally accessible memories (SAMs) and verbally accessible memories (VAMs), which are essentially implicit and explicit memory systems, respectfully. Accordingly, the VAM system involves the hippocampus, while the SAM involves the amygdala.

The heavy emphasis on explicit memory leads to a limitation of the fear network model—conceived as composed of semantic and highly organized memories—but it does not comprehensively account for implicit memory. According to the Dual Representational Theory trauma information can be stored as VAMs on the conscious memory level or SAMs, which are largely nonconscious. Whereas VAMs can be accessed in therapy through deliberate recall, SAMs are only accessible through cues that activate the nonconscious networks (Brewin, Dalgleish, & Joseph, 1996).

Consistent with the dimensions of explicit memory that are cortically and hippocampally driven, the VAM system comprises the narrative memory of the trauma. These memories are autobiographical and can be deliberately retrieved. VAM system memories of the trauma comprise the context, including the past, present, and future.

"These memories are available for verbal communication with others, but the amount of information they contain is restricted because they only record what has been consistently attended to. Diversion of attention to the immediate source of threat and the effects of high levels of arousal greatly restrict the volume of information that can be registered during the event itself" (Brewin, 2005, p. 139).

A traumatized individual uses the VAM system to evaluate the trauma both at the time it is happening, and afterward, as she asks herself how the event could have been prevented and/or the consequences and implications of the experience on the future. Brewin and colleagues refer to the emotions that accompany VAM system memories as "secondary emotions" because they were not experienced at the time of the trauma itself. They are directed at the past (regret or anger about careless risks taken) or the future (sadness at the loss of cherished plans and hopelessness at the thoughts of not finding fulfillment). These secondary emotions involve guilt and shame over the perceived failure of having not prevented the event.

The SAM system, by contrast, contains information that has been obtained from lower-level processing of the traumatic scene which includes sights, sounds, and bodily sensations such as the changes in heart rate, temperature, or pain that were too briefly apprehended to be bound together in conscious memory required for the VAM system. The SAM system is consistent with implicit memory that is largely amygdala driven and accounts for flashbacks that can be triggered involuntarily by situational reminders of the trauma, which may include sights and sounds or physical feelings or emotions.

The interplay between VAMs and SAMs can be influenced by the degree of intensity of emotion. Since VAMs are highly dependent upon the hippocampal-PFC memory system, during periods of intense emotion they can be superseded by lower level systems that involve the SAMs—the hyperactivity of the amygdala. In such situations the SAM system tends to become hyperactive.

Thus, during these periods of intense emotion associated with traumatic experiences, there tend to be a reduction of hippocampally dependent processing of information (underlying the VAMs—explicit memory) and the formation of SAMs due to heightened amygdala reactivity. The increase in SAMs and the decrease in VAMs correspond to increased trauma reminders in the form of flashbacks triggered by sights, sounds, and smells that are experienced as a sense of timeless threat.

Because they are amygdala driven, and part of the implicit memory system, the non–hippocampally dependent memories (SAMs) appear to be more resistant to change and the passage of time. In contrast, VAMs are far more vulnerable to distortion/modification over time. Thus, the SAM system is not restricted to verbally coded memories and is more extensive. Because they are difficult to communicate to a therapist, SAMs (implicit memories) are also difficult to update by a purely verbal based approach. Flashbacks, for example, are spontaneous and difficult to control because it's awkward to attempt to regulate exposure to sights, smells, sounds, and so on that act to trigger them. The emotions triggered have been referred to as "primary emotions," consisting of fear, helplessness, and horror (Grey, Holmes, & Brewin, 2001). The more drawn out and extended the traumatic experience, the more the tendency to experience a range of emotions.

Since the SAM system is largely non-conscious and can involve the fast track to the amygdala, sensory information (i.e., smells or sounds, etc.) goes directly to the amygdala from the thalamus. Meanwhile, high levels of stress result in elevated levels of cortisol, NE, and cytokines, leading to impairment of the VAM system through over-reactivity of the amygdala.

According to Dual Representation Theory, when the client with PTSD deliberately maintains attention on the implicit memories (i.e., the sounds, smells, etc.) content of the flashbacks, and no longer tries to suppress them, the memories encoded in the SAM system become reconsolidated in the VAM system. The timeless qualities of the SAM images and sensations thus become linked with a spatial and temporal context. Through the reconsolidation in the VAM system, when SAMs are triggered, they are put into the context of time and place so that the individual can remind himself that he is now safe and the trauma or threat is in the past. He can feel secure in the present with a sense of safety that the trauma and danger is behind him.

The exposure and reconsolidation process must be repeated multiple times, not only because there generally exists a lot of information in the SAM system to be re-encoded, but also because neuroplasticity necessitates repetition. Rehearsing the new VAM memories long enough will promote easier access to the SAM memories. Thus, Dual Processing Theory envisions the creation of new memories through the VAM (explicit system) that compete with SAM (implicit system memories of the trauma). This perspective acknowledges that original SAM-based memories of the trauma are indelible and that the VAM system memories put the SAM system memories in perspective. This process calms down the activation of the sympathetic nervous system like a thermostat, including how the PFC inhibits the overactivity of the amygdala.

The interaction between the SAM and VAM system can be promoted through exposure and cognitive restructuring processes. Peres and colleagues (2007) have demonstrated cerebral blood flow changes during retrieval of traumatic memories before and after psychotherapy. The narrative organization of memory can be modified by associated experiences of emotional context and the state of consciousness during the recall process (Peres, Mercante, & Nasello, 2005).

The therapeutic integration of SAMs and VAMs is consistent with the Expert Consensus Guidelines series of treatment of PTSD, which states that exposure-based therapy is the treatment of choice for intrusive thoughts, flashbacks, trauma related fears, and avoidance (Expert Consensus Panels for PTSD, 1999). Many CBT approaches to PTSD combine cognitive restructuring methods with exposure (Brewin, 2001). Exposure to the traumatic memories is a well-constructed process that incorporates the emotional content (Littrel, 1998).

The reinterpretation and reconsolidation of traumatic memories, combined with exposure and cognitive restructuring, can alleviate some of the distressing symptoms by challenging the nature of the representations of the traumatic event (Peres, McFarlane, Nasello, & Moores, 2008). The affect shift, combined with new explicit, hippocampally driven memories (VAMs), allows the traumatic and fragmented memories (SAMs) to transform into an integrated implicit and explicit memory that can be more easily managed and available for narrative expression.

This integration of implicit and explicit memory (VAMs and SAMs) via exposure takes place within the "safe emergency" of the therapeutic relationship. The resulting promotion of a moderate degree of anxiety is critical for neuroplasticity. These dynamics include moderated levels of NE to engage the alpha-2A receptors, which engage the PFC (instead of turning it off by excessive amounts of NE which engage the alpha-1 adrenergic receptors), and a moderate increase in glutamate, which engages the NMDA receptors—important for long-term potentiation (LTP).

Indeed, consistent with the dynamics of the inverted U, which aid in effective neuroplasticity and memory, arousal levels must be carefully managed. For example, if arousal levels are too low, the PFC is not engaged, and traumatic images are not accessed. But if arousal levels are too high, the levels of NE are excessive and the adrenergic receptors are activated serving to take the PFC offline. The client begins to dissociate or become so overwhelmed with the traumatic memory, at the expense of contact with the immediate surroundings, strengthening its networks without transferring information from images biased to verbal memory (Brewin, 2005).

Therefore, a graduated and incremental approach is advisable whereby the traumatic SAM system memories are dealt with in smaller units and a hierarchy from less distressing to more distressing is developed, allowing therapist and client an opportunity to break down the levels of distress into "doable" chunks. Most important, the client, rather than waiting to feel comfortable in challenging himself to move out of his comfort zone, needs to understand that a moderate degree of anxiety is therapeutic. Through this process of incremental challenge, the newly constructed VAM system memories can be facilitated by a moderate degree of anxiety accessed through graduated exposure and integration of SAMs—implicit memory.

"Hot spots" are brief moments when emotions are particularly intense and correspond to flashbacks. Hot spots are important points for focus in exposure rather than addressing the entire event (Ehlers & Clark, 2000). Hot spots may correspond to moments where there is maximal functioning separation between visuospatial and verbal processing (Brewin, 2005). This separation can lead to a large discrepancy between the contents of the respective implicit and explicit memory systems (VAM & SAM). These are moments that provide retrieval cues that need reconsolidation into explicit memory so that they do not trigger flashbacks.

It is recommended that therapeutic attention be on the fragmented SAM related flashback memories hot spots. Sustained conscious attention to these memories could potentially promote integration with the VAM system, thereby strengthening coping skills with a new, far more adaptive, narrative. This process enhances inhibitory control over the amygdala and diminishes flashbacks. The restructuring and integration of the memory systems thus promotes a new narrative based on memories of successful self-efficacy prior to the trauma and constructive lessons learned post trauma.

Since traumatic memories are vulnerable to being triggered and reexperienced (i.e., flashbacks) because they are fragmented and disorganized, therapy should be directed toward making those memories coherent and structured to reduce the risk of unwanted intrusions (Ehlers & Clark, 2000; Conway & Pleydell-Pearce, 2000). Traumatic memories can be reactivated through exposure and reconsolidation by incorporating them into more accurate information.

Implicit memories cannot be corrected but can be more efficiently inhibited. Therapists can promote the construction of alternative memories. Theoretically, this is a constructive perspective instead of a connectionist perspective. Newly constructed memories compete with the original memory for control of behavior and attention with the emphasis on self-organization.

Increasing cognitive complexity and self-complexity bolsters one's stress-protective abilities (Tennen & Affleck, 1998). Self-complexity increases as we expand the number of different perspectives we have on ourselves, optimally one of those perspectives is that the self is complex enough to weather the stress.

Therapeutic approaches, therefore, should attempt to integrate implicit and explicit memory of traumatic experience by constructing an adaptive narrative promoting self-organization. It is through this foundation that, as the PTSD symptoms subside, the individual may be inclined to stand back and take a wider look at his/her place in the world and try to derive meaning from that wider perspective. Tainted much less by the emotional pain of the trauma there is the potential to represent a sense of connectedness with people and the world around him/her. The old sense of self ("old me") is lost because the trauma, and the new sense of self ("new me"), can be seen as more open and appreciative of the interdependence of the world.

References

Alderson, A. L. & Novack, T. A. (2002). Measuring recovery of orientation during acute rehabilitation for traumatic brain injury: Value and expectations of recovery. *Head Trauma Rehabilitation, 17*(3), 210–219.

Arden, J. B. & Linford, L. (2009a). *Brain-based therapy with adults: Evidenced-based treatment for everyday practice.* Hoboken, NJ: John Wiley & Sons.

Arden, J. B. & Linford, L. (2009b). *Brain-based therapy with children and adolescents: Evidenced-based treatment for everyday practice.* Hoboken, NJ: John Wiley & Sons.

Baker, D. G., Ekhator, N. N., Kasckow, J. W., Hill, K. K., Zoumakis, E., Dashevsky, B. A., Chrousos, G. P., & Geracioti Jr., T. D. (2001). Plasma and cerebrospinal fluid interleukin-6 concentrations in posttraumatic stress disorder. *Neuroimmunomodulation, 9,* 209–217.

Barlow, D. (2010). Negative effects from psychological treatments: A perspective. *American Psychologist, 65*(1), 13–20.

Beckner, V. L. & Arden, J. (2008). *Conquering post-traumatic stress disorder: The newest techniques for overcoming symptoms, regaining hope, and getting your life back.* Beverly, MA: Fair Winds Press.

Bremner, J. D. (1999). Does stress damage the brain? A review article. *Biological Psychiatry, 45,* 797–805.

Bremner, J. D. (2002). Neuroimaging studies in post-traumatic stress disorder. *Current Psychiatry Report, 4,* 254–263.

Bremner, J. D. (2005). *Does stress damage the brain? Understanding trauma-related disorders from a mind-body perspective.* New York, NY: W. W. Norton.

Bremner, J. D., Krystal, J. H., Southwick, S. M., & Charney, D. S. (1995). Functional neuroanatomical correlates of the effects of stress on memory. *Journal of Psychiatry, 156,* 360–366.

Bremner, J. D., Licinie, J., Dainell, A., Krystal, J. H., Owens, M. J., Southwick, S. M., Nemerhoff, C. B., & Charney, D. S. (1997). Elevated CSF corticotrophin-releasing factor concentrations in posttraumatic stress disorder. *American Journal of Psychiatry, 154,* 624–629.

Bremner, J. D., Staib, L. H., Kaloupek, D., Southwick, S. M., Soufer, R., & Charney, D. S. (1999). Neural correlates of exposure to traumatic pictures and sound in Vietnam combat veterans with and without posttraumatic stress disorder: A positron emission tomography study. *Biological Psychiatry, 45,* 806–816.

Breslau, N., Davis, G. C., Peterson, E. L., & Schultz, L. R. (2000). A second look at comorbidity in victims of trauma: The posttraumatic stress disorder-major depression connection. *Biological Psychiatry, 48,* 902–909.

Brewin, C. (2005). Encoding and retrieval of traumatic memories. In J. J. Vasterling and C. Brewin, Neuropsychology of PTSD: Biological, cognitive and clinical perspectives (pp. 131–157). New York: Guilford Press.

Brewin, C. R. (2001). A cognitive neuroscience account of posttraumatic stress disorder and its treatment. *Behavioral Research Therapy, 39,* 373–393.

Brewin, C. R. (2003). *Posttraumatic stress disorder: Malady or myth?* New Haven, CT: Yale University Press.

Brewin, C. R., Dalgleish, T., & Joseph, S. (1996). A dual-representation theory of post-traumatic stress disorder. *Psychological Review, 106,* 670–686.

Britton, J. C., Phan, K. L., Taylor, S. F., Fig, L. M., & Liberzon, I. (2005). Corticolimbic blood flow in posttraumatic stress disorder during script-driven imagery. *Biological Psychiatry, 57*(8), 832–840.

Brown, D., Scheflin, A. W., & Hammond, D. C. (1998). *Memory, trauma treatment, and the law.* New York, NY: Norton.

Carrion, V. G., Weems, C. F., Eliez, S., Ptwardhan, A., Brown, W., Ray, R. D., & Reiss, A. L. (2001). Attenuation of frontal asymmetry in pediatric posttraumatic stress disorders. *Biological Psychiatry, 50,* 943–951.

Chrousos, G. P. (1995). The hypothalamic-pituitary-adrenal axis and immune-mediated inflammation. *New England Journal of Medicine, 332,* 1351–1362.

Chu, J. A. (1998). *Rebuilding shattered lives: The responsible treatment of complex post-traumatic and dissociative disorders.* New York, NY: John Wiley & Sons.

Clark, C. R., McFarlane, A. C., Morris, P., Weber, D. L., Sonkkilla, C., Shaw, M., ... Egan, G. F. (2003). Cerebral function in posttraumatic stress disorder during verbal working memory updating: A positron emission tomography study. *Biological Psychiatry, 53*(6), 474–481.

Conway, M. A. & Pleydell-Pearce, C. W. (2000). The construction of autobiographical memories in the self-memory system. *Psychological Review, 107,* 261–288.

Dalgleish, T. (2004). Cognitive approaches to posttraumatic stress disorder: The evolution of multirepresential theorizing. *Psychological Bulletin, 130,* 228–260.

Davidson, P. R. & Parker, K. C. K. (2001). Eye movement desensitization and reprocessing (EMDR): A meta-analysis. *Journal of Consulting and Clinical Psychology, 69,* 305–316.

De Bellis, M. D., Baum, A. S., Birmaher, B., Keshavan, M. S., Eccard, C. H., Boring, A. M., Jenkins, F. J., & Ryan, N. D. (1999). Developmental traumatology, part 1: Biological stress systems. *Biological Psychiatry, 45,* 1259–1270.

De Bellis, M. D., Hooper, S. R., & Sapia, J. L. (2005). Early trauma exposure and the brain. In J. J. Vasterling & C. R. Brewin (Eds.), *Neuropsychology of PTSD: Biological, cognitive, and clinical perspectives* (pp. 131–150). New York, NY: Guilford Press.

De Bellis, M. D., Keshavan, M. S., Shifflett, H., Iyengar, S., Beers, S. R., Hall, J., & Moritz, G. (2002). Brain structures in pediatric maltreatment-related posttraumatic stress disorder: A sociodemographically matched study. *Biological Psychiatry, 52,* 1066–1078.

De Decker, A., Hermans, D., Raes, F., & Eelen, P. (2003). Autobiographical memory specificity and trauma in inpatient adolescents. *Journal of Clinical Child Adolescent Psychology, 32*(1), 22–31.

Delahanty, D. L., Nugent, N. R., Christopher, N. C., & Walsh, M. (2005). Initial urinary epinephrine and cortisol levels predict acute PTSD symptoms in child trauma victims. *Psychoneuroendrocrinology, 30,* 121–128.

Ehlers, A. & Clark, D. M. (2000). A cognitive model of posttraumatic stress disorder. *Behaviour Research and Therapy, 38,* 319–345.

Elenkov, I. J., Iezzoni, D. G., Daly, A., Harris, A. G., & Chrousos, G. P. (2005). Cytokine dysregulation, inflammation, and well-being. *Neuroimmunomodulation, 12,* 255–269.

Expert Consensus Panels for PTSD. (1999). The expert consensus guidelines series treatment of posttraumatic stress disorder. *Journal of Clinical Psychiatry, 60*(16), 3–76.

Foa, E. B. & Rothbaum, B. O. (1998). *Treating the trauma of rape: Cognitive behavioral therapy for PTSD.* New York, NY: Guilford Press.

Friedman, M. J. (1997). Drug treatment for PTSD: Answers and questions. *Annals of the New York Academy of Sciences, 821,* 359–468.

Fries, E., Hesse, J., Hellhammer, J., & Hellhammer, D. H. (2005). A new view on hypocortisolism. *Psychoneuroendocrinology, 30,* 1010–1016.

Gilbertson, M. W., Shenton, M. E., Cszewski, A., Kasai, K., Lasko, N. B., Orr, S. P., & Pittman, R. K. (2002). Smaller hippocampal volume predicts pathologic vulnerability to psychological traumatic. *Nature Neuroscience, 5,* 1242–1247.

Grey, N., Holmes, E., & Brewin, C. R. (2001). Peritraumatic emotional "hotspots" in traumatic memory: A case series of patients with posttraumatic stress disorder. *Behavioral and Cognitive Psychotherapy, 29,* 367–372.

Gunnar, M. R. & Vazquez, D. M. (2001). Low cortisol and flattening of expected daytime rhythm: Potential induces of risk in human development. *Development and Psychopathology, 13,* 515–538.

Harvey, A. G., & Bryant, R. A. (1999). A qualitative investigation of the organization of traumatic memories. *British Journal of Clinical Psychology, 38,* 401–405.

Herman, J. L. (1992). *Trauma and recovery.* New York, NY: Basic Books.

Hobson, J. A., Stickgold, R., & Pace-Schott, E. F. (1998). The neuropsychology of REM sleep dreaming. *NeuroReport, 9,* RI–R14.

Hull, A. M. (2002). Neuroimaging findings in post-traumatic stress disorder: Systematic review. *British Journal of Psychiatry, 181,* 102–110.

Karl, A., Malta, L., & Maercker, L. (2006). Meta-analytic review of event related potential studies in post-traumatic stress disorder. *Biological Psychology, 71,* 123–147.

Lang, P. J. (1985). The cognitive psychophysiological of emotion: Fear and anxiety. In A. H. Tuma & J. D. Maser (Eds.), *Anxiety and anxiety disorders* (pp. 131–170). Hillsdale, NJ: Erlbaum.

Littrell, J. (1998). Is the reexperience of painful emotion therapeutic? *Clinical Psychological Review, 8,* 71–102.

Maes, M., Lin, A. H., Delmeire, L., Van Gastel, A., Kenis, G., DeJong, L. R., & Bosmans, E. (1999). Elevated serum interleukin-6 (IL-6) and IL-6 receptor concentrations in posttraumatic stress disorder following accidental man-made traumatic events. *Biological Psychiatry, 45,* 833–839.

Miller, G. E., Chen, E., & Zhou, E. S. (2007). If it goes up, must it come down? Chronic stress and the hypothalamic-pituitary-adrenocortical axis in humans. *Psychological Bulletin, 133*(1), 25–45.

Nelson, J. P., McCarley, R. W., Hobson, J. A. (1983). REM sleep burst neurons, PGO waves and eye movement information. *Journal of Neurophysiology, 50,* 784–797.

Nutt, J. D. & Malizia, A. L. (2004). Structural and functional brain changes in posttraumatic stress disorder. *Journal of Clinical Psychiatry, 65*(Suppl), 11–17.

Papanicolaou, D. A., Wilder, R., Manolagas, S., & Chrousos, G. P. (1998). Roles of interleukin-6 in human disease. *Annuals of Internal Medicine, 128,* 127–137.

Peres, J, Mercante, J., & Nasello, A. G. (2005). Psychological dynamics affecting traumatic memories: implications in psychotherapy. *Psychological Psychotherapy, 78,* 431–447.

Peres, J., Newberg, A. B., Mercante, J. P. P., Simao, M., Albuquerque, V. E., Peres, M. J. P., & Nasello, A. (2007). Cerebral blood flow changes during retrieval of traumatic memories before and after psychotherapy: A SPECT study. *Psychological Medicine, 37,* 1481–1491.

Peres, J. T. P., McFarlane, A., Nasello, A. G., & Moores, K. A. (2008). Traumatic memories: Bridging the gap between functional neuroimaging and psychotherapy. *Australia and New Zealand Journal of Psychiatry, 42,* 478–488.

Phelps, E. A. (2009). The human amygdala and the control of fear. In P. J. Whalen & E. A. Phelps (Eds.), *The human amygdala* (pp. 204–219). New York, NY: Guilford.

Pissiota, A., Frans, O., Fernandez, M., Von Knorring, L., Fischer, H., & Fredrickson, M. (2002). Neurofunctional correlates of posttraumatic stress disorder: A PET symptom provocation study. *European Archives of Psychiatry Clinical Neuroscience, 252,* 68–75.

Pitman, R. K., Sanders, K. M., Zusman, R. M., Healy, A. R., Cheema, F., Lasko, N. B., Cahill, L., & Orr, S. P. (2002). Pilot study of secondary prevention of posttraumatic stress disorder with propranolol. *Biological Psychiatry, 51,* 189–92.

Rauch, S. L. (1996). Symptom provocation study of post-traumatic stress disorder using positron emission tomography and script-driven imagery. *Archives of General Psychiatry, 53,* 380–387.

Sapolsky, R. M. (2003). Stress and plasticity in the limbic system. *Neurochemical Research, 28,* 1735–1742.

Semple, W. E., Goyer, P. F., McCormick, R., Donovan, B., Muzic, R. F., Jr., Rugle, L., ... Schulz, S. C. (2000). Higher blood flow at amygdala and lower frontal cortex blood flow in PTSD patients with comorbid cocaine and alcohol abuse compared with normals. *Psychiatry: Interpersonal and Biological Processes, 63,* 65–74.

Slaikeu, K. A. (1990). *Crisis intervention: A handbook for practice and research* (2d ed.). Needham Heights, MA: Allyn & Bacon.

Teasdale, J. D. & Barnard, P. J. (1993). Affect, cognitive, and change. Hove, UK: Erlbaum.

Tedeschi, R. G. (1999). Violence transformed: Posttraumatic growth in survivors and their societies. *Aggression and Violent Behavior, 4,* 319–341.

Teicher, M. (2000). Wounds that time won't heal: The neurobiology of child abuse. *Cerebrum, 4*(2), 50–67.

Tennen, H. & Affleck, G. (1998). Personality and transformation in the face of adversity. In R. Tedeschi, C. L. Park, & L. Calhoun (Eds.), *Posttraumatic growth: Positive changes in the aftermath of crisis* (pp. 65–98). Mahwah, NJ: Erlbaum.

Thomas, L. A. & De Bellis, M. D. (2004). Pituitary volumes in pediatric maltreatment related to PTSD. *Biological Psychiatry, 55,* 752–758.

Vaiva, G., Ducrocq, F., Jezequel, K., Averland, B., Lestavel, P., Brunet, A., & Marmar, C. R. (2003). Immediate treatment with propranolol decreases posttraumatic stress disorder two months after trauma. *Society of Biological Psychiatry, 54,* 947–949.

Van der Hart, O., Brown, P., & Van der Kolk, B.A. (1989). Pierre Janet's treatment of post-traumatic stress. *Journal of Traumatic Stress, 2*(4), 1–11.

Van der Kolk, B. A. (1993). Group for patients with histories of catastrophic trauma. In A. Alonso & H. I. Swiller (Eds.), *Group therapy in clinical practice* (pp. 289–305). Washington, DC: American Psychological Association.

Van der Kolk, B. A. (1996). The complexity of adaptation to trauma: Self-regulation, stimulation discrimination, and characterological development. In B. A. Van der Kolk, A. C. Mcfarlane, & L. Weisaeth (Eds.), *Traumatic stress: The effects of overwhelming experience on mind, body, and society* (pp. 182–213). New York, NY: Guilford Press.

Van der Kolk, B. A. (2003). The neurobiology of childhood trauma and abuse. *Child and Adolescent Psychiatric Clinics of North America, 12*(2), 293–317.

Van der Kolk, B. A., Burbridge, J. A., & Suzuki, J. (1997). The psychobiology of traumatic memory: Clinical implications of neuroimaging studies. *Annals of the New York Academy of Sciences, 821,* 99–113.

Vyas, A., Bernal, S., & Chattarji, S. (2003). Effects of chronic stress on dentritic arborization in the central and extended amygdala. *Brain Research, 965,* 290–294.

Vyas, A., Mitra, R., Rao, B. S. S., & Chattarji, S. (2002). Chronic stress induces contrasting patterns of dendritic remodeling in hippocampal and amygdaloid neurons. *Journal of Neuroscience, 22,* 6810–6818.

Woon, F. L. & Hedges, D. W. (2008). Hippocampal and amygdala volumes in children and adults with childhood maltreatment-related posttraumatic stress disorder: A meta-analysis. *Hippocampus, 18,* 729–736.

Yehuda, R. (2001). Current status of cortisol findings in PTSD. *Psychiatric Clinics of North America, 25,* 341–368.

Yehuda, R., Boisoneau, D., Lowy, M. T., & Giller Jr., E. L. (1995). Dose response changes in plasma cortisol and lymophocyte glucocorticoid receptors following dexamethasone administration in combat veterans with and without posttraumatic stress disorder. *Archives of General Psychiatry, 52,* 583–593.

Yehuda, R., McFarlane, A. C., & Shalev, A. Y. (1998). Predicting the development of post-traumatic disorder from the acute response to a traumatic event. *Biological Psychiatry, 44,* 1305–1313.

Yehuda, R., Southwick, S., Giller, E. L., Ma, X., & Mason, J. W. (1992). Urinary catecholamine excretion and severity of PTSD symptoms in Vietnam combat veterans. *Journal of Nervous Mental Disorders, 180,* 321–325.

Zoellner, L. A., Fitzgibbons, L. A., & Foa, E. B. (2001). Cognitive-behavioral approaches to PTSD. In J. P. Wilson, M. J. Friedman, & J. D. Lindy (Eds.), *Treating psychological trauma and PTSD* (pp. 159–182). New York, NY: Guilford.

Chapter 4
The Roots of EFT in Medicine and Psychology
Dawson Church

Abstract

A common misperception of Emotional Freedom Techniques (EFT) is that it was developed solely from Thought Field Therapy (TFT). In reality, the roots of both EFT's and TFT's techniques can be found in therapeutic developments that date back to the origins of modern psychology, including Sigmund Freud and Wilhelm Wundt in the 1800s. Some concepts used by EFT date from the discovery of electricity in the 1700s, while others are drawn from concepts prevalent in the worldview of the ancient Arab, Judeo-Christian, and Buddhist cultures. A review of the history of medicine allows us to locate the 48 techniques of Clinical EFT in their proper historical context. The historical trajectory offered by this perspective provides an intellectual framework from which hypotheses about the future clinical application of EFT may be derived.

Keywords: EFT, Emotional Freedom Techniques, psychology, medicine, history

Dawson Church is a health writer and researcher in the field of energy medicine. He is author of the award-winning best-seller *The Genie in Your Genes*, editor of the peer-reviewed professional journal *Energy Psychology*, executive director of the National Institute for Integrative Healthcare (niih.org), and CEO of Energy Psychology Group (EFTuniverse.com). Send correspondence to Dawson Church, 334 Fulton Road, #442, Fulton, CA 95439, or dawsonchurch@gmail.com. The author receives income from books and speaking engagements on the approach described in this chapter.

The quest to relieve mental and emotional suffering is an ancient human enterprise. Twenty-five hundred years ago, the Buddha taught how suffering may be relieved through contemplation and meditation. His near contemporary, the Greek philosopher Epicurus, proclaimed that any philosopher who did not reduce suffering was worthless. Residents of eighth-century Islamic cities recognized the phenomenon of mental illness, and built asylums to care for those suffering from these afflictions. Shakespeare wondered how to "ease the anguish of a torturing hour." In the shortest verse in the Bible, Saint John tells us that "Jesus wept"; anger, grief, and other emotions are vividly portrayed in the Old and New Testaments. Muhammad, after conquering Mecca in a great *jihad* or struggle, then told his followers that the more difficult *jihad* now begins: the one to master our unruly inner states (Smith, 2004). In today's secular world, it is the field of psychology that wrestles with the question of mental and emotional suffering. Many methods have been developed in attempts to reduce that suffering, and the core techniques of EFT can be located within the history of psychology.

Freud, Insight, the Unconscious Mind, and the Neurobiology of Trauma

A great leap in understanding the persistence of human emotional suffering came to Europeans in the late 19th century when Sigmund Freud grasped and explained the significance of the unconscious mind. Ask your friends if they want to be healthy, wealthy, and wise, and they will assure you that they do. Yet we return again and again to behaviors, thoughts, and beliefs that perpetuate our suffering. Freud's emphasis on the unconscious mind demonstrated that despite our attempts at change at the conscious level, there is a well of hidden mental material that may be quite at odds with our good intentions and may perpetuate old patterns of suffering.

Freud produced many brilliant insights, but he was quite incorrect in believing that insight produces change (Breuer & Freud, 1895). Cognitive neuroscience has now shown us that psychological conditions such as phobias and posttraumatic stress disorder (PTSD) are not simply "in the mind," and that mental insight into the origins of trauma does not extinguish it. Emotional trauma conditions the brain in a feedback loop that maintains the emotional problem by adding synaptic connections to oft-used neural pathways. Eric Kandel, who won the Nobel Prize for Medicine or Physiology in 2000, showed that within just 1 hour of repeated stimulation, the number of synaptic connections in a neuronal pathway can *double* (Kandel, 1998). Conversely, unused pathways can decay in as little as 3 weeks. The axon sheaths around brain neurons are completely disassembled by the body and recreated every 10 minutes (McCrone, 2004). Recent discoveries in neural plasticity have upset the previous paradigm that human brains grow till about the age of 17 years and then become fixed anatomy. The brain and nervous system are dynamic structures boiling with change, rewiring themselves second by second on the basis of both internal and external stimuli. If emotional and mental processes are characterized by chronic suffering, stress-regulating structures in the brain's limbic system such as the hippocampus actually shrink as neuronal material is broken down and repurposed to reinforce the circuits that carry stress signals (Felmingham, Kemp, & Williams, 2006). Insight alone is not enough to produce change; the conditioned emotional responses that wire our brain physiology must somehow be counterconditioned.

Behaviorism and Cognitive Therapies

Freud's contemporary Wilhelm Wundt believed that psychology might become a science, modeled after physics or chemistry. In his laboratory in Leipzig, Germany, he laid the foundations for modern experimental psychology, and emphasized the link between consciousness and physiology (Wundt, 1894). Wundt established the first journal devoted to psychological research.

As the 20th century progressed, psychology shifted from Freud's emphasis on exploring the unconscious and took a more concrete turn to examine behavior. Influenced by Ivan Pavlov's experiments showing that conditioned responses could be induced in animals, B. F. Skinner (1938) emphasized that behavior can be altered by the appropriate stimuli. Skinner focused on observable behavior rather than internal mental events such as thought, meaning, and emotion.

Yet it is easily observable that human beings can modify the simple stimulus-response cycle shown in Skinner's experiments, using inner processes such as volition and belief. This led to the rise of cognitive therapies, which displaced behaviorism as the predominant psychological paradigm in the 1960s. Rather than merely seeking insight into a client's cognitive world, psychiatrist Aaron Beck, psychologist Albert Ellis, and others experimented with methods to change those cognitions to produce heal their behaviors. This led to the development of cognitive therapy. Cognitive therapy is results-oriented and present-focused. It has clients assess dysfunctional beliefs, identify unhelpful patterns of thinking, and, when possible, change habitual behaviors and emotional responses to events (Beck, Rush, Shaw, & Emery, 1979).

Counterconditioning

In the 1950s, psychiatrist Joseph Wolpe developed the concept of counterconditioning, in which a conditioned fear response is paired with induced relaxation. Wolpe called his concept "reciprocal inhibition" (Wolpe, 1958). Wolpe was born in South Africa, where, before moving to the United States, he treated patients suffering from "war neurosis," or what is now known as PTSD. It is noteworthy that a number of the break throughs that have occurred in psychology have arisen from attempts to treat PTSD, which is often characterized as a treatment-resistant condition (Bradley, Greene, Russ, Dutra, & Western, 2005).

Initially a dedicated follower of Freud, Wolpe's observation that talk therapy was usually unsuccessful with these patients prompted him to seek more effective methods. Reciprocal inhibition involves deliberately evoking a traumatic response while simultaneously providing a soothing stimulus. He developed this technique to create his most famous method, called "systematic desensitization." This exposes a client to a fear-producing stimulus at a low level, but pairs it with a relaxation technique. Once the client has adjusted to the minimally triggering stimulus, stronger stimuli are applied.

To countercondition or inhibit fearful memories, Wolpe tried various relaxation techniques. He eventually found that diaphragmatic breathing (DB) was the most effective. DB keeps the client focused on the breath while the client reexperiences a traumatic event. As we will see when examining the commonalities between the new schools of psychotherapy, keeping the client "in the body" while he or she reexperiences trauma may be an essential ingredient of successful counterconditioning.

Like Skinner, who broke complex behaviors into simple components, Wolpe had clients first "reciprocally inhibit" small traumatic cues and then, following modest improvements, larger ones. Such counterconditioning breaks the association between the fearful thought and the conditioned activation of the alarm response by the brain's limbic system. Wolpe used an assessment measure he called the subjective units of disturbance (SUD) scale, by which the client rated the degree of distress experienced in the presence of a fear-producing stimulus. This client-rated measure of the success of therapy echoed Carl Rogers's call for "client-centered therapy," which sought to minimize the power differentials between expert therapist and client (Rogers, 1957).

This emphasis on empowering the client can also be seen in schools that became influential along with the rise of the human potential movement, such as humanistic and transpersonal psychology. Abraham Maslow coined the term *self-actualization*—the full use of a human being's talents and potentials—and placed it at the top of his "hierarchy of needs," arguing that once lower-order needs such as survival and reproduction are met, self-actualization is the ultimate human need (Maslow, 1954).

Somatic Stimulation: The Common Element in Innovative Therapies

In the 1970s and 1980s, pioneering clinicians such as Peter Levine, Roger Callahan, John Diamond, George Goodheart, Edna Foa, and Francine Shapiro provided a vital missing piece to the transformational puzzle. Before the psychoneuroimmunologists mapped the dance between cells and feelings and before epigeneticists revealed the interactions between emotions and gene expression, they realized that *the body plays a crucial role in psychological change* and that *somatic stimulation* can influence cognition. By engaging the body during cognitive restructuring, they were able to quickly break the feedback loop that held old psychological problems in place. Their methods, such as Prolonged Exposure (PR; Foa, 1979), Somatic Experiencing (SE; Levine, 1997), Eye Movement Desensitization and Reprocessing (EMDR; Shapiro, 1995) and Thought Field Therapy (TFT; Callahan, 2001), were superficially different. But they all used somatic stimulation to induce psychological change. Wolpe's DB became an integral part of PE. EMDR used eye movements. TFT used fingertip tapping on acupuncture points. SE had clients shake their limbs to mimic the shaking that naturally occurs in stressed muscles after a traumatic event. Other pioneers such as Goodheart (1987) and Diamond (1985) also experimented with acupressure and muscle resistance as paths to healing. These somatic methods underscored the importance of holism, the idea that body, mind, and emotions are a whole. This stands in contrast to reductionism, which seeks to understand a complex organism by reducing it to a collection of smaller parts.

The Evolutionary Basis of Emotion

The understanding that psychology and physiology are holistically linked is not new. A thousand years ago, Muslim physician Ahmed al-Bhakli observed that, "if the psyche gets sick, the body may also find no joy in life and eventually develop a physical illness" (Deuraseh & Abu Talib, 2005; Syed, 2002). Many other scientific authorities understood that emotions are inextricably interwoven with biology. Charles Darwin (1872) was interested in the role of emotions in natural selection, and he presented his observations in his book *The Expression of Emotions in Man and Animals*.

The development of emotions can be viewed through the lens of another new scientific field, that of evolutionary biology (Wilson, 1978). Evolutionary biology asks the questions: How is this behavior helpful? How did it assist our distant ancestors with survival? The answer in the case of emotion is that fear allows us to respond to a threat, increasing our chances of survival. Those primates who had the fastest fear response, whose limbic systems processed a stress signal most efficiently, were the most likely to survive and pass their genes to their offspring.

These traits were then further honed in the next generation, with the individuals with the fastest fear response most likely to survive and reproduce. The process continued generation after generation. Modern humans represent the culmination of hundreds of generations of evolutionary selection based on an excellent stress response. A large part of our central nervous system is devoted to coping with environmental threats such as predators and hostile competitors. Our ability to read emotional cues on the faces of other human beings is the result of natural selection for this trait. Archaic humans who could quickly read threatening intent on the face of a potential enemy tended to live, while those who were inept at this skill perished. Our brains have a highly evolved ability to detect and remember threats, as this skill was adaptive for our ancestors.

Today, living in a world with few of those same objective threats, these same brain structures now have little sensory input to process. They therefore focus on subjective threats: worries, complaints, resentments, and other emotion-laden thoughts. An understanding of evolutionary biology shows us how we developed the emotions we have, why they were adaptive for our distant ancestors, and why we worry even in the absence of objective threats to our survival. We translate those worries into a physiological stress response, generating various physical symptoms. Brain researcher Joseph LeDoux (2002) refers to this as the "hostile takeover of consciousness by emotion."

Holism: The Impact of Trauma on Health

Wundt's students were well aware of the interaction of emotions, consciousness, and physiology, calling his approach "holistic psychology." South African President Jan Smuts (1926) argued for an integrative vision of biology in *Holism and Evolution*. The American Holistic Medical Association was founded in 1980 and the American Holistic Nurses Association in 1981. Early contributors within these organizations included such well-known leaders in the field of holistic health as Norman Shealy, MD, PhD; Andrew Weil, MD; Bernie Siegel, MD; Christiane Northup, MD; Larry Dossey, MD; Barbara Dossey, RN; Candace Pert, PhD; and Joan Borysenko, PhD.

In the 1990s, a large-scale epidemiological study showed the holistic link between adverse emotions and physical health (Felliti, Koss, & Marks, 1998). The Centers for Disease Control, in association with Kaiser Permanente, a hospital chain with 11 million members, examined the link between disease and childhood trauma in 17,421 adults. Called the ACE (Adverse Childhood Experiences) Study, it found an association between traumatic childhood experiences and disease. Many diseases, including the top 10 killers of adults, correlated with unhealed emotional wounds. They included cancer, heart disease, diabetes, high blood pressure, obesity, hepatitis, sexually transmitted diseases, alcoholism, and bone fractures. The higher the number of adverse childhood experiences, the higher the likelihood of each of these diseases. Smoking, intravenous drug abuse, depression, unintended pregnancy, and suicide attempts also correlated with higher ACE scores.

Other studies have also found strong links between emotional trauma and physical disease. Particularly revealing are studies of identical twins. They are born with identical sets of genes, and when DNA microarrays are used to scan their 23,688 genes at birth, their chromosomal maps are virtually indistinguishable. But by the time twins reach the age of 50, their genetic profiles have diverged (Fraga et al., 2005). Epigenetic influences have set them on different courses and, on average, they die more than 10 years apart. One of the most important epigenetic influences is stress (Jirtle & Skinner, 2007). The emotional trauma of stress is now known to affect the expression of over 1,000 genes, including those that influence aging, cancer, and cell regeneration (Dusek et al., 2008; Ornish et al., 2008).

The data from the ACE study lead to the sober conclusion that time does not heal. The mean age of participants in the ACE study was 57 years old, and the emotional trauma they had suffered had occurred a half-century before. Results thus indicate that if emotional suffering is not addressed, it can wreak havoc on the body, even decades later (Kendall-Tackett, 2009). The relief of emotional suffering is not just a luxury for the elites of the world who can afford expensive courses of psychotherapy, it is a public health issue affecting rich and poor individuals and countries alike. The World Health Organization predicts that depression will become the leading cause of disease burden worldwide by 2030, eclipsing heart disease, cancer, and other illnesses (Lepine & Briley, 2011). The authors of the ACE Study likened the reductionistic efforts of the medical establishment to fire fighters pouring their water on the smoke (physical disease) while the flames (emotional trauma) rage unabated. Holistic therapies that counteract emotional trauma by regulating the response of the limbic system to stress give clinicians, for the first time in history, the means to douse the fire from which much ill-health springs.

Energy Psychology

As therapists began to experiment with methods like EMDR and TFT in their practices, innovations spread quickly. New methods such as Emotional Freedom Techniques (EFT; Craig, 2008), Energy Diagnosis and Treatment (EDxTM; Gallo, 2000), and Tapas Acupressure Technique (TAT; Fleming, 1996) developed out of the initial group of somatic-based therapies. Psychologist Fred Gallo coined the term "energy psychology," or EP, to describe this family of therapeutic methods. Though they may use different protocols, what they all have in common is an understanding of the role of the body in psychological healing. Somatic experiencing, EMDR, EFT, and other forms of EP all keep the client "in the body" during there living of trauma, instead of "in the mind" as talk therapy does.

Counterconditioning Trauma by Staying in the Body During Recall

Advocates of body-centered practices such as yoga, qigong, tai chi, mindfulness, and breathwork emphasize the value of these methods for counterbalancing the stress of modern life, and the emotional triggering of traumatic events.

Energy therapies take somatic practice further. Rather than allocating relaxation to one end of the spectrum of experience, stress to the other, and seeking a balance, they bring the relaxation offered by somatic practices into the heart of stress. They encourage the client to stay in the body—through tapping, eye movements, shaking, or breathing—while reexperiencing a traumatic event.

This combination sends two competing signals to the brain. One signal enters the limbic system as the result of a traumatic memory. This signal activates the conditioned stress response. A second and wholly inconsistent signal enters the limbic system in the form of physiological self-soothing through tapping, shaking, breathing, or eye movements. Which of these two competing signals will the limbic system act on? Will it send a fight-flight signal to the hindbrain and autonomic nervous system in consequence of the traumatic thought? Or will it sound the "all clear" in response to the soothing physiological signal?

The physiological signal of safety usually trumps the psychological signal of danger

(Feinstein & Church, 2010). When faced with this conflict, even with a highly conditioned response signal carried through a well-developed stress neural network, the limbic system places a premium on the soothing signal. It recognizes that the paper tiger in your mind is not a real tiger when the image of the paper tiger is accompanied by a concrete physical indication of safety like eye movements, tapping, or DB. Once that conditioned feedback loop is broken, it usually stays broken; thinking about the trauma later no longer evokes a stress response in the brain. These new therapies work directly on the limbic system, which processes emotion, in contrast to talk therapy, which engages the prefrontal cortex, the brain region that processes conscious thought (Phelps & LeDoux, 2005).

The brain's prefrontal cortex represents a recent evolutionary innovation. In its present form it is scarcely 100,000 years old, the blink of an eye in evolutionary terms (Krasnegor, Lyon, & Goldman-Rakic, 1997). By comparison, the brain stem, the part of the brain responsible for keeping us safe and secure, has had some 250 million years of practice in honing survival functions (Shubin, 2009). The limbic system mediates between them. Talk therapies that engage only the parts of the brain responsible for cognition may have some effect, but somatic therapies that engage the limbic system can nullify the fear response quickly and permanently.

Early Research

This combination may account for the startling speed, effectiveness, and durability of energy psychology methods such as EFT. Several seminal studies of EFT were published in the early years of the 21st century as the field progressed from clinical observation to empirical measurement. Rowe (2005) assessed the breadth and intensity of psychological distress of participants in an EFT weekend seminar, as well as the presence of specific symptoms such as anxiety, depression, and paranoia, and found them to be significantly reduced. Not only did the workshop improve psychological functioning, but also 3-month and 6-month follow-ups showed the effect to hold over time. Other studies went on to examine the effect of EFT when delivered to groups, and found it to reduce psychological distress regardless of the practitioner delivering the intervention (Church & Brooks, 2010; Palmer-Hoffman & Brooks, 2011; Church, De Asis, & Brooks, 2012; Church & Brooks, 2013).

Other researchers performed a randomized controlled trial of EFT for specific phobias (Wells, Polglase, Andrews, Carrington, & Baker, 2003). Phobias—in which the stimulus of a thought about a feared object or situation produces a feeling of fear to which the body is conditioned to initiate an alarm response—are a classic Pavlovian reaction. Talk therapies have limited success with phobias. Since phobias are irrational, cognitive arguments against them have little currency in the economy of the brain. Somatic stimulation, however, counterconditions most phobias rapidly. Wells et al. (2003) found that a single 30-minute session of EFT reduced symptoms significantly. At 6-month follow-up, participants retained most of their therapeutic gains. A replication was able to produce the same effect in just 10 minutes of treatment (Salas, Brooks, & Rowe, 2011). An extension of Wells et al. (2003) carefully controlled for confounders such as therapist allegiance, expectancy effects, and other variables that might affect treatment (Baker & Siegel, 2010). It found that the change in phobic symptoms was indeed produced by EFT, rather than experimental artifacts.

Over 50 studies of EFT and TFT have now been performed, and several papers review these (Church & Feinstein, 2013; Feinstein, 2012). One review of energy psychology (Feinstein, 2012) summarizes the state of research as follows: "A literature search identified 51 peer-reviewed papers that report or investigate clinical outcomes following the tapping of acupuncture points to address psychological issues. The 18 randomized controlled trials in this sample were critically evaluated for design quality, leading to the conclusion that they consistently demonstrated strong effect sizes and other positive statistical results that far exceed chance after relatively few treatment sessions. Criteria for evidence-based treatments proposed by Division 12 of the American Psychological Association were also applied and found to be met for a number of conditions, including PTSD."

Church & Feinstein (2013) note the following characteristics of acupoint tapping as it relates to clinical treatment: "(1) The limited number of treatment sessions usually required to remediate PTSD; (2) the depth, breadth, and longevity of treatment effects; (3) the low risk of adverse events; (4) the limited commitment to training required for basic application of the method; (5) its efficacy when delivered in group format; (6) its simultaneous effect on a wide range of psychological and physiological symptoms, and (7) its suitability for non-traditional delivery methods such as online and telephone sessions."

Exposure and Cognitive Acceptance: EFT's Setup Statement

Tasked by Congress with identifying efficacious therapies for PTSD, the U.S. government's Institute of Medicine (IOM) sought to identify their characteristics. The IOM review concluded that the two methods validated in research were cognitive and exposure therapies (Institute of Medicine, 2007). EFT's Setup Statement represents a simple yet elegant combination of exposure and cognition. The first half, "Even though I have (name of problem)" uses exposure to keep the client mentally focused on a traumatic event. The Reminder Phrase "(name of problem)" keeps the client focused on the issue (exposure) while stimulating acupressure points. The second half of the Setup Statement, "I deeply and completely accept myself," is a statement of cognitive acceptance of the problem. Rather than attempting to minimize the problem, comfort the client, reframe the problem, or induce positive thinking, EFT emphasizes acceptance. Carl Rogers referred to this as the paradox of change: In order to change, the first step we must take is to accept circumstances just the way they are.

EFT Practices Drawn from Effective Therapies

EFT borrows from Wolpe, using his SUD scale and emphasis on client-assessed progress. It also adapts the client-centered approach of Carl Rogers, by defining EFT as peer-to-peer coaching, rather than psychotherapy with all the power differentials inherent in that relationship. Clinical EFT techniques such as Daisy Chaining, Ranting and Tapping, and Tell the Story borrow from Freud's "talking cure," allowing the client to verbalize while discharging the emotional intensity of traumatic memories through tapping. Chasing the Pain and Aspects are Clinical EFT techniques that emphasize holism: The treatment target might shift from a physical pain, to an emotion, to a piece of a traumatic memory, to another pain, to a current event, and to a past event, all within the course of a few minutes. These techniques recognize that trauma may be held in any of these parts of the body or psyche, and seek a comprehensive release by exploring any and all possible locations in which trauma may be stored.

Borrowing from cognitive therapies, Clinical EFT practitioners are taught to look for cognitive shifts in clients, such as reframes in language and perspective. However, training emphasizes the value of patience, giving the client time and space to make their own discoveries, rather than supplying the client with reframes originating in the mind of the therapist. This echoes the recommendation of Fritz Perls, the founder of Gestalt therapy, who advocated giving clients time and space to experience their emotions, while the therapist stays present and nonjudgmental of the process (Perls, 1969). Client-generated reframes originate in the client's own neural network and have a potency that observer-generated cognitions cannot possess.

Energy Fields and Electromagnetic EEG Outcomes

Energy psychology also draws on concepts from physics. Albert Einstein linked matter and energy in his equation $e = mc^2$, which places matter on one side of the equation and energy on the other. More recently, string theorists posit that even molecules that physics treats as solid matter are actually minute strings of energy. They hypothesize that what physics measures as solid physical molecules with high mass are actually strings that are vibrating slowly, while what we measure as molecules of low mass are strings that are vibrating fast. Medicine has been fascinated with invisible fields from the time of the first discovery of electricity. By the mid 1700s, electricity was being artificially stored, generated, and transmitted; the book *Electrical Medicine* by Johann Schaeffer appeared in 1752, by which time many physicians were using electricity on their patients (Shealy & Church, 2008).

During energy psychology treatments, psychological change can happen very quickly and be demonstrated by changes in the electromagnetic field of the brain. Several researchers have used electroencephalogram (EEG) readings to explore brain-wave changes that occur concurrently with energy psychology treatment. Diepold and

Goldstein (2008) took qualitative EEG recordings of a client recalling a traumatic memory. They compared these readings with baseline values and found that recall of an emotional trigger produced statistically abnormal EEG readings as the fear response was activated in the client's brain. After TFT treatment, the brain's fear response was extinguished and stayed extinguished, even when the client recalled the same traumatic scene 18 months later.

Lambrou, Pratt, and Chevalier (2004) used EEG readings to compare claustrophobics with a nonclaustophobic population. They then gave the claustrophobics a 30-minute EP treatment and found that their EEGs had normalized. On follow-up 2 weeks later, the EEG readings were still normal. Swingle, Pulos, and Swingle (2004) took a group of auto accident victims with PTSD, measured their EEG readings, and then taught them EFT. After 3 months, Swingle and colleagues found that the EEG readings had improved, as had participants' PTSD symptoms. Acupuncture studies using fMRI technology also show regulation of the fear centers of the brain (Hui et al., 2005, Fang et al., 2009, Napadow et al., 2007). Electromagnetic and other fields demonstrate the energetic dimension of EP treatments.

This research suggested that once an emotional trigger had been neutralized using EP, the conditioned feedback loop was permanently broken. The soothing signal provided by tapping, when reaching a limbic brain processing a fear signal produced by a traumatic memory, in effect cancelled it out. The brain seems to place a premium on the soothing somatic signal, elevating its importance in the survival hierarchy above the fear-producing thought, thus extinguishing the conditioned response loop between fearful thought and the stress response. This extinction of conditioned fear responses shows up in an examination of the brain's electromagnetic signature.

The Future of Energy Psychology

We see from the previous review that EFT draws elements from discoveries made by many different schools of psychology over the past 2 centuries. Table 1 summarizes some of these elements.

The widespread application of EFT represents a logical next step for the healing professions.

Table 1. *EFT Methods, Their Derivations, and Major Proponents*

Clinical EFT Technique	Draws From	Proponent
Acupuncture	Oriental Medicine	Various
Aspects	Behavioral Therapy	Skinner
Chasing the Pain	Holistic Psychology	Wundt
Cognitive Shifts	Cognitive Therapy	Beck, Ellis
Cravings Masking Anxiety	Cravings Masking Anxiety	Callahan
Daisy Chaining	Talking Cure	Freud
Electromagnetic Energy Fields	Electroencephalography	Berger
Energy Field Effects	Quantum Physics	Einstein
Energy Basis of Matter	String Theory	Kaku
Floor to Ceiling Eye Roll	Eye Movements	Feldenkrais
Gentle Techniques	Client Centered	Rogers
Handling Excessive Intensity	Gestalt Therapy	Perls
Molecular Basis of Emotions	Psychoneuroimmunology	Pert
Movie Technique	Neuro Linguistic Programming	Bandler, Grinder
Nine Gamut	Nine Gamut	Callahan
Psychological Reversal	Reversal of Body Morality	Diamond
Reframing	Cognitive Therapy	Beck, Ellis

(continued)

Table 1. (*Continued*)

Clinical EFT Technique	Draws From	Proponent
Reminder Phrase	Exposure Therapy	Foa
Secondary Gain	Secondary Gain	Freud
Setup Statement First Half	Exposure Therapy	Foa
Setup Statement Second Half	Cognitive Therapy	Beck, Ellis
Setup while Tapping	Counterconditioning	Wolpe
Sneaking Up	Reciprocal Inhibition	Wolpe
Somatic Stimulation	Counterconditioning	Wolpe, Levine
Specific Events	ACE Study	Felliti
SUD	Systematic Desensitization	Wolpe
Tail-enders	Neuro Linguistic Programming	Bandler, Grinder
Tapping on Acupoints	Traditional Oriental Medicine	Callahan
Tell the Story, Movie	Talking Cure	Freud
Testing	Client-Centered Therapy	Rogers

It gives them the ability to rapidly remediate both psychological and physiological issues. To whatever degree a problem is related to stress, EFT can address it. To use the analogy of the authors of the ACE Study, EFT fights the fire of emotional trauma at the source of the blaze. It can extinguish the flame of suffering from both childhood and adult events. These events run the gamut of human suffering, and include:

- Bullying
- Test anxiety
- Domestic violence
- Self-esteem deficits
- Accidents and emergencies
- Performance anxiety
- Interpersonal problems
- Negative emotions such as anger, guilt, and shame
- Work-related stress
- Family conflict
- Sports performance
- Natural disasters
- Human-caused disasters
- Political differences
- Cultural and racial conflict

The Buddha's dream of liberating human beings from suffering comes closer with every advance we make in emotional self-management. EFT can play an important role in emotional liberation, both for individuals, and for societies, as it mitigates the stress that inhibits self-actualization. At that point, human creativity and awareness is unlocked, and we become capable of actualizing much more of our potential.

References

Baker, A. H. & Siegel, M. A. (2010). Emotional Freedom Techniques (EFT) reduces intense fears: A partial replication and extension of Wells et al. *Energy Psychology: Theory, Research, and Treatment, 2*(2), 13–30. doi:10.9769.EPJ.2010.2.2.AHB

Bandler, R. & Grinder, J. (1979). *Frogs into princes: Neuro linguistic programming.* Moab, UT: Real People.

Beck, A. T., Rush, A. J., Shaw, B. F., & Emery, G. (1979). *Cognitive therapy of depression.* New York, NY: Guilford Press.

Bradley, R., Greene, J., Russ, E., Dutra, L., & Western, D. (2005). A multidimensional meta-analysis of psychotherapy for PTSD. *American Journal of Psychiatry, 162,* 214–227.

Breuer, A. & Freud, S. (1895). *Standard edition of the complete psychological works of Sigmund Freud, Vol 2.* New York, NY: Hogarth Press.

Callahan, R. J. (2001). The impact of thought field therapy on heart rate variability. *Journal of Clinical Psychology, 57*(10), 1153–1170.

Church, D. (2010). Your DNA is not your destiny: Behavioral epigenetics and the role of emotions in health. *Anti Aging Medical Therapeutics, 13,* 35–42.

Church, D. & Brooks, A. J. (2010). The effect of a brief EFT (Emotional Freedom Techniques) self-intervention on anxiety, depression, pain and cravings in healthcare workers. *Integrative Medicine: A Clinician's Journal, 9*(4), 40–44.

Church, D. & Brooks, A. J. (2013). The effect of EFT (Emotional Freedom Techniques) on psychological symptoms in addiction treatment: A pilot study. *International Journal of Scientific Research and Reports, 2*(2).

Church, D. De Asis, M., & Brooks, A. (2012). Brief group intervention using EFT (Emotional Freedom Techniques) for depression in college students: A randomized controlled trial. *Depression Research and Treatment, 2012,* 1–7. doi:10.1155/2012/257172

Church, D. & Feinstein, D. (2013). Energy psychology in the treatment of PTSD: Psychobiology and clinical principles. In T. Van Leeuwen & M. Brouwer (Eds.), *Psychology of trauma* (pp. 211–224). Hauppage, NY: Nova Science Publishers.

Church, D., Hawk, C., Brooks, A., Toukolehto, O., Wren, M., Dinter, I., & Stein, P. (2013). Psychological trauma symptom improvement in veterans using EFT (Emotional Freedom Techniques): A randomized controlled trial. *Journal of Nervous and Mental Disease, 201,* 153–160.

Craig, G. (2008). *The EFT manual.* Santa Rosa, CA: Energy Psychology Press.

Darwin, C. (1872). *The expression of emotions in man and animals.* London, UK: John Murray.

Deuraseh, N. & Abu Talib, M. (2005). Mental health in Islamic medical tradition. *International Medical Journal, 4,* 76–79.

Dhond, R. P., Kettner, N., & Napadow, V. (2007). Neuroimaging acupuncture effects in the human brain. *Journal of Alternative and Complementary Medicine, 13,* 603–616. doi:10.1089/acm.2007.7040

Diamond, J. (1985). *Life energy.* New York, NY: Dodd, Mead.

Diepold, J. H. & Goldstein, D. (2008). Thought Field Therapy and qEEG changes in the treatment of trauma: A case study. *Traumatology, 15,* 85–93. doi:10.1177/1534765608325304

Dusek, J. A., Out, H. H., Wohlhueter, A. L., Bhasin, M., Zerbini, L. F., Libermann, T. A., & Benson, H. (2008). Genomic counter-stress changes induced by a mind body practice. *PLoS One, 3,* e2576.

Fang, J., Jin, Z., Wang, Y., Li, K., Kong, J., Nixon, E. E., … Hui, K. K.-S. (2009). The salient characteristics of the central effects of acupuncture needling: Limbic-paralimbic-neocortical network modulation. *Human Brain Mapping, 30,* 1196–1206. doi:10.1002/hbm.20583

Feinstein, D. (2008) Energy psychology in disaster relief. *Traumatology, 141,* 124–137.

Feinstein, D. (2010). Rapid treatment of PTSD: Why psychological exposure with acupoint tapping may be effective. *Psychotherapy: Theory, Research, Practice, Training, 47,* 385–402. doi:10.1037/a0021171

Feinstein, D. (2012). Acupoint stimulation in treating psychological disorders: Evidence of efficacy. *Review of General Psychology, 16*(4), 364–380. doi:10.1037/a0028602

Feinstein, D. & Church, D. (2010) Modulating gene expression through psychotherapy: The contribution of non-invasive somatic interventions. *Review of General Psychology, 14,* 283–295. doi:10.1037/a0021252

Feldenkrais, M. (1984). *The master moves.* Cupertino, CA: Meta Publications.

Felliti, V. J., Koss, M. P., & Marks, J. S. (1998). Relationship of childhood abuse and household dysfunction to many of the leading causes of death in adults. The Adverse Childhood Experiences (ACE) Study. *American Journal of Preventive Medicine, 14,* 245–258. doi:10.1016/S0749-3797(98)00017-8

Felmingham, K., Kemp, A., & Williams, L. (2006). Changes in anterior cingulate and amygdala after cognitive behavior therapy of posttraumatic stress disorder. *Psychological Science, 18,* 127–129. doi:10.1111/j.1467-9280.2007.01860.x

Fleming, T. (1996). *Reduce traumatic stress in minutes: The Tapas Acupressure Technique (TAT) workbook.* Torrence, CA: Author.

Flint, G. A., Lammers, W., & Mitnick, D. G. (2005). Emotional Freedom Techniques: A safe treatment intervention for many trauma based issues. In J. Garrick & M. B. Williams (Eds.), *Trauma treatment techniques: Innovative trends* (p. 125–150). New York, NY: Routledge.

Foa, E. B. (1979). Failure in treating obsessive-compulsives. *Behaviour Research and Therapy, 17*(3), 169–176.

Fraga, M. F., Ballestar, E., Paz, M. F., Ropero, S., Setien, F., Ballestar, M. L., … Esteller, M. (2005). Epigenetic differences arise during the lifetime of monozygotic twins. *Proceedings of the National Academy of Sciences USA, 102*(30), 10604–10609.

Gallo, F. P. (2000). *Energy diagnostic and treatment methods.* New York, NY: Norton.

Goodheart, G. J. (1987). *You'll be better.* Geneva, OH: Author.

Hui, K. K.-S., Liu, J., Marina, O., Napadow, V., Haselgrove, C., Kwong, K. K., … Makris, N. (2005). The integrated response of the human cerebro-cerebellar and limbic systems to acupuncture stimulation at ST 36 as evidenced by fMRI. *NeuroImage, 27,* 479–496.

Institute of Medicine, Committee on Treatment of Posttraumatic Stress Disorder. (2007). *Treatment of posttraumatic stress disorder: An assessment of the evidence.* Washington DC: Institute of Medicine. Retrieved from http://www.nap.edu/catalog/11955.html

Jirtle, R. L. & Skinner, M. K. (2007). Environmental epigenomics and disease susceptibility. *Nature Reviews Genetics, 8,* 253–262.

Kandel, E. (1998). A new intellectual framework for psychiatry. *American Journal of Psychiatry, 155,* 457–469.

Kendall-Tackett, K. (2009). Psychological trauma and physical health: A psychoneuroimmunology approach to etiology of negative health effects and possible interventions. *Psychological Trauma: Theory, Research, Practice, and Policy, 1,* 35–48.

Krasnegor, N. A., Lyon, G. R., & Goldman-Rakic, P. S. (Eds.). (1997). *Development of the prefrontal cortex: Evolution, neurobiology, and behavior.* New York, NY: Brookes.

Lambrou, P. T., Pratt, G. J., & Chevalier, G. (2003). Physiological and psychological effects of a mind/body therapy on claustrophobia. *Subtle Energies and Energy Medicine, 14,* 239–251.

LeDoux, J. (2002). *Synaptic self: How our brains become who we are.* New York, NY: Penguin.

Lepine, J-P. & Briley, M. (2011). The increasing burden of depression. *Neuropsychiatric Disease Treatment, 7*(1), 3–7.

Levine, P. A. (1997). *Waking the tiger: Healing trauma: The innate capacity to transform overwhelming experiences.* Berkeley, CA: North Atlantic Books.

Maslow, A. (1954). *Motivation and personality.* New York, NY: Harper.

McCrone, J. (2004). How do you persist when your molecules don't? *Science and Consciousness Review.* Accessed June 1, 2008 at www.sci-con.com/articles/20040601

Napadow, V., Kettner, N., Liu, J., Li, M., Kwong, K. K., Vangel, M., … Hui, K. K. (2007) Hypothalamus and amygdala response to acupuncture stimuli in carpal tunnel syndrome. *Pain, 130*(3), 254–266.

Ornish, D., Magbanua, M. J. M., Weidner, G., Weinberg, V., Kemp, C., Green, C., ... Carroll, P. R. (2008). Changes in prostate gene expression in men undergoing an intensive nutrition and lifestyle intervention. *Proceedings of the National Academy of Sciences USA, 105(24)*, 8369–8374.

Palmer-Hoffman, J. & Brooks, A. J. (2011). Psychological symptom change after group application of Emotional Freedom Techniques (EFT). *Energy Psychology: Theory, Research, & Treatment, 3*(1), 33–38.

Perls, F. A. (1969). *Ego, hunger, and aggression: The beginning of Gestalt Therapy.* New York, NY: Random House.

Phelps, E. A. & LeDoux, J. E. (2005). Contributions of the amygdala to emotion processing: From animal models to human behavior. *Neuron, 48*, 175–187.

Rogers, C. R. (1957). The necessary and sufficient conditions of therapeutic personality change. *Journal of Consulting Psychology, 21*(2), 95–103.

Rowe, J. E. (2005). The effects of EFT on long-term psychological symptoms. *Counseling and Clinical Psychology, 2*, 104–111.

Salas, M. M., Brooks, A. J., & Rowe, J. E. (2011). The immediate effect of a brief energy psychology intervention (Emotional Freedom Techniques) on specific phobias: A pilot study. *Explore: The Journal of Science and Healing, 7*(3), 255–260.

Shapiro, F. (1995). *Eye movement desensitization and reprocessing (EMDR): Basic principles, protocols, and procedures.* New York, NY: Guilford Press.

Shealy, N. & Church, D. (2008). *Soul medicine: Awakening your inner blueprint for abundant health and energy.* Santa Rosa, CA: Energy Psychology Press.

Shubin, N. (2009). *Your inner fish: A journey into the 3.5-billion-year history of the human body.* New York, NY: Vintage.

Skinner, B. F. (1938). *The behavior of organisms: An experimental analysis.* New York, NY: Appleton-Century.

Smith, H. (2004). The news of eternity. In D. Church & G. Gendreau (Eds.), *Healing our planet, healing our selves* (pp. 43-48). Santa Rosa, CA: Elite Books.

Smuts, J. (1926). *Holism and evolution.* New York, NY: Viking.

Swingle, P. G., Pulos, L., & Swingle, M. K. (2004). Neurophysiological indicators of EFT treatment of posttraumatic stress. *Subtle Energies and Energy Medicine, 15*(1), 75–86.

Syed, I. B. (2002). Islamic medicine: 1000 years ahead of its times. *Journal of the International Society for the History of Islamic Medicine, 2*, 7–8.

Wells, S., Polglase, K., Andrews, H. B., Carrington, P., & Baker, A. H. (2003). Evaluation of a meridian-based intervention, Emotional Freedom Techniques (EFT), for reducing specific phobias of small animals. *Journal of Clinical Psychology, 59*, 943–966. doi:10.1002/jclp.10189

Wilson, E. O. (1978). What is sociobiology? *Society, 15*(6), 10–14.

Wolpe, J. (1958) *Psychotherapy by reciprocal inhibition.* Palo Alto, CA: Stanford University Press.

Wundt, W. (1894). Ueber psychische Kausalitat und das Prinzip des psychophysichen Parallelismus. *Philosophische Studien, 10,* 1–124.

Chapter 5
What Does *Energy* Have to Do with Energy Psychology?
David Feinstein

Abstract

An obstacle to professional acceptance of the growing body of research supporting the efficacy of energy psychology is the vague use of the term *energy* in the field's name and explanatory frameworks. This chapter explores whether the concept of "energy" is necessary to fully account for the observed clinical outcomes that follow "energy psychology" treatments. Evidence is presented that shifting 3 types of energy—electromagnetic signals, brain waves, and energy fields—gives energy psychology protocols their advantage in quickly changing longstanding patterns in the brain. *Electromagnetic signals* that reduce threat arousal in the amygdala follow the stimulation of selected acupuncture points (acupoints). Acupoint stimulation also produces delta *waves* that are believed to depotentiate neural pathways that maintain maladaptive fear. Meanwhile, *energy fields* that organize neural activity provide a possible solution to a quandary in neuroscience. Conventional neurological models cannot explain how the diverse brain activities that are involved in information processing are coordinated. Just as electromagnetic fields have been shown to organize cellular activity in wound healing, energy fields are believed to organize neurological processes. The rapid resolution of intrusive, unprocessed memories seen in energy psychology treatments is attributed, in part, to the way acupoint stimulation is able to directly impact these "organizing fields." A working model that attempts to explain energy psychology treatment outcomes contains 3 premises about electromagnetic and more "subtle" energies in psychotherapy: (a) energy is an omnipresent dimension of body and mind that can be influenced to impact each in desired ways, (b) energy carries information, and (c) clinical interventions can draw upon the ways energy fields, through resonance, influence other energy fields as well as neural activity.

Keywords: acupoints, reconsolidation, energy, fields, resonance

David Feinstein, PhD, is a clinical psychologist who has received nine national awards for his books on consciousness and energy healing. Correspondence: 777 East Main Street, Ashland, OR 97520. E-mail: df777@earthlink.net. Acknowledgments: I gratefully acknowledge comments on drafts of this chapter by Maarten Aalberse, doctorandus, John Freedom, Dag Hultcrantz, Douglas J. Moore, PhD, Robert Schwarz, PhD, and Anthony J. Tranguch, MD, PhD. Disclosures: The author derives income from trainings, clinical services, and books and articles related to the approach examined in this chapter. This chapter was published earlier in the journal *Energy Psychology: Theory, Research, and Treatment*.

Introduction

Energy psychology is a psychotherapeutic and self-help approach that combines established clinical methods (such as imaginal exposure and mindfulness) with somatic interventions (such as the stimulation of acupuncture points by tapping on them) for effecting therapeutic change. By using the term *energy* in its name and explanatory models, energy psychology has opened itself to criticisms, conceptual confusion, and skepticism about mobilizing vague forms of energy for healing—skepticism that reaches back at least to the fierce controversies surrounding vitalism (Williams, 2003), ether as a physical medium (Duffy & Levy, 2009), orgone therapy (Reich, 1973), and Franz Anton Mesmer's (1734–1815) "animal magnetism." There is little question that the efficacy claims of energy psychology practitioners—which have been roundly criticized and sometimes ridiculed (e.g., Devilly, 2005; Herbert & Gaudiano, 2001; Lohr, 2001; McCaslin, 2009; McNally, 2001; Pignotti & Thyer, 2009)—would receive a more receptive hearing if the explanatory models were couched exclusively in conventional clinical language. More accepted terminology might include cognitive restructuring, exposure treatment, desensitization, counter-conditioning, information processing, sensorimotor interventions, neural reorganization, or even the modulation of gene expression (Feinstein & Church, 2010), all of which are probably involved.

A survey of 51 peer-reviewed journal articles describing outcomes of energy psychology treatments found that all 51 reported positive changes in symptoms or behavior (Feinstein, 2012). The articles investigated outcomes following Thought Field Therapy (TFT) or Emotional Freedom Techniques (EFT) treatments, the two most extensively practiced and researched energy psychology formats. Each utilizes the stimulation of selected acupuncture points (acupoints) by tapping on them. A critical analysis of the 18 randomized controlled trials (RCTs) in this sample showed that their findings "consistently demonstrated strong effect sizes and other positive statistical results that far exceed chance after relatively few treatment sessions" (p. 14). In three of the investigations—with survivors of genocide or abuse—posttraumatic stress disorder (PTSD) scores dropped from well above to well below clinical PTSD cutoffs on self-inventories or caregiver inventories for a majority of participants after a *single* treatment session (Church, Piña, Reategui, & Brooks, 2011; Connolly & Sakai, 2011; Sakai, Connolly, & Oas, 2010). Sustained improvement was found at 1 year (Sakai et al., 2010) and 2 years (Connolly & Sakai, 2011). These single-session PTSD studies corroborated earlier field reports of successful single-session PTSD treatments with more than 300 disaster survivors (described in Feinstein, 2012). The 51 articles reviewed presented statistically significant evidence regarding nine conditions that responded favorably to energy psychology treatments. In addition to PTSD, these included phobias, specific anxieties, generalized anxiety, depression, weight control, physical pain, physical illness, and athletic performance.

With accumulating evidence supporting the efficacy of energy psychology, the question "if it works, how does it work?" becomes more prominent. Numerous explanations that attempt to account for the neurological mechanisms involved have been proposed (e.g., Alberse, 2012; Feinstein, 2010, 2012; Feinstein & Church, 2010; Lane, 2009; Ruden, 2005, 2010). This chapter examines whether the concept of "energy" increases the explanatory power of existing models.

Existing Explanatory Models and Their Limitations

Explanations by early proponents of the approach (e.g., Callahan & Callahan, 1996) focused on hypothesized "thought fields" and principles of acupuncture that traced to traditional Chinese medicine. Laboratory findings in areas germane to energy psychology have since made it possible for explanatory models to be better informed by empirical evidence. For instance, a number of studies have identified physiological changes that correlate with the observed clinical improvements. Acupoint stimulation has been shown in published or pilot studies to reduce levels of the stress hormone cortisol, activate stress-reducing genes, normalize aberrant brain wave patterns, and increase production of serotonin, opioids, and other neurotransmitters associated with pleasure (summarized in Church & Feinstein, in press).

Physiological correlates of subjective and behavioral improvements are not, however, mechanisms of action. Studies using electroencephalogram (EEG), functional magnetic resonance imaging (fMRI), and positron emission tomography (PET) scans have revealed two *mechanisms* that are presumably involved in the established psychological effects of acupoint stimulation.

An ongoing research program at Harvard Medical School using fMRI and PET scans has conclusively shown that stimulating selected acupoints produces extensive deactivation in the amygdala and other areas of the limbic system (Dhond, Kettner, & Napadow, 2007; Fang et al., 2009; Hui et al., 2000, 2005). Energy psychology protocols combine acupoint tapping with the activation of unwanted emotions through imaginal exposure, usually by bringing to mind a problematic memory or trigger. This simultaneously *increases* arousal (through the imaginal exposure) while at the same time *decreasing* arousal (through electromagnetic signals sent to the limbic system via acupoint tapping). In reconciling these opposing signals, the brain is ultimately able to engage the memory or trigger without limbic arousal. While the Harvard researchers used traditional acupuncture needling as their primary means of stimulating the acupoints they examined, various other investigators have found a normalization of brain wave patterns following acupoint tapping for anxiety-related or neurological disorders (Diepold & Goldstein, 2009; Lambrou, Pratt, & Chevalier, 2003; Swingle, 2010; Swingle, Pulos, & Swingle, 2004). A double-blind study comparing penetration by acupuncture needling with nonpenetrating pressure also found equivalent clinical improvements for the two interventions (Takakura & Yajima, 2009). Whether using needles, tapping, or other means, the process starts with acupoint stimulation generating piezoelectricity (electricity produced by mechanical pressure), the same principle that causes the spark that lights a cigarette lighter or a propane barbecue. Electrical currents are then sent to cells, organs, and other biological systems via the body's connective tissue (Oschman, 2003).

So a relatively well-established mechanism of action in energy psychology protocols is that electrical signals produced by tapping on selected acupoints during imaginal exposure reduce limbic arousal. A second process, this one involving brain waves, has also been identified. Repetitive sensory stimulation, in this case tapping on acupoints, generates large increases in the amplitude of delta waves in areas of the brain involved in fear memories, as detected by EEG readings. After several minutes of stimulation, these amplified delta waves have been shown to disrupt activated memory networks, reminiscent of the "natural memory editing system" found in delta wave of sleep (Harper, 2012, p. 61). Specifically, glutamate receptors on synapses that mediate a fear memory are believed to be "depotentiated by these powerful waves of neuronal firing" (p. 61). When the neural circuits in the amygdala that maintain the threat response are deactivated in this manner (during virtually *any* exposure therapy protocol that employs repetitive psychosensory stimulation on upper parts of the body, according to Harper's findings), "the material basis of the fear memory has been removed" (p. 64). Ruden (2010) has incorporated this and related neurological findings into a sophisticated protocol for trauma treatment.

Sending *deactivating signals* to the amygdala and generating *delta waves* that disrupt activated memory networks are two ways acupoint tapping appears to evoke *energies* that impact brain activity in therapeutic ways. These mechanisms suggest a logical neurological sequence in the treatment of serious disorders such as PTSD. The sequence progresses from (a) PTSD involving, at its psychophysiological core, a proclivity for amygdala hyperarousal, to (b) the stimulation of acupoints generating (c) deactivating signals and depotentiating brain waves while the threat response has been triggered by imaginal exposure, (d) turning off the threat response and possibly eradicating neural pathways, in a manner that (e) permanently changes the conditioned response to the trigger or memory. This formulation offers a plausible rationale for the distinctive ways acupoint stimulation serves as an active ingredient in energy psychology protocols beyond the other elements that are found in most therapies (therapeutic alliance, empathic communication, etc.).

While this account is consistent with established neurological principles, it has some gaps and limitations. First, controversy exists about whether "sham points" may be as clinically effective as the points used in traditional acupuncture, with some evidence suggesting that the traditional points are more effective (Lang et al., 2007) and other studies suggesting that sham points may be equally effective (Haake et al., 2007).

Second, although the model is consistent with existing physiological and clinical data, it has not been scientifically tested. Imaging equipment is available that could confirm or disconfirm each stage of the hypothesized sequence described earlier, but these studies are yet to be conducted. And even if imaging studies were to confirm that the neurological processes involved in treating PTSD have been accurately anticipated, the range of disorders that appear to respond to essentially the same acupoint tapping protocols (Feinstein, 2012) requires explanation.

Third, the surprising speed and power observed during energy psychology treatments themselves pose a challenge to existing paradigms (Feinstein, 2009). Anyone who knows someone struggling with longstanding PTSD or who is familiar with the professional literature on treating the disorder will do a double-take on hearing of the studies referred to earlier in which a vast majority of subjects who had scored above PTSD cut-offs on standardized measures were substantially below those cut-offs after a single session. In fact, in an informal survey of 265 energy psychology practitioners, less than 1% said they believed that the primary active ingredient in energy psychology treatments can be explained exclusively in conventional terms (reported in Feinstein, 2004). Might the "energy" dimension of energy psychology play a more systemic role in these surprising outcomes than the relatively confined effects of generating electromagnetic deactivating signals and memory-disrupting delta waves?

Does "Energy" Have a Legitimate Role in Explanatory Models?

While scientific frameworks in conventional Western thought are still dominated by a rigid materialism and mechanistic worldview, leading-edge scientists, studying topics from neurology to quantum mechanics, are finding them inadequate for addressing some of the most pressing questions in their respective fields (Laszlo & Dennis, 2012). Nowhere is this more evident than in medicine. Bruce Lipton, a cell biologist who did some of the pioneering work on stem cells and on gene expression while on the medical school faculties at Stanford and at the University of Wisconsin, has suggested that medicine is a century behind modern physics in utilizing the realization that the universe is most fundamentally made—not of seemingly separate billiard ball-like atoms and molecules suspended in empty space—but of energy:

> Quantum physicists discovered that physical atoms are made up of vortices of energy that are constantly spinning and vibrating … The fact that energy and matter are one and the same is precisely what Einstein recognized when he concluded: $E = mc^2$. … The Universe is *one indivisible, dynamic whole* in which energy and matter are so deeply entangled it is impossible to consider them as independent elements (Lipton, 2005, pp. 100–102).

Conventional medicine focuses first on the chemical side of illness and healing, largely from a Newtonian "poolball" perspective; energy medicine and energy psychology focus first on the energy side.

Strengths of an Energy-Attuned Model

Lipton (2005) pointed out that a linear, mechanistic understanding of the complex information exchanges involved in the body's normal functioning cannot "even come close to giving us an accurate understanding of disease" (p. 103) while "hundreds upon hundreds of … scientific studies over the last fifty years have consistently revealed that 'invisible forces' of the electromagnetic spectrum profoundly impact every facet of biological regulation" (p. 111).

Two clinically vital qualities that distinguish energy from chemistry are speed and responsiveness. With 50 to 100 trillion cells comprising the human body, survival depends upon the speed and efficiency of signal transfer. The act of walking requires communication among millions of cells. While chemical signals proceed at less than 0.5 in./s and much of the signal's energy is lost in the heat generated by thermochemical coupling (Lipton, 2005), electromagnetic signals travel through nerve fibers at up to 500 feet/s, and energy fields can "broadcast" information to other energy fields at the speed of light's 186,000 miles/s. Lipton (2005) described research suggesting that "energetic signaling mechanisms such as electromagnetic frequencies are a hundred times more efficient in relaying environmental information than physical signals such as hormones, neurotransmitters, etc." (p. 112). Biologists have also repeatedly demonstrated the extraordinary sensitivity and responsiveness organisms have to tiny signals in the environment (Oschman, 2000, 2005), including an ability to detect extremely weak electromagnetic fields and discriminate them from background "noise" involving much stronger signals (Adey & Bawin, 1977). Recognizing this sensitivity to gradients of electromagnetic information fills a gap in our understanding of the complex information processing accomplished by the human brain.

Six strengths of utilizing an energy medicine framework have been identified as involving its abilities to (a) address biological activities at their energetic foundations; (b) regulate physiological processes with precision, speed, and flexibility; (c) foster healing and prevent illness with interventions that can be readily, economically, and noninvasively applied; (d) include methods that can be utilized on an at-home, self-help basis, fostering a stronger patient and practitioner partnership in the healing process; (e) adopt nonlinear concepts consistent with distant healing, the healing impact of prayer, and the role of intention in healing; and (f) strengthen the integration of body, mind, and spirit, leading not only to a focus on healing but to achieving greater well-being, peace, and passion for life (Feinstein & Eden, 2008). These strengths have led nationally prominent physicians such as Christiane Northrup (2008), Norm Shealy (1998), and Mehmet Oz (2007) to publicly predict that energy medicine will play a central role in the future of medicine. According to Dr. Oz (2007), "Energy medicine is the last great frontier in medicine!"

Energy Psychology's Three Primary Energy Systems

Energy psychology is a branch of energy medicine in a manner somewhat analogous to the way psychiatry is a branch of conventional medicine. Psychiatry applies medical principles and procedures for enhancing mental health; energy psychology applies energy medicine principles and procedures toward the same objective. Complementing the familiar energies that fall within the electromagnetic spectrum, energy healing practitioners believe they are also working with energies that involve a "subtle" dimension that is not easily detected or measured (Collinge, 1998). The Association for Comprehensive Energy Psychology (www.energypsych.org) identifies three subtle energy systems that may be addressed by energy psychology interventions: (a) energy pathways, such as "meridians"; (b) energy centers, such as "chakras"; and (c) the energy field surrounding the body, known scientifically as the "biofield," or in healing and spiritual traditions as the "aura."

All three forms of subtle energy—meridians, chakras, and biofields—have been independently discovered and worked with by healers throughout the world over the millennia. At least 97 cultures refer to the human aura, each calling it by their own name (White & Krippner, 1977). The chakras, according to Collinge (1998), are

> major centers of both electromagnetic and vital energy [which] are recognized in indigenous cultures the world over. In the Huna tradition of Hawaii, they are called auw centers; and in the Cabala, they are the "tree of life" centers. In the Taoist Chinese traditions the term is dantien, and in yogic theory they are called "chakras" (p. 35).

"Vital energy" is also believed to flow throughout the body along an unseen network of pathways, which are called "meridians" in traditional Chinese medicine and "nadis" in the yogic tradition of ancient India. Each of these energy systems—the aura, chakras, and meridians—is thought of as involving electromagnetic as well as subtle energies.

Empirical Support for the Existence of Subtle Energies

Not only are the existence of the aura, chakras, and meridians corroborated across cultures, but each has been distinguished by electromagnetic measures and other physical verifications. Hundreds of experiments using dozens of unconventional instruments, in fact, have pointed to the existence of energies that are not described within conventional frameworks (Church, 2009; Collinge, 1998; Dale, 2009; Gerber, 2001; Oldfield & Coghill, 2011; Swanson, 2003, 2010; Tiller, 1997). For instance, a vivid demonstration of subtle energy in a lab setting, originally conducted in Russia, has been followed by collaborative experiments between the Institute of Heartmath in California and the Institute of Biochemical Physics of the Russian Academy of Sciences (Poponin, 2002). A laser beam sent through a vacuum showed distinct patterns in the vacuum's energy field after a sealed container holding DNA was placed in the vacuum. After the DNA was removed, with strict vacuum conditions maintained, the laser beam was again passed through the vacuum. This time, patterns of light oscillation that were not in the vacuum prior to the insertion of the DNA were found after the DNA was removed. These remaining oscillations have been interpreted as being the subtle energy imprint of the DNA. Had they been electromagnetic imprints, which propagate at the speed of light, any such traces would have quickly left the chamber or been absorbed. But, as Swanson (2010) commented, these traces had "an independent, stable existence" (p. 128).

Holding that such energies are more than mere artifacts of nature, Swanson (2010) proposed that "subtle energy modifies the familiar forces of electromagnetism, gravity, and the nuclear forces [and] appears to be the source of auras and chakras and the qi [life force] which flows through the acupuncture system of the body" (pp. 48–49). Perhaps the most provocative quality of subtle energy for psychotherapists, however, is that "it responds to and interacts with thought" (Swanson, 2010, p. 50). The influence of intention on plant growth (McTaggart, 2007; Tompkins & Bird, 1973) and healing (Schmidt, 2012), as well as on mechanical instruments (Nelson, Bradish, Dobyns, Dunne, & Jahn, 1996; Tiller, 1997), has substantial empirical support, and some form of subtle energy appears to be mediating (Dale, 2009).

A Working Model for Energy Psychology

That memories, beliefs, feelings, thoughts, and habits of behavior are coded in the brain is well established. Also unquestioned is the fact that energy can carry information, as in the light waves that are bringing these words to your eyes, sound waves, radio waves, and other electromagnetic frequencies such as x-rays. Not so familiar is the way these electromagnetic energies may interact in coordinating psychological processes, with energy fields organizing the brain's neurons in coding information.

The original explanatory model within energy psychology was Roger Callahan's formulation of the "thought field." Callahan viewed a thought field as a "force field" in the body that "carries thoughts and information" (Callahan & Callahan, 2011, p. xxi). Callahan's Thought Field Therapy instructs the client in ways of tuning into the thought field associated with a psychological problem. Tapping on specific acupuncture points after this thought field has been mentally activated is believed to resolve energy disturbances that were involved with that problem. The desired result of this sequence is that the thought field that was sustaining the problematic emotional responses, behaviors, and ways of thinking will be altered.

How the Brain Processes Disturbing Experiences

Before addressing how energy fields might be able to therapeutically impact emotions, thought, and behavior, we will first review current understanding of the ways the brain manages distressful experiences. Ecker, Ticic, and Hulley (2012) summarized recent findings about how the brain stores and revises emotional learning. Core beliefs and mental models formed in the presence of intense emotion during childhood or later "are locked into the brain by extraordinarily durable synapses" (p. 3) that normally persist for the remainder of the person's life. Neuroscience research since 2004 has, however, demonstrated that—by facilitating a specific sequence of experiences—it is possible to activate targeted emotional learnings and chemically unlock their synapses "for prompt dissolution of those retrieved learnings at their emotional and neural roots" (p. 8). Through this process of "depotentiating" (deactivating at the synaptic level) the neural pathways maintaining emotional learnings that are at the basis of psychological problems, "major, longstanding symptoms can cease [because] their very basis no longer exists" (p. 4). When synapses are temporarily unlocked during the precise set of conditions described below, neural pathways that sustain old emotional learnings may be altered or totally eradicated.

The key involves the way the brain first *consolidates* emotionally charged experiences (translating them into memory) and may then, after such experiences have been recalled, *reconsolidate* them (reintegrate retrieved memories into the memory system in a way that maintains or modifies the memory). Experiences become consolidated into working memory within seconds, and then into short-term memory within minutes to hours, through the synthesis of proteins that form synaptic pathways between neurons ("synaptic consolidation"), a hippocampus-mediated process. Over time they are further consolidated with other memories ("systems consolidation"), a process that involves the neocortex (Roediger, Dudai, & Fitzpatrick, 2007). Memories are formed by separate memory systems into two basic layers, implicit and explicit memories. Implicit memories do not involve conscious recall of an event. They are, rather, encoded as behavioral learnings, emotional reactions, perceptions of the outer world, and bodily sensations, as well as "generalizations across experiences, summarizing elements of lived moments into schema or mental models of events" (Siegel, 2010, p. 63). While implicit memories do not bring the earlier experience into conscious memory, they can impact current experiences without the person's recognition of their influence. This can be useful. The implicit memory system, in fact, plays a central role in daily functioning, from navigating one's way through repetitive choice points without having to seek a new solution each time, to routine procedures such as tying one's shoes or driving a car. We don't think about the steps or where we learned them. We simply do them, with our minds free to focus on other concerns.

Explicit memory involves the more familiar conscious recall of facts and events. First encoded by the hippocampus, memories of one's experiences subsequently become integrated as autobiographical memory at the neocortical level. Compared with the emotional or procedural learnings in the implicit memory network, which are stored in the subcortical limbic system and right cortical hemisphere, explicit memory

> is more flexible and gives us the factual scaffold of our understanding of the world as well as weaving a set of autobiographical puzzle piece assemblies. In other words, implicit memory provides the pieces; explicit memory assembles them into fuller pictures of the whole (Siegel, 2010, p. 64).

But when a memory is based on trauma or other difficult experiences, this integration of the implicit and explicit memory systems may not occur. Ecker et al. (2012) have explained that implicit memories of highly charged emotional events may, in fact, "underlie and generate" a large proportion of the symptoms people present in psychotherapy (p. 14), including symptoms that are often attributed to genetic and other factors, such as many forms of depression. They propose that the implicit memory system generates coherent mental models that "make deep sense in light of actual life experiences and are fully adaptive in how they embody the individual's efforts to avoid harm and ensure well-being" (p. 7). Symptoms, they feel, are best understood as emerging from mental models that reflect "adaptive, coherent strivings" (p. 7) from an earlier time rather than in the pathologizing terms found in much of the clinical literature. However, when these models are imposed on new circumstances, they are often limiting or harmful and may become the source of a range of psychological difficulties.

The Cost of Unprocessed Memories

Implicit body-level memories and learnings can influence perceptions, thoughts, and behavior in ways that produce psychological symptoms or are otherwise costly to the person's ability to thrive, and they tend to persist. If, however, the experience that evoked the implicit memory is paired with an experience that is in conflict with the person's predominant mental models, the conflict may enter consciousness in ruminations, mental enactments of what might have been done or said differently, or in dream content. Sleeping and dreaming are among the ways the brain attempts to reconcile implicit memories with experiences that challenge them (Walker & van der Helm, 2009). Conscious and unconscious mental activities converge to make sense of unsettling experiences, to put them into perspective by comparing them with related experiences from the past, and to glean learnings that can be applied when similar situations are encountered.

Some experiences, however, overwhelm a person's ability to integrate them with existing neural networks, and they are consolidated in the implicit memory system without subsequent integration by the neocortex. Traumatic experiences may actually be stored in fragments—as sensations, perceptions, emotions, thoughts, and impulses to react, such as to flee the situation—that can re-emerge and impact current perceptions and behavior with no conscious recognition of their origin. PTSD, stemming from intense trauma, has received the greatest attention, but many typical childhood or subsequent experiences—such as severe humiliation, betrayal, embarrassment, criticism, or a major loss or threat—can also create implicit memories and learnings that reactivate in the present and dominate information processing. Rather than being stored in the fragmentary manner seen in PTSD, these experiences tend to be coded in the implicit memory system as isolated but coherent internal schema for avoiding harm or adapting to difficult situations. Because they were formed to cope with circumstances that are usually no longer current, they may be at the root of automated, self-limiting thoughts, perceptions, and behavior. Such unprocessed implicit emotional learnings become intertwined and confused with the current experience, causing responses that are invisibly linked to the past while preventing desired outcomes in the present.

Most people, even those who are coping relatively well, carry numerous implicit memories that are echoed in their current behavior in ways that are self-limiting. If a male teacher who had bushy eyebrows was sexually provocative toward you, you may find yourself reflexively shying away from bushy-eyebrowed men. Sensory aspects of the original experience—smells, sounds, tastes, skin sensations, or images such as bushy eyebrows—can become triggers that evoke an old emotion or bodily response and result in your projecting it onto the current situation. Another person's tone of voice, gesture, or facial expression may cause you to overlay your emotions and responses from an early experience onto what is happening now. Resolving unprocessed memories through reconsolidation is a path out of these difficult and often self-defeating scenarios.

How the Brain Updates Emotional Learnings

Despite the stubborn tenacity of these deep emotional learnings, nature has established a mechanism for "updating existing learnings with new ones" (Ecker et al., 2012, p. 26). After an emotional memory has been brought to mind—in response to cues, triggers, context, or suggestion—the memory can, for a brief period, be reconsolidated in a new way. If, during this "reconsolidation window," which can last for several hours, a second vivid experience is introduced that differs significantly "from what the reactivated target memory expects and predicts about how the world functions" (p. 21), the original learning can be revised or completely eliminated. The old learning is replaced by a new experience that first challenged and then "disconfirmed" the outdated beliefs, models, and interpretations. This new, incompatible experience produces a neural mismatch that chemically "unlocks" the synapses of the earlier memory and "renders [its] circuits labile," that is, susceptible to change by "a new learning experience that contradicts (for erasing) or supplements (for revising) the labile target knowledge" (p. 27). For the synapses to "unlock," the disconfirming experience must be evoked while the original learning is still in a reactivated condition. For the memory to be reconsolidated in a new way, the same disconfirming experience must be repeated, or another experience that contradicts the mental model that grew from the original memory must be introduced, during the reconsolidation period.

Demonstrated first in animal studies and then in humans, this process can rapidly and permanently change "learnings formed in the presence of intense emotion" that, until recently, had appeared to psychotherapists as well as brain researchers to be so indelible that it seemed, after they had been established, that "the brain threw away the key" (Ecker et al., 2012, p. 3). We now know a great deal about the brain's keys for unlocking the synapses that maintain emotional memory. Ecker et al. (2012) summarized the clinical implications of these developments: "With clear knowledge of the brain's own rules for deleting emotional learnings through memory reconsolidation, therapists no longer have to rely largely on speculative theory, intuition, and luck for facilitating powerful, liberating shifts" (p. 4). Understanding the memory reconsolidation process has made it possible for clinicians to more systematically transform the core beliefs and mental models formed in response to earlier life experiences.

Therapeutically Resolving Unprocessed Memories

A century of psychotherapy has been dedicated to freeing people from old, dysfunctional patterns that are rooted in the past, allowing them to reach potentials that would otherwise remain beyond their grasp. Ways of overcoming limitations that trace to childhood were pioneered by psychodynamic therapists and have been refined by cognitive-behavioral therapists. Newer "power therapies" introduce additional therapeutic elements that are believed to enhance the speed and efficiency by which old habits and conditioned reflexes can be interrupted and new ones established (Commons, 2000). These "power therapies"—claimed by their proponents to be unusually effective in interrupting old habits of thought, feelings, and behavior and in establishing new ones—share in their use of somatic interventions. Along with energy psychology, prominent therapies utilizing somatic interventions include Eye Movement Desensitization and Reprocessing (Shapiro, 2001), Gestalt Therapy

(Polster & Polster, 1973), Hakomi (Kurtz, 2007), Sensorimotor Psychotherapy (Ogden, Kekuni, & Pain, 2006), and Somatic Experiencing (Levine, 2010).

In introducing the earliest energy psychology protocols, Callahan (1985) formulated a set of procedures that were remarkably attuned to the findings about memory reconsolidation that would emerge two decades later. The sequence of experiences necessary for systematically evoking the reconsolidation process to transform a target emotional learning, regardless of the form of therapy, has been described by Ecker et al. (2012): (a) vividly accessing emotional memories or learnings that are involved in the targeted symptom, (b) concurrently activating an experience that contradicts implicit models or conclusions that were drawn from the original experiences—which Ecker et al. termed a "juxtaposition experience," and (c) verifying that the change has occurred. During these steps, implicit memories and learnings enter the neocortex-mediated explicit memory system and integrate with neural pathways that support established coping strategies, their earlier adaptive functions are examined and appreciated, and their automated, unrecognized influence on current perceptions, thoughts, and behaviors are eliminated. This is how unprocessed implicit emotional memories and learnings are "processed."

In a typical energy psychology protocol, the initial rounds of acupoint tapping most often involve activating the symptom or presenting problem and the emotional learnings underlying it via imaginal exposure. The client calls up the issue using images, evocative phrases, or a felt sense of the problem. When the tapping has removed some of the emotional edge of the current problem, childhood memories that play into the current problem often spontaneously emerge, and as they become the new focus, their adaptive historical function can usually be discerned. Techniques for bridging to earlier memories, such as following a current feeling back to one of the first times that feeling was experienced, may also be used.

The second set of sequences—generating an experience that disconfirms the earlier learnings—is the most complex stage for most reconsolidation-oriented therapies, but it is where energy psychology protocols show their greatest advantage. Because stimulating selected acupoints almost instantly reduces limbic arousal (see Fang et al., 2009; Hui et al., 2005), the emotional landscape changes *during* the exposure. A traumatic memory or trigger that produced a physiological threat response is vividly imagined, but the disturbing physiological response is no longer present. The brain is experiencing a mismatch. The memory or trigger created a strong expectation that the implicit emotional learnings would be evoked, but the expected emotional reaction did not occur because acupoint stimulation had temporarily deactivated the limbic system. The juxtaposition of holding the troubling scene simultaneous with no physiological arousal is the mismatch that is the necessary ingredient for the scene that was mentally activated to be reconsolidated in a new way.

In this juxtaposition stage, energy psychology protocols closely mimic the early laboratory experiments with animals in which the role of reconsolidation was discovered. For instance, a red light in the cage of an experimental animal would glow just before a foul odor was administered. Once the implicit learning that the red light meant the odor was coming had been established, the red light alone would cause the animal to try to avoid the odor. But if the expected odor is not released following the appearance of the light, a mismatch between expectations and perceptions is created: "The synapses of the schema's neural circuit [are] molecularly unlocked, like an unlatching of train cars still sitting in place [so] the schema can be modified or erased permanently" (Ecker, 2010, p. 45). These conditions can be easily created in the laboratory, but they are more challenging to create in a clinical setting. The mismatch in energy psychology treatments, however, is generated by simply tapping on the skin, almost too easy to believe. The required mismatch or "disconfirming experience" is effected by bringing the trigger to mind while preventing the threat response from occurring via the deactivating signals the acupoint stimulation sends to the amygdala. Other therapies often have to work much harder to create suitable mismatch experiences.

For Ecker et al.'s (2012) third stage (verifying that the change has occurred), energy psychology practitioners use SUD (subjective units of distress) ratings to provide both the clinician and the client not only a way of readily verifying that the desired outcomes have occurred but also a gauge that can be frequently called upon to determine which elements of the treatment need adjustment or repetition. A single experience that contradicts an old learning can unlock the synapses, launching reconsolidation, but it usually must be repeated several times for unlearning to occur. The process of assigning the rating is essentially a mindfulness task that often also uncovers salient aspects of the situation that then receive attention.

The observations of Ecker et al. (2012) regarding therapeutic change, based on an understanding of the reconsolidation of emotional learnings, are consistent with the clinical and research findings emerging from within energy psychology. One of the most controversial but most significant of these is that "transformational change through the erasure sequence does not rely on extensive repetition over time to effect change" (p. 32). The rapid outcomes seen in energy psychology treatments are consistent with Ecker et al.'s observations about "the swiftness with which deep, decisive, lasting change occurs through the therapeutic reconsolidation process" (p. 32). This of course "challenges traditional notions of the time required for major therapeutic effects to come about" (p. 32), as reports of the single-session energy psychology treatments of PTSD discussed earlier have tended to do. Another pertinent observation is that the "mismatch" component—the visceral experience that contradicts the client's existing emotional knowledge and becomes the basis for the new learning—"must feel decisively *real* to the person based on his or her own living experience ... it must be experiential learning as distinct from conceptual, intellectual learning, though it may be accompanied by the latter" (p. 27). One of the most satisfying and frequently repeated experiences for energy psychology practitioners is watching the astonished expression on a person's face when bringing to mind a memory or trigger or entering an *in vivo* situation that 15 min earlier was met with the physiological components of terror but is now unable to produce any emotional charge whatsoever.

Variables that impact treatment speed and outcome include the age of the problematic emotional learning, its intensity, the context in which it was formulated, and the frequency of the experiences that led to and reinforced the emotional conclusions (Ecker et al., 2012). In discussing the durability of new learnings that are based on reconsolidation, Ecker et al. noted that new learning of any kind of course "creates brain change in the form of new neural connections," but "it is *only* when new learning also unwires old learning that *transformational* change occurs" (p. 33). In therapies that take advantage of the natural reconsolidation process, the "new learning directly impinges upon and revises the circuits of the old learning, rewiring and updating them" (p. 33). Eliminating the old learning through reconsolidation is necessary for clinical outcomes where "symptom cessation is rapid and complete, not subject to relapse, [and] remaining symptom-free is effortless" (p. 33). Such changes are of a different order than "extinction training," where learned responses are challenged and temporarily overridden by—but are *not* fundamentally changed or erased by—new conditioning. In reconsolidation, the original memory pathways are *themselves* changed. In extinction training, the new learnings are formed "in a physically separate memory system" that competes with "the target learning" (p. 16). As a result, extinction training has less power and the symptoms it does extinguish are subject to return.

Of particular interest with reconsolidation-informed therapies is the way that when an old emotional learning "is erased, erasure is limited to precisely the reactivated target learning, without impairing other closely linked emotional learnings that have not been directly reactivated" (p. 25). Consistent with reports from energy psychology practitioners, after the learned fear response has been eliminated, "subjects still remembered the experiences in which they had acquired the conditioned fear response, as well as the fact of having had the fear, but the fear was not re-evoked by remembering those experiences" (p. 25). In fact, energy psychology training programs teach practitioners to challenge positive outcomes (Adams & Davidson, 2011), asking the client to try to reproduce the fear, pain, anger, or other disturbing emotion associated with the target memory or trigger. If they can, the treatment is not complete. The speed with which an unwanted emotion can be decisively, experientially eliminated is one of the aspects of energy psychology treatments that clients find most convincing.

One final observation from Ecker et al. (2012)—that the treatment leads to an "increased sense of unified self and wholeness" (p. 33)—is also consistent with the outcomes reported by energy psychology practitioners. More than just overcoming symptoms, when outdated emotional learnings are transformed, eliminating their limiting beliefs and mental models, new connections with neural networks that support optimal functioning are formed. With little prompting, clients talk about themselves and their situations in more adaptive ways. Their view of their world and their place in it becomes more complex yet more coherent and empowering. In a comprehensive study of the developing mind, Siegel (2012) found increasing integration and coherence to be the hallmarks of healthy development. Such self-organization is reinforcing. Siegel explained that "a positive emotion arises with increases in integration, whereas a negative emotion occurs with decreases in integration" (p. 338). This impulse toward greater integration and health is organic. While self-limiting emotional memories that have not been processed interfere with the movement toward increased integration and coherence, they forcefully reveal themselves in symptoms, waking imagery, dreams, and problematic behavioral patterns. It is as if they push for expression in the psyche's calculus for promoting self-healing and personal evolution until they have been adequately processed.

Unanswered Questions

In discussing possible mechanisms of action in the "power therapies," Commons (2000) suggested that they work at the "subcortical level of brain activity," delaying conditioned stimuli from directly eliciting negative emotional responses "until the frontal lobes can perform their interpretive function" (p. 137). While this is consistent with current neurological understanding of what occurs when problematic implicit memories have been successfully processed, it does not address an even more basic question for the "power therapies," or any other form of psychotherapy for that matter.

No one knows how all the parts of a single memory are coordinated in the brain. Various brain structures work simultaneously in creating a memory, and that memory seems to be distributed over many areas of the brain. A visual image may be stored here. A physical sensation there. A judgment about the experience somewhere else. How they are integrated is unknown. Moreover, after trying for more than two centuries to locate just where and how memory is stored, neuroscientists are still unable to fully explain a most curious finding by the French physiologist Jean Pierre Flourens in the early 1800s (Yildirim & Sarikcioglu, 2007), revisited by the American psychologist Karl Lashley in the 1940s (Lashley, 1950). Lashley, and Flourens before him, surgically removed various parts of the brains of laboratory animals and watched the effects on their behavior. For instance, after training a rat to perform a complex task, Lashley would remove a part of its cerebral cortex, the region of the mammalian brain involved in the higher functions of the nervous system, and observe whether it could still do the task. What was most perplexing is that not only could up to half the cortex be removed without curbing the ability to do the task, it did not matter *which parts* of the cortex were removed. Independent of the specific areas of the cortex that were left intact, as long as at least half the cortex remained, the rat could still do the task. The same finding in different animals by subsequent researchers led one of them to famously state in *Scientific American* the enigmatic observation that "memory is both everywhere and nowhere in particular" (Boycott, 1965, p. 48).

What Is Added by an "Organizing Field" Hypothesis?

Lashley (1950) speculated that recall must involve "some sort of resonance among a very large number of neurons" (p. 479), but the enigma remained of how memory fragments stored throughout the brain are organized into a single experience at the time of recall (known to neurologists and consciousness researchers as the "binding problem"; Revonsuo & Newman, 1999). In 1981, the British biologist Rupert Sheldrake proposed that morphic (form-generating) fields organize the actions of neurons in forming thought as well as all other biological processes (Sheldrake, 1981). Fields (think of iron filings taking shape on a piece of paper with a magnet beneath it) are "lines of force" whose nature has been debated since Michael Faraday's studies of electromagnetism in the 1830s. Sheldrake built his morphic field hypothesis on the ways that quantum fields affect subatomic particles and extended the concept to atoms, molecules, cells, and more complex structures. The brain's morphic field, in this theory, organizes the neurons responsible for memory into a coherent system in ways that obviously occur but no one has adequately explained. The field's "lines of force," according to Sheldrake, operate through "resonance" (as Lashley had suggested) rather than a direct exchange of energy, much as the electrical field of a person's brain will start to resonate with the electromagnetic field of a nearby person's heart (McCraty, 2004).

Sheldrake emerged as a hero within the holistic healing community while being discounted or worse by mainstream scientists. In a scathing critique shortly after his book came out, the senior editor of *Nature* suggested that "This infuriating tract ... is the best candidate for burning there has been for many years" (Maddox, 1981, p. 246).

Nonetheless, energy fields have been shown to organize the activity in cells and group of cells. For example, after a wound, the immune system sets into motion a complex array of cascading chemicals to protect the body from further harm and to fix what has been damaged. At the same time, electrical currents connecting enormous numbers of cells are produced, *acting upon the body to stimulate growth and repair* (Liboff, 2004; Oschman, 2000). Oschman (2000) explained that an electrical field is generated at the site of a wound, and it remains until the repair is complete, attracting mobile skin cells, white blood cells, and fibroblasts that close and heal the wounds. Finally, as the tissue heals, the current changes and "feeds back information on the progress of repair to surrounding tissues" (p. 94). This remarkable level of orchestration between energy fields and cells operates—according to Sheldrake (1981), McTaggart (2008), and others—not only with the cells involved in immune and repair responses but also with the neurons involved in learning.

An early description of how organizing fields influence health, dating back to the 1930s, emerged from the research of Harold Burr, a neuroanatomist at the Yale School of Medicine. Burr measured the electrical field around an unfertilized salamander egg and found that it was shaped like a mature salamander (Burr, 1972), as if the blueprint for the adult were already there in the egg's energy field. The electrical axis that would later be aligned with the brain and spinal cord was already present in the unfertilized egg, as measured by a vacuum-tube voltmeter with extremely sensitive, nondistorting, silver/silver-chloride electrodes to detect microvolt differentials (devices that a contemporary engineer, after examining Burr's scientific papers, described in a peer-reviewed journal as having been both reliable and "remarkable for their time"; Matthews, 2007, p. 55). Burr went on to find electrical fields surrounding numerous organisms, from molds to plants to frogs to humans, and he was able to describe electrical patterns that distinguished health from illness. In a hospital-based study conducted in the 1940s, voltage abnormalities around the cervix were found to predict malignancies with 85% accuracy in more than 1000 women presenting with gynecological symptoms (Langman & Burr, 1947).

Burr demonstrated not only correspondences between specific pathologies and electrical characteristics of related organs but also that physical illness is *preceded* by changes in an organism's electromagnetic field (Burr & Northrup, 1935), a potentially cardinal finding for preventive medicine and a core principle of energy medicine.

The unanswered question in Burr's and Sheldrake's theories (as well as in other notable formulations or speculation about an *underlying reality*, such as Plato's "Forms," William James's "subtler forms of matter," Carl Jung's "archetypes," David Bohm's "implicate order," and Ervin Laszlo's "interconnected universe") is "what is the nature of this hypothetical medium" (Radin, 2006, p. 234) by which the underlying reality and the world as we see it are intertwined? The idea of some sort of "ether"—which was prevalent until experiments in the 1880s by Albert Michelson and Edward Morley failed to detect an "ether wind" from the Earth's movement—keeps reemerging. Underlying influences of invisible fields in organizing physical phenomena have, in fact, been independently proposed within a variety of disciplines, including physics, medicine, neurology, and physiology (McTaggart, 2008). Consider "zero-point energy," for instance. Formulated in a 1913 paper by Einstein and Otto Stern that built on the work of Max Planck, zero-point energy is the lowest possible energy a quantum mechanical system can have. It suggests that the vacuum, "the space between particles," is not empty! Rather, there is "an ocean of microscopic vibrations in the space between things ... the very underpinning of our universe [is] a heaving sea of energy" (McTaggart, 2008, p. xxvii). While the standard model of quantum physics leaves unanswered questions (Kane, 2005), zero-point energy has been supported by a number of experiments and is generally accepted, even if not entirely understood (Davis et al., 2005).

It is not necessary, however, to explain mysteries of nature that still elude quantum physicists in order to recognize that if resonance is the best explanation available for the attunement that occurs between one person's heart and another's brain as well as a host of other observable phenomena, that: (a) some medium is required, and (b) its nature would involve some sort of energy or line of force that we do not yet know how to detect directly. Returning to the way neurons are organized during complex processes such as consolidating or retrieving a memory, a 2001 paper introducing the concept of a "brainweb" (Varela, Lachaux, Rodriguez, & Martinerie1, 2001) was, a decade later, the most frequently cited article published that year in *Nature's* prestigious specialty journal on neuroscience (Luo et al., 2010). Attempting to explain how "scattered mosaics" of information over many brain regions are coordinated into a unified experience, the investigators suggest that "frequency bands" (think of how a radio tunes into a particular frequency) synchronize cognitive activities throughout the brain. Neurologists at Stanford had previously proposed a "neural broadcasting theory" to explain, on a smaller scale, how neurons appear to influence neighboring neurons even when there is no electrochemical connection via axon and dendrite (Schuman & Madison, 1994). In all three theories—morphic fields, the brainweb, and neural broadcasting—the neurons *resonate* to a field or a frequency that coordinates their activities. Thomas Insel, the Director of the National Institute of Mental Health (2012), has, in fact, pointed to accumulating evidence that the synchronization of "large scale electrical oscillations across distant brain regions" allows content-specific information to be transmitted (p. 1). Laboratory studies have, for instance, shown that individual neurons in the prefrontal cortex are synchronized by oscillations in the brain's electromagnetic fields, demonstrably impacting thought and behavior (Buschman, Denovellis, Diogo, Bullock, & Miller, 2012). Neurons resonate with brainwaves.

Resonance implies vibration. The vibratory nature of biological structures has been described by Oschman (2000, 2005). Every component of the body—from units within the cell; to the cell; to the organs; to complex structures such as the cardiovascular, respiratory, or collagen systems— is "immersed in, and generates, a constant stream of vibratory information" (Oschman, 2000, p. 71). Oschman suggested that a requirement for "complete health" is "total interconnection" of all the body's systems at this vibratory level. These connections can become impaired by physical damage or emotional trauma, making the person vulnerable to disease and dysfunction. Interventions, including "acupuncture and other energy therapies," however, "restore and balance the vibratory circuitry" (p. 71).

Building upon the morphic resonance, brainweb, and neural broadcasting theories and combining them with the role of energy psychology in facilitating emotional learning through reconsolidation as described earlier, the following formulation for explaining the role of energy fields in energy psychology treatments is derived: *Organizing fields* that (a) *coordinate* neural activity are (b) *impacted* via energy psychology interventions to (c) *orchestrate* information-processing in ways that (d) *enhance* integration and coherence.

Visualizing an "Organizing Field" in a Clinical Situation

Acupoint stimulation presumably enhances clinical outcomes at several levels. The brain imaging studies discussed earlier show that stimulating certain acupoints sends deactivating signals directly to the amygdala and produces brainwave patterns that reduce learned fear. As a result, cortisol and other stress chemicals are not released, the hippocampus and higher cortical regions stay online, and formative experiences can be reconsolidated in a manner that updates internal models and links them with adaptive neural networks. This formulation is useful as far as it goes. But—just as it is still a mystery how neural activity is coordinated in memory formation—the coordination of neural shifts following energy psychology treatments is yet to be decisively explained. Both point to the hypothesis of an organizing field that directs neural activity. That is, in addition to generating electromagnetic signals and brain waves that impact the amygdala, acupoint stimulation appears to also work at a more global level. While other "power therapies" may enhance the adaptive capacities of organizing fields in their own distinctive ways, acupoint stimulation works directly with the meridian system, bringing balance to the body's energy pathways and then, by resonance, to its entire "vibratory circuitry" (Oschman, 2000, p. 67), including the energy fields that organize neural activity.

In energy psychology sessions, the client is invited to think about a memory or a trigger that brings up a troubling emotion. This, according to the hypothesis proposed here, activates the organizing field that connects the memory, the trigger, and the emotion. Rather than immediately attempting to process the memory, energy psychology protocols next stimulate acupoints to enhance the balance and coherence of the organizing field. While the concept of an organizing field may seem ephemeral and abstract—you cannot grasp it through your senses any more than you can visualize the concepts of magnetism or gravity—such fields are nonetheless believed to act upon matter, specifically in this case, neurons and neural pathways. The potential roles of fields and frequencies in neural operations have been proposed in the morphic resonance, brainweb, and neural broadcasting theories discussed earlier. Even if we cannot see them, we can imagine them and speculate about their nature.

To turn this speculation into a more palpable experience, imagine that you have goggles that allow you to view the energy fields that organize neural activity. As sci-fi as that sounds, the claims of some healers that they "see" the energies they work with have been indirectly verified (Gerber, 2001; Hunt, 1995), perhaps representing an ability to perceive frequencies outside the normative range, analogous to the way dogs can hear sounds that humans cannot hear. So with our imaginary energy-sensitive goggles, we can speculate about the actions of energy fields in an energy psychology treatment session.

> A new client, Richard, comes to you with concerns that his emotional reactions to his boss may be about to cost him his job. Virtually any evaluative comment about his performance, however respectfully delivered or constructively intended, causes Richard to feel severely criticized, become angry, and have difficulty maintaining a civil tone in his responses. His heart begins to beat more quickly, his breathing becomes shallow, and his hands start to tremble. During his first session with you, after a few rounds of tapping acupoints while recalling a recent incident with his boss, he quiets himself and scans his inward sensations to give a rating to the amount of distress the incident still evokes. This mini-mindfulness procedure often brings up earlier experiences related to the current situation, and an image arises of his father watching him play baseball on a playground and yelling at him in front of his friends when he misplays a ground ball. His humiliation around this incident is rated as an 8 on the 0–10 subjective units of distress scale. After several rounds of tapping, it is down to a 0. Two additional incidents, both of greater intensity and emblematic of his father's charged criticism, next come to mind and are in sequence tapped down from 10 to 0. The incident with his boss is then quickly brought to 0. The next week, he proudly recounts two situations that would have triggered him but did not. Table 1 speculates on how the organizing fields governing Richard's relationship to criticism might have appeared through our magical goggles.

The Model in a Nutshell

Explanations in the behavioral sciences are progressing toward increasingly precise and subtle frameworks, from the psychological to the biological to the neurochemical to the quantum mechanical to the realm of subtle energies. It may, however, only be at the energetic levels that we can begin to explain the speed and coordination of millions of extremely subtle and sophisticated processes occurring simultaneously. Acupoint stimulation, in addition to producing electromagnetic signals and brain waves that reduce activation in the brain's emotional centers during the reconsolidation window, apparently impacts the "organizing fields" that govern neural activity. This brings momentary balance and harmony to the body's energy pathways, and the brain's organizing fields resonate with this balance. This enhances their capacity to orchestrate the resolution of intrusive, unprocessed memories. Resolving unprocessed experiences not only eliminates intrusive fragments from implicit memory, supporting the emergence of coherent explicit memories. It allows this more coherent narrative to network with other memories into neural networks that provide more adaptive guidance. In the model presented here, this ongoing process of the integration of new experiences and the reconsolidation of old learnings, vital in maintaining mental health, is directed by fields of energy, lines of force that carry information and organize neural activity.

Three Core Premises of an "Organizing Field" Model

While scientific substantiation of this model may have to wait until instruments have been developed that can detect and track changes in organizing fields, the model is (a) congruent with constructs that have been scientifically established or reasonably well-established, (b) straightforward enough to be useful in guiding the practitioner, and (c) sophisticated enough to guide research (see **Conclusion**). The model is based on three core premises about energy, discussed in the following sections.

Table 1. *Speculation on the Role of "Organizing Fields" in an Energy Psychology Treatment*

The Experience	The Organizing Field
Richard is calmly going through his day.	The fields organizing Richard's neural circuitry are, for the moment, relatively integrated and balanced.
Richard's boss makes a constructive suggestion about one of Richard's projects. Richard has a strong, negative, kneejerk reaction.	An organizing field has linked the neurons being fired by the current situation to memory fragments of his father's fierce criticism. Richard's meridians resonate with this memory and become disturbed, as they were in the original event.
"Implicit" (unrecognized) memories of hurt and unfairness from childhood are imposed onto the situation, impacting Richard's perceptions, emotions, and behavior, though he is not consciously recalling the earlier experiences.	The disturbed meridians, through resonance, impact the organizing field so its state shifts to that of the earlier time. It activates additional implicit learnings from the playground and related incidents with accelerating power.
As Richard becomes calmer with the initial tapping, and mindful while assessing his distress level, the "playground" memory enters his conscious awareness.	The initial tapping and mindfulness create another state change in the meridians, causing the organizing field to become focused and able to accesses details of the earlier memory in a more coherent manner.
Richard begins to tap acupoints with the memory active and quickly feels more peaceful. Holding the scene simultaneously with no physiological arousal contradicts the expectations of Richard's internal model, producing the mismatch necessary for the old learnings to be reconsolidated in a new way.	The acupoint stimulation brings balance to the meridians that had become disturbed during the recall of the playground and related incidents. The organizing field resonates with the restored balance and flow of energy, allowing it to bring the old learnings into explicit memory, to transform them, and to connect them with more adaptive organizing fields and neural networks.
The memories are now cohesive rather than emerging as intrusive perceptions, images, and emotions. The next time his boss makes a suggestion about one of his projects, Richard receives it with no emotional overlay.	The organizing field has orchestrated a reconsolidation of the old learnings. The unprocessed implicit learnings have been integrated into adaptive networks and are no longer there for Richard's organizing field around criticism to activate.

Energy Is an Omnipresent Dimension of Body and Mind That Can Be Influenced to Impact Each in Desired Ways

Like a miniature battery, each of the body's cells stores and emits electricity. Information processing within a cell and communication among cells is achieved through electrical activity. Memories, feelings, and thoughts are encoded in patterns of tiny electrical impulses. Every breath, every muscle movement, and every morsel of food being digested, in fact, involves electrical energy. These electrical and electrochemical processes, along with more subtle energies, form the foundation of an energy-attuned model of health and healing.

Subtle energies share a property with gravity, which is that neither can be seen or photographed or in any other way directly perceived through mechanical extensions of our senses. While the Earth's gravity field remains invisible to our most delicate instruments, its effects are so easily demonstrated that its existence seems obvious. Like gravity, the human "life force" that is the focus of energy healing practitioners has never been directly imaged by scientific instruments. Unlike gravity, however, this "life force" is not accepted within conventional science. Yet its effects can also be easily demonstrated. If you have it, you are alive. If you do not, you are dead. It is that simple. Energy medicine and conventional medicine would enter into an easier dialogue if the implications of this single fact were more widely recognized. If conventional medicine were more focused on the body's life force, it would first approach an illness with non-invasive energy interventions, and it would be more adept in preventing disease. Consider, for instance, modern thermography, where emanations in the infrared range of the electromagnetic spectrum detect the precursors of illness (Diakides & Bronzino, 2007) or Burr's (1972) early finding that disturbances may show up in an organism's energy field months before they manifest as tumors.

While the "life force" has not yet been detected by conventional scientific instruments, it contains an obvious essential property: the ability to sustain life. Many cultures have concepts and vocabularies for describing this "life force" or "vital energy," such as the Sanskrit *prana*, the Greek *pneuma*, the Japanese *ki*, and the Chinese *chi* or *qi* (pronounced "chee"). Though these terms have often been translated as "energy" in the West, each depicts a larger construct than electromagnetic energy. The concept of qi, for instance, provides the main theoretical basis for traditional Chinese medicine, philosophy, culture, and natural science (Jonas, 2003). Jonas explained (2003) that while it "has characteristics of energy such as the ability to work, to be accumulated, stored, discharged and projected from the body, qi also has characteristics of intelligence and information" (p. 103). Prana, a core concept in yoga and ayurvedic medicine, is understood as the life-sustaining energy that permeates the aura, the chakras, and the nadis, the subtle network of energy channels similar to the Chinese concept of meridians (Co & Robins, 2011).

Just as human anatomy contains many systems and structures, energy manifests in the body in many forms. Some of these energies have been measured by existing instrumentation. Others (subtle energies) have not been. Such energies are, however, said to be known for their effects: "Healers through the ages have perceived subtle energies intuitively and proven them through application" (Dale, 2009, p. 422). Dale explained, "Subtle doesn't mean delicate. In fact, science is beginning to suggest that the subtle—the as yet immeasurable—actually directs" (p. xxi) the energies that are more familiar. So, for instance, the electromagnetic fields that appear to shape an organism's growth (e.g., Burr, 1972) may shadow more subtle information-laden energies that are actually influencing the electromagnetic field being detected. The role of energy fields in mental and physical health has been established in a number of arenas (Oschman, 2000, 2003). For instance, the human heart, which emits an electromagnetic field that is approximately 5,000 times as powerful as the electromagnetic field of the brain, surrounds the entire body, and extends 8 to 10 feet beyond it (Childre & Martin, 2000). This field governs an array of physiological processes, and its strength and coherence correspond with a person's physical and mental well-being (McCraty, Atkinson, Tomasino, & Bradley, 2009).

Healing applications of electrical stimulation and energy fields have also been documented. TENS (transcutaneous electrical nerve stimulation; Johnson & Martinson, 2006) and PEMS (pulsed electromagnetic field stimulation; Markov, 2008) machines are entering the medical mainstream. In an early meta-analysis of 15 studies, chronic wounds exposed to electrical stimulation healed 144% faster than comparable wounds that did not receive this treatment (Gardner, Frantz, & Schmidt, 1999). A progression of studies demonstrated that the electrical frequency of a chemical could have the same effect as the chemical itself. For instance, histamine increases heart rate, atropine decreases heart rate. Researchers exposed a beating heart to the *electrical frequency* of the histamine molecule and the heart rate increased; the electrical frequency of atropine decreased heart rate. While these findings are still controversial, the study, originally conducted in France, was replicated by independent research teams in Canada, Italy, and Israel before being published in *Nature* (Davenas et al., 1988). The electrical frequencies of the compounds were having the same effects as the compounds themselves! The principle has been extended to healing. Pancreatic tissue from healthy rats was scanned with a laser, and the information was converted into a wide bandwave signal. Rats that had been given a lethal dose of a toxin that destroys the pancreas were exposed to these bandwave signals. In the original experiment in Moscow, and two replications by other teams in other countries, all the rats receiving the toxin without subsequent treatment died within 4 days; 90% of the rats exposed to the bandwave signals survived (Gariaev, Friedman, & Leonova-Gariaeva, 2006). Their stem cells were stimulated and they regenerated pancreatic tissue.

Church (2009), in reviewing evidence from a vast array of sources, summarized, "Energy is the currency in which all transactions in nature are given or received" (p. 114). Physiological processes in the brain and the body are influenced by a complex system of energy flows and fields, some of which we can readily detect and measure with existing instrumentation and some of which we cannot. The healing traditions of most cultures that live in closer harmony with nature than ours hold that bringing these energies into balance and harmony enhances health.

Energy Carries Information

Information is carried by energy in countless devices, from wireless routers to cell phone towers. Energy has, in fact, been described as "information that vibrates" (Dale, 2009, p. 4), with changing amplitudes and frequencies being capable of coding information that can be "stored or applied" (p. 5). Electromagnetic waves extend from low frequencies, such as radio waves, whose wavelengths can extend over thousands of miles, to high frequencies, whose wavelengths are a fraction of the size of an atom.

Energy psychology interventions are believed to produce shifts in the energy systems that code psychological information, particularly the meridians, the chakras, and the biofield that surrounds the body. For instance, the chakras are an interrelated set of energy fields that—according to the energy healers who work with them—play a key role in processing memories and maintaining psychological patterns (Judith, 1987). The detail and subtlety of the information carried by such energies may be surprising, as in this account by energy healer and intuitive Donna Eden (2008):

> Each chakra spirals down seven layers into the body. ... If I move into the field deeply enough, and reach the fourth, fifth, and sixth levels, I get images and stories. When I tell the stories, the person usually responds with a surprised confirmation. Working with the heart chakra of a morose 36-year-old woman, I related, "I feel I am looking out at the world from the age of about 7, and I have just lost someone I love dearly. It is not a parent, perhaps a sibling? My grief is too much to bear. My heart is closing down." Her startled and tearful reply: "That's when Robert, my older brother, was accidentally shot by a neighbor boy who was playing with his father's gun. He died 2 days later" (pp. 155–156).

Beyond the memory carried in her chakra's energy field were instructions that kept the woman, Gail, from risking deep intimacy. Implicit learnings are, in this rendition, coded in the energy field as well as the neurons. After her brother's death, Gail had never again been able to allow herself to love that deeply. After the energy techniques brought balance and restoration to the disturbed energies locked in her heart chakra, there was an internal shift on this issue. The same reconsolidation sequence occurred as described earlier, but this time the energy intervention involved the heart chakra instead of acupoint stimulation. The pain of her brother's death was activated, Gail's heart chakra was simultaneously brought into balance, and being able to recall her brother's death without pain in her heart was the juxtaposition experience that allowed her reflexive fear of intimacy to be eradicated and more adaptive strategies to develop. In fact, Gail reported a "breakthrough," with her marriage entering deeper levels of intimacy, during the week following the session. While this may of course have been a coincidence, correspondences between shifts in core issues during energy healing sessions and changes in emotional and behavioral patterns are frequently reported.

The chakras, according to Eden (2008), carry psychological information, storing memory in a separate system that parallels, influences, and somewhat duplicates the memory stored in the brain's neurons. Strange as this sounds to Western ears, "mental" processes are no longer believed to be limited to the brain. Neuroscientists have established that memory and intelligence are distributed throughout the body in a vast network of mind–body cellular communication (Pert, 1999).

If the first premise for a model of the mechanisms at play in energy psychology is the concept that energies that can be influenced impact health and mental health, the second premise is that energy carries information. To the degree that energy psychology practitioners can influence the body's energies, they can alter stored information that underlies psychological processes.

Clinical Interventions Can Draw upon the Fact That Energy Fields, Through Resonance, Influence Other Energy Fields as well as Neural Activity

Individuals resonate with one another energetically. A person's EEG (brain wave) patterns are, as we have seen, influenced by the EKG (heart wave) patterns of a nearby individual, even though there was no conscious intention to send or receive a signal (McCraty, 2004). These experiments led McCraty and his colleagues to conclude that "the nervous system acts as an antenna, which is tuned to and responds to the magnetic fields produced by the hearts of other individuals" (p. 549). McCraty and Childre (2010) also presented evidence that information encoded in the heart's magnetic field "is communicated throughout the body and into the external environment" and, in fact, creates "bidirectional feed-forward and feedback loops" with the Earth (pp. 20–21).

Resonance is (as in the way that plucking a guitar string tuned to C will cause the C string of another guitar across the room to vibrate) emerging as a unifying concept for understanding a range of unexplained phenomena. Sheldrake's (1981) morphic resonance hypothesis is the most comprehensive formulation, extending from subatomic particles to the evolution of culture. The concept has been applied by others to systems ranging from neural networks (Lashley, 1950; the "synchrony" of Varela et al., 2001) to human/environment interactions (McCraty & Childre, 2010). Of greatest relevance for understanding the effects of energy psychology interventions are the resonances (a) between acupoint stimulation and the body's energy pathways or meridians, (b) between the meridians and the "organizing fields" that orchestrate psychological processes, and (c) between these organizing fields and neural activity. In brief, acupoint stimulation impacts the meridian system, which through resonance, impacts organizing fields that, again through resonance, impact neural activity. This apparent ability of acupoint tapping to readily establish harmony and alignment at these three levels may be the source of its demonstrated ability to achieve a range of clinical objectives with unusual speed and power.

Conclusion

Three ways that energy psychology protocols impact the body's energies have been proposed: (a) electrochemical impulses reduce arousal in the limbic system during the reconsolidation window, which allows neural pathways maintaining outdated emotional learnings to be revised or eliminated; (b) delta waves are generated, which are also involved in depotentiating maladaptive emotional learnings; and (c) balancing the body's meridian energies by stimulating acupoints brings greater order and coherence to the organizing fields that regulate neural activity. By stimulating acupoints while problematic memories or triggers are mentally activated, the synapses maintaining the implicit learnings related to those memories or triggers are unlocked and reconsolidation can occur. The limbic system's reduced arousal (due to the acupoint stimulation) while the memory or trigger is still active becomes the "new normal."

This formulation has both research and clinical implications. The conceptual framework held by a researcher or clinician determines the questions that will be asked and the avenues that will be explored. If the framework excludes the role of the body's energies in psychological processes, the subsequent conclusions will be skewed toward aspects of the therapy that are not related to these underlying energy dynamics. Each of the premises of the working model, however, raises salient questions that can be investigated. If energy can be influenced to optimize mind and body (Premise 1), what are the most direct ways of engaging that energy and the most effective ways of influencing it? If energy carries information (Premise 2), can that information be accessed; can maladaptive information be altered? If energy fields, through resonate, influence one another as well as neural activity (Premise 3), what are the most effective ways to leverage this principle for therapeutic gain?

As an energy perspective is brought into research and treatment settings, new and extremely practical glimpses into nature's enigmas emerge. The tension between "expanded horizons" and critical thinking can, however, be challenging in any field, and markedly so when attributing controversial outcomes whose causes are difficult to determine to energies that are difficult to detect. Nonetheless, empirical support for the existence and relevance of energies not usually considered in clinical practice—as surveyed in this chapter—is there for anyone to review. Despite its controversies, unexplained mechanisms of action, and push against the boundaries of conventional clinical frameworks, energy psychology is proving to be a potent intervention for health and well-being as well as a bridge into the mysterious world of subtle energies.

References

Adams, A. & Davidson, K. (2011). *EFT level 1 comprehensive training resource*. Fulton, CA: Energy Psychology Press.

Adey, W. R. & Bawin, S. M. (1977). Brain interactions with weak electric and magnetic fields. *Neurosciences Research Program Bulletin, 15*, 1–129.

Boycott, B. B. (1965). Learning in the octopus. *Scientific American, 212*(3), 42–50. doi:10.1006/ccog.1999.0393

Buschman, T. J., Denovellis, E. L., Diogo, C., Bullock, D., & Miller, E.K. (2012). Synchronous oscillatory neural ensembles for rules in the prefrontal cortex. *Neuron, 76*, 838–846. doi:10.1016/j.neuron.2012.09.029

Burr, H. S. (1972). *The fields of life*. New York, NY: Ballantine.

Burr, H. S. & Northrup, F. S. C. (1935). The electro-dynamic theory of life. *Quarterly Review of Biology, 10*, 322–333. doi:10.1006/ccog.1999.0393

Callahan, R. J. (1985). *Five minute phobia cure: Dr. Callahan's treatment for fears, phobias and self-sabotage*. Wilmington, DE: Enterprise.

Callahan, R. J. & Callahan, J. (1996). *Thought Field Therapy (TFT) and trauma: Treatment and theory*. Indian Wells, CA: Thought Field Therapy Training Center.

Callahan, R. & Callahan, J. (2011). *Tapping the body's energy pathways*. Indio, CA: Callahan Techniques.

Childre, D. L. & Martin, H. (2000). *The HeartMath solution: The Institute of HeartMath's revolutionary program for engaging the power of the heart's intelligence*. New York, NY: HarperCollins.

Church, D. (2009). *The genie in your genes: Epigenetic medicine and the new biology of intention*. Santa Rosa, CA: Elite.

Church, D. & Feinstein, D. (in press). Energy psychology in the treatment of PTSD: Psychobiology and clinical principles. In N. Gotsiridze-Columbus, *Psychology of trauma*. Hauppauge, NY: Nova.

Church, D., Piña, O., Reategui, C., & Brooks, A. (2011). Single session reduction of the intensity of traumatic memories in abused adolescents after EFT: A randomized controlled pilot study. *Traumatology, 18*, 73–79. doi:10.1177/1534765611426788

Co, S. & Robins, E. B. (2011). *The power of prana: Breathe your way to health and vitality*. Boulder, CO: Sounds True.

Collinge, W. (1998). *Subtle energy: Awakening to the unseen forces in our lives*. New York, NY: Warner Books.

Commons, M. L. (2000). The power therapies: A proposed mechanism for their action and suggestions for future empirical validation. *Traumatology, 6*, 119–138. doi:10.1006/ccog.1999.0393

Connolly, S. & Sakai, C. (2011). Brief trauma intervention with Rwandan genocide survivors using Thought Field Therapy. *International Journal of Emergency Mental Health, 13*, 161–172.

Dale, C. (2009). *The subtle body: An encyclopedia of your energetic anatomy*. Boulder, CO: Sounds True.

Davenas, E., Beauvais, F., Amara, J., Oberbaum, M., Robinzon, B., Miadonnai, A., … & Benveniste, J. (1988). Human basophil degranulation triggered by very dilute antiserum against IgE. *Nature, 333*, 816–818. doi:10.1038/333816a0

Davis, E. W., Teofilo, V. L., Haisch, B., Puthoff, H. E., Nickisch, L. J., Rueda, A., & Cole, D. C. (2005). Review of experimental concepts for studying the quantum vacuum field. In M. S. El-Genk (Ed.), *Space technology and applications international forum* (pp. 1390–1401). Melville, NY: American Institute of Physics.

Devilly, G. J. (2005). Power therapies and possible threats to the science of psychology and psychiatry. *Australian and New Zealand Journal of Psychiatry, 39*, 437–445. doi:10.1080/j.1440-1614.2005.01601.x

Dhond, R. P., Kettner, N., & Napadow, V. (2007). Neuroimaging acupuncture effects in the human brain. *Journal of Alternative and Complementary Medicine, 13*, 603–616. doi:10.1006/ccog.1999.0393

Diakides, N. A. & Bronzino, J. D. (2007). *Medical infrared imaging*. Boca Raton, FL: CRC Press. doi:10.1006/ccog.1999.0393

Diepold, J. H. & Goldstein, D. (2009). Thought Field Therapy and QEEG changes in the treatment of trauma: A case study. *Traumatology, 15*, 85–93. doi:10.1177/1534765608325304

Duffy, M. C. & Levy, J. (Eds.). (2009). *Ether space-time and cosmology. Vol. 2: New insights into a key physical medium*. Montreal, Canada: C. Roy Keys.

Ecker, B. (2010). Unlocking the emotional brain: Finding the neural key to transformation. *Psychotherapy Networker, 34*(5), 43–47, 60.

Ecker, B., Ticic, R., & Hulley, L. (2012). *Unlocking the emotional brain: Eliminating symptoms at their roots using memory reconsolidation*. New York, NY: Routledge.

Eden, D. (2008). *Energy medicine* (2nd ed.). New York, NY: Tarcher/Penguin.

Fang, J., Jin, Z., Wang, Y., Li, K., Kong, J., Nixon, E. E., & Hui, K.-S. (2009). The salient characteristics of the central effects of acupuncture needling: Limbic-paralimbic-neocortical network modulation. *Human Brain Mapping, 30*, 1196–1206. doi:10.1006/ccog.1999.0393

Feinstein, D. (2004). *Energy psychology interactive: Rapid interventions for lasting change*. Ashland, OR: Innersource.

Feinstein, D. (2009). Facts, paradigms, and anomalies in the acceptance of energy psychology: A rejoinder to McCaslin's (2009) and Pignotti and Thyer's (2009) comments on Feinstein (2008a). *Psychotherapy: Theory, Research, Practice, Training, 46*, 262–269. doi:10.1037/a0016086

Feinstein, D. (2010). Rapid treatment of PTSD: Why psychological exposure with acupoint tapping may be effective. *Psychotherapy: Theory, Research, Practice, Training, 47*, 385–402. doi:10.1037/a0021171

Feinstein, D. (2012). Acupoint stimulation in treating psychological disorders: Evidence of efficacy. *Review of General Psychology*. Advance online publication. doi:10.1037/a0028602

Feinstein, D. & Church, D. (2010). Modulating gene expression through psychotherapy: The contribution of non-invasive somatic interventions. *Review of General Psychology, 14*, 283–195. doi:10.1037/a0021252

Feinstein, D. & Eden, D. (2008). Six pillars of energy medicine: Clinical strengths of a complementary paradigm. *Alternative Therapies in Health and Medicine, 14*(1), 44–54.

Gardner, S. E., Frantz, R. A., & Schmidt, F. L. (1999). Effect of electrical stimulation on chronic wound healing: A meta-analysis. *Wound Repair and Regeneration, 7*, 495–503. doi:10.1006/ccog.1999.0393

Gariaev, P. P., Friedman, M. J., & Leonova-Gariaeva, E. A. (2006). Crisis in life sciences: The wave genetics response.

Journal of Non-Locality and Remote Mental Interactions, IV. Retrieved from http://www.emergentmind.org/gariaev06.htm

Gerber, R. (2001). *Vibrational healing* (3rd ed.). Rochester, VT: Bear & Co.

Haake, M., MüLler, H.-H., Schade-Brittinger, C., Basler, H. D., SchäFer, H., Maier, C., ... & Molsberger, A. (2007). German acupuncture trials (GERAC) for chronic low back pain: Randomized, multicenter, blinded, parallel-group trial with 3 groups. *Archives of Internal Medicine, 167*, 1892–1898. doi:10.1001/Archinte.167.17.1892

Harper, M. (2012). Taming the amygdala: An EEG analysis of exposure therapy for the traumatized. *Traumatology, 18*(2), 61–74. doi:10.1006/ccog.1999.0393

Herbert, J. D. & Gaudiano, B. A. (2001). The search for the Holy Grail: Heart rate variability and Thought Field Therapy. *Journal of Clinical Psychology, 57*, 1207–1214. doi:10.1002/jclp.1087

Hui, K. K. S, Liu, J., Makris, N., Gollub, R. W., Chen, A. J. W., Moore, C. I., ... & Kwong, K. K. (2000). Acupuncture modulates the limbic system and subcortical gray structures of the human brain: Evidence from fMRI studies in normal subjects. *Human Brain Mapping, 9*, 13–25. doi:10.1006/ccog.1999.0393

Hui, K. K.-S., Liu, J., Marina, O., Napadow, V., Haselgrove, C., Kwong, K. K., & Makris, N. (2005). The integrated response of the human cerebro-cerebellar and limbic systems to acupuncture stimulation at ST 36 as evidenced by fMRI. *Neuro Image, 27*, 479–496. doi:10.1006/ccog.1999.0393

Hunt, V. (1995). *Infinite mind: The science of human vibrations*. Malibu, CA: Malibu Publishing.

Johnson, M. & Martinson, M. (2006). Efficacy of electrical nerve stimulation for chronic musculoskeletal pain: A meta-analysis of randomized controlled trials. *Pain, 130*, 157–165. doi:10.1016/j.pain.2007.02.007

Jonas, W. B. (2003). Qigong: Basic science studies in biology. In W. B. Jonas & C. C. Crawford (Eds.), *Healing intention and energy medicine: Science, research methods and clinical implications* (p. 103). Philadelphia, PA: Elsevier. [Editors' introduction]

Judith, A. (1987). *Wheels of life: A user's guide to the chakra system*. Woodbury, MN: Llewellyn.

Kane, G. (2005). The dawn of physics beyond the standard model. *Scientific American, 15*(1), 4–11.

Kurtz, R. (2007). *Body-centered psychotherapy: The Hakomi method* (rev. ed.). Mendocino, CA: LifeRhythm.

Lambrou, P. T., Pratt, G. J., & Chevalier, G. (2003). Physiological and psychological effects of a mind/body therapy on claustrophobia. *Subtle Energies & Energy Medicine, 14*, 239–251.

Lane, J. (2009). The neurochemistry of counterconditioning: Acupressure desensitization in psychotherapy. *Energy Psychology: Theory, Research, and Treatment, 1*(1), 31–44. doi:10.9769.2009.1.1.JRL

Lang, T., Hager H., Funovits, V., Barker, R., Steinlechner, B., Hoerauf, K., & Kober, A. (2007). Prehospital analgesia with acupressure at the Baihui and Hegu points in patients with radial fractures: a prospective, randomized, double-blind trial. *American Journal of Emergency Medicine, 25*, 887–893. doi:10.1016/j.ajem.2007.01.016

Langman, L. & Burr, H. S. (1947). Electrometric studies in women with malignancy of cervix uteri. *Science, 105*(2721), 209–210.

Lashley, K. S. (1950). In search of the engram. In *Physiological mechanisms in animal behavior* (Society for Experimental Biology Symposium IV, pp. 454–482). Oxford, England: Academic Press.

Laszlo, E. & Dennis, K. L. (Eds.). (2012). *The new science and spirituality reader*. Rochester, VT: Inner Traditions.

Levine, P. A. (2010). *In an unspoken voice: How the body releases trauma and restores goodness*. Berkeley, CA: North Atlantic Books.

Liboff, A.R. (2004). Toward an electromagnetic paradigm for biology and medicine. *Journal of Alternative and Complimentary Medicine, 10*, 41–47. doi:10.1006/ccog.1999.0393

Lipton, B. H. (2005). *The biology of belief*. Santa Rosa, CA: Elite.

Lohr, J. M. (2001). Sakai et al. is not an adequate demonstration of TFT effectiveness. *Journal of Clinical Psychology, 57*, 1229–1235. doi:10.1002/jclp.1089

Luo, L., Rodriguez, E., Jerbi, K., Lachaux, J.-P., Martinerie, J., Corbetta, M., ... & Craig, A. D. (2010). Ten years of *Nature Reviews Neuroscience*: Insights from the highly cited. *Nature Reviews Neuroscience, 11*, 718–726. doi:10.1038/nrn2912

Maddox, J. (1981). A book for burning? *Nature, 293*(5830), 245–246.

Markov, M. S. (2008). Expanding use of pulsed electromagnetic field therapies. *Electromagnetic Biology & Medicine, 26*, 257–274. doi:10.1006/ccog.1999.0393

Matthews, R. E. (2007). Harold Burr's biofields: Measuring the electromagnetics of life. *Subtle Energies & Energy Medicine, 18*(2), 55–61.

McCaslin, D. (2009). A review of efficacy claims in energy psychology. *Psychotherapy: Research, Practice, Training, 46*, 249–256. doi:10.1006/ccog.1999.0393

McCraty, R. (2004). The energetic heart: Bioelectromagnetic communication within and between people. In P. J. Rosch & M. S. Markov (Eds.), *Clinical applications of bioelectromagnetic medicine* (pp. 541–562). New York, NY: Marcel Dekker.

McCraty, R., Atkinson, M., Tomasino, D., & Bradley, R. T. (2009). The coherent heart: Heart–brain interactions, psychophysiological coherence, and the emergence of system-wide order. *Integral Review, 5*(2), 100–115.

McCraty, R. & Childre, D. (2010). Coherence: Bridging personal, social, and global health. *Alternative Therapies in Health and Medicine, 16*(4), 10–24.

McNally, R. J. (2001). Tertullian's motto and Callahan's method. *Journal of Clinical Psychology, 57*, 1171–1174. doi:10.1002/jclp.1083

McTaggart, L. (2007). *The intention experiment: Using your thoughts to change your life and the world*. New York: Free Press.

McTaggart, L. (2008). *The field: The quest for the secret force of the universe* (Rev. ed.). New York, NY: HarperCollins.

National Institute of Mental Health. (2012, November 1). *In-synch brain waves hold memory of object just seen* [Press release]. Retrieved from http://www.nimh.nih.gov/science-news/2012/in-sync-brain-waves-hold-memory-of-objects-just-seen.shtml

Nelson, R. D., Bradish, J., Dobyns, Y. H., Dunne, B. J., & Jahn. R. G. (1996). Field REG anomalies in group situations. *Journal of Scientific Exploration, 10*, 111–142.

Northrup, C. (2008). Foreword. In D. Eden, *Energy medicine for women* (pp. xv–xx). New York, NY: Tarcher/Penguin.

Ogden, P., Kekuni, M., & Pain, C. (2006). *Trauma and the body: A sensorimotor approach to psychotherapy.* New York, NY: Norton.

Oldfield, H. & Coghill, R. (2011). *The dark side of the brain: Major discoveries in use of Kirlian photography and electrocrystal therapy.* Pontypool, Wales: Coghill Research Laboratories.

Oschman, J. L. (2000). *Energy medicine: the scientific basis.* New York, NY: Harcourt.

Oschman, J. L. (2003). *Energy medicine in therapeutics and human performance.* New York, NY: Elsevier.

Oschman, J. L. (2005). Energy and the healing response. *Journal of Bodywork and Movement Therapies, 9*(1), 3–15. doi:10.1006/ccog.1999.0393

Oz, M. (2007, November 20). *The Oprah Winfrey Show* [television broadcast]. Chicago, IL: American Broadcasting Company.

Pert, C. B. (1999). *The molecules of emotion: The science behind mind-body medicine.* New York, NY: Simon & Schuster.

Pignotti, M. & Thyer, B. (2009). Some comments on "Energy Psychology: A Review of the Evidence." Premature conclusions based on incomplete evidence? *Psychotherapy: Research, Practice, Training, 46,* 257–261. doi:10.1006/ccog.1999.0393

Polster, E. & Poster, M. (1973). *Gestalt therapy integrated: Contours of theory and practice.* New York, NY: Brunner-Mazel.

Poponin, V. (2002). *The DNA phantom effect: Direct measurement of a new field in the vacuum substructure.* Retrieved September 4, 2012, from http://www.bibliotecapleyades.net/ciencia/ciencia_genetica04.htm

Radin, D. (2006). *Entangled minds: Extrasensory experiences in a quantum reality.* New York, NY: Simon & Schuster.

Reich, W. (1973). The function of the orgasm: Sex-economic problems of biological energy (V. R. Carfagno, Trans.). In W. Reich, *The discovery of the orgone* (Vol. 1). New York, NY: Farrar, Straus and Giroux.

Revonsuo, A. & Newman, J. (1999). Binding and consciousness. *Consciousness and Cognition, 8,* 123–127. doi:10.1006/ccog.1999.0393

Roediger, H. L., Dudai, Y., & Fitzpatrick, S. M. (2007). *Science of memory concepts.* New York, NY: Oxford University Press. doi:10.1006/ccog.1999.0393

Ruden, R. A. (2005). A neurological basis for the observed peripheral sensory modulation of emotional responses. *Traumatology, 11,* 145–158. doi:10.1177/153476560501100301

Ruden, R. A. (2010). *When the past is always present: Emotional traumatization, causes, and cures.* New York, NY: Routledge.

Sakai, C. S., Connolly, S. M., & Oas, P. (2010). Treatment of PTSD in Rwandan genocide survivors using Thought Field Therapy. *International Journal of Emergency Mental Health, 12*(1), 41–50.

Schmidt, S. (2012). Can we help just by good intentions? A meta-analysis of experiments on distant intention effects. *Journal of Alternative and Complementary Medicine, 18,* 529–533. doi:10.1089/acm.2011.0321

Schuman, E. E. & Madison, D. V. (1994). Locally distributed synaptic potentiation in the hypocampus. *Science, 263,* 532–536. doi:10.1006/ccog.1999.0393

Shapiro, F. (2001). *Eye Movement Desensitization and Reprocessing (EMDR): Basic principles, protocols, and procedures* (2nd ed.). New York, NY: Guilford Press.

Shealy, N. (1998, June 20). *Acceptance speech upon receipt of the Alyce & Elmer Green Award for Excellence.* Eighth Annual Conference of the International Society for the Study of Subtle Energies and Energy Medicine, Boulder, CO.

Sheldrake, R. (1981). *A new science of life: The hypothesis of morphic resonance.* Rochester, VT: Park Street Press.

Siegel, D. J. (2010). *The mindful therapist: A clinician's guide to mindsight and neural integration.* New York, NY: Norton.

Siegel, D. J. (2012). *The developing mind: How relationships and the brain interact to shape who we are* (2nd ed.). New York, NY: Guilford Press.

Swanson, C. (2003), *The synchronized universe: New science of the paranormal.* Tucson, AZ: Poseidia.

Swanson, C. (2010). *Life force, the scientific basis: Breakthrough physics of energy medicine, healing, chi and quantum consciousness.* Tucson, AZ: Poseidia.

Swingle, P. G. (2010). Emotional Freedom Techniques (EFT) as an effective adjunctive treatment in the neurotherapeutic treatment of seizure disorders. *Energy Psychology: Theory, Research, and Treatment, 2,* 27–37. doi:10.9769.EPJ.2010.2.1.PGS

Swingle, P. G., Pulos, L., & Swingle, M. K. (2004). Neurophysiological indicators of EFT treatment of posttraumatic stress. *Subtle Energies & Energy Medicine, 15,* 75–86.

Takakura, N. & Yajima, H. (2009). Analgesic effect of acupuncture needle penetration: A double-blind crossover study. *Open Medicine, 3*(2). Retrieved from http://www.openmedicine.ca/article/view/189/235

Tiller, W. A. (1997). *Science and human transformation: Subtle energies, intentionality and consciousness.* Walnut Creek, CA: Pavior.

Tompkins, P. & Bird, C. (1973). *The secret life of plants: A fascinating account of the physical, emotional, and spiritual relations between plants and man.* New York, NY: Harper & Row.

Varela, F., Lachaux, J.-P., Rodriguez, E., & Martineriel, J. (2001). The brainweb: Phase synchronization and large-scale integration. *Nature Reviews Neuroscience, 2,* 229–239. doi:10.1038/35067550

Walker, M. P. & van der Helm, E. (2009). Overnight therapy? The role of sleep in emotional brain processing. *Psychological Bulletin, 135,* 731–748. doi:10.1037/a0016570

White, J. & Krippner, S. (1977). *Future science: Life energies and the physics of paranormal phenomena.* New York, NY: Anchor.

Williams, E. A. (2003). *A cultural history of medical vitalism in Enlightenment Montpellier.* Burlington, VT: Ashgate.

Yildirim, F. B. & Sarikcioglu, L. (2007). Marie Jean Pierre Flourens (1794–1867): An extraordinary scientist of his time. *Journal of Neurology, Neurosurgery, and Psychiatry, 78,* 852. doi:10.1136/jnnp.2007.118380

Chapter 6
Energy Healing at the Frontier of Genomics
Garret Yount

Abstract

Modern genomics has revealed that the biological source of human complexity is in the regulation of gene expression, or the process of turning genes "on and off" and modulating their products. This chapter describes molecular road maps that could potentially link the effects of healing energy interventions with recently discovered molecules that are potent regulators of gene expression, called microRNAs. Since there are more than a thousand human microRNAs and each of them is believed to be able to regulate the expression of hundreds of target genes, these molecules have wide-ranging influence in biological processes. As an example, molecular routes are described that start with EFT-induced changes in cortisol levels and follow various established signaling pathways leading to the modulation of gene expression that contributes to cancer biology.

Keywords: EFT, gene expression, genomics, epigenetics, microRNA, non-coding RNA, cortisol, inflammation

Garret Yount, PhD, is a molecular biologist who leads the Mind-Body Medicine Research Group at the California Pacific Medical Center Research Institute in San Francisco. Send correspondence to Garret Yount, 475 Brannan Street, Suite 220, San Francisco, CA 94107, or yountg@cpmcri.org.

The growing body of evidence that energy healing modalities such as Emotional Freedom Techniques (EFT) and qigong can have profound health-promoting effects compels a search for biological processes that might underlie this influence. This chapter describes speculative road maps for pursuing such mechanistic insights via a route that includes molecules at the cutting edge of genomics. The latest discoveries in genomic science have been brought to light through techniques called "next generation sequencing," which have allowed scientists to rapidly decode, or sequence, large stretches of deoxyribonucleic acid (DNA) base pairs spanning entire genomes. Information from such studies has explained the initially perplexing fact that humans do not have more genes than do less complex organisms, such as sponges.

Sponges are an ancient group of animals that are similar to humans in that their protoplasmic mass, constituting the egg, is converted into a multitude of cells, which are metamorphosed into the tissues of the body. One would be hard pressed to find similarities beyond this, which is not surprising since sponges struck off on their own branch of the evolutionary tree and diverged developmentally from other animals over 600 million years ago. The surprise came when the genome of the sponge was sequenced and we realized that they have approximately 18,000 to 30,000 genes, which is a similar ranges estimated for humans and other mammals (Srivastava et al., 2010). Beyond the similarity in number of genes, there is remarkable similarity in the sequences of the genes themselves. Most strikingly, many of the genes shared between humans, sponges, and other animals are genes involved in cancer.

We now understand that the source of our complexity is in the regulation of gene expression, the process of controlling gene expression and modulating their products, rather than in the genes themselves. Much of the molecular machinery for conducting this epigenetic regulation is contained in the part of the genome that lies in between the genes that encode proteins—in the noncoding regions of the DNA (Taft, Pheasant, & Mattick, 2007). Important components of this gene-regulating machinery are the ribonucleic acid (RNA) molecules transcribed from noncoding DNA. Many of these so-called noncoding RNAs act to regulate the expression of coding genes in a highly dynamic process that is constantly occurring in virtually every cell of the body and is responsive to information in the cellular environment. This chapter describes the most well studied family of noncoding RNAs, microRNAs, as an example to illustrate just one route whereby energy healing interventions might utilize genomic regulatory systems to affect health and healing. The ability to influence the development of cancers, or oncogenesis, is chosen as the destination point.

MicroRNAs are short noncoding RNA molecules of 20–25 nucleotides in length that regulate gene expression in animals and plants. More than a thousand human microRNAs have been identified and many of these have been shown to regulate the expression of target genes (Bentwich et al., 2005). Interaction with target genes typically results in the inhibition of gene expression, but induction of expression can also occur (Orom, Nielsen, & Lund, 2008). MicroRNAs regulate gene expression at the post-transcriptional level, which means that they interfere with the process of gene expression at the point after genetic information is transcribed from DNA to a messenger RNA (mRNA), and before the mRNA is translated into a protein.

Each microRNA can regulate the expression of hundreds of target genes. They can do this by being promiscuous at the molecular level. That is, they can bind to and regulate target gene mRNA molecules without requiring exact matches between the nucleotide pairs (Bartel, 2009). This is different from the interaction when two strands in a DNA molecule are held together by hydrogen bonds between complementary base pairs (i.e., A-T and C-G). Due to their ability to bind with imperfect complementarity, microRNAs are able to regulate more than one third of all cellular mRNAs and thus have wide-ranging influence in biological processes (Rossbach, 2010).

Our road map of potential molecular pathways linking energy healing with the regulation of microRNAs begins with a recently published randomized controlled trial of EFT demonstrating that a single EFT intervention can reduce cortisol levels in healthy adults (Church, Yount, & Brooks, 2012). Church and colleagues tested for changes in cortisol levels in saliva samples collected from subjects immediately before and 30 minutes after receiving an hour-long therapeutic intervention. Subjects were randomly assigned to either an EFT group, a psychotherapy group receiving a supportive interview, or a control group receiving no treatment. The researchers also assessed subjects' psychological distress symptoms in parallel. The results showed clearly that the EFT group experienced a statistically significant decrease in cortisol levels compared with the psychotherapy and no treatment groups. Moreover, the decrease in cortisol levels in the EFT group mirrored observed improvements in psychological distress that included a significant decrease in the subjects' feelings of anxiety. This is exciting because it is the first clinical trial to evaluate a physiological biomarker such as cortisol levels and it yielded robust positive effects. It sets the stage for further research to explore whether EFT affects other physiological systems, including the regulation of genes.

Cortisol is a master hormone mediating the human stress response and several pathophysiological conditions, including cancers, have been associated with its deficiency, excess, or dysregulation (Spiegel, 2012). One theory related to oncogenesis posits that elevated cortisol levels, associated with the persistent activation of the hypothalamic-pituitary-adrenal axis caused by chronic stress, impair the immune response and contribute to the development and progression of cancers (Reiche, Nunes, & Morimoto, 2004). This theory is supported by evidence that psychological and psychopharmacotherapeutic interventions that reduce affective distress showed beneficial effects in cancer patients (Reiche, Morimoto, & Nunes, 2005).

The effects of cortisol are mediated through binding with the glucocorticoid receptor and forming an activated hormone-receptor complex. The glucocorticoid receptor is expressed in almost every cell in the body and a variety of synthetic glucocorticoids are used clinically to mimic the endogenous activity of cortisol. Hydrocortisone is the name used for pharmaceutical preparations of cortisol. Prednisone is a potent synthetic member of the glucocorticoid class of drugs that is used to certain inflammatory diseases and cancers but has many significant short-term and long-term adverse effects (Clarke & Kirwan, 2012; Bergmann, Barraclough, Lee, & Staatz, 2012; Mardjuadi et al, 2012; Bruce & Kupersmith, 2012).

Cortisol diffuses through the cell membrane and binds to the glucocorticoid receptor in the cytoplasm of the cell. One of the primary activities of the activated hormone-receptor complex is to move into the cell nucleus, where it binds to glucocorticoid response elements in the promoter region of target genes and influences their expression. Alternatively, the activated hormone-receptor complex can influence the expression of genes by remaining in the cytoplasm and preventing other proteins from moving into the nucleus that would otherwise regulate the expression of target genes. As part of these activities, the glucocorticoid receptor interacts with many helper proteins (e.g., coactivators and corepressors) that modulate the outcomes of its function.

The activated glucocorticoid receptor can regulate microRNA expression (Yang & Wang, 2011). One example of a microRNA that has been shown to be regulated by the glucocorticoid receptor is microRNA-223 (Rainer et al., 2009) and this microRNA is known to be dysregulated in numerous cancers, including chronic lymphocytic leukemia (Stamatopoulos et al., 2009), acute lymphoblastic leukemia (Chiaretti et al., 2010), acute myeloid leukemia (Pulikkan et al., 2010), ovarian cancer (Laios et al., 2008), and hepatocellular carcinoma (Wong et al., 2008). A search for downstream targets of microRNA-223 hepatocellular carcinoma cells identified the Stathmin 1 (STMN1) gene as one of the genes targeted by microRNA-223 for regulation (Wong et al., 2008).

Stathmin, the protein encoded by the STMN1 gene, is an important part of the cellular cytoskeleton. As such, it plays a key role in cell growth, division (mitosis), and cell migration. Interference with expression of stathmin can lead to unregulated cell growth characteristic of cancer cells (Cassimeris, 2002). Indeed, the expression of stathmin has been shown to be dysregulated across a broad range of human malignancies, including leukemia, lymphoma, neuroblastoma, mesothelioma, and lung, ovarian, prostatic, and breast cancers (Rana, Maples, Senzer, & Nemunaitis, 2008). Thus a molecular pathway has been described whereby EFT-induced changes in cortisol levels could possibly impact molecules involved in oncogenesis (see Figure 1).

The microRNA-15b/16 family of microRNAs represents another example of a microRNAs that can be regulated by the activated glucocorticoid receptor (Rainer et al., 2009) and could therefore potentially be influenced by the effects of EFT. Regarding cancer, these microRNAs have been investigated most extensively in models of prostate cancer and chronic lymphocytic lymphoma and have been shown to target multiple genes involved in oncogenesis, including BCL2 (Bonci et al., 2008; Aqeilan, Calin, & Croce, 2010). The BCL2 gene encodes the Bcl-2 (B-cell

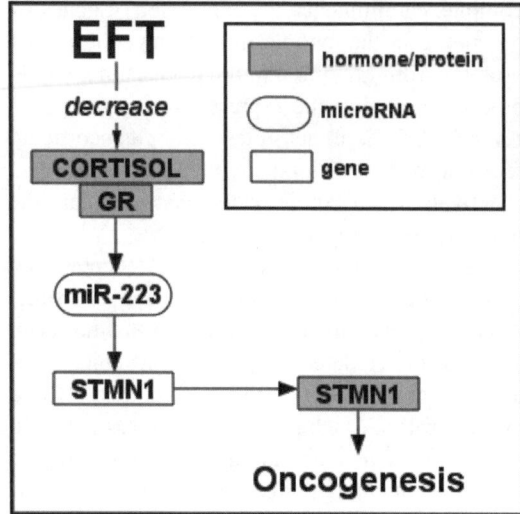

Figure 1. Molecular Pathway Linking the Influence of EFT Intervention and Oncogenesis Through microRNA-223.
GR: Glucocorticoid Receptor; miRNA: microRNA; STMN1: Stathmin 1.

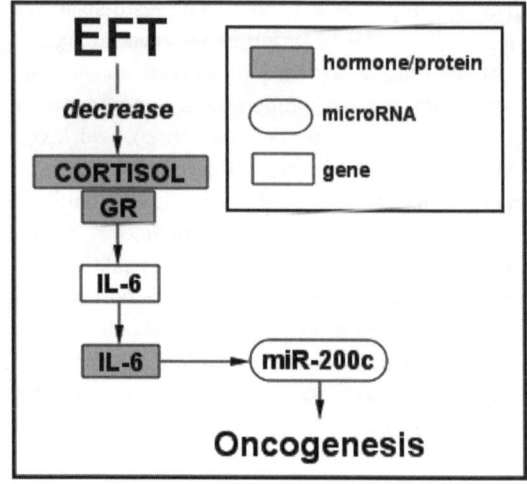

Figure 2. Molecular Pathway Linking the Influence of EFT Intervention and Oncogenesis Through microRNA-200c.
GR: Glucocorticoid Receptor; IL-6: Interleukin-6; miRNA: microRNA.

lymphoma 2) protein, which plays a key role in programmed cell death and is therefore crucial for both the development of cancers as well as the responsiveness of tumors to therapy.

Aside from microRNAs, important gene targets of the activated glucocorticoid receptor complex are those encoding the interleukin-6 (IL-6) family of proinflammatory cytokines (Nissen & Yamamoto, 2000). Increased levels of proinflammatory cytokines can contribute to tumor cell growth in some cancers and there is a growing consensus in the field that this is because inflammation is a critical component of tumor progression (Coussens & Werb, 2002). The idea is that tumors are sustained and promoted by inflammatory signals from the surrounding microenvironment, including IL-6 (Bromberg & Wang, 2009).

IL-6 has been shown to regulate the expression of several microRNAs associated with the development of cancer. For example, IL-6 inhibits expression of microRNA-200c in breast cancer cells and this inhibition promotes activation of an inflammatory signaling circuit that is believed to stimulate breast cancer tumor growth (Rokavec, Wu, & Luo, 2012). This example illustrates a second type of route whereby molecular signals initiated by EFT could travel and, ultimately, influence tumor cell biology (see Figure 2).

Studies of other cancers have identified additional microRNAs that could be placed on our road map proximate to IL-6 as depicted in Figure 2. Elevated IL-6 levels have been shown to reduce expression of microRNA-370 in cholangiocarcinoma cells, for example, which leads to the release from inhibition of the oncogene (cancer-promoting gene) mitogen-activated protein kinase kinase kinase 8 (Meng, Wehbe-Janek, Henson, Smith, & Patel, 2008). Another example is microRNA-148a, which is inhibited by IL-6 in models of biliary tract cancer and contributes to the overexpression of the oncogene DNA methyltransferase-1 gene (Braconi, Huang, & Patel, 2010). Interestingly, this same microRNA acts to decrease the expression of the oncogene beta-catenin in models of hepatocarcinoma (Yuan et al., 2012). These findings illustrate that the molecular pathways and the interrelationships between the signaling molecules downstream of cortisol and glucocorticoid receptor activation are highly complex and dependent on the cellular context.

While this chapter focuses on molecular pathways involved in oncogenesis, it is worth noting that similar road maps could be generated regarding other diseases. As one example, EFT-induced changes in cortisol levels could influence the pathogenesis of pulmonary hypertension through regulation of microRNA-17/92. Similar to the road map depicted in Figure 2, microRNA-17/92 regulation occurs proximate to IL-6 (Brock et al., 2012). Brock and colleagues found that IL-6 can induce expression of microRNA-17/92 and lead to dysregulated expression of the BMPR2 gene. The BMPR2 gene encodes the bone morphogenesis protein receptor type II and dysregulated expression of this protein is a hallmark of pulmonary hypertension.

Regardless of the end point, an interesting byway can be added to these road maps by looking upstream of cortisol, as the link between EFT intervention and altered cortisol levels is unknown. Cortisol is produced in the adrenal cortex through a series of biosynthetic reactions that involve an enzyme in the cytochrome P450 superfamily. The P450 enzyme is encoded by the cytochrome P450, family 11, subfamily B, polypeptide 1 (CYP11B1) gene, and recent studies at the University of Glasgow indicate that the CYP11B1 is a target for regulation by microRNA-24 (Wood, 2012). This evidence for the regulation of cortisol expression being proximate to a microRNA prompts the intriguing hypothesis that the influence of EFT on cortisol levels may be mediated through this and/or other microRNAs (see Figure 3).

Positioning microRNAs ahead of cortisol level changes in the pathways mediating the effects of EFT intervention is highly speculative; however, a recent study evaluating stress-related changes in levels of microRNAs measured in blood samples from healthy adults supports the possibility. Katsuura and colleagues measured microRNAs levels in whole blood collected from medical students 7 weeks before, 1 day before, immediately after, and 1 week after a nationally administered examination for academic promotion (Katsuura et al., 2012). Using the samples obtained 1 week after the examination as baseline controls, they evaluated whether the stress of examination was associated with changes in microRNA levels and found a significant elevation of microRNA-144/144* and microRNA-16 levels immediately after finishing the examination. As microRNAs constitute an early part of the physiological response to stress, they might play a similar role in the relief from stress and be one of the earliest detectable biomarkers for the effects of EFT and other therapeutic interventions.

The molecular pathways described in this chapter provide plausible signaling routes by which the effects of EFT might tap in to a vast, previously hidden, layer of RNA regulatory mechanisms to exert their influence on health and healing. The example that was fleshed out began with EFT-induced changes in cortisol levels and followed known pathways that enable inflammation-associated cytokines to epigenetically modulate gene expression and directly contribute to the cancer biology. Networks of interconnected pathways could be built by following any other of the many downstream consequences of cortisol regulation. It would be interesting to overlay the pathways involved in depression, for example, since cortisol plays a multifaceted role in major depression disorder (Herbert, 2013) and there is evidence for the effectiveness of EFT as a treatment for this disease (Church, De Asis, & Brooks, 2012). Future research aimed at testing mechanistic hypotheses such as those explored in this chapter will be a critical step in leveling the playing field, in the arena of biomedical research, for energy healing modalities in relation to conventional medicines such as pharmaceutical drugs.

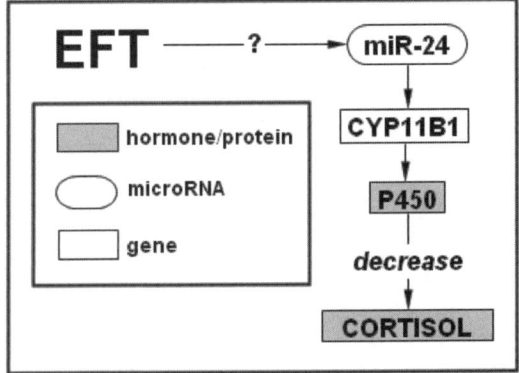

Figure 3. Molecular Pathway Linking EFT Intervention and Cortisol Biosynthesis Through microRNA-24. miRNA: microRNA; CYP11B1: cytochrome P450, family 11, subfamily B, polypeptide 1; P450: cytochrome p450 enzyme.

References

Aqeilan, R. I., Calin, G. A., & Croce, C. M. (2010). miR-15a and miR-16-1 in cancer: Discovery, function and future perspectives. *Cell Death and Differentiation, 17*(2), 215–220.

Bartel, D. P. (2009). MicroRNAs: Target recognition and regulatory functions. *Cell, 136*(2), 215–233.

Bentwich, I., Avniel, A., Karov, Y., Aharonov, R., Gilad, S., Barad, O.,... Bentwich, Z. (2005). Identification of hundreds of conserved and nonconserved human microRNAs. *Nature Genetics, 37*(7), 766–770.

Bergmann, T. K., Barraclough, K. A., Lee, K. J., & Staatz, C. E. (2012). Clinical pharmacokinetics and pharmacodynamics of prednisolone and prednisone in solid organ transplantation. *Clinical Pharmacokinetics, 51*(11), 711–741.

Bonci, D., Coppola, V., Musumeci, M., Addario, A., Giuffrida, R., Memeo, L., ... De Maria, R. (2008). The miR-15a-miR-16-1 cluster controls prostate cancer by targeting multiple oncogenic activities. *Nature Medicine, 14*(11), 1271–1277.

Braconi, C., Huang, N., & Patel, T. (2010). MicroRNA-dependent regulation of DNA methyltransferase-1 and tumor suppressor gene expression by interleukin-6 in human malignant cholangiocytes. *Hepatology, 51*(3), 881–890.

Brock, M., Trenkmann, M., Gay, R. E., Michel, B. A., Gay, S., Fischler, M., ... Huber, L. C. (2009). Interleukin-6 modulates the expression of the bone morphogenic protein receptor type II through a novel STAT3-microRNA cluster 17/92 pathway. *Circulation Research, 104*(10), 1184–1191.

Bromberg, J. & Wang, T. C. (2009). Inflammation and cancer: IL-6 and STAT3 complete the link. *Cancer Cell, 15*(2), 79–80.

Bruce, B. B., & Kupersmith, M. J. (2012). Safety of prednisone for ocular myasthenia gravis. *Journal of Neuro-ophthalmology, 32*(3), 212–215.

Cassimeris, L. (2002). The oncoprotein 18/stathmin family of microtubule destabilizers. *Current Opinion in Cell Biology, 14*(1), 18–24.

Chiaretti, S., Messina, M., Tavolaro, S., Zardo, G., Elia, L., Vitale, A., ... Foà, R. (2010). Gene expression profiling identifies a subset of adult T-cell acute lymphoblastic leukemia with myeloid-like gene features and over-expression of miR-223. *Haematologica, 95*(7), 1114–1121.

Church, D., De Asis, M. A., & Brooks, A. J. (2012). Brief group intervention using EFT (Emotional Freedom Techniques) for depression in college students: A randomized controlled trial. *Depression Research and Treatment, 2012,* 1–7.

Church, D., Yount, G., & Brooks, A. J. (2012). The effect of Emotional Freedom Techniques (EFT) on stress biochemistry: A randomized controlled trial. *Journal of Nervous and Mental Disease, 200,* 891–896.

Clarke, L. & Kirwan, J. (2012). Efficacy, safety and mechanism of action of modified-release prednisone in rheumatoid arthritis. *Therapeutic Advances in Musculoskeletal Disease, 4*(3), 159–166.

Coussens, L. M. & Werb, Z. (2002). Inflammation and cancer. *Nature, 420*(6917), 860–867.

Herbert, J. (2013). Cortisol and depression: Three questions for psychiatry. *Psychological Medicine, 43*(3), 449–469.

Katsuura, S., Kuwano, Y., Yamagishi, N., Kurokawa, K., Kajita, K., Akaike, Y., ... Rokutan, K. (2012). MicroRNAs miR-144/144* and miR-16 in peripheral blood are potential biomarkers for naturalistic stress in healthy Japanese medical students. *Neuroscience Letters, 516*(1), 79–84.

Laios, A., O'Toole, S., Flavin, R., Martin, C., Kelly, L., Ring, M., ... O'Leary, J. (2008). Potential role of miR-9 and miR-223 in recurrent ovarian cancer. *Molecular Cancer, 7,* 35.

Mardjuadi, F., Medioni, J., Kerger, J., D'Hondt, L., Canon, J. L., Duck, L., ... Machiels, J. P. (2012). Phase I study of sorafenib in combination with docetaxel and prednisone in chemo-naive patients with metastatic castration-resistant prostate cancer. *Cancer Chemotherapy and Pharmacology, 70*(2), 293–303.

Meng, F., Wehbe-Janek, H., Henson, R., Smith, H., & Patel, T. (2008). Epigenetic regulation of microRNA-370 by interleukin-6 in malignant human cholangiocytes. *Oncogene, 27*(3), 378–386.

Nissen, R. M. & Yamamoto, K. R. (2000). The glucocorticoid receptor inhibits NFkappaB by interfering with serine-2 phosphorylation of the RNA polymerase II carboxy-terminal domain. *Genes and Development, 14*(18), 2314–2329.

Orom, U. A., Nielsen, F. C., & Lund, A. H. (2008). MicroRNA-10a binds the 5'UTR of ribosomal protein mRNAs and enhances their translation. *Molecular Cell, 30*(4), 460–471.

Pulikkan, J. A., Dengler, V., Peramangalam, P. S., Peer Zada, A. A., Muller-Tidow, C., Bohlander, S. K., ... Behre, G. (2010). Cell-cycle regulator E2F1 and microRNA-223 comprise an autoregulatory negative feedback loop in acute myeloid leukemia. *Blood, 115*(9), 1768–1778.

Rainer, J., Ploner, C., Jesacher, S., Ploner, A., Eduardoff, M., Mansha, M., ... Kofler, R. (2009). Glucocorticoid-regulated microRNAs and mirtrons in acute lymphoblastic leukemia. *Leukemia, 23*(4), 746–752.

Rana, S., Maples, P. B., Senzer, N., & Nemunaitis, J. (2008). Stathmin 1: A novel therapeutic target for anticancer activity. *Expert Review of Anticancer Therapy, 8*(9), 1461–1470.

Reiche, E. M., Morimoto, H. K., & Nunes, S. M. (2005). Stress and depression-induced immune dysfunction: Implications for the development and progression of cancer. *International Review of Psychiatry, 17*(6), 515–527.

Reiche, E. M., Nunes, S. O., & Morimoto, H. K. (2004). Stress, depression, the immune system, and cancer. *Lancet Oncology, 5*(10), 617–625.

Rokavec, M., Wu, W., & Luo, J. L. (2012). IL6-mediated suppression of miR-200c directs constitutive activation of inflammatory signaling circuit driving transformation and tumorigenesis. *Molecular Cell 45*(6), 777–789.

Rossbach, M. (2010). Small non-coding RNAs as novel therapeutics. *Current Molecular Medicine, 10*(4), 361–368.

Spiegel, D. (2012). Mind matters in cancer survival. *Psychooncology, 21*(6), 588–593.

Srivastava, M., Simakov, O., Chapman, J., Fahey, B., Gauthier, M. E., Mitros, T., ... Rokhsar, D. S. (2010). The Amphimedon queenslandica genome and the evolution of animal complexity. *Nature, 466*(7307), 720–726.

Stamatopoulos, B., Meuleman, N., Haibe-Kains, B., Saussoy, P., Van Den Neste, E., Michaux, L., ... Lagneaux, L. (2009). microRNA-29c and microRNA-223 down-regulation has in vivo significance in chronic lymphocytic leukemia and improves disease risk stratification. *Blood, 113*(21), 5237–5245.

Taft, R. J., Pheasant, M., & Mattick, J. S. (2007). The relationship between non-protein-coding DNA and eukaryotic complexity. *Bioessays, 29*(3), 288–299.

Wong, Q. W., Lung, R. W., Law, P. T., Lai, P. B., Chan, K. Y., To, K. F., & Wong, N. (2008). MicroRNA-223 is commonly repressed in hepatocellular carcinoma and potentiates expression of Stathmin1. *Gastroenterology, 135*(1), 257–269.

Wood, S. (2012). *Regulation of adrenal corticosteroidogenesis: The role of microRNAs in the control of aldosterone synthase and 11β-hydroxylase expression* (Doctoral dissertation, University of Glasgow). Retrieved from http://theses.gla.ac.uk/3252/

Yang, Z. & Wang, L. (2011). Regulation of microRNA expression and function by nuclear receptor signaling. *Cell & Bioscience, 1*(1), 31.

Yuan, K., Lian, Z., Sun, B., Clayton, M. M., Ng, I. O., & Feitelson, M. A. (2012). Role of miR-148a in hepatitis B associated hepatocellular carcinoma. *PLoS One, 7*(4), e35331.

Chapter 7
The Curious Phenomenon of Surrogate Tapping
David Feinstein

Abstract

A psychotherapeutic approach that combines cognitive techniques with the stimulation of acupuncture points by tapping on them has been gaining increased attention among clinicians as well as among laypersons using it on a self-help basis. It is called energy psychology. Thirty-six peer-reviewed studies published or in-press as of April 2012—including 18 randomized controlled trials—have found the method to be surprisingly rapid and effective for a range of disorders. More surprising are reports of "surrogate tapping." In surrogate tapping, the practitioner taps on him- or herself and applies other elements of energy psychology protocols as if he or she were the person whose problem is being addressed, all the while holding the intention of helping that person. Essentially long-distance healing within an energy psychology framework, successful reports of surrogate tapping have been appearing with some frequency within the energy psychology practitioner community. A search of the literature and pertinent websites, combined with a call for cases involving surrogate tapping, produced the 100 anecdotal accounts described here where an apparent effect was observed. Studies of other long-distance phenomena, such as telepathy and distant healing, are reviewed to put these reports into context. The paradigm challenges raised by reports of positive outcomes following surrogate treatments are considered, and conclusions that can and cannot be legitimately reached based on the current data are explored.

Keywords: acupoints, distance healing, energy psychology, entanglement, surrogate tapping

David Feinstein, PhD, is a clinical psychologist who has received nine national awards for his books on consciousness and healing. Correspondence: df777@earthlink.net. 777 East Main St, Ashland, OR 97520. Acknowledgments: Comments on drafts of this chapter by John Freedom, CEHP, Dag Hultcrantz, Douglas J. Moore, PhD, and Gwyneth Moss, MA, are gratefully acknowledged. Special thanks to Sandra Shipp for her assistance in collecting and analyzing the data reported here. Disclosures: The author receives income from energy psychology publications and trainings. This chapter was published earlier in the journal *Energy Psychology: Theory, Research, and Treatment*.

After a slow and reluctant entry into energy psychology, I found that the responses of my clients to acupoint tapping turned me into an enthusiastic proponent (Feinstein, 2004, 2009, 2010, 2012a, 2012b). My first impressions were not unusual. The procedures look strange; no credible research had (at the time) been produced, and the prevailing explanations made little sense. The fact that it happens to work so frequently and rapidly was, however, a cause for not a little cognitive dissonance.

I began to speculate upon and then lecture about possible mechanisms. If I was speaking to a group that included energy psychology practitioners, someone would invariably ask about "surrogate tapping." Reported with some frequency within the energy psychology community, surrogate tapping is essentially long-distance healing within an energy psychology framework. The practitioner taps on him- or herself and applies other elements of energy psychology protocols as if he or she was the person whose problem is being addressed, all the while holding the intention of helping that person. Often the other person would not even be in the same location. Tapping on acupoints to produce psychological change had been quaint enough. These reports seemed to stretch all credibility. Oddly, however, surrogate tapping seemed to produce the desired outcomes more often than one might expect! For instance, an 11-year-old boy whose nighttime bed-wetting was persistent despite a good deal of therapeutic intervention was not making progress in his current therapy. His mother was in treatment with another therapist, a psychologist trained in Thought Field Therapy (TFT). During their sessions, he had the boy's mother stimulate her own acupoints and use wordings as if she were her son. The boy's enuresis quickly remitted (described in Feinstein, 2004). Such accounts of surrogate tapping have been reported with the person present or at a distance and with the person knowing or not knowing the procedure was being used. Other instances have involved animals and infants.

My reply to the questions about this phenomenon during my lectures would be some version of "It is hard enough to explain to my psychologist colleagues why tapping on the skin seems to do something to the brain that brings about the rapid resolution of PTSD. Can we please just leave claims that tapping on oneself can do something to *someone else's brain* out of the discussion for now!" But I knew that this anomaly had to be addressed eventually and sensed that it would provide a challenge that might move the field beyond the "amygdala deactivation model" (Feinstein, 2010) I was advocating. Focusing on the deactivating signals that are sent to the amygdala by the stimulation of acupoints provides a view of a very complex process through a neurological lens. Surrogate tapping, if it really does what is being reported, would clearly call for a different lens, or atleast a wider one.

My curiosity eventually overcame my resistance to acknowledging the accumulating reports of successful surrogate tapping. In the spring of 2012, I conducted a literature search and put out a request to the energy psychology community via e-letters and e-lists for case descriptions of surrogate tapping. I had been able to locate only one peer-reviewed journal report describing the process (McCarty, 2006), but 54 reports were found on various websites. The request for cases led to 24 additional replies. An additional 114 written reports were generously provided by an Emotional Freedom Techniques (EFT) practitioner, Jack Schulz, who was writing a book on the topic and had accessed a database I had not searched. Of the total of 193 unique cases identified from the literature, websites, direct requests, and shared data, all reported positive outcomes, and exactly 100 met the following criteria:

- A "sender" had applied an energy psychology protocol to him or herself with the intention of being helpful to a "receiver."
- The sender did not physically tap on the receiver but may have been in the same room (as is often the case with infants or animals) or the two may have been isolated by distance.
- The receiver did not apply the protocol to him or herself.
- The positive outcome was attributed to the surrogate tapping.

Of the 100 reports, 28 indicated that the receiver was an adult, 15 that the receiver was a child or adolescent, and 15 that the receiver was an infant; age was not specified in three of the reports. In the other 39 cases, the receiver was an animal. Surrogate sessions may be the most feasible way to use energy psychology protocols with infants, animals, or others who are themselves unable to carry out the tapping or verbalizations.

A positive outcome was attributed to the surrogate tapping in all 100 cases. The sender wrote the report in all 100 instances. In 48 of the 100 cases meeting the selection criteria, evidence of the positive outcome was based on the sender's observations. In 19 cases, the sender also related a direct account from the receiver. This account had been unprompted by the sender in 11 of these 19 instances. In the remaining 33 cases, the improvements were reported by a party other than the sender or the receiver (e.g., a medical caregiver, a parent whose infant was the receiver while someone else was the sender, or the owner of a pet when someone else was the sender).

The surrogate tapping effects reported included both physical and emotional/behavioral changes. Examples of physical changes included: improving dementia and eliminating incontinence in a 90-year-old woman, appearing to arrest a grand mal seizure in an adult male, a "miraculous" hiatus in the side effects of chemotherapy, continued stability of white blood cell counts in a cancer patient, stopping an attack of chronic pulmonary obstruction disorder, eliminating severe diaper rash in an infant, cessation of a serious case of hiccups in an infant, eliminating a rapidly growing bone cancer in a pet, eliminating overnight an oozing sore in a show dog allowing him to compete the next day, eliminating residual heartworm in a dog, greatly reducing chronic diarrhea in an adult horse, and improving the quality and extending the life of several dogs and cats beyond the hopes expressed by their veterinarians.

Examples of emotional or behavioral shifts that were reported included calming rage in an adult male, reducing anxiety and pain in several circumstances, decreasing an elderly woman's extreme agitation about being placed in a nursing home, accommodating a request for help from a male alcoholic who had been adamant about not wanting treatment until just after surrogate tapping of which he was not aware, eliminating training barriers in an iron man triathlete, eliminating fear of heights in a female adult, and eliminating fear of vacuums and thunder in household pets. Of course, alternative, more mundane explanations could explain the changes in each of these situations, but as a group, with the desired outcomes quickly following the interventions, cause–effect possibilities warrant exploration.

An issue for those who practice surrogate tapping, as well as remote diagnosis and other forms of distance healing, is the need to obtain permission. While no uniform or widely accepted ethical guidelines address this issue directly, questions about the need to inform the receiver in advance of a remote intervention and to obtain permission are being debated (Feinstein, 2011). In 59 of the 100 reports, permission could be assumed or was clearly not required (e.g., the surrogate tapping was requested by the receiver, a father was tapping for his infant son, a woman was tapping for her cat). In five other cases, it could not be determined from the report whether permission could be assumed or was clearly not required. In nine of the remaining 36 cases, permission was explicitly sought, and in another instance, permission was obtained through the practitioner's alleged sense of clairvoyantly contacting the client to gain permission. In the remaining 26 cases, there was no mention of permission having been requested.

Examples of Surrogate Tapping

Three of the cases are presented here to provide a sense of the way surrogate tapping is conducted. A woman reported using surrogate tapping on her brother:

> He has had cancer and is also a severe alcoholic who really doesn't seem to care if he lives or dies. It is truly heartbreaking. He effectively shuts himself away from everyone and does not want help. During his radiation treatment for cancer, he was so ill he told our mother that he was "in hell." I began tapping in desperation, putting my heart and soul into helping him. I tapped without anyone knowing.

She tapped for over an hour late one night, upon learning of his being in extreme distress, using statements that addressed his physical discomfort, his hopelessness, and his wanting to die. The next morning she phoned her sister, who, not knowing anything about the surrogate tapping, told her "We can't believe it! Jerry looks and says he feels so good. He is feeling really positive and up and about. It seems like a miracle." The evening before, he had been so sick after a particular radiation treatment that he was vomiting and curled up on the floor in so much pain he believed he was dying. That is what had prompted the woman to, "in desperation," begin the surrogate tapping. She continued to privately use it from time to time. She reported, "After that day, he continued to feel really good, and 18 months later he was clear of cancer."

A college athlete called her mother, crying and frustrated because she felt that no matter what she did, she could not lose extra weight that was limiting her success in her sport. She complained that all of her mother's suggestions were making her feel much worse. Having offered everything else she could think of, the mother decided to try surrogate tapping. She reported,

> The next day, my daughter called me to let me know that she seemed to have lost her ravenous appetite … for no reason. Two weeks later, she comes home for a visit and she has lost the 10 pounds she was struggling to lose. She said she just wasn't as hungry and was craving fruit instead of candy and the weight just seemed to have melted off somehow. … I did not tell her I did this surrogate tapping protocol for her.

A more critical problem around food involved a 6-year-old boy who had a phobic concern about putting anything in his mouth, resulting in daily fear, fights, and dread about eating. His weight at the time of the session was less than that of an average 4-year-old, and doctors were considering more invasive interventions. He never asked for food, would eat only four foods, and these only after a daily struggle. There was no sense of any normal hunger–eating–satiation cycle. The practitioner, Wendy Anne McCarty (2006), frequently utilizes surrogate tapping on behalf of infants and children while working with their parents. Her published account of this case is quite detailed and instructive about the procedure. It is condensed here in a manner approved by McCarty (personal communication, July 8, 2012):

> I asked the mother if it was all right for me to tune into her son energetically. I closed my eyes and with my intention made contact with her son [who was at home, several miles away] and got a sense of his energy field. I asked the mother to also get more settled and quiet within herself and then to tune in to her son and share with me as we went along what she felt or noticed. I quietly spoke out loud my communication with the boy, my impressions, and what I sensed from him, so that the mother would be included and the two of us could connect more fully. I introduced myself to the boy and explained that his mother was concerned about him and was asking me for help. I energetically sensed his field and asked him if we could help with his difficulty with food. His trepidation about any change struck me. I explained to him that he didn't need to change, nor would we ask him to do anything differently than he felt he needed to do; but asked if we could see how we may help it be less scary, painful, or difficult for him. I felt a softening, a receptivity. With that sense of permission, we began the work with his energetic presence being an integral part of the session.
>
> When I asked the mother if eating, food, or weight had been an issue during her childhood, she said yes, they had. She related that her father then and now was "cruel" and "demeaning" to her mother and the girls in the family concerning weight and attractiveness. If they gained weight or ate foods he disapproved of, he would suggest that no one would ever want them. Clearly, that was a strong family dynamic that was a possible contributor to the boy's pattern. I energetically intuitively checked in with the son to ask if this was at the heart of the matter and "no" was the response.
>
> The mother then related that she was always dieting, but still eating more than she "should." Clearly the ambivalence and attention around eating was a life issue for her, yet as I checked in again, that did not seem to be at the core of her son's issue. So, here we were—the son's current pattern and a three-generational pattern on line as we were working. Yet, the core had seemingly not emerged in my assessment.
>
> I quieted and asked the son energetically, where is the heart of this issue? I immediately was inspired to ask about his birth and if there was talk about eating and food at that time. The mother acted surprised and said, "Yes, just before I was going to give birth … I gained so much weight during the pregnancy and then was pre-ecliptic. I was huge. I was in the delivery room and I pulled the doctor over and said, rather dramatically, 'Don't ever let me eat again! I never want to eat again! I'm so big! Don't let me ever put a thing in my mouth again!'"
>
> Shortly after this emphatic plea, she had her baby boy. With this birth moment

acknowledged and put on line, everything felt as if it fell into place with this as the heart of the current problem. Now we could utilize EFT to help shift the patterns. With the remaining 30 min, I briefly explained EFT to her and suggested I surrogate the tapping on myself for her son, while she held her attention on the particular aspect of the pattern during each tapping sequence. (Other times, when there is more time, I teach parents how to surrogate with their body for their baby or child's issue.)

I first applied EFT with the mother to address the abusive, demeaning behavior she experienced with her father concerning weight and eating. We then moved on to her personal food–weight pattern. After she reported that the related emotions had shifted to close to neutral, we came back to the son. I had the mother picture him expressing his anxiety, dread, and fear of food. As I resonated with the pattern, I tapped on my body for him, "Even though I am sooooo afraid to eat and afraid somebody will try and make me eat, I'm a good kid." With this, we both felt a lessening of the intensity, yet more was still there.

I then went to the messages at birth. In front of the mother, I spoke out loud what I was communicating to her son nonlocally. "You know, sometimes babies when they are born hear things and take them on as if the message was for them. I think that happened at your birth. Your mother made some very strong statements about her weight and her not wanting to eat again. I think you took that message as if it was for you, but it wasn't. It was meant only for her. You are a growing little boy and it is good for you to eat and gain weight and get bigger. That is what you are supposed to do as you are growing up. I think your system got this confused back when you were a baby being born. So, we are going to help that baby not hold that message anymore, since it wasn't meant for him."

With that, I asked the mother to go back to the image of her making that emphatic statement in the birthing room as I tapped on myself for her son and for the baby in her womb. "Even though I heard those statements about never eating again and being too big and got confused and took them on as mine, I deeply and completely love and accept myself and *now can let those go and find my own relationship with food, enjoying food and eating, and growing bigger*."

Both the mother and I felt a dramatic shift with the whole pattern seemingly dissipated when we tried to focus on it after tapping that round. I asked the mother to sense into his dread, anxiety, fear of eating pattern. Neither one of us could feel any charge in it now. The old pattern was not accessible. She was stunned that she could sense the change—an empowering moment.

I explained that with my experience with EFT, when an old pattern lets go, the person *organically* changes, from inside out, and has new ideas, notions, thoughts, feelings, and actions—a new experience of the issue. Thus I encouraged her to not try to coax him to eat as usual and to just be receptive to see what he would do now after the session.

The next day I received a message from the mother. The mother said that the family felt "a miracle had happened." She related that within one hour of her returning home, for the first time in his entire life, her son spontaneously said, "Mama, I'm hungry. Would you feed me?" Never before had he requested food, wanted food, or even expressed the sense of being hungry.

This report described communication with the receiver that is far more elaborate than in most of the cases that met the selection criteria. The case was presented for its intimate glimpse into the thought processes of a practitioner who is known as being proficient with surrogate tapping. Most often the procedure involves tuning into the receiver and the symptoms that are of concern while tapping on a standard set of acupoints and using verbalizations that reflect an empathic understanding of the receiver's situation. While the 100 anecdotal reports do not prove that surrogate tapping has positive clinical effects, they do suggest that some people may be able to evoke positive clinical effects from a distance and that tapping may be involved in these outcomes.

Evidence Corroborating Reports of Distant Surrogate Effects

These accounts, of course, raise many questions. Anecdotal reports are only a preliminary stage in establishing the efficacy of a treatment, but systematic studies of surrogate tapping are yet to be conducted. Another way to form a framework for interpreting the various reports of positive outcomes following surrogate tapping is to see if analogous phenomena have been documented in other contexts.

A sizable literature has addressed the question of effects at a distance (more than a thousand studies are summarized in books such as Benor, 2001; Dossey, 1995; Jonas & Crawford, 2003; McTaggart, 2008, 2011; Radin, 1997, 2006; Swanson, 2003, 2010; Targ, 2012; Tart, 2009; and Tiller, 1997). Benor (2001) reviewed 191 controlled studies of healing with no physical intervention that had been published up to 2000. The healing was conducted through nontouch "laying-on-of-hands" or through mental influence alone, with the targets including human subjects, animals, plants, bacteria, yeasts, cells in cultures, enzymes, and DNA. Significant effects were found in 124 of the 191 studies, with the distance between the healer and the recipient ranging from a few inches to thousands of miles. Benor has continued to track studies of distance healing and posts them online at http://www.wholistichealingresearch.com/StudiesandProgressNotes.html. Schmidt (2012), after reviewing three meta-analytic studies of distant effects involving hundreds of trials, concluded that the evidence is strong that "benevolent intention" (p. 529) can produce positive outcomes in the receiver. Braud and Schlitz (1997) conducted a review and meta-analysis of 30 studies in which individuals attempted to influence autonomic nervous system activity in another person at a distance (usually measured by skin conductance) and found a robust effect size across the studies. Meanwhile, the effects of focused intention on seed germination and plant growth have long been established (reviewed in McTaggart, 2007; Tompkins & Bird, 1973).

While this literature is not without adamant critics (e.g., Ernst & Singh 2009; Park, 2000; Wanjek, 2002), a few of the individual investigations into healing effects at a distance are briefly described here to provide the reader a better sense of the phenomena being reported. For instance, scientists at the University of California (UC), Irvine, exposed a lethal dose of gamma radiation to live cells in Petri dishes. Half the cells died within 24 hr. When "healing energy" was sent to the Petri dishes of the same type of cell before and after the exposure to the same type of radiation, 88% survived. It did not matter whether the healers were in the next room or thousands of miles away. After describing the UC Irvine trials, Swanson (2010) noted that "this experiment has been repeated more than 100 times with consistent results" (pp. 24–25).

Medical qigong, an ancient Chinese practice that involves controlling and directing energy for healing purposes, has been shown to be able to, from a distance, "protect normal cells from harmful assaults, increase anti-tumor immunity, reduce tumor metastases, promote cell death of tumor cells, and increase survival time of tumor-embedded animals" (Yan, Lu, & Kiang, 2003, p. 105). For instance, a qigong master named Jixing Li was able to *selectively* kill human cancer cells in a laboratory 3,000 miles away. The cells, placed in a growth medium within an incubator at Penn State University, were focused upon by Li while in California. The cells Li targeted died. A second set of cancer cells, only a few inches away, continued to grow rapidly (Neely, 2008). Yount et al. (2012) measured the effect of a healer's efforts to diminish the growth of human cancer cells in a culture and found that the number of sessions (one, two, or five) correlated with decreased viability of the cancer cells. The positive effects were independent of the distance between the healer and the cells (0.25, 25, or 2000 meters). Experiments with human cells have shown that nontouch energy treatments can also stimulate the proliferation of healthy human cells in a culture (Gronowicz, Jhaveri, Clarke, Aronow, & Smith, 2008).

In another distant healing experiment with cancer, people given brief training in an energy healing technique were able to dramatically raise the remittance rate of mice infected with incurable cancer to above 70%. Meanwhile, none of the mice in a control group that received no treatment survived (Bengston & Krinsley, 2000). It did not matter whether the healer believed the intervention would work. Another series of experiments found one salient characteristic of the practitioner that did appear to matter. The effects of a person's directed intention toward others at a distance compared favorably with the person's ability to mentally influence his or her own physiology (Braud & Schlitz, 1983). Swanson (2010), after an extensive review of distant healing research, suggested that the higher the practitioner's "consciousness"— which he defines in terms of "coherence of the mind" (p. 616)—the greater the ability to exert physical influences from a distance.

Distance effects of intention and consciousness are also well-documented in areas other than healing. Declassified Central Intelligence Agency documents have revealed that hundreds of "remote viewing" experiments sponsored by the agency and conducted at the Stanford Research Institute produced remarkable results, such as a "remote viewer" in Palo Alto, who after only being given the geographical coordinates, made an accurate drawing of a multistory crane located at a Soviet weapons laboratory 10,000 miles away (Puthoff, 1996). In a series of provocative (and controversial) demonstration projects, crime rates were reported to have decreased significantly within weeks after large numbers of meditators temporarily moved into a neighborhood (Hagelin et al., 1999). Providing possible insight into these outcomes, 11 individuals who claimed an ability to produce nonlocal effects were able to successfully influence the brain activity of participants from whom they were isolated, as detected by functional magnetic resonance imaging (Achterberg et al., 2005). Friends who are apart from one another can also, in some instances, send thoughts that measurably impact each other's brain waves (Standish, Kozak, Johnson, & Richards, 2004). Resonance between twins was reported in a provocative study of electroencephalogram (EEG) correspondences between twins separated by distance, published in *Science* (Duane & Behrendt, 1965) and can be found in a rich folklore of dramatic accounts, such as when a 4-year-old girl burned her hand and her twin sister at another location simultaneously developed a blister of the same size in exactly the same place (Playfair, 2009). The abilities of some individuals to influence physical events—such as to get a silver dollar to land "heads-up" 100 times in a row (Tart, 2009)—have also been repeatedly demonstrated, along with putative telepathy and other at-a-distance effects (Radin, 1997, 2006; Targ & Katra, 1999; Targ, 2012). For instance, patterns in random number generators are slightly but reliably influenced when a crowd is mentally and emotionally focused on the same event, whether a touchdown at a football game or a national tragedy (Nelson, Bradish, Dobyns, Dunne, & Jahn, 1996).

Some controlled investigations have failed to find an effect for distant healing interventions (e.g., Koenig, 2007), and others have identified secondary factors that affect outcomes, such as knowledge or belief about the treatment (e.g., Easter & Watt, 2011). A systematic review of 23 randomized trials investigating clinical outcomes of prayer, distance healing, or other noncontact forms of healing—involving 2,774 patients—found that 57% of the studies yielded statistically significant treatment effects (Astin, Harkness, & Ernst, 2000). Performing a meta-analysis on more than 1,000 controlled studies of distant effects, Radin (1997) found that the combined odds against the reported outcomes being due to chance, even after statistical adjustments for potential selective reporting biases, are 10^{104} to 1.

Paradigm Challenges Posed by at-a-Distance Effects

In short, documented cases of surrogate tapping leading to desired effects add to a substantial body of evidence that (a) physical influences from a distance occur and (b) that conditions can be established for atleast some practitioners in which distance healing occurs with reasonable frequency. Newtonian/reductionist scientific frameworks cannot, however, begin to explain how this might work.

When new data does not fit existing paradigms, the first impulse is to ignore or discount the data (Kuhn, 1996), as I baldly did in fielding the theoretically inconvenient audience questions about reports of successful surrogate tapping. I was not alone in using such a strategy when facing cognitive dissonance. Many journal editors have systematically excluded even the most well-designed studies of telepathy and distant effects—research that, if accurate, requires that the "laws of physics will have to be rewritten" (Broughton, 1992, p. 76). An *American Psychologist* article focused on a scientifically rigorous 10-year research program demonstrating dream telepathy as a case in point. It highlighted this program in tracing the systematic bias in professional psychology publications against anomalous observations such as extrasensory perception (Child, 1985). Child concluded that, although the research program was rigorous and "widely known and greatly respected" among scientists active in parapsychology, the experiments received no mention in reviews to which they are clearly pertinent or have been condemned based on entirely erroneous assertions. "Insofar as psychologists are guided by these reviews," Child observed, *"they are prevented from gaining accurate information about research"* that might significantly impact their worldview (p. 1219). Balanced presentations of parapsychological research have, in fact, despite a few notable exceptions (e.g., Bem & Honorton, 1994; Rao & Palmer, 1987), mostly been excluded from mainstream psychological journals.

But the evidence for distance healing and other so-called "paranormal" phenomena mentioned above, while remaining controversial (e.g., Dossey, 2006), is not going away. Rather it is showing up in yet another arena, this time in energy psychology, with the reports of improvements following surrogate tapping. But how can surrogate tapping produce the outcomes being reported? How can my unannounced tapping beneath my eye (the first acupuncture point of the stomach meridian) while I am in Oregon help relieve my grandson's stomachache after he was too enthusiastic with a giant pastrami sandwich at Carnegie Deli in New York City? The options available to anyone who is paying attention to these strange occurrences include (a) accept mainstream understanding of time and space and discount the findings on distance healing, (b) accept both and live with mutually incompatible conclusions, or (c) be open to the findings on distance healing and reconsider one's worldview accordingly. To revise a longstanding way of viewing the world is not an easy process for an individual or for a discipline that is invested in established models, but mainstream scientific and medical paradigms are being confronted with serious challenges that strain their most basic premises (Laszlo & Dennis, 2012). Radin (2006) went so far as to say that rather than thinking of experiences such as telepathy as mysterious powers of the mind, they may prove to be "the initial stages of awareness of deeper levels of reality" (p. 277).

Expanding the Paradigm to Accommodate at-a-Distance Effects

The prevailing paradigm in medicine remains curiously Newtonian. Lipton (2005), a cell biologist who did some of the early work on gene expression while on the faculty of Stanford University's School of Medicine, has suggested that physics is a century ahead of medicine. Specifically, quantum physics recognizes that the universe is not made of matter suspended in empty space but of energy. After enumerating the modern technological miracles whose invention depended on the application of quantum mechanics—from cell phones to space ships—Lipton turns to the advances in biomedical science that can be attributed to quantum physics. "Let's list them in order of their importance," he prepares his readers, and then answers: "It is a very short list—there haven't been any" (p. 109).

The property of quantum systems that is of most direct relevance to surrogate tapping and distance healing is called nonlocality or entanglement, which Einstein famously referred to as "spooky action at a distance." The theory of entanglement proposes, and many experiments have verified, that if two subatomic particles such as photons or electrons have interacted, what happens to one will simultaneously influence the other, even if they are separated by great distances (Fraser & Massey, 2008). Pointing to this theory to explain distance healing has been regarded as naïve since quantum mechanics applies to the unimaginably small world of subatomic particles, not to macrosystems like human brains or bodies. However, the brain is a system of communication among billions of neurons with trillions of synapses sharing a common mechanism: an electrochemical wave reaches a neuron's synapse causing channels to open that allow calcium ions to enter, which when they reach a critical number, cause the neuron to release neurotransmitters, the building blocks of cell communication. The quantum element "enters at the ion channels," which are at some points less than a billionth of a meter in diameter, a scale at which "quantum effects become quite noticeable" (Radin, 2006, p. 258, reporting findings by Stuart Hameroff). Quantum effects in macrosystems are, in fact, now taken for granted by physicists, and the dividing line between classical and quantum physics has been breaking down. In an article in *Nature*, Vedral (2008) noted that over the course of "less than a century, researchers have moved from distrusting entanglement because of its 'spooky action at a distance' to starting to regard it as an essential property of the macroscopic world" (p. 1004).

Vedral (2009) defined entanglement as a degree of observable correlation that "exceeds any correlation allowed by the laws of classical physics" (p. 1005) and presented evidence that entanglement "can exist in arbitrarily large" systems involving not just two photons or electrons but millions of atoms (p. 1007). Macrosystem applications of entanglement can already be found in solar technology and in the fledgling field of quantum computing, which utilizes quantum properties, including nonlocal effects, to represent and perform operations on data. Experiments have already been carried out in which quantum computational operations were successfully executed.

The effects of entanglement in nature are generally quite weak, though Vedral (2008) explained that with "a great deal of effort" it is possible to create "high overall entanglement and connectivity" (p. 1006). The two basic approaches to generating large-scale entanglement are: "bottom up" and "top down" (p. 1006). The bottom-up approach may be what is occurring with surrogate tapping. It involves "gaining precise control of a single system" (tapping on one's own body) and "then extending that control to two systems" (the targeted benefactor of the process). In the top-down approach, an intervention in the environment (sometimes as simple as changing the temperature) can initiate entanglement in entities within that environment. This may be what is occurring when crime rates decrease after large numbers of meditators have entered a community. While Vedral noted that it is still an open question whether macroscopic entanglement operates in living systems, the fact that the property is now widely recognized in complex nonorganic systems involving solar technology and quantum computing points in that direction.

The medium that would account for distant influences such as entanglement is yet to be detected by scientific instruments. No one has explained the precise mechanisms that allow two photons or two people to physically influence one another, even when separated by large distances, though theories abound (e.g., Jahn & Dunne, 2011; Leder, 2005; Radin, 2006; Sheldrake, 2009). The Higgs field, a ubiquitous energy field (described throughout the Internet as "the energy of the vacuum from which all else came"), is believed to give elementary particles their mass and has been confirmed through the probable verification of the boson, the so-called "god particle" (Than, 2012). Zero-point energy, formulated in a 1913 paper by Einstein and Otto Stern that built on the work of Max Planck, is the lowest possible energy a quantum mechanical system can have. It suggests that the "vacuum," the space between particles, is not empty but is an energy field! While zero-point energy is still generally accepted, the standard model of quantum physics has left some unanswered questions (Kane, 2005).

For instance, it has been able to conceptually unite three of the four fundamental forces of nature—electromagnetism and the "weak" and "strong" quantum forces—but not the fourth, gravity. "String theory," which proposes that the electrons and quarks within an atom are one-dimensional lines of vibration ("strings") in a multidimensional universe, attempts to reconcile this by providing a self-contained mathematical model that describes all the fundamental forces and forms of matter (Becker, Becker, & Schwarz, 2007). A holographic model in which "all parts of a greater universe are expressed fractally in each smaller part" posits an invisible field of information that is believed to give form to all physical structures (Kelly, 2011, p. 25). A theory proposed by a group of Russian physicists attempts to explain anomalous phenomena by positing "torsion fields," which can carry information at speeds far faster than the speed of light (Akimov & Shipov, 1996), explaining apparent simultaneous effects across distances. A "synchronized universe" model has been proposed by Swanson (2003, 2010), also to account for observations of such phenomena as telepathy, remote viewing, distant healing, out-of-body experiences, and, most significantly, consciousness itself.

Interpreting the Surrogate Tapping Reports

If a cause–effect relationship between surrogate tapping and positive clinical outcomes is scientifically established, another bit of evidence will have been added to the ledger calling for such expanded models as those described above. How strong is the evidence? Anecdotal reports are considered "heuristic" in science, enough to guide further investigation but in themselves not interpretable as evidence. From the 100 reports collected that suggest there is an effect following surrogate tapping, we do not know if most people who have tried the method obtained results similar to those in the reports or if the ratio is closer to 1 in a 1,000, suggesting that the hits were due to factors other than the tapping. Nor are there any controls on the assessments of those reporting, who would likely have been predisposed to see improvement. When my grandson's tummy ache improved at the same moment I was doing the surrogate tapping, I found myself willing to let our daughter know what I had been up to and take the credit.

The accumulated reports are, however, provocative enough to call for further research into what could be a paradigm-challenging, not to mention highly useful, procedure. While not without design challenges, research on surrogate tapping could be patterned after the first published randomized controlled trial investigating an energy psychology treatment (Wells, Polglase, Andrews, Carrington, & Baker, 2003), which has been corroborated by two partial replications (Baker & Siegel, 2010; Salas, Brooks, & Rowe, 2011). Similar procedures for client selection, randomization, and pre-/postassessments of targeted symptoms could be utilized; but during the period the participants in the original research was receiving the energy psychology treatment, a task with no known clinical benefit, such as working a puzzle, could be performed. Meanwhile, the treatment would be conducted through surrogate tapping by a practitioner in another room or another location. Variables that might be investigated in the first or subsequent studies include the amount of distance between the participant and the practitioner, whether the participant and practitioner had been introduced or had formed some sort of relationship, whether the practitioner had previous success with surrogate tapping (various reports suggest that some people are more highly proficient than others), and the exact procedures used by the surrogate practitioner. Directly following the treatment, and on subsequent follow-up, the initial assessments of targeted symptoms would be repeated. A control group would be led through an identical protocol except the surrogate tapping would be omitted. Informed consent would need to delicately address ethical issues regarding permission for remote interventions while adequately disguising the nature of the investigation.

Even in the absence of such investigation, however, when the anecdotal reports are placed into the larger context of (a) established evidence for at-a-distance effects and (b) the models that have been proposed by credible sources to explain them, speculation on cause–effect relationships between surrogate tapping and the reported outcomes gains credibility. The observed effects are consistent with the data on distant healing, intercessory prayer, and other nonlocal influences (e.g., Cardeña, Lynn, & Krippner, 2000). The outcomes in the 100 cases that were collected seem unlikely to have all occurred by chance. Striking results have, in fact, been described frequently enough that surrogate tapping is assumed to be a viable intervention by many within the energy psychology community. While research is needed to scientifically establish whether this practice is more than wishful thinking, it is appealing to have a formula for directing your good intentions when your grandson is in trouble. And for family members who are separated by miles and feeling helpless when a loved one is suffering, there is just enough indication that it works to consider giving it a try.

References

Achterberg, J., Cooke, K., Richards, T., Standish, L. J., Kozak, L., & Lake, J. (2005). Evidence for correlations between distant intentionality and brain function in recipients: A functional magnetic resonance imaging analysis. *Journal of Alternative and Complementary Medicine, 11*, 965–971. http://dx.doi.org/10.1089/acm.2005.11.965

Akimov, A. E. & Shipov, G. I. (1996). *Torsion fields and their experimental manifestations*. Moscow: International Institute for Theoretical and Applied Physics (preprint 4a, Russian Academy of Natural Sciences).

Astin, J. A., Harkness, E., & Ernst, E. (2000). The efficacy of "distant healing": A systematic review of randomized trials. *Annals of Internal Medicine, 132*, 903–910.

Baker, A. H. & Siegel, M. A. (2010). Emotional Freedom Techniques (EFT) reduces intense fears: A partial replication and extension of Wells et al. *Energy Psychology: Theory, Research, & Treatment, 2*(2), 3–30.

Becker, K., Becker, M., & Schwarz, J. H. (2007) *String theory and M-theory: A modern introduction*. Cambridge, England: Cambridge University Press.

Bem, D. J. & Honorton, C. (1994). Does psi exist? Replicable evidence for an anomalous process of information transfer. *Psychological Bulletin, 115*, 4–18. http://dx.doi.org/10.1037/0033-2909.115.1.4

Bengston, W. & Krinsley, D. (2000). The effect of laying-on of hands on transplanted breast cancer in mice (letter to editor). *Journal of Scientific Exploration, 14*, 353–364.

Benor, D. J. (2001). *Spiritual healing: Scientific validation of a healing revolution* (Healing research, Vol 1). Southfield, MI: Vision Publications.

Braud, W. & Schlitz, M. (1983). Psychokinetic influence on electrodermal activity. *Journal of Parapsychology, 47*, 95–119.

Braud, W. & Schlitz, M. (1997). Distant intentionality and healing: Assessing the evidence. *Alternative Therapies in Health and Medicine, 3*(6), 62–73.

Broughton, R. S. (1992). *Parapsychology: The controversial science*. New York, NY: Ballantine.

Cardeña, E., Lynn, S. J., & Krippner, S. (Eds.) (2000). *Varieties of anomalous experience: Examining the scientific evidence*. Washington, DC: American Psychological Association.

Child, I. L. (1985). Psychology and anomalous observations: The question of ESP in dreams. *American Psychologist, 40*, 1219–1230. http://dx.doi.org/10.1037/0003-066X.40.11.1219

Dossey, L. (1995). *The power of prayer and the practice of medicine*. New York, NY: HarperCollins.

Dossey, L. (2006). Prayer experiments: Science or folly? Observations on the Harvard prayer study. *Network Review, 91*, 22–23.

Duane, T. D. & Behrendt, T. (1965). Extrasensory electroencephalographic induction between identical twins. *Science, 150*, 367. doi:10.1126/science.150.3694.367

Easter, A. & Watt, C. (2011). It's good to know: How treatment knowledge and belief affect the outcome of distance healing intentionality for arthritis sufferers. *Journal of Psychosomatic Research, 71*, 86–89. http://dx.doi.org/10.1016/j.jpsychores.2011.02.003

Einstein, A. & Stern, O. (1913). Einige Argumente für die Annahme einer molekularen Agitation beim absoluten Nullpunkt [Some arguments for the existence of molecular agitation at absolute zero]. *Annalen der Physik, 345*, 551–560. doi:10.1002/andp.19133450309

Ernst, E. & Singh, S. (2009). *Trick or treatment: The undeniable facts about alternative medicine*. New York, NY: Norton.

Feinstein, D. (2004). *Energy psychology interactive: Rapid interventions for lasting change*. Ashland, OR: Innersource.

Feinstein, D. (2009). Facts, paradigms, and anomalies in the acceptance of energy psychology: A rejoinder to McCaslin's (2009) and Pignotti and Thyer's (2009) comments on Feinstein (2008a). *Psychotherapy: Theory, Research, Practice, Training, 46*, 262–269. doi:10.1037/a0016086

Feinstein, D. (2010). Rapid treatment of PTSD: Why psychological exposure with acupoint tapping may be effective. *Psychotherapy: Theory, Research, Practice, Training, 47*, 385–402. doi:10.1037/a0021171

Feinstein, D. (2012a). Acupoint stimulation in treating psychological disorders: Evidence of efficacy. *Review of General Psychology, 16*, 364–380. doi:10.1037/a0028602

Feinstein, D. (2012b). What does *energy* have to do with energy psychology? *Energy Psychology: Theory, Research, and Treatment, 4*(2), 59–80.

Feinstein, D. (with Eden, D.) (2011). *Ethics handbook for energy healing practitioners*. Fulton, CA: Energy Psychology Press.

Fraser, P. H. & Massey, H. (2008). *Decoding the human body-field: The new science of information as medicine*. Rochester, VT: Healing Arts Press.

Gronowicz, G., A., Jhaveri, A., Clarke, L. W., Aronow, M. S., & Smith, T. H. (2008). Therapeutic touch stimulates the proliferation of human cells in culture. *Journal of Alternative and Complementary Medicine, 14*, 233–239.

Hagelin, J. S., Rainforth, M. V., Orme-Johnson, D. W., Cavanaugh, K. L., Alexander, C. N., Shatkin, S. F., ... & Ross, E. (1999). Effects of group practice of the *Transcendental Meditation* program on preventing violent crime in Washington, DC: Results of the national demonstration project, June–July 1993. *Social Indicators Research, 47*, 153–201. http://dx.doi.org/10.1023/A:1006978911496

Jahn, R. G. & Dunne, B. J. (2011). *Consciousness and the source of reality*. Princeton, NJ: ICRL Press.

Jonas, W. B. & Crawford, C. C. (Eds.). (2003). *Healing intention and energy medicine: Science, research methods and clinical implications*. Philadelphia, PA: Elsevier.

Kane, G. (2005). The dawn of physics beyond the standard model. *Scientific American, 288*(6), 68–75.

Kelly, R. (2011). *The human hologram: Living your life in harmony with the unified field*. Santa Rosa, CA: Elite Books.

Koenig, H. G. (2007). Religion and remission of depression in medical inpatients with heart failure/pulmonary disease. *Journal of Nervous and Mental Disease, 195*, 389–395.

Kuhn, T. S. (1996). *The structure of scientific revolutions* (3rd ed.). Chicago, IL: University of Chicago Press.

Leder, D. (2005). "Spooky actions at a distance": Physics, psi, and distant healing. *Journal of Alternative & Complementary Medicine, 11*, 923–930. http://dx.doi.org/10.1089/acm.2005.11.923

Lipton, B. H. (2005). *The biology of belief*. Santa Rosa, CA: Elite Books.

McCarty, W. A. (2006). Clinical story of a 6-year-old boy's eating phobia: An integrated approach utilizing prenatal and perinatal psychology with energy psychology's Emotional Freedom Techniques (EFT) in a surrogate nonlocal application. *Journal of Prenatal & Perinatal Psychology & Health, 21*(2), 117–139.

McTaggart, L. (2007). *The intention experiment: Using your thoughts to change your life and the world*. New York, NY: Free Press.

McTaggart, L. (2008). *The field: The quest for the secret force of the universe* (Rev. ed.). New York, NY: HarperCollins.

McTaggart, L. (2011). *The bond: Connecting through the space between us*. New York, NY: Free Press.

Neely, J. E. (2008). Laboratory observations in distance healing: The rocky marriage of mechanism and vitalism. Accessed Jan 5, 2013 at: http://www.inter-disciplinary.net/ptb/mso/hid/hid7/Neely%20Paper%202008.pdf

Nelson, R. D., Bradish, J., Dobyns, Y. H., Dunne, B. J., & Jahn, R. G. (1996). Field REG anomalies in group situations. *Journal of Scientific Exploration, 10*, 111–142.

Park, R. L. (2000). *Voodoo science: The road from foolishness to fraud*. New York, NY: Oxford University Press.

Playfair, G. L. (2009). *Twin telepathy* (2nd ed.). Charleston, SC: History Press.

Puthoff, H. E. (1996). CIA-initiated remote viewing program at Stanford Research Institute. *Journal of Scientific Exploration, 10*(1), 63–76.

Radin, D. (1997). *The conscious universe: The scientific truth of psychic phenomena*. San Francisco, CA: HarperCollins.

Radin, D. (2006). *Entangled minds: Extrasensory experiences in a quantum reality*. New York, NY: Simon & Schuster.

Rao, K. R. & Palmer, J. (1987). The anomaly called psi: Recent research and criticism. *Behavioral and Brain Sciences, 10*, 539–551. http://dx.doi.org/10.1017/S0140525X00054455

Salas, M., Brooks, A., & Rowe, J. (2011). The immediate effect of a brief energy psychology intervention (Emotional Freedom Techniques) on specific phobias: A pilot study. *Explore: The Journal of Science and Healing, 7*, 155–161. http://dx.doi.org/10.1016/j.explore.2011.02.005

Schmidt, S. (2012). Can we help just by good intentions? A meta-analysis of experiments on distant intention effects. *Journal of Alternative and Complementary Medicine, 18*, 529–533. doi:10.1089/acm.2011.0321

Sheldrake, R. S. (2009). *Morphic resonance: The nature of formative causation* (4th ed.). Rochester, VT: Park Street Press.

Standish, L. J., Kozak, L., Johnson, L. C., & Richards, T. (2004). Electroencephalographic evidence of correlated event-related signals between the brains of spatially and sensory isolated human subjects. *Journal of Alternative* and *Complementary Medicine, 10*, 307–314. http://dx.doi.org/10.1089/107555304323062293

Swanson, C. (2003), *The synchronized universe: New science of the paranormal.* Tucson, AZ: Poseidia.

Swanson, C. (2010). *Life force, the scientific basis: Breakthrough physics of energy medicine, healing, chi and quantum consciousness.* Tucson, AZ: Poseidia.

Targ, R. (2012). *The reality of ESP: A physicist's proof of psychic abilities.* Wheaton, IL: Quest.

Targ, R. & Katra, J. (1999). *Miracle of the mind: Exploring nonlocal consciousness and spiritual healing.* New York, NY: New World Library.

Tart, C. T. (2009). *The end of materialism: How evidence of the paranormal is bringing science and spirit together.* Oakland, CA: New Harbinger.

Than, K. (2012, July 4). "God Particle" Found? "Historic Milestone" From Higgs Boson Hunters. *National Geographic News.* Retrieved from http://news.nationalgeographic.com/news/2012/07/120704-god-particle-higgs-boson-new-cern-science/

Tiller, W. A. (1997). *Science and human transformation: Subtle energies, intentionality and consciousness.* Walnut Creek, CA: Pavior.

Tompkins, P. & Bird, C. (1973). *The secret life of plants: A fascinating account of the physical, emotional, and spiritual relations between plants and man.* New York, NY: Harper & Row.

Vedral, V. (2008). Quantifying entanglement in macroscopic systems. *Nature, 453,* 1004–1007. doi:10.1038/nature07124

Wanjek, C. (2002). *Bad medicine: Misconceptions and misuses revealed, from distance healing to vitamin O.* New York, NY: Wiley.

Wells, S., Polglase, K., Andrews, H. B., Carrington, P., & Baker, A. H. (2003). Evaluation of a meridian-based intervention, Emotional Freedom Techniques (EFT), for reducing specific phobias of small animals. *Journal of Clinical Psychology, 59,* 943–966. doi:10.1002/jclp.10189

Yan, X., Lu, P. Y., & Kiang, J. G. (2003). Qigong: basic science studies in biology. In W. B. Jonas & C. C. Crawford (Eds.), *Healing intention and energy medicine. Science, research methods and clinical implications* (pp. 103–137). Philadelphia, PA: Elsevier. http://dx.doi.org/10.1016/B978-0-443-07237-6.50014-0

Yount, G., Patil, S., Dave, U., Alves-dos-Santos, L., Gon, K., Arauz, R., & Rachlin, K. (2012). Evaluation of biofield treatment dose and distance in a model of cancer cell death. *Journal of Alternative and Complementary Medicine.* doi:10.1089/acm.2011.0950

Psychological Trauma

Chapter 8
Energy for Healing Trauma: Energy Psychology and the Efficient Treatment of Trauma and PTSD
Fred P. Gallo

Abstract

Recently there has been increasing interest in investigating energy psychology theoretically and as clinical intervention. This chapter provides an overview of energy psychology, including its history, theory, active ingredients, and empirical research on the effects in general and for the treatment of trauma and PTSD. Personal and case vignettes are also provided to illustrate the treatment process. The therapeutic effects are also discussed with respect to neuroscience, cognitive restructuring, reciprocal inhibition, genetics, distraction, placebo effect, memory reconsolidation, and energetic and spiritual considerations.

Keywords: energy psychology, trauma, PTSD, Thought Field Therapy, Emotional Freedom Techniques, midline energy treatment, energy diagnostic and treatment methods

Fred P. Gallo, PhD, has been a clinical psychologist for 36 years. He is a member of APA and PPA and is on the board of directors of ACEP. He wrote the first professional book on energy psychology and coined the term. He has published eight books to date and presents on energy psychology internationally. Send correspondence to Fred P. Gallo, PhD, Gallo and Associates Psychological Services, 60 Snyder Road, Hermitage, PA 16148, or fgallo@energypsych.com. Comments and editing assistance on this chapter by Dawson Church, PhD; Ralph P. Davis, DCH; and Maarten Aalberse, clinical psychologist, are gratefully acknowledged. By way of disclosure of potential conflicts of interest, the author conducts trainings, provides clinical services, and has written books and articles related to the approach examined in this chapter.

Traumatic events, the memories of them, and trauma itself entail some obvious yet often elusive distinctions. While many rightly feel that they suffer because of the traumatic event, it is also clear that the event is over, although there may be real physical and psychological consequences to deal with. Others who suffered traumatic events may feel that it is the memory itself that torments, although the memory often feels like the event is happening now, rather than merely being a memory. And others do not even recall the event, yet are plagued by disconcerting emotions and physical sensations that have their roots in trauma.

The distinction among traumatic event, the memory, and trauma becomes clear after the emotional distress is dissipated. Complete resolution means that the trauma is gone and all that remains is a memory, albeit often a distant and possibly vague memory. While it would be surreal to look back on certain kinds of traumatic events with pleasure, it is not at all uncommon to experience relief, serenity, and even interest and awe about the event after the distress is gone. And for those who have gone through and resolved trauma, experiences like these can often lead to a deeper understanding and positive transformation, even spiritual renewal. Often meaning or a revised meaning prevails, and the survivor may find ways to make a contribution to others as a result of having suffered tribulation.

Grief Trauma

Most people are not strangers to traumatic events and trauma. Either they have personal experience or know others who have suffered in this way. For me, trauma began at a young age. Though I do not consciously remember the proverbial birth trauma, I do recall many painful medical treatments and some other painful events from childhood. Some were relatively minor as I think back on them now, and others were absolutely devastating. I've lost to death many loved ones, including parents, two brothers, grandparents, and more.

When I was 11, my mother was diagnosed with breast cancer. She died in 1959, when she was only 43. I was 12, my sister was 10, and my three brothers were 7, 5, and 1. Our father was 37.

The cancer spread aggressively throughout her body. She underwent several surgeries and radiation treatment. I watched and ached as the mother we loved, and knew to be passionate and vibrant, withered away. She suffered immensely and we suffered with her in our own ways. In those days, cancer patients mostly remained at home with insufficient pain medication to the end, which meant intense pain. Dad confided in me that she was going to die months before she did, and he told me to keep it a secret. I recall that strong electrical charge, the bolt of lightning that surged throughout my body when he told me she was going to die. There was no hope.

Although she wasn't supposed to know, I'm sure that she did. But she kept the secret too; we didn't talk about it. As a child, I frequently cried myself to sleep and prayed that she would be cured or at least not suffer. As a good Catholic boy, I even tried to relieve her pain by placing a holy scapular at various locations on her body where she felt pain. She told me that it helped, but the pain kept traveling. There was no keeping up with it! I felt dejected, helpless, and hopeless, and I was convinced that my efforts were not helping. Now I believe that she found some solace in my attempts and even some pain relief. But I felt dejected when the pain let up at one location and moved on to another. I recall crying with hopelessness, "This isn't working!" She tried to console me. "It helps where you put it, Freddy. It just moves on. It helps." Of course, my three brothers and my sister were also tormented by her illness and death. And our father's heartbreak was surely the greatest of all, although I couldn't understand that at the time.

For me, my mother's illness and death were both agonizing and numbing. And this trauma interfered with my ability to relate well to others for many years. I had complex grief and I tried to cope by emotional reliving or avoiding or suppressing, but ultimately none of this helped. I don't think it occurred to me that my grief could be eliminated by anything other than the passage of time. Yet time was not healing these wounds, and I had to wait nearly four decades for relief through other means. To my amazement, each resolution of a traumatic scene and the traumatic distress took a few minutes. The method is detailed later in this chapter.

Physical Injury Trauma and Panic

Another significant trauma occurred when I was 21. I had just graduated from Duquesne University in Pittsburgh, Pennsylvania, where I majored in philosophy and psychology. The day after graduation, I had an automobile accident that nearly claimed my life. It was early June 1968, and I was driving my red Volkswagen Bug to the university student union to meet friends when a large car smashed into mine and ripped off the driver's side door. The impact sent the car spinning around in a jerking motion. The windshield seemed to shatter slowly and then I was jettisoned from the car and sent flying through the air, in what seemed to be *slow motion,* into some wooden steps that my body broke. I bounced over a banister, slid along the sidewalk, and rolled over before coming to an abrupt halt. I tried to get up, and at that moment I could feel a sharp pain and an oozing sensation in my left side. Then I rolled over and looked up at the sky, terrified that I was going to die. "No! I'm not going to die! No! I'm not ready." My determination may have been key to my survival.

I suffered many injuries, including a bruised kidney and ruptured spleen. I had surgery, received six pints of blood, and my life hung in the balance for several days. I was in the intensive care unit for the first four days and in the hospital for 10 days altogether. I learned to cope with the severe pain between morphine injections. I realized that the pain after surgery was different from the pain I felt in the emergency room; this was healing pain and the pain in the ER was dying pain. While both pains may have been objectively equally severe, this realization made a big difference since pain is subjective. It made the pain more acceptable. I could focus on it with some degree of gratitude, and that made it manageable. Also when it occurred to me several days later that I was asking for those euphoric morphine shots even when I wasn't in pain, obviously becoming addicted, I decided to stop then and there. It took a few years to get over the cravings. If I even talked about the experience of morphine, I felt light-headed and even high. But I never went out looking for it.

Over the next 2 months, I recovered at home. During that time, I also had thyroid surgery. Even though my physical condition improved quickly after the surgeries, I continued to experience psychological trauma for many years: fear when I was driving, generalized anxiety, flashbacks and frequent episodes of panic with the feeling that I was going to die.

I resolved that driving phobia over a period of time by learning to relax my hold on the steering wheel while driving and assuring myself that the car would not go out of control. It took quite some time, but eventually I was able to drive with comfort and even enjoyment.

And I resolved the panic disorder by riding out a severe panic attack one evening about 10 years after the accident. Back then I had many panic attacks, and this final one lasted for over 2 hours. I tried everything I could think of to get rid of it: praying, pacing, rubbing my hands together, breathing in a paper bag, taking a warm shower, taking a cold shower, drinking a shot of whiskey, and then even running down the street and back to my house. Finally, in defiance, I tried to intensify the panic. I lay face down on my bed, closed my eyes, and tried to go into the panic—into the terror and abyss. With insolence, I spoke to the panic, "Come on and get me! Go ahead, get me!" The curious result was that the opposite occurred; the panic vanished instantly. I had come face-to-face with my fear, stared it straight in the eye, did not waver, and the panic disappeared.

About a week later, the aura of another attack started. Again I simply relaxed into the sensations. Almost immediately, the panic sensations dissipated. I searched for any inkling of panic and anxiety in my body, but it was gone. Such satisfaction and excitement about this serendipitous discovery! From then on, I no longer lived in dread of panic. Even if a twinge of anxiety occurred, I faced it, observed it, stepped into it, and it would disappear.

I also knew that this approach could not be used in an attempt to outwit or try to get rid of panic, since *it* would surely *know.* It couldn't just be a technique; I had to be for real. I had to truly want to immerse myself in the experience, no matter what. With this, my confidence grew, and I came to understand the sources of my panic. It was partly about something I concluded while flying out of the car in June 1968. I had forgotten this. As I slid along the sidewalk, I had the rather detached thought, "Am I going to die now or after I stop sliding?" It was not a matter of *if* I was going to die; dying was imminent. It was just a matter of how soon. When I stopped sliding along the sidewalk, my demise was inevitable at any moment. The panic always carried with it the sense that I was going to die *now* and I had to fight to stay alive. Though it was good to decide not to die at the time of the accident, somehow I took this out of context. In a sense the accident and dying were ever present, or nearly so. And as much as it seemed like panic was happening to me, I was actually the author of the panic.

Traumatic stress is created the moment we say no to the traumatic event and the flow of life energy is blocked. The ancient Chinese called it stagnant chi. If experience of the traumatic event is accepted in the moment, then life energy flows instead of becoming stuck. As the old saying goes, what you resist persists.

Eventually, I understood that panic—that strong electrical charge—was also connected to when my father told me of my mother's inevitable death. To some, resolution of a trauma can be a long-drawn-out process, but when an effective method is applied, very little time is needed. We shall discuss more about effective methods, but first some additional reflections on the phenomenon of trauma.

What Is Trauma?

The Buddha maintained that life is suffering because of our attachment to the notion that we should not become ill, age, and die. The solution is to not be seduced by this view but instead embrace life as it is, accepting our humanness, accepting both the ups and downs of life, and realizing that everything is essentially impermanent. This spiritual principle is also germane to various religions. In Christianity, Christ states that His kingdom is not of this Earth. Since trauma is so prevalent, these spiritual dictums might be amended by stating that life is suffering because of trauma. Yet trauma is not simply about awful events. Trauma is intensified by two other factors: resistance to accepting the trauma on the one hand, and attachment to it on the other.

Although there is a conscious attachment to the memory and its meaning, trauma is also an unconscious attachment, so that what fuels trauma is not so much what is remembered as what is forgotten. It was Freud's fundamental insight that psychological disorders are a function of unconscious material, information that has been suppressed or repressed. So trauma is about being blind to certain information and not coming to terms with it. "Coming to terms with" can involve recovering the misplaced information and understanding it from a wider perspective, from a higher level of consciousness. Given this understanding, one approach involves an archeological expedition to uncover the lost material and resolve the unfinished business. While abreaction is a way of experiencing and discharging emotion associated with a traumatic event, many patients become retraumatized because reliving the experience activates the sympathetic nervous system. So trauma can build on trauma.

Characteristics

Although memory is involved with trauma, it is the implicit (nondeclarative) memory rather than the explicit (declarative) memory that matters most. Again this is the distinction between unconscious and conscious. There are many aspects to consider when we examine trauma.

Trauma has many highly visible features. The landscape can be painted with a fine brush or a broad one. With a fine brush, there is posttraumatic stress disorder (PTSD), dissociative disorders, and many other diagnoses described in the DSM. PTSD is trauma in its most pronounced form. It's composed of the traumatic event, the fear, and the helplessness. The event itself is tragic enough, although the aftermath, which is rightly called traumatic stress, is what torments. That torment includes any number of symptoms such as intrusive recollections, distressing dreams, flashbacks, avoidance, emotional numbing, splitting, and more. The distinction can also be made between posttraumatic stress (PTS) and PTSD. PTS is a significant source of distress, but does not fulfill all the criteria of PTSD.

These are the conditions and the symptoms of obvious trauma that can be a single incident, multiple incidents, and complex trauma. However, with a broad brush, even less obvious traumas can have a major impact. Many psychological, physical, and societal problems are rooted in trauma. Consider the societal trauma that has haunted German society since WWII, even though most of the people who participated in or who were witness to the Holocaust have passed on. And America continues to struggle with the ghosts of slavery. Also, the individual's resources and perceptions are essential to the impact of the event. Some obvious traumatic events are tolerated well by some people and other seemingly inconsequential events are highly damaging to others.

The individual's background is significant in developing ongoing traumatic stress or being able to traverse it. If the person exposed to a traumatic event had a healthy developmental history and secure attachment with a loving caregiver, the chances of developing PTSD and other traumatic sequelae are profoundly reduced. And if PTSD has developed with such individuals, the effectiveness and brevity of treatment is greatly enhanced. Having an insecure attachment with little resilience makes it difficult for treatment to proceed efficiently in many instances (Schore, 1994).

Theories

There are many theories about trauma, each involving a different slice or angle. To the cognitivetherapist, trauma is attachment to distressing memories and thoughts. The goal is to reframe thoughts in a more rational direction or to become aware of one's ability to dismiss thought. Consistent with this is the knowledge of being the thinker and having the ability to let go of traumatic memories and the associated distress. This is certainly worth recognizing and often an important avenue to healing from trauma. Some discover that it is possible to not take trips into the painful memories, and also to alleviate traumatic stress.

To the behaviorist, trauma is conditioning attachment and extinction is the goal. Treatments have involved exposure, either flooding or gradual exposure. Frequently, this process itself can be traumatizing if the therapist or client is uncomfortable with strong emotion. Also, negative consequences of flooding exposure have been reported (Pitman et al., 1991). Nevertheless, some degree of exposure is generally essential to overcome trauma, although that degree need only be subtle, or what might be referred to as attunement. Attunement involves simply bringing the memory to mind without getting caught up in any associated distressing emotion.

Integrating the approaches of the cognitive and behavior therapists, the traumatic memory is exposed and processed. Exposure and processing can be described in terms of desensitization, habituation, and disassociation. Essentially, the distress is removed by overcoming avoidance and no longer associating to the memory. The distress is alleviated as you step back from the traumatic memory and view it from a distance. This alters the structure of the memory in the brain, allowing the hippocampus to record it as just a memory. Additionally, cognitive restructuring often follows as a result of emotion modulation or is offered to the client for consideration. This is similar to the psychoanalytic process of offering an interpretation when the client is able to accept it.

The systemic aspects of trauma and treatment involve relationships. Trauma is often intertwined with relationships that cause or enable the person to remain a trauma victim. The solution becomes one of shifting the relationship in a healthy direction, away from an unhealthy attachment or entanglement. Additionally, the therapist's interaction with the client is imperative in this regard. The therapist's view of the client invariably influences the outcome. If the client and therapist are attached to a view of victimhood, this can stifle positive results.

The neuroscientist sees trauma as attachment involving sympathetic nervous system activation, including hypervigilance of the amygdala and the hypothalamus-pituitary-adrenal axis. At the same time, the dissociation and numbing effects of trauma is a parasympathetic response of the dorsal vagal complex (Porges, 2011). Trauma also disables the hippocampus, the brain structure involved in emotionally experiencing the event as in the past. Thus trauma becomes ever present, not completed in time. The goal is to calm the amygdala, HPA axis, and dorsal vagal complex, allowing the hippocampus to record the event as finished.

To the chemist, trauma is chemical attachment. Traumatic stress raises cortisol, glutamate, and adrenalin; it also lowers GABA and serotonin. The goal is chemical balance, maybe via medication. However, any effective trauma treatment will result in neurochemical changes as well.

To the body worker, trauma may be attached to the muscles, and the goal becomes one of awareness and release through massage and movement.

Trauma can also be seen as an ego attachment that interferes with one's spiritual connection and true Self. Some forms of meditation make it possible to transcend ego and trauma by not over-engaging, avoiding, or suppressing the traumatic scenes. The goals are decentering, a fluid rather than rigid sense of self, and well-being.

The shaman says that the soul leaves the body during a traumatic event and soul retrieval is needed. The shaman may travel to upper and lower worlds to escort the soul back to the body. Is this a metaphor for the dissociative process evident with trauma or is it something much more profound?

Bioenergy

Trauma is also and fundamentally an energetic attachment: an energetic block or imbalance, a disturbed and perturbed vibration of energy, a resonating energy field that goes on and on within the traumatized person and resonates outward to others.

Considering Albert Einstein's formula $E = mc^2$, matter and energy are interconvertible. Matter is fundamentally dense energy. Quantum physics has suggested that energy and consciousness are interrelated and that energy behaves in ways that are consistent with consciousness and choice (Bohm & Hiley, 1993).

Matter and energy are not so different; they are only different forms of the same reality. Thus the unconscious, conscious cognitions, chemistry, brain, muscles, and so on are energy in distinct forms. Superstring theory holds that even quarks, the fundamental particles that constitute electrons and protons, are really vibrating strings of energy (Greene, 2003). And it would seem that consciousness and spirit are intimately involved with energy as well.

Even living bodies are composed of these vibrating little strings of energy. Fritz-Albert Popp found that cells emit photons and that there is a difference between the frequencies of healthy and unhealthy cells (Popp & Beloussov, 2003). Perhaps this is the biological equivalent of a fiber-optic communication network carrying subtle energies and information throughout our cells and outward to others.

Once an energetic configuration or field is established, it seems to have a proclivity to replicate and perpetuate itself. This is essentially about memory and form. In this respect, Jung (1968) discussed the collective unconscious and archetypes, which are informational and influential fields not limited by space and time. In similar and distinct ways, Sheldrake (1981, 1988) posited formative causation, morphic resonance, and morphogenetic fields, which he says account for animate and inanimate forms, and even behavior. And in the 1970s, Harold Saxon Burr discussed Life-fields (L-fields), which he detected around rocks, trees, salamanders, and humans (Burr, 1972). Life-fields account for form. This is perhaps why the human body maintains its form even though all of the atoms are recycled every 4 to 7 years. It is suggested here that what holds the material body together is an energy field. Yet as the years go on, gravity does take its toll.

These findings have a 7,000-year history that goes back to India, where it was believed or discovered that the body has a life force—prana—and this energy is evident in chakras and auras. Five thousand years ago in China, meridian systems of chi (equivalent to prana) were described, and acupuncture was developed as a way of regulating chi and thus health. Chi and prana can be translated as energy, influence, power, mind, and spirit.

In the 1970s, research by Becker and Reichmanis revealed a lower electrical resistance at many acupoints, suggesting that meridians and acupoints are electrical (Becker & Selden, 1985). In the 1980s, French researchers injected radioactive technetium in specific kidney meridian acupoints on 330 patients and observed how the isotopes traveled the kidney meridian (Darras, de Vernejoul, & Albarede, 1992). Though this research has not been replicated, it may offer support for a bodily energy system that has subtle and electromagnetic qualities.

Often findings raise important questions as data accumulate and theories become challenged. For example, the largest study on acupuncture found that acupuncture and sham acupuncture were superior to standard medical treatment for certain kinds of back pain (Haake et al., 2007). The effectiveness of both was also found for the treatment of myofascial pain (Goddard et al., 2002). The conundrum is that both "real" and "sham" acupuncture worked similarly in these studies, perhaps suggesting that it does not matter where the needles are placed or even if acupuncture needles pierce the skin. This raises the question about the reality of meridians. It has also been proposed that the mechanism of acupuncture is not a function of chi, but rather the result of stimulating endorphins (Stux & Pomeranz, 1995; Pomeranz, 1996). Although there are questions about the mechanisms of acupuncture, this does not preclude energetic factors involved in energy psychology (EP). After all, EP does not utilize needles in treatment, and even many of the acupuncture studies still involved at least touching acupoints. It seems that these studies only demonstrate that needles piercing the skin are not necessary in order to stimulate meridians and whatever else is involved in the treatment effects.

History

Trauma involves traumatic events, perception, neurology, chemistry, information, energy, consciousness, and spirit. If the structure of the trauma energy field can be substantially altered or collapsed, the trauma can be eliminated. And this appears to be what occurs when applying energy psychology (Callahan, 1995; Callahan & Turbo, 2002; Craig & Fowlie, 1995; Craig, 2011; Gallo, 1997, 1999, 2000, 2002, 2003, 2005).

EP's more recent history dates back to the early 1960s, when chiropractor Dr. George Goodheart founded applied kinesiology (Goodheart, 1987), an approach that employs manual muscle testing and holistic concepts to address physical problems. Goodheart pioneered therapy localization, which involves touching specific bodily locations while applying manual muscle testing (Kendall, Kendall, & Wadsworth, 1971). This approach provided the needed diagnostic information to correct some otherwise intractable problems. Goodheart explored a variety of therapeutic options, including spinal and cranial adjustments, neurolymphatic and neurovascular reflexes, nutrition, herbs, homeopathy, flower essences, stimulating acupoints, and more.

Whereas Goodheart discovered a connection among specific muscles, reflexes, and meridians, others explored applied kinesiology to treat psychological problems. Psychiatrist John Diamond (1985) explored the emotion-meridian connection and the use of affirmations, music, and other media for treating psychological issues. Along similar lines, psychologist Roger J. Callahan developed a treatment method that involves attuning psychological problems such as phobias and traumas and then tapping on specific acupoints (Callahan, 1985; Callahan & Turbo, 2002). Later related approaches were developed by Craig (Craig & Fowley, 1995; Craig, 2011), Gallo (1999, 2000, 2005, 2007), and others (Gallo, 2002; Diepold, Britt, & Bender, 2004; Mollon, 2008; Benor et al., 2009).

Personal Experiences

When I first encountered energetic approaches, I was skeptical. The idea of treating a psychological problem by tapping on the body was foreign to me. Of course, I knew about acupuncture, Reichian therapy, and Rolfing, as one of my graduate professors used to undergo Rolfing sessions regularly and return to class after the weekend rather beaten up. At the time that seemed odd to me.

Nonetheless, I decided to give it a try. I used to have a fear of heights; I eliminated this problem within a few minutes. The same applied to trauma concerning my mother's death. All I had to do was tap on specific acupoints while bringing the memory to mind, or when I was in a situation that triggered emotional distress. Initially, I assumed that the benefits were simply the result of distraction. When the fear of heights did not return, however, and when the traumatic memories forever ceased to be distressing, the distraction theory was readily discarded. A better explanation was needed.

The essential features of the treatment involve attuning to (thinking about) the issue and then stimulating the body in specific ways, such as by tapping on acupoints. Although I overcame panic by staying present, observing the panic and trying to intensify it, most of my clients were unable or reluctant to approach panic in this way. But tapping somehow makes it easier to stay the course, and clients usually report that they feel calm and relaxed. Yet the results are not limited to relaxation; there is also a shift in understanding and consciousness, a cognitive restructuring. After treating trauma in this way, people often shift out of ego attachment and became more philosophical and spiritual about what happened to them. "It doesn't bother me anymore. Oh, it's just something that happened. I don't know why it bothered me for so long. The anger and resentment are gone. I feel lighter, more at ease, more at peace." These are typical comments from people who were previously tormented by trauma after receiving EP treatments.

Case Example

Amanda, a 19-year-old university student, was referred to me because of PTSD after an automobile accident in 1999. The driver in the other car crossed over the medial strip and struck her vehicle head on, killing both of his passengers and himself. Amanda was pinned under the dashboard for several hours while a rescue team struggled to cut her out of the crushed car. She had multiple injuries and was in the hospital and then spent several months in a rehabilitation center. I saw her a year after the accident. She was having frequent nightmares, flashbacks, panic, anxiety, and guilt feelings. She was also abusing alcohol.

Initially, we focused on her memory of being pinned under the dashboard. After she thought about it and rated the subjective units of distress (SUD) as a 9 or 10, I asked her to place the memory in an imaginary container. I then guided her through the midline energy treatment (MET), a procedure that involves tapping at four specific areas on the head and chest (Gallo, 2005; Gallo & Vincenzi, 2008). After about five rounds of tapping, she was able to recall the event vividly without distress. Follow-up sessions at 1 week, 2 weeks, and 2 months revealed that after the initial session, her distress about the event, her nightmares, and her flashbacks no longer occurred.

In the course of treatment, other aspects of the trauma were treated, including guilt feelings concerning the people who died. This distress was also resolved in one session by using MET and a couple of related treatments.

Later in therapy, she reported that a relative molested her from age 5 to 12. Using a more specifically focused treatment involving manual muscle testing, other locations for her to tap were determined in order to efficiently eliminate this sexual abuse trauma. After distress of various memories was efficiently treated, she reported a lingering feeling of worthlessness, including a "dirty and disgusting" feeling in the lower abdomen. Similar treatment was applied to eliminate this sensation and her belief about not being worthwhile. Follow-up several months later revealed ongoing relief on all aspects treated.

Research

Many practitioners find that EP approaches are highly effective in view of the large number of case reports and their clinical experiences. Though case reports are interesting and essential in the early phases of development, empirical research is needed to discern if the therapeutic results are due to a significant extent to the method itself. What follows is a partial review of the research. It should be noted, however, that while empirical studies aim to discern the effectiveness of the procedures themselves, the therapeutic relationship is of utmost importance (Norcross, 2011).

In addition to effectively treating a variety of conditions, including anxiety, phobias, depression, and physical pain (Wade, 1990; Leonoff, 1995; Carbonell, 1997; Darby, 2001; Wells et al., 2003; Lambrou, Pratt, & Chevalier, 2003; Darby, 2001; Schoninger, 2001; Salas, Brooks, & Rowe, 2011; Sakai et al., 2001; Pignotti, 2005; Church & Brooks, 2009), the efficiency of energy psychology in treating trauma and PTSD has become increasingly established over nearly two decades (Figley et al., 1999; Diepold & Goldstein, 2000, 2008; Johnson et al., 2001; Green, 2002; Sakai, Connolly, & Oas, 2010; Church et al., 2009; Church, 2009; Church, Piña, Reategui, & Brooks, 2010; Church, Geronilla, & Dinter, 2009; Burk, 2010; Church, Yount, & Brooks, 2012; Church et al., 2013). Studies using EP in treating PSTD are particularly interesting, since generally PTSD has been considered a treatment-resistant and refractory condition. Some have argued that it may be incurable, and should be regarded as a condition that can only be managed (Johnson et al., 2004; Phelps, 2009). I hypothesize that EP approaches may actually eliminate the trauma by activating the implicit memory associated with amygdala neurons and permanently altering their connections or wiring (Hebb, 1949). While more EP studies are covered in other chapters of this anthology, a few studies addressing trauma follow.

The Figley et al. (1999) study was a systematic clinical demonstration project that evaluated the effectiveness of Thought Field Therapy (TFT) and three other treatments for PTSD (see Table 1). Detailed evaluative measures at follow-along and follow-up were included. Follow-up evaluations within the 4-to 6-month range revealed that all of the approaches yielded sustained reduction in subjective units of distress. Although evaluation time frames and the number of subjects varied across treatment conditions, respective mean group treatment times and posttreatment follow-up SUD ratings provided preliminary data on the effects of the treatments. While all of the approaches demonstrated effectiveness, TFT was the most efficient in terms of both speed and reduction in SUD.

Diepold and Goldstein (2000, 2008) conducted a case study of TFT with evaluation by

Table 1. *Florida State University Active Ingredients Project Data*

Method	Subjects	Time (min)	Pre-SUD	Post-SUD
V/KD	8	113	4.75	3.25
EMDR	6	172	5.00	2.00
TIR	2	254	6.50	3.40
TFT	12	63	6.30	3.00

quantitative electroencephalogram (qEEG). Statistically abnormal brain-wave patterns were noted when the patient thought about a trauma compared to a neutral baseline event. The qEEG evaluation while the subject thought about the traumatic memory immediately after TFT diagnosis and treatment revealed no statistical abnormalities. An 18-month follow-up indicated that the patient continued to be free of emotional upset regarding the treated trauma. This study supports the hypothesis that negative emotion has a measurable effect, and also objectively identified an immediate and lasting neuroenergetic change in the direction of normalcy and health after TFT.

Church, Yount, and Brooks (2012) examined cortisol levels in 83 subjects randomly assigned to a single session of EFT, talk therapy, or rest. Cortisol is the "master hormone" regulating many aspects of the body's stress response mechanisms, especially those associated with the autonomic nervous system. Therefore the authors proposed that successful therapy would result in lower stress that would be reflected in reduced salivary cortisol. Their investigation found that cortisol levels in the rest and therapy groups declined at approximately the same rate, but that cortisol in the EFT group declined significantly more. The decline in this physiological marker of stress was also significantly correlated with a decline in anxiety, depression, and other psychological conditions. Since cortisol levels of PTSD patients are elevated as well, effective treatment with EFT would likely lower cortisol levels with such patients.

Johnson et al. (2001) reported on uncontrolled treatment of trauma victims in Kosovo with TFT during five 2-week trips in the year 2000. Treatments were given to 105 Albanian patients with 249 separate violent traumatic incidents. The traumas included rape, torture, and witnessing the massacre of loved ones. Total relief of the traumas was reported by 103 of the patients and for 247 of the 249 separate traumas treated. Follow-up data averaging 5 months revealed no relapses. While this data is based on uncontrolled treatments, the absence of relapse ought to pique our attention, since a 98% spontaneous remission from PTSD is unlikely.

Sakai et al. (2001) reported on an uncontrolled study of 1,594 applications of TFT in the treatment of 714 patients with PTSD and many other disorders. Paired t tests of pre- and posttreatment subjective units of distress were statistically significant at the .01 level in 31 categories.

Several other EP approaches have been subjected to experimental tests. Efficacy in reducing or eliminating symptoms of PTSD, such as anxiety, depression, and phobias, has been demonstrated in several studies of Emotional Freedom Techniques (EFT) (Rowe, 2005; Wells et al., 2003; Church & Brooks, 2010).

An early EFT study focused on subjects who had been involved in motor vehicle accidents and who experienced PTSD associated with the accident (Swingle & Pulos, 2000). All subjects received two treatment sessions; all reported improvement immediately following treatment. Brain-wave assessments before and after treatment indicated that subjects who sustained the benefit of the treatments had increased 13–15 Hz amplitude over the sensory motor cortex, decreased right frontal cortex arousal, and an increased ratio of 3–7 Hz: 16–25 Hz in the occipital region.

The most extensive longitudinal clinical study on the effectiveness of EP was conducted in South America over 14 years with 31,400 patients (Andrade & Feinstein, 2004). A substudy of this group took place over 5½ years with 5000 patients diagnosed with PTSD and many other psychological disorders. Only those conditions in which EP and a standard of care control group (cognitive behavior therapy plus medication when indicated) could be used were included in the substudy. At the end of treatment and at follow-up periods of 1 month, 3 months, 6 months, and 12 months, the patients were interviewed by telephone by interviewers that had not been involved in the patients' treatment. These follow-up interviews revealed a 90% positive clinical response and 76% complete elimination of symptoms with EP alone, and a 63% positive response and 51% complete elimination of symptoms with CBT/medication ($p < .01$). These results are highly significant, suggesting that EP was superior to CBT/medication for a wide range of psychological disorders. Furthermore, while the average number of sessions in the CBT/medication group was 15, the average number in the EP group was only three.

As I stated earlier, studies using EP to treat PSTD are particularly interesting, as PTSD is often considered to be treatment-resistant condition. Some reviews have even argued that it may be incurable, and should be regarded as a condition that can only be managed at best (Johnson et al., 2004). Yet in several studies, EP has successfully brought PTSD scores from clinical to subclinical levels. In a within-subjects study, Sakai, Connolly, and Oas (2010) used TFT with a population of genocide orphans in Rwanda, and found statistically significant reductions in symptoms in a single session. In a second uncontrolled trial, Stone, Leyden, and Fellows (2009) found reductions in PTSD symptoms in genocide survivors in a different Rwandan orphanage, using two group sessions plus a single individual session with the most traumatized individuals.

Church, Piña, Reategui, and Brooks (2009) performed a randomized controlled trial with 16 abused male children aged 12 to 17 in a group home. The experimental group of eight received EFT, while the control group of eight received no treatment. A 1-month follow-up was performed, which found that the PTSD levels of all eight of the EFT group had normalized, while no member of the control group had improved ($p < .001$).

EFT has been used to successfully reduce PTSD symptoms in two pilot studies with war veterans (Church, 2009; Church, Geronilla, & Dinter, 2009). In the first study, 11 veterans and their family members received a weeklong EFT intensive consisting of 10 to 15 sessions. Their average scores dropped from clinical to subclinical levels, as did their other psychological symptoms such as hostility, psychosis, phobic anxiety, and depression. Three follow-ups, including at 1 year, found them stable, having maintained the gains they experienced in the weeklong intensive. In the second study, veterans received six sessions of EFT, with similar results.

These studies led to a full RCT with a much larger group of subjects (Church et al., 2013). The results from this study again showed that symptoms in a wait-list control group did not diminish over time, while six sessions of EFT produced drops to subclinical levels of PTSD, with the average subject remaining subclinical at 3- and 6-month follow-up. The vets were randomized to EFT ($n = 30$) or standard of care wait list ($n = 29$). Intervention consisted of six hour-long EFT coaching sessions concurrent with standard care. The EFT subjects evidenced significantly reduced psychological distress ($p < 0.0012$) and PTSD symptom levels ($p < 0.0001$) after the intervention. Additionally, 90% of the EFT group no longer met criteria for PTSD, compared with 4% in the control group. After the wait period, the controls received EFT. In a within-subjects longitudinal analysis, 60% no longer met PTSD criteria after three sessions, which increased to 86% after six sessions for the 49 subjects who received EFT. Benefits remained at 86% at 3 months and at 80% at 6 months. By comparison, a similar PTSD study of cognitive behavioral therapy showed that only 40% of veterans improved after treatment (Monson et al., 2006).

Theoretical Reflections

Extensive clinical experience and experimental studies support the effectiveness of EP in treating trauma-based and other conditions. Though there are other approaches to addressing the energy substrate, how can we account for the therapeutic results of stimulating acupoints while attuning a psychological problem, such as trauma? What does the tapping really do? There are many possible explanations.

Placebo effect is one suggested mechanism, although that applies to all treatments to some extent. However, since EP treatments produce statistically significant results when tested against other therapies in randomized trials that control for the placebo effect, it would seem that placebo has less to do with it than the methods themselves.

Distraction. Another explanation is that tapping simply distracts the patient. Though it is difficult to maintain complete focus on the problem while tapping, this explanation is insufficient because relief continues after the treatment has been completed.

Reciprocal inhibition. Namely anxiety-provoking stimuli occurring simultaneously with an anxiety-inhibition response (e.g. relaxation) such that the link between the stimulus and the anxiety is weakened—is another plausible explanation, as clients report a relaxation response after the tapping. However, it is also conceivable that the relaxation response is secondary to reduced stress and not a result of neutralizing stress by instilling relaxation.

Cognitive restructuring is another explanation, since changes in thought and perception regularly occur with these treatments. However, with EP treatments the cognitive shifts occur after the negative emotions have been relieved, rather than the cognitive reappraisal causing the emotional relief. While a positive shift in cognition can serve to support healthy psychological functioning, and positive cognitions can be installed through EP processes as well, EP treatments do not appear to directly address cognition as the initial lever for change.

Neurochemicals. Neurotransmitters and endorphins may play a role in EP treatment effects, similar to what has been proposed with acupuncture (Stux & Pomeranz, 1995; Pomeranz, 1996). This does not preclude energetic effects, however. Even with antidepressants, chemical change is not sufficient to account for symptom reduction; the chemical change occurs quickly, and the depression usually diminishes weeks later as a result of neurogenesis and synaptogenesis. The effects of tapping are often quite rapid, faster than chemical and neuronal changes can be expected to occur; so other factors are likely involved. Also, neurotransmitter changes will probably dissipate quickly, whereas the effects of tapping appear to be long lasting.

Brain structures are also involved in the treatment effects. Trauma entails an activation of the amygdala and HPA axis such that internal and external triggers perpetuate the stress reaction. Also, the hippocampus appears to be prevented from processing the event as completed in time, as simply a memory. Successful treatment involves deactivation of the stress reaction so that the information can be processed through the hippocampus, thus alleviating the trauma.

Memory reconsolidation. Similar to the now-debunked long-held neuroscience dogma that the brain cannot grow new neurons, for some time it was believed that a memory remains stable once it has been consolidated into long-term storage. It was assumed that long-term memory was similar to ROM (read only memory), like on a CD ROM. Once something has been recorded, it is the same every time the CD is played. The hypothesis of memory reconsolidation is radically different, since it proposes that the very process of remembering alters the memory. Recall Heraclitus's doctrine of change, stating that you can't step in the same river twice. The very act of memory retrieval renders memories fragile, subject to change and perhaps erasure. This hypothesis also has enormous implications for the treatment of PTSD, and for many other psychological disorders. Depending on how the memory or the state is recalled, alteration can be in a healthy or pathologic direction. Retrieval combined with a strong sympathetic nervous system response can pathologically alter the memory; whereas recall with a calming parasympathetic response can alter the memory in a healthier direction. To some extent, this is what EP treatments do; they substantially alter the memory.

Genes represent another important variable in psychological functioning and many psychological disorders. Strong memory of a traumatic event is thought to contribute to the development of PTSD, with genetic variability of the gene encoding PKCα (PRKCA). The gene is associated with memory capacity, including aversive memory, in nontraumatized subjects of European descent. This finding was replicated in an independent sample of nontraumatized subjects. Functional magnetic resonance imaging (fMRI) revealed PRKCA genotype-dependent brain-activation differences during successful encoding of aversive information. Further, the identified genetic variant was also related to traumatic memory and to the risk for PTSD in heavily traumatized survivors of the Rwandan genocide. The results indicate a role for PKCα in memory and suggest a genetic link between memory and the risk for PTSD (De Quervain et al., 2012). There is also evidence that successful psychotherapy in general, including EP results in alteration of gene expression (Rossi, 2002; Church, 2007).

Other Views

My preferred explanation is that many layers are involved with EP treatments. While brain structures, neurochemistry, genes, developmental history, unconscious dynamics, and cognition are implicated in trauma and other psychological problems, these conditions are also energetic, if we can assume that everything in our physical reality is fundamentally energy.

Energetic information. Trauma is energetic information, similar to the electromagnetic information adhering to audiotapes and computer hard drives. Imagine that a traumatic event is like throwing stones into a pond and that trauma is the resultant splashing and ripples. Of course, ponds are highly proficient at getting over the impact quickly, while humans are proficient at capturing and maintaining trauma. It is as if people are ponds that freeze at the moment of impact and the informational ripples become frozen in time. The nervous system, cells, and energy system capture and store the trauma information. Since nature constructs complex structures from simple fractals, trauma is an energetic field at the most basic level.

By disrupting the stability of the field, the system reassembles at a higher, healthier, more evolved order (Prigogine & Stengers, 1984).

This informational field is also called a thought field that is hypothesized to have a physical reality and to be composed of subtle energetic markers or perturbations that are the basic cause of negative emotions (Callahan, 1995; Callahan & Turbo, 2002; Gallo, 2005). Perturbations are similar to what theoretical physicist David Bohm called active information (Bohm & Hiley, 1993; Rubik, 1995). When the trauma thought field is attuned, these perturbations are available for treatment. Simultaneously, all of the aspects involved in trauma are activated. This includes brain structures, neurochemistry, genes, unconscious dynamics, cognition, behaviors, energy, and so on. With EP it is possible to elicit the thought field, analyze its structure, and subsume the perturbations (Gallo, 2000).

Mindfulness. Another feature of EP is that tapping facilitates mindfully observing the traumatic memory and reactive emotional sensations, also called somatic markers (Damasio, 1994). Mindfulness enhances functioning of the prefrontal cortex (PFC) and anterior cingulate cortex (ACC), as well as reducing activity of the amygdala and other structures involved in emotions and stress activation (Hölzel et al., 2011). This nonjudgmental observational process also appears to improve attention, emotion regulation, bodily awareness, a fluid sense of self, and a state of well-being. When tapping is done mindfully, meaning simply observing the state without judgment or prejudice, I propose that this accelerates the effects that are observed through mindfulness meditation alone. Interestingly, both meridians and mindfulness have ancient roots, which are being revisited now from our scientific perspectives.

A higher order. Thought fields, similar to other systems, are maintained within a range of energy balance; too much or too little energy causes a loss of order. A loss of order is a loss of information. Physically tapping on acupoints (and possibly other locations) disrupts the system by overloading the adhesive energetic field. The trauma system loses its order and collapses or transitions to varying degrees of entropy. The pond with its informational ripples begins to thaw and change form. The traumatic event can now be viewed calmly and the calmness is incorporated into one's life. The basic memory is the same; the emotional experience and meaning has changed.

So a revised memory structure prevails: a memory with a different emotional attachment. The client comes to view the event from a higher or broader perspective, with neutrality or deeper positive feelings. Mindfulness prevails. The shaman might declare that the soul has returned home.

References

Andrade, J. & Feinstein, D. (2004). Energy psychology: theory, indications, and evidence. In D. Feinstein, *Energy psychology interactive* CD. Ashland, OR: Innersource.

Becker, R. O., & Selden, G. (1985). *The body electric*. New York, NY: Morrow.

Benor, D. J., Ledger, K., Toussaint, L., Hett, G., & Zaccaro, D. (2009). Pilot study of Emotional Freedom Techniques: Wholistic hybrid derived from Eye Movement Desensitization and Reprocessing and Emotional Freedom Techniques, and cognitive behavioral therapy for treatment of test anxiety in university students. *Explore: The Journal of Science and Healing, 5,* 338–340.

Bohm, D. & Hiley, B. J. (1993). *The undivided universe: An ontological interpretation of quantum theory*. London: Routledge and Kegan Paul.

Burk, L. (2010). Single session EFT (Emotional Freedom Techniques) for stress-related symptoms after motor vehicle accidents. *Energy Psychology: Theory, Research, & Treatment, 2*(1), 65–72.

Burr, H. S. (1972). *Blueprint for immortality: The electric patterns of life*. Essex, England: Saffron Walden.

Callahan, R.J. (1985). *Five minute phobia cure*. Wilmington, DE: Enterprise.

Callahan, R. J. (1995, August). A Thought Field Therapy (TFT) algorithm for trauma: A reproducible experiment in psychology. Paper presented at the Annual Meeting of the American Psychological Association, New York.

Callahan, R. J., & Turbo, R. (2002). *Tapping the healer within*. New York, NY: McGraw-Hill.

Carbonell, J. (1997). An experimental study of TFT and acrophobia. *Thought Field, 2*(3), 1–6.

Church, D. (2007). *The genie in your genes*. Santa Rosa, CA: Energy Psychology Press.

———. (2010). The treatment of combat trauma in veterans using EFT (Emotional Freedom Techniques): A pilot protocol. *Traumatology, 16*(1), 55–65.

Church, D. & Brooks, A. J. (2010). The effect of a brief EFT (Emotional Freedom Techniques) self-intervention on anxiety, depression, pain and cravings in healthcare workers. *Integrative Medicine: A Clinician's Journal, 6,* 40–44.

Church, D., Geronilla, L., & Dinter, I. (2009). Psychological symptom change in veterans after six sessions of EFT (Emotional Freedom Techniques): An observational study. *International Journal of Healing and Caring, 9*(1), 1–14.

Church, D., Hawk, C., Brooks, A., Toukolehto, O., Wren, M., Dinter, I., & Stein, P. (2013). Psychological trauma symptom improvement in veterans using Emotional Freedom Techniques: A randomized controlled trial. *Journal of Nervous and Mental Disease, 201*(2):153–160.

Church, D., Piña, O., Reategui, C., & Brooks, A. (2012). Single session reduction of the intensity of traumatic memories in abused adolescents after EFT: A randomized controlled pilot study. *Traumatology, 18*(3), 73–79. doi:10.1177/1534765611426788

Church, D., Yount, G., & Brooks, A. J. (2012). The effect of Emotional Freedom Techniques (EFT) on stress biochemistry: A randomized controlled trial. *Journal of Nervous and Mental Disease, 200*(10), 891–896.

Connolly, S. & Sakai, C. (2011). Brief trauma intervention with Rwandan genocide survivors using Thought Field Therapy. *International Journal of Emergency Mental Health, 13*(3), 161–172.

Craig, G. & Fowlie, A. (1995). *Emotional Freedom Techniques: The manual.* Sea Ranch, CA: Author.

Craig, G. (2011). *The EFT manual.* Fulton, CA: Energy Psychology Press.

Damasio, A. R. (1994). *Descartes' error: Emotion, reason, and the human brain.* New York, NY: Putnam.

Darby, D. (2001). *The efficiency of Thought Field Therapy as a treatment modality for individuals diagnosed with blood-injection-injury phobia.* Unpublished doctoral dissertation. Minneapolis, MN: Walden University.

Darras, J. C., De Vernejoul, P., & Albarede, P. (1992). Nuclear medicine and acupuncture: A study on the migration of radioactive tracers after injection at acupoints. *American Journal of Acupuncture, 20*, 245–256.

De Quervain, D., Kolassa, I. T., Achermann, S., Aerni, A., Boesiger, P., Demougin, P., ... Papassotiropoulos, A. (2012, May 29). PKCα is genetically linked to memory capacity in healthy subjects and to risk for posttraumatic stress disorder in genocide survivors. *Proceedings of the National Academy of Sciences USA, 109*(22), 8746–8751. doi:10.1073/pnas.1200857109

Diamond, J. (1985). *Life energy.* New York, NY: Dodd, Mead.

Diepold, J. H. & Goldstein, D. (2000). *Thought Field Therapy and qEEG changes in the treatment of trauma: A case study.* Moorestown, NJ: Author.

———. (2008). Thought Field Therapy and qEEG changes in the treatment of trauma: A case study. *Traumatology, 15*(1), 85–93. http://dx.doi.org/10.1177/1534765608325304

Diepold, J. H., Britt, V., & Bender, S. S. (2004). *Evolving Thought Field Therapy: The clinician's handbook of diagnoses, treatment, and theory.* New York, NY: Norton.

Feinstein, D. (2010). Rapid treatment of PTSD: Why psychological exposure with acupoint tapping may be effective. *Psychotherapy: Theory, Research, Practice, Training, 47*, 385–402.

Feinstein, D. (2012). Acupoint stimulation in treating psychological disorders: Evidence of efficacy. *Review of General Psychology.* doi:10.1037/a0028602

Figley, C. R., Carbonell, J. L., Boscarino, J. A., & Chang, J. A. (1999). Clinical demonstration model of asserting the effectiveness of therapeutic interventions: An expanded clinical trials method. *International Journal of Emergency Mental Health, 2*(1), 1–9.

Gallo, F. (1997). A no-talk cure for trauma: Thought Field Therapy violates all the rules. *Family Therapy Networker, 21*(2), 65–75.

Gallo, F. P. (2000). *Energy diagnostic and treatment methods.* New York, NY: Norton.

———. (2002). *Energy psychology in psychotherapy: A comprehensive source book.* New York, NY: Norton.

———. (2003). Meridian-based psychotherapy. In E. Leskowitz (Ed.), *Complementary and alternative medicine in rehabilitation* (pp. 215–225). New York, NY: Churchill Livingstone.

———. (1999). *Energy psychology: Explorations at the interface of energy, cognition, behavior, and health* (1st ed.). Boca Raton, FL: CRC Press.

———. (2005). *Energy psychology: Explorations at the interface of energy, cognition, behavior, and health* (2nd ed.). Boca Raton, FL: CRC Press.

———. (2007). *Energy tapping for trauma.* Oakland, CA: New Harbinger.

Gallo, F. P. & Vincenzi, H. (2008). *Energy tapping: How to rapidly eliminate anxiety, depression, cravings, and more using energy psychology.* Oakland, CA: New Harbinger.

Goddard, G., Karibe, H., McNeill, C., & Villafuerte, E. (2002). Acupuncture and sham acupuncture reduce muscle pain in myofascial pain patients. *Journal of Orofacial Pain, 16*(1), 71–76.

Goodheart, G. J. (1987). *You'll be better.* Geneva, OH: Author.

Greene, B. (2003). *The elegant universe: Superstrings, hidden dimensions, and the quest for the ultimate theory.* New York, NY: Vintage.

Haake, M., Müller, H. H., Schade-Brittinger, C., Basler, H. D., Schäfer, H., Maier, C., ... Molsberger, A. (2007). German acupuncture trials (Gerac) for chronic low back pain. *Archives of Internal Medicine, 167*(17), 1892–1898.

Hebb, D. O. (1949). *The organization of behavior: A neuropsychological theory.* New York, NY: John Wiley.

Hölzel, B. K., Lazar, S. W., Gard, T., Schuman-Olivier, Z., Vago, D. R., & Ott, U. (2011). How does mindfulness meditation work? Proposing mechanisms of action from a conceptual and neural perspective. *Perspectives on Psychological Science, 6*, 537–559.

Johnson, D. R., Fontana, A., Lubin, H., Corn, B., & Rosenheck, R. A. (2004). Long-term course of treatment-seeking Vietnam veterans with posttraumatic stress disorder: Mortality, clinical condition, and life satisfaction. *Journal of Nervous and Mental Disease, 192*, 35–41.

Jung, C. (1968). *Collected works of C. G. Jung.* NJ: Princeton University Press.

Kendall, H., Kendall, F., & Wadsworth, G. (1971). *Muscle testing and function* (2nd ed.). Baltimore, MD: Williams and Wilkins.

Lambrou, P. T., Pratt, G. J., & Chevalier, G. (2003). Physiological and psychological effects of a mind/body therapy on claustrophobia. *Subtle Energies and Energy Medicine, 14*, 239–251.

Leonoff, G. (1995). The successful treatment of phobias and anxiety by telephone and radio: A replication of Callahan's 1987 study. *TFT Newsletter, 1*(2).

Mollon, P. (2008). *Psychoanalytic energy psychotherapy.* London: Karnac.

Monson, C. M., Schnurr, P. P., Resick, P. A., Friedman, M. J., Young-Xu, Y., & Stevens, S. P. (2006). Cognitive processing therapy for veterans with military-related posttraumatic stress disorder. *Journal of Consulting Clinical Psychology, 74*(5), 898–907.

Norcross, J. C. (2011). *Psychotherapy relationships that work: Evidence-based responsiveness.* New York, NY: Oxford University Press.

Phelps, E. A. (2009). The human amygdala and the control of fear. In P. J. Whalen & E. A. Phelps (Eds.), *The human amygdala* (pp. 204–219). New York, NY: Guilford.

Pignotti, M. (2005). Thought Field Therapy voice technology vs. random meridian point sequences: A single-blind controlled experiment. *Scientific Review of Mental Health Practice, 4*(1), 72–81.

Pitman, R. K., Altman, B., Greenwald, E., Longpre, R. E., Macklin, M. L., Poiré, R. E., & Steketee, G. S. (1991). Psychiatric complications during flooding therapy for posttraumatic stress disorder. *Journal of Clinical Psychiatry, 52,* 17–20.

Pomeranz, B. (1996). Acupuncture and the raison d'etre for alternative medicine. *Alternative Therapies, 2*(6), 84–91.

Popp, F. A. & Beloussov, L. (2003). *Integrative biophysics: Biophotonics.* Boston, MA: Kluwer Academic Publishers.

Porges, S. (2011). *The polyvagal theory: Neurophysiological foundations of emotions, attachment, communication, and self-regulation.* New York, NY: Norton.

Prigogine, I. & Stengers, I. (1984). *Order out of chaos: Man's dialogue with nature.* New York, NY: Bantam.

Rossi, E. L. (2002). *The psychobiology of gene expression: Neuroscience and neurogenesis in hypnosis and the healing arts.* New York, NY: Norton.

Rowe, J. E. (2005). The effects of EFT on long-term psychological symptoms. *Counseling and Clinical Psychology, 2,* 104–111.

Rubik, R. (1995). Energy medicine and the unifying concept of information. *Alternative Therapies, 1*(1), 34–39.

Sakai, C. S., Connolly, S. M., & Oas, P. (2010). Treatment of PTSD in Rwandan genocide survivors using Thought Field Therapy. *International Journal of Emergency Mental Health, 12*(1), 41–50.

Sakai, C., Paperny, D., Mathews, M., Tanida, G., Boyd, G., Simons, A., ... Nutter, L. (2001). Thought Field Therapy clinical application: Utilization in an HMO in behavioral medicine and behavioral health services. *Journal of Clinical Psychology, 57,* 1215–1227. doi:10.1002/jclp.1088

Salas, M., Brooks, A., & Rowe, J. (2011). The immediate effect of a brief energy psychology intervention (Emotional Freedom Techniques) on specific phobias: A pilot study. *Explore: The Journal of Science and Healing, 7,* 155–161.

Schoninger, B. (2001). Thought Field Therapy in the treatment of speaking anxiety. Unpublished doctoral dissertation. Cincinnati, OH: Union Institute.

Schore, A. (1994). *Affect regulation and the origins of the self.* Hillsdale, NJ: Lawrence Erlbaum.

Sheldrake, R. (1981). *A new science of life.* Los Angeles, CA: J. B. Tarcher.

———. (1988). *The presence of the past.* New York, NY: Times Books.

Stone, B., Leyden, L., & Fellows, B. (2010). Energy psychology treatment for orphan heads of households in Rwanda: An observational study. *Energy Psychology: Theory, Research, &Treatment, 2*(2), 31–38.

Stux, G. & Pomeranz, B. (1995). *Basics of acupuncture* (3 rd ed.). New York, NY: Springer.

Swingle, P. G., Pulos, L., & Swingle, M. K. (2004). Neurophysiological indicators of EFT treatment of posttraumatic stress. *Subtle Energies and Energy Medicine, 15*(1), 75–86.

Wade, J. F. (1990). *The effects of the Callahan phobia treatment techniques on self concept.* San Diego, CA: Professional School of Psychological Studies.

Wells, S., Polglase, K., Andrews, H. B., Carrington, P., & Baker, A. H. (2003). Evaluation of a meridian-based intervention, Emotional Freedom Techniques (EFT), for reducing specific phobias of small animals. *Journal of Clinical Psychology, 59,* 943–966.

Chapter 9
The Physiology of Trauma: The "Freeze" Response and the Trauma Capsule
Rob Nelson

Abstract

Emotional trauma occurs when an unexpected threat to our survival or identity is met with a feeling of isolation and powerlessness to cope with it. Using a hypothetical tiger attack as an illustration, this chapter explains the physiological process underlying trauma and the role of the parasympathetic freeze response in encapsulating the experience in procedural memory. The difference between stress and trauma is examined, along with the role of kindling in exacerbating traumatic symptoms over time. The inability of conventional "talk" therapy to fully discharge procedural memories is understood as the failure of words alone to register with the more primitive limbic system of the brain.

Keywords: trauma, emotional trauma, amygdala, dissociation, freeze response, trauma capsule, procedural memory

Rob Nelson, MS, is a certified EFT and Matrix Reimprinting trainer and practitioner. Based in Santa Rosa, California, Rob teaches nationally and internationally, and offers sessions worldwide via Skype. Correspondence to Rob Nelson, 850 Third Street, Santa Rosa, CA 95404, or robnelson.eft@gmail.com. www.TappingtheMatrix.com.

The Stress Response

Imagine encountering a tiger in the wild. Let's say you're out for a lovely stroll through the jungle one day, minding your own business, when suddenly this tiger comes loping around a bend in the trail, sees you, and stops in his tracks. His tail begins to lash, he stares right into your eyes and a low growl meets your ears. What happens next in your brain and body—the fight-or-flight response—is the product of millions of years of evolution and quite beyond your conscious control. Let's take a look at what happens.

A staggering amount of sensory data is flowing in through your eyes, ears, nose, and skin at all times, channeled to the amygdala, the part of your brain tasked with deciding what's a threat and what's benign. The amygdala is the gatekeeper and activates fight or flight whenever it perceives a threat.

With a large, ferocious, hungry-looking tiger sizing you up, it's a safe bet that your amygdala is going to throw the switch, which really means activating the sympathetic half of your autonomic nervous system (ANS). The job of the ANS in general is to keep your body in a balanced state (homeostasis), continually alternating between arousal and relaxation—imagine a nice smooth sine wave (Scaer, 2012).

The sympathetic half of your ANS is in charge of arousal and keeps you on your toes, mobilizing the energy and resources needed to deal with challenging situations. It doesn't take a tiger. It doesn't even take a real-world event. Just thinking about past struggles or worry over imaginary problems of the future is enough to ramp up the sympathetic stress response.

Face to face with a real tiger, though, your body instantly reacts. Adrenaline and cortisol are pumped into the bloodstream and sent coursing to your muscles, especially your arms and legs, for action. Blood pressure increases along with glucose levels. Your eyes dilate, respiration rate shoots up, perception of pain diminishes, and your rational mind is effectively bypassed.

You have now entered "fight or flight." This sudden intense one-pointed focus, totally energized and free of pain—this is the rush that daredevil athletes get hooked on. You feel so alive! If only you weren't about to be ripped apart by that tiger (Science Daily, n.d.).

This state of arousal is not meant to be a long-term condition. All that cortisol and adrenaline is corrosive and all that blood going to your arms and legs has to come from somewhere—that somewhere being your digestive, reproductive, and immune systems, along with the frontal lobes of your brain. Healing a cut on your toe is a low priority if your leg is about to be torn off. And digesting breakfast can wait if you're about to be lunch for the tiger. And you certainly don't need to waste any time pondering the meaning of life when your life will be over soon if you don't climb that tree right now!

The stress response evolved as a short-term survival strategy. Ongoing long-term exposure to stress, real or imagined, is the likely underlying cause for many diseases (Levine, 1997).

The Freeze Response

With the tiger about to charge, no weapon at hand, and no way to "fight," all your bodily resources are mobilized for "flight." But what if you can't get away? You've run the wrong way and now your back is to the wall and there's no escape. Fight or flight has totally failed—here comes the tiger. You're going to die and there's nothing you can do about it.

At this point something very interesting happens. The parasympathetic half of your autonomic nervous system now kicks in. All of the resources mobilized for fight or flight are instantly redirected in a drastic way (Levine, 1997). Generally, the parasympathetic system is in charge of relaxation—balancing out the arousal of the stress response. But in the face of imminent death (real or perceived), relaxation doesn't look like chilling out at the beach. This is where the "freeze response" switches on. Think of a deer caught in the headlights. Or an opossum "playing dead."

The opossum isn't actually playing. It doesn't get to decide when to collapse. The freeze response is an involuntary state that suddenly takes over. It's unfortunate that people who freeze are often judged as weak and cowardly, as if they'd made a decision about not fighting back or trying to get away. This extra burden of shame is entirely unfair. The freeze response is a sudden, drastic relaxation—a precipitous drop in heart rate and blood pressure, a letting go of muscle contraction in the bladder and bowels. Your eyes will dilate; you may start drooling (Science Daily, n.d.).

Psychologically, it's a state of shock, enhanced by a massive dose of endorphins in the bloodstream. As the tiger approaches, you become dissociated from your body. Numb and floating. Detached from reality. That's really helpful, because when the tiger rips you apart, you won't even feel it (Spiegel, 1997).

The Difference Between Stress and Trauma

But let's just say the tiger *doesn't* attack you. Perhaps he's already eaten a few people today and is too full to bother. Perhaps your sudden lack of motion as a result of the freeze response (part of its evolutionary survival value) makes the tiger lose interest and it simply wanders off. Hooray! You survived!

So what happens now? After a time, you'll come back to your senses. If you were a wild animal, you'd begin to shake and tremble. Your body would replay or reenact the same physical movements you'd engaged in during your flight. This is known as the "freeze discharge" (Levine, 1997).

Because this encounter with the tiger may have survival value in the future, your brain has recorded the whole experience into what is known as "procedural memory." This type of memory is used to keep knowledge current. Think about learning to ride a bike. Once you've learned how, you never forget. This is another example of information stored in procedural memory. Even if it's been 20 years since you've ridden a bike, you can just hop on and start riding (Scaer, 2012).

When a wild animal is shaking during the freeze discharge, it's clearing the procedural memory by completing the physical actions of fight or flight. This tells its brain that the whole thing is over, and the distress is actually transformed into increased resilience.

As a rational human being, it's unlikely that you'll be able to shake off the tiger attack and discharge your own freeze response. This means the whole thing will likely be stored for you, in procedural memory, *as if it's still happening!*

And this is the difference between regular garden-variety stress and emotional trauma. Both are very serious. Prolonged stress has a highly corrosive effect on the body and is implicated in many disease processes—it's a real problem. But if the actual stressors are removed—the check clears, the biopsy comes back negative, your nasty coworker gets transferred, you finally get a good night's sleep—then you can relax, your autonomic nervous system returns to homeostasis, and health and well-being are restored (Sherwood, 2008).

When the freeze response causes an overwhelming experience to be stored in procedural memory, the stressor becomes internalized. Even if the original stressor is gone, the memory, or aspects of the memory, can become a hair trigger for reactivating fight, flight, or freeze. You can tell a Vietnam veteran, "Hey, the war is over—get over it!" but that isn't going to clear the veteran's PTSD (Procedural memory, n.d.).

The Trauma Capsule

Procedural memory storage happens whenever the freeze response is triggered, because the event is perceived as having crucial survival value and a kind of snapshot is taken of all the external information coming in through our senses, and all of the information from our internal landscape.

The external snapshot of our tiger incident might include the particular color of his fur and eyes, the deep sound of his growl, or ambient sounds from the jungle. Your brain might register the scent of the tiger or of a flower nearby, or the particular combination of heat and humidity on your skin. A vast array of subliminal inputs is recorded as part of an instinctual survival strategy. Because you do survive, these will be used as cues in the future, alerting your amygdala to danger.

The internal snapshot will include your emotional state (stark terror) along with the corresponding sensations in your viscera and muscles. It will also contain—and this becomes key—whatever thoughts and beliefs were occurring to you in that moment to make sense of the situation.

These internal and external snapshots are stored in procedural memory but *encapsulated* in a sense by a layer or coating of numbness—the dissociation of the freeze response. Trauma authority and neurologist Robert Scaer, MD, refers to this as the "trauma capsule" or "dissociation capsule." The function of the capsule is to help us carry on and survive by shielding us from the intensity of the experience, by acting as a kind of barrier to our conscious awareness of the contents (Scaer, 2007).

To the extent that the trauma capsule is working, we may never fully experience the intensity of the trauma on a conscious level. Unfortunately, for the subconscious level—as represented by the limbic system of the brain—the experience is held as a current event. We never really stop experiencing it.

So to use our example, just below the surface of your awareness, within the thin walls of that capsule of dissociation, you are still being chased by a tiger.

Breaching the Capsule

After a little while the whole tiger encounter may seem to lose its charge. Perhaps it becomes a popular story you tell at parties. The trauma capsule and all of the feelings it contains, however, remain strong. This may explain why many people seem to remember little or nothing of their childhood. Dissociation from early traumas seems to generalize and occlude most other memories, even neutral or happy ones.

Over time the capsule walls seem to grow thin. Whether by loss of general vitality through aging or because a new stressor taxes the system, the dissociative protection begins to fail. Cues in the environment that match the contents of the trauma capsule may begin to provoke a reaction from the amygdala (Scaer, 2007).

Perhaps you see an orange and black sweater out of the corner of your eye. Or the low growl of a motorcycle hits your ears. Perhaps the subtle smell of some perfume resembles a tropical flower that was blooming in the jungle as you ran past. Cues like this—even if they don't register on a conscious level—can act as triggers, evoking the unfinished memory, activating the original emotional distress and sending your system back into fight or flight. Suddenly, your heart is pounding, you're sweating and anxious, and you have no idea why.

Kindling

The old expression "Time heals all wounds" may not apply to emotional trauma. Through a process known as "kindling," new environmental cues can become associated with the memory, even cues unrelated to the original experience. So now it's not just the scent of that one specific tropical flower anymore, it's any tropical flower, and then any flower at all (Scaer, 2012).

The snowball effect of kindling makes the world seem progressively more dangerous and may account for the some of the more severe symptoms of PTSD. More and more environmental cues are able to breach the trauma capsule, leading to hypervigilance and avoidance. Your world is now full of tigers and when the original memory gets triggered, you are right back in the jungle, running for your life. Your here-and-now experience has been hijacked.

The Challenge of Healing Emotional Trauma

As EFT practitioners, our clients come to us with all sorts of problems and issues. Sometimes they're aware of specific traumatic events in their past and eager to resolve them. This can make our work wonderfully straightforward and lead to rapid success. Unfortunately, this isn't always the case. Many people have life issues or dysfunctional patterns without recognizing the origin of the problem. To the extent that a trauma capsule is working, our client might not even remember the original event! Even when a memory is known, dissociation can make it seem relatively minor to the client. Getting to the root of client's problem may be essential for being effective, but how do we know when any particular memory is likely traumatic?

The Perfect Storm: Conditions That Trigger the Freeze Response

The word *trauma* often brings certain situations to mind, including rape and violent assault, natural disasters, terrible automobile accidents, war, kidnapping and terrorism, and child abuse and molestation. These overwhelming experiences have in common an immediate threat to life, safety, and/or identity. They also represent a state of helplessness on the part of the victim.

This combination of factors—a threat to survival or identity, combined with a sense of helplessness or powerlessness—is precisely what triggers the freeze response and this is the basis for emotional trauma.

Two additional factors that are often present in trauma seem to play an important role. The first is the unexpectedness of the event—it's a surprise, a shock, unforeseen, out of the blue. The second factor is a sense of isolation, being cut off, on your own, no one there to help you or take your side.

To summarize, the four conditions that trigger the freeze response, according to Robert Scaer (2007), are:

- A threat to one's safety or identity
- A sense of powerlessness

- The unexpected nature of the experience
- A sense of isolation.

These elements can provide clues as to whether a particular life event triggered the freeze response. They are often reflected in the language that clients use in speaking of an event. This can be very helpful in identifying specific memories to tap on.

A "Small T" Trauma

Two-year-old "Sarah" wanted to snuggle with her mother on the couch, but Mom was not in the mood and when Sarah climbed up and leaned up against her, Mom turned away and gave her the cold shoulder. This was the first time Sarah had ever felt rejected by her mother.

Was this a trauma? Obviously this wasn't life threatening. A casual observer might not have even noticed. For a child that young, however, almost entirely dependent on her mother, it was terrifying. It was a sudden and unexpected threat to Sarah's identity as Mommy's beloved little girl.

Did she feel powerless? Absolutely. She had no resources to cope with this. An older child might ask her mom, "Hey, is something bothering you?" Sarah was 2 years old and could barely talk. And finally, was there a feeling of isolation? Again, a very strong yes. There was no one else there to comfort her.

Children are especially apt to experience the freeze response. They lack resources and coping skills and their identity is still forming and easily threatened. They lack experience, so bad happenings are more unexpected. Childhood traumas often occur prior to the development of language and speech, making it more difficult, but no less important, to locate them.

Encapsulated Beliefs

Could such a small event as Sarah being snubbed by her mother be significant? This one incident actually set the stage for a lifetime pattern of painful relationships. It surfaced during a session with a client in the midst of her third divorce and feeling terrible rejection.

Recall the "snapshot" that's taken during the Freeze response. A key component of the trauma capsule is cognitive: whatever beliefs formed in that moment to make sense of what was happening, beliefs about oneself or about life that offered an explanation, however random or illogical. These beliefs become our perceptual filters.

For little Sarah that belief was "I am unlovable," and that belief became encapsulated along with her emotional distress and certain visual and auditory cues. Over time, through the process of kindling, the number of cues likely grew, adding opportunities to feel rejected and unlovable. New experiences were perceived (or misperceived) through this filter, reinforcing and compounding Sarah's negative perception of herself and her place in the world. Our beliefs affect our behavior and often become self-fulfilling prophecies. Sarah's feeling of being unlovable increased over the years and she attracted a series of terrible boyfriends and husbands who matched and reinforced her expectations. Any prospective suitor who expressed genuine love for her was likely overlooked—or dismissed as crazy.

The Dog Brain—Why Words Alone Aren't Enough

For most EFT practitioners, the tool of choice for dealing with a highly charged, specific traumatic memory is the Tell the Story or Watch the Movie Technique (see Chapter 20), which work by providing a safe structure—a container—for opening the trauma capsule and carefully discharging the contents bit by bit, stopping to tap for every single spike in emotional intensity as the story goes along.

Although the Story Technique, in particular, relies on talking, it should be clear that words alone aren't enough to discharge the memory. Your client may have told that same story a hundred times, to friends, to family, or in conventional "talk therapy." Tapping makes all the difference, but why?

The amygdala, the gatekeeper for fight, flight, and freeze, is centered in the limbic system of the brain. This "mammalian brain" developed millions of years before the newer centers of the brain that handle spoken language. It doesn't respond to words (Scaer, 2012)!

The limbic system is sometimes called "the dog brain." If you've ever had a dog, imagine he's in the house, standing by your front door, and growling like crazy because someone is coming up the walkway. You might explain to your dog that the person approaching is actually Aunt Martha and she's really an awfully nice person and there's no reason to worry, and so forth. What effect is this rational explanation going to have on the dog? Likely none at all. But what happens if you reach down and pat the dog on his head? You might say something like "Good dog, good boy, it's okay." The soothing tone of your voice, combined with the reassuring pats on his head, will calm him right down. You can probably picture him sitting there, tongue hanging out, tail wagging.

This is very much what we're doing with EFT. We're patting the dog brain. Our tapping tells the amygdala, "Everything's okay, there's no danger here, time to relax."

Languaging and Presence

The function of our language in EFT is primarily to elicit and highlight specific triggers so that the tapping can downregulate or disengage the response of the amygdala. With traumatic memories, we're basically exposing the contents of the trauma capsule piece by piece, discharging the associated emotions.

This is why talk therapy is largely ineffective for any kind of real trauma. No matter how insightful or intuitive the therapist, or how deep the insights go, *words don't register with the amygdala.*

There are aspects of conventional talk therapy that do register on the mammalian brain. Reassuring visual cues of the therapist's facial expressions and body language affect the right orbitofrontal cortex, one of the brain centers tasked with regulating the amygdala. The calm and soothing tone or pitch of the therapist's voice does register and help somewhat, but these aspects of therapeutic "presence" are generally insufficient to actually discharge the procedural memory, even after years of therapy.

When we throw tapping into the mix, however, we contact the amygdala directly and are often able to extinguish the distress in a matter of minutes.

Review

Emotional trauma occurs when an unexpected threat to our survival or identity is met with a feeling of isolation and powerlessness to cope with it. Our autonomic nervous system, triggered by the amygdala, shifts from the sympathetic fight-or-flight response to the parasympathetic freeze response (a state of shock and dissociation). During the freeze response, the brain records a snapshot of our internal and external landscape, and this is encapsulated into procedural memory. Our conscious awareness is shielded by dissociation from the event at the same time it is kept current in the subconscious for its survival value.

Environmental cues matching the content of this "trauma capsule" may retrigger the recorded emotional distress, activating a fight, flight, or freeze reaction. This may happen on a subliminal level with little or no awareness of the real cause of distress.

Emotional trauma is different from the stress response. The latter may be resolved simply by removing the stressor from the environment. With trauma, the stressor has been internalized, stored in procedural memory, and is prone to activating the amygdala, until it can be discharged.

As time goes by, the process of "kindling" may add new triggering cues and sensitivities. Because this is all happening in the limbic (or mammalian) part of the brain, which predates spoken language, words alone cannot fully discharge the traumatic procedural memory. This is why we use tapping.

References

Levine, P. (1997). *Waking the tiger: Healing trauma*. Berkeley, CA: North Atlantic Books

Procedural memory. (n.d.). In *Wikipedia*. Retrieved from http://en.wikipedia.org/wiki/Procedural_memory

Scaer, R. C. (2007). *The body bears the burden: Trauma, dissociation, and disease* (2nd ed.). New York, NY: Haworth Medical Press.

Scaer, R. C. (2012). *8 Keys to brain-body balance*. New York, NY: W. W. Norton.

Science Daily. (n.d.). *Sympathetic nervous system*. Retrieved from http://www.sciencedaily.com/articles/s/sympathetic_nervous_system.htm

Sherwood, L. (2008). *Human physiology: From cells to systems* (7th ed.). Stamford, CT: Cengage Learning.

Spiegel, D. (1997, June). Trauma, dissociation, and memory. *Annals of the New York Academy of Sciences, 821*, 225–237. doi: 10.1111/j.1749-6632.1997.tb48282.x

Chapter 10
Integrating EFT and Traditional Trauma Treatment: A Four-Stage Model for Safely Treating Trauma
Mary T. Sise

Abstract

Increased understanding of the brain's response to trauma has led to a shift in the way clinicians view trauma treatment, and an explosion of new techniques. However, energy psychology methods, such as EFT, must be delivered in a safe and structured manner to severely traumatized patients, especially those traumatized in childhood, while the brain is still developing. This requires an understanding of the delicacy of the traumatized brain, especially the impact of early childhood fragmentation. Without the appropriate training in the foundations of traditional trauma therapy, the EFT practitioner may inadvertently retraumatize or quickly overwhelm the client. This chapter provides an integrated approach that honors traditional thinking, brain research, and a safe way of using EFT.

Keywords: trauma, abuse, fragmentation, four-stage model

Mary T. Sise is a licensed clinical social worker with a private practice. Past president of the Association for Comprehensive Energy Psychology and coauthor of the book *The Energy of Belief: Psychology's Power Tools to Focus Intention and Release Blocking Beliefs,* she has been teaching about healing trauma for over 20 years. Send correspondence to Mary Sise, 596 New Loudon Road, Latham, NY 12110, or MarySise100@gmail.com. www.MarySise.com.

EFT is a potent therapeutic method that can rapidly process traumatic events and empower clients with a technique they can use outside the office.

For many clients, EFT techniques are straightforward. The process can even seem miraculously simple and the sequel of the trauma—anxiety, nightmares, and flashbacks—are oftentimes eliminated in one or two sessions. This often happens with single-incident traumatic events (car accidents, assaults, etc.) that occurred in adulthood. For clients who have experienced multiple traumatic events in childhood, however, EFT is not so straightforward. When a client has had a lifetime of traumatic experiences and childhood abuse, treatment must be carefully tailored and the EFT methods we, as clinicians, have come to know and depend on must be used judiciously. For these clients, we must focus the goal of treatment to "do no harm."

To understand traumatic experiences and why something is coded as a trauma is beyond the scope of this chapter other than to say what is obvious: that the brain of a young child is very different from the brain of an adult. We know that children have the ability to dissociate and live in a world of fantasy much easier than adults do. For example, if a 4-year-old child has an imaginary friend, we usually laugh and play along. If a teenager has an imaginary friend, we suspect psychosis and quickly seek professional help. When traumatic events happen to young children (mostly under the age of 7), they are able to dissociate and split off the event from their consciousness much easier than older children can. Young children are able to make as if the traumatic event is happening to some other little girl or boy. If the event is a frequent, repeated abuse, such as by a family member in the home with easy access to the child, the young child can actually create parts to take the abuse and give these parts quite a bit of her own energy. The consciousness of the child fragments to survive the pain and at times even the knowledge of these events is repressed. If the traumas continue, especially with a repetitive pattern, the child will create walls of separation between the parts, in a presentation of dissociative identity disorder—where one part is completely unaware of what the other part knows.

This is in contrast to what often happens when the abuse starts at an older age, for example, a young girl at the age of 13. At this age, with a more developed brain, the child is unable to completely dissociate, and so she will exhibit more "borderline type" behaviors, because although she is aware of what she is doing or saying, she cannot easily control her different selves. This type of client usually has some awareness that abuse has occurred and with whom, versus those clients for whom the abuse happened at a very young age.

When new clients come to you, they may not let you know (or they may not be aware) that they had a traumatic childhood, but for good clinical care, it is critical that you have this information. This became clear to me in my early years of energy psychology work. I had learned EFT and had a large trauma caseload when, in my eagerness to convert all of my colleagues to learning EFT, I offered to see any of their clients and do an EFT session as long as the clinician came with the client. There were many successful cases until one man who was having trouble with anxiety after a car accident 3 years earlier came in with his therapist. Thinking this would be an easy case, I began to target the anxiety of him having been being hit from behind by another car. Next thing I knew, he was in a flashback of being raped as a young boy (from behind); he was seeing blood (which was not part of the car accident story) and thought he was back in the basement of the apartment he lived in as a young child. I had no idea of his history and, worse yet, I had no relationship with him. His eyes were wild, his therapist was no help, and it took me several hours and every clinical skill I had (including using EFT) to treat that rape. He has ended up being a client of mine for years and we successfully treated his multiple traumatic events. However, I will never forget how much he suffered that day, due to my arrogance that I could quickly treat his trauma from his car accident. From that point forward, I made it my policy to do my own full intake on every client, so that I could treat each person in the safest, most humane way possible.

As trauma was a relatively new field of study and certainly not taught in graduate school, I had attended numerous conferences, workshops, and trainings prior to learning EFT in 1997. I had studied Shapiro's EMDR (Shapiro, 2001), Linehan's dialectical behavior therapy (DBT; Linehan, 1993), and Judith Herman and Bessel van der Kolk's teachings on a four-stage model of trauma treatment (Herman, 1992; van der Kolk, McFarlane, & Weisaeth, 1996). In addition, my clients taught me the importance of the energy of the therapist-client relationship. I found that EFT and all energy psychology methods worked with rapid speed and safety when I combined them with listening and opening my heart. Over the past 15 years, I have integrated this four-stage model of trauma treatment with EFT and safely assisted hundreds of clients in transforming their lives.

Stage 1: Evaluation Stage

The main goals of this stage are:

- Gather intake information without client destabilization.
- Assess the client's ego strength.

I use the entire hour of the first session to do a full intake. I ask the general intake questions about who lives with the patient and what medications she might be taking, and then go further to ask questions about her history of previous hospitalizations, any substance abuse history, nightmares, suicidal ideation, or eating disorder history. I note when the problem began, as that will indicate to me when this person could no longer cope with what was happening. Instructing the client to give me a brief overview of her life (the key word here is "brief," as many clients believe that by finally telling their story they will be healed), I ask her to tell me which incidents stand out for her. I ask questions about who was there for her as a child. Did anyone leave her? Support her? I watch her closely to make sure she is not getting retraumatized. Are her eyes glazing over; is she getting anxious? If I see she is getting overwhelmed, we stop the process and do some gentle breathing or a grounding exercise that the client indicates she already uses when she gets upset. I do not use EFT yet, as I haven't had a chance to explain it, so there is no informed consent.

Primarily, I am trying to discern whether or not this client has a history of early childhood trauma, or if she has been relatively high functioning and happy and a current stress or trauma has brought her to treatment.

The other thing that needs to be assessed, primarily with a person who has been multiply traumatized, is whether or not this person has the necessary resources of friends, family, and financial stability to do the intense work they may need to do.

To recap, the key factors that guide the pacing of the therapy for me include:

1. If there is a trauma, is it a single adult incident or has this person gone through numerous traumatic episodes (i.e., domestic violence, childhood abuse)?
2. How old were they when the trauma began—how healthy is their brain?
3. How much of the trauma involved the body? (If the body was hurt, this will indicate to me that there is a higher likelihood of dissociation.)
4. What is the relationship to the perpetrator? Is it a family member? Was it a medical trauma or a car accident? If a family member or other person who was supposed to protect them, there is usually more difficulty with trusting others (including the therapist).

EFT at Stage 1

In this first session, I do not teach EFT to the client. Depending on how long the intake session is, I might begin a brief explanation about EFT, the brain, and trauma. Most traumatized individuals are (rightfully so) quite suspicious of what you are doing. They know from their traumatic experiences that things are often not what they seemed; a seemingly harmless trip for ice cream ended up being something else. They will benefit from a slow introduction, with enough information for them to make their own informed choice about this "strange" treatment. Most important, you do not want to open up any doors that you won't have time to close safely in the first session.

If the person is relatively healthy and this is a single incident trauma, then in the second session I move forward by explaining the neurobiology of trauma and teaching the steps of EFT, and we begin using EFT to process the trauma. These clients are relatively easy to work with and the treatment usually goes smoothly.

Stage 2: Stabilization and Safety

The main goals of this stage are:

- Build ego strength to do the work.
- Build a life worth living.
- Build a relationship to do the work.

Using the information I've received in the intake, I look at the areas of the client's life that need to be strengthened. So, for example, if she is not working, we use EFT to help her envision herself on a job interview. If that is too difficult, we use EFT to help her go to the store and ask a clerk for something. Each time we make strides toward making her current life run well, rather than opening the doors to the past.

Several things happen with this approach. The client begins to see that you, the therapist, really do care about her, which makes her feel safe in the room with you. An energetic bond forms, which will be there when you eventually do go back into those traumatic childhood memories. The second thing that happens is the client begins to see that EFT really works. She begins to feel empowered to change her emotional state rather than being a victim of it.

I also teach clients about the neurobiology of trauma: how they have a limbic brain and a rational brain. I show them pictures of the brain, and explain how their amygdala acts as a smoke detector to signal them when there is danger. They begin to call themselves "limbic" or "triggered," rather than "stupid." This understanding and self-compassion is very freeing for them.

Some seriously multiply traumatized clients will remain in this stage for years, making slow and steady progress. One of my most seriously traumatized clients who has a diagnosis of dissociative identity disorder and 50 psychiatric hospitalizations, with whom I have worked for over 20 years, is finally able to work on the horrific trauma she endured as a child, mainly because her life is worth living now.

It is also important to note that some multiply traumatized clients will only be able to take the SUD (subjective units of distress) level down a few points—for example, fear from a 10 SUD rating to a 6. Do not push such clients to go further. The main purpose is to teach them that they can have a feeling and reduce it, so they realize they have a choice. If you have them go too fast, you might trigger the traumatic event before they are ready to deal with it, and retraumatize them.

EFT at Stage 2

Try to stay in present time and combine EFT with visualization to have the client imagine what she would like to be, do, or have. Using EFT, have her tap as she imagines a safe space in her mind, such as a beach where she can relax and be safe. Develop healthy energy practices; for example, teach her energy medicine strategies such as Donna Eden's 5-minute routine to keep the body healthy (Eden, 2008). Combine EFT with visualization to help her get a job, take a class, rescue a pet, do volunteer work—all the things that make life worth living. If the SUD level doesn't lower all the way to 0, don't continue to push the client.

Stage 3: Trauma Processing

The main goals of this stage are:

- Process the memories as they surface.
- Keep the client stable during this process.

Once there is some stability—the client is functioning fairly well in her daily life, her environment is safe, and she feels you are on her side—the client will begin to bring in situations that are linked to the original traumatic event. At this point you will start with the current trigger and then link it to when the client felt like this before, by adding a few questions such as:

- Is there anything about this that feels familiar?
- Have you felt this way before?
- How old do you feel?

The therapist can also have the client close her eyes, feel the distress in her body, give it a phrase or a color or a shape (e.g., "red ball in my belly" or "a black lump in my throat") and a belief (e.g., "I am not enough," "I am ugly," or "I am a failure"), and then trace it back to an earlier time with questions such as:

- Where do you see yourself with that point of view?
- Where did you get that idea?

Clients will often report things like "I see myself in high school, the male teacher is taunting me, looking at my breasts, the boys are laughing." The therapist can then instruct the adult self to walk into the classroom and go to the younger self. It is imperative here that the older self be able to tolerate for a few seconds feeling the shame and humiliation that the younger one was feeling. Using EFT, you begin to tap on whatever emotion is surfacing first. For some clients, it is anger; for others, it is humiliation and shame. Once the initial feelings have lowered, the therapist asks the client: "What does the younger part of you need to know from the adult you?" Sometimes, it can be as simple as "It is over" or "He was a jerk."

After all the energy is released from here, you invite the younger part to move forward in life to today, to see how life turned out. (Skip over the lousy parts if you wish!) The important thing is for the client's younger part to see that today she has more options: She doesn't have to go to high school; she has her own car and credit card; she can speak up. You invite the child part to come to today and look out the eyes to see you. Encourage her to look around the room, and to breathe deeply for the body. At this point, you combine EFT with a positive statement of the client's choosing such as "I forgive myself" or "I did the best I could."

This type of work is similar to soul retrieval work. When we are overwhelmed in a trauma, a part of the very fiber of our being splits off and stays in the past. We abandon ourselves in order to survive. When speaking with my clients, I normalize this coping strategy and honor it as a wonderful plan, as it helped her survive back then. Once the younger child part returns and reintegrates, clients often report that they feel fuller, more whole, and more peaceful. It is not unusual to have a period of stability for the client, until the next triggering event. Do not push the client to go too fast, allow her to savor this peaceful time. Honor the client's own guidance system to let you know when the next trauma needs to be processed.

A recent example demonstrates this process. Joe, age 25, had a severe early history of abuse and was placed in foster care by age 5. As a teen, he frequently went into rages and became violent whenever he witnessed someone being bullied. He confessed that he had no idea what he even did in these rage states—and felt guilty afterward, as he usually hurt the bully more than the bully hurt the other person. When I saw him as a teenager, we targeted a bullying incident and brought his SUD level from a 10 to a 5. From that point forward, the rages improved. He was in Stage 2 of treatment, and that was an improvement.

Recently, Joe returned to treatment asking for help with his reactions to authority figures. He was starting a new job, and didn't want to ruin it with his pattern of making impulsive comments when he felt someone else was being mistreated. I explained to him that I viewed rage as two energies: anger and helplessness. We discussed the violent incidents of his teen years, and had him connect with the visceral reactions he has to bullying. I then asked him to trace this energy back further to an earlier time. He saw himself at age 5, in his house as his father was beating up the family pet. The rage—anger plus helplessness—was at a SUD level of 8. We did one round of EFT targeting this event, and the SUD level lowered to a 4. He then visualized his older self of today walking into the room, and picking up his younger self. He began to shake and cry. We used EFT at this point, lowering the SUD score further. He then spoke sternly to the father, and imagined himself walking out of the house with his younger self. He showed his younger self how he did get out of that home and was adopted by a very loving mom, and he never has to go back there again. His new affirmation was "There are many good people in this world." He placed his younger self in his heart, and his entire face lit up. "I feel safe," he reported. His SUD level was now 0.

EFT at Stage 3

Start with a triggering event or theme. Use EFT on that issue. Ask the client questions to suggest a connection to the past or a limiting belief she might have. Find the original trauma and then feel the original pain briefly. Use EFT here. Bring the adult part to the child part, allowing them to connect and bring the child part to today. Use EFT to install something positive that the client requests, such as "I am safe now."

Stage 4: Reconnecting and Future Pacing

The main goals of this stage are:

- Move forward without the trauma.
- Make some meaning out of the experience.
- Reconnect with Source.

This stage is probably the most rewarding of all. The traumas are released and a whole new world opens up for the client. We can use visualizations with EFT to help the client see herself in a new job. Many clients will go back to school, get married, or start a new hobby. Oftentimes their old friends just don't fit anymore, and you will need to normalize this and help them move forward and make new friends. Clients will often report that, because of the trauma, they had not seen themselves as reaching certain milestones, so they lost the ability to dream. This stage is when the dreaming happens and the client is able to see and fulfill her soul's destiny.

This is the stage where you can begin to make some meaning out of what the client has been through. It is important to help her to manage her fear about when the other shoe will drop, or her fear of success. Talk about God, and help her identify new avenues for community and meaningful living. It is important to note that if clients try overly hard to make meaning in the earlier stages of the trauma, it may be "spiritual bypass"—meaning the client is doing this in order to avoid feeling something (usually their anger!)—and it will keep them stuck. Save those discussions until this stage.

EFT in Stage 4

Use EFT to process any lingering beliefs the client has regarding her lack of worthiness. Combine EFT with visualization to help her start a new career, or begin to date. Use EFT to eliminate the fear of success and the belief that when good things happen, something bad will soon happen.

Important EFT Additions

I have found three very important additions to the EFT protocol when working with clients, especially traumatized clients. I have written further about them in the book *The Energy of Belief: Psychology's Power Tools to Focus Intention and Release Blocking Beliefs* (Bender & Sise, 2008).

1. Before taking a SUD rating, I have the client note where she is feeling the distress in her body. Traumatized clients are frequently "out of the body" and often EFT treatments won't work when they are not in the body. This additional statement puts the client in the body and the SUD reading is more accurate.
2. I rub both of the neurolymphatic (NLR) drainage points for the acceptance affirmation. I have the client cross her arms over her chest and rub both NLR spots while saying: *Even though I have this problem, belief, or fear* (name it), *I accept myself.*

Note: At times, trauma patients will not touch the NLR area of the body because it is triggering them to the trauma of being touched. Since it is important to move the lymph, I have them rub the back of their necks and their shoulders while they are saying their affirmation.

3. I instruct the client to tap the Karate Chop spot (Small Intestine meridian) and state her intention with this format: *I am choosing to release this problem, belief, or fear* (name it), *all the roots, origins, and all that it means and does to me.*

I find that this extra wording focuses the treatment. And by adding the phrase about roots and origins, the treatment attains a deeper level of healing.

Conclusion

Clients who have experienced multiple traumatic childhood events must be approached differently from clients who have experienced single traumatic events in adulthood. Using the four-stage traditional trauma-processing model, which focuses on thorough evaluation and stabilization prior to trauma processing and reconnection, a practitioner can minimize suffering and avoid inadvertently retraumatizing the client. EFT, when properly integrated into each stage, plays a critical role in the healing of trauma.

As a species we have begun to realize that the legacy of untreated traumatic events has global implications. Generations of traumatized individuals go on to traumatize their offspring. Wars beget wars. Trauma knows no boundaries, no race, no color, no economic specialness. Traumas continue long after the event has passed in the mind and psyche of the individual, weighing heavily on the survival of our species. Humane trauma treatment is possible, and our clients deserve the very best of care in the process. Our future depends on it.

References

Bender, S. S. & Sise, M. T. (2008). *The Energy of belief: Psychology's power tools to focus intention and release blocking beliefs.* Santa Rosa, CA: Energy Psychology Press.

Donna Eden, D. (2008). *Energy medicine: Balancing your body's energies for optimal health, joy, and vitality.* New York, NY: Jeremy P. Tarcher/Penguin.

Herman, J. (1992). *Trauma and recovery.* New York, NY: Basic Books.

Linehan, M. M. (1993). *Cognitive behavioral treatment of borderline personality disorder.* New York, NY: Guilford Press.

Shapiro, F. (2001). Eye Movement Desensitization and Reprocessing (EMDR): Basic principles, protocols, and procedures (2nd ed.). New York, NY: Guilford Press.

Van der Kolk, B. A., McFarlane, A. C., & Weisaeth, L. (Eds.). (1996). *Traumatic stress: The effects of overwhelming experience on mind, body, and society.* New York, NY: Guilford Press.

Chapter 11
The Affect Bridge in EFT: A Reliable Method for Finding Core Issues

Brigitte Hansoul and Yves Wauthier

Abstract

In most EFT sessions, a key factor to success resides in the ability of the practitioner to identify the core issues provoking the client's present symptom. With long-term practice, the EFT professional may be able to reach this goal through clinical sense and intuition. As mentors and teachers, however, we often witness practitioners who make an incomplete or inaccurate assessment of the core issues. The client's present problem may therefore be unresolved, or only seemingly resolved, leading to a reappearance of the problem, as the causal roots were not addressed. The technique we present in this chapter provides a clear protocol that will allow any EFT practitioner to precisely and correctly identify and treat the causal root of the client's issue. The affect bridge, which originated as a hypnotic regression technique, allows one to trace the present affect back to the past. In this application of the method to EFT, the goal is to find the initial causal situation of the problem currently presented by the client. The problem can then be addressed by tapping on the past conditioning event until it is resolved. The present event is therefore desensitized and the symptom does not reoccur. This chapter discusses the mode of action of the technique, explores the mechanisms of conditioning and deconditioning, explains what a full regression bridge is, provides a detailed protocol of the affect bridge, and illustrates its use in EFT with a clinical case transcription.

Keywords: affect bridge, core issues, hypnotic regression, protocol

Brigitte Hansoul, founder of the Training Institute for Psychotherapy Therapeutia in Belgium, has been a clinical psychologist and a psychotherapist for more than 15 years. A past president of APEC (French-speaking Association for Clinical Energy Psychology), she coauthored *EFT, Tapping, and Energy Psychology* and adapted the French version of *The EFT Manual*.

Yves Wauthier, president of the Training Institute for Psychotherapy Therapeutia, Belgium representative to ACEP, and president of APEC, is a psychotherapist specializing in brief therapy and posttraumatic stress management. He coauthored *EFT, Tapping, and Energy Psychology* and adapted the French version of *The EFT Manual*.

Send correspondence to Brigitte Hansoul or Yves Wauthier, 25 rue Félix Bovie, 1050 Bruxelles, Belgique, or info@therapeutia.com.

Objective of the Affect Bridge Technique

The affect bridge was originally a hypnotic regression technique (Watkins, 1971). Its aim is to trace the thread of the affective component of current experience to the initial event of the past that conditioned it. As its name suggests, the technique makes a bridge between the affect of the *present* and the identical one of the *past*. The goal is to find the initial causal situation of the problem currently presented by the client; this would, in the language of EFT, be called the "core issue." The problem can be resolved at the level of the conditioning event in the past, so that it does not happen again in the present.

Mode of Action: Conditioning and Deconditioning

The effectiveness of the technique is based on the Pavlovian conditioning process and its extinction by deconditioning. After conditioning dogs to pair the sound of a bell with the arrival of food (the past), it was sufficient for Pavlov to ring the bell in the present for the dogs to salivate. The bell became a trigger with the power to cause the conditioned response (salivation).

Because it is associated (conditioned) to the event, each sensory aspect of the initial situation of the *past* (visual, auditory, olfactory, kinesthetic) can constitute a trigger afterward, in the *present*. This means that every aspect of a situation in the *present* similar or identical to the same aspect of the painful experience in the *past* can constitute a bell reminding the limbic brain of this situation in the past, and trigger the same conditioned response (affective, cognitive, and physiological) as the earlier event.

A painful experience can condition the emotional brain and create a trigger in two ways:

- Through a single but strong impact; the trauma marks the limbic system in one blow, as in a car accident.
- Through repetition; trauma by toxicity marks the limbic system in the long term, as in bullying or repeated deprecation.

Often the triggering stimulus remains unconscious. When the trigger is activated, the individual involved finds him or herself feeling anxious, depressed, or uncomfortable for no apparent reason. With no understanding of what is happening, the person's reactions therefore seem irrational or disproportionate.

Example 1: A client had a serious car accident. Just before impact, the other driver attempted to avoid it by braking suddenly. The noise of the braking became associated with the trauma of impact, resulting in the creation of a bell/trigger. Therefore when, years later, the client heard the squeal of brakes while walking in the street, he felt a surge of panic, began to sweat, and felt frozen, unable to move and think (conditioned physiological response). The client did not make the link between the brake noise and the accident, which he no longer thought about, as it had occurred years before. He did not understand what was happening.

Example 2: A client was scared (conditioned response) by her boss because the boss's tone of voice (bell/trigger) unconsciously reminded her of her overly severe father. Not noticing the element that her boss and her father had in common, she thought she was frightened by the boss and sought help with this issue. In reality, it was her father that she had always been frightened of: her limbic brain triggered a fear response to whatever reminded her of her father.

To ensure that the trigger has no more effect in the present, we must deactivate it in the past. In the example of the boss, if we treat only the current emotion (fear of the boss), the client will see her fear of her boss dissolve, but the trigger of the past will not be disabled, so the next person who reminds her of her father will trigger the same conditioned response (fear).

Hence, in EFT the therapist is invited to search for the core issues. In this case, identifying the fear of the father as the core issue, we can allow the limbic brain of the client to rehabilitate by deconditioning the fear reaction relative to the perceived severity of the father in the past. In this way, the client will no longer perceive a sign of severity as danger, and no severe person in the present will cause her to be afraid.

Looking for Core Issues

A simple way to find a core issue is to:

- Identify the feeling of the client in the current situation
- Then use that feeling as "the golden thread" to go back to the past.

To follow the golden thread, the practitioner asks the client if the current feeling reminds him of an earlier time in his life. It is preferably childhood that is concerned, because it is rare that the roots are in adulthood, except in cases of accidents or traumas that occurred in adulthood and that people remember well.

The question can be formulated, for example, as follows: "When you are connected to this feeling, and you let yourself go back in time as far as possible, what does it take you back to?"

This is the principle of the affect bridge: Regress from present to past, following the thread of emotional reaction.

This invitation to the client to see what it reminds him of in the past, brings us to the method Freud used in psychoanalysis to discover the unconscious origins of his patients' troubles. He knew that it was the subconscious of the patient, rather than the conscious mind, that would lead to the source of the problem. This is why the basic rule of psychoanalysis is free association, which is to "say everything that comes to mind." This process activates the limbic brain, the emotional rather than rational mind.

The American psychologist John G. Watkins (1971) noted the importance of reaching the point where the client has limbic rather than mental access to his memories. That is why he developed the technique of the affect bridge, under hypnosis, by which the subconscious activated by the trance can be ordered to regress to the past and see what the current feeling state reminds him of. Specifically, the hypnotherapist invites the client in trance to focus on his emotion (affect) in the current situation, and then directs the subconscious to follow the thread toward this emotion from the past to find the event when this emotion was triggered and felt for the first time.

Full Regression Bridge and Affect Bridge

When a real-life situation activates a trigger, the conditioned response that is triggered consists of emotions, physical sensations (physiological response), and thoughts (cognitions) experienced by the client. A "full regression bridge" consists of using all of these elements to induce a regression. The technique of the affect bridge uses only the component of *emotion*. The regression bridge (taking into account not only emotion, but also the physical sensations and cognitions) is more reliable than the affect bridge. It is featured in our book *Clinical EFT Protocols* (Hansoul & Wauthier, 2014). Under hypnosis, in fact, even if the hypnotherapist focuses the client's attention on emotion through trance, the subconscious focuses on all the elements (emotions, sensations, cognitions).

It is, indeed, clear that if the current emotion is fear, there are different past events that caused fear. The client in the earlier example was afraid of her father, but she probably was also afraid, for example, of the dark or of not being good enough. If the subconscious returns to the situation with the father and not to the fear of the dark, it is because all the other elements of connection (especially cognitions) between the present and past events were taken into account. Thus, under hypnosis, making a bridge that seemingly uses only the affect, actually makes a full regression bridge, and results in finding the correct origin of the problem.

But in EFT, this is not necessarily true, because a real trance is absent. When clients are associated with the past, when they are really reliving it, they have a slightly altered state of consciousness—a light trance. But, if the client is not sufficiently engaged in the scene, if it is just intellectual thoughts and *not* lived in the senses, the affect bridge can lead to a memory associated with the same emotion, but not located at the root of the causal axis of the current event. In our example, it could lead to a memory of fear of the dark from the client's childhood, which is not the origin of her current fear of her boss.

The technique of the full regression bridge requires detailed technical prerequisites that are not the subject of this chapter. We therefore describe the affect bridge by giving a simple clinical example. We follow this case, however, with another transcript of a session using the technical elements of the full regression bridge and other advanced techniques used with clients with complex traumas. A detailed description of the full regression bridge can be found in *Clinical EFT Protocols* (Hansoul & Wauthier, 2014).

How to Use the Affect Bridge in EFT

The simplest use of the affect bridge in EFT consists of focusing on the current emotion while making a regression:

Step 1: Engage the client in the current event. Ask for the SUD level of the event (intensity of emotional distress from 0 to 10).

Step 2: Identify the current emotion.

Step 3: Ask "When is the first time you felt this emotion (name the emotion) in the past?" or "When you are connected to this emotion (name the emotion) and let yourself go back in time as far as possible, what does it take you back to?" Ask for the SUD level of the event.

Step 4: Decondition the past event by tapping with EFT until SUD = 0 (emotion fell to 0).

Step 5: Check the *current* event: Is it really deactivated (SUD = 0: emotion has disappeared).

We have seen that it is by staying connected to the emotional brain, the limbic brain, corresponding to the activation of the subconscious in hypnosis, that the client will access the right information. Otherwise, the cognitive mind of the client will provide an intellectual response of little value. Without access to trance in EFT, how can you access the limbic brain rather than the cognitive brain of the client? The art is to associate clients with their emotions and properly ask the questions cited here.

Let's review the details of each step using our client example of fear of her boss.

Step 1: Engage the Client in the Current Event

This is to allow the client to get back into *reliving* the situation, as if she is reliving it now. Her experience would be: "*Now* I put myself back into the memory of the present (recent past) as if I'm there once again. I am therefore now in the memory of the present." This is called being 'associated' to the memory: reliving it. This reliving is identifiable by the fact that the client speaks in the present tense: "I am very afraid" (*now*, when I am in the present/recent past). It is not an intellectual memory, which can be identified by the client speaking in the past tense instead of the present: "I was scared" (in the past).

We can say to the client: "Put yourself back in the moment when you are facing your boss, as if you are there right now" (note the intentional use of the present tense). "Are you there?" Wait for confirmation and ask for the SUD level.

Step 2: Identify the Current Emotion

Ask the client: "Now that you are at this moment in front of your boss, what emotion do you feel?"

Step 3: Ask the Connecting Questions

Ask: "When is the first time you felt this fear in the past?" or "When you are connected to this fear, and let yourself go back in time as far as possible, what does it take you back to?"

Here, the art of the therapist is to keep the client connected to her emotion, reliving the scene. One has to avoid asking in a way that activates the cognitive mind of the client, such as: "When do you *think* you felt this fear before?" It is not a question of thinking or reflecting, but *letting emotion take us back*.

In this case, the client responded with a scene with her father, raising his voice in a stern tone: "I see myself in the kitchen with my father, he speaks in a very harsh tone."

It is important to verify that the client has the same emotion in this event, in this case, fear. Otherwise, it is not the root. The client has found an answer with her mind, or was not sufficiently engaged in the scene. (If this happens, start again. In case of persistent difficulty, a full regression bridge is necessary.) Ask for the SUD level.

Step 4: Decondition the Past Event

You do this by tapping until the SUD level goes down to 0 (emotion fell to 0.) Tap the scene from the past (in the kitchen with the father) to complete desensitization.

Step 5: Check the Present Event

Check the present event (facing the boss): Is it really deactivated (SUD = 0)? If the affect bridge is properly executed, this is usually the case. In rare cases, something of low intensity remains, which tapping can reduce to 0. If the SUD level of the present event has little or no reduction, it is because:

- The event in the past was not the root of the present situation, or
- The root is constituted by more than one event.

Indeed, as stated previously, a painful experience can create a trigger in two ways:

- Through a single but strong impact, as in a car accident.
- Through repetition as in bullying or repeated deprecation.

A case like this one (fear of the father) is more likely to belong to the second category.

Each event of the repetition contributes to the root; that's why taping on one of them generally doesn't annihilate the trigger. Nevertheless, it is usually sufficient to tap on the most important ones to reach a SUD of 0 regarding the present event. To identify these events in this case, one could ask: 'When you think to the fear of your father, what are your worst memories?' See our book *Clinical EFT Protocols* (Hansoul & Wauthier, 2014) for a detailed description of the protocol used when the root is composed by multiple events.

Advanced Notes on Connecting the Client to Reliving the Scene

Good knowledge of a client's history (anamnesis) is more than useful. To help clients connect with their emotions, you will need to determine whether they tend to be associated or disassociated from their emotions. Basically, is the person emotional or cognitive?

Clients dissociated from their emotions. If clients are cognitive, avoid tapping while you ask them to explain their problem. As they do, look for the specific target of where to start. With this type of client, you want to get them to contact their emotions with the greatest possible intensity because they have a tendency to dissociate. You are seeking to stimulate and activate their sympathetic nervous system (corresponding to the accelerator in a car) so as to connect them sufficiently to the problem. Avoid tapping at this stage because tapping activates the parasympathetic system (equivalent to the brakes in a car) and calms the nervous system. Basically, if you are tapping at the same time, you are pressing both the accelerator and the brake (Hansoul & Wauthier, 2010). It is good to ask such clients for as much detail as possible in order to connect them to the scene they are describing. If they have trouble identifying the emotion, you can help here by suggesting a palette of emotions that appear to you to best represent the problem to be treated or resonate the most with it. Be careful to keep your suggestions as proposals, so as to avoid leading clients away from what they would choose themselves. If clients are unable to connect to their emotions, it may be necessary to help by putting yourself into the client's emotion and expressing it, for example, by emphasizing how it could be difficult or hard or sad or scary for the client.

Clients too associated with their emotions. If, on the other hand, a client tends to be too emotional, you will need to stay in a comfort zone (do not enter overly into emotion) in order to correctly identify and make the affect bridge.

A Simple Case of Using the Affect Bridge in EFT

Martine, during her training for mental health professionals, proposed herself as a guinea pig. She asked to work on a phobia and panic that seized her every year when she had to take her medical examination and a CT scan (*present*). Just the idea of being locked in this machine, in the tube, and unable to move triggered a wave of anxiety. This caused an acceleration of her heart rate and her breathing; she began to panic, broke out in a sweat, and had uncontrollable thoughts of immediate danger (*conditioned response*).

Step 1: Martine was asked to get back to the moment when she had her last scan (*recent past taken as equivalent to the present*) and to assess the SUD level, which was 8 out of 10.

Step 2: She was asked what emotion she felt when reliving the scene. It was anxiety.

Step 3: Martine, with eyes closed, was asked: "When you are connected to the anxiety and let yourself go back in time as far as possible, what does that bring you back to?" She remembered suddenly that, a year before the onset of the symptoms, she'd had to have an abortion. She'd had several miscarriages and had also lost a child a few months after his birth. Since the time of the abortion, she said she had suffered from agoraphobia in addition to her claustrophobia. For example, if she saw people boarding a train and coming toward her, she would panic and leave the train quickly, even going so far as to push her way out.

To identify the past event, Martine was asked what was the most difficult memory regarding the abortion. She said it was the moment she had to confirm to the doctor her decision to go ahead with the procedure. The SUD level for this event was 9.

Step 4: Decondition the past event by tapping the EFT until SUD = 0. We conducted several rounds of tapping with the keyword she chose: *"waste."* After a few rounds of tapping, her SUD rating was at 1. She was asked where she could feel the distress in her body. It was at her heart level. The thinking associated with this sensation was that it could not be set to 0 without fear of forgetting. She could not risk forgetting these children without disloyalty, or without feeling the sense of betraying them. We then conducted a round of tapping on this idea. Her SUD level then dropped to 0.

Step 5: Check the event of the present: Is it really disabled (SUD = 0)? I asked Martine to think again about the CT machine. Her SUD level was at 0. She went home by bus and has never again suffered either agoraphobia or claustrophobia.

Conclusion

In this chapter, the authors have provided a clear ready-to-use protocol of the hypnotic affect bridge technique adapted for EFT. This protocol allows the practitioner to identify reliably the core issue underlying the client's present symptom, often decreasing the length of intervention and considerably enhancing its effectiveness. Tracking the affect back to the past, the core issue is treated and the present symptom effectively removed. When learned, this technique becomes an indispensable everyday tool for the EFT practitioner.

References

Hansoul, B. & Wauthier, Y. (2010). *EFT, tapping, and energy psychology.* Labege, France: Edition Dangles.

Hansoul, B. & Wauthier, Y. (2014). *Clinical EFT protocols.* Labege, France: Edition Dangles.

Watkins, J. G. (1971). The affect bridge: A hypnoanalytic technique. *International Journal of Clinical and Experimental Hypnosis, 19*(1), 21–27.

Chapter 12
How Childhood Experiences Shape Adult Attachment
Alina Frank

Abstract

We are born with an innate need for loving and nurturing social interaction. If our early experiences with caregivers provide this, they impart to us a sense of a kind and safe world. When our childhood relationships are less than adequate, we build up emotional and physical defenses, which weaken the body over time. Science continues to find evidence to validate this in research, as in the Adverse Childhood Experiences (ACE) Study conducted by the U.S. Centers for Disease Control and Prevention (CDC) and Kaiser Permanente. Emotional Freedom Techniques (EFT) has been shown to lower cortisol (stress hormone) levels, as well as slow brain waves to the lower frequencies associated with relaxation. EFT neutralizes the pain and disharmony from negative childhood experiences by breaking the neural connections between the originating wounds and current life situations.

Keywords: EFT for negative childhood traumas, EFT and ACE study, childhood experiences and EFT, Adverse Childhood Experiences Study, ACE Study

Alina Frank is a master life coach, who has been a top trainer of EFT and Matrix Reimprinting since 2006. In her private practice, she specializes in romantic relationships and sexuality. Send correspondence to Alina Frank, 1093 Village Loop, Langley, WA 98260, or alina@tapyourpower.net. www.tapyourpower.net.

When we are born, we are hardwired to connect with our caregivers. Unlike other mammals, we mature slowly, our brains learn through social interaction at a slow rate, and we are dependent on our parents for survival for a longer time than any other mammal. When our early connections with our caregivers are loving and nurturing, the result is health, vitality, and a strong sense of self. When our early attachments lack those qualities, the result can be poor health, a fragile ego, or a belief that we aren't enough or the world is unsafe.

Science continues to validate the vital link between our environment and our health. Research exploring the role of adverse childhood experiences in the outcome of adult lives now shows that neglect or abuse in childhood correlates with brain changes, including a measurable reduction in the size of the hippocampus (Frodl et al., 2010; Teicher, 2002). The main role of the hippocampus is to form and store memory; it also has the ability to assist one in envisioning the future based on the past. A smaller hippocampus leaves the individual less able to deal with stress. Chronically elevated levels of stress hormones can literally kill off cells in the area of the brain that helps regulate stress. This then leads to the nervous and hormonal systems being on perpetual high alert, which then creates a positive feedback loop. This is akin to the thermostat in your home turning up the heat in your home when it's getting hotter and the air conditioner kicking on as it gets cold. In other words, positive feedback loops overwhelm the system. Brain scans of children from abusive households actually look similar to those of combat soldiers. These children are vigilant at detecting threats in their environments in the same way a soldier is trained to look for enemy combatants (McCrory et al., 2011, p. 947).

Certain ways in which the most important part of our bodies, the brain, exhibits childhood wounds demonstrate the truth of the statement "Our biographies affect our biology." Research has shown that traumatic stress, including stress caused by sexual abuse, can cause important changes in how the brain functions and develops (Siegel, 1999; Perry & Szalavitz, 2006). Other studies offer evidence that severe child sexual abuse may have a significantly damaging effect on the brain's development. In addition to the research on the hippocampus already noted, Anderson et al. (2002) recorded abnormal functioning of the cerebellar vermis (the brain area assisting in proprioception, or awareness of one's body in space) in adults who had been sexually abused in childhood. Teicher et al. (1993, 2004) found that child sexual abuse was associated with a lesser corpus callosum volume (the area of the brain that aids in processing social cues).

One of the most comprehensive and ongoing scientific explorations regards the correlation between childhood trauma and adult health and lifestyle choices. Between 1995 and 1997, the Adverse Childhood Experiences (ACE) Study was conducted by the U.S. Centers for Disease Control and Prevention (CDC) and Kaiser Permanente (Felitti et al., 1998). The researchers sent 12,494 questionnaires to Kaiser HMO patients, and 9,508 responded, with 8,056 being included in the study. They were queried about their childhood and about their adult health and lifestyle habits. The average respondent age was 56 years old. The study concluded that the higher the incidence of these adverse experiences, the more they were likely to die younger than their non-ACE peers. An ACE score of 6 or higher led to death an average of 20 years sooner.

What constituted an adverse childhood experience? The categories used for the study were physical, psychological, or sexual abuse; violence against the mother in the family; or residing with household members who were substance abusers, mentally ill or suicidal, or ever imprisoned.

The high ACE scorers were more likely to be obese, to abuse substances, and to smoke early in life, all of which are high risk factors for a number of health conditions. Researchers also found "a significant dose-response relationship between the number of childhood exposures and the following disease conditions: ischemic heart disease, cancer, chronic bronchitis or emphysema, history of hepatitis or jaundice, skeletal fractures, and poor self-rated health" (Felitti et al., 1998, p. 250).

Other adverse childhood experience studies have validated their findings, including one performed in Minnesota that confirmed that, as the number of adverse events increases, the risk for health problems increases in a strongly correlated way in areas such as alcohol and substance abuse, depression, anxiety, and smoking (Minnesota Department of Health, 2011). A strong correlation has also been demonstrated between being abused or mistreated as a child and suffering from migraines as an adult, as well as several other medical and psychiatric disorders (Jones, 2011).

Given the evidence of the connection between adverse childhood experiences and later health, one might conclude that only in cases of severe dysfunction, such as categorized in the studies, would one be at risk. Unfortunately, that isn't the case. The physical and psychological damage caused by "Big *T*" traumas such as serious accidents, rape, and psychological, physical, or sexual abuse is widely recognized, but "small *t*" traumas can have the same effect of creating dysfunctional behaviors that impact negatively on physical and emotional health. "Small *t*" traumas may be memorable incidents involving a critical father, an overprotective mother, or a denigrating teacher. These experiences form the basis for belief systems and worldviews that create major limitations and dysfunctional patterns of behavior.

The most important time in our lives, in terms of building and formulating our beliefs, is the first 6 years of life. The raw materials for these beliefs come primarily from our family of origin. The human brain emits four different types of brain waves, each with a distinct frequency: beta (13–30 cycles per second), alpha (8–12 cycles per second), theta (4–8 cycles per second), and delta (0.05–4 cycles per second). Theta brain waves occur when we are in a state of deep meditation, or dreaming. Delta brain waves occur when we are sleeping without dreams. Before the age of 6, we spend the vast majority of our waking lives in theta and delta states, which are primarily hypnogogic or akin to a hypnotized state of mind.

Brain-wave states are significant when we understand that they can be altered. Our ability as adults to change our brain-wave state to a slower frequency through inducing relaxation (e.g., through meditation) can have healing effects. Our brain-wave states are affected both by traumatic experiences and by healing interventions such as EFT. Researchers have studied the brain-wave states of traumatized subjects before and after energy psychology (EP) interventions, using the electroencephalogram (EEG) for objective measurement. Lambrou, Pratt, and Chevalier (2003) tested a group of subjects with claustrophobia and found a reduction in the brain-wave frequencies associated with fear post EP. Swingle, Pulos, and Swingle (2004) found similar positive improvements in the brain states of auto accident victims with PTSD after they received EFT. Swingle (2010) demonstrated a post-EP increase in the low-frequency brain waves associated with relaxation.

While in the deeply receptive theta and delta states, we receive impressions and form perceptions about the world, especially as small children. We take in impressions of our surroundings in order to learn rapidly about how the world operates without the benefit or addition of critical thinking skills. We need to learn that we must hold onto our mother's hand when we cross a busy street or the result is disaster. If we weren't in this receptive state, we might question our mother's authority, want to see if we could walk across alone, or start analyzing different strategies regarding where to cross. Being in this state saves us time and energy from having to relearn these lessons. This sort of association (busy street requires attention) works to our benefit, but other lessons may not be so useful.

Using the previous example, let's imagine that you want to dance and sing across the street while holding your mother's hand. Your mother notices that one of her more pretentious and judgmental acquaintances is standing on the same corner. In an effort not to look like a mother with an out-of-control child, your mother grabs you roughly by the hand and says, "Why can't you behave like a good girl?" This message goes directly into programming your subconscious mind with all sorts of limiting beliefs, such as you can't be physically expressive, you have to be "normal," you are a bad person, you don't deserve your mother's (therefore anyone else's) love, or you need to always be concerned with how others see you. That event is a perfect example of a "small *t*" trauma.

Our experiences in these early critical years are the primary determinants of our sense of who we are, our view of the world as a safe or a scary place, and our belief that we deserve or don't deserve to have our dreams fulfilled. With EFT, we can easily diminish the profound impact that seemingly insignificant events from this time period had on us. It's important to note in the use of EFT that no one can determine what was traumatic for someone else. For example, if your parents were "helicopter" parents, that is, they constantly hovered and came to your rescue at the slightest impediment you faced, then the "small *t*" traumas of such incidents may have left you with the impression that you aren't capable of surviving on your own. Perhaps you decided that you can't make it without a romantic partner, or you are frozen by the thought of taking even the smallest risk in business. If, however, your parents were on the opposite end of the spectrum (not abusive, just not very present), then your "small *t*" traumas may have created in you the feeling that no one will ever meet your needs in a romantic relationship, or maybe you engage in extremely risky social behaviors in an attempt to finally be noticed.

Case Histories of Overcoming Early Childhood Trauma

The following are four brief case histories of using EFT to overcome childhood trauma.

Casey grew up in a family in which substance abuse was ever-present until she was 9 years old, at which point her parents got divorced and her mother joined Alcoholics Anonymous. Casey's core issue was abandonment. As an adult, on a subconscious level, she felt unable to attract a partner and believed that, even if she could find the right guy, he would leave her. Through EFT, these beliefs became conscious, which led to her tapping on specific instances in which one or both of her parents had been too drunk to make dinner for her. Within a few months of her EFT sessions to clear these early traumas, Casey met Larry, and they remain happily married.

Trisha's father was demanding and controlling, always insisting that all the children in the family needed to be perfect. Trisha learned early in her life that if she wanted his approval and love she needed to dismiss her own needs in favor of his. This led to a lifelong pattern of always placing others' needs before her own—the stereotypical people-pleaser. She became a nurse and worked intensely in the care of her patients. This pattern continued when she started her own family; she took less and less care of her own needs. In her 30s, Trisha contracted fibromyalgia. With EFT, Trisha discovered that she was very uncomfortable setting limits with others, and that some part of her enjoyed having the chronic pain in order to point to a physical reason why she couldn't help others (secondary gain). It was as if her body created boundaries for her because she couldn't do this herself by simply saying no. Using EFT to clear her fears around setting clear boundaries, and finding out what she really wanted to be doing with her time, Trisha overcame all the symptoms of fibromyalgia. She is now a raw food caterer and is completely pain free.

Jerry's mother was emotionally violent and unpredictable. At an early age, he knew that his situation was volatile. In his words, "The shit could hit the fan at any moment." Jerry learned to be hyper-aware of how his mother was feeling, of her moods, and he tried as much as possible to avoid her. Jerry ended up marrying a woman who was exactly like his mother. In his 40s, Jerry developed allergies that left him debilitated most of the time. Jerry's EFT coach zeroed in on key events in his childhood involving his mother. Most were brief "small *t*" memories such as a look she gave him or the tone of voice she used with him. After a few months of EFT sessions, Jerry's allergic reactions are mostly gone and he has filed for divorce.

Jason's father controlled his mother in every imaginable way. He didn't allow her to drive a car, to work outside the home, or even to visit her own family during holidays. On the rare occasions that she asked for something, his father's reaction left the household shaking. Jason came to EFT at the insistence of his boss. Jason had been having angry outbursts and had left several people in his firm in tears during staff meetings. Jason had learned from his family that you had to be strong and that no one should ever be able to have the appearance of exerting power over you, or you'd risk being squashed. After four sessions, Jason resolved his anger management issue and was no longer at risk of losing his job.

In these four case histories, we see examples of stressful childhood family experiences that may have altered the adult nervous system response to stressful situations. In addition to the research cited earlier regarding brain waves, studies have explored the role of EFT in being able to reduce cortisol, one of the most important of the body's stress hormones. For example, Church, Yount, and Brooks (2012) examined cortisol levels in 83 subjects randomly assigned to a single session of EFT, talk therapy, or rest. Cortisol is the "master hormone" regulating many aspects of the body's stress response mechanisms, especially those associated with the autonomic nervous system. Their investigation found that anxiety and depression symptoms declined more than three times as much in the EFT group as in the talk therapy group. Cortisol levels in the rest and therapy groups declined at approximately the same rate, while cortisol in the EFT group declined significantly more. It may be that the effect that EFT has on reducing such stress hormones facilitates the individual's ability to downregulate his or her fight-or-flight response in stressful situations and perhaps take the opportunity to self-reflect and make healthier behavioral choices.

As these brief case histories demonstrate, disruptions to healthy connections and inner peace are imprinted in our minds at the deepest levels. These injuries have an innate desire to be understood, processed, and integrated into the whole of who we are through the lessons we learn from them. This occurs through a phenomenon known as recapitulation, reenactment, or repetition compulsion. We re-create similar experiences in our lives on a subconscious level, in an attempt to integrate these old experiences. Reenactment (as illustrated in the cases) can look like choosing the wrong romantic partners (with behaviors similar to that of their parents) or attracting employers or jobs that are less than ideal. When we use EFT to remove the charge from those childhood traumas, we leave behind the need for reenactments. Another way of stating this is that we are no longer in vibrational alignment with those events and therefore will not need to attract similar events to limit who we can ultimately become—fully actualized human beings.

Consistent application of EFT may neutralize negatively impacting events from our past and offer us the opportunity of seeing that many of these experiences have shaped us in positive ways as well. We can begin to see that we learned valuable lessons from those experiences. When we are able to discover this, we may well find that "it's never too late to have a happy childhood."

References

Anderson, C. M., Teicher, M. H., Polcari, A., & Renshaw, P. F. (2002). Abnormal T2 relaxation time in the cerebellar vermis of adults sexually abused in childhood: Potential role of the vermis in stress-enhanced risk for drug abuse. *Psychoneuroendocrinology, 27*, 231–244.

Church, D., Yount, G., & Brooks, A. (2012). The Effect of Emotional Freedom Techniques on stress biochemistry: A randomized controlled trial. *Journal of Nervous and Mental Disease, 200*(10), 891–896.

Felitti, V. J., Anda, R. F., Nordenberg, D., Williamson, D. F., Spitz, A. M., Edwards, V., Koss, M. P., & Marks, J. S. (1998). Relationship of childhood abuse and household dysfunction to many of the leading causes of death in adults, the Adverse Childhood Experiences (ACE) Study. *American Journal of Preventive Medicine, 14*(4), 245–258.

Frodl, T., Reinhold, E., Koutsouleris, N., Reiser, M., & Meisenzahl, E. M. (2010, October). Interaction of childhood stress with hippocampus and prefrontal cortex volume reduction in major depression. *Journal of Psychiatric Research, 44*(13), 799–807. doi:10.1016/j.jpsychires.2010.01.006.

Jones, A. (2011). Adverse childhood experiences are associated with risk for migraine later in life. *Neurology Reviews, 19*(5), 24–29. Retrieved from http://www.neurologyreviews.com/Article.aspx?ArticleId=z0t4yGrRnCk=&FullText=1

Lambrou, P. T., Pratt, G. J., & Chevalier, G. (2003). Physiological and psychological effects of a mind/body therapy on claustrophobia. *Subtle Energies & Energy Medicine, 14*, 239–251.

McCrory, E. J., De Brito, S. A., Sebastian, C. L., Mechelli, A., Bird, G., Kelly, P. A., & Viding, E. (2011, December 6). Heightened neural reactivity to threat in child victims of family violence. *Current Biology, 21*(23), R947–948. doi:10.1016/j.cub.2011.10.015

Minnesota Department of Health. (2011). Executive summary. *Adverse Childhood Experiences in Minnesota: Findings & recommendations based on the 2011 Minnesota Behavioral Risk Factor Surveillance System.* Retrieved from http://www.health.state.mn.us/divs/chs/brfss/ACE_ExecutiveSummary.pdf

Siegel, D. (1999). *The Developing Mind: How relationships and the brain interact to shape who we are.* New York, NY: Guilford Press.

Swingle, P. G. (2010). Emotional Freedom Techniques (EFT) as an effective adjunctive treatment in the neurotherapeutic treatment of seizure disorders. *Energy Psychology: Theory, Research, and Treatment, 2*(1), 27–37.

Swingle, P. G., Pulos, L., & Swingle, M. K. (2004). Neurophysiological indicators of EFT treatment of posttraumatic stress. *Subtle Energies & Energy Medicine, 15*(1), 75–86.

Perry, B., & Szalavitz, M. (2006). *The boy who was raised as a dog: And other stories from a child psychiatrist's notebook—What traumatized children can teach us about loss, love, and healing.* New York, NY: Basic Books.

Teicher, M. H. (2002, March). Scars that won't heal: The neurobiology of child abuse. *Scientific American, 286*, 68–75.

Teicher, M. H., Dumont, N. L., Ito, Y., Vaituzis, C., Giedd, J. N., & Andersen, S. L. (2004, July 15). Childhood neglect is associated with reduced corpus callosum area. *Biological Psychiatry, 56*(2), 80–85.

Teicher, M. H., Glod, C. A., Surrey, J., & Swett, C. (1993). Early childhood abuse and limbic system ratings in adult psychiatric outpatients. *Journal of Neuropsychiatry and Clinical Neurosciences, 5*(3), 301–306.

Chapter 13
Resolving the Frozen Forms of Parents and Children: Energy Treatment Focused on Archaic States and Their Triggers

Willem Lammers

Abstract

This chapter describes archaic roots of trauma, phobias, and addictions in terms of the Inner Parent and the Inner Child, with the help of psychoanalytical and transactional analysis theory. The chapter also introduces techniques for the resolution of these roots with the help of energy psychology treatment methods. The concepts presented here will support professionals in analyzing and processing traumatic events of their clients, on a deeper level than the treatment on the level of single symptoms. The concepts and methods presented here are applied in the context of a stable working alliance. Direct treatment of underlying aspects of the client's issues by means of energy approaches seems to add to the long-term effectiveness of energy psychology treatment. Compared to traditional models of psychotherapy, results seem to be achieved more rapidly—with less pain. This model can be applied in combination with any system of energy psychology, like Emotional Freedom Techniques (EFT), Thought Field Therapy (TFT), Be Set Free Fast (BSFF), Tapas Acupressure Techniques (TAT), Energy Diagnostic and Treatment Methods (EDxTM; Gallo, 1999, 2000). With the help of Logosynthesis (Lammers, 2008) distinct energetic representations of the Inner Parent can be completely resolved. An earlier version of the model described in this chapter was published in Fred Gallo's *Energy Psychology in Psychotherapy* (Lammers, 2002).

Keywords: archaic state, introject, inner parent, inner child, logosynthesis

Willem Lammers, MSc, DPsych, TSTA, is a chartered psychologist and psychotherapist, specializing in the boundaries of body, mind, and spirit. He is founder, author, and trainer of Logosynthesis, an energy treatment system based solely on the power of words. Send correspondence to Willem Lammers, Pardellgasse 8a, 7304 Maienfeld, Switzerland, or info@logosynthesis.net.

Ego States

The concepts of Inner Child and Inner Parent are derived from Eric Berne's transactional analysis (TA), in which they are referred to as Child and Parent ego states. Because in TA the Child and the Parent ego states also refer to social roles, I prefer the use of the terms "Inner Child" and "Inner Parent" for the purpose of this chapter. They refer to a phenomenological reality in which the person meets the demands of daily life from different attitudes:

- An adult position firmly rooted in the sensory, emotional, and cognitive reality of the present;
- An archaic position that contains reactivated and reexperienced events: the Inner Child;
- An archaic position containing or embodying introjected material from significant others in childhood: the Inner Parent.

The purpose of any form of coaching, counseling, and psychotherapy is to reduce the influence of archaic positions in the perception and interpretation of the here-and-now.

The Inner Child

The roots of the Inner Child concept are located in psychoanalysis, especially in the work of Paul Federn and Edoardo Weiss (Berne, 1961; Stewart, 1992). They used the term *ego state* for the totality of a person's mental and bodily experience at any given moment. Federn (1952) suggests that people may sometimes reexperience ego states dating from earlier stages in their lives. He introduced two types of ego states:

- The first state is an autonomous set of feelings, attitudes, and behaviors that are adaptive to the current reality. In transactional analysis, this set is referred to as the Adult ego state (Berne, 1961).
- In the second state, earlier developmental stages are reexperienced. This state consists of archaic relicts from any given moment in the person's childhood. It corresponds with the Child ego state in transactional analysis.

Transactional analysis (Berne, 1961) developed these concepts for use in the consulting room. Goulding and Goulding (1979), integrating theory and techniques from TA and Gestalt therapy started to treat the Inner Child as a more or less separate client. The approach of Goulding and Goulding contained three steps:

1. They asked the client to go back to the moment in childhood when he formed a belief or made a decision about himself, other people, or the quality of life.
2. They invited him to review this decision on the basis of new information provided by the therapist and by adult parts of the client.
3. They invited the client to "re-decide" and to create a new belief based on the revised frame of reference.

Since the work of the Gouldings and other colleagues, the treatment of archaic states has become part of many schools of guided change.

The Inner Parent

Eric Berne (1961) observed a third set of ego states in which experiences and behaviors seemed to be copied from someone else: the Parent ego state—Inner Parent for the purpose of this chapter. Berne (1966, p. 366) called this a "borrowed" ego state: the person seemed to copy the thoughts, feelings, and behaviors of parental figures. This concept was adapted from Fairbairn (1952, p. 171), who assumed an antilibidinal ego, opposed to the libidinal ego, which represented the part of the self that is oriented toward fulfillment of biological and psychological needs. John McNeel (1976) developed the Parent interview to explore the contents of this Parent ego state as a therapeutic technique. Sharon Dashiell (1978) went one step further, and started to treat the archaic representations of the parental figures as if they were real clients. From McNeel and Dashiell, the use of energy psychotherapy procedures to change Inner Parent states is a logical next step.

McNeel's Parent Interview

John McNeel (1976) developed a technique to work with introjects of significant others, which allows for a cognitive restructuring of Inner Parent contents. His *parent interview* is a specific form of the psychotherapeutic two-chair technique, as developed by Frederick Perls (1969). In this method, the therapist sets up a role-play with the client, in which the latter acts as a significant other. The most common way to begin this interview is to ask the client to take the role of the parent for the duration of the interview, and then to ask, "What's your name, Mom?" or "What's your name, Dad?" Then the therapist elicits the parent's feelings and thoughts in response to the son's or daughter's needs. In the course of the process the client discovers how his own needs or behavior were once challenging to the parent, or that the latter was involved in personal, family, or work issues, which led to neglect of the needs of the child. The technique is based on the assumption that the original parent did not act with malice, but from a threatened or exhausted position (McNeel, 1976, p. 66). The parent interview provides the client with a visceral appreciation of the experience of the significant other and starts to appreciate the parent as a separate human being with an idiosyncratic frame of reference. Due to his interpretation of parental messages, the Inner Child may have held beliefs such as "I'm unlovable" or "There's something wrong with me" or "It's my fault," which are contradicted by the information from the Inner Parent in the interview. Clients have learned to limit their own behavior in reaction to these amplified misperceptions of their parents' behavior. The parent interview helps clients realize that their negative beliefs were based on a misunderstanding of the world of their parents at the time, thus enabling them to change to a more realistic perspective. The technique allows the client to replace the previous conflict between a powerless, vulnerable Inner Child and an overly powerful Inner Parent by adequate reality testing. This leads to cognitive restructuring of the clients' frame of reference regarding his past and his relationships to significant others.

Dashiell's Parent Resolution Process

Sharon Dashiell's method goes one step further: into actual psychotherapy with the parental introject as if he or she were a client. She suggests that the Inner Parent can be accessed, offered new information, and thus be helped to transform unresolved stored feelings. This allows the Inner Parent to react in a healthy way to the Inner Child, which changes the internal dialogue between Parent and Child from repressive conflict to support and contact. The process is not limited to introjects of natural parents; it can also reveal and resolve issues from the psychological presence of peers in the family and in school, and of individuals from previous generations. The issues treated in this "psychotherapy with the Inner Parent" are limited only by the content of the therapy contract with the actual client.

The following techniques are firmly rooted in the tradition of humanistic psychology. For the experienced professional in energy psychology, they offer a bridge from traditional psychotherapy to the energy psychology methods in this book.

Operating Assumptions and Theory

McNeel's and Dashiell's work contain the assumption that when a child is not able to process threatening, confusing, or stressful information from the environment, this information is transformed into a separate part: an *introject* (Ferenczi, 1916). Such an introject stores the sensory information from the environment in the moment of distress. In time, an Inner Parent develops. The Inner Parent consists of myriad parts: all introjects, all parental representations, in the life of the client. Each introject or Inner Parent part is connected to a corresponding Inner Child part, which cannot process the information from the parent. This part is frozen, and child development comes to a stop. In terms of Goulding and Goulding (1979), the child makes a survival decision to manage the complex information from the outside world. The psychoanalyst Kernberg (1975) would describe this structure of an introject in combination with a stereotyped reaction as an *object relation*.

In an energy psychology frame of reference, the Inner Parent as well as the Inner Child are more or less coherent sets of thought fields (Callahan, 1985) or frozen energy structures. They're limiting the free flow of energy within people and between people and the world around them.

In energy psychology terms, the Inner Parent can be seen as a set of energy structures representing frozen sensory representations of people, objects, and events, which couldn't be processed by the person at a certain age. The Inner Child is a corresponding set of energetic representations of a child of that age, bound within the energy system of an adult person, with a full spectrum of emotions, thoughts, values, and behaviors. By definition, this means that parts of the person are developmentally arrested at a specific age—by traumatizing events.

Trauma Between the Inner Parent and the Inner Child

In trauma, parts of the Inner Parent trigger stereotyped reactions of parts of the Inner Child. The processing of significant events is locked in a repetitive dialogue between those parts. Adult parts may not suffer from this blockage, their energy will flow freely, and the person will still continue to develop. Every human being has developmentally arrested parts due to unprocessed traumatic events. In the brain, an important role seems to be played by the limbic system (Van der Kolk, MacFarlane, & Weisaeth, 1996).

Many methods for trauma processing focus on the Inner Child and leave neglecting or abusive Inner Parent structures in place. They engage adult ego states as sources of new information or as mediators in the internal dialogue. This works fine as long as stress levels are average. Whenever stress levels rise again, however, the internal dialogue between the oppressive Inner Parent and the vulnerable Inner Child will be resumed as long as treatment of the Inner Parent has not taken place.

The procedures introduced here are designed to resolve these frozen structures, and restore the free flow of energy within the person and in the interaction with his environment.

Inner Parent Resolution as an Option for Treatment

To deal with the Inner Child, the most effective way is the neutralization or even the complete resolution of the Inner Parent. The Inner Child is divided into thousands of aspects, and each one is firmly connected to specific aspects of the Inner Parent. When these introjects are neutralized, nothing can activate the contents of the Inner Child anymore, and the treated aspects of the Inner Child will be resolved, replaced by free flowing adult energy.

Inner Parent Resolution is based on McNeel and Dashiell's work in the sense that parts of the Inner Parent are treated as if they were clients, in different ways:

- The Inner Parent can be accessed to provide information to the client to resolve conflicts or confusion in the Inner Child;
- New information can be made available to the Inner Parent, which allows for a change in the introject's frame of reference;
- The Inner Parent can go through a therapeutic change itself, and be treated for issues like phobias or psychic trauma;
- The Inner Parent is resolved as a whole.

In general, Inner Parent Resolution work is remarkably easy compared to addressing Inner Child parts. The Inner Parent structures are frozen thought forms installed at a certain age of the client. Clients perceive them as being different from themselves, while they directly identify with Inner Child structures: These feel "real" for the client, even though these structures are completely out of touch with the current potential of the person.

Inner Parent Resolution: Treatment Steps

To dissolve introjects you need a strong working alliance. The client must feel at ease in the working relationship and be willing to look beyond the surface of his daily life. Then you can identify and address issues like limiting beliefs, fears, or traumatic events. Once you have a clear issue to work with, you let the client go back in time and find a situation, which involved a parent and which is related to the client's issue. Then you guide the client through the following steps:

1. Let the client take a position in space or sit in a dedicated chair for the child that made the experience, and ask the person to "be" the child.
2. Now explore and activate the experience of the child, the accompanying pain and suffering, and the corresponding 0–10 score on the scale for subjective units of discomfort/distress (SUD). Stay in this position only as long as necessary to assess the experience and the SUD level, and from there ask the client to find a position in space for the parent.
3. When you've found this position in space, let the client go there and assume a typical body position of the parent involved, and to *become* this parent. You can also assign a dedicated chair for the parent and let the client move to that chair.
4. Make contact with the parental introject by saying hello, and asking, "What's your name, Mom/Dad?"

5. Ask the client as the parent to tell you about thoughts and feelings, especially regarding the client as a child, in the situation the client identified.
6. Ask the parent to describe her/his own life circumstances that led to the reaction that was so painful for the child.
7. Identify from this information a basic treatment issue of the Inner Parent, like a traumatic event or a phobia.
8. Treat this issue with energy-based methods like EFT, TFT, BSFF, TAT, or Logosynthesis.
9. When the SUD levels are down significantly, ask the parent to look at the child the sequence started with, and to tell the child how he/she thinks and feels about this child now.
10. Thank the parent for the cooperation, let the client leave the Inner Parent seat or position, and change to the Inner Child's, with the words "Now be you as a child again."
11. Ask the client how this makes a difference for him/herself as a child. Usually, the client experiences enormous relief, and is able to relate to the parental figure in a new way.
12. Let the client leave the position or the chair of the Inner Child and move to a new position, representing the client in the here-and-now. Let the client look back at the incident from an adult perspective, and allow for cognitive integration of the experience and future pacing for the type of circumstances that had triggered the symptom.

Usually there is a deep relief after the treatment of introjects. Once one aspect of the Inner Parent has been treated, other aspects or parental figures can be addressed as well. Also issues of peers, friends, school comrades, grandparents, and earlier generations can be resolved this way. It is amazing to see how parents' repressive or destructive behaviors appear in earlier ancestors. Because these are all "just" rigid energy structures, they tend to be resolved at an amazing pace.

The treatment continues through new cycles until a new kind of dialogue between the Inner Parent and the Inner Child becomes possible. This might take several sessions.

During this process, unconditional support of the Inner Child by the therapist is essential, as the Inner Parent can be really nasty at times.

The Inner Child as a Set of Frozen Reactions to Triggers from the Inner Parent

Many clients present symptoms that don't seem to relate to their present environment. They fear entering an elevator, they react as if their boss is going to beat them up, or as if the next board meeting will decide about life and death. Such events trigger stereotyped emotions, physical symptoms, and limiting beliefs. In reality, these symptoms are aspects of the Inner Child: frozen reactions to parental introjects, activated by people or events in the client's current life. To identify and access the corresponding introjects you will usually start with an exploration of Inner Child experiences, focusing on recurrent emotions or bodily sensations.

Flash Questions

Once a recurrent physical or emotional symptom has been identified, for example, a pit in the stomach, I use *flash questions* to let the client access traumatic memories without rational interference. I tell the client that I will ask a question, and that the client should give an immediate reaction, a yes or a no, without thinking. Here is an example for a client with stage fright:

Have you experienced this sensation before you were 12? Yes or no?
Yes.
Before 6? Yes or no?
Yes.
Before 3? Yes or no?
No.
So there's something between 3 and 6. Is it before 4?
Yes.
So you were 3 when you had these sensations for the first time. What's the first thing that comes up when you imagine you're 3 years old now and you have this feeling?
My mother.

Here we have discovered a frozen connection at the age of 3—between an introject of the client's mother as a trigger and the tension in the pit of his stomach as a reaction. The introject is activated unconsciously in the client's adult life, in this case when he's asked to present in the boardroom. There it will lead to the stage fright reaction pattern. Once a childhood experience has been identified, you ask the client to be the child he has been in that concrete situation and describe it with the help of concrete perceptual labels, like:

> *Your mother is there. Where is she in the room? In front of you? Behind you? Above you? Below you? More left? More right?*
> *She's right in front of me.*
> *How do you know she's there? Do you see her? Hear her? Feel her?*
> *I see her standing right in front of me. She's very tall.*
> *What do you feel when you see her in front of you?*
> *I'm very scared, my heart is palpitating, and I've this knot in my stomach.*

Resolving Childhood Trauma

Childhood trauma often consists of an undifferentiated lump of sensory perceptions, emotions, and cognitions, from which reactions can be triggered by occasions only remotely reminiscent of the event, as in the board meeting. The first steps in resolving such a lump are differentiations:

1. Between triggers and reactions. Triggers are introjects, frozen energy structures of what the person sees, hears, senses, smells, or tastes in the moment of a traumatic incident. The emotions and physical sensations of the client are reactions to the original triggers, frozen in the moment of that incident.
2. Between the present and the past. The client tends to react to incidents in the present as if something terrible is threatening him now. In fact, the current situation is not dangerous at all, but it reactivates painful memories of past incidents.
3. Between what really happened and what could have happened. Many memories become traumatic, because they activate fantasies of what could have happened, not because of what actually happened.

When people learn to differentiate between the frozen perception of an incident and their frozen reactions to it, they can start to really live in the present—not in the past or in a fantasy. People will stop suffering once the original trigger—the archaic memory or fantasy—is separated from the original reaction, as well as from the present reality.

There are different ways to reduce the triggering influence of an introject:

- Interpretation is the classical way to disconnect the past from the present. The client learns to understand what happened in a new way.
- Treatment of the symptom that appears in reaction to the trigger. This is the common way used now in EFT, EMDR, and other systems of trauma treatment.
- Addressing the trigger directly. This intervention was developed in Logosynthesis, but you can use it just as well with EFT. Once the trigger has been neutralized or even completely resolved, the reaction of the client will weaken or disappear. The present environment of the client will not reactivate the trigger anymore, and in the end the client will fulfill his adult task in the boardroom.

Jackie's Fantasies

Jackie (all case names have been changed) suffered from a severe acrophobia for many years. She had to work on a ladder from time to time, and this was agonizing for her. When, in the session, she imagined standing on a ladder, she felt a strong tension in her neck and shoulders. When I asked her to go back in time and to find earlier occasions in which she experienced this sensation, Jackie became aware of memories of a traffic accident and of a panic attack on the top of a high tower. The earliest incident she could identify was at age 6, when she had fallen from a balcony through the glass roof of a conservatory. In the memory of this incident there were various scenes: She fell through the glass roof, she saw her bleeding feet surrounded by broken glass, and the most significant moment was when her mother came in and screamed at her, "You could have died!" In a flash, she saw her dead body, a small corpse in a white coffin, with her mum crying her heart out. When this scene was reactivated, the SUD level was at 10.

When this scene had become active for Jackie, I asked her to "become" her mum. In the following parent interview, "Mum" told me how she was shocked by the image of her little daughter bleeding, with broken glass spread all over the place. I then went through a tapping sequence with "Mum" for this image. During the first cycle, she was already relieved: "Indeed! Jackie could have died, but that scene looked much worse than it actually was, with all the blood and broken glass!" I thanked "Mum" for the interview and let Jackie be her own self again, as a 6-year-old. The SUD level was down to 0.

When we went back on the timeline, the disturbing incidents we had found before had also lost their emotional charge. When Jackie now thought of standing on a ladder again, the SUD rating for the fear was down to 0.

This example illustrates how a client can freeze in reaction to the introject of a shocked mother. Little Jackie had hoped that her mother would comfort her in her distress, but she was screamed at instead. The real trauma was not caused by falling through the glass roof, but by Mum's unexpected reaction. As a consequence the image and voice of Mum were stored as introjects, static energy structures, which triggered fear as soon as Jackie was standing on the ladder. Unconsciously, the ladder activated Jackie's memory of the childhood trauma.

In this case I treated the mother introject as if it were a client, with a normal EFT procedure. This resolved the frozen connection between the trigger introject and the fear reaction. As a result, the memory of her mother's panic was not reactivated when she was standing on a ladder.

Memories that at first sight do not contain traumatic material can trigger catastrophic fantasies. In this case, the mother's reaction triggered an inner fantasy video in which the client was lying dead in the midst of splinters, found by a mother in deep sorrow. For the Inner Child of a certain age there is no difference between real life events and fantasies about what could have happened. Therefore, imagined traumatic events must be treated the same way as events that actually happened.

Treating Inner Child Reactions Through the Inner Parent

The effective treatment of Inner Child states needs to involve the Inner Parent. If the Inner Parent contains disturbed or traumatized states, the development of the child will be arrested in reaction to thought fields, the frozen energy structures of those states. Treating the Inner Parent brings relief to an anxious or confused Inner Child, and its original reaction will not be triggered anymore. When the person is asked to identify with the Inner Parent and tap, problems disappear very easily. The reason for this is that the Inner Parent is a set of relatively simple energy structures: It's the composite of the frozen perceptions of a historical person at different times and places. It's not a real person; it's an energy structure built up as a reaction to the child's intuitive, but often distorted logic in the unexpected experience or painful situations. Sometimes the parental introject cannot cope or does not want to cope with the needs of the child. Once treated, the Inner Parent can let go of such an attitude, and thus free the person from the developmental arrest. The Inner Child follows changes in the Inner Parent. Once the repetitive inner dialogue between an all-powerful Inner Parent and a wounded Inner Child is interrupted, the deepest cause of the client's symptom disappears. This becomes clear when the client becomes aware of the present for the first time, with the whole of its potential. Inner Parent Resolution contains the following steps:

1. Identify, along a timeline, a number of significant incidents in the past.
2. Ask the client to feel the way he or she felt at the time of each incident.
3. Find the earliest incident.
4. If the child did not get sufficient support, contact and treat the introject to a point where the Inner Parent is able to positively support the young child.
5. Move to the Inner Child position, and check if it can make a positive contact with the Inner Parent.
6. Move back to the here-and-now situation of the client, for integration and future pacing.

Inner Parent Resolution is particularly useful to relieve trauma, phobias, and addictions rooted in early childhood, in distress or disturbances of parents, or in a family tradition.

Cathy's Concert

My musician friend Cathy called me because she was very nervous about her performance that night—her first solo performance in front of a large audience. A few weeks before she had given a performance that failed. She plays a very subtle instrument and the people in the hall were very noisy, so that she had not been able to build up a real contact with her audience. Cathy was very afraid this would happen again. During the conversation, I picked up a fear of not being heard. I asked a few flash questions about the age at which this had started, and we ended at 5. At that time, something had happened that had made her decide to stop talking, and she hadn't said a word for half a year. Then she was guided into speaking again by a very gentle teacher. When I asked her to be the 5-year-old child, Cathy felt very distressed by her mother. I asked her to become her mother, who was then interviewed. The Inner Parent felt very bad and helpless about not being able to make contact with her daughter, and showed this to her daughter as anger. I guided the mother introject through a number of EFT sequences for that, and she softened toward the child. In order to construct a positive and supportive inner dialogue, the client switched back and forth between Inner Child and Inner Parent a number of times. Every time the mother introject was treated, a dialogue between Parent and Child was invited, until the mother was able to really see and hear the 5-year-old. The little girl reacted by becoming confident and being able to speak. I then guided her back to the present and to the recent concert and checked how that felt now for her: There was no problem at all. When I asked her about the concert that evening, at first she couldn't believe that the fear was gone, then she started laughing. The concert was a success.

Resolving the Inner Parent with the Help of Logosynthesis

In the previous examples, we applied EFT to the Inner Parent, to neutralize the negative charge of the introject. You can also go one step further and dissolve the energy structure of the Inner Parent altogether, with the help of Logosynthesis (Lammers, 2008; Lammers & Fredi, 2010). Logosynthesis is a treatment model that dissolves frozen energy structures in and around the client by applying the power of words: The client says specific sentences, which have the effect of moving energy and dissolving archaic energy structures. In this application of the Logosynthesis treatment system, the client explores a traumatic event and identifies the accompanying representation of the Inner Parent. The client perceives the parental figure of that moment as an image, a sound, or a felt energy in space—above or below, left or right, in front of or behind the client. This representation of the parent triggers an Inner Child reaction in the client, as physical sensation or a painful emotion, which can be expressed in a SUD score. When the representation of the Inner Parent of that traumatic moment has been identified, the client can disempower it or even dissolve it by simple speaking three sentences, with a processing pause after each one. These sentences are:

1. *I retrieve all my energy, bound up in this representation of this person, and take it back to the right place in my Self.*
2. *I remove all energy of this person, related to this representation, from all of my cells, all of my body and my personal space, and send it back to where it truly belongs.*
3. *I retrieve all of my energy, bound up in all my reactions to this representation of this person and take it back to the right place in my Self.*

As a result of speaking the sentences and letting them work, the distressing representation of the parent will change or disappear completely. If it changes, the procedure is repeated for each new image, until the distress has been dissolved or reduced to a bearable level for the client. If the representation of the Inner Parent doesn't lead to inadequate reactions anymore, the client will have access to all available resources as an adult person.

References

Berne, E. (1961). *Transactional analysis in psychotherapy.* New York, NY: Grove Press.

Berne, E. (1966). *Principles of group treatment.* New York, NY: Grove Press.

Callahan, R. (1985). *The five minute phobia cure.* Wilmington, DE: Enterprise.

Dashiell, S. (1978). The parent resolution process. *Transactional Analysis Journal, 8*(4), 289–294.

Fairbairn, W. R. D. (1952). *Psychoanalytic studies of the personality.* London, UK: Tavistock.

Federn, P. (1952). *Ego psychology and the psychoses.* New York, NY: Basic Books.

Ferenczi, S. (1916). Introjection and transference. In S. Ferenczi, *Contributions to psychoanalysis* (Ernest Jones, trans.; pp. 30–80). Boston, MA: Richard G. Badger. (Original work published 1909).

Gallo, F. P. (1999). *Energy psychology: Explorations at the interface of energy, cognition, behavior, and health.* Boca Raton, FL: CRC Press.

Gallo, F. P. (2000). *Energy diagnostic and treatment methods.* New York, NY: W. W. Norton.

Gallo, F. P. (Ed.) (2002). *Energy psychology in psychotherapy: A comprehensive sourcebook. The Norton energy psychology series.* New York, NY: W. W. Norton.

Goulding, R. & Goulding, M. (1979). *Changing lives through redecision therapy.* New York, NY: Brunner-Mazel.

Kernberg, O. F. (1975). *Borderline conditions and pathological narcissism.* New York, NY: Aronson.

Lammers, W. (2002). Inner child, inner parent resolution. In F. P. Gallo (Ed.), *Energy psychology in psychotherapy: A comprehensive sourcebook. The Norton energy psychology series.* New York, NY: W. W. Norton.

Lammers, W. (2008). *Logosynthesis: Change through the magic of words.* Maienfeld, Switzerland: IAS Publications.

Lammers, W. & Fredi, A. (2010). *Restoring the flow* [e-book]. Retrieved from http://www.logosynthesis.net/docs/logosynthesis.primer.pdf.

McNeel, J. (1976). The parent interview. *Transactional Analysis Journal, 6*(1), 61–68.

Perls, F. S. (1969). *Gestalt therapy verbatim.* Lafayette, CA: Real People Press.

Stewart, I. (1992). *Eric Berne.* London, UK: Sage.

Van der Kolk, B., MacFarlane, A. C., & Weisaeth, L. (Eds.). (1996). *Traumatic stress.* New York, NY: Guilford Press.

Chapter 14
Important Aspects of the Healing Relationship in EFT: Bringing the Unconscious into Consciousness
Judith H. Frost

Abstract

Emotional Freedom Techniques (EFT) has been rapidly gaining popularity over the last several decades. It's been a heady and exciting time for those leading the way in this cutting-edge healing field. Now EFT is coming of age with the establishment of Clinical EFT, which has been validated extensively in research studies to meet the designation of "evidence-based" practice. Extensive trainings in the methodology of Clinical EFT are being conducted all over the world, turning out fine practitioners, among them mental health clinicians, coaches, and lay people, who perform Clinical EFT in a technically excellent way. One area that has not yet been widely attended to, however, is that of the role of the healing relationship between practitioner and client. Many studies have shown the vital importance of the healing relationship in achieving the best treatment outcomes. This chapter is intended to explore one of the least understood aspects of that relationship: the interplay between client transference and practitioner countertransference. Many practitioners are not aware of the dynamic process of transference and countertransference that is present in the treatment room during EFT sessions. This chapter particularly focuses on the recognition and use of countertransference to help practitioners take advantage of the opportunities it provides and the pitfalls that should be avoided.

Keywords: EFT Expert, trauma, energy psychology ethics, transference, countertransference, healing therapeutic relationship

Judith H. Frost, MSW, LiCSW, is a therapist and nationally respected EFT Expert on a mission to help people heal. A certified clinical trauma professional, her passion is assisting people who have experienced severe trauma including rape, accidents, and war. She is an EFT Universe trainer and enthusiastic dog lover. Send correspondence to Judith H. Frost, 2330 North Narrows Drive, Tacoma, WA 98406, or Judith@tap4healing.com.

Introduction

Emotional Freedom Techniques (EFT) has been rapidly gaining popularity over the last several decades. It's been a heady and exciting time for those leading the way in this cutting-edge healing field. Practitioners have experimented with adding and subtracting tapping algorithms and looked for new applications for the tapping. Now EFT is coming of age with the establishment of "Clinical EFT," which has been validated extensively in research studies to meet the designation of "evidence-based" practice. Clinical EFT has been shown to be effective in a variety of emotional and physical conditions, including posttraumatic stress disorder (PTSD) and anxiety (Church, 2013).

Extensive trainings and mentoring in the methodology of Clinical EFT are being conducted all over the world, turning out fine practitioners, including mental health clinicians, coaches, and lay people, who perform Clinical EFT in a technically excellent way. One area that has not yet been widely attended to, however, is that of the role of the healing relationship between practitioner and client. Many studies have shown the vital importance of the healing relationship in achieving the best treatment outcomes (Horvath & Symonds, 1991).

In recognition of the importance of the healing relationship, Feinstein (2011, pp. 142–145) devoted four pages of his *Ethics Handbook for Energy Healing Practitioners* to proper aspects of creating and maintaining a healing relationship within the context of energy work. It goes far beyond just creating rapport with a client, and clearly describes the responsibilities of the practitioner in creating a safe healing relationship. It is a "must study" document for all Clinical EFT practitioners.

This chapter is intended to explore one of the least understood aspects of that relationship: the dynamic interplay between client transference and practitioner countertransference. It is important to note that, although this article addresses trauma treatment specifically, the principles apply equally to all Clinical EFT treatment for any other issue.

Even licensed mental health clinicians get sweaty palms thinking about issues of transference and countertransference, so it is unrealistic to think that lay people who practice EFT will fully understand their implications. Sigmund Freud (1977) coined these terms at the dawn of psychoanalysis, yet these concepts still have enormous value to practitioners of every sort of modality today. They refer to the unconscious processes and energy exchanges that are present in every healing relationship that, if understood and used appropriately, can augment the healing effects of any therapeutic method. If not understood and attended to, the action of these processes can cause unnecessary rifts in the healing relationship and even harm to the client (Dalenberg, 2010).

Transference and Countertransference in the Context of Trauma Work

In practical terms, *transference* refers to the client's bringing his feelings, ideas, and beliefs about other important figures from his past and projecting them onto the practitioner. Transference is often manifested as a sexual attraction toward a practitioner, but it can show up in many other forms such as rage, mistrust, or extreme dependence. Another manifestation of transference is idolizing the practitioner, placing her on a pedestal or conveying "guru" status upon her. Since few people can actually live up to these expectations, it is particularly insidious because not managing this well sets the client up for disappointment and replication of prior betrayals (Dalenberg, 2010, p. 6).

Since practitioners are human beings too, *countertransference* will also occur. This happens when the practitioner unconsciously brings her feelings, ideas, and beliefs about other important figures from her past and projects them onto the client. Add to that the energetic attunement that EFT practitioners already have with their clients. The practitioner's awareness of her own countertransference is even more critical than understanding the client's transference. Not only does this understanding help practitioners regulate their emotions and actions in the healing relationship, but also their attunement to their own feelings makes them aware of any issues they may need to process on their own or in their own healing work (Dalenberg, 2010, pp. 7–11).

Because of the intense emotional content of much trauma work, countertransference tends to be even more intense than in other types of healing work (Brown, 2012; Dalenberg, 2010). In addition, countertransference issues appear to develop more rapidly in energy work than in traditional therapies because the practitioner's intuition is much more engaged (Hover-Kramer, 2002, p. 96).

Yet another type of energy exchange is present in trauma work. *Trauma-specific* transference and countertransference occurs in the context of treating both acute stress and post-traumatic stress (Dalenberg, 2010). This kind of transference and countertransference may manifest in powerful feelings and beliefs evolved from the trauma itself, combined with those from life pretrauma. Traumatic events are, by definition, fraught with powerful feelings and beliefs for both the practitioner and the survivor. Often the practitioner has a strong emotional response to the fact of the trauma as well as to its effect.

EFT practitioners are human beings with their own healed and unhealed traumas, and, as a result, it is virtually impossible not to be triggered at times during trauma work. If the practitioner is unaware of, or chooses to ignore, feelings that arise during treatment, her judgment and attunement to the client may be impaired, resulting in less effective treatment. On the other hand, an aware practitioner's use of such feelings and beliefs can greatly enrich the client's healing experience. The difference is the practitioner's awareness of her own experience so she can use this information to make appropriate therapeutic choices on behalf of the client.

Countertransference has traditionally been seen as something practitioners needed to "root out" or prevent. The more recent view of countertransference, however, is that it's a valuable tool that a fully aware practitioner can use to enrich the work. Powerful, uncharacteristic feelings that arise toward a client are a signal that countertransference is afoot (Dalenberg, 2010, pp. 5–6).

Case Study: Julia

Ron became very angry with his client, Julia, as she recounted a difficult interaction with her son during an EFT session. Ron flushed with anger and had sharp feedback for Julia about her interaction with her son. Julia left bathed in guilt and tears, shocked by the harshness of her practitioner's comments.

During consultation, Ron was asked about his relationship with his own mother, and he talked about things she had said that were traumatic. He was near tears as he told his story. He had unknowingly been hearing his own mother's voice from a place of the old, unhealed wounds of a 6-year-old child. His uncharacteristic anger was a signal that powerful countertransference was at work.

EFT practitioners sometimes believe that Clinical EFT is such a powerful healing tool that they won't be subject to these reactions because tapping with the client will dissolve any issue of their own that arises as well as the client's. Although this is sometimes the case, issues are multifactorial with many aspects and, therefore, complacency does not serve either practitioner or client. The ethics of the profession dictate that practitioners must not use client interaction to work out their own issues, as the client's interests are always primary. The best practice is to develop a keen awareness of familiar feelings (anger, helplessness) and unaccustomed feelings (rage, contempt) that come up during healing sessions (Feinstein, 2011, p. 15).

Ron did not understand that even EFT practitioners are not immune to being unconsciously triggered by their own past trauma or by their interaction with the client's trauma. It was Ron's unawareness of his countertransference that caused his harmful reaction to the client's statements. Had he been aware of, or even just curious about, his unaccustomed anger, he might have prevented a serious therapeutic error.

Consider that even our everyday relationships are full of the effects of everyone's transferential experiences from the past. It would be naïve to think that healing interactions won't be. Practitioners who underestimate the power of these interactions leave themselves open to making therapeutic errors, even creating the environment for lawsuits (Vesper, 1998, p. 5). Becoming aware of the potential for therapeutic error means developing intentional awareness and curiosity about your own responses to a client's material. It also means regularly engaging in consultation with other professionals to get a clearer vision of what may be going on.

Countertransference in Single-Session EFT

A unique feature of Clinical EFT is the rapidity with which clients can get relief from their trauma symptoms. In an article in *Energy Psychology,* Larry Burk (2010) described the rapid recovery from stress-related symptoms experienced by three different clients after motor vehicle accidents. This is not uncommon for clients to experience with skillfully applied Clinical EFT.

Even when practitioners work with clients for such a short time, it's still important to stay alert to the effects of countertransference. The relationship need not be long and complicated for countertransference to occur. Clients will benefit from working with a fully aware practitioner even in the briefest of treatment situations.

The Therapeutic Relationship in Trauma Work

We all need and want a variety of relationships throughout our life. Although this primary need is biologically determined to promote survival of the species, the exact nature of the relationships we actually have depends on early experiences. For example, attachment research has demonstrated that the effect of the parent's attitude toward the infant predisposes the child's later behavior with the parent (Fonagy, Steele, & Steele, 1991, p. 901). The child's secure or insecure experience in infancy is highly predictive of the quality of later relationships with people other than the parents (Sroufe, 1983, p. 5).

In new situations, we transfer those early-formed expectations onto the other person. Present behavior combines a set of realistic perceptions, thoughts, and feelings about today mixed with the understandings and beliefs developed from prior traumatic and nontraumatic experiences (Hughes, 1999). Most practitioners recognize these realities with the client in relation to their interactions in the outside world, but fail to understand them in the context of the therapeutic relationship. In addition, they fail to understand these realities regarding *themselves* within the therapeutic relationship.

Case Study: Christine

Tony watched his client, Christine, sob heavily after recounting her fears after being kidnapped and raped by three armed men. She had been held for three days, repeatedly abused and threatened with a knife. The men told her if she told anyone they would kill her. Tony felt protective of Christine, wanting to shield her from the fear and from the men. She had no place to go where she felt safe. The treatment helped her calm down but did not allay her fears. Tony wrestled with his fear for her as she left. He knew there was nothing he could do, and he felt helpless.

At 10 years old, Tony had been designated the "man of the family," responsible for three younger siblings after his father's death. As a result, "helpless" was a familiar and intolerable feeling for him. He found himself obsessing about what might happen to Christine. It occurred to him that his mother, who lived in the next town, had a spare room and that Christine would be safe there. He decided that the perfect solution was for her to stay with his mother until the police found the perpetrators. His mother generously agreed to the arrangement, and he called Christine to offer her the room.

Tony was unaware of the countertransference that led him to "rescue" his client and commit serious boundary and ethics violations. Was that the first time he had acted on such feelings, or was this an ongoing issue for him in dealing with his clients? Tony certainly would have benefited from continued work on his unhealed trauma, but his real error was being unaware that his powerful feelings were about his issues and not about Christine. It is the practitioner's responsibility to be aware of the countertransference and to seek some form of consultation to help him deal with it (Hover-Kramer, 2002, p. 97).

Constance Dalenberg (2011), one of the foremost researchers in the field of countertransference issues in the treatment of trauma, stated that "trauma victims figure prominently in virtually every well-known therapeutic dilemma or disaster associated with strong countertransference reactions" (p. 12). She goes on to say that "psychopractitioners often have countertransferential reactions to the *fact* of the trauma…the psychopractitioner's pre-existing thoughts and beliefs about the trauma may affect the course of therapy greatly" (p. 13, italics in original).

The practitioner is often responding to her own feelings in the presence of the client's powerful feelings. While Clinical EFT offers more hope for healing than treatments of the past, practitioners can still experience strong feelings from just knowing the person had to endure the horror of the trauma.

Recognizing Countertransference as Emotional Response

Pope and Tabachnick (1993), in their article, "Practitioners' Anger, Hate, Fear and Sexual Feelings" reported that more than 80% of their participants, all practicing psychologists, reported experiencing each of these fears with at least one client, and most with many of their clients. These emotions are normal, no matter what the client's issues may be. However, trauma brings up a whole additional set of emotions.

Listening to a client recount hearing the screams of men burning to death in a locked troop carrier, or of seeing blood pooling around the bodies of dead children in a classroom in Connecticut, are difficult to bear witness to. At least if it's on the news, you can change the channel. The horrible sense of helplessness that is a key part of what makes traumatic events traumatic infects not only the survivor but also her practitioner. Even using Clinical EFT's "Gentle Techniques," practitioners are exposed to some truly terrible things in hearing clients' stories. Not only is it possible that a piece of one's own story might be triggered, but also the empathy that the practitioner feels for the client creates emotional responses in the practitioner.

Laura Brown (2012) wrote that the practitioner might unconsciously engage in one or more of these common countertransference reactions: numbing and avoidance, avoidant disbelief, morbid curiosity, and blaming and shaming the victim.

Numbing and Avoidance

One of the most common countertransference responses that practitioners have to their clients' traumatic stories is the desire not to hear or know the details. It literally mirrors the numbing and avoidance that trauma survivors use as coping mechanisms. Dalenberg (2010) discusses a number of cases of trauma-related countertransference in which the practitioners were so numb to survivors' stories that they repeatedly failed to listen to the client, or forgot painful details that the client had related. Sometimes they discouraged clients from telling their stories even when the client wanted to disclose. Although the Clinical EFT client does not always have to disclose details for the healing to take place, many have been carrying the pain for so long they want to share their stories. Silencing clients if they want to tell their stories "constitutes a form of retraumatization and empathetic failure" (pp. 12–13).

When survivors do disclose, they deserve to be heard and empathized with. The truth is that no practitioner is immune from unconsciously using the protective shield of numbing and avoidance, but awareness of this mechanism can help practitioners make choices about how to proceed.

Avoidant Disbelief

Some things are so difficult to hear that the practitioner begins to believe that the client's stories did not really happen at all, or that the events were not really "that bad," (minimization). This is especially true when the traumatization exceeds the boundaries of the practitioner's own emotional capacities. If the trauma client is a survivor of severe, repeated childhood abuse or torture, or was trafficked to several men before the age of 10, for instance, the practitioner may not believe the stories. Often trauma survivors report seemingly impossible events because of the developmental stage at which the abuse occurred and the context of the trauma. Such unlikely parts of the client's stories only reinforce the practitioner's tendency toward avoidant disbelief (Brown, 2012, pp. 5–7).

Consider the following. If the Nazis had not kept such meticulous records of their atrocities, would we believe Holocaust survivors' stories? If the horrors of Rwanda had not been thoroughly documented by international agencies after their occurrence, would we believe that human beings were truly capable of such behavior? Practitioners are not the arbiters of what is true or not true. If you find yourself doubting that "such a thing could ever have happened," seek consultation and consider the possibility that avoidant disbelief is at work.

Case study: Sophie. Anna had been seeing 26-year-old Sophie for anxiety, depression, and posttraumatic stress for about 3 months and was growing weary of Sophie's tales of the sexual sadism she had endured at the hands of her father and his friends. When Sophie began to talk about the "other children" who had not survived, Anna felt she had to intervene. "It sounds like these are very scary dreams," she said sympathetically to Sophie. "No wonder you're so frightened." Sophie insisted that these were real events and real people. Anna could not wrap her head around the story that Sophie was telling; it was too bizarre and horrible. She simply didn't believe that such things could happen in the middle-class neighborhood in which Sophie grew up.

After her session, Anna reflected on what she had heard and how she was feeling. She realized she felt angry and afraid in a way that seemed over the top. She called a colleague for a consult and realized that she was using avoidant disbelief to protect herself. Whatever the literal truth was in Sophie's original traumas, it did not serve her for Anna to disbelieve her. At the next session, Anna apologized for not believing, sharing how difficult it was to hear Sophie's story. She talked about how brave Sophie was to work toward healing.

Anna avoided a serious therapeutic mistake by examining her reactions and feeling, and by seeking consultation about her reactions. Sophie felt validated with more trust of her therapist and made good progress in her healing.

Morbid Curiosity

The fascination with the "gory details" of high-profile crimes, such as the recent case of the three women held in a house in Cleveland for 10 years, show how interested people are in the intimate and shocking details of other people's lives. Think also of "reality" TV, which feeds the public's desire to peer into others' lives. As a society, our fascination with horror in novels, movies, and video games seems never ending.

Practitioners are not immune to such interest, and have been given license to ask intrusive questions as part of the therapeutic interaction. An embarrassing truth of trauma work is that some practitioners find the details of clients' traumas exciting, titillating, or even arousing (Brown, 2012, p. 47).

There's a fine line between getting enough information to do the work and digging for gratuitous details. Clinical EFT generally does not require that the practitioner understand all the details, although it is important to find and clear all the aspects. Although certain details are essential to the healing process, the practitioner needs to be sure that pursuing the details is in the service of client healing and not in self-interest. This is where a fully aware practitioner will notice the countertransference and take corrective action.

Another ugly side to the countertransferential demand for more details is the human desire to share a bizarre story with friends and colleagues for self-importance (Brown, 2012). While it may seem all right because no names or identifying information are used, *telling any part of the client's story to anyone outside of formal consultation* is a serious breach of professional boundaries and ethics (Feinstein, 2011, p. 18).

Blaming and Shaming the Victim

Working with trauma survivors is a difficult business. They don't easily trust the practitioner, they are often hypersensitive to a careless comment, or they may become dependent and helpless while resisting the practitioner's best efforts to help.

Practitioners can naturally become frustrated and begin to blame the client for "not wanting to get better" (Brown, 2012, p. 51). Though these feelings are normal, when the practitioner acts on them, they interfere with or derail the healing.

The anger often manifests as subtle blame and a call for the client to "do it right." This may be couched in phrases such as "you need to take responsibility for your life," or "you need to forgive your mother." A Clinical EFT practitioner may attempt reframes that have an edge of blame in them. Sometimes practitioners attempt to apply "positive" frames long before the client is ready to hear them. The client gets the covert message that she is not "doing it right" or feeling the "right feelings," which only replicates the messages she is getting from the outside world that she should "just get over it." The healing relationship and the client suffer as a result.

Physical Manifestations of Countertransference

Although countertransference has traditionally been thought of as a solely emotional response to a client, physical reactions are now being recognized as independent of one's own physiology. Egan and Carr (2008) found high levels of body-centered countertransference, also called "somatic transference," in female trauma therapists in Ireland.

Booth, Trimble, and Egan (2010) found somatic countertransference among clinical psychologists of both sexes. Interestingly, they found that the clinicians with the highest-reported incidents of somatic countertransference were the highest rated among their peers for quality work. The studies found a wide range of ways that somatic countertransference expressed itself. They studied a 16-item list of somatic expressions. It is probable that there are more, but these are the ones the study authors chose to use. These sensations in the practitioner's own body are literally tools to alert them that something is going on to which they need to pay attention. The five highest-ranking somatic expressions were sleepiness, muscle tension, yawning, unexpected shift in body, and tearfulness, with 71–92% of clinicians experiencing one or more episodes within the prior 6-month period. The next five most common were headache, stomach disturbance, throat constriction, dizziness, and raised voice. These were experienced by 26–54% of the clinicians in that 6-month period. Even the symptoms that were the least experienced (i.e., loss of voice, sexual arousal, aches in joints, nausea, numbness, and genital pain) were experienced by as many as 32% of the clinicians studied.

It is not surprising to energy workers and Clinical EFT practitioners that the body would be so strongly affected by somatic countertransference. What may be surprising to some are the number and variety of bodily sensations that practitioners experience in response to their clients.

Case Study: Jo

EFT practitioner Barbara reported that she always felt tired when she saw a particular client, Jo. She found herself stifling yawns and surreptitiously pinching herself to stay awake. Week after week, the same thing happened.

Barbara tried taking brisk walks at lunch before her afternoon appointment with Jo. She gulped down coffee she didn't want. She felt fine for the clients preceding Jo and following her, but during that hour with Jo, Barbara always fought to stay awake. She called for consultation after she saw Jo at 9 a.m. one day and she realized the same thing happened.

In talking about the client's history, Barbara remarked how similar Jo's early abuse mirrored her own, and how uncomfortable it would make her when they worked on that issue. She admitted that she even steered Jo away from that issue with the belief that the client wasn't ready to address it. In consultation, Jo realized her tiredness had nothing to do with being tired and everything to do with avoiding dealing with her own childhood abuse.

As Barbara realized, everything that happens in a client session is a clue that a good detective will take note of and examine. Often it's good practice to share your physical sensations with the client as a tool to further the client's work. For instance, when working with a person who is minimizing the actual, current physical danger that he's in, it might be useful to share the nervous, squiggly feeling in your stomach as he talks. In Barbara's case, the "tiredness" was a signal to her that her own issue was getting in the way of Jo's ongoing progress, and would not have been appropriate to share with Jo. Once Barbara began to address her own issue with her own Clinical EFT practitioner, she no longer stood in the way of Jo's addressing hers.

Every itch or twitch a practitioner experiences in a session is not necessarily countertransference from the client's material. For a fully aware practitioner, however, both emotional and body sensations invite curiosity.

Good Boundaries Guard Against Impulsive Action

Good boundaries create a safe, stable place for trauma survivors and practitioners to do their work. When a trauma client walks into the practitioner's office, it means coming into a safe space bounded by integrity, reliability, and predictability (Brown, 2012, pp. 59–60).

The boundaries around not having social or sexual relationships with clients are in place to protect both the client and practitioner from the transference issues that frequently show up in the course of treatment. Boundaries demonstrate the practitioner's respect for the client and the therapeutic relationship that is critical to healing.

Conscious adherence to good boundaries and ethics gives the practitioner space to make reasoned judgments in the presence of strong countertransference instead of taking an impulsive step based on it.

Conclusion

Transference and countertransference are present in nearly every interaction a Clinical EFT practitioner will have with a client. Countertransference is not something to be afraid of. It's an opportunity that fully aware practitioners will be able to take advantage of to help their clients. The key is remaining aware and seeking consultation when needed.

References

Booth, A., Trimble, T., & Egan, J. (2010). Body-centred countertransference in a sample of Irish clinical psychologists. *Irish Psychologist, 36*, 284–289.

Brown, L. S. (2012). *Emotional and cultural competence in the trauma-aware therapist* [Continuing Education online course]. Retrieved from http://www.socialworkcoursesonline.com/active/courses/course074.php?Help

Burk, L. (2010). Single session EFT (Emotional Freedom Techniques) for stress-related symptoms after motor vehicle accidents. *Energy Psychology: Theory, Research, & Treatment, 2*(1), 6572. doi:10.9769.EPJ.2010.2.1.LB

Church, D. (2013). Clinical EFT as an evidence-based practice for the treatment of psychological and physiological conditions. *Psychology, 4*(8), 645654. doi:10.4236/psych.2013.48092

Dalenberg, C. (2010). *Countertransference and the treatment of trauma.* Washington DC: American Psychological Association.

Egan, J. & Carr, A. (2008). Body-centred countertransference in female trauma therapists. *Irish Association of Counselling and Psychotherapy Quarterly Journal, 8,* 24–27.

Feinstein, D. with Eden, D. (2011). *Ethics handbook for energy healing practitioners.* Fulton, CA: Energy Psychology Press.

Fonagy, P., Steele, M., & Steele, H. (1991, October). Maternal representations of attachment during pregnancy predict the organisation of mother-infant attachment at one year of age. *Child Development, 62*(5), 891–905.

Freud, S. (1977). *Introductory lectures on psychoanalysis.* New York, NY: Norton.

Horvath, A. & Symonds, B. (1991, April). Relation between working alliance and outcome in psychotherapy: A meta-analysis. Journal of Counseling Psychology, 38(2), 139–149. doi:10.1037/0022-0167.38.2.139

Hover-Kramer, D. (2002). *Creative energies: Integrative energy psychotherapy for self-expression and healing.* New York: W. W. Norton.

Hughes, P. (1999). *Dynamic psychotherapy explained.* Oxford, UK: Radcliffe Medical Press.

Pope, K. & Tabachnick, B. (1993, May). Therapists' anger, hate, fear, and sexual feelings: National survey of therapist responses, client characteristics, critical events, formal complaints, and training. *Professional Psychology: Research and Practice, 24*(2), 142–152. doi:10.1037/0735-7028.24.2.142

Sroufe, L. (1983). Infant-caregiver attachment and patterns of adaptation in pre-school: The roots of maladaptation and competence. In M. Perlmutter (Ed.), *Minnesota symposium in child psychology* (pp. 41–91). Hillsdale, NJ: Erlbaum.

Vesper, J. (1998). Mismanagement of countertransference in posttraumatic stress disorder: Ethical and legal violations. *American Journal of Forensic Psychology, 16*(2), 5–15.

Chapter 15
EFT for Stress-Related Symptoms after Motor Vehicle Accidents
Larry Burk

Abstract

Motor vehicle accidents (MVA) are a common cause of posttraumatic stress disorder (PTSD). Energy psychology (EP) approaches such as EFT (Emotional Freedom Techniques) are a new form of exposure therapy used to treat PTSD arising from a variety of causes. These techniques provide an attractive alternative to more established approaches such as cognitive behavioral therapy (CBT) because of their potential for accelerated healing similar to that demonstrated with Eye Movement Desensitization and Reprocessing (EMDR). There are only a few reports in the literature of the use of EP for the treatment of PTSD resulting from MVA. This clinical report presents three case histories documenting the use of single-session EFT for the treatment of acute psychological trauma immediately after a car accident, urticaria as a component of acute stress disorder (ASD) 2 weeks after a car accident, and PTSD and whiplash syndrome 11 months after a car accident. These cases are discussed in the context of a review of the current literature on PTSD after MVA and are followed by recommendations for future research.

Keywords: motor vehicle accident, PTSD, posttraumatic stress disorder, stress, urticaria, whiplash, trauma

Larry Burk, MD, CEHP, is a musculoskeletal teleradiologist and a medical acupuncture practitioner with a part-time private practice specializing in EFT (www.orientalhealthsolutions.com). He was formerly associate professor of radiology at Duke University School of Medicine and cofounder and director of education of the Duke Center for Integrative Medicine. Send correspondence to Larry Burk, 907 Broad St, Durham, NC 27705, or burk0001@yahoo.com.

Over 2.3 million people in the United States were injured in 2008 from serious motor vehicle accidents (MVA; USDOT, 2008). Posttraumatic stress disorder (PTSD) can occur in people involved in up to half of serious car accidents, making MVA a leading cause of PTSD in the general population (Blanchard & Hickling, 2003). Symptoms of traumatic stress include persistent reexperiencing of the traumatic event, persistent avoidance of stimuli associated with the trauma and numbing of general responsiveness, and persistent symptoms of increased arousal. Symptoms that last between 2 days and 1 month after the accident can be diagnosed as acute stress disorder (ASD), whereas symptoms that last longer than 1 month can qualify as PTSD (Schupp, 2004, pp. 19–20).

Cognitive behavioral therapy (CBT) has been shown to be superior to supportive psychotherapy in the treatment of PTSD after MVA (Blanchard et al., 2003). The Dresden study (Maercker, Zöllner, Menning, Rabe, & Karl, 2006) showed similar results in 8 to 12 sessions that combined well-established CBT techniques (imaginal or in-vivo prolonged exposure and cognitive restructuring) with additional procedures, such as writing assignments, social sharing, and facilitation of posttraumatic growth. Novel approaches such as virtual reality exposure therapy have recently been developed (Beck, Palyo, Winer, Schwagler, & Ang, 2007). Acupuncture has been used for treatment of emotional blocks in whiplash syndrome that resulted in myoclonic shaking, emotional releases, and regression (Greenwood, Leong, & Tan, 1988). Acupuncture has also shown comparable results to CBT for treatment of PTSD in a randomized controlled trial that included a wait-list control group (Hollifield, Sinclair-Lian, Warner, & Hammerschlag, 2007).

The features of acupuncture and exposure therapy have been combined in energy psychology (EP) approaches such as EFT (Emotional Freedom Techniques) by subjects self-tapping on acupuncture points during the repetition of a reminder phrase summarizing a traumatic event (Craig, 2008). Subjective units of distress (SUD) that can range from 0 to 10 are assessed before and after a round of tapping, which usually consists of a generic sequence of eight or more major acupuncture meridian endpoints on the face, chest, and hands. The Reminder Phrase may be adjusted on subsequent rounds to address other components of the trauma, which are commonly referred to as "aspects." EFT can be incorporated into standard individual psychotherapy or taught in groups as a method of self-care. Thousands of laypersons and non–mental health practitioners around the world have learned it, and it thus has potential use as a form of "do-it-yourself" psychological first aid (Craig, 2009).

EFT was shown to be effective in significantly reducing PTSD scores in 11 military veterans and family members during a week of intensive therapy that involved from 10 to 15 individual treatment sessions (Church, 2010). Similar results were obtained in a study of seven veterans treated with EFT for six sessions each, with all subjects showing statistically significant decreases in PTSD, anxiety, and depression (Church, Geronilla, & Dinter, 2009). The only study of EFT for PTSD after a motor vehicle accident correlated SUD scores and a questionnaire assessing avoidance of driving and riding in a motor vehicle (Swingle, Pulos, & Swingle, 2004). All nine subjects reported moderate to severe traumatic stress, with a SUD average of 8.3, which was reduced to a statistically significant average of 2.5 after two treatment sessions. A case report that used another EP acupoint tapping technique, negative affect erasing method, resolved nightmares and flashbacks related to a near fatal accident after only one treatment session (Gallo, 2009).

These published studies of rapid and dramatic improvement in PTSD after only a limited number of sessions of EFT or other EP techniques have contributed to the controversy surrounding these approaches in the mainstream psychological community. A randomized controlled trial of EFT versus a wait list with 16 abused adolescents showed a statistically significant reduction in intrusive memories and avoidance symptoms after only one session (Church, Piña, Reategui, & Brooks, 2012). In contrast, one of the strongest studies demonstrating the efficacy of CBT in PTSD showed that 60% of 60 veterans still met the criteria for PTSD after 12 sessions, and 50% demonstrated no improvement at all (Monson et al., 2006). These conflicting results and the unfamiliar claim that tapping on the skin may accelerate the clearing of severe psychological traumas without a well-defined scientific mechanism of action have created a significant amount of cognitive dissonance among conventionally trained therapists (Feinstein, 2009). The three case histories in this clinical report contribute further support to these claims, as immediate results were again obtained in single-session treatments.

Case 1: First Aid for Immediate Psychological Trauma after Car Accident in One Session

A 39-year-old female laboratory researcher at a major university was in a head-on hit-and-run car accident, which I witnessed. She was stopped in the left-turn lane at an intersection waiting for the light to change when a car turning from the crossing road hit her car in the left front bumper, careened off, and drove away. Her air bag deployed, and she got out of the car within a few minutes. She was calling the police on her cell phone when I approached to offer assistance. She had minor bleeding from her right hand but no other significant injuries. However, she was visibly shaking and distressed from the acute trauma.

After identifying myself as a physician who treats traumatized patients and volunteering to stay with her until the police arrived, I offered to help relieve her distress by guiding her through EFT tapping. She began tapping while recounting the experience of seeing the car turn the corner and immediately had an exacerbation of her stress, so I instructed her to stop talking and keep tapping until ready to go on to the next part of the story. She then described the car impact and the air bag expanding. In this way, distress associated with each aspect of the accident was reduced. She tapped until she could tell the whole story without distress. When the police arrived, she was able to describe the situation in a coherent fashion.

The woman then went on to say that she had just had $1,200 worth of work done on the car that morning in preparation for moving across country to a new laboratory position at another research university in a few days time. A month later I received a follow-up e-mail expressing gratitude for the timely EFT first aid. She was able to get a new car, drive to her new home, and start her new job without any concerns about the trauma of the car accident. As a basic science researcher, she was unfamiliar with EFT or EP, but she was appreciative of the serendipity of the intervention and its impact on her rapid recovery.

Case 2: Relief of ASD and Urticaria at 2 Weeks Post–Car Accident in One Session

A 21-year-old female college student was enrolled in a stress management class I taught at a major university. She complained of severe hives for 2 weeks after a car accident during which she lost control while driving in the rain, spun around several times, and hit a telephone pole. The constant itching for which the student health clinic had prescribed antihistamine medication had compromised her studying. The medicine relieved the hives but made her too drowsy to study, so she quit taking it, and the hives came back. She was quite frustrated with her inability to resolve the situation.

I had introduced the class to EFT after downloading the EFT manual from the Internet and offered to work with her individually after class as my first trial of EFT. She had only 20 minutes before her next class but was desperate for relief. She picked "scary car accident" as her Reminder Phrase, which yielded a 6/10 SUD rating. Adding "thought I was going to die" made it 8/10. She tapped one round of EFT, and her SUD score went down to 4/10. Upon inquiry about other aspects, she then changed the Reminder Phrase to "guilty about totaling my dad's car," which was "an 11" on the 0-to-10 scale. Another round of tapping reduced the SUD rating to 2/10 and provided obvious physical signs of relief.

I instructed her to stop taking the medication but continue to tap as needed. She returned to class 2 days later quite pleased to report that she had not had any more hives. She had felt occasional itching, which additional tapping relieved. She then mentioned that she had also spontaneously tapped while reviewing previous car accidents and had recovered her confidence in driving. She had not mentioned these issues during the earlier brief intervention. At the end of the semester, she reported that she had not had any more hives and that learning EFT had been her most valuable experience of the semester.

Case 3: Relief of PTSD and Whiplash Syndrome 11 Months after Car Accident in One Session

A 52-year-old woman complained of neck stiffness and fear of driving in stop-and-go situations on city streets. She had been rear-ended while stopped at an intersection 11 months previously. The woman was a college acquaintance of mine. We reconnected for the first time in 32 years at a conference on healing. I observed that she drove very slowly through the city during the conference, far below the speed limit. She had particular difficulty at intersections and had limited range of motion in her neck, which further impaired her driving abilities.

She rated her fear of being rear-ended again at 10/10 on the SUD scale and reported having been frozen by fear at the intersection at the time of the accident while watching the oncoming car in her rearview mirror. She had been taken to the emergency room and treated for a whiplash injury. A round of EFT reduced her SUD score to 5/10, but she then experienced a flashback to another car accident 29 years before. That accident had been more serious, resulting in a pneumothorax, rib fractures, and a concussion, as well as the near death of her boy friend. She described driving and being frozen in the middle of an intersection when a speeding car struck her vehicle on the passenger's side.

Although she reported losing consciousness after the crash, her memories of being unable to get out of the intersection in the few seconds before the accident were intense, with especially vivid auditory sensations of the oncoming car revving its engine. She tapped several rounds on "being frozen with fear" and then on the stiffness in her neck. Her fear diminished to 0/10, and she was able to drive through the city later that day and stop at intersections without the paralyzing fear of being rear-ended. Eight months later she reported that her neck mobility was significantly improved, that her fear was still gone, and that she had gotten one speeding ticket, indicating that she was no longer driving as slowly as before the EFT session.

Discussion

The EP approach in these case reports, EFT, produced effective results for symptoms of stress-related symptoms after MVA in single-session treatments. The treatments were performed informally outside the clinic in everyday situations including a car accident scene, a classroom, and a healing conference. These dramatic results are supported by a growing number of scientific studies of EP in the treatment of PTSD from a variety of causes, including military combat, childhood abuse, and community disasters, some of which utilized Thought Field Therapy, a precursor of EFT (Feinstein, 2008b). These findings have potential implications for the use of EP techniques for first aid and for the treatment of ASD and PTSD.

Exposure plus CBT is widely accepted as the standard of care for PTSD in conventional psychology, although early studies recommended 10 treatments sessions or more (Marks, Lovell, Noshirvani, Livanou, & Thrasher, 1998). In contrast, early claims of successfully treating PTSD in one session were made for Eye Movement Desensitization and Reprocessing (EMDR), a form of exposure therapy related to EP in utilizing bilateral visual, auditory, or tactile stimulation (Shapiro, 1989). A later PTSD wait-list comparison study of 72 patients, including 17 survivors of MVA, showed slightly better results for EMDR than for CBT, using an average of 4.2 sessions compared with an average of 6.4 sessions of exposure therapy plus cognitive restructuring (Power et al., 2002). A recent study of four sessions of EMDR versus wait list in 27 children with PTSD following MVA showed significant improvement in 75% of the subjects after EMDR compared with no improvement on the wait list (Kemp, Drummond, & McDermott, 2010).

EMDR has moved from the fringes of psychotherapy toward the mainstream due to the publication of a significant number of scientific studies showing its effectiveness for PTSD (Shapiro, 2002). In common with EP, the unfamiliar approach, confusing name, and uncertain mechanism of action of EMDR contributed to conventional therapists resisting its acceptance. Subsequently, theoretical models based in part on brain-imaging studies have been developed that offer support for the premise that bilateral stimulation can have an effect on memory processing in the hippocampus and amygdala (Stickgold, 2002). Related models proposed by Lane (2009) for the mechanism of action in EP indicate that acupoint stimulation produces opioids, serotonin, and gamma-aminobutyric acid (GABA) and regulates cortisol, thereby inducing a relaxation response. This relaxation response counter conditions anxiety and changes memory processing in the midbrain, particularly the amygdala. These data from acupuncture brain-imaging studies may assist in greater acceptance of EP in mainstream practice (Napadow et al., 2008).

The connection to acupuncture research is an important one for EP, since acupuncture is now an accepted facet of integrative medicine due in part to an extensive scientific evidence base (NIH Consensus Development Panel on Acupuncture, 1998). It has been used as an integrative treatment for PTSD in the military at Fort Bliss Restoration and Resilience Center in Texas (Chang, 2009). Ear acupuncture was used in New York City at Saint Vincent's Hospital on 99 survivors of 9/11 and showed a statistically significant reduction in self-rated stress (NADA, 2007). A multidisciplinary pain program utilizing acupuncture in Victoria, British Columbia, achieved a 68% success rate in the treatment of 100 patients with whiplash syndrome, which is also referred to as "accident neurosis" and shares many of the features of PTSD in physical form (Nunn & Greenwood, 1991). If, as Bessel van der Kolk (1994, p. 253) states, "the body keeps score," perhaps the acupuncture meridians are the scorekeepers and the limbic system is the scoreboard.

First Aid for Psychological Trauma

As illustrated in the first case, EFT has the potential to be used as a form of first aid for immediate trauma. One difference between EFT and EMDR is that EMDR is only taught to licensed mental health professionals, whereas EFT has been taught to a broad variety of health care practitioners as well as to lay people. EFT training could be made widely available to paramedics and other first responders to accident scenes and disasters. A related approach using acupressure administered by paramedics was shown to be effective for reducing pain and anxiety in a randomized controlled trial during the transportation of 60 patients after minor trauma (Kober et al., 2002). In stable patients, for whom the emotional trauma may be greater than the physical trauma, EFT could be used in the ambulance, on the battlefield, or at a disaster scene.

Whether such early intervention is a good idea is open to debate, as the most widely used conventional method, psychological debriefing, has shown disappointing results (McNally, Bryant, & Ehlers, 2003). The motivation to potentially prevent the development of PTSD has obvious merit, but usually only a minority of those who experience acute trauma go on to develop ASD or PTSD. Most people cycle between phases of avoidance and phases of processing in the aftermath of a significant trauma (Pennebaker & Harber, 1993), so any intervention would likely need to be adapted to the particular coping style of the individual. The rapidity of EP in reducing anxiety may speed up that processing. Lane (2009) has noted that the reduction in anxiety activates different neural networks and gives people greater access to higher levels of cortical thinking to reevaluate traumas. Perhaps similar to the impact of the addition of EP to exposure therapy, success in psychological debriefing could be increased with the addition of EP. Feinstein (2008b) has documented the effectiveness of EP through systematic observation in several disaster relief circumstances and noted that three international humanitarian relief organizations have adopted EP as a treatment in post-disaster missions.

Acute Stress Disorder

The second case occurred in the context of a group stress management class, which highlights another significant difference between EMDR and EFT: EFT can be easily taught to groups, whereas EMDR is most frequently a component of individual psychotherapy. The ability to offer EFT in a group setting presents obvious advantages in terms of cost effectiveness, and a group model for CBT has been previously described for PTSD after MVA, which emphasized the potential for building group cohesion and increased social support (Beck & Coffey, 2005). Based on this concept, a randomized controlled trial comparing EFT to CBT for prevention of PTSD could be designed by recruiting patients with ASD from hospital trauma wards to attend outpatient groups after discharge.

This case also focused on a physical manifestation of ASD in the form of hives, a less common occurrence than whiplash syndrome and one without a direct relation to bodily injury. Most studies of psychosomatic illnesses focus on chronic urticaria lasting longer than 6 weeks rather than on the acute form of hives, as in this case. Early descriptions refer to a "psychosomatic formula" in which "the bodily process emerged, or recurred, on meeting an emotionally upsetting event" (Mitchell, Curran, & Myers, 1947, p. 185). The incidence of PTSD was found to be higher among patients with chronic idiopathic urticaria than it was in a matched control group of allergy patients, suggesting that traumatic memories or emotions could be manifested through the skin (Chung, Symons, Gilliam, & Kaminski, 2010). Although no studies of urticaria and EFT have been performed yet, EFT seems particularly well suited for addressing such physical manifestations of stress.

PTSD

The third case is similar to the second case in that both involved women with a history of previous MVA. In one study, a history of prior MVA was a predictor of acute stress severity in survivors of car accidents, suggesting the possibility of identifying those who may benefit from early treatment (Harvey & Bryant, 1999). In a study of victims of violent crime, the incidence of PTSD was higher in women than men (38% vs. 14%), and a diagnosis of ASD led to an eventual diagnosis of PTSD in 83% of the victims (Brewin, Andrews, Rose, & Kirk, 1999). The woman in the third case had no history of treatment for stress following either of her two car accidents. Perhaps her PTSD could have been prevented if, as in the second case, early intervention with EP had been offered. Randomized prospective controlled trials of EP versus CBT versus EMDR will be required to answer such questions, but there are indications that all of these techniques have some level of effectiveness.

The third case showed dramatically the ability of EFT to resolve long-term symptoms of PTSD and whiplash syndrome following a car accident in a single session. The potential for EFT and other EP approaches such as Thought Field Therapy and negative affect erasing method to accelerate the healing of PTSD merits further study in comparison to other more established techniques. Thus far, few randomized controlled trials of EFT have been performed, with the initial one being a favorable comparison of single-session EFT to diaphragmatic breathing for phobias of small animals (Wells, Polglase, Andrews, Carrington, & Baker, 2003). A more recent single-session study showed better results for EFT than progressive muscle relaxation for test anxiety (Sezgin & Özcan, 2009). As Feinstein (2008a) indicated, the accumulated body of evidence for the efficacy of EP is rapidly expanding, and the treatment of PTSD after MVA is fertile ground for further research.

Conclusion

The three case reports of rapid relief of stress-related symptoms after MVA with EFT presented in this chapter highlight the potential for the use of EP approaches in the settings of immediate psychological trauma, ASD, and PTSD. The possibility for significantly shortening the length of treatment should be intriguing to health policy analysts who are charged with allocating limited health care resources. Similar to the logic expressed by Sugarman and Burk (1998) that physicians have an ethical obligation to learn about alternative medicine to safeguard the best interests of their patients, a case can logically be made that psychologists and other mental health professionals have an ethical obligation to learn about EP. Whether or not they choose to incorporate such corporal methods into their practice is up to them, but preliminary research indicates that their patients are likely to benefit from the use of EP.

References

Beck, J. G. & Coffey, S. F. (2005). Group cognitive behavioral treatment for PTSD: Treatment of motor vehicle accident survivors. *Cognitive and Behavioral Practice, 12*, 267–277. doi:10.1016/S1077-7229(05)80049-5

Beck, J. G., Palyo, S. A., Winer, E. H., Schwagler, B. E., & Ang, E. J. (2007). Virtual reality exposure therapy for PTSD symptoms after a road accident: An uncontrolled case series. *Behavior Therapy, 38*, 39–48. doi:10.1016/j.beth.2006.04.001

Blanchard, E. B. & Hickling, E. J. (2003). *After the crash: Assessment and treatment of motor vehicle accident survivors* (2nd ed.). Washington, DC: American Psychological Association.

Blanchard, E. B., Hickling, E. J., Devineni, T., Veazey, C. H., Galovski, T.E., Mundy, E., Malta, L. S., & Buckley, T.C. (2003). A controlled evaluation of cognitive behavioural therapy for posttraumatic stress in motor vehicle accident survivors. *Behavioral Research and Therapy, 41*, 79–96. doi:10.1016/S0005-7967(01)00131-0

Brewin, C. R., Andrews, B., Rose, S., & Kirk, M. (1999). Acute stress disorder and posttraumatic stress disorder in victims of violent crime. *American Journal of Psychiatry, 156*, 360–366.

Chang, J. C. (2009, Fall) Integrative PTSD outpatient programs. *Journal of the American Association of Integrative Medicine, 1*, 2–3. Retrieved from http://www.aaimedicine.com/pdf/JAAIM_fall09.pdf

Chung, M. C., Symons, C., Gilliam, J., & Kaminski, E. R. (2010). The relationship between posttraumatic stress disorder, psychiatric comorbidity, and personality traits among patients with chronic idiopathic urticaria. *Comprehensive Psychiatry, 51*, 55–63. doi:10.1016/j.comppsych.2009.02.005

Church, D. (2010). The treatment of combat trauma in veterans using EFT (Emotional Freedom Techniques): A pilot protocol. *Traumatology, 16*, 55–65. doi:10.1177/1534765609347549

Church, D., Geronilla, L., & Dinter, I. (2009). Psychological symptom change in veterans after six sessions of Emotional Freedom Techniques (EFT): An observational study. *International Journal of Healing and Caring, 9*(1). Retrieved from http://www.patclass.com/Marshall%20Published.pdf

Church, D., Piña, O., Reategui, C., & Brooks, A. (2012). Single session reduction of the intensity of traumatic memories in abused adolescents after EFT: A randomized controlled pilot study. *Traumatology, 18*(3), 73–79. doi:10.1177/1534765611426788

Craig, G. (2008). *The EFT manual*. Santa Rosa, CA: Energy Psychology Press.

Craig, G. (2009). *EFT for PTSD*. Santa Rosa, CA: Energy Psychology Press.

Feinstein, D. (2008a). Energy psychology: A review of the preliminary evidence. *Psychotherapy: Theory, Research, Practice, Training, 45*, 199–213.

Feinstein, D. (2008b). Energy psychology in disaster relief. *Traumatology, 14*, 124–137. doi:10.1177/1534765608315636

Feinstein, D. (2009). Controversies in energy psychology. *Energy Psychology: Theory, Research and Treatment, 1*, 45–56.

Gallo, F. P. (2009). Energy psychology in rehabilitation: Origins, clinical applications, and theory. *Energy Psychology: Theory, Research and Treatment, 1*, 57–72.

Greenwood, M., Leong, L. A., & Tan, W. C. (1988). Traditional acupuncture treatment for whiplash syndrome. *American Journal of Acupuncture, 16*(4).

Harvey, A. G. & Bryant, R. A. (1999). Predictors of acute stress following motor vehicle accidents. *Journal of Traumatic Stress, 12*, 519–525. doi:10.1023/A:1024723205259

Hollifield, M., Sinclair-Lian, N., Warner, T., & Hammerschlag, R. (2007). Acupuncture for posttraumatic stress disorder: A randomized controlled pilot trial. *Journal of Nervous and Mental Disease, 195*, 504–513. doi:10.1097/NMD.0b01 3e31803044f8

Kemp, M., Drummond, P., & McDermott, B. (2010). A waitlist controlled pilot study of eye movement desensitization and reprocessing (EMDR) for children with posttraumatic stress disorder (PTSD) symptoms from motor vehicle accidents. *Clinical Child Psychology and Psychiatry, 15*, 5–25. doi:10.1177/1359104509339086

Kober, A., Scheck, T., Greher, M., Lieba, F., Fleischhackl, R., Fleischhackl, S., Randunsky, F., & Hoerauf, K. (2002). Prehospital analgesia with acupressure in victims of minor trauma: A prospective, randomized, double-blinded trial. *Anesthesia & Analgesia, 95*, 723–727. doi:10.1097/00000 539-200209000-00035

Lane, J. R. (2009). *The neurochemistry of counter conditioning: Acupressure desensitization in psychotherapy*. Energy Psychology: Theory, Research and Treatment, 1, 31–44.

Maercker, A., Zöllner, T., Menning, H., Rabe, S., & Karl, A. (2006). Dresden PTSD treatment study: Randomized controlled trial of motor vehicle accident survivors. *BMC [BioMed Central] Psychiatry, 6*, 29. doi:10.1186/1471-244X-6-29

Marks, I., Lovell, K., Noshirvani, H., Livanou, M., & Thrasher, S. (1998). Treatment of post-traumatic stress disorder by exposure and/or cognitive restructuring. *Archives of General Psychiatry, 55*, 317–325. doi:10.1001/archpsyc.55.4.317

McNally, R. J., Bryant, R. A., & Ehlers, A. (2003). Does early psychological intervention promote recovery from posttraumatic stress? *Psychological Science in the Public Interest, 4*, 45–79.

Mitchell, J. H., Curran, C. A., & Myers, R. N. (1947). Some psychosomatic aspects of allergic diseases. *Psychosomatic Medicine, 9*, 184–191.

Monson, C. M., Schnurr, P. P., Resick, P. A., Friedman, M. J., Young-Xu, Y., & Stevens, S. P. (2006). Cognitive processing therapy for veterans with military-related posttraumatic stress disorder. *Journal of Consulting and Clinical Psychology, 74*, 898–907. doi:10.1037/0022-006X.74.5.898

Napadow, V., Ahn, A., Longhurst, J., Lao, L., Stener-Victorin, E., Harris, R., & Langevin, H. M. (2008). The status and future of acupuncture mechanism research. *Journal of Alternative and Complementary Medicine, 14*, 861–869. doi:10.1089/acm.2008. SAR-3

National Acupuncture Detoxification Association (NADA). (2007, November 30). 9/11 survivors receiving NADA treatment show lower stress symptoms. *News from NADA*. Retrieved from http://acudetox.com/news/?p=21

NIH Consensus Development Panel on Acupuncture. (1998). Acupuncture. *JAMA, 280*, 1518–1524. doi:10.1001/jama.280.17.1518

Nunn, P. J. & Greenwood, M. T. (1991). Whiplash syndrome: A transformational approach. *Humane Medicine, 7*, 173–181.

Pennebaker, J., W. & Harber, K., D. (1993). A societal model of collective coping: The Loma Prieta earthquake and the Persian Gulf War. *Journal of Social Issues, 47*, 125–145.

Power, K., McGoldrick, T., Brown, K., Buchanan, R., Sharp, D., Swanson, V., & Karatzias, A. (2002). A controlled comparison of eye movement desensitization and reprocessing versus exposure plus cognitive restructuring versus waiting list in the treatment of post-traumatic stress disorder. *Clinical Psychology and Psychotherapy, 9*, 299–318. doi:10.1002/cpp.341

Schupp, L. J. (2004). *Assessing and treating trauma and PTSD*. Eau Claire, WI: PESI Publishing and Media.

Sezgin, N. & Özcan, B. (2009). The effect of progressive muscular relaxation and Emotional Freedom Techniques on test anxiety in high school students: A randomized blind controlled study. *Energy Psychology: Theory, Research and Treatment, 1*, 23–29.

Shapiro, F. (1989). Efficacy of the eye-movement desensitization procedure in the treatment of traumatic memories. *Journal of Traumatic Stress, 2*, 199–223. doi:10.1002/jts.2490020207

Shapiro, F. (2002). EMDR 12 years after its introduction: Past and future research. *Journal of Clinical Psychology, 58*, 1–22. doi:10.1002/jclp.1126

Stickgold, R. (2002). EMDR: A putative neurobiological mechanism of action. *Journal of Clinical Psychology, 58*, 6175. doi:10.1002/jclp.1129

Sugarman, J. & Burk, L. (1998). Physicians' ethical obligations regarding alternative medicine. *JAMA, 280*, 1623–1625. doi:10.1001/jama.280.18.1623

Swingle, P. G., Pulos, L., & Swingle, M. K. (2004). Neurophysiological indicators of EFT treatment of posttraumatic stress. *Subtle Energies & Energy Medicine, 15*, 75–86.

U.S. Department of Transportation (USDOT). (2008). *Traffic Safety Facts annual report*. National Highway Traffic Safety Administration, Washington, DC. Retrieved from http://www-nrd.nhtsa.dot.gov/Pubs/811170.PDF

Van der Kolk, B. A. (1994). The body keeps the score: Memory and the evolving psychobiology of posttraumatic stress. *Harvard Review of Psychiatry, 1*, 253–265. doi:10.3109/10673229409017088

Wells, S., Polglase, K., Andrews, H.B., Carrington, P., & Baker, A. H. (2003). Evaluation of a meridian-based intervention, Emotional Freedom Techniques (EFT), for reducing specific phobias of small animals. *Journal of Clinical Psychology, 59*, 943–966. doi:10.1002/jclp.10189

Chapter 16
Energy Psychology with Rwandan Orphans
Barbara Stone, Lori Leyden, and Bert Fellows

Abstract

A team of four energy therapy practitioners headed by Dr. Lori Leyden, founder of the nonprofit organization Create Global Healing, visited Rwanda in 2009 to conduct trauma remediation programs with two groups of orphan genocide survivors with complex posttraumatic stress disorder (PTSD). The team used multiple energy psychology interventions without isolating the variables in this pilot study, as the goal of the team was to provide as much emotional relief as possible. Both groups showed a significant reduction of symptoms as measured by the Child Report of Posttraumatic Symptoms (CROPS). At a residential high school orphanage with 550 students, N = 34 students with clinical PTSD scores completed a pre and post-test, showing an average reduction in symptoms of 18.8% ($p < .001$). The second group of orphans had been young children during the genocide. When they lost their parents, they had each become the head of their household, caring for younger siblings. Of these orphan heads of household who were living independently in the capital city of Kigali, N = 28 scored in the PTSD range on the pretest. N = 21 completed post-tests at 1 week, N = 18 completed 3- month post-tests, and N = 10 completed 6-month post-tests. Their average overall reduction in PTSD symptoms was 37.3%, showing statistical significance. This chapter includes three case reports and focuses on the complexity of the background trauma in these orphans and the symptoms of catastrophic loss. It includes assessing the efficacy and limits of energy psychology in remediating PTSD symptoms, addressing the long-term needs of this population, and presenting Dr. Leyden's vision for world healing.

Keywords: energy psychology, TFT, Thought Field Therapy, TAT, Tapas Acupuncture Technique, genocide, Rwanda, trauma, PTSD, posttraumatic stress disorder

Barbara Stone, PhD, LISW, DCEP, is an ACEP certification consultant, professor at Energy Medicine University, bilingual psychotherapist, developer of Soul Detective protocols, and author of *Invisible Roots: How Healing Past Life Trauma Can Liberate Your Present* and *Transforming Fear into Gold*. She holds a doctorate in clinical psychology. Send correspondence to Barbara Stone, 1817 State Route 83, Unit 513, Millersburg, OH 44654, or contact@souldetective.net.

Lori Leyden, PhD, MBA, is a psychotherapist, humanitarian, author of *The Grace Process Guidebook* and *The Stress Management Handbook,* and founder of the nonprofit Create Global Healing and Project LIGHT: Rwanda. She holds a doctorate in psychoneuroimmunology. Send correspondence to Lori Leyden, 2424 De La Vina Street, Unit B, Santa Barbara, CA 93105, or Lori@CreateGlobalHealing.org.

Bert Fellows, MA, is director emeritus of psychological services at the Pain Management Center of Paducah, managing editor of *Pain Physician,* and author/coauthor of over 50 published articles. Retired after 40 years of clinical practice, he is now devoted to education, global humanitarian work, consciousness-raising, spiritual/energetic interventions, and hypnotherapy. Send correspondence to Bert Fellows, Pain Management Center of Paducah, 2831 Lone Oak Road, Paducah, KY 42003, or bert06@embarqmail.com.

Genocide Background

On June 12, 1994, while the American public was glued to their television sets watching the news about the deaths of Nicole Brown Simpson and Ronald Goldman and seeing O. J. Simpson accused of their murder, across the Atlantic Ocean another blood bath was in full swing in Rwanda, a tiny central African country slightly smaller than the state of Maryland. Rwanda is bordered on the west by the Democratic Republic of the Congo, on the north by Uganda, on the east by Tanzania, and on the south by Burundi. Long-standing enmity between two groups of Rwandans with a common language and common culture erupted in civil war on April 6, 1994, when an airplane carrying the Rwandan President General Juvénal Habyarimana and Burundi President Cyprien Ntaryamira, who were returning from peace talks in Tanzania, was shot down as it was trying to land in Kigali, the capital of Rwanda.

The civil war in Rwanda resonated back to the enmity between Cain and Abel, the first two children of Adam and Eve. In the Biblical account, Abel, the shepherd, was more highly praised for the fruits of his labor than his brother Cain, the farmer. The underdog Cain felt angry and killed Abel. In the Sumerian records (Sitchin, 2002), the story is expanded to Abael (Abel) boasting to his brother month after month that the Lord favored him over his brother Ka-in (Cain). Abael's taunting culminated in a boundary violation when Abael used Ka-in's irrigation ditches to water his herds. In a fit of rage, Ka-in hit Abael on the head with a rock and killed him.

Herders Versus Farmers

The conflict between the two major groups in Rwanda, the Tutsi and the Hutu, went back many centuries. The Tutsi were herders and were generally taller than the Hutu farmers, with the average height for the Tutsi being 5'8" and the average height for the Hutu 5'6", a better height to work the land. Intermarriage in the royal Tutsi family yielded Tutsi kings that were over 6'6" tall, with some reaching a height of over 7 feet (Slothrop, 2011). As with any ruling elite class, the minority Tutsi rulers oppressed the Hutu group, which made up about 88% of the population of Rwanda. When the colonial powers divided up Africa after the end of World War I, Rwanda went to Belgium.

The motto of colonialism was to divide and conquer, so the Belgians fostered enmity between these two main groups in Rwanda. They sided with the ruling Tutsi and used them as administrators to force the Hutu peasants to devote a certain percentage of their land to growing coffee for the colonialists. The Belgians also got interested in the eugenics movement and labeled the Tutsi group as racially superior since their skulls were bigger, they were taller, and they had lighter skin than the Hutus. The Belgians measured skulls and gave each Rwandan an ethnic identity card of Tutsi, Hutu, or Twa ("History of Rwanda," n.d.). The Twa Pygmies make up only about 1% of the population of Rwanda ("Rwanda Civil War," n.d.). When parents of different groups intermarried, the child was assigned the ethnic identity of the father.

Simultaneous with the internal conflict, anti-colonialist sentiment was rising in Africa. The ethnic divisions angered the Rwandan king, Rudahigwa Mutara III, who took the Christian name of Charles. The king wanted to end the system of forced labor and wanted total independence from Belgian colonial occupation (Stephen, 2008). In July of 1959, King Rudahigwa Mutara III died suddenly following a routine vaccination. The press blamed Belgium. "Though the assassination was disguised as a clinical accident by his doctor, Julien Vinck, the reality is that the king was eliminated under orders from the Belgians" (Stephen, 2008). The country went into a period of turmoil in which the Belgians withdrew and government rule went to the Hutu majority. Thousands of Tutsi were killed. Thousands more fled the country, marking the start of the 1959 to 1961 "Hutu Peasant Revolution," which ended Tutsi domination. Rwanda was declared a republic in 1961, and 1962 saw the first elected president of Rwanda, Gregoire Kayibanda, leader of the PARMEHUTU majority party ("Rwanda Profile," 2013). "By 1962, when Rwanda gained independence, 120,000 people, primarily Tutsis, had taken refuge in neighboring states to escape the violence which had accompanied the gradual coming into power of the Hutu community" ("Outreach Programme," n.d.). Some Tutsi later organized in the neighboring country of Uganda under the name of the Rwandan Patriotic Front (RPF) with the goal of returning to their homeland. Meanwhile, corruption infiltrated the Hutu government, subverting its peaceful ideals. The military seized power on July 5, 1973, under the leadership of Major General Juvenal

Habyarimana. The military abolished the National Assembly, the PARMEHUTU Party, and all political activity ("Rwanda Civil War," n.d.).

Subsistence Farming

Rwanda is called "the land of a thousand hills" because of its beautiful, rolling hills. Agriculture in the form of subsistence farming is the main economic activity, as Rwanda does not have minerals, oil, or natural resources other than its fertile soil. From 1934 to 1989, the population in Rwanda increased from 1.6 million people to 7.1 million, so competition increased for land to grow the crops necessary for survival. At 408 inhabitants per square kilometer, Rwanda's population density is among the highest in Africa. Overpopulation may have added more pressure to the civil war (Prunier, 1995).

In 1990 the RPF invaded Rwanda from western Uganda in an effort to reclaim their homeland and to make the Rwandan President General Habyarimana share power with the Tutsi minority. Habyarimana called on foreign support, particularly from France, and contained the invasion, using it as an excuse to fuel anti-Tutsi sentiment. The radical Hutu government in Rwanda laid out a plan to eliminate every single Tutsi in the whole country of Rwanda. They thought they could get away with their plan because if they killed all the Tutsi, nobody would be left to oppose their actions. Somehow they forgot about the several hundred thousand Tutsi refugees in neighboring countries. This extremist "Hutu Power" group used radio, the main means of dissemination of information in Rwanda, to fuel racial tension. They launched a new radio station called Radio-Television Libre des Mille Collines (RTLMC) in June of 1993 that began broadcasting hatred of the Tutsi, dehumanizing them by labeling them "cockroaches," blaming them for all the problems in the country, and calling for their "extermination" (Cotton, 2010).

The Complexity of the Trauma

The Hutu genocide plan included not only every Tutsi in the country, but also the Hutu moderates who believed in peaceful coexistence between the two groups. Immediately after the assassination of the Rwandan president, the genocide plan went into action with its death lists of all the Tutsi and moderate Hutus in the country.

Government-Sponsored Killing

The government forced everybody to participate in some way. By forcing moderate Hutus to murder a Tutsi or be killed themselves, they included as many people as possible in the genocide guilt, exacerbating the trauma in the country (Hatzfeld, 2006). What is a law-abiding Hutu citizen supposed to do when ordered by the government, upon peril of his own life, to kill his Tutsi wife or neighbor? This moral dilemma is captured dramatically in the movie *Hotel Rwanda* (George, 2005), the story of Hutu hotel manager Paul Rusesabagina, who was ordered to shoot his Tutsi wife. Fortunately, he found a way to subvert this command.

Machetes

The method of killing added to the trauma. Since machetes were a household item for farmers and were cheaper than guns, in 1993, businessmen close to General Habyarimana imported $750,000 worth of machetes from China, enough for one new machete for every third male in the entire country (Melvern, 2006). The government distributed these machetes to civilian militia groups called the "Interahamwe," meaning those who stand/work/fight/attack together. The Interahamwe civilian militia was responsible for much of the killing. Resenting the dominance of the taller Tutsi, the Hutu militia first cut off the legs of the Tutsi to "cut them down to size" and then continued the slow, painful, brutal process of hacking the body apart until the person died. Of an original population of about 7.5 million, over one million Rwandans were killed, mostly by machete, in just 100 days (Gourevitch, 1998, p. 3).

Other Damage

Another aspect of Hutu power was dehumanization of Tutsi females by systematic rape. Estimates are that 250,000 to 500,000 women and girls in Rwanda were raped, and of the women who survived, 70% of them are HIV positive. "Almost all of the women who did survive the genocide were victims of sexual violence or were profoundly affected by it" (Chu & de Brouwer, 2009).

Some of the parents of the students at the orphanage did not die immediately from the genocide, but died after it was over from their physical and emotional wounds. One parent was still living but was incapacitated from losing both arms. Others survived their physical wounds, but the stress of witnessing their children and other family members being massacred drove them into insanity.

Ending the Genocide and Rebuilding the Country

The RPF, under the leadership of Paul Kagame, went into action as soon as the genocide started and marched into the country from Uganda. The RPF took control of the capital city of Kigali on July 4, 1994, which stopped the bulk of the killing as the genocidaires fled the country and took refuge mostly in the Congo. The war ended on July 16, 1994. One of the first actions of Paul Kagame was to abolish the ethnic identity cards. Now all Rwandans are just Rwandans without ethnic division. With an infrastructure that had been demolished, Kagame started the process of rebuilding. In 2003 the first elections since the genocide gave General Paul Kagame a 7-year presidential term, and he was reelected in 2010 with 93% of the vote. "Kagame transformed his country, turning it into one of the fastest growing nations in Africa and—in the view of some—a model of economic and social development" (CNN wire staff, 2010). Immediately following the genocide, Rwanda's population was 70% female, and women currently occupy 56% of the seats in Rwanda's parliament and own 41% of Rwandan businesses (Chu & de Brouwer, 2009). Rwanda is now listed by the U.S. Department of State as having a low threat of terrorism and being one of the safest African countries to visit.

Catastrophic Loss

A single incident of trauma like a car accident or being robbed is called simple trauma and usually resolves with a small number of energy psychology sessions. Often one traumatic memory can be resolved in a single session, a statistic reported in psychologist Carl Johnson's work in war-torn countries (Johnson, Shala, Sejdijaj, Odell, & Dabishevci, 2001). Dr. Johnson's amazing statistics are that out of a total of 337 subjects in Kosovo, South Africa, Rwanda, and the Congo, 334 of them were treated successfully. They reported 1016 traumas, and 1013 of these were treated successfully in a single session intervention. When trauma has been repeated, as in a teenager being raped over and over, or when a person experiences multiple traumas at the same time, the situation is called "complex trauma." Many of the orphans we worked with had lost not only their parents, but also many or all of their siblings and sometimes their entire extended family network. Of the surviving family members, many were so traumatized that they were unable to provide any emotional or physical support. Genocide survivors also lost their homes and land as the militia looted their possessions and confiscated their property. They lost their emotional security, with many still fearing for their lives if they were to return to the areas where they had lived. Some lost their health, purposely infected by HIV or crippled by machete wounds.

While the newcomers on our humanitarian team were prepared to witness the horror of the genocide, we were not prepared for feeling the anxiety and hopelessness about the future the orphans at the residential high school faced as they entered the age when they should be moving out on their own. With no family, no higher education, no money, no land in a society based on subsistence farming, and no job skills in a difficult economy, most of the students faced living on the streets when they graduated from high school. Not surprisingly, some students were in their mid to late 20s and just could not seem to pass their exams to graduate. At least at the orphanage, they had a roof over their heads, meals, and supportive people around them. The orphan heads of household we worked with in Kigali were already out on the streets, often struggling for daily survival.

Methods

We used a variety of means to establish rapport with the orphans and to meet their physical, emotional, and spiritual needs.

Spiritual Faith

Calling on transpersonal help in the form of their Christian faith is the cornerstone of healing for these orphans and gives them strength to go on under extremely difficult life circumstances. At the beginning of our trip, we arrived at the residential high school on a Sunday morning. Our first activity was worshipping together with the students and teachers. We could hear the music and feel the building rocking long before we got to the meeting room! We really enjoyed the singing, dancing, and instrumental music in the service.

Several choirs, self-taught, performed beautiful, soulful music for us.

The headmaster asked Dr. Stone to speak to the group during the worship service. She shared the following experience of praying for help in 1991 when she had been diagnosed with breast cancer.

"As I was praying to Jesus, the face that God wears for me since I was raised in a Christian family, I felt Jesus tap on my sternum communicating the complete thought, 'I now heal your soul.' That was my first experience with tapping, and I felt a deep wound heal up in my soul with that touch. I had not realized I brought ancestral pain with me into this incarnation, but with the touch of the Master, something deep in my soul healed, and I absolutely knew I would survive the cancer. I feel so grateful for getting back my health and wrote my doctoral dissertation on the emotional factors influencing cancer survival" (Stone, 1994). One of the key factors with those who survive this illness is a direct encounter with a transpersonal being of Light who imparts help.

The emotional response of the students to her story moved her heart deeply. They understood the principle of turning to a higher power for spiritual, emotional, and physical strength.

Providing Food

At the residential high school orphanage, Dr. Leyden bought a cow and served a meal that included meat, which the orphans there get only a few times a year. In our workshop with the orphan heads of household, we provided lunch, a great incentive for the students to attend, as some of them have many days with no food at all. Trauma relief is more than just energy tapping. How can a hungry person focus on the tapping procedure? One must first meet the immediate physical needs.

Multiple Energy Psychology Interventions

In addition to this "nutrition therapy," we taught the orphans multiple stress reduction methods in groups. At the high school we did group interventions of exercises for breathing, centering, and gratitude. We did laughter yoga with the group, and we led them in a group tapping sequence for the trauma of the genocide. We interviewed students to assess those in greatest need and did some individual sessions with the most traumatized students. The previous year, Dr. Leyden had provided special training to leaders she identified in the group, including teaching them EFT, so these leaders could help others after the first team left. We added further training for leaders in the group and provided them with support materials.

At the smaller group of 33 orphan heads of household located in Kigali, our translator led the group in a warm-up of singing, dancing, and clapping—great fun! We gave the group the CROPS test at the beginning of the workshop and from the results identified the most traumatized orphans. We were able to add individual sessions for eight of the most traumatized students. We taught the group diaphragmatic breathing, yoga, gratitude exercises, and laughter yoga. Team member Bert Fellows taught the group a modified version of Tapas Acupressure Technique (TAT), developed by Tapas Fleming (www.tatlife.com). We then split the group in half and Dr. Leyden led one part in a Grace Process Forgiveness exercise, and Dr. Stone taught the other half the TFT sequence for genocide trauma. Then we traded groups so each student got both methods. We left laminated diagrams of the tapping points and treatment sequences so they could continue to practice the methods after we left. When Dr. Leyden returned to the orphanage the following year, the whole atmosphere had changed. During our visit in 2009, decorations consisted of some toilet paper strewn over the beams. In 2010, the energy at the school was brighter, and the decorations were beautiful cloth drapes. One student verbalized the internal change she experienced in a touching manner. She said, "At first when you told me to rub my heart and say that I love myself, I didn't love myself. But as I have practiced what you taught us, I realize that now, I do love myself!"

PTSD Measure

The measure we used to assess the level of trauma in the orphans we worked with was a translation into their language of Kinyarwanda of the Child Report of Posttraumatic Symptoms (CROPS), developed by Ricky Greenwald, PsyD, founder and director of the Trauma Institute and Child Trauma Institute. (The CROPS assessment instrument is available through the institute's website, www.childtrauma.com). We chose this measure to replicate studies previously done in Rwanda

Table 1. *Average (Mean ± SD) CROPS Score Changes at the Residential High School Orphanage*

Sample Size	CROPS Pretest	CROPS Post-test	Score Difference	Average % Drop	Significance
$n = 34$	34.5 ± 7.7	28.0 ± 11.2	6.53 ± 8.75	18.8%	$t = 4.348$ $p < .001$

by the Thought Field Therapy teams headed by researchers Carl Johnson and Caroline Sakai. We wanted to add Greenwald's Parent Report of Post-traumatic Symptoms (PROPS), as Sakai's group found the children tended to underestimate their own level of stress, but with their parents missing, nobody knew our orphans well enough to complete this second measure. The CROPS test has 26 statements reflecting symptoms of trauma, depression, and anxiety. The respondent can answer each statement with none for 0 points, some for 1 point, or lots for 2 points, so the maximum score is 52. Any score of 19 or more indicates clinical posttraumatic stress. Test items include difficulty concentrating, worry about the future, avoidance of reminders of bad things that have happened, insomnia, physical symptoms, low energy, feeling different from others and alone, and feeling jinxed, depressed, and/or nervous.

Results
Residential High School Orphanage

Janette (all names have been changed to protect confidentiality), a student at the high school who carried great sadness, felt very surprised to find herself in a group learning self-help energy psychology methods. She believed that speaking relieved a person, but when someone asked her about her problems, her sorrow welled up so much that she was unable to talk. The first aspect of her trauma she wanted to focus on was having no stable place to live or to go to during school vacations when she could not stay at the orphanage. Her beginning subjective units of disturbance (SUD) level was 10, which dropped all the way down to 0 after tapping for her fears. She left with a huge smile! Her initial CROPS score was 39, and at 1 week after our intervention, her score had dropped down to 24.

The average initial score of the orphans we worked with at the residential high school was 30.9, far above the cutoff of 19. Of the 34 students who started out with scores greater than 19 and completed a post-test, the average score was 34.5 (see Table 1). When these students took a post-test a week after our intervention, their scores had dropped down to an average of only 28 (Stone, Leyden, & Fellows, 2009).

Orphan Heads of Household

The orphan heads of household we worked with in Kigali had to struggle with the additional stressor of finding daily food and shelter. In this group, N = 28 with clinical PTSD scores completed a pretest. N = 21 completed post-tests at 1 week, N = 18 completed 3-month post-tests, and N = 10 completed 6-month post-tests. Whereas the initial CROPS average from the high school was 30.9, the initial scores in the groups below were slightly higher, ranging from 32.6 to 34.6. Table 2 shows that the students who were motivated to complete more of the follow-up measures were the ones who had started out with higher scores.

The average overall reduction in PTSD symptoms was 37.3%. Note that without any further intervention, the CROPS scores dropped steadily,

Table 2. *Average PTSD Symptom Reduction for Orphan Heads of Household*

Scores Indicating PTSD	Avg. Initial CROPS Score	Avg. CROPS Score after 1 wk.	Avg. CROPS Score after 3 mos.	Avg. CROPS Score after 6 mos.
$n = 28$ out of 33	32.6			
$n = 21$ reporters at 1 month	32.7	29.5		
$n = 18$ reporters at 3 months	33.3	30.1	27.3	
$n = 10$ reporters at 6 months	34.6	31.9	28.8	21.7

indicating that the students were continuing to practice the energy psychology self-help methods they learned. All of the various ways the results were analyzed showed statistically significant improvement ranging from *p* values of <0.009 to 0.001 (Stone, Leyden, & Fellows, 2010).

Trauma Outbreaks During the Night

In the high school orphanage, students slept in one large room with bunk beds arranged in rows with two single bunk beds placed side by side, with two persons sleeping on each single mattress, so four students slept in a row on each level. The girls' room had about 250 females and the boys' room about 300 males. Before our team leader Lori Leyden first went to Rwanda, the headmaster reported that at least once per week, someone in the dorm would have a nightmare or flashbacks, dissociate, and feel like he or she was back experiencing the genocide. Once one person started screaming, others were triggered and soon the whole dorm would be hysterical. Sometimes the school would have to call in the military to come and take some students to a hospital. On her first visit, Dr. Leyden taught the students a variety of self-help therapies including EFT, TAT, and her own work, which she calls the Grace Process. After that first visit, the headmaster reported that these trauma outbreaks of screaming had decreased by 90%.

Three Case Reports from Dr. Stone

The following three case reports of Dr. Stone's individual work with students demonstrate various aspects of the complexity of trauma and catastrophic loss these orphans experienced.

Simone

Simone had a good life before the genocide, which came when she was 11 years old and in the fourth grade. Simone's mother, father, and five siblings went to the health center to hide when the militia came to their village. Although the health center was supposed to be a safe zone, the militia threw a grenade into the building, resulting in high fatalities. Simone does not know how she got out of the health center. Both of her parents, her sister, and three brothers died there. She fled the health center and went to the Catholic Church, which was also supposed to be a safe zone. The militia came to the church and started killing everyone. Simone was left for dead, with bodies stacked on top of her. The following morning, she went out and hid in the bush. The militia returned, but they did not see her.

A Hutu man found her and put her with other children he was hiding, refusing to disclose their presence to the Hutu militia. When the RPF soldiers came, they protected Simone. After some weeks, she found that one of her brothers had survived the grenade attack. He was hurt so badly with head wounds that he was unable to care for himself, so at 11, Simone became an orphan head of household looking after herself and her brother. As he grew to adulthood, her brother was unable to handle the level of undigested trauma in his system, both physical and emotional, and Simone described him as "going mad." He was spending his adult life in bars, living alone and homeless.

After the genocide, Simone could not return to school. In Rwanda, as in most third world countries, students must pay to go to school and need to buy the uniforms the school children wear. Stricken by poverty, Simone had nobody to pay her school fees. At age 26, she still found reading and writing difficult. She reported that her genocide memories returned every time her landlord came for her rent money.

During our session Simone had a headache from remembering the noise of the grenades and guns. We cleared reversals and tapped on her anger and rage at the catastrophic loss she experienced. To her surprise, her headache went away after our tapping. She was then able to verbalize, "God wants me to live a better life, to do better things." She felt that since her parents died without sin, they went to heaven. In her dreams at night she would see her parents coming and paying her school fees so she could continue her education and would see her siblings around her. But every time she woke up from these dreams, she would feel worse, realizing that her brother, the only family member who had also survived, was mentally deranged and that she still was not able to complete her education.

Simone's initial trauma score on the CROPS was 42 out of a possible 52. After 1 week her score dropped to 40, after 3 months to 39, and after 6 months her score dropped down to 30.

Esther

Esther's teachers identified her as one of the most traumatized at the high school orphanage. She sometimes dissociated, ran off into the forest by herself, and had to be brought back by force. Esther refused to come to our group sessions, but she was willing to come for an individual session. I asked Esther to rate her initial distress about the genocide trauma on the SUD scale of 0 to 10, with 10 being the worst trauma possible. Esther reported that her initial rating was 100, going "way beyond all numbers." After clearing reversals, her disturbance level came down to 90.

Esther's mother was Hutu and her father was Tutsi. She was conceived out of wedlock, and during her mother's pregnancy, her father left to join the RPF. Esther was only 6 years old when the genocide hit. Her mother was not hurt because she was Hutu, but because Esther's father was Tutsi and her identity card said Tutsi, Esther was repeatedly raped by older men. Esther's mother committed suicide in 1998, which was 4 years after the genocide ended. At age 10, Esther was forced to live in a household that included one of her perpetrators. He continued to rape her, threatening to kill her if she told anyone about the sexual abuse. When she finally disclosed what was happening, she was blamed. Her father abandoned her and moved out of the country. Having no place to go, Esther was taken in by the residential high school.

The core of her wound was repeated rape by multiple abusers. After tapping on her rape memories, she felt somewhat better, but her continued disturbance was palpable. She was still feeling the presence of her perpetrators around her, and she felt physical pain in her tailbone. We did further healing work on her lower spine with an energy psychology technique of a chakra pullout using counterclockwise motions to release the trauma and then clockwise motions to restore well-being to the lower part of her spine. As we were doing this work, heavy rain began to fall, making a lot of noise as it hit the tin roof over our heads. I asked her to visualize standing in the rain and letting this rain wash away all of the pain of her sexual abuse, washing her clean on the inside and restoring her innocence. I learned this intervention of imagining being under a cleansing waterfall from molecular biologist and naturopath Adam McLeod (2006). We then prayed, thanking God for healing her pain and asking for angels to walk with her always, on all four sides, plus above and below. This visualization brought her a great deal of emotional relief and completely resolved her physical pain. We made a strong, intense empathic connection.

The following day Esther was radiant. She showed up in the group smiling, laughing, and participating wholeheartedly! The entire team noticed this positive change. Esther asked me to be her "grandmother." At first I thought that her request meant that she recognized that my heart had opened deeply to her, like it opens to my grandchildren. Through the translator, I acknowledged this connection. Then when I brought this request up to our team leader, I found out that what Esther had meant by asking me to be her grandmother was a request to establish contact between us through e-mail and for me to provide ongoing emotional and financial support, as in a third-world child sponsorship program. At that point, we did not have a sponsorship program set up for the orphanage, and I had to let Esther know that neither I nor anybody else on our team could commit to becoming a grandparent sponsor. Setting that boundary was difficult for me, but it was crushing for Esther. The loss of this hope added to her feeling of abandonment by her father's exit and her mother's suicide. While most of the other orphans at the school showed a significant decrease in their trauma rating scales after our interventions, Esther's trauma score went up slightly. Her CROPS pretest score was 37, and her score after this disappointment rose to 39.

I learned a powerful lesson from this incident. Esther's needs went way beyond desensitizing her trauma with tapping. She needed a social support system, job training, and financial support to move out into the world once she graduated from high school. She needed an ongoing supportive connection, which I could not provide.

Helen

Helen's father had seven children with her mother plus several children by another wife. Helen's uncle loved her very much, took her places, and paid her school fees so she could get an education. The militia attacked her village the second week of the genocide, killing her parents and some of her siblings in their own home. Helen and her uncle escaped and hid in the marshes until they got word that coming out was safe. When they came out of the marshes, they discovered that the message of safety was a trick by the militia, who immediately captured them and hacked them with machetes. Helen fainted. The militia laid their bodies down in trenches and then buried them, not caring whether people were dead or alive. When she regained consciousness, heavy mud weighed down her body, and breathing was extremely difficult. When insects started crawling into her ears, she tried to get out. Even though she was only 8 years old, by mustering all of her strength, she was able to wiggle one elbow to break a hole through the earth. She was able to get out her left arm and her head, and then she dragged out the rest of her body. Knowing the militia would return, she bent over to cover up the hole where she had escaped. As she leaned over, she felt as if her head were falling off. Up until this point, she had not realized that her neck had been cut. With one hand holding her forehead to keep her head attached, she rearranged the soil so her exit would not be detected and hid in the bushes. Then she heard her uncle crying out for help and witnessed the militia return, go to the location of her uncle's cries, and poke spears through the dirt until her uncle was dead.

Five aspects of Helen's trauma.
1. *Guilt.* She did not think of helping her uncle at the time because she was badly wounded and the situation was unsafe. Later, however, she was haunted by flashbacks of her uncle's cries and visions of him standing before her. Because she loved him so much, she felt tremendous guilt that she had not helped him.
2. *Intrusive images.* After Helen escaped, she was haunted by images of her deceased mother and siblings. She went back to her home and covered the bodies of her family members with pieces of cloth and banana leaves. Visions of their corpses still haunted her.
3. *Homelessness.* After the genocide, Helen lived with a surviving half-sister who kicked her out when she reached the age of maturity, telling her, "You can go back to where you lived, or you can commit suicide. I don't care about you." This rejection left Helen homeless, and at the time of treatment, she was squatting in a house that was under construction and was extremely unsafe.
4. *Scars.* Helen still carried scars of machete wounds on her neck, hands, and ankles, as they had tried to cut off her feet. Genocide survivors feel ashamed of these scars, which mark their place on the death lists.
5. *Exile.* Because Helen knew the identity of the people who had killed her family, she feared she would be recognized and assassinated if she returned to her village.

Individual treatment. We started treatment with tapping on the trauma of seeing her family's corpses. Next we tapped on her guilt over not helping her uncle. Other counselors had tried to help her get through her guilt, but she was not able to let it go until we tapped on this specific issue, including tapping on the index fingernail point for the Large Intestine meridian, identified by John Diamond as the meridian where we hold guilt (Diamond, 1985, p. 134). After tapping, I asked Helen what would have happened if she had tried to rescue her uncle when she first heard his voice crying for help. She responded that if she had gone to help him, the militia would have killed her too when they returned because she did not have enough time to get him out. This cognitive reframing intervention helped her realize that rescuing her uncle had been impossible.

Next we used prayer, the intervention Helen and the Christian agency where we were working used the most. Helen prayed for God to forgive her for not saving her uncle, and she sensed that she was forgiven. She also prayed for God to help all of her family members who had died in the genocide, especially her uncle. As she was praying with great emotion, I silently added a prayer from my own belief system for Archangel Michael to gather up the spirits of any of them who might still be earthbound and take them into the next world to rejoin their loved ones (Stone, 2008). With this intervention, Helen felt a huge emotional shift, and the burden lifted from her heart. We shouted, "Hallelujah!"

The following day in class, Helen was radiant. She had practiced her centering techniques overnight, and her perspective on her situation had gone through a major shift. Within a few days, Dr. Leyden and the Christian agency teamed up to help Helen get into safer housing.

Helen's initial CROPS score out of a possible 52 points was 43, which was the third highest score in the group of 33 students. After one week, Helen's score dropped to 40, after 3 months to 39, and after 6 months to 33, showing a lasting benefit of the trauma healing work our team did and indicating that she may have been continuing to use the self-help healing tools we taught the group.

The Treatment Method
EFT and TFT
Gary Craig originally trained with psychologist Roger Callahan, PhD, in the method Callahan developed and called Thought Field Therapy (TFT; Callahan, 2001). Craig simplified TFT into Emotional Freedom Techniques (EFT) to make it easier to learn, and EFT is the energy psychology method that has reached the masses. EFT is much easier to master as a self-help tool than the more complicated method of TFT.

Replication
One of the principles used to evaluate research is replication. If two independent researchers can use the same methods and get similar results, the study is taken more seriously. Since Dr. Leyden had already taught both groups of orphans in Rwanda EFT, our team replicated the TFT protocol that researchers Carl Johnson and Caroline Sakai had used. Sakai published the results of an excellent, successful study they did with Rwandan orphans, which was controlled, using a wait-list method to isolate the amount of improvement that came from just using the TFT algorithms for trauma, rage, anger, sexual assault, and survivor guilt (Sakai, Connolly, & Oas, 2010).

Culturally Sensitive Interventions
We needed to stay within the belief systems of the evangelical Christian agencies we were working with. The people in Rwanda believed in two methods of healing. One was letting a person tell their whole story, beginning to end, without interruption. Many of the orphans we worked with had never disclosed their stories. While we longed to honor them all by listening to what happened to them, we only had time to hear a few accounts. We selected the most traumatized of the orphans and gave them an individual session in which they could tell their stories, as in the case histories just reported. The theory of this method of healing is that "remembering is releasing," the same principle used in hypnosis. With extreme cases of trauma, however, remembering an event can trigger violent unresolved feelings and retraumatize the client. In our individual sessions, when a person became visibly upset, we used energy tapping to calm the person down and desensitize the trauma.

The other intervention the group believed in was prayer, calling on the power of the spiritual figure of Jesus Christ. They did not have a belief system that tapping on an acupressure point could bring emotional relief, so we added two features to the protocol to fit the therapy into their belief system:

1. After an initial SUD assessment, including a nonverbal happy face to sad face spectrum, we began and ended the treatment with prayer.
2. In the initial reversal clearing statements of love and acceptance, we added two statements that Dan Benor, MD, uses in his Wholistic Hybrid of EMDR and EFT (WHEE) method, "Jesus loves and accepts me" and "God loves and accepts me" (see Dr. Benor's website www.wholistichealingresearch.com).

Affirmations Versus Tapping
When the energy therapies involving affirmations and tapping were first being developed, innovators Roger Callahan and John Diamond disagreed on why the methods worked. Psychiatrist John Diamond believed that the affirmations resolved the problem. Psychologist Roger Callahan felt that tapping the right point released the emotional disturbance. Both methods appear to work. If a person taps the right point, a negative emotion seems to dissolve. If a person says the right affirmation to release the negative and install the positive, the negative emotion also seems to dissolve. EFT uses affirmations throughout the tapping process. The tapping sequence in EFT is designed as a single sequence to cover all the major meridian end points, regardless of the issue. TFT does not use affirmations. Over thousands of cases, Roger Callahan has refined the most likely sequence of meridian points needed to unlock each negative pattern. TFT is like a rifle aimed at a very specific target point. In the chart that we replicated from the TFT researchers (see Step 6 in the TFT treatment protocol that follows), one can see the points we used for each of the negative emotions included. If we felt the subject needed additional support, we sometimes added the affirmations.

Thought Field Therapy (TFT) Treatment Protocol for Trauma

1. **Rate how much the problem you have selected hurts:**

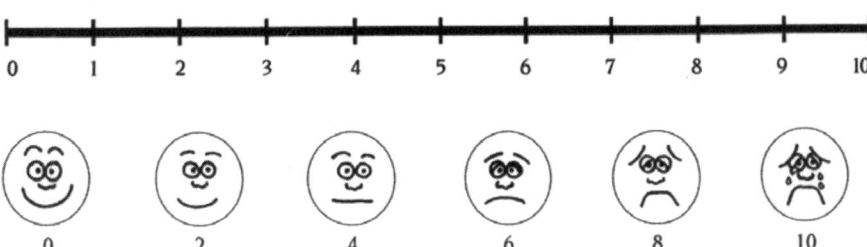

Show how much it hurts, either by showing with how far apart your hands are (close together is not very much pain, wide apart is a lot of pain) or by picking a number above from 0–10.

2. **Pray, asking God for help and asking Jesus into your heart to help heal the problem.**
3. **Heart circle**
   Put your right hand over your heart and rub in a clockwise circle while saying,
   - I accept all of my feelings about all of my problems.
   - I love and accept myself (or I wish I could love and accept myself).
   - God loves and accepts me.
   - Jesus loves and accepts me.
4. **Focusing exercise**
   Put your finger in your bellybutton and at the same time tap or rub:
   - Both collarbone points, then
   - Under the nose and
   - Under the lips
   (You can do under the nose and under the lips at the same time.)

5. **Eliminating blocking beliefs**
   Tap the side of the hand while saying several times:

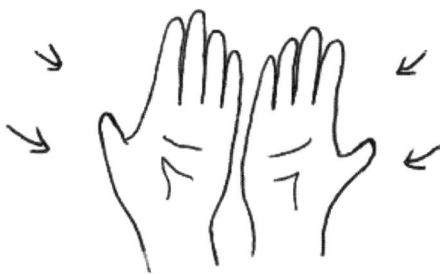

   - *Whether or not I feel getting over this trauma is possible, I love and accept myself, and God loves and accepts me.*
   - *Whether or not I feel getting over this trauma is safe for me and/or for others, I love and accept myself, and Jesus loves and accepts me.*
   - *Whether or not I feel I deserve to get over this trauma, I love and accept myself, and God loves and accepts me.*
6. **Tap this series of points:**

Emotion Treated	Tapping Points	Optional Affirmation for the First Round	Optional Affirmation after the 9 Gamut
Trauma	Eyebrow Under Eye Under Arm Collarbone	"It's over now."	"It's over now."
Rage	Outer Eye Collarbone	"I accept all of my rage about what happened."	"I forgive myself for not being able to stop it."

(continued)

Emotion Treated	Tapping Points	Optional Affirmation for the First Round	Optional Affirmation After the 9-Gamut
Anger	**Little finger** **Collarbone**	"I accept all of my anger about what happened."	"I forgive myself for not being able to stop it."
Sexual Assault	**Middle finger** **Collarbone**	"I call back my life energy/ power from the past!"	"I call back my life energy/ power from the past!"
Guilt	**Index finger** **Collarbone**	"I accept how guilty I feel for surviving."	"I forgive myself for feeling guilty. It was not my fault."

7. **Do the 9 Gamut Procedure**
   Tap the Gamut point with:
   - Eyes closed
   - Eyes open
   - Eyes down to the right
   - Eyes down to the left
   - Eyes circling in one direction
   - Eyes circling in the opposite direction
   - Hum a few notes
   - Count to 5
   - Hum a few notes
8. **Tap the same series of points again** (eyebrow, under eye, under arm, etc.).
9. **Rate how much the problem hurts now.**
10. **Next step:** If the problem still hurts quite a bit, you can do this whole process over again. If the problem is a lot better, then pray and thank God for the healing!

Summary

Tapping interventions are the gold standard for releasing traumatic imprints, and we saw marked upward shifts in emotional functioning once these orphans embraced the variety of self-help energy psychology methods we brought to them. This emotional healing is a vital part of recovery for people with catastrophic loss and complex trauma, but survivors need more than just emotional relief from traumatic memories. Maslow's hierarchy of needs places physical needs at the foundation of the pyramid of developmental psychology. People need food and shelter before they can address their higher-level needs for safety, love/belonging, esteem, and self-actualization, in that order (Maslow, 1943). Although the students at the residential high school orphanage had their physical needs met during the time school was in session, they knew that once they left school, they would be presented with the same daily struggle for basic physical necessities that the orphans in Kigali faced. We needed to provide food for the day for both groups of students as we were teaching them energy psychology self-help methods, but all of the students needed a means to be able to provide for the basic necessities of life for themselves in the future.

Needs Assessments

One of the most beautiful things about Dr. Leyden's humanitarian work is that she asks the people she serves what they most need. The previous year the needs assessment at the high school orphanage chose getting running water at the school as the top priority. They had been carrying water uphill by oxcart from a well 3 kilometers away. Dr. Leyden did a fundraiser to raise money for the well, and our team member Bert Fellows was the major contributor to that project. That first day we had a ribbon-cutting ceremony for the dedication of the well, and the whole school rejoiced as we splashed each other with water! During our visit in 2009 the orphanage chose getting electricity as the top priority need. By 2010, Dr. Leyden's fundraising had provided electricity to the classrooms so the students could study after dark and get computers.

The biggest need all of the students had was job training so they could provide for themselves as they were propelled into being on their own after school. Our team leader Lori Leyden responded to this need for economic security and in 2011 launched Project LIGHT: Rwanda (LIGHT stands for Leadership, Inspiration, Global Healing, and Transformation; see projectlightrwanda.com), a new form of humanitarian aid that includes trauma healing, leadership, and entrepreneurship skills training. The program started with a group of 12 "ambassadors" and had great success. Dr. Leyden's vision is to have international youth healing centers all over the world in communication with each other, interfacing with donors, students, businesses, and charities for an impact for lasting, sustainable change (see the YouTube video *Project LIGHT Rwanda*).

Guidelines for Humanitarian Workers

1. Go where you are invited and have an in-country host to sponsor you and mobilize the population to be treated.
2. Know the history of the country/culture/disaster situation in as much detail as possible.
3. Find out the cultural and societal norms of wherever you are going. When in Rome, do as the Romans do, or at least be aware when you are stepping outside these norms and have calculated the risks.
4. Know the language of the participants or have translators available. If you are using support materials, get them translated into the language of the recipients.
5. Plan carefully and whenever possible, use a model by which you train participants in the method you use so your programs become self-sufficient.
6. In spite of all the preparation you do, know that you may still experience culture shock. Be prepared for all scenarios, make plans, and then be absolutely prepared to drop those plans in favor of the needs that arise for what is best for the individual and the group you are serving.
7. Be prepared for extremes of weather, poor accommodations, inadequate food supplies, lack of luxury items, and challenging Internet connection. Humanitarian work is physically demanding, but immensely satisfying and fun. Being in good physical health will help your adjustment. If you have serious health issues, you may need to limit your involvement to financial contributions or background support.
8. Committing to your own self-healing work is crucial so you know your own trauma triggers. Have self-care skills you can use to stay in balance during your trip.

The Importance of Invitation

One needs an invitation from an in-country group. An unfortunate circumstance happened when a person with great heart flew a team of relief workers to the site of the tsunami in Indonesia. This group never got to get off the plane because no arrangements were in place to get the team to the people who needed help. Plugging into an organization that is already in gear saves an enormous amount of footwork. If someone wants to do humanitarian work in a certain area of the world, the person can check on the Internet for NGOs (non-governmental organizations) that are already involved in the area and doing a similar mission.

Be sure you are wanted in the area, and respect the culture you are serving. A well-meaning Christian organization did relief work after the tsunami and raised money to build an orphanage for around 100 of the children who had lost both parents. Though the intent was good, this action produced an outcry against these children, who had been raised in Muslim homes, being put into an evangelical Christian agency. The plan had to be abandoned because it violated religious boundaries.

Become involved only upon invitation and seek invitations from stable, mature organizations that have the resources to mobilize the target population and support them before, during, and after your interventions.

Meeting Basic Needs

Unless the basic survival needs of the target population are met, any trauma relief will probably be short-lived or minimized. That is why having a host organization that can provide food, water, shelter, clothing, transportation, medical care, and social support alongside the trauma specialist interventions is so important.

Energy interventions are primarily targeted toward emotional trauma relief with the end result of mental and physiological homeostasis.

An extremely simple trauma "first aid" intervention such as the work being done by trauma therapist and trainer Gunilla Hamne of the Peaceful Heart Network has been remarkably impressive. The extent to which recipients of the trauma interventions are supported by some kind of social structure, be it their own community, a charitable or church organization or a government program, determines the quality and longevity of the interventions. The best plan is an approach that is as holistic as possible, addressing as many legitimate challenges to normal functioning as possible without creating unnecessary dependency and without disturbing the social value system of the participants or their sponsors.

Teamwork

The challenges of language, cultural, and social differences require great maturity and flexibility on the part of the humanitarian workers. A person going alone needs to be exceptionally confident in his or her skills and ability to adapt. Going in a group provides more structure and emotional support for the challenges that arise. Trust the inner wisdom and innate healing abilities of those you are serving. Adopt an attitude of partnership with them and remember that you will be receiving a great deal in return. The reward of seeing lives change and feeling the gratitude coming from the people served opens the heart.

Research

Getting feedback on the effectiveness of humanitarian interventions is important to evaluate the project. Workers can collect data for a pilot study by something as simple as recording the SUD level of each subject before and after an intervention. A full-scale research study is very complicated and requires the approval of an institutional review board (IRB), something that is difficult and expensive to get if a person is not part of a university that has an IRB. For good research, the intervention needs to be a single intervention systematically applied by all members of the intervention team, such as the very successful work published by Caroline Sakai and the TFT group (Sakai, Connolly, & Oas, 2010). In Rwanda, Sakai and her group had to get a second IRB from the government in Rwanda before they were permitted to do their study. Doing research requires a funding source.

Other long-term projects such as Dr. Leyden's Project LIGHT: Rwanda are more diverse, with multiple interventions used to meet the needs of the population served. This model does not fit well into scientific study for which one needs to isolate the variables, but it matches multifaceted need with a multifaceted intervention.

Credentials

In general, the more sophistication, training, and experience the workers have, the more successful the emotional trauma relief will be. Having credentials such as being EFT certified or ACEP certified or having a professional license in the area of intervention builds credibility and opens doors to NGOs. But there is also a place for non-credentialed helpers if they are proficient in the role assigned to them on the team. One successful team delegated one team member just to collect data.

Project Categories

The following list can help divide planning a humanitarian project into discrete categories to get an overview of the project.

- Long-term/short-term
- Group/single
- First aid/ongoing
- Single intervention/multiple intervention
- Research/non research
- Funded/unfunded
- Passport/no passport
- Visa/no visa

Many humanitarian projects will require many months or up to a year of preparation. Be sure to give yourself plenty of time.

Hope for World Peace

In the process of Dr. Leyden's Create Global Healing humanitarian venture to relieve suffering in one of the most traumatized places on our planet, we were all deeply moved and inspired by the courage and resilience of these amazing young people. We got back more than we gave—their openhearted love and appreciation for our help and their beautiful, self-taught soulful music, clearly audible in Dr. Stone's YouTube video *Trauma Healing in Rwanda*. Dr. Leyden says in her YouTube video *EFT with Orphan Genocide Survivors in Rwanda: A Create Global Healing Program,* "These orphan genocide survivors inspire in me a true knowing that world healing is possible. I came away saying that if these survivors could forgive, now we've got a template for world peace. Because if they can forgive, we can bring this model all over the world, and now we really have something to offer."

References

Callahan, R. (2001). *Tapping the healer within: Using Thought Field Therapy to instantly conquer your fears, anxieties, and emotional distress.* Chicago, IL: Contemporary Books. See also www.rogercallahan.com

Chu, S. K. H. & de Brouwer, A-M. (2009). Rwanda genocide victims speak out. In Chu and de Brouwer (Eds.), *The men who killed me: Rwandan survivors of sexual violence.* Vancouver, BC: Douglas & McIntyre. Retrieved from http://www.herizons.ca/node/334

CNN wire staff. (2010, August 11). Kagame wins re-election in Rwanda, official results show. *CNN World.* Retrieved from http://articles.cnn.com/2010-08-11/world/rwanda.elections_1_hutus-tutsis-polling-stations?_s=PM:WORLD

Cotton, S. (2010, December 31). Where radio is king: Rwanda's hate radio and the lessons learned. Retrieved from http://friendsofevil.wordpress.com/2010/12/31/where-radio-is-king-rwanda%E2%80%99s-hate-radio-and-the-lessons-learned

Diamond, J. (1985). *Life energy: Using the meridians to unlock the hidden power of your emotions.* St. Paul, MN: Paragon House.

George, T. (Director). (2005). *Hotel Rwanda* [Film]. Los Angeles, CA: MGM.

Gourevitch, P. (1998). *We wish to inform you that tomorrow we will be killed with our families: Stories from Rwanda.* New York, NY: Farrar, Straus & Giroux.

Hatzfeld, J. (2006). *Machete season: The killers in Rwanda speak.* New York, NY: Picador.

History of Rwanda. (n.d.). Retrieved from http://www.historyworld.net/wrldhis/plaintexthistories.asp?historyid=ad24

Johnson, C., Shala, M., Sejdijaj, X., Odell, R., & Dabishevci, K. (2001, October). Thought Field Therapy—soothing the bad moments of Kosovo. *Journal of Clinical Psychology, 57*(10), 1237–1240.

Maslow, A. H. (1943). A theory of human motivation. *Psychological Review, 50*(4), 370–96.

McLeod, A. (2006). *Just for the health of it.* Presentation at the Prophets Conference, Boulder, CO, May 19–21, 2006. See also Adam McLeod's website: www.dreamhealer.com

Melvern, L. (2006). *Conspiracy to murder: The Rwandan genocide.* Brooklyn, NY: Verso Books.

Outreach Programme on the Rwandan Genocide and the United Nations. (n.d.). Retrieved from http://www.un.org/en/preventgenocide/rwanda/education/rwandagenocide.shtml

Prunier, G. (1995). *The Rwanda crisis, 1959–1994: History of a genocide* (2nd ed.). London, UK: C. Hurst.

Rwanda civil war. (n.d.). Retrieved from http://www.globalsecurity.org/military/world/war/rwanda.htm

Rwanda profile. (2013, February 5). *BBC News Africa.* Retrieved from http://www.bbc.co.uk/news/world-africa-14093322

Sakai, C., Connolly, S., & Oas, P. (2010, winter). Treatment of PTSD in Rwandan child genocide survivors using Thought Field Therapy. *International Journal of Emergency Mental Health, 12*(1), 41–50.

Sitchin, Z. (2002). *The lost book of Enki: Memoirs and prophecies of an extraterrestrial god.* Rochester, VT: Bear & Co.

Slothrop, T. (2011, November 6). The Tutsi, giants of Central Africa? Giants of Palestine? Retrieved from http://remnantofgiants.wordpress.com/2011/11/06/tutsi-giants

Stephen, R. (2008, July 30). Remembering King Rudahigwa Mutara III, 49 years on. New Times: Rwanda's First Daily. Retrieved from http://www.newtimes.co.rw/news/index.php?i=13607&a=8300

Stone, B. (1994). *Cancer as Initiation: Surviving the fire.* Chicago, IL: Open Court Publishing.

Stone, B. (2008). *Invisible roots: How healing past life trauma can liberate your present.* Santa Rosa, CA: Energy Psychology Press.

Stone, B., Leyden, L., & Fellows, B. (2009, November). Energy psychology treatment for posttraumatic stress in genocide survivors in a Rwandan orphanage: A pilot investigation. *Energy Psychology: Theory, Research, and Treatment, 1*(1). doi:10.9769.EPJ.2009.1.1.BS

Stone, B., Leyden, L., & Fellows, B. (2010, November). Energy psychology treatment for orphan heads of households in Rwanda: An observational study. *Energy Psychology: Theory, Research, and Treatment, 2*(2). doi:10.9769.EPJ.2010.2.2.BS

Chapter 17
EFT-Centered Humanitarian Work: Opportunities and Challenges for Nonprofit Organizations
Carrie McCabe

Abstract

EFT Global, a 501(c)(3) registered foundation, is dedicated to bringing the enormous benefits of Emotional Freedom Techniques (EFT) to assist and empower three primary populations: those affected by natural and human-caused disasters, those living among weakened social and political systems, and other humanitarian workers. Ultimately, EFT Global exists because of the generous donation of time and resources from those who believe in the healing power of EFT. Yet there are at least six issues inherent to any nonprofit organization that impact its ability to recruit, prepare, and retain volunteers and other skilled workers, skill, with EFT Global being no exception. These include: leadership, time constraints, skills and expertise, financial resources, technology and infrastructure, and an organization's value proposition. Although these issues are really no different for for-profit organizations, it can be argued that the impact on nonprofit organizations is greater, especially for those organizations in which the vast majority of human resources serve on a volunteer basis. Relative to EFT Global, the leadership team faces ongoing challenges relative to raising and leveraging funds, recruiting people with high-demand skills and qualified EFT practitioners in sufficient numbers and in areas of the world where they are needed most while ensuring their time, energy, and contributions are appreciated sufficiently. In the early stages, nonprofit organizations such as EFT Global will gain enough forward momentum to move the organization to the next critical level of development as it gains increased visibility and cachet, a small cadre of sustaining donors, and a strong enough infrastructure and leadership team such that no single leader is critical to its survival. Further, as familiarity and application of EFT continues to grow, so too will organizations such as EFT Global, enabling them to help increasing numbers of people impacted by emotional and traumatic stress around the world.

Keywords: EFT Global, humanitarian organization, nonprofit organization, all-volunteer organization

Carrie McCabe, MA, MA, leads EFT Global, Change By Design, and Carrie McCabe Coaching. She has over 20 years of global experience assisting individuals and organizations in growing and achieving their personal, leadership, and organizational development goals. Carrie holds dual master's degrees in counseling psychology and human resources and industrial relations. Send correspondence to Carrie McCabe, 5103 Garfield Ave., Minneapolis, MN 55419, or cmccabe@eftglobal.org.

Nonprofit organizations are generally founded to serve humanitarian or environmental needs, channeling all income into programs and services aimed at meeting these unmet or under-met needs such as hunger, emergency relief, health, education, deforestation, clean water, or the like. Often, a nonprofit organization fills a gap between services provided by governments and activities from which for-profit organizations make money. Take, for example, services for those impacted by natural and human-caused disasters or to ensure clean air. Though governments around the world may have enacted legislation providing some assistance, regulation, or oversight and for-profit industry might legitimately say they are "committed to reducing air pollution" or "helping disaster survivors," most of the actual work and direct services provided are performed by nonprofit organizations. This space is where nonprofits thrive.

Nonprofits today face both numerous opportunities and challenges. Many people have an interest in being a part of a nonprofit organization because nonprofits generally offer an opportunity to engage in meaningful, rewarding work that makes a difference in the lives of others and reflects their personal beliefs and values. Nonprofit work can also afford people the opportunity to work with other caring, dedicated, diverse, and like-minded people who share the same excitement about an organization's mission. Also, because nonprofits frequently employ only a small paid staff and rely extensively on a corps of volunteers to provide services, both staff members and volunteers can gain new skills and experience they may not be able to gain elsewhere.

Nonetheless, nonprofit organizations can also face many challenges. For example, many nonprofit workers face tough working conditions, offer services in inhospitable and dangerous places, and experience high levels of stress and even trauma. While many challenges relate to the financing of nonprofits, other challenges are endemic to the traditional volunteer structure and organization of nonprofits. In addition to the services offered by many nonprofits, stress levels among staff members and volunteers can be further exacerbated due to high levels of ambiguity, disorganization, inefficiency, inconsistent decision-making processes, and makeshift work environments.

Regardless of the opportunities or challenges faced, at the heart of these you'll find people. Any great nonprofit organization operates because it has dedicated and committed people with a combination of experience and skills that helps propel the organization forward while working toward meeting the unmet or under-met needs that fuel the staff members, the volunteers, and ultimately the organization's mission.

This chapter explores six issues inherent to any nonprofit organization that impact its ability to recruit, prepare, and retain volunteers and other skilled workers. These include: leadership, time constraints, skills and expertise, financial resources, technology and infrastructure, and an organization's value proposition. Although these issues are really no different for for-profit organizations, it can be argued that the impact on nonprofit organizations is greater, especially for those organizations in which the vast majority of human resources serve on a volunteer basis. To illustrate these issues, I will discuss the impact of each on EFT Global, an actual early stage nonprofit organization.

First, let's consider EFT Global's mission, services, structure, and evolution. A 501(c)(3) registered foundation that was launched on October 31, 2011, EFT Global is dedicated to bringing the enormous benefits of EFT to assist and empower three primary populations: those affected by natural and human-caused disasters, those living among weakened social and political systems, and other humanitarian workers.

- **Those affected by natural and human-caused disasters**

When skillfully applied, energy psychology based exposure treatments including EFT have shown to be particularly effective in relieving the emotional distress typically experienced by disaster survivors. In a recent study involving 77 Haitian seminarians after the 2010 earthquake, 62% exhibited scores in the clinical range on the posttraumatic stress disorder (PTSD) checklist (PCL). After receiving 2 days of instruction in EFT, none of the 77 participants scored in the clinical range on the PCL. Further, posttest PCL scores decreased an average of 72%, ranging between a 21% reduction to a 100% reduction in symptom severity. These results are consistent with other published reports of EFT's efficacy in treating PTSD symptoms among traumatized populations including war veterans and genocide survivors (Gurret et al., 2012; Feinstein, 2012).

Energy psychology treatments such as Thought Field Therapy (TFT) and EFT have also been used effectively, in Rwanda with child and teenage victims of the 1990s genocide and rape, with Iraq war veterans suffering from PTSD, with Christ church earthquake survivors, and with hurricane evacuees in Atlanta, Georgia, among others (Church, 2010; Stone, Leyden, & Fellows, 2009; Feinstein, 2008).

While the application of EFT following a disaster must be calibrated to the unique cultures, needs, and constraints of the individuals being treated as well as appropriately timed to provide maximum assistance, if properly applied, field reports show a pattern of strong outcomes following the use of EFT immediately after a disaster and longer term in the subsequent treatment of PTSD (Feinstein, 2008). During the early stages of a disaster, EFT has been enormously helpful in rebuilding trust, hope, and connection while dramatically reducing and even completely resolving traumatic symptoms. According to Feinstein (2008), there are four tiers of energy psychology intervention: 1) immediate relief/stabilization, 2) extinguishing conditioned responses, 3) overcoming complex psychological problems, and 4) promoting optimal functioning. Immediately following a disaster, application of psychological first aid using EFT would be characteristic of the first tier of intervention with the subsequent tiers being introduced over a period of time to assist as needed. Because EFT is so scalable, it is very well suited for large disaster situations, especially when taught by experienced EFT practitioners who can ensure the techniques are being applied effectively and efficiently.

EFT Global volunteer teams led and/or supervised by EFT experts facilitate recovery of local populations from the traumatic impact of natural and/or human-caused disasters through application of specific EFT techniques and by empowering survivors to learn and apply simple self-help EFT techniques.

- **Those living among weakened social and political systems**

A weakening or total collapse of common social and political structures is often experienced by local populations as a progression of vulnerability to emotional and physical distress. Often people and entire communities living among weakened social and political systems face persistent and chronic vulnerabilities due to a long-term pattern of fundamental needs going unmet such as adequate food and shelter, proper health care, safety and security, and stable employment opportunities. This pattern is generally accompanied by feelings of helplessness and hopelessness about the future. Living with these chronic issues often manifests in a variety of ways: fear, overwhelm, apathy, numbness, insecurity, shock, anger, rage, sadness, isolation, hypervigilance, racing thoughts, tightness in one's stomach, an elevated heart rate, ongoing anxiety, restlessness, insomnia, headaches, and the like. These emotional and physical symptoms can generally be reduced or cleared through proper application of specific EFT techniques.

EFT Global provides community support services to facilitate recovery of individuals experiencing an increased vulnerability to emotional and physical distress as a result of weakened social and political structures. This is accomplished through delivery of EFT support services and by empowering community members to learn and apply simple self-help EFT techniques. Examples of community support include service delivery and education on EFT to community leaders and affected members as well as working with professionals in local associations, schools, social welfare agencies, and other non-governmental organizations (NGOs).

- **Other humanitarian workers**

In 1998, half of the respondents in a World Health Organization survey of active aid workers reported they were unable to function well on the day they were interviewed. Six out of 10 interviewed reported general fatigue and one half reported frequent headaches as well as high rates of sleeping difficulties, irritability, and anger (Lovgren, 2003). Another 2001 study published in the *Journal of Traumatic Stress* showed that 30% of returning humanitarian workers reported stress symptoms and about 10% could have been diagnosed with PTSD (Eriksson et al, 2001).

The Antares Foundation and the U.S. Centers for Disease Control and Prevention (CDC) collaborated on a series of research studies examining stress and adjustment among a large group of expatriate humanitarian aid workers and among three separate groups of national staff in Jordan, Uganda, and Sri Lanka. High percentages of both expatriates and national staff showed signs of significant emotional distress (Antares Foundation, 2012). For example, a PTSD prevalence of 25% existed for rescue personnel responding to events such as earthquakes, plane crashes, and bomb explosions as compared to 4% in the general population. After Hurricane Katrina, the prevalence of PTSD among New Orleans police officers was 19%. Elevated levels of depression, anxiety, and other psychological distress have also been reported. Several studies have shown that volunteers working in disasters have even higher levels of distress than those for whom disaster response is part of their regular job (Antares Foundation, 2012). The adverse psychological consequences of working with traumatized individuals on an ongoing basis have been described in multiple ways: secondary traumatic stress disorder (STSD), compassion stress, compassion fatigue, and vicarious traumatization (McCann & Pearlman, 1990; Pearlman & Saakvitne, 1995).

Regardless of how we refer to these adverse psychological consequences, researchers contend that humanitarian organizations must do a better job of first selecting and then preparing their staff before sending them into crisis situations. They must also offer better psychological support for humanitarian workers while they're in the field (Shah, Garland, & Katz, 2007; McFarlane, 2004). Though it's not possible to eliminate stress experienced by humanitarian workers, some stress can be prevented or reduced, and the effects on individual members, their team, and on the larger organization of which they are a part can be lessened. This requires action to be taken at all levels—by the individual, his/her teammates, manager/supervisor, and the organization as a whole.

Although stress management guidelines are broadly applicable to all kinds of humanitarian workers, several categories of workers warrant special attention. Those identified as middle managers such as project leaders/managers have been found to be especially vulnerable to stress. They experience the same "on-the-job" and community based stress as other types of workers, but they have the added responsibility of both ensuring that the work of their staff is accomplished and providing support for their staff. They also experience pressures from their own supervisors. Yet, unlike the staff they supervise, it was found that they may not have peer support close at hand (Antares Foundation, 2012). Non-professional staff members are often an overlooked group. This group may include office workers, drivers, logistical people, and so on. Though their jobs may be less visible than that of field staff, their jobs are essential for the organization to fulfill its mission. As such, they too experience workplace and non-workplace stresses. Lastly, despite their importance, volunteers are often seen as less closely tied to an organization than paid staff. As a result, their needs may be neglected. In many cases, volunteers are themselves survivors of the humanitarian emergency and are selected based on urgent need and immediate availability as opposed to experience, training, and skill. Yet their experience in the field and their needs are similar to other humanitarian-based workers. In fact, in many cases, their need is greater if they too are survivors of the immediate situation at hand (Antares Foundation, 2012).

EFT Global assists all levels of employees and volunteers of other humanitarian organizations in preparing for, minimizing, and/or recovering from the impact of emotional and traumatic stress encountered as a result of working in difficult field conditions and crisis situations. Services before, during, and after field missions and crisis situations are offered as follows:

- **Before field missions:** EFT Global has developed a specific support program to prepare humanitarian workers psychologically and emotionally before leaving for a potentially traumatic field mission. Humanitarian workers gain education about stress, how to reduce the effects of stress, the stress factors anticipated in a specific job or assignment, and how to help themselves and their colleagues reduce the traumatic impact of working in an ongoing crisis situation.
- **During field missions/crisis situations:** EFT Global has developed specific EFT trauma-related protocols and services to provide psychological and emotional support for local staff and field workers. Services can be provided in person or remotely via Skype. These services provided by EFT practitioners trained to deal with stress and trauma create another avenue for humanitarian organizations to monitor the well-being of their field staff while on assignment as well as those helping to support field staff remotely.
- **After field missions/crisis situations:** The challenges of an assignment ending, returning home, or transferring to a new assignment are often underestimated

(Antares Foundation, 2012). EFT Global provides one-on-one and group EFT services to home office staff, returning staff, and field humanitarian workers. These services are effective for both those specifically reporting emotional and traumatic stress symptoms and for those who haven't reported any symptoms but whom others believe may benefit from assessment and possible assistance.

Structure of EFT Global

EFT Global is currently an all-volunteer organization with the exception of the services it offers other humanitarian organizations. EFT practitioners delivering services to other humanitarian organizations receive a reduced fee for their services with the understanding that the difference between what EFT Global charges and their compensation helps to offset other types of EFT Global projects, that is, projects focused on natural and human-caused disasters and community support. As such, practitioners delivering EFT-related services to other humanitarian organizations may or may not provide services to the other two populations served by EFT Global.

EFT Global is led by the author (USA), Diane von der Weid (Switzerland), and David MacKay (Mexico), under the auspices of leading clinical researcher, author, and EFT expert Dawson Church, PhD. Each member of this team brings a range and depth of expertise and experience that complements the others.

I have over 20 years of experience working across the globe assisting individuals and organizations to grow and achieve their personal, leadership, and organizational goals. Diane von der Weid is an EFT trainer and stress consultant with over 20 years of professional experience managing small and large-sized corporations, both Swiss and international, and served for eight years as the political advisor to the United Nations High Commissioner for Human Rights (OHCHR) in Geneva. David MacKay, president of the Hispanic EFT Association, is a leading expert in EFT for the Hispanic community and has helped define Hispanic EFT training and certification standards.

Project team structure is the same for both EFT Global projects in support of natural and human-caused disasters and for those living among weakened social and political structures. Each project team is led by an EFT Global Trainer. After meeting a series of selection criteria such as EFT Intermediate Practitioner Level certification from a reputable EFT-certifying body, more than 3 years' experience in a supervisory capacity, and more than 1 year of experience providing direct EFT services, a trainer is then qualified to lead a given project and expected to both train and supervise EFT Global teachers and helpers. New EFT Global Trainers either contact the organization and express interest in volunteering or are recruited by the EFT Global leadership team to volunteer on the organization's behalf. Prior to any fieldwork, EFT Global Trainers are required to complete trauma training developed and taught by EFT Global.

EFT Global Teachers teach others to serve in a facilitator and emotional helper role. As is true for EFT Global Trainers, teachers are also required to complete trauma training before being able to volunteer and must also meet predetermined selection criteria. EFT Global Teachers either contact the organization wanting to volunteer or EFT Global Trainers or members of the organization's leadership team recruit them. If possible, EFT Global Teachers come from the general area or local community being served.

EFT Global Facilitators (Emotional Helpers) are also required to complete a course in trauma offered by EFT Global before being able to assist those impacted by trauma. Facilitators or Emotional Helpers either volunteer or are recruited by members of the EFT Global project team. Emotional Helpers generally come from the local community being served by EFT Global. As members of the local community, language and cultural barriers are typically not an issue. Ideally, Emotional Helpers are well known and respected in their communities. In turn, this helps make rapport and trust building easier across the community for the EFT Global Facilitator as well as other members of the project team.

EFT Global Helpers are responsible for coordinating and managing project logistics and are generally recruited from the local community being served. Logistics include both project coordination as well as coordination with other NGOs. To work effectively in many disaster situations, a joint effort with other trauma experts, humanitarian organizations, and local people and groups is required. Collaboration helps accelerate access to people, information, and resources necessary to assist those in need. As such EFT Global Helpers will often receive direction and support from EFT Global project team members as well as EFT Global partners.

All EFT Global volunteers providing direct services to the populations served by the organization are rigorously screened and trained in all areas associated with working in a traumatic, disaster, or chaotic situation. As much as is possible, this ensures they are "on the ground ready" and can withstand the stress of difficult field conditions while adhering to the highest ethical standards and elite standard of care practices.

In addition to direct project delivery roles, EFT Global has many other challenging and meaningful volunteer and contract needs in areas such as fundraising, research, public relations, marketing, administrative support, web/technical support, curriculum development, and EFT outreach. Many of these needs exist sporadically and are filled as they arise.

Six Common Issues Impacting a Nonprofit's Volunteer Base

Ultimately, EFT Global exists because of the generous donation of time and resources from those who believe in the healing power of EFT. Yet, as mentioned previously, there are at least six issues inherent to any nonprofit organization that impact its ability to recruit, prepare, and retain volunteers and other skilled workers, with EFT Global being no exception. These include: leadership, time constraints, skills and expertise, financial resources, technology and infrastructure, and an organization's value proposition. EFT Global leadership team members have considered and continue to be mindful of the impact and importance of these issues when making both short-term and longer-term organizational decisions. Additionally, EFT Global project team leaders must look carefully at how each of these issues affects their ability to attract and retain the volunteers who make up their teams. While it is important to understand the combined impact of these six interrelated issues, each will be discussed sequentially.

1. Leadership

Ineffective leadership is still a major constraint to effective humanitarian action and is frequently cited as one of the most critical issues facing humanitarian organizations today (Harvey et al., 2009). Recent research suggests that leading through influence as opposed to authority vested in a position or status is essential for success at the operational level of leadership. Operational leadership is defined as leadership in-country responsible for providing clear vision and objectives for the response to a specific crisis, focused on the affected population and building a consensus that ultimately serves to bring humanitarian workers together around that vision and objectives. As such, five qualities have emerged as essential for strong operational leadership to exist: strategic leadership skills or the ability to see and relate to the bigger picture; relationship building and communication skills; decision-making and risk-taking skills; management and organizational skills; and personal qualities such as self-awareness, self-confidence, being principled, and acting with integrity. Together, these qualities point to the importance of "relational leadership" based on networking, communication, and strong team building that brings out the leadership potential of others (Buchanan-Smith & Scriven, 2011).

The relational nature of humanitarian leadership is underscored when looking at a leader's ability to build consensus across agencies and nonprofit organizations, to know when to bring in others before making a clear decision, and to know where and when to give staff members space to operate. The importance of relational leadership is especially relevant for EFT Global. In the recruitment and selection of qualified individuals to serve in the roles of EFT Trainer, Teacher, and Facilitator (Emotional Helper), candidates must meet a minimum level of training, education, and experience as well as possess certain personal and leadership qualities and characteristics. Although these characteristics are more difficult to assess and measure than specific training and educational credentials, they are as, if not more, important. In light of the difficult field conditions often associated with EFT Global projects, a practitioner's level of self-awareness, emotional self-control, adaptability, and general willingness to accept feedback and coaching, for example, can make the difference between project success or not. Although many leadership skills can be taught, for those serving in a trainer role and assuming responsibility for leading the overall project team, it's expected that a threshold level of leadership experience and characteristics already exists. For those working in a teacher or facilitator capacity, an opportunity to develop and hone these skills and gain additional leadership experience is one of the benefits of serving on behalf of EFT Global. Nonetheless, even for these roles, certain personal and leadership characteristics are required for selection. These requirements are in place because the cost of not possessing a threshold level is just too high, both for the individuals involved and for the people EFT Global serves.

2. Time Constraints

Consistently, a lack of time is identified as the number one barrier or obstacle to volunteering cited by both volunteers and non-volunteers a like (Peter D. Hart Research Assoc., 2006). Whether economics, family demands, or other pressures are the issue, volunteer organizations must consider time constraints when recruiting and making use of volunteers. While volunteer rates continue to increase year after year, at least in the United States, there is also a trend toward more episodic or short-term volunteer engagements, making longer-term projects and commitments as well as leadership roles much more difficult to fill (U.S. Bureau of Labor Statistics, 2011; Corporation for National and Community Service, 2006). Although these are U.S.-based statistics, it is assumed that competing demands for people's limited time and a resulting desire to engage in shorter-term volunteer engagements are characteristic of other developed countries.

Lack of time is an enormous issue for a nonprofit organization such as EFT Global. Generally, the recovery process from natural and human-caused disasters takes many months, often years, and volunteers servicing these populations need to travel to the impacted area and be willing to commit a week or more of concentrated time assisting survivors. Time required for volunteers engaging in community support work may not be as intense, but the investment is still quite significant. As a result, many otherwise-qualified EFT practitioners simply cannot make the time requirements work, given their already very busy personal and professional lives. Even though EFT Global has incorporated into its delivery model a strong preference for in-country/region/area EFT practitioners and support-related volunteers for as many roles as possible, a general lack of qualified EFT experts in many regions of the world is a reality, particularly in developing countries. This creates an over reliance on qualified practitioners from the Western world.

Because EFT Global makes a significant investment in the preparation and training of volunteer EFT practitioners, the organization requires in exchange a minimum of 10 days of service over an 18-month period. Presently a large percentage of those volunteering are self-employed and, as a result, do not have paid time off. Therefore, 10 days of required service can be significant in terms of both time and lost income. As stated previously, the goal is to leverage in-country/region/area EFT practitioners whenever possible because this reduces travel and acclimation time. Additionally, the impact of language and cultural barriers is significantly reduced or ceases to be an issue at all. But, as previously discussed, this is often not possible. Nevertheless, the lack of qualified EFT practitioners around the globe will likely improve over the next 5–10 years. As the number of qualified EFT practitioners continues to grow, EFT Global expects to encounter new time-related issues. For example, as demands on time increase and people's lives become more complex in developing countries, people's ability to volunteer for EFT Global could potentially be impacted. Additionally, the concept of time and the role it plays in different cultures will likely influence how EFT Global approaches its work in various parts of the world.

3. Skills and Expertise

As is true of for-profit organizations, one of the most significant challenges facing humanitarian organizations is the ability to attract and retain staff and volunteers with the requisite education, skills, and personal characteristics needed to successfully deliver on the organization's mission. Humanitarian organizations are now looking to the private sector to fill vacancies, especially for many competitive and hard-to-fill roles such as IT, finance, and even leadership. Securing hard-to-find talent can have a significant impact on overall results. For example, highly skilled IT professionals can dramatically and rapidly change how an organization both operates in the field and raises funds through strategic technology implementation and integration (Center for Creative Leadership & People in Aid, 2010).

But even if an organization is able to fill open positions with qualified individuals, are they able to retain them? Data suggest that this is becoming a bigger and bigger challenge for NGOs despite the current economic climate. In fact, recent reports of many humanitarian organizations suggest that as many as 50% of new recruits quit after the first or second field mission (Center for Creative Leadership & People in Aid, 2010).

For small nonprofits, particularly those that have no paid staff or a very small number of paid staff, the ability to attract on a project or contract basis qualified volunteers and specialized experts such as web developers, technical support, and accounting professionals is particularly challenging and yet critical to the survival of the organization. Retention then becomes paramount once volunteers are trained and highly skilled contractors have started an assignment. For example, once EFT Global invests the time and resources into preparing and training volunteer staff, the organization cannot afford to have them fail to honor their commitment to the organization. This is also true for specialized workers hired to complete projects requiring specific skills and expertise (e.g. web development) that current organizational members don't possess or that are not readily available as a volunteer arrangement. Whether the position is filled on a voluntary or contractual basis, onboarding consumes time and resources that could be spent elsewhere. As such, each selection decision is important because it either helps build organizational capacity or depletes it. When relying primarily on volunteer staff, resource decisions might be even more critical to the future of an organization as compared to organizations in which staff members are paid and resources and budgets are greater.

4. Financial Resources

Consistent with other nonprofits, particularly those in the early stages of formation, funding issues are an ever-present challenge. Without funding, it's hard to accomplish the organization's goals and objectives, even with an all-volunteer staff. On the other hand, a limited budget can help organizational members think and act creatively to obtain the services and support they need to be successful. If an organization is able to navigate through the early stages of formation when funding is often limited, increased commitment to the organization's mission often results. This is certainly true for EFT Global. The leadership team has not allowed limited funds to become a barrier.

Instead, team members have looked for creative solutions when faced with potential obstacles. This has proved to be a very successful model and has served to increase members' commitment to the mission and vision of the organization.

A key question many leaders of humanitarian organizations are now asking themselves centers on how similar to the for-profit sector they can ever afford to be. In other words, where should the line be drawn between being a humanitarian organization, with the culture and type of staff that entails, and being super efficient and profit-driven like big business? Today, there seems to be little doubt that many of the most successful humanitarian organizations have shifted their operational model closer to the private sector than ever before. Yet it also seems that there is a line that should not be crossed. The trick, of course, is knowing where that line is today and how far you can move it in the future, without "losing your soul" (Center for Creative Leadership & People in Aid, 2010). While there are no easy answers, there's no doubt that NGOs are being forced to run leaner, more efficient organizations than ever before due to mounting financial pressures. This is unlikely to let up in the foreseeable future.

As a way to maximize EFT Global's limited financial resources, the leadership team made the decision to leverage technology as a means to build community and infrastructure. For example, due to time constraints and limited resources, it's not feasible for the organization to consistently provide face-to-face training to volunteers who may be located in many places around the world. To address this issue, EFT Global integrated Moodle, a learning management system, into the organization's web platform to give us the tools to manage, promote, and deliver training to volunteers, regardless of their location, time zone, and language preference. In addition to reducing overall training costs, the use of an online learning management system also allows EFT Global to maximize the numbers it can train at any given time; that is, Moodle can scale to accommodate very large educational deployments.

As a means of raising smaller amounts across a larger number of donors, EFT Global has also incorporated crowd-funding technology into its website. The leadership team is hopeful that this, in combination with other strategies, will reduce the organization's overall reliance on grants and large donors. Other means for raising funds outside of the more traditional methods include charging a fee for services provided to other humanitarian organizations as well as collecting a small service fee from other EFT-centered humanitarian organizations using EFT Global's crowd-funding technology. In turn, these funds will be allocated to projects for which it's not possible to charge for services, such as natural disasters.

5. Technology and Infrastructure

Technology has introduced the world to new ways of working and communicating. Business models for humanitarian as well as other types of organizations continue to evolve as a result of thinking differently about how technology can be used to reduce costs and increase scale where it wasn't possible in years past. For humanitarian organizations, technology has expanded the pool of potential employees and volunteers, increased the speed in which many things get accomplished, and, at least in part, reduced overall costs. On the other hand, humanitarian organizations face the dual challenge of leveraging technology while still meeting the "human" needs of their members.

Members of any organization or human system require a sense of place. This offers members somewhere to gather, to connect, to belong. In the digital age, chat rooms, forums, and online communities often serve as that place for members. Whether an organization has a physical address, a universal resource locator (URL), or both, a sense of place helps to provide structure and legitimacy to an organization. Organizations lacking a credible address, website, or both are generally viewed with skepticism. For example, potential donors often evaluate an organization's website to determine its legitimacy as a first step when conducting due diligence.

For EFT Global as well as many other newer humanitarian organizations, place is largely online. As such, the EFT Global leadership team set out to create a website where volunteers, donors, researchers, partners, and service recipients as well as anyone and everyone committed to EFT can find information, share knowledge, interact, learn from one another, and ultimately extend the global reach of both the organization and EFT more generally. All visitors can join EFT Connect, EFT Global's social community, where they can interact in the forum, post their profile, start a group or conversation, or host a blog. In addition, they can make use of EFT Global's crowd-funding technology and direct their hard-earned dollars to a project of their choosing or express interest in becoming a volunteer, "like" the site, and more. They can participate as much or as little as they desire. The aim of all these tools is the same: to create a sense of place where participation and community are encouraged across a group of otherwise dispersed people.

An additional means for encouraging participation through technology is the option for anyone interested to create and host, at no charge, a practitioner blog. This is an especially attractive option for new practitioners who aren't yet generating much, if any, income; for those who want to share their views about EFT with others but may not have the disposable income to host a blog themselves; or for those who reside in areas of the world where lack of infrastructure or income would otherwise prevent them from sharing their views, perspectives, or services relative to EFT.

EFT Global's investment in technology also enables the organization to engage in crowd-funding to raise funds for EFT Global projects as well as other EFT-centered humanitarian efforts. This is consistent with the direction many fundraising efforts are moving—people want to have a choice as to where their funds are being directed. Crowd funding enables organizations to offer that while also gathering information about what types of projects donors prefer to support. Information collected could influence the type of projects and services the organization chooses to fund in the future. In the case of EFT Global, we made a conscious choice to allow other EFT-centered organizations to raise funds on our site as a way to model the core principals of EFT, create a partnership with other organizations, raise a small amount of money to help offset our project costs, and create a larger EFT-oriented presence in the world.

Because EFT Global provides services across the globe, visitors to the website can translate content into more than 25 languages. While the translation is basic, it does offer assistance to those who do not speak English. Additionally, EFT Global offers an "official blog" posted in English, French, and Spanish. To truly create a global community, it needs to be accessible to all people; the goal is to incorporate more and more features, over time, to ensure accessibility.

With the integration of a learning management system, EFT Global is able to train volunteers located anywhere in the world simultaneously, using a "classroom" style environment. This significantly reduces costs associated with training volunteers and makes it feasible to provide training more often and to smaller groups of people. Recognizing that face-to-face training is also important, both private and public/private trainings are offered. In a public/private offering, fees are collected for a certain number of paying attendees, which helps offset the training costs of EFT Global volunteers.

For project teams, EFT Connect enables a team leader to create a private group where project details and information, logistics, check-in procedures, cultural information, and the like can be accessed and shared. Assuming members have access to the Internet, they can stay up to date on projects of which they are a part and communicate with team members easily.

Because EFT Global doesn't have a physical location, its website essentially serves as a digital infrastructure providing volunteers, researchers, partners, donors, and site visitors/members a sense of place and structure. EFT Global.org ultimately serves as an online gathering place for all those interested in how EFT is being used to promote and contribute to world peace.

6. Value Proposition

Humanitarian organizations making use of volunteers are well advised to understand the primary needs and drivers (motivations) of their volunteers. Once this is well understood, the organization must also identify the benefits it promises volunteers in return for their time, energy, and contributions.

Perhaps the biggest benefit people get from volunteering is the satisfaction of incorporating service into their lives and making a difference at the local, national, and/or global level. Beyond the obvious reasons people most often cite for volunteering such as being able to help others, convenience, devotion to the cause, and having free time available, there are many other reasons people volunteer (McCabe, 2012). Often, volunteers want to acquire new skills and experience to shift careers or go further in their present career, make new contacts and build new networks, make in roads for the possibility of a new job, use their gifts and talents in a way they are not currently being utilized, and contribute to the transformation of their own lives as well as the lives of others. People also volunteer to increase their level of confidence, overall life satisfaction, and sense of accomplishment and pride.

Volunteer drivers and needs vary by generation. For example, members of Generation Y frequently cite a desire to give time to more entrepreneurial organizations as opposed to large, bureaucratic structures. As such, they are seeking the freedom to try new things in new ways while putting their often highly sought-after skills, especially technical and communication, to work on the organization's mission (McCabe, 2012). They are also more interested in professional development than other generations. Boomers are more interested in putting to use the depth of their existing skills and experiences. Each generation has different expectations about volunteer service; the challenge is to bring these diverse generations together through multiple options and opportunities.

Understanding and appreciating the unique drivers and needs of volunteers in an all-volunteer organization is absolutely essential. By doing so, the organization can ensure volunteers are being recognized and appreciated adequately so as to encourage them to contribute to the organization's mission in the future. In addition to the drivers often cited for volunteering such as being able to make a direct contribution to their communities or being of service to others, many EFT practitioners volunteering for EFT Global cite traveling to areas of the world they would otherwise not see and experience, building a broader network of professional colleagues and friends, being exposed to multiple cultures, and gaining greater experience and skills. Volunteer practitioners and other types of volunteers often receive many forms of recognition and appreciation as a result of their contributions. For example, gratitude is often conveyed many times over by those they are assisting. Publicity about specific projects can also serve as recognition and reward. Often, the reputation of volunteer practitioners is greatly enhanced among peers, those seeking to hire EFT experts, and those seeking assistance and advice. Ultimately, gratitude, flattery, and enhanced reputation can serve as powerful reinforcement for continued service to an organization. From an EFT Global perspective, this is certainly a positive for the volunteers, the organization as a whole, and the people the organization serves.

In addition, volunteers, regardless of role, have the opportunity to make a real impact on the way EFT Global operates and how it will evolve to meet future needs. For many, this is the first real opportunity to have their voice heard within the structure of a formal organization. Many find this empowering, which serves as a catalyst for other positive changes in their lives. EFT Global's leadership team is firmly committed to ensuring that the experiences of EFT Global volunteers are positive and their contributions, big or small, are genuinely acknowledged and appreciated.

The Future of EFT in the Nonprofit Sector

Ultimately, all organizations, including humanitarian organizations, must gain a certain momentum before there is enough energy and resources enabling them to survive. Until such time, each decision relative to staff, paid or unpaid, and how precious time and dollars are invested either contributes to the organization's forward momentum or not. All these decisions are directly tied to the six issues impacting a non-profit organization's ability to recruit, prepare, and retain volunteers and other skilled workers as detailed in this chapter (leadership, time constraints, skills and expertise, financial resources, technology and infrastructure, and an organization's value proposition). Although these issues are common to all non-profits, how each deals with them will depend on the organization's mission, breadth of services and delivery model, structure, unique characteristics of the leader(s), and influence from the Board of Directors, donors, partners and sponsors. Successful organizations exist in many forms; there is no right way or best way to build and lead a nonprofit. The ultimate goal for any nonprofit organization is to fulfill its mission—to thrive—in a manner consistent with the organization's culture and values.

In terms of EFT Global, the organization has not yet reached sufficient momentum to guarantee survival. It's unlikely that it will until several things happen: increased visibility and cachet enabling it to have more volunteer interest than need, a small cadre of sustaining donors, and a strong enough community to reach out to when increased funds are required in a short period of time as well as a strong enough infrastructure and leadership team such that no single leader is critical to the survival of the organization. Frequently, many of these things happen at about the same time, which, of course, helps to create the momentum to move an organization to the next, critical level of development. EFT Global is likely 9–12 months away from gaining the momentum it needs to move to the next phase in its development.

Since it launched a little over a year ago, EFT Global has faced many challenges just as any other nonprofit organization. Undoubtedly, it will face more going forward. Nevertheless, the ability to make a difference by sharing and applying EFT to help individuals and communities across the world heal from emotional and traumatic stress and transforming the lives of those we serve as well as our own far outweighs any challenges. As familiarity and application of Emotional Freedom Techniques continues to grow, so too will EFT Global. This will increase the organization's ability to attract and retain qualified EFT practitioners in countries and regions of the world where none exist today. In turn, this will make service delivery for EFT Global less expensive and more effective and efficient. As this happens, the organization will build more capacity, allowing it to scale services to help increasing numbers of people. Essentially, by leveraging momentum, EFT Global will be able to do more and more good in the world with the ultimate aim of actually averting human-caused disasters in the future—now that's exciting to think about! Our goal of attracting high-quality EFT experts and practitioners, putting in place the needed systems and infrastructure to enable the organization to help heal the world for years to come, and making a real difference in the lives of survivors and other humanitarian workers experiencing emotional and traumatic stress makes leading EFT Global both a privilege and an honor.

References

Antares Foundation. (2012). *Managing stress in humanitarian workers: Guidelines for good practice* (3rd ed.). Retrieved from http://www.antaresfoundation.org/download/managing_stress_in_humanitarian_aid_workers_guidelines_for_good_practice.pdf

Buchanan-Smith, M. & Scriven, K. (2011, June 9). *Leadership in action: Leading effectively in humanitarian operations.* London: Overseas Development Institute (ODI)/Active Learning Network for Accountability and Performance in Humanitarian Action (ALNAP). Retrieved from http://www.alnap.org/node/7579.aspx

Center for Creative Leadership & People in Aid (2010). *Leadership and talent development in international humanitarian and development organizations: A Center for Creative Leadership/People In Aid review of current and future practice and expectations.* Brussels, Belgium: Center for Creative Leadership.

Church, D. (2010, March). The treatment of combat trauma in veterans using EFT (Emotional Freedom Techniques): A pilot protocol. *Traumatology, 16*(1), 55–65.

Corporation for National and Community Service (2006). *Volunteer growth in America: A review of trends since 1974.* Retrieved from http://www.nationalservice.gov/pdf/06_1203_volunteer_growth.pdf

Eriksson, C., Vande Kemp, H., Gorsuch, R., & Hoke, S. (2001). Trauma exposure and PTSD symptoms in international relief and development personnel. *Journal of Traumatic Stress, 14*(1), 205–212.

Feinstein, D. (2008). Energy psychology in disaster relief. *Traumatology, 14*(1), 124–137.

Feinstein, D. (2012). Acupoint stimulation in treating psychological disorders: Evidence of efficacy. *Review of General Psychology, 16,* 364–380.

Gurret, J-M., Caufour, C., Palmer-Hoffman, J., & Church, D. (2012). Post-earthquake rehabilitation of clinical PTSD in Haitian seminarians. *Energy Psychology: Theory, Research, and Treatment, 4*(2), 33–40.

Harvey, P., Stoddard, A., Harmer, A., & Taylor, G. (2009). *The state of the humanitarian system. Assessing performance and progress. A pilot study.* ALNAP, London: ODI.

Lovgren, S. (2003, December 3). Aid workers, too, suffering post-traumatic stress. *National Geographic News.* Retrieved from http://news.nationalgeographic.com/news/2003/12/1203_031203_aidworkers.html

McCabe, S. (2012, May 14). *Motivation and retention strategies for reaching volunteers across generations* (MSW clinical research paper, St. Catherine University and University of St. Thomas, Minneapolis, MN). Retrieved from http://sophia.stkate.edu/cgi/viewcontent.cgi?article=1121&context=msw_papers

McCann, I. & Pearlman, L. (1990). Vicarious traumatization: A framework for understanding the psychological effects of working with victims. *Journal of Traumatic Stress, 3,* 131–149.

McFarlane, C. (2004). Risks associated with the psychological adjustment of humanitarian aid workers. *Australian Journal of Disaster and Trauma Studies, 1,* 22–31.

Pearlman, L. A. & Saakvitne, K. W. (1995). Treating therapists with vicarious traumatization and secondary traumatic stress disorders. In C. R. Figley (Ed.), *Compassion fatigue: Coping with secondary traumatic stress disorder in those who treat the traumatized* (pp. 150–177). New York, NY: Brunner/Mazel.

Peter D. Hart Research Associates. (2006). Volunteer Match User Study: Findings from quantitative and qualitative opinion research conducted June to August 2006 for Volunteer Match. Retrieved from http://cdn.volunteermatch.org/www/nonprofits/resources/hart_presentation.pdf

Rosenthal, R. (2012). Trends in volunteering. Minnesota Association of Volunteer Administration. Retrieved from http://www.mavanetwork.org/resources/Documents/TrendsinVolunteeringRosenthal.pdf

Shah, S. A., Garland, E., & Katz, C. (2007). Secondary traumatic stress: Prevalence in humanitarian aid workers in India, *Traumatology, 13*(1), 59–70.

Stone, B. Leyden, L., & Fellows, B. (2009). Energy psychology treatment for posttraumatic stress in genocide survivors in a Rwandan orphanage: A pilot investigation. *Energy Psychology: Theory, Research, & Treatment, 1*(1), 73–82.

U.S. Bureau of Labor Statistics (2011). Volunteering in the United States–2011. Retrieved from http://www.bls.gov/news.release/archives/volun_02222012.pdf

Fundamental Techniques of Clinical EFT

Chapter 18
Finding Core Issues
Peter Donn

Abstract

Many of the standard EFT protocols, such as the Movie Technique or Chasing the Pain, have a fairly straightforward procedure that can be followed to get a defined outcome (such as freedom from a specific trauma or a physical pain). When working with core issues, however, EFT becomes more like an art that develops with experience and often involves persistence, patience, and detective-like skills. Working with core issues can also reap great dividends for your clients. Sometimes a core issue blocks achieving success with a more superficial issue in EFT and so there is a great opportunity to address something deeper and more foundational. It is as though there is something in that moment that is saying, "Now is the time to tackle something really important!" We all experience themes in our lives that replay over and over. These represent what are known as our *core issues:* fundamental patterns we run that cause continual disappointment, frustration, emotional pain, and self-esteem issues, for which we compensate in avoidance and self-defeating behavior patterns. Examples are themes of success and failure, abandonment and aloneness, never feeling good enough, betrayal, chronic illness, feeling a fraud, addictions, and the feeling of always being knocked down every time you get going. Examples of core beliefs that could support the previous are: "I am not good enough," "Life is a struggle," "I am a failure," "I am bad," or "No one is here for me." Working with core issues is one of the most powerful ways to use EFT, and the most potentially transformational. This chapter discusses ways to find and treat core issues. Asking the right questions to discover important early events or experiences, thereby tracking down the birth of core issues, is key to success.

Keywords: core issues, core beliefs, life themes, beliefs, behavior patterns, trauma, art of EFT, life decisions

Peter Donn, Bsc (Hons), has a decade's professional experience practicing and training others in EFT. He is partner at the EFT Training Centre and coauthor of *Birth Freedom Techniques (BFT): Applying the Groundbreaking Technique of EFT to Conception, Pregnancy, Birth, and Beyond*. Send correspondence to Peter Donn, 2 Love Lane, Kings Langley, Hertfordshire WD4 9HN, UK, or peter@donn.biz. www.donn.biz.

The Creation of Core Issues

Core issues tend to come into realization in the life of an individual in the early years (usually pre 7 years old) when the child is absorbing information like a sponge and interpreting life events from a limited context. Within this context, even small upsetting events can lead to the formation of foundational beliefs about life, which become generalized and affect large sections of the child's worldview. The effect is a form of disempowerment or limited version of reality. As an example, if an adult experiences his mother leaving the room and not coming back for an hour, there is (usually!) no disempowering interpretation. If a 6-month-old baby experiences the same thing, the unconscious effect of the experience could be the creation of such beliefs as "I am not important," "I can't trust those close to me for my survival," "I am alone in the world," or one of many other possibilities. Once created, these beliefs remain intact, influencing behaviour, coloring outlook, and triggering negative emotional states in specific correlating situations even when the original experience has long been forgotten.

In my work with clients, I find that core issues also often develop at or before birth, with particular focal areas being around conception, at key points during the time in the womb (based usually on what was happening in the life of the parents), and during the birth process. Many clients find themselves going back to traumatic past lives. It is not up to practitioners to judge whether or not such a concept exists, but rather to treat what the client reveals like any other experience. I have had much success with individuals treating their experience of past lives.

There are also many cases in which clients appear to inherit foundational life perspectives from parents and other important authority figures in their early years. I find that these are crystalized in the lives of individuals through key personal experiences. Although those events are good ones to work with, I find it particularly powerful for my client to represent his or her mother, for example, and we do an EFT treatment as if I am treating the mother. This appears to have the effect of releasing inherited issues and beliefs, although there may still be some clearing needed on specific relevant events in the life of the individual.

Core issues tend to take the form of beliefs, but they are deeply rooted and usually feel true *to the core*, even if only within a specific context or even if to the conscious mind they appear ludicrous. Sometimes a core issue can feel like an identity, as in "I am [intrinsically] unlovable." Ultimately, core issues are at the foundation of most of our negative reactions and behavior. For example, a core issue of fear of abandonment might cause clinginess in a relationship and generate fear when a partner is "out with his mates" for too long.

Examples of Core Issues

Core issues can take many forms. Here are some common examples:

- Life is a struggle.
- Life doesn't support me.
- Life is against me.
- Life has let me down.
- I am alone.
- I am bad.
- I am a failure.
- I am unwanted.
- I have been abandoned (and therefore could be again).
- I am a fraud.
- I am unsafe.
- I am unloved/unlovable.
- I am unlucky.
- I am cursed.
- I can't have what I want.
- I am responsible for others (and therefore there is no time for me).
- I am special (as in "diva" special!).
- Men/women are not to be trusted.

Summary of Steps to Finding and Treating Core Issues

The following are the key steps for working with core issues in an EFT session (this is a practitioner-client session; self-treatments are possible but can be very hard to administer).

Note that in the example that follows I make use of the VOC 0–10 scale. VOC stands for "validity of cognition" and refers to the degree to which something feels true; 0 signifies it doesn't feel true at all and 10 signifies it feels completely true. The VOC scale is most often used in the context of beliefs. In my case, I use it to check the degree to which a client believes a core issue statement, as you will see in steps 5 and 6.

1. *Identify the gateway issue.* Identify the presenting issue/challenge to be treated using EFT and, if it is appropriate, work deeply with this.
2. *Deepen into the problem.* Ask your client to focus on the problem, and report on the feelings, emotions, and body sensations that it brings up in the body.
3. *Ask key questions to find a core event.* Ask questions to help guide your client back in time to a core event or experience that contains those same feelings.
4. *Treat the event while identifying core issues.* Use EFT to treat all the emotional layers and aspects from that contributory event/experience and, during the process, become aware of the core issue(s) created or confirmed. The next step will intersect with this step.
5. *Identify and treat core issues, beliefs, and other disempowering structures created.* Find and release beliefs, vows, decisions, and new "characters" or personalities developed as a result of the event/experience.
6. *Test the VOC (validity of cognition) level of the core issue.* Do not skip this step. If some truth remains, continue with the next step.
7. *Treat other similar events.* Identify other events that follow a similar theme, and treat these as per the previous two steps.

Working with Core Issues: The Steps in Detail

To go into detail with each of these steps, I'll use an example client, whom I will call Marilyn. In the notes that follow, "P" represents the practitioner and "M" Marilyn. The statement *"I deeply..."* is short for *"I deeply and completely love and accept myself"* or whatever you may be using that is appropriate. "Tap, tap, tap" implies a round or more of EFT tapping treatment using basic EFT tapping. This example is typical of a real session. It is important to read through all the steps in advance before actually guiding a client through the process, as things often don't happen in a sequential order.

Preparation

Suppose that Marilyn comes for a consultation, arriving stressed and wanting to share many things that are bothering her. In this state of being, it is going to be difficult to get clarity on how we are to make a start, much less deepening into a core issue. We need to do some initial EFT to help her feel calm right now.

P: How are you feeling generally, Marilyn?

M: Stressed and overwhelmed.

P: Let's do some general tapping on this: *Even though I feel stressed and overwhelmed, I deeply...* Tap, tap, tap.

P: How do you feel now?

M: Much better. I feel calm and centered.

Step 1: Identify the Gateway Issue

Now that Marilyn is in a calm space, we are able to find a starting point. When we have an initial problem to work with, there are two ways we can work. One way is to treat just the presenting issue and the other way is to identify and treat a foundational core issue. As this chapter is about core issues, that is the way we will proceed. It may be, however, that your client will not wish to work in this way, particularly if this is her first experience of EFT, or she is not feeling safe, or if she just came to treat a fear of spiders and has no interest in working with an existential trauma issue from her time in the womb! You need to decide your approach on a case-by-case basis, but explaining in advance a little about the benefits of working with core issues can help clients feel it is worthwhile to explore deeper territory.

P: Great, now tell me, what is your biggest issue or challenge right now, or what you would like to work on?

M: I am really worried about my daughter. She is out a lot with the wrong friends and I am concerned she is going to get into trouble and make a mess of her life.

Step 2: Deepen into the Problem

For the best chances of finding key core experiences quickly and effectively, it is important to help the client become aware of the feelings (e.g., dragging feeling, feeling pushed, heaviness), emotions, and body sensations (e.g. head tension, achy hips) that arise when the client focuses on the problem. Each one of these sensory elements is a window into the subconscious mind, providing a clue about a specific past memory or sense of something that is related. For example, pressure on the shoulder could go back to being led out of the room in disgrace by an angry teacher or it could represent the burden of responsibility a young boy may feel if his father suddenly leaves home.

    P: Please bring your attention deeply into your body. When you think about your daughter getting in with the wrong friends and making a mess of her life, what feelings, emotions, and body sensations are you aware of?

    M: I feel a shortness of breath, heaviness in my chest, and I feel like a dark cloud is enveloping me. I feel like something is holding me down and I can't get up.

    P: What else are you feeling?

    M: I feel ashamed and powerless and like I can never hold my head high again.

Step 3: Ask Key Questions to Find a Key Event

Probing questions and detective work are important here, but there are some simple questions that are consistently effective (list to follow).

    P: What would happen if you did hold your head high after that point in time?

    M: I would be cut down or rejected.

    P: Marilyn, when was the first time in your life you remember feeling shortness of breath, heaviness in your chest, like a dark cloud is enveloping you, feeling held down and powerless, and maybe this came about because you held your head high? (This is a key question to ask.)

    M: I was in school, around age 6. I answered a question in class and I was feeling good about myself. Then afterward in the playground these bullies in my class surrounded me and jumped on me and said I was teacher's pet and a swot [geek or nerd] and that I wasn't cool.

So we now have an important event to work with. Before continuing, however, let's look at some other effective questions you could ask to help your client get back to a core event:

- What do these feelings [list feelings] remind you of?
- When was the first time you remember feeling this way?
- What person or event would you like to have missed? Although this is a general question, the subconscious mind will often find something that is directly relevant to the context of the current feelings.
- What event do you never want to remember?
- [If nothing comes to mind] If you were to make up a past event that could have given rise to these feelings, what would you invent? Feel free to use your imagination.

The following questions can elicit greater clarity about the event once there is at least a general sense. Allow some spaciousness and time with each of these:

- What age do you appear to be?
- Who is around you? Are you alone?
- Are you inside or outside? Upstairs or downstairs? What's the weather like?
- What else are you feeling?
- What else are you aware of?
- What do you need to do?
- What can't you do?

What happens if, despite asking questions, no event comes to mind? In this case, do some tapping on the feelings, emotions, and body sensations that are present. This will allow a further deepening into relevant material and the arising of new feelings and awareness that could be a closer match to relevant events from the past. You can then again ask the list of questions. I suggest you try this before asking your client to invent a matching event.

What if an event comes to mind, but it is quite recent? Ideally, you are looking for an upsetting event from early childhood, so you could ask if there is an earlier event. If none comes to mind, you can start with the one you do have, start to treat it, and then ask after some time if there is an earlier instance of this same theme.

Step 4: Treat the Event While Identifying Core Issues

The event can now be treated with EFT, using any of the standard trauma protocols: Tell the Story Technique, Watch the Movie Technique (see Chapter 20), or Tearless Trauma Technique (see Chapter 28), depending on the severity of the trauma. The latter two protocols allow the charge to be cleared from severely traumatic events, with little or no emotional pain. Another way is to ask, "What is the worst thing about what happened?" while tapping away the resulting emotions and feelings, then asking the question repeatedly, tapping away the emotional content between each time.

Telling the Story is important to achieve completion, as it can reveal much more detail about the ongoing effect of this event on the client. This is what we are going to need to bring awareness to and treat the client's behavior patterns and beliefs, which since the originating event have formed the client's reality, usually up until the present moment in time.

As the treatment progresses, we are interested in the conclusions drawn by the client (beliefs created and decisions made) as a result of the experience, and which usually represent core issues that we need to treat. These are important structures that affect how the clients see the world and how they behave and react in the world. Although it is written as another step after this one, this information could arise while the charge is cleared from the event. Thus it is as well to keep an eye out for it and jot it down for clearing later.

> P: Marilyn, I'd like to work with you to gently release all the upset from this experience. Is that okay with you, and is it something you think you could easily tell me about? If not, that is completely fine.
> M: It's a bit upsetting now I am thinking about it, but I can tell you what happened.
> P: Okay, we're going to use the Movie Technique, which makes things much gentler for you. If this event were a movie, what would its title be?
> M: "The End of Marilyn the Swot."
> P: *Even though I have this "End of Marilyn the Swot" movie, I deeply...* Tap, tap, tap.

See the Movie Technique chapter for details of this technique, and make sure you end up by using the Telling the Story Technique to clear all the charge on every element of the event until it feels peaceful, light, and clear.

Step 5: Identify and Treat Core Issues, Beliefs, and Other Disempowering Structures Created

This is probably the most important step, as it involves identifying the mental structures that are limiting your client the most. You ask questions to bring these to the surface, but usually some are revealed during the previous step when you are clearing the charge on the event. If you spot one, you can highlight it to your client and see if it feels true. For example, your client may be saying, "I don't feel safe." You can ask questions to determine the scope of this, for example, whether one core issue is that the world isn't safe, that is, that the feeling of lack of safety in that specific incident was generalized.

When you are asking questions, make it clear that the question is to be answered not from your client's present-moment awareness but from the time the event happened.

As there can be different sections to the story of the event, you may need to break it down and ask questions after emotional peak points, as each section will reveal new structures (beliefs, decisions, etc.) created. As the structures arise, write them down to treat later.

> P: What beliefs about life or God or the universe did you create from the event?
> M: Confusion about whether I should be a good girl and try hard to do well like my parents encouraged me to do or if I should give up doing well and be cool and part of the gang, as no one likes clever people.
> P: So what beliefs came out of that confusion?
> M: That if I am a swot or try hard, I will be alone and not be part of the group. In order to have friends, I need to stop being too clever.
> P: So what was the effect on you of carrying those beliefs from that point on?
> M: Not knowing how hard to try. Actually just getting by to keep my parents believing I was doing well, but all the time making sure I never stood out.
> P: So that was the decision you made, to just "get by"?
> M: Yes.
> P: So just for clarity, what core belief about life did you create that has always affected you since then?
> M: That life doesn't like smartasses and will reject them, making them feel alone and isolated.
> P: What do you think the effect of that belief was on you as you moved forward in your life?

M: To always hold back from being the best I can. Actually, as soon as I try to learn something, I find it such a struggle—like part of me is rebelling. This explains a lot.

P: Marilyn, I want to check something with you. Please say the following and tell me if you resonate with it: *I have to be small to avoid being rejected by Life or people.*

M: Yes, I definitely resonate with this.

P: [Asking for a VOC level] How true does that statement feel to you on a 0 to 10 scale?

M: For both *Life* and *people* they both feel about an 8/10.

Core Issue: I have to be small to avoid being rejected by Life/people.

What happened is that Marilyn made the decision to hold back her potential because of a fear of being alone and ousted from her peer group. It is possible she had had earlier upsetting experiences of being rejected or alone or isolated, possibly even for the same or similar reason of standing out or expressing herself authentically.

P: [Checking the VOC on a potential core issue that comes into the mind of the practitioner] Please say the following and tell me if you resonate with it: *I am alone in this world.*

M: Yes, that's true. That feels so painful. (Tears come to her eyes.)

With this reaction it is clear that the VOC on this belief must be a 10 or close to it!

Core Issue: I am alone.

This confirms that there is something around this that is an important issue for Marilyn. Another piece of work after this would be to find and treat events that resulted in this feeling of aloneness.

P: What was the effect on you over the course of your life of the decision to be small to avoid being rejected?

M: It has affected me so much I can't even imagine. Without it I would have achieved so much. I have been so stressed throughout my life. I now realize that I was never able to be myself and had to double-check everything I did to make sure it was never too good. I didn't realize how much I was holding myself back. Now thinking back I feel really angry with those bullies for destroying all my future potential—I'm getting angrier by the minute! I'm also angry with myself for letting them do that to me. And also, why didn't I talk to my parents about it?

P: *Even though I feel so angry with the bullies for destroying my future, I deeply...* Tap, tap, tap.

P: *Even though I am angry with myself... letting that happen...* Tap, tap, tap.

P: *Even though I didn't talk to my parents...* Tap, tap, tap.

P: How are you feeling?

M: Much better.

It's also good for clients to be aware of the positive effect that a so-called negative experience had on them.

P: Looking over the course of your life, what did you gain out of having such an experience?

M: Nothing!

P: Okay, let's put it another way. In which way did you become stronger or be motivated to make things better for yourself or others?

M: Funny you should say that. Actually, I am really good at motivating children to achieve their potential. I go round to schools and help the kids enjoy learning. I have got a good reputation. People send me their kids! I love what I do! And I now realize why I was very scared that my daughter is getting in with the wrong crowd. I was scared she would be led by them, and end up losing the chance to make the best of herself, which is what I did. But I can also feel her aloneness, so I can understand why she is doing what she is doing.

P: Yes, we still have some more clearing to do on these elements.

P: *Even though I have to be small to avoid being rejected by life, I deeply...* Tap, tap, tap.

P: How do you feel now?

M: That feels completely untrue now. In fact, you are more likely to be rejected by life by being small and insignificant. It is about allowing yourself to be yourself.

All the new elements that arise after this would be treated in the same way, including other structures that this example hasn't highlighted. The following questions can help bring these to light so they can be treated directly with EFT. Some of these may require a complete session, as there could be other important events that were the source of their creation:

- What beliefs about life/God/the universe did you create?
- What beliefs about Self did you create?
- What decisions did you make?
- What vows (if any) did you make?
- What character did you have to become in order to deal with and survive the situation in which you found yourself from that point on? (Example: *I had to be an ordinary human being who just got by intellectually.*)
- What behaviors did you adopt in order to keep yourself safe in the future? (Example: *I had to be just mediocre in order to avoid rejection.*)

More questions are asked and more answers are given and EFT is used to treat the elements revealed.

What happens if another event comes to mind while treating the original event? If the new event is earlier in time and represents the same theme, I would suggest shifting to that earlier event, as it is likely to be more foundational. You can ask the client if that event feels more foundational and if it feels right to move to it. The client will usually know what to do. Regardless, return to the unprocessed event later to test it (see next step).

Step 6: Test the VOC Level of the Core Issue

Once again, use the VOC (validity of cognition) 0–10 scale to check how the client is doing from the perspective of the core issues revealed and the original presenting issue. It is good to mentally try out challenging scenarios to confirm whether the clearing is complete. The past self who was going through the event needs to be checked as well as the present-day self.

P: Marilyn, from the perspective of the You who was going through the event, how true is the following belief to her, on a scale from 0 to 10, with 10 being the most true? *I have to be small in order to avoid being rejected.*

M: It doesn't feel true at all for her. I can see her throwing a glass of water over the bullies now and going inside to study!

P: And from your perspective?

M: I do get a slight sense of that, but it definitely feels clearer and I can feel myself wanting to challenge myself more now. That feels quite exciting.

P: There is probably another experience we need to visit to completely release that.

Actually, although that would be the deepest way to work, it may not be necessary to reach a cleared state on that belief. You could just tap directly on the belief and potentially clear it completely. The disadvantage is that the belief or feeling could potentially come back in the future in a context that unconsciously reminds the client of the untreated past event. But this may never happen.

P: Let's try tapping on that directly. *Even though I have to be small to avoid rejection, I deeply…* Tap, tap, tap.

P: How true does that feel now?

M: Completely untrue. I feel like I've shed a layer of suppression and I can't wait to get out there and study everything I've been putting off learning!

P: The feeling "I am alone"—how does that feel to you and the earlier you?

M: Yes, that is still there. Not quite as strong.

P: Would you like to schedule a session to work on that core issue?

M: Yes, please.

P: And how do you feel about the original issue about your daughter mixing with the wrong friends at school? When you think about that, how do you feel in your body?

M: All those negative feelings are gone. I do have some concern and I think it is something to do with her feeling alone like I did. I now understand why I felt so worried. I'm motivated to tell her my story and make sure she feels heard and understood by me, as I wasn't able to tell my parents about it. Maybe I can do some EFT on her!

P: That would be a great idea if she is willing!

P: I want to check something with you. Imagine you are in an evening class and you have done the best in the class at the exam and everyone is looking at you with nasty angry expressions on their faces. How do you feel?

M: That that is their issue! I feel great that I have studied hard and have reaped the benefits. And even as I say that, I can see they are now looking at me with admiration—their expressions were mock anger, like they were pretending to be jealous when in fact they were delighted for me.

P: So how are you left feeling?

M: I feel great, such a worry lifted. Thank you. Let's schedule the next session to work on the aloneness/rejection issue that came up.

P: Yes, let's do that.

Step 7: Treat Other Similar Events

In order for the client to feel completely clear on the core issue, it may be necessary to treat other events in which the theme of the core issue is highlighted. As each event is treated, the now-moment level of reality or truth of the core issue will continue to reduce. It isn't usually necessary to treat all events that have the core issue theme. At a certain point, your client won't be able to attribute any truth or reality to the core issue and you know you are complete. It is good, however, to try out future scenarios that stand the greatest chance of retriggering the beliefs and feelings, as I did by asking Marilyn how she would feel with classmates after getting the best score on an exam.

If the core issue hasn't completely gone, go through the whole protocol again, but this time use the core issue itself as the gateway issue (focusing on the core issue and becoming aware of all the feelings, sensations, and emotions) to find other contributory events. As many core issues could arise from a specific past event, this could need a series of sessions.

Summary

Finding and treating core issues is rewarding work. Any good practitioner and willing client should be using these techniques to effect profound, foundational shifts in behavior, outlook, and even what clients perceive as their identity or personality. Working in this way dramatically increases the likelihood of a more permanent solution to the client's specific life themes. Though more involved than using EFT in its more superficial form, it is a highly efficient way to work. Using EFT to help find and treat core issues is one of its most transformational applications and is when its true power can be harnessed, with deep results for your client.

Chapter 19
Aspects
Karin Davidson and Kathryn B. Sherrod

Abstract

While some people describe EFT as a miracle treatment that requires only one session (referred to as a "one-minute wonder"), experienced practitioners recognize that treatment often requires more than one session and possibly many sessions. In the growing body of research on EFT, only four studies used a one-session model and those targeted specific issues (three on phobias, one on posttraumatic stress disorder, PTSD). The other more than 20 outcome studies involved multiple sessions, from several to 15, with promising results. The problems with which clients usually present for treatment require multiple sessions. Why would this be? This occurs because only some issues are simple enough to be resolved quickly, while other issues are far more complex, involving various components or dimensions, each of which might require treatment. That is, traumas, memories, emotional wounds, and negative beliefs that clients carry inside them are often multifaceted, composed of what are termed "aspects." Aspects are individual pieces of a larger issue. In order to establish complete resolution, these individual pieces must be identified and addressed as relatively separate entities.

Keywords: aspects, complex issues, layers, peeling an onion, generalization effect, extinction

Karin Davidson, CHT, is an international trainer and speaker for EFT and other energy psychology modalities. She coauthored the *EFT Comprehensive Training Resource Level 1 (& 2)* for EFT certification and maintains an EFT practice. An award-winning producer, she has produced over 500 television and DVD training programs. Send correspondence to Karin Davidson, 303 North Providence Road, Media, PA, 19063, or info@howtotap.com.

Kathryn B. Sherrod earned a PhD in 1972. In her 40-year career, she has published 23 articles, written five books, and taught several graduate courses in psychology. Dr. Sherrod has lectured and provided consultation in the US and the UK. Send correspondence to Kathryn B. Sherrod, 2400 Crestmoor Road, Nashville, TN 37215, or drks@bellsouth.net.

What Are Aspects?

The term "aspects" refers to the facets or pieces comprising an issue. The aspects of an issue or event can include emotional components, sensory triggers, physiological responses, earlier related memories, and negative beliefs that are associated with the presenting problem—all of which need to be identified and addressed individually before the issue can be truly resolved.

Why Be Specific?

EFT works best when it is applied to very specific events, memories, or feelings. Attempting to work with large, global concepts is ineffective. Inexperienced practitioners sometimes try to work on too large an issue and, not succeeding in doing the impossible, they convince themselves that EFT itself is ineffective. Similarly, ignoring complicating aspects can leave unresolved portions of issues, again leading inexperienced individuals to conclude that EFT is ineffective.

Most issues that clients bring to therapy are complex. Treatment for these complex conditions typically requires multiple sessions. Rather than being discouraged by the fact that new aspects appear to arise after prior ones have been resolved, it is possible to appreciate the reality that clients are benefiting by having many layers of their issues resolved. In the treatment of complex conditions, it is important to be aware that it is necessary to identify and treat, one by one, numerous thoughts, emotions, and beliefs that might appear to be unrelated to each other but are connected at some level. Complex problems can include triggers for the problematic response, early experiences associated with the problematic situation, irrational beliefs that maintain the problem, or highly specific elements of a traumatic memory, such as the sound of screeching tires prior to an automobile collision (Feinstein, Eden, & Craig, 2005).

How Clients View Their Issues

Most people do not break their issues into aspects or pieces. They generally view their issues as huge challenges that they believe could feel as overwhelming to clinicians as to themselves. Clients might voice their concern that their problems are so huge that they are too much to work with or they might quietly worry that they will be rejected. They live within their issues, feel surrounded by their issues, and are often afraid of their issues. For example, clients have said, "If I tell you what I did, you won't want to see me anymore." Or they might ask, "That's probably the worst thing you've ever heard, isn't it?" Or they might comment, "I don't know how you listen to people's problems all day long; you must be depressed, too." They lack the objective perspective that clinicians have due to viewing these issues from the outside because of not being personally involved in the issues.

More important, clinicians have worked on their own problems and have worked on other clients' problems, so clinicians have seen people get past their issues. Clinicians are aware that our issues do not define us. Our issues affect us, but we define ourselves. By breaking issues into aspects, clinicians can help clients recognize that their issues have manageable parts. As some of those parts are resolved and clients experience success in the therapeutic situation, clients become more willing to tackle the larger parts that were initially of too great a magnitude to imagine them being resolved. That is, clients learn to trust the process when they experience it working for them.

Types of Aspects That May Be Relevant

Most clinicians are aware of some types of aspects without necessarily considering other types of aspects. Aspects can involve any portion of how organisms function. For example, aspects can involve changes or reactions in any of the following categories of functioning:

- Cognitive reorganization and clarification (from a cognitive perspective).
- Altering conditioning attachments and allowing extinction (from a learning theory or behavioral perspective).
- Reconnecting with people in new ways or possibly disconnecting from people who were involved in the incident in some way or who seem connected in some way with the incident (from a systems theory perspective).
- Calming the amygdala or enhancing the communication among various central nervous system areas (from a neurological or neurobiological perspective).

- Allowing changes in the neurochemical reactions of the nervous system, either sympathetic or parasympathetic systems (from a biochemical perspective).
- Adjustment of hormonal actions and reactions (from an endocrinological perspective).
- Being in the present moment and experiencing feelings that fit the current situation rather than having emotional reactions that are historically driven (from an emotional or "mindful" perspective).
- Breathing deeply and abdominally rather than shallowly (from a breath pattern perspective).
- Releasing tight muscles that have been retaining body memories or holding emotional tension (from a perspective involving bodywork, including clinicians who intentionally notice body language, such as in Gestalt therapy).
- Altering the way the body deals with disease processes (from an immunological perspective).
- Releasing "stuck" chi and allowing recovery of fluidity of movement in chakras, meridians, or auras (from an energy perspective).

How Information Storage Helps Us

Why might there be so many different ways in which memories can be recorded and stored for later retrieval, with those memories sometimes reappearing at what appear to be the most inopportune times? Why are there so many different aspects of events that are encoded in people's psyches, bodies, and approaches to their social network? Remembering events and experiences that were dangerous or that appeared to be dangerous is logically related to survival. It is likely that survival is far more important to our species than is comfort.

When experiences occur that we consider significant enough to threaten our safety, we humans, from a survival perspective, have redundant ways of encoding those experiences. By having redundancy in how our memories are recorded, we have multiple ways to keep ourselves safe. We have a built-in system of checks and balances on which we rely to protect ourselves. This means that, if we somehow forget one of the aspects encoded in our many different redundant systems and begin to allow ourselves to wander back into dangerous situations, we stop ourselves in various ways. Our danger-alert system is too often stuck on high alert. In that way, if we forget or ignore one portion of our warning system, we remember or subconsciously respond to another portion of our warning system. That is, we humans remain programmed to avoid potentially harmful experiences and sometimes we allow our programming to keep us in a state of constant vigilance. EFT is helpful in allowing us to learn more effectively when we need to be vigilant versus when we are safe enough to appreciate our companions and surroundings.

Many of us have a tendency to encode various events as dangerous and as worth remembering throughout our systems. Others of us appear to be somewhat psychologically hardier and react less intensely to events. How we, as individuals, are affected by experiences is influenced by our genetic and prior conditioning, as well as by the quality and intensity of the experience (Mineka & Zinbarg, 2006).

For example, if we lived in a jungle containing saber-toothed tigers, it would probably have been necessary to have such amazing redundancy that we would remember dangers that are life threatening. We would have wanted to learn how to avoid tigers and keep ourselves safe. Because the programming that is intended to keep us safe is so powerful, it sometimes surfaces and we apply it in situations that are not truly dangerous. It is often possible to develop the same levels of redundant encoding that could be useful in life-threatening situations, and apply that redundant encoding to events that are more embarrassing or uncomfortable than dangerous.

What Clients Do with Their Pain

How intensely anyone reacts to events or situations is complicated by the fact that some people show their reactions externally and are obvious in how they react, while others "shut down" and make efforts to suppress their reactions. Clients come in all types, from those whose reactions are obvious to those whose reactions are fairly well hidden. Virtually all clients who come for treatment are afraid of being hurt again, like a person who has a thorn embedded in a hand who wants the thorn removed but does not want to offer up the hand so that someone can remove the thorn. Luckily, EFT is a treatment that removes thorns with relatively little pain. After clients have benefited from having some aspects of painful memories resolved, they become much more willing to request assistance and to notice where they have pain rather than attempting to hide it.

Negative Self-Beliefs Arise from Trauma

Having a danger-alert system is only part of holding onto painful memories, whether those memories are conscious or subconscious. A major part of why clients generally retain painful memories about experiences is because they erroneously interpret these experiences as indicating something flawed or damaged or horrible about them. Clients can feel diminished, demeaned, worthless, bad, stupid, unlovable, out of control, or something else that feels intolerable. Again, these memories, whether contained in the body, in hormonal messengers, in neurochemicals, embedded in thoughts, or woven into feelings are kept around to keep us safe. Keeping us emotionally safe is as important as keeping us physically safe. Emotional rejection can cause the same types of central nervous system reactions that physical pain causes (Kross, Berman, Mischel, Smith, & Wager, 2011). This means that emotional pain and physical pain have some common representation in the brain. Not only can sticks and stones hurt my bones, but words can definitely also hurt me. These painful memories and the solutions we developed in reaction to those memories once served a purpose. That purpose is no longer being served; we have outgrown our earlier solutions. A new resolution is needed. Unfortunately, what we developed earlier as solutions have now become part of the problem.

Aspects Are Unique to the Individual

Clients can vary in the number of aspects related to any given trauma, event, or memory. Some clients develop unique aspects, based on their perceptions, histories, and sensitivities. Because aspects can be unique to each client, it is helpful for clinicians to be sensitive to the information clients are providing rather than assuming that one type of trauma, for example, an automobile accident, leads to certain symptoms, while personal betrayal leads to certain other symptoms. Even though there are commonalities among the symptoms associated with particular types of trauma, no type of trauma always leads to certain symptoms. The lists of symptoms or aspects regarding various types of trauma have been compiled to create a beginning point rather than to establish a definitive set of symptoms.

In addition to the existence of different types of aspects, aspects vary in levels of intensity. Some aspects of one traumatic event can be at a particular intensity level while other aspects of the same event are at a different intensity level. Aspects can include ways in which clients currently restrict themselves in terms of what they allow themselves to do socially, in their careers, and regarding balancing work and relaxation. It is generally considered most effective if the client taps on one aspect at a time until the SUD (subjective units of distress) level for each aspect is reduced to 0 intensity.

Likewise, aspects, while each playing a role in the makeup of the overall trauma, are relative in perceived importance. Some aspects are more critical to resolving the issue than others. These critical aspects are typically referred to as "core issues." During EFT, clients are often not aware that they are noticing part of a core issue. For example, clients often comment, "Well, this doesn't seem important or relevant, but I just remembered something that happened when I was 6." Recollections that clients suddenly remember are usually very important.

Often when a core issue is resolved, many of the other related smaller pieces no longer seem so formidable because their intensity has been reduced by tapping on the more fundamental parts. Sometimes, as core events and issues are resolved, clients also resolve many related aspects spontaneously. In EFT, as in basic learning theory, this phenomenon is called the "generalization effect."

Can Old Traumas Really Be Resolved?

A question even among many therapists relates to whether traumas and memories can actually be resolved. If clients have retained stored memories related to traumas for decades, is it actually possible to relieve that stored pain? Researchers used to believe that once memories were created by the hippocampus, they were consolidated in the brain, being stored as proteins in the cortex. After memories were stored in protein form, they were considered somewhat immutable. That is, they were not going to change. If, once people learned something, they were not able to unlearn that information or have available brain space within which to encode and store new information, the possibility of being stuck in the painful past could lead to remarkable rigidity and inflexibility. In reality, although we humans can sometimes be rigid and inflexible, we can also be remarkably resilient and creative.

To be resilient and creative implies that clients can learn new information to replace old information without reviewing all the old information each time they want to access the new information. This could be viewed as similar to needing to find a way around an obstacle in our path. In terms of how unresolved problems function as obstacles, a painful memory can block the pathway to success or to intimacy in relationships or it can block the ability to function in the current moment. When we have those obstacles, sometimes we have to take long detours around those obstacles to find success, enjoy our relationships, stay healthy, or sleep peacefully. Once an obstacle is removed, however, we would want to retain only the efficient way to get to our goal, not remembering the detour in detail with all its now unnecessary information. Through EFT, we can free ourselves from old painful memories and the obstacles they create, rather than being burdened by them, allowing ourselves to follow efficient and enjoyable pathways to find resources and to connect with people in satisfying relationships.

Psychologist John Arden (see Chapter 3) presents a clear and compelling explanation of how traumatic memories are stored and how they can be amenable to change. He differentiates between traumatic memories that are accessible verbally (which are the ones amenable to "talk therapy") versus the memories that are not accessible verbally. EFT is an approach that works to reduce the trauma associated with both types of memories. Arden posits that the most effective therapeutic approaches would integrate explicit and implicit memories of traumatic events by helping clients organize their thoughts and feelings rather than being lost in the fragmentation that often accompanies trauma.

Redefining Ourselves as Okay Instead of Damaged

Neuroscientists have now discovered that memories are definitely not immutable, but can be changed or reconsolidated (Hardt, Einarsson, & Nader, 2010; Sara, 2000). This is what all forms of psychological therapy focus on: the client no longer being bound by painful memories and, instead, finding ways to approach life and relationships differently. Scientists now recognize that when memories are brought back to consciousness, those memories can be altered or re-encoded (Nader & Einarsson, 2010), which is the mechanism by which clients can change the way they view the past and the way they view themselves.

As the aspects of a trauma or event are systematically and individually addressed, whether specific pieces of the original trauma, supporting negative beliefs, or related events, the brain has the ability to relearn and recategorize what may have previously seemed insurmountable (Garelick & Storm, 2005). An important aspect of the recategorization process involves clients' views of themselves. If they have previously categorized themselves as unlovable, they can now perceive themselves as lovable to some people if not to everyone. If they have categorized themselves as stupid, they can perceive themselves as competent in some areas if not in all areas. If they have categorized themselves as bad, they can perceive themselves as solid, decent humans. The practitioner's understanding of how to identify and address each aspect individually is vital to the potential of complete and lasting recovery.

Getting to the Core Issue

The metaphor of peeling an onion is often used to describe the process of working through the layers of issues surrounding a single event, trauma, or memory. The more complicated an issue, the more layers, or aspects, it may contain. "Peeling off" these layers, one by one, is important for a complete resolution. Each aspect has a different feeling to it, even if the difference is slight. Each of these aspects must be addressed separately in EFT. Clients simply continue tapping on each layer as it is revealed, until all layers are resolved.

Although EFT does not directly cure people of their painful memories, it helps clear interferences with the basic healing power of the body and thus releases the body and mind to function effectively. In the absence of energy work, clients' psyches can be so clogged up and restricted by the stuck energy or painful memories that they do not function well in life or in relationships. As aspects of issues are resolved, and the healing power of the body becomes less burdened, later aspects are usually easier to resolve.

Reactions to an Automobile Accident

In a discussion involving coping with traumatic events and PTSD, Ed Beckham, PhD, and Cecilia Beckham, LCSW, BCD, noted different types of psychological symptoms in reaction to a singular event, such as a car accident (2004). It is helpful to be aware of the types of specific symptoms that can exist. Here is a list the Beckhams developed of possible aspects of trauma within an individual:

- Fear.
- Difficulty riding in automobiles.
- Belief that one is going to die.
- Difficulty driving.
- Negative reactions to the presence of other cars.
- Self-blame for reacting slowly and not avoiding the accident.
- Anger or resentment at the driver who hit them.
- Anger or stress involving subsequent lawsuits.

Other aspects that may present using the example of the car accident are:

- Guilt if others were injured.
- Feeling trapped.
- The sound of the accident.
- The inability to avoid the accident; loss of control.
- The sound of a song playing on the radio at the time of the accident.
- Visual images or memories of the accident.
- Fear that another accident will occur.
- Physiological responses at the time of the accident; tightness in chest, difficulty breathing, etc.
- Difficulty driving in challenging conditions such as rain, snow, etc.

Possible Aspects in Fear of Flying

In a different type of potential trauma, such as fear of flying, there are also layers of aspects that need to be individually resolved. This is illustrated in Table 1. With some beliefs and traumatic experiences, it can take longer to address all aspects. Persistence is critical.

Possible Layers in Relationship Issues

The benefits of persistence are demonstrated in a situation involving a woman concerned about her relationship with her husband. Suppose, for instance, a client finds a text message from an unknown woman on her husband's cell phone. Her most noticeable initial feeling may be anger. She taps on the anger and it begins to resolve. After the resolution of the feelings of anger, the next aspect that may surface is the fear that he may love the other woman more than her. Resolving this fear might then lead to sadness, then to betrayal, then to lack of self-worth, and so on. Each of these aspects must be addressed separately. The client simply continues tapping on each layer as it is revealed, until all layers are resolved. Once these layers are all resolved, the client can find opportunities to clearly address the issues between her husband and herself. She is no longer hindered or confused by these emotional reactions that might possibly cloud conversations with her husband about what is happening. She can focus clearly on what she wants to be happening in their relationship so she

Table 1. An Example of Aspects of "I'm Afraid of Flying"

Thanatophobic (Fear of death)	Mysophobic (Fear of germs)	Loss of control	Claustrophobic (Fear of small spaces)	Phonophobic (Fear of loud noises)	The plane shakes
- It will be painful.	- I will get sick.	- It's dangerous to give up control.	- I can't get out.	- I'm in danger.	- We'll fall out of the sky.
- What about my children?	- No fresh air.	- The pilot might be tired.	- We'll run out of air.	- No control.	- I can't do anything about it.
- What if I go to hell?	- The restrooms are dirty.	- If something goes wrong, I can't do anything about it.	- The seats are too close.	- We're being attacked.	- We'll get caught in a storm.

can determine whether she believes her husband also wants to work on their relationship.

Why Are We Afraid of Change?

In addition to the multiple aspects that may present within the direct context of a single event or memory, some aspects can also present as issues related to change and identity. Clients may be ambivalent about letting go of chronic issues, their identity may be wrapped up in a particular issue, or they may become attached to various elements of their story. That is, even when clients truly want to change, there is often an unconscious fear of that change that must also be addressed. They might be unaware of benefits they are enjoying from their present behavior or issues. Change often generates some degree of discomfort and resistance, even when it is "positive," because it represents the unknown.

The degree to which a change in a positive direction can lead to massive discomfort and the need for psychological reorganization is exemplified by one young woman who was emotionally strong in the face of being expected to die from organ damage. Suddenly, and unexpectedly, she received a reprieve in the form of a heart-lung transplant. Her reaction was to become depressed because she was used to receiving accolades for being strong in the face of her breathing restrictions and the possibility of dying at any moment. After her surgery healed, she looked like everyone else and she no longer received attention just for breathing and refusing to give up. She commented, "Now, I can walk up a flight of stairs and no one appreciates me for doing that. I can read a book and no one notices my persistence. I'm no longer blue from lack of oxygen." She explained, "When I was in college, my doctors had written letters saying that I could not walk up any stairs, so if one of my classes was scheduled to be on the second floor of a building that had no elevator, the class had to be rescheduled to a first floor room to accommodate my needs. My whole world revolved around my illness and limitations." She summarized, "I have to develop a whole new identity as a healthy person and it's just weird." EFT is used for these aspects as well.

The Relevance of Earlier Events

It can be helpful to ask clients if they remember a similar event or a time when they felt the same emotion as the one they feel in reaction to their presenting issue. The reason for asking about earlier events is that these earlier events sometimes lay the groundwork for current beliefs, interpretations, and struggles. Later events often reinforce the response or belief created at that first event. Earlier events can be viewed as the roots of the problem, while the presenting issues are the obvious part of the problem. For anyone who has ever pulled weeds, the leaves of the weeds are the presenting problem while the earlier events are the roots of the weeds. Unless weeds are pulled up by their roots, they can regrow.

In some cases, clients can clear a specific incident with all its known aspects but still not feel the issue is resolved. Usually, this signifies that other related incidents or issues are still affecting the presenting one. A metaphor for this is a table; the problem is the tabletop and the aspects are the table legs holding up the problem (see Chapter 26). If the presenting problem is not resolved by clearing the earliest related event, it is important to keep questioning and then tapping for all the aspects of related events. Fortunately, psychological extinction often occurs while using EFT with related events so that often not all related events need to be addressed to resolve the presenting problem (see Chapter 25, "The Generalization Effect").

Treating Children

In treating complex issues, clinicians need to be aware that children sometimes have issues and/or manifestations of traumas that are different from those observed in adults (Spates, Waller, Samaraweera, & Plaisier, 2003). Perry (2000) observed that millions of children have been traumatized. It appears imperative to find rapid and effective ways of helping them resolve their trauma. Church and colleagues (2012a, 2012b) have published two studies on using EFT with adolescents, one addressing depression and the other PTSD; their research demonstrates rapid reduction in symptoms and distress.

When treating children for trauma, it is helpful to realize that their parents might have been vicariously traumatized by being aware of their children's emotional pain. Similarly, when treating parents for trauma, their children might have been vicariously traumatized. This occurs because family members are emotionally connected with each other. The most thorough solution is to use EFT with all involved.

Because children are often remarkably sensitive to situations and to the people around them, children are sometimes traumatized by events that others deem minor. Fortunately, however, children are also remarkably resilient when someone helps them resolve those traumas. The aspects that are part of children's issues are often different from adult aspects. It is important for clinicians to listen carefully to children and to watch their body language to notice reactions these young clients might not be willing to express directly. By being aware of the aspects that might be relevant to children at different developmental levels, clinicians can be more helpful to young clients.

One of the differences between the way children express aspects and the way adults express aspects of trauma is that children often rely on describing pieces of events to "explain" what happened. For example, a child who got into a physical fight on the playground might say, "He hit me and I hit him." If an adult probes for more information about what happened, the child might add, "I had a bloody nose." The adult might ask, "What else happened?" or "What else do you remember?" The child might answer, "My shirt got torn and my mom was going to yell at me." Each detail is an aspect that needs to be addressed. Similarly, a child who was rejected at the school cafeteria might say, "She wouldn't sit with me and I cried." The adult might ask, "What happened next?" The child might say, "I was alone at my table." The adult might ask, "What happened while you were alone at your table?" The child might answer, "I wasn't hungry and I didn't eat my lunch." Again, each of these issues has aspects that can be addressed. Children are less likely to talk about their feelings regarding what happened than are adults.

Children are also less likely to "go back to the beginning of the story," often relying on telling about the specific and intense moments to convey their experiences. In contrast, adults often want to tell the whole story to provide a full context to the experience. For this reason, adults sometimes benefit from being encouraged to focus on one experience while children benefit from being encouraged to provide more contextual information.

The younger the child, the more likely the child is to lack effective words to convey what happened. Toddlers and young elementary school children might do much better with stuffed animals of different sizes to act out with the animals what occurred. For example, young children might be given an opportunity to show the therapist what one person did to another person by holding one stuffed animal and having that animal do something to another animal or say something to another animal. Sometimes children take on the behavior of an adult by doing something an adult has done to them. The child might hit the stuffed animal or scold the stuffed animal, acting out what has happened to the child. Children sometimes prefer to identify with the stronger, more powerful person than with themselves (especially if they view themselves as weak, powerless, or inadequate in some way). Sometimes, to get to the aspects of a difficult situation for a child, it is helpful to allow the child to show what happened.

Children sometimes want to tap on stuffed animals rather than tapping on themselves. Because of having mirror neurons in our brains, tapping on someone else or something else can have similar effects as tapping on ourselves. That is, when we tap on someone else (or a stuffed animal), some of the same areas of the brain that are activated are the areas that are activated when we tap on ourselves. Similarly, when we watch someone else tapping (whether they are tapping on themselves, on someone else, or on a stuffed animal), some of the same areas of the brain are activated as when we tap on ourselves. This appears to be related to how we have information that we use to develop empathy as well as helping us learn by watching what other people do. Although this is a complicated and controversial area of neurology (Heyes, 2010; Hickok, 2009), there is little doubt that, in some manner, we facilitate our own learning by watching other people do things.

One of the benefits of having stuffed animals for children to tap on is that sometimes when children get upset, they remain capable of focusing on how upset their stuffed animals might be, even when the children are having trouble focusing on their own distress. For example, one little boy, Ricky (not his real name), who was diagnosed with an autistic spectrum disorder, had a very difficult time with transitions. Struggling with transitions is typical for children who feel emotionally vulnerable for any reason. Aspects of transitions could include feeling anxious about getting out of the car, worrying about what to say to other kids, worrying about dropping the ball in sports, not knowing how to ask someone for help, or needing protection from a bully. Keeping a stuffed tapping animal in the family car allowed Ricky to tap on the animal on the way to school, while riding to day camps, or when going to birthday parties so he was calm enough when he got there to pay attention to classwork at school or to enjoy the fun activities that were planned for him and the other children.

Children generally like games and fantasies. For this reason, encouraging children to tap on the "magic buttons" on their bodies is a helpful way for them to view tapping as a game. One child who had been awakened by a nightmare of being chased by a polar bear agreed to tap on her magic body buttons while she talked with her mother about the dream. Initially, the child talked really fast about how the bear was huge with green teeth and big claws, but eventually the bear had no teeth and his claws were covered with ice so he could not effectively claw anyone. The child finally said, "It was only a dream, Mom," in that exasperated tone of voice children do so well.

By the end of this tapping time regarding the dream, the child apparently decided to try to appear to be still scared to get more attention. This can happen in exactly the same way that a child needs a drink of water, needs to go to the bathroom (again), or needs to tell you something important at bedtime. It often really means that the child does not want to go to sleep right now and is looking for an excuse to delay the inevitable.

Though recognizing that even tapping can become a way of manipulating parents to get some extra attention at inappropriate times may be an important part of learning for parents and their children, it is important not to be too quick to consider manipulation as the underlying motivation when children seem to be just seeking attention. That is, children naturally seek attention and that is just a part of what they need as they grow.

Tapping with children who just want some attention can be a way to connect with children. Sometimes during the day a child might want some tapping time as a way to connect with a parent and be noticed. This can function as a warm and wonderful bonding time. While a child is tapping with a parent, something might come up that the child wants to clear. It is also possible that nothing specific will come up and the child might simply benefit from realizing that his or her needs are noticed and valued by a parent. Such respectful and loving recognition and appreciation of a child's needs is a very important aspect of nurturing children. Similarly, a practitioner might become aware that a child is requesting a session with the practitioner as a way to get some one-on-one time with a nurturing adult.

Children need nurture and they ask for it in various ways. Often, it is possible to provide the requested nurture so the child can feel supported, even if the child is asking for one thing while really desiring another.

Conclusion

In summary, aspects are the individual facets of a problem. While EFT and other energy-related modalities have been shown to be highly effective in resolving trauma and negative beliefs and memories, EFT is used at its fullest potential when the issues addressed are highly specific, and when the myriad aspects related to any potential issue are addressed individually. The ability to identify, understand, and work effectively with aspects leads to thorough and lasting results. Rather than clients being mired in past painful events or lost in current perplexing and challenging situations, clients can be free to explore ideas, connect with people in authentic satisfying relationships, and reach their potential.

References

Beckham, E. & Beckham, C. (2004). *A personal guide to coping* (Chapter 11: Coping with trauma and posttraumatic stress disorder). Retrieved from http://www.drbeckham.com/handouts/CHAP11_COPING_WITH_PTSD.pdf

Church, D., De Asis, M. A., & Brooks, A. J. (2012a). Brief group intervention using EFT (Emotional Freedom Techniques) for depression in college students: A randomized controlled trial. *Depression Research and Treatment, 2012*, 1–7. doi:10.1155/2012/257172

Church, D., Piña, O., Reategui, C., & Brooks, A. (2012b). Single session reduction of the intensity of traumatic memories in abused adolescents after EFT: A randomized controlled pilot study. *Traumatology, 18*(3), 73–79. doi:10.1177/1534765611426788

Feinstein, D., Eden, D., & Craig, G. (2005). *The promise of energy psychology: Revolutionary tools for dramatic personal change*. New York, NY: Jeremy P. Tarcher.

Garelick, M. G. & Storm, D. R. (2005). The relationship between memory retrieval and memory extinction. *Proceedings of the National Academy of Sciences of the United States of America, 102*(26), 9091–9092. Retrieved December 18, 2012, from http://www.pnas.org/content/102/26/9091.full

Hardt, O., Einarsson, E. O., & Nader, K. (2010). A bridge over troubled water: Reconsolidation as a link between cognitive and neuroscientific memory research traditions. *Annual Review of Psychology, 61*, 141–167.

Heyes, C. (2010). Where do mirror neurons come from? *Neuroscience and Biobehavioral Reviews, 34,* 575–583.

Hickok, G. (2009). Eight problems for the mirror neuron theory of action understanding in monkeys and humans. *Journal of Cognitive Neuroscience, 21*(7), 1229–1243.

Kross, E., Berman, M., Mischel, W., Smith, E. E., & Wager, T. (2011). Social rejection shares somatosensory representations with physical pain. *Proceedings of the National Academy of Sciences USA, 108*(15), 6270–6275.

Mineka, S. & Zinbarg, R. (2006). A contemporary learning theory perspective on the etiology of anxiety disorders: It's not what you thought it was. *American Psychologist, 61*(1): 10–26.

Nader, K. & Einarsson, E. O. (2010). Memory reconsolidation: An update. *Annals of the New York Academy of Sciences, 1191,* 27–41.

Perry, B. D. (2000). Traumatized children: How childhood trauma influences brain development. *Journal of the California Alliance for the Mentally Ill, 11*(1), 48–51.

Sara, S. J. (2000). Retrieval and consolidation: Toward a neurobiology of remembering. *Learning and Memory, 7,* 73–84.

Spates, C. R., Waller, S., Samaraweera, N., & Plaisier, B. (2003). Behavioral aspects of trauma in children and youth. *Pediatric Clinics of North America, 50*(4), 901–918.

Chapter 20
"Tell the Story" and "Watch the Movie" Techniques
Rue Anne Hass

Abstract

The Tell the Story and Watch the Movie techniques add depth, creativity, and mastery to EFT. With this approach to tapping, you can safely invite further clarity and even intensity associated with a difficult event to surface. These techniques allow the story of experiencing the event to ease toward resolution of the anxiety or trauma associated with it. The techniques have the additional benefit of not requiring clients to share the content of their tapping. This becomes important for clients who regard the details of their memories or events as too disturbing, embarrassing, or shameful for them to voice to anyone (e.g., the EFT practitioner). This chapter details how to do the techniques step by step and then provides case examples of using them to transform traumatic events/memories. The cases illustrate clearing a frightening experience at the dentist, an auto accident, a severe spider phobia, and a dangerous skiing accident. The chapter also provides a longer case example of how a client used the Movie Technique, silently, to resolve a severe childhood trauma that she had not realized was still unresolved and affecting her relationship with her son.

Keywords: tell the story, watch the movie, story technique, movie technique, trauma, specific, dentist, accident, phobia, skiing accident, worry, embarrassment

Rue Anne Hass, MA, is a spiritual life path coach and intuitive mentor, author, ordained minister, and EFT Master Practitioner. She is the author of *EFT for the Highly Sensitive Temperament*. Her background includes extensive training in psychospiritual philosophy and energy psychology therapies. Send correspondence to Rue Anne Hass, PO Box 17653, Boulder, CO 80308-0653, or rue@intuitivementoring.com. www.IntuitiveMentoring.com.

After you learn the basics of EFT, there are many techniques that will lend elegance and mastery to your work. The Watch the Movie and Tell the Story Techniques are two of these. They follow the same basic procedure, using two different perceptual systems. Watch the Movie is usually experienced internally, silently, while Tell the Story is done out loud, offering two different ways to capture an emotional response so that you can resolve it with EFT.

I first describe how to do each technique and then give case examples of how it can be used. Before you begin to follow the steps for each technique, check in with your client. If your client is feeling nervous about even approaching the topic, tap first for how your client is feeling right now and clear any upset before you start. The following steps are addressed to the client.

How to Do the Movie Technique

1. Find a specific traumatic event that you can imagine as a brief story, movie, or video. Think of an event that was traumatic for you. If you are dealing with a particular life theme, core issue, or belief, such as "I am not good enough," be more specific by trying to recall a key memory that fits into this theme. Think of the event as though it were a scary movie. Make sure it's an event that lasts just a few minutes; if your movie lasts several hours or days, you've probably picked a general pattern. Try again, selecting a different event, till you have a movie that's just a few minutes long.

Here is an example from the EFT Universe Tutorial on the Movie Technique that will help you to find a specific event to tap on:

> This example is a man whose general issue is "Distrust of Strangers." We trace it to a particular childhood incident that occurred when the man, who we'll call John, was 7 years old. His parents moved to a new town, and John found himself walking to a new school through a rough neighborhood. He encountered a group of bullies at school but always managed to avoid them. One day, walking back from school, he saw the bullies walking toward him. He crossed the street, hoping to avoid their attention. He wasn't successful, and he saw them point at him, then change course to intercept him. He knew he was due for a beating. They taunted him and shoved him, and he fell into the gutter. His mouth hit the pavement, and he chipped a tooth. Other kids gathered round and laughed at him, and the bullies moved off. He picked himself up and walked the rest of the way home.
>
> If John were to apply EFT to his general pattern, "Distrust of Strangers," he would be tapping generally—and ineffectually. When instead you focus on the specific event, you're honing in on the life events that gave rise to the general pattern. A collection of events like John's experience with the bullies can combine to create a general pattern. ("The movie technique," n.d.)

2. Give your movie a title. One good way to find a title is to notice the worst part of the specific event, and come up with a few vivid words to describe it. Let these words come from your gut or your heart. Or how would your 10-year-old self say this? John might call his movie "The Bullies."
3. Rate the degree of your emotional distress around just the title, not the movie itself. For instance, on the SUD (subjective units of distress) scale of 0 to 10 where 0 is no distress and 10 represents maximum distress, you might be an 8 when you think of the title "The Meeting." Write down your movie title, and your SUD number.
4. Create an EFT Setup Statement using your movie title. It might sound something like this: *"Even though I have this movie _____ [insert your movie title here], I deeply and completely accept myself."*
5. Tap on the EFT acupressure points, while repeating the Setup Statement three times. Your distress level will typically go down. You may have to do EFT several times on the title for it to reach a low number like 0 or 1 or 2.
6. Think of the "neutral point" before the bad events in the movie began to take place. For John in the previous example, the neutral point was when he was walking home from school, before the bullies saw him.
7. Once you've identified the neutral point of your own movie, start running the movie through your mind, until you reach a point

where the emotional intensity rises. In John's case, the first emotionally intense point was when he saw the bullies.
8. Stop at this point and assess your intensity number. It might have risen from a 1 to a 7, for instance.
9. Perform a round of EFT on that first emotional crescendo. For John, it might be, *"Even though I saw the bullies turn toward me, I deeply and completely accept myself."* Use the same kind of statement for your own problem: *"Even though* [first emotional crescendo], *I deeply and completely accept myself."* Keep tapping till your number drops to 0 or near 0, perhaps a 1 or 2.
10. Now rewind your mental movie to the neutral point, and start running it in your mind again. Stop at the first emotional crescendo. If you sail right through the first one you tapped on, you know you've really and truly resolved that aspect of the memory with EFT.
11. Go on to the next crescendo. For John, this might have been when the bullies shoved him into the gutter. When you've found your second emotional crescendo, repeat the process. Assess your intensity number, do EFT, and keep tapping till your number is low. Even if your number is only a 3 or 4, stop and do EFT again. Don't just push through low-intensity emotional crescendos; since you have the gift of freedom at your fingertips, use it on each part of the movie.
12. Rewind to the neutral point again, and repeat the process.
13. When you can replay the whole movie in your mind, from the neutral point, to the end of the movie when your feelings are neutral again, you'll know you've resolved the whole event. You'll have dealt with all the aspects of the traumatic incident. The end of the movie is usually a place where the bad events come to an end. For John, this might be when he picked himself off the ground and resumed his walk home.
14. Test yourself. To truly test yourself, run through the movie, but exaggerate each sensory channel. Imagine the sights, sounds, smells, tastes, and other aspects of the movie as vividly as you can. If you've been running the movie silently in your mind, speak it out loud. When you cannot make yourself upset, you're sure to have resolved the lingering emotional impact of the event. The effect is usually permanent.

When you have worked through enough individual movies in this way, the whole general pattern that the events contributed to creating often vanishes. Perhaps John had 40 events that contributed to his distrust of strangers. He might need to do the Movie Technique on all 40, but experience with EFT suggests that when you resolve just a few key events, perhaps 5 or 10 of them, the rest fade in intensity, and the general pattern itself is neutralized.

How to Do the Story Technique

The Tell the Story Technique is similar to EFT's Movie Technique. Make sure you're familiar with the Movie Technique first, because most of the instructions are the same as for Tell the Story. The main difference between the two is that the Movie Technique is usually performed silently, while the Story Technique is spoken out loud. Here are the steps:

1. Identify a specific event, like you do in the Movie Technique. Give the story a title, and rate the emotional charge of the title alone. Use the 0-to-10 scale, with 0 being no emotional intensity, and 10 being the maximum possible intensity.
2. Use EFT on the story title alone, till the intensity level drops to a low number—0, 1, or 2.
3. Then start telling the story from the beginning. That beginning should be a neutral point. If the story is about being shouted at by a teacher in school at the age of 6, for instance, start at the point just before, when the room was calm, before the shouting began.
4. Stop whenever you reach an emotionally intense part of the story, which is easy because you'll feel your intensity number going up, for example to a 5 or 7 or even 10. (Note: As a practitioner working with a client, you need to stop the client if you believe the client's intensity number is rising, even if the client doesn't stop on his or her own. Clients are often so used to just pushing through the tough feelings, they don't realize they can stop, and resolve

them using EFT. Find out just how high the client's number is.)
5. When you reach that first rise in intensity and stop, create an EFT Setup Statement targeted to that particular emotional crescendo: *"Even though* [emotional crescendo], *I deeply and completely accept myself."* Tap on all the EFT acupressure points while repeating the statement, and repeat several times if necessary, till the intensity level drops to a low number—0, 1, or 2.
6. Start telling the story again. Stop at the next intense moment, and repeat the process.
7. When the whole story has been told, and all emotional crescendos have been tapped down to low numbers, test your results. Tell the story emphatically. Exaggerate. Raise your voice. Imagine each sensory channel—sights, sounds, smells, tastes—as strongly as possible. Try to get upset during the emotional crescendos. When you fail to elicit an emotional response, you'll know you've truly eliminated the emotional sting of this event. ("Tell the story," n.d.)

Case Example: Car Accident

Dawson Church, PhD, gives a clear example of using both techniques to resolve trauma from a car accident:

> I worked with a female client in her twenties during an EFT workshop. Her issue was a car crash. We searched for aspects. We used the Tell the Story Technique, recounting the event out loud, and the Movie Technique, which is playing the event mentally without words.
>
> Aspects are pieces of an event or problem. They may involve different sensory channels, such as sight, smell, hearing, taste, and touch. They may also be emotions or physical sensations. They may also be cognitions, phrases, or images. Here are some of the aspects we discovered.
>
> As she began to tell her story, her first words were: "I looked down for a second." I treated that statement as an aspect, and asked for her SUD level. It was a 10, so we used the phrase in a Setup Statement. We tapped and it quickly went to 0.
>
> I noticed she seemed edgy, so I asked her how she felt. She said she felt a lot of nervous energy, and it came to focus up and down the front of her throat. So we treated that as Aspect #2, created a new Setup, and just a single round of tapping brought the sensation under control.
>
> You start telling the story, or running the movie in your head, from a neutral point. I asked her to pick a neutral point and it was "It was a nice day in San Francisco." We then went through her describing the moment she looked down without a rise in her SUD level, and she told the story through the moment of the crash itself.
>
> The impact threw her body forward, and we treated the physical shock as a kinesthetic aspect.
>
> She remembered the noise of the crash, and tapped on that, after which she switched aspects to remembering the smoke coming out from under the hood of the car. When she got out of the car, her first thought was "There goes $5,000." It was her dad's car, and she knew she would have to buy him a replacement. Then she pictured telling him. She said he was the anxious type, and he'd be freaked out by the news.
>
> We did rounds of EFT on each different aspect. After clearing each one, she rewound the movie in her mind and played it from the beginning. You can also have a client imagine that they have a remote control that controls playback. They can rewind or fast forward if they wish, for example, to get quickly through a part of the story that clearly no longer holds emotional charge. I also ask clients to hit the "pause" button during an emotional peak, and fully experience the emotion. This is opposite to our usual tendency to rush through bad feelings. With EFT we stay with those feelings till they're all tapped away.
>
> The next emotional peak in the story was the memory of the other driver yelling at her that his wife was pregnant. Her numbers didn't go down as we tapped on that, so we performed several rounds of the 9 Gamut Procedure. I suspected this was not the first time in her life she'd been yelled at, so we generalized to "People yell at me." Eventually her SUD went down for both this phrase and the memory of the other driver. The end of her

story was the ambulance taking the pregnant woman away. (Church, n.d.)

Variation: Create a Fictional Story or Movie

Actual tapping sessions may not fit neatly into the "recipe." Be alert to and aware of the nuances of your experience, your clients' small clues about their inner experience, and their reported SUD levels, and let these be your guide. Sometimes it is useful to make modifications. One of the most useful modifications is to create a fictional story or movie that relates the event in an indirect way.

If it is too uncomfortable for the client to think of or to describe what happened, or if the client doesn't know what happened, the client can "make up" a story or movie that contains the main elements and emotions of what happened, but tell it as a "once upon a time" story. The client can be the main character of this created story, or can invent a character that the story happens to. Do the story/movie process in the same way as detailed previously.

Case Example: Spider Phobia

EFT Master Gwyneth Moss gives a good example of making up a movie, describing a client, Elaine, who had a terror of tarantulas:

> Tapping helped her to say the word "tarantula," but looking at a photograph of a tarantula brought all of her fear response back. I asked her if she could remember any experience in her life that could be the root of this fear or could explain it, and she responded that she could not. So I took a different tack and asked her to imagine herself to be the director of a fictional movie in which a fear of tarantulas would make sense. That movie could be set in another country, in another time and the actors could be a different age and sex. Elaine invented a movie about a teenage boy in Tudor times, hundreds of years ago, and gave it the title "Death in the Night." As she began to construct the movie in her mind, I could see she was getting distressed, so we started with several rounds of silent tapping.
>
> In EFT we use words to tune in emotion and tapping to clear or calm emotion. When the emotion is strongly present, we do not need words to tune it in, and silent tapping can help a person calm down enough to continue. We then started to sneak up on the problem: "Even though I've made this movie and there's some very scary bits in it…" And after a few rounds we got to tapping for the title of the movie, "Death in the Night," until Elaine felt comfortable to narrate her movie.
>
> She started with the opening scene where the young man who has had to leave his home and family is alone in a straw hut in the night. Then the tarantulas sneak into the hut. At this moment her fear rose visibly so we started tapping with *"Even though they started to come under the door…"* and *"Even though there were hundreds of them…"* Then to *"Even though they crawl up on the bed…"* It took several rounds of tapping to clear each step through the movie, as she would hit the top of the scale on each one. But clear they did and, after each, we rewound to the beginning and started the narration again. I have to say that this took a great deal of bravery from Elaine and sometimes she could only have me tap on her fingers.

Moss described how she tapped with her client through the most terrible aspects of the invented story, and completed her narration with this comment:

> If you use the technique of the fictional movie, then you simply use it just as you do for a real memory. However, we do need to be very clear that it is fiction and that the imagined events are simply a means of tuning in the emotional disturbance so that it can be cleared. If we get too close to reality, we could be in danger of creating a memory where there was none. To create a fiction, you can change place and time; all that needs to fit is the emotion. Your test is first to be able to narrate the fiction and then to be able to face what was previously triggering. (Moss, n.d.)

Other Modifications

After you have done the Story and Movie techniques a number of times, and you have a sense of how they flow, you can create modifications in the moment as needed. The following are accounts from my own experience and from my work with clients.

Case Example: Traumatic Dental Experience

I suffered through a 3-hour appointment that involved removing three old crowns. It was an invasive, painful, intensely physical procedure that required lots of muscular wrenching on the part of the dentist, as well as loud noises. I had to use all my energy tricks and wisdom to stay present and still. It was overwhelming.

Tapping was a great help to me. Typical of the sensitive person, I held it together while I was still at the dentist's office, smiling and nodding as I made the next appointment, driving myself carefully home. Once I was safe at home, though, I couldn't stop crying. I shook and cried and tapped. The shaking was important for my body to feel. Shaking after a shock is the return of movement and flow, where before there was freeze.

Because I was so deeply immersed in the present feeling of what had happened, I didn't stop to do the EFT Setup Statements. I just tapped. The images, sensations, feelings, and memories were right there. I was just telling the story to myself, and tapping through the points, pausing when something particularly difficult came to mind, and focusing on that until the feelings subsided.

I tapped while I remembered the experience.

I tapped while I talked to myself about what had happened.

I tapped while I re-felt all the *fear* and *pain* and emotions of *helplessness, trapped-ness,* and *being a victim.*

I tapped for the *invasive wrenching* that I had felt.

I tapped for all the *threatening noises.*

I tapped for *how my mouth felt,* especially after the anesthetic wore off.

I tapped for the effects of the anesthetic chemicals in my body.

I tapped and cried for most of the night.

I felt much more balanced the next day. I was able to think of what had happened without going back into trauma. Later I was able to talk calmly to the dentist about my experience of her work. I was able to return to the subsequent appointments and stay relaxed and calm. Going to the dentist will never be easy for me, and this was the worst dental experience that I had ever had, but tapping through the story of what happened while acknowledging and honoring my feelings helped me feel supported and returned me to a sense of ease.

This way of doing the Story Technique is useful when the issue you are tapping about is so "up" that it could be cumbersome to stop and do the EFT Setups. In general, however, and particularly when you are learning EFT, it is best to use the Setup Statements and follow the Basic Recipe.

Note: People who are used to numbing what they feel should use clear Setup Statements and be sure to approach their traumatic experience gently and respectfully. In such cases, it is very useful to work with an experienced and skilled practitioner.

Case Example: Skiing Accident

My daughter was 28 when she had a serious accident on the ski slope. She caught an edge of her ski on a crust of snow, lost her balance, and slammed headfirst into a tree, denting and cracking her helmet. Two weeks after the event, I spent an afternoon tapping with her.

I started the tapping by talking very slowly, speaking softly, watching her closely for shifts in her experience, seeking to move her body's awareness past the *bracing*, and past the moment of *impact with the tree*, toward returning to positive movement inside.

The worst part for her, she said, was *seeing her cracked and dented helmet*, and realizing that *it had saved her life*. She had her helmet there as we were tapping, and we tapped a long time for even *being able to look at her helmet*, until she could do that without crying, slowly becoming able to talk about *what it represented*.

We tapped further on:

How I came to consciousness again after I hit the tree…
…and cried (a good release)
…took my skis off
…called my husband on my cell phone
…he didn't answer
…he must be still skiing down the mountain
…how I waited, bravely
…checked my body for injuries
…a lot of pain and shock but no serious injuries
…called him again, starting to worry about **him.**

And then we tapped for how she *pulled herself together to stand and ski shakily* the rest of the way down the mountain *"on my own,"* finally being *met by the emergency rescue team* and *taken care of.*

At the end of this session, she was able to talk about the whole event with ease. She hasn't gone skiing much since that incident, but when she did, she found she was able to head down the mountain with caution, but without fear.

Case Example: A Silent Movie Technique Session

An event might be too triggering, embarrassing, or emotionally overwhelming to be spoken aloud. A powerful benefit of the Movie Technique done silently is that clients do not have to share the event featured in the movie. This has particular relevance for traumatized groups who might not want to disclose the details and fail to seek help out of fear that they will have to talk about the trauma. Rape victims, war veterans, and both victims and perpetrators of abuse may fall into this category. Or the upsetting events may have involved great embarrassment or shame. Whatever the reason for the reluctance to speak about an event, the Movie Technique allows clients to clear the disturbing emotions without speaking about what happened.

Knowing this was useful in my session with Estelle who had no idea that an event in her childhood was still distorting her current emotional life. Her story seemed quite simple on the surface. She was worried about her 26-year-old son, who had moved into his own apartment with three other young men. She wanted him to be independent, but she worried obsessively about him all the time. In this session we didn't tap directly on her worry issue but on an event at the source of her worry. Not only did our tapping have a powerful effect on Estelle's generalized worry, it also significantly changed her perception of the triggering event.

When Estelle was 5 years old, a "terrible trauma" had befallen her suddenly. She said, "I had been going along as a happy energetic child, a cheerful free spirit, and then a dreadful experience happened to me out of the blue. After that, I knew that anything could happen at any time, even when things are going fine, and I had to be on the lookout for it, always. It is decades later now, and I still can't stop worrying."

We did a whole tapping session on her inner "movie" of this event. She did not share with me the details of what actually happened.

Estelle reported that she had done quite a lot of work on the incident. "It's mostly just the worry now," she said. "I just have some feelings stuffed down inside about it. It feels like a habit—a way of being or perceiving things."

I could tell that it hadn't occurred to Estelle to connect her constant worrying with her stuffed feelings from the earlier trauma. As we talked a bit about that, Estelle said, "This thought just popped into my head: *Life is not safe.*" She felt this statement as fear and anxiety. In her body, she felt "a tightness and pressure in my abdomen, a light fluttery feeling above my navel, and a hollow echo-y feeling in my center up to my throat. I can't breathe." The SUD numbers were 8–10, sometimes feeling like they were over 10.

Thinking about what she described as a "hollow place" in her center, connected to the traumatic experience, I suggested, "Sometimes, when a really scary unexpected thing happens to a child, it is as if a part of them leaves their body. Psychologists call this dissociation. Estelle, if you could locate, in your own personal space around yourself, the part of you that 'left,' where would it be?"

I had prefaced this question by acknowledging that this might be a weird question to her, so she should only answer it if it felt accurate. But Estelle responded right away, saying definitively, "It is above my head, about 6 feet up and back a little, right over my crown chakra, and it is hovering."

Before we tapped, I asked Estelle to touch gently into all the feelings in her around that event, and notice what the intensity of them was on the 0–10 scale. She said it was a 9.

Now we tapped:

Even though I have this belief that life is not safe, that started a long time ago with a dreadful experience, I accept myself anyway, and I accept that there is a part of me that is thinking and feeling this way.

Even though I can't stop worrying, and worrying is deeply embedded in my family, I accept that there is something in me that feels that way and is kind of programmed to be that way, and I honor myself for how hard this has been.

Even though something in me believes that life is not safe, I accept that is the way it was, and I am ready to bring healing to this. I want to know if there is a different way to think about all this.

Tapping through the points:

Something in me believes that life is not safe.

That scary thing that happened when I was a little girl, when everything had been going fine, and then something terrible happened all of a sudden.

That made me believe for the rest of my life that life was not safe.

I have a lot of fear that is buried inside.

That experience scared me and I feel like some part of me left, and I have this hollow echo-y empty space in my center.

This feels like fear to me.

This empty feeling fear.

I don't feel safe.

I can't stop worrying.

Something dreadful can happen at any moment.

I know this because I experienced it.

This fear.

Life is not safe.

I can't stop worrying.

I asked Estelle to pause here, tap on her collarbone point, and take some deep breaths, all the way down into her abdomen. "See how deep your breath can go...Imagine that you can fill your center all way down to your abdomen with breath, moving all the way down."

She said that now her center felt "not echo-y, not hollow, not empty." I asked, "If it was not all those things, what was it?"

Suddenly, she had tears. "My center now has some life in it," she said shakily.

I asked, "How do you experience 'life in your center'?"

"Gosh," Estelle said. "A bit of solidity?"

So we did some more tapping, starting with those inner sensations:

Especially because I am no longer feeling echo-y or hollow in my center, I accept myself, and I appreciate that feeling of solid life that is expanding there.

Even though I have these tears... ("If these tears had words, what would they would be saying?" I asked.)

...these tears are saying, "You deserve to live and you deserve to be happy!"... I accept that I have these tears and I love hearing that voice in me that says, "You deserve to live."

I didn't know that I could deserve to live!

Something about that experience made me believe that I didn't deserve to live.

I thought I didn't deserve to live—I thought it was all my fault.

And nobody understood.

Nobody even knew because I couldn't tell.

I have been holding all those feelings in ever since.

There was nobody I could tell, and I forgot about the feelings, the whole thing.

Those feelings have been stuffed down in there ever since, and I thought I forgot about them.

But all the rest of my life I have been worrying.

I had a thought. I told Estelle that I was just going to say what was coming into my mind; she could go with it if it felt right, or change it. I asked her to tap on the back of her hand on the 9 Gamut point while I talked. This is a location in the energy meridian system that talks to our fight-flight-freeze response. When tapping on this point calms our energy system, we are able to think more clearly, disengage from stuck fear-based responses, and make different choices.

I said, "Imagine that you can bring your adult self back to your child self, just before the moment that this terrible thing happened. There she is, going along, things are fine, she is a cheerful little free spirit...Now, in some way pull her into your lap, or just be there with her, reaching for a feeling of comfort in yourself and holding this for her.

"We will explain to her as we tap that something is going to happen to her that will be really scary and dreadful, and she *will* be able to deal with it. Tell her that you, as her grown-up self, will be there to help her. Let her know that she has the resources inside to deal with it and to stay in her body. You might imagine picking up her hand and tapping on it."

I am going back now in time to my little girl self, and I'm letting her know that I am here for her. Right now everything is just fine in her life, and I am letting her know that there is a change coming.

You, my dear little girl self... you are feeling happy now and life is going well, I want you to know that something scary is about to happen ... and I am here with you. I am your grown-up self, and we are going to go through this together. I will be right with you, and I want you to know that you have everything inside that you to need to take care of yourself when this happens.

> *Something scary is about to happen.*
> *You are okay deep inside.*
> *I am right here with you.*
> *You are not alone.*
> *I am right here with you.*
> *You are not alone.*

After this tapping, all of Estelle's physical symptoms of the worried state were gone.

I continued, "Now tap on your collarbone point, Estelle, and take a moment to reexperience that event, in imagination, being with your little girl self during this experience, holding her, talking to her, telling her the truth about herself, letting her know that she can manage this and she can talk to you about it. There won't be people in her life that she can share this with, but she can talk to you about it."

"I was called Judy then," Estelle said.

"Okay. In a moment I will be quiet here… Now, I am holding you, Estelle, in this space, while you are holding Judy, your little girl self, in spacious comfort, a safe deep inner knowing of resource, while you tap on your collarbone point.

"Let Judy reexperience what happened while knowing that you are there, she is not alone, she is safe. It is hard, it is scary, it is dreadful, *and she will be all right.* You are living proof that she deserves to live.

"Let your story go on for a little while after that experience, so that little Judy knows that she survived, she is okay, even though it was awful, she is okay, she is never alone. Let me know when your internal experience of this is complete."

There was a long silence. Then Estelle spoke: "I took her to the lake, we went into the lake, and she had a big cry and I held her. At the end she had a big sigh, looked up at me, and hugged me. She knows that I am there and she is not isolated. She knows that there is a big person who knows, and who is safe, and who loves her."

I said, "Still tapping on your collarbone point, invite her to come back inside your heart, where her home is, even though she hasn't been there since that bad experience. Ask her if she would like to grow up to be her adult self in you, knowing that she brings all of her childlike joy and innocence and free spirit, while you offer to her your experience and wisdom about being in the world. Is she willing to come home?"

When Estelle said her child self was happy about coming home, we continued tapping through the points, saying things like:

(I said, "Letting her float down now…that 6 feet…into the crown of your head, coming into your heart…However you imagine this happening, it is okay.")

> *I am inviting my child self to come home.*
> *I am Judy, and I am coming home into my Estelle self…nestled up near her heart.* (Estelle added this phrase.)
> *I am Judy and I am coming home into my heart, in my grown-up Estelle self.*
> *I am Estelle/Judy and I am whole and healed.*
> *I am Estelle/Judy and my heart is happy.*
> *I know that dreadful things can happen at any time.*
> *I know that I will be able to deal with them.*
> *I have Judy's sunshine in my heart*
> *And Judy has my adult awareness of the world.*
> *And I, Estelle, have a sun and a son in my heart.*
> *I had been worried about him.*
> *And he, being part of the ancestral lineage in my family, is a worrier too.*
> *But as worry heals in me it heals in him.*
> *I want him to know that he is able to deal with his situation.*
> *I know that dreadful things can happen at ay time, and I know that I will be able to deal with it.*
> *Now I can let my son know that truth too.*
> *I know that I will be able to deal with whatever happens, and I know my son will too.*

After we completed this round of tapping, I asked Estelle to say the phrase "Life is not safe" to herself and notice her internal response. I asked her to feel into the way she had been holding the situation before we tapped, and how she was holding it now.

Estelle said, "It is like that whole worry issue about my son is back over there geographically at his house, not anywhere near me. I am comfortable that it is *his* thing. I don't even need to say,

"It will be fine," because that isn't even a part of it. Of course it will be fine. I feel it; I don't need to say it." Her SUD level was now at 0.

When I contacted Estelle two years later for an update, much in her life had changed. She was no longer worrying so obsessively. Her son had moved through the challenges he had been facing and was on a good life path. She wrote: "It's almost like I've been given a new past. On an intellectual level, I know what happened, but on an emotional level, my past is sunny and bright.… If I think of the event, it is the picture that I created during our session that comes to my mind, and I don't know if you can have any idea what an amazing gift that is!"

Conclusion

The Tell the Story and Watch the Movie techniques are safe and gentle ways to add depth, subtlety, and effectiveness to your tapping. It is not necessary to share the story of the difficult event with anyone, even the person with whom you are tapping. A good example is a teenage boy I tapped with who had had an acutely embarrassing event from which he wanted to gain some emotional distance. He was so glad he didin't have to talk about it to me. He felt much better after addressing the story and his reactions using this technique. I never did learn what happened to him, but I could gauge his reaction to the story by observing the changes in his face and body language and his SUD ratings as we tapped.

Another benefit of the Tell the Story and Watch the Movie techniques is that they invite creative flexibility with the basic EFT recipe, while staying true to the essence of the tapping structure. The story is right there for you to make use of, in the client's or your own words. You don't have to worry about coming up with the "right words" to tap on, because you are simply incorporating the name of the emotional crescendos into a Setup Statement.

The Tell the Story and Watch the Movie techniques provide a simple yet profound and elegant way to tap.

References

Church, D. (n.d.). Aspects of a car crash: EFT's movie technique, with rewind and pause. Retrieved from http://eftuniverse.com/index.php?option=com_content&view=article&id=10905

Moss, G. (n.d.). Creative uses of the EFT movie technique, Part 4 of 4: Fictional movie for tarantula terror. Retrieved from http://eftuniverse.com/index.php?option=com_content&view=article&id=3224

The movie technique. (n.d.). Retrieved from http://eftuniverse.com/index.php?option=com_content&view=article&id=9210

Tell the story. (n.d.). Retrieved from http://www.eftuniverse.com/index.php?option=com_content&view=article&id=9211

Chapter 21
Being Specific
Ann Adams

Abstract

The biggest mistake practitioners make in using EFT is being too general. Often, clients present with large, global feelings and issues; however, these larger issues are actually a culmination of specific memories, events, and aspects. The ability to identify and address these specifics is vital to the success of EFT. This chapter offers several easy ways to get specific: using a constricted breathing exercise, noticing and using the emotional response in your body, fully addressing physical discomfort, and using investigative questions such as who, what, when, where, and how and questions involving the five senses to develop a specific Setup. Specificity is central to the effective use of EFT.

Keywords: specific, getting specific in EFT, being specific in EFT, constricted breathing, chasing the pain, asking questions in EFT

Ann Adams, LCSW, teaches EFT and mentors practitioners internationally. She created EFT4PowerPoint.com, a comprehensive training program used by EFT trainers all over the world, coauthored *EFT Comprehensive Training Resource Level 1 (& 2),* and codirected the EFT Masters Program. Send correspondence to: Ann Adams, 46 Ridgeview Drive, Silver Creek, GA 30173, or master@eft4powerpoint.com.

One of the core concepts in EFT is the importance of being specific. EFT instructs us to:

1. Pick a specific event, or define a physical feeling.
2. Measure the intensity of the emotion or feeling.
3. Create a Setup consisting of a specific problem statement and an acceptance statement.
4. Use EFT to address all the details, or aspects, of the issue being addressed.
5. Measure intensity again.
6. Modify Setup as aspects change.
7. Repeat EFT sequence.
8. Continue to measure intensity, clarify changes, and modify Setup until the intensity is gone.

Though EFT represents a process through which one must pass, it is relatively straightforward and seems simple, particularly to practitioners coming from a background of working with other modalities or with more traditional training. Then why is the most common problem among even experienced EFT practitioners the tendency to address a general issue rather than find specifics?

The answer is that most individuals approach their presenting problem as a single, broad issue, rather than as a series of problematic events. People rarely contact me saying they want to deal with a specific event such as flashbacks from an automobile accident. Nor do they tell me that they want to resolve several childhood events that are causing their current angst. No, they call with many other reasons, such as: They are unhappy, depressed, can't find the right guy, or want to develop more confidence; they eat too much, are always angry, are unhappy with their spouse and they wonder if they should leave; they are always getting in trouble in school or with their boss; or they have a medical issue and are wondering if EFT can help.

Let's be clear that EFT does not cure any medical issue, acquire boyfriends, save marriages, make people happy, or bring about promotions. At times, these things do happen after using EFT, but EFT did not make it happen—*the client* did. When EFT is used as a tool to work through the associated events and emotional drivers behind the presenting problem, energy is freed and one's body is allowed to heal. In doing so, individuals are enabled to make better decisions, try new ways of looking at themselves and the world, and explore new ways of behaving. In essence, clearing the specificities driving a presenting problem allows a client to think more clearly about his or her situation and life.

Specific Memories and Events

One of the earliest psychological approaches that embraced the role of specific events and memories in understanding and addressing one's current situation was Alfred Adler's Early Recollections approach (Feist, 2009, p. 86). Alfred Adler believed that individuals are essentially self-determined; in other words, an individual's personality, behavior, and sense of self is shaped by the meaning one gives to one's experiences. Adler also believed that "interpretations of experiences are more important than the experiences themselves" (Feist, 2009, p. 95); and he often asked his patients about their early recollections in order to gain an understanding of their personality, insisting that early recollections are always consistent with an individual's present life. Although most professionals today do not strictly subscribe to Adler's theories, research has demonstrated that there is merit in the emphasis Adler placed on these early recollections and how they shape perceptions, attitudes, and beliefs.

Psychologist Daniel Kahneman, Nobel Prize winner and one of the founders of behavioral economics, explains human memory and the way individuals assign value to their experiences in his concept of the "two selves": the "Experiencing Self" and the "Remembering Self" (Murray, 2012). According to Kahneman, the "Experiencing Self" lives in the present and is constantly processing input and information from one's physical and social environments. The "Experiencing Self" views life as a series of moments of experience; however, once a moment of experience has passed, it is often lost forever. Through his research, Kahneman calculated that the psychological presence of most experiences lasts about 3 seconds (Murray, 2012). The "Remembering Self," on the other hand, is drawing from the countless, minute-to-minute and day-to-day experiences one has and writing a story of things remembered. Kahneman suggests that the experiences that make it from the "Experiencing Self" to the "Remembering Self" are marked by change; individuals remember the experiences that are new, novel, surprising, unexpected, and have greater significance.

Furthermore, the experiences that are remembered are not necessarily recorded by the mind in their entirety, or in 100% accuracy; rather, the things remembered are done so based on the perception of the individual and what value he or she places on distinct pieces of the memory. In fact, research has found that memory often outweighs experience. Kahneman says, "We make our decisions in terms of our memories and basically, we maximize remembered utility, not the actual total utility" (Chernoff, 2013). For instance, a person, Casey, is flying on a particular airline for a business trip. The staff was courteous, the flight was on time, and she is generally very comfortable during her time on the airplane. Casey is pleased with her flying experience. At the end of the flight, however, a steward trips and spills hot coffee onto Casey's lap, ruining her clothes and leaving her with minor burns and discomfort. Most likely, Casey's positive experience of the flight up until the point of the accident will be overwritten by her negative, even traumatic experience with the hot coffee.

In the case of EFT, therefore, approaching a presenting problem as a broad issue would be akin to approaching an issue through the "Experiencing Self," when it is the "Remembering Self" that holds the information that informs patterns, behaviors, and presenting problems EFT is designed to address.

Not only is identifying specific events or memories vital to the success of EFT, and truly reflective of how the human brain categorizes memories and learns, but the specifics of the specific events are also important. Each individual piece of a single memory or event can hold energy that needs to be released. For example, one of the most commonly cited triggers to memory and recall is smell. Researchers know that one of the reasons smell is such a powerful memory trigger is because the olfactory nerve is located in close proximity to both the amygdala, the part of the brain associated with emotional memory, and the hippocampus, also associated with memory (Stafford, 2012). So, when addressing a specific event with EFT, that memory will likely need to be addressed in even smaller pieces, the details, such as the associated smell of the memory. In EFT, these pieces, or specifics of the specifics, are often referred to as "aspects" and are discussed in greater detail later in the chapter.

Constricted Breathing

This chapter will apply the concept of getting specific from the most simple to the more complex. It is not always simple or easy to identify events or remembered specifics behind our presenting problems. One of the best ways to begin the process of being specific is to stay with the here and now, in the moment, physical experience of the impact of the problem. A simple way to identify that in-the-moment physical experience is to identify how well you are breathing. When we are upset or in pain, we tend to breathe much more shallowly than when we are relaxed. The following exercise demonstrating how addressing a very small, specific piece of a much larger problem not only allows EFT to be more effective, but can also help you or a client gain some perspective and calm that can then be applied to the process of identifying and working through the rest of a larger issue.

Begin the Constricted Breathing exercise by taking three slow deep breaths to help stretch your lungs. On the last breath, assess what percentage of a true full breath you were able to take.

Create a Setup using that percentage and an acceptance statement such as *"Even though I am only breathing at 65% of my capacity, I deeply and completely accept how I am breathing right now."* Then, as you focus on your less-than-full breath, tap through all the points, at least twice, simply saying your percentage at each point (e.g., 65%). Don't worry about the exactness of your percentage or number; it is only a baseline to measure progress. After tapping, stop and take another slow deep breath. If it's not up to 100%, continue with the same process until it is; or if something specific pops up, you can choose to begin EFT on that specific.

Using the Constricted Breathing exercise by itself is extremely powerful. I teach it to all my clients as a quick method for self-calming. As they tap for their breathing, they are also addressing whatever is creating the shallow breathing. Your client's day and life will be significantly calmer if, several times a day, the client checks his or her breathing and taps for whatever percentage it may be below 100%. This exercise demonstrates the efficacy of EFT, and it can also serve as an illustration for addressing something highly specific, in this case the percentage of one's breath capabilities.

Noticing the Emotional Response in the Body

The second easiest way to begin to be specific is to notice feelings of any emotion, upset, or physical discomfort in the body. It is certainly easier for an individual to identify where he or she *feels* an emotion in the body than to figure out which, of probably many, events and feelings could be behind the presenting issue. Ask your client to take that slow breath again, close his or her eyes, and pay attention to where in the body, at this exact moment, the client *feels* the strongest physical sensation of emotion or discomfort. Most everyone can do this.

The physical feeling *is* the emotion. After all, if you didn't have any feeling or response physically, how would you know you were having an emotion?

Encourage your client to be as descriptive as possible in pinpointing the feeling, for example, "the tightness in my throat," "the suffocating feeling in my chest," "my upset stomach," "this ache behind my eyes," "my lower back throbs" or "my knees shake." The most benefit will come from focusing on the one physical feeling that is strongest in the moment. Now assess how intense that feeling is for your client on the 0-to-10 scale. Create the Setup from that feeling. Examples:

> *Even though I feel like I am going to throw up, I deeply and completely accept myself anyway.*
> *Even though my throat is tight and feels restricted, I am alright.*
> *Even though my shoulders feel they are carrying the weight of the world, I fully accept that is how I feel right now.*

Tap the points as you focus on the specific physical response to the emotion. Use the client's definition(s) of the physical feeling as the Reminder Phrase as you tap the points, for example, "throat constriction."

Especially when one is just starting with EFT, simply using the same word, or words, at each point is entirely acceptable. Actually, using the same words is just fine even if a person has years of experience. If you do choose to use different words, select them from the complete physical description at the various points. For instance, depending on the description and the "story," the EFT script could progress, at different points, with phrases such as "my stomach," "all sour," "want to throw up," "it aches," and "rumbling, rolling feeling."

Other EFT books and recorded EFT sessions, will offer a wide variety of words to say at each point. Generic scripts use different words at each point; after all, they don't know what *each* specific event or feeling is, which is, of course, the limitation of such a script. Creativity and coming up with different words for each point, or developing very creative Setups is not necessary. EFT works when it is kept *simple and focused on the physical manifestation of the current upset.* In this approach, the physical feeling is the specific. Repetition of what is there is helpful *and* there is no need to be sidetracked by the challenge of "What words should I use?" You change the description of the physical feeling as that physical feeling changes.

In reality, as long as one is totally focused and tuned in to the feeling, tapping without words can also be effective. Words are helpful, yes, but not essential. Focus on the feeling, measure, tap, check the intensity and whether the feeling has changed, modify the Setup and Reminder Phrase as it changes, and repeat until the feeling is at 0—with or without words.

Physical Discomfort

EFT can also be used when the body experiences pain. As in the previous section, your job as a practitioner is to help your client clearly define what he or she is feeling physically. There may or may not be an obvious emotion associated with the physical discomfort. Continue to ask questions to define the specifics of what exactly is being addressed. Tapping on "I don't feel well" is not specific enough and will not garner the results of which EFT is capable. Common pinpointing questions are:

- Where *exactly* is the discomfort? Get very specific. Instead of describing the location as "my hand" or "my head," encourage the client to provide details such as "On the back side of my right hand running from my wrist halfway down my fingers."
- What *kind* of discomfort is it? Common definitions of pain are: aching, burning, crushing, cramping, dull, deep, electric,

gnawing, knot-like, pressing, pinching, pulsing, pounding, pins and needles, prickling, shooting, sharp, stabbing, sore, stretching, tender, throbbing, tight, tense.

- What is the *intensity?* Comparing the discomfort to the worst it has ever been, a 10 on the 0-to-10 scale, what is the intensity now?

An effective alternative is to describe the feeling as a metaphor. Using metaphors can be fun and often helpful: "like a rake is digging and scraping in my head," "like a grey mushy amoeba about the size of a grapefruit," or "like a red-hot poker stabbing in my head." Metaphors can help a client describe a sensation or feeling that is abstract by using language, representations, and descriptors that are more meaningful to them. These metaphors can provide valuable information when gathering specifics, and the more vivid they are to the client, the more effective they will be.

Help your clients develop a clear description of their discomfort by asking them to describe it in detail. Most people are able to give a color and other details to their feelings and, amazingly, as the intensity lessens, the color and details seem to change as well. Here are some helpful questions:

- What color is this physical feeling?
- How big is it? What is the shape?
- What does the sensation of it feel like?
- Is it solid? Is it moving?
- Does it remind you of something?

Additional information may also be helpful. Other good questions are:

- When did this start?
- What was happening in your life around that time?
- If there were an emotional reason for this, what would it be?
- How do you feel about having this?
- Does it change locations or stay in the same place?
- When and what makes it worse?
- What does it keep you from doing?
- What does it mean to you to feel this?

Remember to write down the intensity of the discomfort before beginning to tap. Then develop a Setup using one or several of the descriptive characteristics: *"Even though I have this fat, black, sharp ball with spikes rattling around in my stomach, I deeply and completely accept myself and my body now."* The Reminder Phrase could utilize the entire description: *"This 8 intensity, fat, black, sharp ball with spikes rattling around in my stomach."* Or it can be divided into one or more parts of the description at each point:

Head: *fat, black*
Eyebrow: *sharp ball with spikes*
Side of Eye: *rattling around*
Under Eye: *in my stomach*
Under Nose: *it's an 8.*

Keep repeating until the rest of the points are covered. Tap two or three rounds of the points and check the intensity and the description.

Modify the Setup and Reminder Phrases as the description changes. Ask additional questions if there is no change or more information is needed. The "pain" may move around as the session continues. Just follow where it goes, using their descriptions as you go. This technique is called "Chasing the Pain."

Notice in this example that the session is focused and specific as various parts of the description or aspects are addressed. Throughout the session, the progress is also being evaluated, or tested. This chapter is about the concept of being specific, but it is not possible to separate being specific, addressing aspects, and evaluating intensity. In EFT these three concepts are intrinsically linked.

The Puzzle

As mentioned earlier, rarely does a client present with a specific event to be resolved. People typically turn to EFT for a general problem rather than a specific event. Think of the presenting problem as a jigsaw puzzle that needs to be put together. The pieces of the puzzle are the events that make up the picture on the lid of the puzzle box; that picture is how the client sees themselves and the world. The part (i.e., the sides) of the puzzle piece that fits to the other pieces can be likened to the involved aspects that make up the event. Puzzle pieces, like problems, come in all sizes and shapes; therefore the sides (the aspects) can be different from one piece (event) to another. Address all the sides (aspects) of the pieces (events) that are a part of the puzzle (presenting problem) and watch as the picture on the puzzle box (views of self and world) changes.

Tapping for a general presenting issue—that picture on the puzzle box—is rarely effective.

After all, the presenting picture on the puzzle box is rarely the real picture. Using the presenting problem as a Setup, *"Even though I eat too much, I deeply and completely accept myself,"* can help a person become calmer and report "feeling better." In addition, such generic tapping can have the benefit of bringing up some of the involved events or related details. It is rare for a generic tapping script to *totally* clear a presenting problem. Any tapping can calm your energy system temporarily—one may feel better for a while. But since all the pieces of the puzzle were not addressed, the problem has not been thoroughly resolved. It really is true, "For results that are terrific, it helps to be specific" (Adams, 2011).

A key benefit of tapping for a specific aspect of a specific event and evaluating as the session progresses is that the resolution of the issue will usually be apparent, allowing the session to then move on to the next aspect or event. It is much easier to evaluate a specific; progress can be readily measured.

Specific Events

Though there are good reasons for getting to a specific, it is not always easy to uncover a specific event. It is not always possible to see the cause and effect of past events on one's current presenting problem. Asking the right question can lead to a specific event.

As an EFT practitioner, the job is very much like that of an investigative reporter. Apply the questions reporters ask (who, what, when, where, how) to the presenting problem:

- Who does that remind you of?
- What does that make you think of?
- When was another time you felt this way?
- Where did you learn that?
- How do you know you have this problem?
- How long have you had this problem?
- When did it start?
- What was going on then?

Or the age-old default therapy question: How do you feel about that?

Other good questions that create specificity revolve around the five senses to describe how you see the current "picture" of the event:

- What do you see?
- What are you hearing?
- What are you feeling/thinking?
- Are there any smells or tastes involved?

All of these questions create the opportunity to focus clearly on an event. There are many effective questions that can help find specific events and core issues (one such list is available at www.FromtheDeskofAnnAdams.com).

Many specific events begin with some variation of "The time when…" After identifying a specific event, it is often important to figure out how long that "time when" lasted. Although the duration of one event may have been long, the specific action that caused the negative emotion during the event often lasted for only a few seconds. A useful method for making sure the event is short enough to be manageable as one piece of the puzzle is to use the metaphor of a movie.

The "Time when…" movie should not exceed 3 minutes and should not have more than a couple of high-intensity segments. If it does, the movie needs to be broken down into smaller scenes. Give the movie a title. This makes it easy to create a Setup—just use the title of the movie. *"Even though I have this 'Teacher slapped my hand' movie, I accept myself anyway."* The movie approach is helpful for finding and then using specific events to address problems.

When identifying a specific event is difficult, using the Constricted Breathing approach or focusing on the physical manifestation of an emotion or on physical discomfort is a useful alternative. Another option is for clients to simply make up a story or to just pretend that they know what the details are. Whatever they come up with is still part of their internal makeup. Whatever comes out will be meaningful to the presenting issue.

Whichever technique is used in getting specific, be sure to clear all the aspects—both emotional and physical—involved in the event before moving on to the next related "piece of the puzzle."

There are times, however, particularly with very high intensity events, when starting out with specifics can seem counterintuitive. If an event is, or could be, extremely upsetting, it is helpful first to address the fears around bringing up the event. Tap for the fears, or use the Constricted Breathing exercise or the current feelings in the body. Another alternative is to imagine the event is locked in some container or moved across the street. Then tap for *"what is in the box"* or *"that event that is far, far away."*

Just because EFT can work quickly does not mean that practitioners should work quickly. The speed of the client should always dictate the speed of the session. People and situations are often complex. A sense of safety is extremely important, and clients need to have good rapport with their practitioner to facilitate their willingness to delve deeply into painful issues.

Conclusion

The power of being specific in EFT is undeniable. This chapter provides some useful background and questions that can assist the client in identifying a specific related event. Getting to a specific related event when someone presents a general issue can, however, be difficult and challenging at times. Sometimes the specific can mean simply using the specific physical responses such as breathing, or the physical feelings that represent emotions or the physical discomfort in the body. This approach can help the client identify related memories and an issue can frequently be resolved by addressing the body's response.

References

Adams, A. (2011). *EFT 4 PowerPoint Comprehensive Training Program, slide #51*. Rome, GA: www.EFT4PowerPoint.com, self-published.

Chernoff, N. N. (2002, May/June). Memory vs. experience: Happiness is relative. *Observer, 15*(5). The Observer.

Feist, J. (2009). *Theories of personality* (7th ed.). New York, NY: Holt, Rinehart, and Winston.

Murray, P. N. (2012, October 3). How memories of experience influence behavior. *Psychology Today*. Retrieved from www.psychologytoday.com/blog/inside-the-consumer-mind/201210/how-memories-experience-influence-behavior

Stafford, T. (2012, March 13). Why can smells unlock forgotten memories? *BBC Future*. Retrieved from http://www.bbc.com/future/story/20120312-why-can-smells-unlock-memories

Chapter 22
Testing Your Results and Why
Charles B. Crenshaw, Jr.

Abstract

Why is testing important, what is testing, and how do you test during an EFT session? These are critical questions for the clinical EFT practitioner. The sources from which EFT has arisen include techniques that often produce subtle results. Therefore it is imperative that we have some way of analyzing the impact of EFT on clients and research subjects. Testing via the subjective units of distress (SUD) scale is that means. The act of checking our work by asking clients to rate their discomfort on the 0-to-10 SUD scale might seem unimportant for the casual user of EFT, but for practitioners it is vital. Testing during sessions enhances our ability to help our clients by providing direction in a session and feedback on its efficacy. This chapter covers why it is imperative to test, the role of testing in energy psychology modalities, how the mind gives a SUD rating, and how to test for the future effects of an EFT intervention.

Keywords: testing, SUD, subjective units of distress, energy body, NLP, neuro-linguistic programming

Charles B. Crenshaw, Jr., MS, MDivW, is a certified EFT practitioner, ordained interfaith minister, meditation teacher, and yoga teacher and trainer. A certified consulting hypnotist, Master NLP practitioner, and certified instructor of NLP and hypnotists, he is on the College of Humanities faculty at the University of Phoenix. Send correspondence to Charles Crenshaw, 8238 Ames Street, Indianapolis, IN 46216, or charles@tapTFJL.com, charles@EasilyStopSmokingNow.com.

Let's consider what testing is practically. Simply stated, it is checking your results to determine whether or not you are making progress. If you are a practitioner, the standard feedback mechanism from the client in front of you is verbal report. We check or test for several reasons in an EFT session. The primary test is to gauge clients' discomfort by asking them to rate their level of emotional or physical pain on a scale of 0 to 10, thereby establishing their subjective units of distress (SUD) level, how sad or angry they are, or their general level of discomfort or pain. This establishes a baseline against which to measure changes.

The SUD scale is a very practical tool developed by Joseph Wolpe, MD, a psychiatrist whose conception we employ universally in EFT. Here is an excellent way to think about the scale as you work with clients in a session, in the words of Wolpe (1990): "Think of the worst anxiety you can imagine and assign it a number...Then think of being absolutely calm—that is, no anxiety at all—and call this a 0. Now you have a scale of anxiety...How do you rate yourself at this moment?" (p. 91).

Children may find it difficult to apply a number to their discomfort, but if you use visual testing and make a game of it, you can get a good reading. For example, you can have children show you with their hands how much they feel the pain or discomfort —hands far apart for a SUD level of 10 and moving closer and closer for lower SUD levels, until they touch to indicate that a SUD level is 0.

In addition to establishing a baseline, it is important for a practitioner to test as an aid in uncovering aspects of a person's presenting problem. In this case, not testing at intervals could hinder a successful outcome. Keeping good notes is important in testing, especially in complicated cases with numerous aspects.

Testing aspects can be tricky and complicated, which is why you want to keep good notes even if you think you have a good memory. The thing about testing aspects is that you don't know that aspects are there until they show up. They are hidden under other layers of emotional pain. For example, a client's SUD drops to 5 from 10 based on the sadness around some personal experience; it then mysteriously jumps back up to a level higher than 5. This is an indicator that there is an aspect of the problem that must be handled. We have to stop there and get what the other emotional pain is, the aspect, and what it is related to. The aspect has a SUD level all its own that must be addressed. In this example, the aspect might be anger at something surrounding the hurt. Once this anger aspect is resolved to 0, often the original issue (sadness) could either go to a lower level, in which case you continue your work with the sadness, or even disappear altogether, your work being done. A challenging component of aspects is when there is more than one aspect to deal with, and when an aspect has an aspect. Again, keeping track with good notes is a key factor. Without proper testing, you would be unaware that such transitions have taken place or be confused by the course of events. This lack of awareness or confusion can produce poor results in an EFT session. All of the previous points to the need for continuous testing.

Testing is a way for us to check whether what we have done has achieved its goal, that is, that the client's emotional upset or physical pain has been lessened or alleviated. In some cases, the effects might be overlooked due to their subtlety or a phenomenon called the Apex Effect. The Apex Effect is a common occurrence in EFT work and refers to individuals tending to dismiss the effects of EFT. This may occur when clients are completely cleared of their previous distress such that they can barely recall being upset and so conclude that "nothing happened" in the session. The Apex Effect may also occur as a result of the subtlety of EFT's effects on the body-mind continuum. Clients, unable to discern the subtle effects, assume nothing happened due to the EFT intervention. They believe that they recovered from their situation on their own or that the change would have happened anyway, with EFT playing no part at all in the change.

To understand how the Apex Effect can exist, we need only recall that the primary presupposition of EFT is that interference in our energy body is associated with the emotional pain. Most people from Western culture have no understanding of, belief in, or experience with the energy body—*prana, chi,* vital force—something that is taken for granted in the East. This then presents a mindset, a belief system, that is unwilling or unable to accept the subtlety of what has happened, the cause-and-effect relationship between the tapping and the change. Dawson Church (2009) elaborates on the role energy plays in the body in his excellent book *The Genie in Your Genes*.

The possibility of the Apex Effect occurring is another reason why it's important for

EFT practitioners to test and record clients' SUD ratings. When clients insist that nothing happened, the SUD ratings provide evidence to the contrary.

The Role of Testing in Energy-Based Modalities

Jerry, Jerry, & Bharati (2007) note that the roots of EFT and other energy psychology modalities can be traced to kinesiology, traditional Chinese medicine (TCM), modern psychology (including behavioral-environmental, cognitive, and neurological branches, among others), neuro-linguistic programming (NLP), Eye Movement Desensitization and Reprocessing (EMDR), yoga, and modern physics. In the past, people did not regard TCM or yoga as modalities associated with testing or consider them related to science, at least not in the same way as they thought of modern psychology or physics. This was a misconception, however. The ability to test the health effects of TCM, yoga, EFT, and other energy-based modalities is now well established and the body of scientific research validating these methods continues to grow. As practitioners, we benefit the field as a whole when we approach our sessions with a professionalism that includes testing our results.

When working directly or indirectly with physical pain, it is easy to test the results. Working directly with pain can be as simple as asking clients if they have any minor pain or discomfort and where that is located in their bodies. If they do, you can simply tap through the basic points a few times and then ask: "How is the pain or discomfort now?" or "Is the pain or discomfort still there?" If the answer is no, you are finished. A possible explanation for this is that the client has experienced a relaxation response associated with the lowering of the cortisol level in the bloodstream, cortisol being one of the stress-related hormones that EFT has been scientifically proven to lower. My experience and the experience of many of my clients is that you need not do Setup Statements or affirmations to experience a level of relaxation. It is well known that tense muscles or holding tension unconsciously can be a source of pain.

Getting a yes response to your question about pain or discomfort indicates that you are beyond the realm of simple physical tension. With a yes answer, you would then ask the client to rate the intensity of the pain on the SUD scale. Now you are moving into the realm of working on the physical pain indirectly because the physical pain is associated with emotional pain. As EFT practitioners have been taught, and acupuncturists report, 30–70% of physical pain is emotional. Current research verifies this. Among other research, a study of health care workers (including physicians, chiropractors, and alternative health care practitioners) it was seen that a significant reduction in physical pain correlated with a decrease in psychological distress (Church & Brooks, 2010). Emotional pain is where the SUD levels really help us gauge the work that is done. By helping people lower their SUD levels, we help them alleviate their pain. This is especially obvious when you run through the Movie Technique with a client and afterward the client is able to view all the previously disturbing events without a trace of the emotional pain experienced before. Thus another reason for testing is to verify that release from this emotional pain has taken place in the client.

Case Example: Reducing Physical Pain Indirectly

Here is an example from my case files of physical pain being reduced indirectly. Samantha (not her real name) is a talented classical musician who also teaches piano. While in a group retreat I was leading, she suddenly felt pain in her wrist.

> Samantha: My wrist hurts when I am doing what you showed us.
> Me: Alright, Samantha, let's just tap through the points a few times. (We tapped two times through the basic points). How does your wrist feel?
> Samantha: It still hurts pretty much the same.
> Me: Really, you notice no difference at all in how it feels?
> Samantha: No, not really.
> Me: So, on a scale of 1 to 10, how much pain is there in the wrist?
> Samantha: It's a 9, I can't put pressure on the wrist.
> Me: Okay. You know the tapping points and procedure, so let's go through this together. "Even though my wrist hurts, I accept and respect myself."

Samantha, tapping the Karate Chop point, immediately started to cry as a memory from her childhood popped up, even before starting the Setup Statement.

> Me: What is the sadness or hurt Samantha? On a scale of 1 to 10, how much sadness or hurt is there?
> Samantha: It is both and the level is 10!

We spent 20 minutes exploring the emotional pain that was the cause of Samanatha's physical pain, which she had no idea was connected to her learning to play the piano as a child. When the SUD levels of the emotional pain from childhood related to feeling inadequate as a pianist and a few other aspects related to this situation dropped to 0, Samantha was completely pain free. The pain never returned.

The Mind's Distress-Rating Mechanism

The question arises: How can people really know how emotionally upset they are about something? More interesting, how can they know how upset they are about something that happened in the past? Our mind processes our emotions; our memories hold those emotions.

Try this experiment. Imagine that you are holding half a lemon in your hand. Smell the lemon, notice the fragrance of the pulp and the essential oils released from the rind of the cut lemon. In your mind's eye, raise that half lemon to your mouth and suck on it; really be there sucking on that lemon. Stop. Your mouth may have puckered or at least watered a bit; your face may have contorted some. On a scale of 0 to 10, how much did sucking that imaginary lemon make you pucker or respond in some other way? For most of us, the puckering effect of sucking on that imaginary lemon in this experiment is as real as actually doing it.

It is the same with emotions. Our remembered image or movie of an event is just as powerful as the event itself, *as powerful emotionally as the event in real time.*

Our ability as humans to recall things is the basic premise on which establishing a SUD level is based. We use the SUD level to get an idea of the emotional intensity clients have attached to something in their minds, in their reality, and then to test again to determine whether that intensity has been reduced. It should be noted that there are other methods of receiving feedback other than verbal report. There are those who have developed skill with testing methods such as muscle testing, an excellent tool for testing SUD levels. Muscle testing is time consuming to learn, however, and requires a certain finesse to execute.

As a practitioner, you need to be diligent in testing the results of the work you do with clients. In addition to SUD testing or the visual testing you might use with children, in vivo testing ensures that you have cleared the problem. For example, if your client's problem was claustrophobia, especially in elevators, taking him out to the elevator in your office building is an in vivo test to see if the phobia is resolved.

Testing for Future Situations

There is one final role for testing in an EFT session: to determine whether the positive results the client experienced in the session will carry over into the future when the client encounters what was formerly a trigger to upset or pain. To illustrate, here's an example from my case files of a client who sought help with stuttering in the presence of authority figures. As a realtor, this problem was detrimental to his work.

> Me: Can you recall the last time you had that embarrassing stutter? What happens just before the stuttering begins?
> Joe: My breathing gets restricted and my throat sort of freezes up.

We did standard EFT and discovered that the originating glitch in the energy body, the original emotional upset being held in the energy body, was an event related to being embarrassed by an older sibling after having urinated in a neighbor's pool while swimming. We got the SUD level related to fear and embarrassment down to 0.

> Me: Joe, can you imagine the next time you will have to interact with someone in authority at work?
> Joe: I don't have to imagine it. There is going to be a meeting with the regional division manager coming up this week, and I am going to have to interact with that manager.
> Me: Okay Joe, are you familiar with the place where you are going to be meeting with this manager?
> Joe: Yes.
> Me: Can you describe the room to me?
> Joe: Sure, it is the conference at our office. It is a spacious wood-paneled room with an oval

table in the center the color of the wood panel, with black leather swivel chairs.

Me: Okay, imagine that it is the designated day and time, and you are there in that room. Can you imagine that? What would be going on in the room at this time? Who are the people who would be there?

Joe: The room would look the same, but there is the smell of coffee and donuts. There is the feeling of camaraderie with my coworkers, and, naturally, the regional division manager is there.

Me: Do you know this manager, have you met before?

Joe: Yeah.

Me: Okay Joe, can you walk up to the manager there in your mind's eye in the future meeting and begin a conversation with him? [Pause] Do you have any emotions when speaking to the person? Do you stutter?

It is at this point that you see whether the change in your client stands up to real world testing. If you question the validity of this proposition, how this type of challenge could possibly be effective, then think about a future imaginary lemon and suck on it!

If your client's answer to questions regarding imagining a future situation is "No, I'm fine," then your work is done. If the answer to these questions is yes, then you can be certain there is more work to do. In addition to testing the stability of the results, having the client envision a future situation is an excellent way to test for hidden aspects, things that might retrigger the person's negative emotions. You can use exaggeration, vivid imagination, and confrontive questions to test whether the work on a particular problem is truly complete. In the case of Joe, a clearly confrontive question was the one asked while he envisioned the situation of talking with his manager, which had previously been a cause for stuttering: "Do you stutter?" For testing purposes, it was necessary to have him vividly imagine the future circumstance that could possibly produce the unwanted response. He did just fine. An exaggeration in Joe's case would have been to have him imagine speaking to the president of the company, or speaking to the president of the United States.

Conclusion

The ways of testing can be as simple as tapping away an immediate emotional situation and seeing the countenance of a client change or getting his or her self-report. They can be as complicated as following the trail of aspects, continuously checking for SUD level updates throughout the process. We may need to be creative when getting information from and testing children, by making the SUD scale a visual game, for instance. Finally, to ensure that clients are completely cleared of the disturbance we tapped on, we have to challenge, to test, our clients in the moment, use in vivo testing, or employ visualization (imagination) to test for future situations that might trigger the disturbance. Aside from this, we need to be prepared for the client who experiences the Apex Effect, for which recorded SUD level testing provides written evidence to the client of beginning disturbance and ending calm. Testing can take many forms, but it must be conducted to provide direction in an EFT session and to track progress.

References

Church, D. (2009). *The genie in your genes* (2nd ed.). Santa Rosa, CA: Energy Psychology Press.

Church, D. & Brooks, A. J. (2010). The effect of a brief EFT (Emotional Freedom Techniques) self-intervention on anxiety, depression, pain and cravings in healthcare workers. *Integrative Medicine: A Clinician's Journal, 9*(4), 40–44.

Jerry, M., Jerry, M., & Bharati, S. V. (2007). *Chariots of sadhana*. Bloomington, IN: Unlimited Publishing.

Wolpe, J. (1990). *The practice of behavior therapy* (4th ed.). New York, NY: Pergamon Press.

Chapter 23
Why EFT Focuses on Negative Cognitions First
Valerie Lis

Abstract

To be effective with EFT, it is important to understand the difference between negative and positive cognitions and when they should be used. In general, negative cognitions are recommended. Although it seems more compassionate to tap with positive statements, they do not provide lasting results. Tapping negative cognitions before positive ones is often compared to cleaning a wound before applying the bandage or needing to mop the floor where it is dirty. Rather than focusing on affirmations, for example, the focus should be on the associated tail-enders (see Chapter 27). Positive statements make effective tapping phrases only if they are emotionally charged. This seems to be especially true for clients who are psychologically reversed. Mastering these essential EFT concepts will bring faster, more consistent results.

Keywords: negative cognition, positive cognition, affirmation, depression, addiction, tail-enders, Choices Method

Valerie Lis, MA, EFT-EXP, offers certification workshops through EFTuniverse.com, customized group training, and individual sessions. She teaches and trains corporate, business, and sales leaders, health professionals, and college students. Send correspondence to Valerie Lis, 33 Fourth Street NW, Osseo, MN 55369, or valerie@valerielis.com.

Practitioners, clients, and consumers who are familiar with the benefits of EFT know that the focus is usually on negative cognitions. People who are new to EFT, however, are often surprised. Amateur tappers may think that stating a negative phrase will make their problem worse. Or they may be afraid of "tapping in something bad." Positive statements and affirmations are often used in tapping scripts and videos; this creates even more confusion. It is important to understand the difference between negative and positive cognitions and when they should be used. Mastering this EFT concept will bring faster, more consistent results.

Optimism and positive thinking are strong values for many people. The use of negative cognitions may seem to go against this philosophy. Western culture places a value on positive thinking, while encouraging the suppression of negative emotions. Suppressed emotions become part of the shadow. Many clichés dramatize this, such as "Big boys don't cry," "I'll give you something to cry about," and "If you don't have something good to say, don't say anything at all." In essence, we want to emphasize the positive because it makes us feel good.

On the surface, it may seem more compassionate to focus on positives rather than negatives. During an EFT session, however, the opposite is true. An EFT session provides an opportunity to relieve negative emotions that have never been processed or integrated into the narrative of self in a healthy way. Often an EFT session is the first time in a client's entire life that the person has had permission to review an unhealed early trauma. Tapping provides a safe environment to do so.

Focusing on negative cognitions is often compared to cleaning a wound before applying the bandage. Although there is a small amount of discomfort that is essential to the healing process, a cover-up would merely create more harm than good. Another analogy is the need to "mop the floor where it is dirty." Hiding the dirt or pretending that it is not there will not lead to a clean floor.

A savvy practitioner recognizes that a client who experiences emotional distress, perhaps even a crying spell, will have better results during a tapping session. Negatives, rather than positives, are more likely to produce the intense, profound, lasting clearings that have been the hallmark of EFT.

As part of the process, positive cognitions that are authentic to the client's neural network often arise spontaneously after the negative has been processed. This usually brings a sense of peace. Clients may claim that what previously caused them distress now just seems "silly." After working on anger about an act of violence, for example, a client may experience a sense of forgiveness toward the perpetrator. Core beliefs may also shift. For example, in tapping on a childhood event that created helplessness, the helplessness may evolve into feelings of empowerment. Near the close of an EFT session, clients will often experience a burst of inspiration or an "aha" moment. When the focus throughout the session is on negative cognitions, positive cognitions arise naturally.

The focus on negative emotions may also be questioned by proponents of the Law of Attraction who believe that individuals attract or magnetize future events based on thought patterns. Some fear that the use of negative statements in an EFT session will attract more negative events into their lives. The following three concepts may help to bring understanding in support of the use of negative cognitions:

1. It is impossible to "not think" a negative thought. (Try to "not think" about a purple elephant.) Resisted thoughts actually become more pervasive. Negative thoughts, even when in the background, will continue to sabotage an individual's emotional and physical health.
2. The negative focus is temporary; it lasts only a minute or two. All of the other moments in a person's life, outside of the EFT tapping process, can be centered on the positive.
3. EFT neutralizes the negative thought, so that the subconscious releases control. As a result, positive thinking and the Law of Attraction actually become more effective.

One reason why EFT focuses on negative cognitions is simply because *that is how it works*. Similar to exposure therapy, the negative (thought) is combined with therapy (tapping) to neutralize the stress response. As a general rule, the more intense the reaction, the better and faster the results. Memories or thoughts that create an intense response are often resolved more quickly than those with a mild response. For example, EFT has been found effective for the intense stress associated with posttraumatic stress disorder (PTSD) and phobias. By contrast, some of the most challenging cases for EFT are when the client is calm or does not react at all.

Many EFT practitioners use positive tapping phrases with affirmations or Dr. Patricia Carrington's Choices Method (in which the words "I choose" are placed before each positive tapping phrase). An affirmation is a positive personal goal or attribute that is stated in the present tense. When used as tapping phrases, affirmations may not have much effect. A more direct approach would be to discover and work on the tail-enders associated with the affirmation.

Although the focus has been on negatives, there are a few circumstances in which positives can be used effectively, especially if the words carry an emotional charge. For example, "I am ugly" creates discomfort for some clients. "I am beautiful" creates discomfort for others. Although "I am beautiful" is positive, if it carries a charge it can be a good tapping phrase. "I am" statements are especially effective. Exaggerating the phrase, even to the point of sarcasm, works extremely well.

Positive phrases may be more charged than negative phrases for clients who are psychologically reversed. This category may include individuals suffering from depression, addictive patterns, or chronic pain. For example, depression implies an inability to experience happiness. The phrase "I am so happy!" is highly charged, and induces anger, frustration, resentment, and sadness. Using it as a tapping phrase may create an opening and begin the process of breaking through the depression. In the same context, "I have a perfect life!" and "I have an exciting future ahead of me!" can be good tapping phrases for clients who suffer from addictive patterns. When global core belief statements are highly charged, the EFT process is especially effective. After these statements have been neutralized, it may be worthwhile to identify and work on related tail-enders.

It may also be effective to move back and forth between negative and positive phrases, especially when working with limiting beliefs and polar opposites. An example is "I hate myself!" and "I love myself!" Going back and forth may neutralize both tapping phrases while eliminating the resistance to self-love.

Some EFT practitioners like to conclude a session with a few rounds of positive affirmations. This can be a way to test results after working on a limiting belief. As long as it is not overdone, there can be value to ending with positive phrases. It will not create new cognitive shifts, but it sets a pleasant tone on which to end a session.

In summary, savvy EFT practitioners understand the need to focus on negative cognitions. In general, it is ineffective and inefficient to use affirmations and positive cognitions unless the word or phrase carries an emotional charge. Understanding the difference between negative and positive cognitions and when they should be used will produce faster, more consistent results with EFT.

Chapter 24
Treating Psychological Reversal and Secondary Gain to Ensure Lasting Client Results

Betsy Bartter Muller

Abstract

Emotional Freedom Techniques (EFT) has earned a reputation for producing rapid and lasting results for clients suffering from stress, trauma, painful memories, and physical symptoms. There are occasions, however, when EFT doesn't seem to work, clients experience only minimal change, or the problem returns after a brief period of relief. Identifying the client's psychological reversals and/or secondary benefits, as well as applying processes for treating these blocks, is a critical practitioner competency. Psychological reversal (PR) has been most simply defined as a form of internal conflict the client holds that opposes or interferes with the desired outcome. Secondary gain, a form of reversal, can occur as a significant impediment when the client has one or more benefits connected with keeping all or part of the problem. One of the most effective ways to ensure relief as well as lasting results is to explore and integrate corrections for PR and secondary gain as part of the EFT treatment. This chapter defines PR and secondary gain, allowing practitioners to more quickly recognize, explore, and clear these impediments to treatment to bring about the desired outcome. Case examples, including the treatment of weight loss resistance, business growth stress, and a writer's creative block, are examined as common situations in which reversals may exist.

Keywords: reversals, secondary gain, secondary benefit syndrome, self-sabotage, subconscious resistance, inner conflict, relapse, EFT, tapping, fear, emotions, chronic illness

Betsy Bartter Muller, MBA, ACP-EFT, CEHP, CEC, is a coach, professional speaker, best-selling author, and certified EFT practitioner in private practice. Her popular women's events, retreats, and Energy Makeover programs have brought healing, productivity, inner peace, and business success to thousands of lives. Send correspondence to Betsy Bartter Muller, 20771 Westminster Drive, Strongsville, OH 44149, or betsy@theIndigoconnection.com.

Background and History

On a personal level, most people know that if change were easy, we would all be at our ideal weight and every stress, pain, or fear that we desired to release would be gone. Unfortunately, life is more complicated than that. On some level, there are hidden forces preventing most individuals from fully embracing the changes they say they desire. As practitioners, we observe that clients can clearly articulate what they want, yet simultaneously create ways to destroy the outcome they seek. Treatment failure often arises in situations in which accomplishing the goal creates a potential danger or puts something important to the client at risk. This well-known psychological phenomenon is referred to as *psychological reversal (PR)*. Another term often associated with PR is *secondary gain*, a situation in which the benefits of having a problem outweigh the benefits of healing the problem.

Some common examples of PR include:

- An obese woman who loses 25 pounds, then immediately gains the weight back because she carries memories causing her to fear that she will attract dangerous attention from the opposite sex if she maintains the slender body.
- A business owner who lands an important and lucrative speaking opportunity, only to become seriously ill on the morning of the speech.
- A woman with severe back pain from a work-related injury who lives quite comfortably while receiving paid time off for the disability.
- A woman who was raped as a teen continues to identify herself as a victim, even though it happened years ago.

The standard setup built into the basic EFT procedure (rubbing the Sore Spot or Karate Chop point while saying the Setup Statement three times) is designed to address some of the underlying PR connected to the client's stated goal. That is why many beginners to EFT achieve profound change in just a few short minutes of meridian tapping. Unfortunately, there are also those who experience little or no shift at all or find themselves relapsing after a brief period of relief. Failure is only feedback! EFT works and lasts when additional measures to explore and clear PR are taken. Understanding PR is the key to better, faster, and lasting outcomes, whether you are using EFT for your own self-care or applying it in professional client care settings.

What Exactly Is Psychological Reversal?

Roger Callahan, the creator of Thought Field Therapy (TFT) from which EFT is derived, is credited with creating the term *psychological reversal* (Callahan 1985) to describe a condition in which the electrical polarity of the body's energy meridian system is reversed. In more general terms, PR has also been called a subconscious condition of self-sabotage in which individuals act in ways that oppose their goals, even when they clearly know they are doing so. EFT founder Gary Craig states that PR is the most common reason tapping does not work, blocking the change process for as many as 40% of all issues being treated (Craig, 2008, p. 56). PR can occur in spite of a client's knowledge, resources, and ability to attain a goal. When someone has experienced a problem for an extended time, whether it is obesity, anxiety, fear of speaking, or a chronic health condition, it may become part of that person's identity and personality. Because PR often exists at the subconscious level, practitioners must be compassionately aware and proactive when creating treatment approaches. Instead of blaming people for laziness, character flaws, or low motivation, consider the possibility that a PR is operating in the background, just like a computer virus that prevents the software from properly functioning. It is interesting to note that Gary Craig has eliminated the term "psychological reversal" from his current EFT tutorial, placing focus on secondary gain as *the* reason clients resist change (Craig, 2013).

Many energy psychology pioneers have hypothesized that PR interrupts healthy human energy flow. Craig referred to the human energy system as a set of subtle energy circuits, explaining that the setup process included at the beginning of every EFT treatment helps to orient the energy system in a way that flow is balanced and restored to clear electromagnetic interference as well as the energy disruptions caused by negative thoughts or emotions (Craig, 2008, p. 55). Using the analogy of flashlight batteries to make the point, Craig compares PR to the situation that arises when the batteries are put in backward: the light won't work. David Gruder, PhD, later coined the term *psychoenergetic reversal* to better convey that PR encompasses both psychological blocks and blocks held in the body's energy system (Gruder, 2006).

Knowing How to Work with PR: A Critical Practitioner Skill

Developing client rapport helps to pave the way for the effective treatment of PR. Full attention to body language, breath, vocal tone, and listening for the specific words used by the client to define the problem, practitioners can craft customized and highly effective Setup Statements and Reminder Phrases. For example, if a client says he is "an outrageous procrastinator," simply weave those words into the Setup: *Even though I am an outrageous procrastinator, I deeply love and accept myself.* Doing so builds rapport, honors the client, and facilitates treatment. It is also important to listen for words regarding reversals or secondary gains that may be preventing the client from releasing the problem. These phrases can be worked into the Setup and treatment statements as well. Practitioners are wise to take notes as clients discuss their present and desired states, as this provides the perfect language for crafting treatment phrases as well as affirmations for reinforcing positive change. Keep in mind that treating PR does not fix the issue. It simply removes the block to releasing the problem. Application of several rounds of EFT tapping should follow treatment of the PR in order to bring about the desired outcome.

Clues That PR May Be Interfering with Treatment

The most common clue that PR exists comes when treatment progress grinds to a sudden halt. When this happens, it is likely that the original PR cleared during the basic Setup has reemerged. Listening and visual observation will provide many clues regarding the nature of the PR interferences. Pay attention to vocal tone, breathing, and posture, as well as the verbal feedback the client provides. Often there is resistance to being "completely over" the problem. This is extremely common in cases in which the issue has become closely linked to the individual's identity. The subconscious may actually be more comfortable living with the problem than considering life without it. EFT Master Lindsey Kenny refers to this subconscious identity attachment as *secondary benefit syndrome* or SBS (Kenny, 2006, p. 54). In order to clear PRs, wording and vocalization become very important. A small adjustment to the Setup Statement and urging a more emphatic vocalization can nudge the treatment flow back into the positive direction. It is important to shift the focus to the *remainder* of the problem as each step of progress is noted:

> *Even though it* still *doesn't feel completely safe to speak in front of people, I deeply love and accept myself.*
> *Even though keeping* some *of this back pain makes my life easier and pays the bills, I deeply love and accept myself.*
> *Even though I don't know who I will become when I* completely *forgive the rapist, I deeply love and accept myself.*

Tapping Reminder Phrases must also be modified to reflect the *remainder* of the problem by using words such as *"remaining speaking fear"* or *"remaining back pain."*

Common Situations in Which PR Is Likely to Surface

Roger Callahan proposed, "Psychological reversals are usually confined to a particular area of one's life, but may occur in any areas such as personal relationships, athletics, love, sex, or health" (Callahan, 1991, p. 221). EFT Master Loretta Sparks, MA, a practitioner with extensive experience using EFT to treat addictions, states that PR "is rarely present when addressing cravings and urges or withdrawal but is prevalent in all other aspects of treating addiction" (Sparks, 2006, p. 39).

David Feinstein (2004, p. 79) identifies two main types of PR to watch for:

- **Global PR,** which involves the desire to be happy. This variation of PR involves issues such as self-esteem, confidence, or core beliefs that have a global or large-scale impact on the client's life experience. A global PR left untreated will sabotage *all* efforts to clear other forms of PR. The following Setup phrase (repeated at least three times while tapping the side of the hand or rubbing the Sore Spot on the chest) would be appropriate for clearing a global

PR: *Even though I don't want to be happy, I deeply and completely love and accept myself.*
- **Specific Context PR,** which is a reversal linked to specific goals or problems the client wants to focus on, such as weight loss, smoking cessation, forgiveness, or fear of public speaking.

Although not part of the EFT procedure per se, the use of applied kinesiology, also referred to as *muscle testing* or *energy checking,* is often integrated by practitioners to test for Global and Specific Context PR. Energy flow and thereby the presence of a PR disruption can be measured by applying light pressure to a specific muscle affected by a meridian. Many practitioners compare muscle response before and after treating the PR, although several studies demonstrated that the statistical reliability of applied kinesiology was no more accurate than random guessing (Lüdtke et al., 2001; Staehle, Koch, & Pioch, 2005; Kenney, Clemens, & Forsythe, 1988; Wüthrich, 2005). Nevertheless, those practitioners using it find that it offers feedback to specify and expedite the clearing of PR, though, again, muscle testing is not a required part of the treatment process. There are many workshops, resources, and professional certification training programs through which proficiency in energy checking can be obtained (Feinstein, 2004; Gruder, 2006).

Table 1 provides a list of some of the most common PRs and accompanying Setup Statements for practitioners to check and correct.

Case Examples
Case 1: Weight Loss Jeopardizes Marriage

Kerry, a business owner in her late 40s came to me seeking guidance for using EFT to facilitate weight loss. During the past 5 years her weight had increased significantly. She now weighed 100 pounds over the healthy number that her doctor recommended. Knee and back pain, low energy, and poor self-esteem in business situations had accompanied the weight gain as well. She admitted that she used food to calm her stress and to give her energy for household chores in the evening.

During initial questioning about potential reversals, one significant issue emerged: safety. Specifically, it was not safe for her or her husband if she lost the weight! Further discussion revealed that 6 years earlier she had achieved a healthy weight loss through diet and exercise, and at about the same time had engaged in an affair that nearly destroyed her marriage. She and her husband filed for divorce but eventually came back together through counseling and were now very happy. Could it be that her marriage would be placed at risk if she were to lose the weight again? We worked with statements that included:

Even though it is not safe for my husband if I release this weight, I deeply love and accept myself.
Even though I would put my marriage in jeopardy if I released this weight, I deeply love and accept myself.
Even though I might attract other men and be tempted to cheat if I released this weight, I deeply love and accept myself.
Even though I could add more stress to my life and marriage if I released all of this extra weight, I deeply love and accept myself.

Kerry reported a sense of calm and a SUD (subjective units of distress) score of 0 on a scale of 0 to 10 as a result of moving through all of the variations of her fear, followed by tapping on *"weight loss fear"* as the Reminder Phrase. Energy checking now gave a strong response on the statement: *"It is safe for me, my husband, and my marriage to release 100 pounds."* Her confident vocal tone confirmed this shift in her orientation to the goal.

We closed the session by tapping to positive affirmations that included the client's own words:

I deserve a healthy body and a happy marriage.
I have learned from the past to nurture my marriage AND care for my health.
My husband will benefit from healthier meals and a more energized wife when I reach and maintain my ideal weight.
I know how to release weight. I did it before and I can do it again in a safe way.

Kerry was able to achieve outstanding results with a healthy exercise and diet plan. Three years have passed. She has released the excess weight and her marriage remains firmly in place. Kerry is thriving in new directions, as she has recently pursued professional speaking to build new business. Kerry reports that she is confident in front of others and has more energy than she could imagine.

Table 1. *Psychological Reversals (PRs) to Check Early in the Treatment Process*

Type of PR	To check	Correction
Global PR	I want to be happy *or* I want to live	Even though I don't want to be happy, I love and accept…
Specific Context PR	I want to be over this problem	Even though I don't want to be over this
Safety	It's safe for me to be over this	Even though it's not safe for me to be over this
Safe for others	It's safe for others if I get over this	Even though it's not safe for others
Healthy	It's healthy if I get over this	Even though it's not healthy for me to get over this
Possible	It is possible for me to get over this	Even though it's not possible
Good for me	Getting over this problem will be good for me	Even though it's not good for me to get over this
Willing to	I am willing to get over this problem	Even though I'm not willing to get over this
Deserving	I deserve to get over this problem	Even though I don't deserve to get over this
Doing all that it takes	I will do all that is necessary to get over this	Even though I won't do what is necessary to get over this
Losing identity	I will lose my identity if I get over this	Even though I'll lose my identity if I get over this
Vengeance	Someone gets away with hurting me it if I get over this	Even though it lets my tormenter off the hook
Benefits/secondary gain	I am willing to get over the benefits of having this problem	Even though I'll lose benefits if I get over this
Completely	I can get completely over this problem	Even though I can't completely get over this

Case 2: Business Growth Stress

Carol, a holistic practitioner in private practice, had read about EFT and called asking for assistance on something she had noticed on and off over the past 15 years. She shared that whenever she successfully filled vacancies in her schedule through reaching out to attract new clients, she would subsequently come down with a mysterious illness that would keep her bedridden for many days. The cancellations and rescheduling that followed made her reconsider whether marketing was worth it. Carol was concerned that something in her subconscious was triggering these illnesses. The potential for income and to help people were strong motivating factors for scheduling more clients. Carol clearly had room in her practice and sincerely loved her work. Carol wanted and deserved more business, and also believed growth was possible. "Filling vacancies in my schedule with new clients is dangerous to my health" emerged as a statement that described the reversal. We treated the statement with this Setup: *"Even though new clients are dangerous to my health, I completely love and accept myself."*

Suddenly, Carol remembered a scene from her past, which involved a scolding from her mother for taking on an extra credit assignment during high school. Her mother's words rang in her memory: "Just watch, you'll get sick if you don't allow enough time to relax. You know I'm right."

Our treatment then focused on the following statements:

Even though I proved my mother right by taking on new clients and getting sick, I deeply love and accept myself.
Even though my mother taught me I would get sick if I added new things to my schedule, I deeply love and accept myself.

As Carol demonstrated greater comfort with the idea that she was in control of the choice to bring in new clients, the way they were scheduled and blocking out time for relaxation and exercise, she became excited about ways to move forward without fear of getting sick. Eventually, we integrated tapping with affirmation statements:

I am in charge of my schedule, filling it in ways that are healthy, relaxing, and safe.
My clients bring joy, health, and abundance to my life.
I have a plan for filling my schedule that allows room for relaxation.
I am grateful for my ability to attract health and prosperity simultaneously.

Several months later Carol reported that her practice had increased by 20% and that she had remained healthy throughout this period of growth. She attributed her success to EFT, as she boasted that she had a waiting list and scheduled carefully to make sure there was room for relaxation to honor her health and well-being.

Case 3: The Hidden Writer

Joel, an avid reader and extremely successful business professional, had always silently dreamed of writing a book. Joel knew that I had helped others release their fears about writing and publishing through a popular "Artist's Way with EFT" seminar I had been leading. Joel was too shy to enroll in the group program and instead requested private coaching. At our first meeting, Joel shared that he wrote every day. He showed me stories and articles he had written yet never shared with anyone. They were excellent. I knew he had strong author potential and was excited for him. I urged him to start a blog and post some of his work online, and also suggested he join a professional writers group in the area. Immediately, I noticed his face go pale with the extreme discomfort he felt about that idea. When asked why he reacted to my suggestion, his response was that he wanted to be published, *but*:

"It's not safe to share my thoughts with strangers."
"I will be criticized and ridiculed for the way I write."
"I will never measure up in the presence of trained writers."

The benefit he gained by not sharing his work with others was avoiding pain of criticism and harsh judgment. Nevertheless Joel was open to exploring these PRs. His love of writing and admiration of authors compelled him to overcome his fear and accomplish the goal of becoming a published author. To test his SUD at the beginning of our session, I asked how uncomfortable he would be about publishing one of his articles to a popular online site for freelance writers. His SUD rated 9 on a scale of 0 to 10. After checking to confirm there was not a Global PR, we proceeded to treatment with the following Setup Statements:

Even though it's not safe to share my thoughts with strangers, I deeply love and accept myself as a writer.
Even though I will be criticized and ridiculed for the way I write, I deeply love and accept myself as a writer.
Even though I might never measure up in the presence of trained writers, I deeply love and accept myself as a writer.

When asked whether he had any specific memories involving writing critics, he mentioned a painful moment during his freshman year of college. He recalled that a professor had severely criticized one of his papers in front of the entire class. The emotion was embarrassment with a SUD score of 9. We completed several rounds of tapping using the Reminder Phrase *"freshman embarrassment,"* before stopping to reassess. Joel was noticeably more relaxed as I inquired whether his SUD level remained at 9. He stated that he was now at a 2. When asked why it was a 2 and not 0, he responded that he was uneasy about which venue would be best for sharing his first release. We then tapped on the theme *"Even though I don't know where to publish first"* and included the 9 Gamut procedure, tapping on the Triple Warmer meridian on the back of the hand (the Gamut point).

After this session, Joel made good on his promise to publish something online and even shared the article with a few business friends on social media that week. He returned the following week pleased with himself and also happy that supportive comments had come to him from complete strangers. Joel is now part of a writers support group and regularly shares his stories and articles. He continues to use EFT to release fears and anxious feelings that emerge and will soon publish his first book.

Conclusion

A wide variety of opinions continue to emerge regarding the nature and definition of psychological reversal (PR). Blocks to recovery are widely recognized, and will continue to be part of the challenge every practitioner will face as they seek to apply EFT as a healing tool. EFT founder Gary Craig's public change of opinion with the announcement that PR does not exist has brought even the most seasoned practitioners into a widespread debate. Blocks are an invitation to practitioners to develop safety, compassion, and even greater rapport with their clients. Whether or not a client's block is defined as energetic, psychological, or otherwise, it may not be relevant to the healing that follows. EFT works best when practitioners are client-centered, focus on guiding treatment progress, and have the curiosity to explore the source of the blocks to ultimately facilitate healing.

References

Callahan, R. J. (1985). *Five minute phobia cure: Dr. Callahan's treatment for fears, phobias, and self-sabotage*. Wilmington, DE: Enterprise Publishing.

Callahan, R. J. (1991). *Why do I eat when I'm not hungry?* Indian Wells, CA: Doubleday.

Cameron, J. (1992). *The artist's way*. New York, NY: Penguin Putnam.

Craig, G. (2008). *The EFT manual*. Santa Rosa, CA: Energy Psychology Press.

Craig, G. (2013). The EFT tutorial. Retrieved Jan. 29, 2013, from http://www.emofree.com/eft/eft-tutorial.html

Feinstein, D. (2004). *Energy psychology interactive: Rapid interventions for lasting change*. Ashland, OR: Innersource.

Gruder, D., Stoler, L., Hover-Kramer, D., Nicosia, G., et al. (2006). *ACEP comprehensive energy psychology certification module 2*. Santa Barbara, CA: Association for Comprehensive Energy Psychology.

Kenney, J. J., Clemens, R., & Forsythe, K. D. (1988, June). Applied kinesiology unreliable for assessing nutrient status. *Journal of the American Dietetic Association, 88*(6), 698–704.

Kenny, L. (2006). Alleviating anxiety. In Ball, R. (Ed.). *Freedom at your fingertips* (pp. 54–56). Fredericksburg, VA: Inroads Publishing.

Lüdtke, R., Kunz, B., Seeber, N., & Ring, J. (2001, September). Test-retest-reliability and validity of the Kinesiology muscle test. *Complementary Therapies in Medicine, 9*(3), 141–145.

Sparks, L. (2006). Addictions. In Ball, R. (Ed.). *Freedom at your fingertips* (pp. 40–42). Fredericksburg, VA: Inroads Publishing.

Staehle, H. J., Koch, M. J., & Pioch, T. (2005, November). Double-blind study on materials testing with applied kinesiology. *Journal of Dental Research, 84*(11), 1066–1069.

Wüthrich, B. (2005). Unproven techniques in allergy diagnosis. *Journal of Investigational Allergology and Clinical Immunology, 15*(2), 86–90.

Chapter 25
The Generalization Effect
Suzanne D. Alfandari

Abstract

When a person has experienced a multitude of traumatic events, it can seem overwhelming and time consuming to consider using the Emotional Freedom Techniques (EFT) process to help the individual resolve each event. Fortunately, practitioners have found that the generalization effect, a phenomenon commonly observed in other psychotherapeutic interventions, has applicability in EFT as well. When clients following the EFT protocol tap on just a few events with enough commonality or bundle them into a trauma or tapping tree, it often happens that the remainder of the related events lose their power of emotional disruption. There are several metaphors used in teaching the generalization effect, the most common being the "forest and trees" and the "tabletops and table legs." EFT work with veterans has provided dramatic examples of the generalization effect. In addition, there is a growing body of research on the generalization effect in EFT and its possible mechanisms. Studies on brain functioning may explain why multiple memories that are bundled together can effectively be altered when focusing on a few; evidence suggests that this may be due to the processes of memory reconsolidation and neural plasticity. One way of changing the brain's interpretation of past events and improving one's life is through the EFT technique called the Personal Peace Procedure (see Chapter 38). This technique is a daily practice in which individuals systematically tap on and thus resolve the effects of all troublesome memories. The generalization effect can help this practice proceed swiftly. A children's version of the Personal Peace Procedure can reduce the layering of issues that support negative core beliefs, or "truths," and send children into adulthood with self-confidence and a sense of inner peace. By tapping and neutralizing those issues that skew our perspectives, we can change individually and collectively, which in turn provides hope that a peaceful world can exist. The generalization effect helps the individual process multiple issues that have commonality, without the need to tap on each issue individually, moving the process along rapidly.

Keywords: generalization, generalization effect, tapping with children, acupoints, tapping tree, Personal Peace Procedure, trauma tree

Suzanne D. Alfandari, MS, MFT, has a private practice as a marriage and family therapist and EFT Expert practitioner, works at Marin Community Mental Health, and teaches EFT to organizations. Send correspondence to Suzanne D. Alfandari, PO Box 150605, San Rafael, CA 94915, or Suzanne@MarinTherapy-Associates.com.

When people who are learning Emotional Freedom Techniques (EFT) come to realize that there may be hundreds of events (i.e., multiple memories of trauma or repetitive negative early childhood events) supporting their adverse symptoms, they might get discouraged. There is no need for discouragement because there is a phenomenon known as the generalization effect, which has frequently been observed in other psychotherapeutic interventions and has applicability to EFT as well.

Mosby's Medical Dictionary defines "generalization" as "the ability of a patient to apply knowledge and skills learned in therapy to a variety of similar but new situations" (Generalization, 2009). In some types of therapy, for example, Parent-Child Interaction Therapy (PCIT), which helps parents in vivo with young behavior-challenged children, the generalization effect is evident in the transference of treatment outcomes from the home setting to the school setting. In their study of PCIT, McNeil, Eyberg, Hembree Eisenstadt, Newcomb, and Funderburk (1991, p. 147) concluded that "the successful treatment of home behavior problems using PCIT is associated with improvements in certain behaviors in the school setting," when no treatment had been given in the school setting.

Similarly, in EFT, generalization occurs when treatment aimed at reducing a client's distress in response to one particular traumatic memory or problem then resolves the distress associated with other, related memories or problems. Again, there has been no specific treatment to address these related problems, but EFT enacts a neutralizing process that starts to generalize to them. For example, if someone has dozens of traumatic memories of being abused, after using EFT to neutralize only a few of them, the negative effects stemming from the rest of the memories often vanish as well. Multiple events (i.e., memories) involving similar emotions, people, places, and circumstances can share enough commonality that after tapping on just a few, generalization occurs to release all of them.

In the course of EFT therapy, it is helpful to introduce the generalization effect to those clients who have long histories of childhood abuse, suffer from other series of traumatic incidents, or have a singular complex traumatizing event or memory (e.g., as a victim of a violent crime). Knowing that it is not usually necessary to tap on each individual traumatic incident or aspect to resolve its associated effects can help reduce the risk that clients may feel overwhelmed by the demands of the EFT protocol.

As Church (n.d.-c) notes, "You don't have to use EFT... [for] every single event that contributes to the global theme.... Memories that are similar lose their impact once the most vivid memories have been neutralized with EFT." Just as the generalization effect makes it unnecessary to tap for all challenging events, it also helps address multiple memories that may have created a global problematic limiting belief. For example, if a parent has told a child over many years that he or she is bad for different reasons, this can lead to the global limiting belief that the person inherently feels never good enough. Sometimes after the energy is balanced around a few of the related memories or aspects that created the limiting belief, the entire issue is balanced (Adams & Davidson, 2011a).

Lindsay Kenny has expanded on the generalization effect with several powerful advanced techniques that include bundling. One bundling technique is the trauma tree, which can be used for, but not limited to, issues related to childhood, marriage, work-life conflict, and traumas. The trauma tree, also called the tapping tree, incorporates into one image all the events (trunk), limiting beliefs (roots), emotions (branches), and symptoms (leaves) to be tapped on as one tree. Kenny has observed that this advanced process of bundling is very effective in work with veterans, allowing them to discharge the collective traumas before dealing with any outstanding events. By dealing with any remaining distress associated with a significant specific event, the tree collapses completely (Kenny, n.d.). In referencing the tapping tree, Ortner states, "You may discover that when you tap on one part of the tree, another part gets handled. For example, tapping on a 'root' limiting belief may also have profound effects on a 'leaf' symptom or side effect" (Ortner, 2013, p. 25). This is likely due to the generalization effect.

Metaphors for the Generalization Effect

Perhaps because the idea is somewhat challenging to describe, in EFT the generalization effect is taught primarily through metaphor, as is evident in Kenny's (n.d.) "trauma tree." This use of figurative language goes back even further, however, to the first formalized manuals for EFT. In order to best explain the generalization effect, it was initially taught with imagery of a forest and trees: "EFT often clears out a whole forest after cutting down just a few trees" (Craig, 2011, p. 104).

Clients recognize when EFT has eliminated a negative tree from their global forest by reviewing their rating of subjective units of distress (SUD) and noticing when it has diminished from a 10 to a 0. As each tree is removed and the forest thins out, clients will notice that they are no longer hindered by so many issues (trees) and can see more clearly a way out of their habituated false core beliefs (forest). Presenting problems—synonymous with aspects, specific events, or physical symptoms—are all "trees" that create a global "forest"—synonymous with core limiting beliefs or personal "truths." Fortunately, a client does not usually need to cut down the trees one at a time. With the generalization effect, if one taps down several of the biggest trees (presenting problems), similar trees are knocked down in the process, often clearing the entire forest. Or, if using the paradigm of the trauma tree, the tree encapsulates the generalization of all similar trees in the forest, leaving only a few specific trees to tap on.

More recently, EFT practitioners have tended to use the metaphor of a tabletop and table legs to describe the generalization effect. Here the table legs represent the trees or the specific events, and the tabletop, like the forest, represents global or core issues that include the interpretations we make about ourselves and others. In the course of a lifetime, the interpretations we make become our individual "truths" or tabletops, which might be supported by hundreds or more specific negative events. Not every leg needs to be collapsed before the whole tabletop holding our truth topples. When the table legs cave in, although the memory of the event or events remains, the acuity of the emotional pain dissolves. For the generalization effect to occur, the biggest table legs are knocked out, leading to a collapse of the tabletop(s)—that is, the core issue(s). Adams and Davidson (2011b, p. 67) explain further:

> The beauty of the Tabletop metaphor is that a "core issue" or belief must have experiences to support it, to hold it up. The metaphor helps us visualize the specifics that prove the belief or make it real to us as the "legs" holding up the belief or problem. The specific legs can be anything from a feeling in the pit of the stomach to the memory of something someone said.... The Tabletop metaphor is useful in imagining, for instance, the legs of one table collapsing leaving only Tabletops (core beliefs) atop one another.... Several underlying tabletops may need to collapse before the major tabletop is finally able to fall.

In the EFT training materials she created with Ann Adams, Karin Davidson describes the generalization effect as a beaver dam. She likens the logs to trees or table legs. When breaking up a beaver dam, only a few key logs need to be removed before the whole thing washes away. Here the lower logs in the dam represent childhood events and the upper logs represent more recent events. When dealing with childhood issues first, by removing the lower logs, the dam is broken sooner without having to tap on all the "logs" or events regarding similar issues (Adams & Davidson, 2011a, p. 60).

Lindsay Kenny compares the generalization effect to a game of dominoes, where the dominoes are representative of similar, recurring events, such as being abused over many years by an uncle. When one "domino" is tapped on, usually the first or most troubling, all the others collapse (L. Kenny, personal communication, January 31, 2013).

A more humorous metaphor comes from Brad Yates, who describes the generalization effect as taking out the garbage: "Sometimes... you take the bag and just throw it out into the big can, and you don't need to go back through and identify every piece of trash that you've thrown out" (Yates, n.d.).

Examples of the Generalization Effect

The generalization effect has been seen vividly in cases with veterans. The diagnosis of posttraumatic stress disorder (PTSD) represents a global issue composed of many specific events that need to be addressed; there likely will be fewer specific events to tap on if they are first addressed and bundled in a trauma tree. If a traumatized veteran identifies specific war-related events and begins addressing them one at a time or begins addressing them by bundling them in a trauma tree, after enough have been neutralized, the symptoms of PTSD no longer have a reason, or table legs, to stand on and the tabletop falls.

Carol Look has described using EFT with 26-year-old veteran Carlin, who on his two tours of duty in Iraq was exposed to numerous traumatic circumstances. Although observing that he appeared "stone cold" on the first night of a veterans' retreat, after one short session of EFT, Look reported that Carlin's previously unmovable blunted affect, demeanor, voice, and attitude were vastly improved. Carlin reported being able to go to sleep without the aid of alcohol for the first time in months, and he observed that he felt peaceful and relaxed. His mother, also present at the retreat, described Carlin's progress as "noticeable and uplifting" (Look, n.d.).

How might these effects of PTSD been resolved so rapidly for Carlin? Often the various specific events underlying a trauma (or table legs beneath the tabletop) have some common themes among them, so that removing one or more legs has an effect on those remaining. Carlin likely had many specific events underlying his PTSD. It is possible that all of these events tended to involve similar memories—comprising the same troops, enemies, equipment, sights, sounds, and smells—thus featuring enough commonality among them to generalize relief over most of the other distressing thoughts and symptoms. The generalized relief from tapping on a few events assisted the return of long-lost peaceful and relaxed feelings.

The next two examples come from my therapy practice; names and identifying details have been masked. The generalization effect is evident in the case of Claire, a 70-year-old woman who presented with relationship problems with her spouse, who was verbally and emotionally abusive to her. Claire complained of headaches, of wanting to sleep often and feeling a pervasive desire to withdraw, and of having no energy to do the creative things she enjoyed. Claire's history included growing up with brothers and a father who ignored or disparaged both her and her mother. The men in her family had encouraged her to believe that girls were not as smart as boys. At the beginning of treatment, Claire was distraught and did not relish the idea of tapping on all specific memories of her husband's nasty barbs or the hopelessness, shame, or grief she felt stemming from her childhood. But because Claire's issues were based on similar negative experiences with composite emotions, she was able to bundle the events, emotions, symptoms, and limiting beliefs into a trauma tree and tap down the intensity. A few specific memories continued to elicit a high SUD rating, for example, the first time she recalled her father ridiculing her accomplishments. However, the distress she felt in response to the whole conglomeration of events and feelings greatly dissipated after tapping down the other few specific events. After EFT, Claire was no longer triggered by her past memories, reported having more energy and few headaches, had started on a creative project, and was learning and practicing improved communication skills to express her feelings and needs, which included refusing to accept verbal or emotional abuse. In order to save the marriage, her husband entered his own therapy to address the root causes of his behavior, and in couples counseling they were able to communicate and extinguish the abuse in the relationship. Fortunately, as a likely beneficiary of the generalization effect, Claire did not have to spend time on every difficult memory to experience these good results.

Another example from my therapy practice was Jim. Jim came in with hopelessness and anger toward his 12-year-old son, who was becoming more and more aggressive. Jim had a long list of his son's bad behavior: He was rude, he cursed, he did not listen, he had trouble with peers and at school, and his verbal attacks often cruelly targeted Jim's vulnerabilities and got under his skin. We made a list of several of these events and Jim's feelings about them, gave them a name, "this bundle of frustration," and tapped the intensity from a SUD level of 9 down to 3. What then remained was Jim's sadness for his son, which we subsequently tapped down to a 0. At this point Jim shared his belief that his son was a great kid who came around in the end on his own terms. Jim did not have to tap on every event that upset him about his son's behaviors. With the help of the generalization effect, he was able to bundle the problems and reduce the remaining intensity to a few issues that quickly blew away, allowing him to feel more compassionate and hopeful and to deal more evenhandedly with his son. After his experience with EFT, Jim reported that he was able to hold clear limits about acceptable behavior from his son without becoming overly reactive the way he had before. Possibly in response to Jim's ability to change his own strong reactions while simultaneously acting as the parent in charge, his son asked to attend family therapy, wherein he expressed his thoughts and feelings in respectful ways.

How Does the Generalization Effect Work?

We now understand that many events that are imbued with similar emotional content can be completely neutralized by tapping on a small portion of the events. Although many EFT practitioners offer anecdotal evidence (such as can be found on EFT websites, including EFTUniverse.com) that the generalization effect occurs, more studies are needed to better understand why this works.

One hypothesis is based on how the brain functions. Joe Dispenza's explanation of the principle in neuroscience called Hebb's law offers insight into how the generalization effect might work. The basis of Hebb's law is: "Nerve cells that fire together, wire together." This means "that if you repeatedly activate the same nerve cells, then each time they turn on, it will be easier for them to fire in unison again...The more these networks of neurons fire, the more they wire into static routes of activity. In time, whatever the oft-repeated thought, behavior, or feeling is, it will become an automatic, unconscious habit" (Dispenza, 2012, p. 45). This is what is presumed to happen with the symptoms and coping mechanisms that those experiencing PTSD develop.

Conversely, according to the theory of Hebbian learning, nerve cells that no longer fire together, no longer wire together either (Dispenza, n.d.), potentially breaking the repetitive negative cycle permanently. In cases in which there are many specific events underlying PTSD, such as was likely true of Carlin's experience as a soldier in Iraq, it is postulated that the first traumatic event created a small neural pathway in the brain. Many therapists working with veterans who suffer from PTSD symptoms have noted that most of this population also reports having experienced childhood traumas (where the neural pathways likely began). When repeated similar events occur, what could have developed as a small pathway from one event eventually builds to a "super freeway" composed of negative thoughts, emotions, behaviors, physical symptoms, or attitudes, resulting in automatic reactions. The rapid results from the generalization effect that follow when targeting only a few specific events by tapping on EFT acupoints suggest that the prevailing quality of these neural bundles are being changed, thereby extinguishing the emotionally laden parts. Tapping leads to desensitization of each stress-producing event, so that it becomes newly associated with a state of relaxation. Because neurons that fire together wire together, the whole bundle may become associated with a state of relaxation, neutralizing the upset feelings and often the physical symptoms as well. The emotional retraumatization is no longer refiring or rewiring together, changing the previously automatic reactions and allowing new, natural, healthy choices and responses. Lane (2009) describes the mechanisms further:

> The acupressure desensitization therapies of energy psychology utilize acupressure to produce a biochemical relaxation response which counter-conditions anxiety-producing stimuli and traumatic memories. Anxiety-producing stimuli that were previously associated with the sympathetic nervous system's FFF [fight-flight-freeze] response, are re-associated with the parasympathetic nervous system's relaxation response.

Herrera (n.d.) speculates that "During an EFT treatment, serotonin (a neurotransmitter) is released in our brain which soothes us.... The result is that emotional issues... are cleared, so then you can feel genuinely positive and permanently empowered with that issue or experience." The resultant soothing effect from serotonin appears to generalize when enough similar issues are cleared. Perhaps this is what happened when Claire neutralized her trauma tree; her headaches stopped and she regained renewed energy for her creativity and her marriage.

Church (n.d.-b) suggests that once the negative charge has been removed from the memories, the negativity does not return. He further elucidates:

> This implies that new synaptic pathways ... are subsequently being reinforced. Other scientific work in the field of memory reconsolidation shows that there are periods during a therapeutic experience when a window of "lability" opens up, and long-standing behaviours can be disrupted. Once the association between a traumatic memory and the body's stress response is broken, it stays broken. Neural networks then begin to rewire themselves to carry new and more supportive behaviours and thoughts. (Church, n.d.-b)

When Carlin neutralized his stress response from a few of his specific war memories by tapping on them, it is possible that could have rewired his neural networks, changing the automatic reactions he developed from coping with the traumas that had become associated with his drinking and insomnia, to feelings of peace and relaxation.

Personal Peace Procedure and the Generalization Effect

The Personal Peace Procedure, an often-used EFT technique, consists of listing every specific troublesome event in one's life and systematically using EFT to tap away the emotional impact of these events. By tapping on a few events daily, all the trees in the forest or all the table legs supporting the tabletops are toppled, removing significant sources of both emotional and physical distress. Some find it helpful to begin the process in a very gentle way by using the bundling technique to resolve many of these issues at once, leaving far fewer on the list and less opportunity for possible retraumatization. The Personal Peace Procedure, which can improve one's work and home relationships, school and work performance, health, and nearly any other area of daily living, can add to individuals' quality of life, ultimately propelling them toward personal peace. Many EFT practitioners agree that if a critical mass of people were to undertake the Personal Peace Procedure, the world would be a better place (Church, n.d.-d).

Tapping on large numbers of events one by one might seem like a daunting task, but because of EFT's generalization effect, where tapping on one issue reduces the intensity of similar issues, the Personal Peace Procedure typically goes much faster than one might imagine.

Children and the Generalization Effect

There is a striking link between childhood stress and later disease. The Adverse Childhood Experiences study at Kaiser Permanente Hospital in San Diego, California, in collaboration with the U.S. Centers for Disease Control and Prevention, showed a strong link between early life stress and an adverse effect on emotional well-being, health, and longevity. This study emphasized that there are some negative experiences that we do not "get over" and that time does not heal (Church, 2009, pp. 60–61). Lipton (2009) explained why this might be so:

> [I]magine the consequences of hearing your parents say you are a "stupid child," you "do not deserve things," will "never amount to anything," "never should have been born," or are a "sickly, weak" person.... Such comments are downloaded into subconscious memory as absolute "facts" just as surely as bits and bytes are downloaded to the hard drive of your desktop computer.... Once programmed into the subconscious mind, however, these verbal abuses become defined as "truths" that unconsciously shape the behavior and potential of the child through life. (Lipton, 2009, p. 134)

These are the same "truths" EFT practitioners talk about alternatively as negative core beliefs, as forests, or as tabletops. Each harsh comment becomes a tree in the forest or a table leg holding the tabletop of these "truths." These "truths" acquired in childhood can have repercussions for adulthood:

> [T]he fundamental behaviors, beliefs, and attitudes we observe in our parents become "hard-wired" as synaptic pathways in our subconscious minds. Once programmed into the subconscious mind, they control our biology for the rest of our lives... unless we can figure out a way to reprogram them. (Lipton, 2009, p. 134)

EFT can be a way to reprogram the subconscious mind. With the knowledge that what is learned in childhood begins the path to creation of a super freeway bundling of neurons in the brain, leading to automatic thoughts and reactions, it becomes vitally apparent how important it is not only to remove our own root causes to distress, but also to teach children how to do so for themselves. One way to do this is to use a form of the Personal Peace Procedure with children. Each night before a child goes to sleep, parents ask their children to describe the good and bad thoughts they experienced and what good and bad things happened to them that day, while the parent or child gently taps on the child's EFT acupoints. Crucially, what this does is prevent the maladaptive neural bundling from ever occurring. Parents, teachers, or anyone else who is in close contact with children can use this technique. Such an approach has the potential for long-term consequences for, as Hanson notes, "Every time you calm the autonomic nervous system through stimulating the parasympathetic nervous system, you tilt your body, brain and mind increasingly toward inner peace and well-being" (Hanson, 2009, p. 96). By addressing issues in children as each day unfolds, the generalization effect could become unnecessary when these children reach adulthood. "This technique could send our children into adulthood with well-developed self-confidence and the ability to feel inner peace" (Church, n.d.-a).

Hope and a Way to Change the World

The great explorers of science and of the mind may be driven by a desire for truth, freedom, and peace. "Civilization's quest for freedom has permeated the history of the world. ... Now, a different type of freedom is evolving. ... It is freedom from limiting and unwanted subconscious programming" (Lipton & Bhaerman, 2009, p. 350). I have shown how one of EFT's techniques, the generalization effect, can neutralize related experiences and emotional content without needing to spend time on every single event. This leads to the release of global negatively experienced core beliefs stored in an individual's brain and moves the person toward experiencing emotional freedom. The removal of the underlying subconscious freeways in the brain of "truths" we inherited and expanded on, can now, via the generalization effect, be neutralized much more quickly than we imagined. Fortunately, these "truths," or limiting subconscious programming, can be changed with a shift in our beliefs. Some scientists, such as Greg Braden, believe that a shift in our beliefs can literally alter the experience of our lives:

> In the instant of our first breath, we are infused with the single greatest force in the universe: the power to translate the possibilities of our minds into reality of our world. To fully awaken our power, however, requires a subtle change in the way we think of ourselves in life, a shift in *belief*." (Braden, 2008, dedication page)

Once we drop our limiting negative beliefs, the so-called truths we collected from our childhoods and reinforced in our adult lives, we grow into emotional freedom, allowing new beliefs and a new perspective. EFT is a remarkable way to shift our beliefs, and the generalization effect helps do that swiftly. Some project that if enough people shift their beliefs, the collective individual shift toward emotional freedom can add to a more peaceful worldly existence. "Wholesome changes in the brains of many people could help tip the world in a better direction" (Hanson, 2009, p. 20). Through the generalization effect we can make great strides in changing the early imprints in our brains that may be restricting our productivity and creativity. With the benefits of EFT, we start building the neural pathways that boost us to our greatest individual potential and offer our unique gifts toward generating a peaceful world.

References

Adams, A. & Davidson, K. (2011a). *EFT comprehensive training resource: Level 1*. Fulton, CA: Energy Psychology Press.

Adams, A. & Davidson, K. (2011b). *EFT comprehensive training resource: Level 2*. Fulton, CA: Energy Psychology Press.

Braden, G. (2008). *The spontaneous healing of belief: Shattering the paradigm of false limits*. Carlsbad, CA: Hay House.

Church, D. (2009). *The genie in your genes: Epigenetic medicine and the new biology of intention*. Santa Rosa, CA: Energy Psychology Press.

Church, D. (n.d.-a). The daily Peace Procedure for children. Retrieved from http://www.eftuniverse.com/index.php?option=com_content&view=article&id=9219:eft-tutorial-center-daily-peace-procedure-children&catid=42:tutorial759&Itemid=3276

Church, D. (n.d.-b). The dark side of neural plasticity. Retrieved from http://www.eftuniverse.com/index.php?option=com_content&view=article&id=10814

Church, D. (n.d.-c). The importance of being specific. Retrieved from http://www.eftuniverse.com/index.php?option=com_content&view=article&id=9208:eft-tutorial-center-importance-of-being-specific&catid=42:tutorial759&Itemid=3265

Church, D. (n.d.-d). The Personal Peace Procedure. Retrieved from http://www.eftuniverse.com/index.php?option=com_content&view=article&id=9214

Craig, G. (2011). *The EFT manual* (2nd ed.). Santa Rosa, CA: Energy Psychology Press.

Dispenza, J. (2012). *Breaking the habit of being yourself: How to lose your mind and create a new one*. Carlsbad, CA: Hay House.

Dispenza, J. (n.d.). The four pillars of healing. Retrieved from http://www.drjoedispenza.com/joedispenza/ctab/TyV-COCVFMiVCQw==/The-Four-Pillars-of-Healing

Generalization. (2009). *Mosby's medical dictionary* (8th ed.). Retrieved from http://medical-dictionary.thefreedictionary.com/generalization

Hanson, R. (2009). *Buddha's brain: The practical neuroscience of happiness, love, and wisdom* (Kindle ed.). Oakland, CA: New Harbinger Publications.

Herrera, A. (n.d.). Why do we use negatives in the EFT setup statement? Retrieved from http://www.eftuniverse.com/index.php?option=com_content&view=article&id=3493:o-we-use-negatives-in-the-eft-setup-statement&catid=47:refinements-to-eft758&Itemid=3093

Kenny, L. (n.d.). Working with vets: My experience while filming the veterans PTSD documentary "Operation Emotional Freedom: The answer." Retrieved from http://www.lifecoachingwithlindsay.com/downloads/Vets_article_2of2.pdf

Lane, J. (2009). The neurochemistry of counterconditioning: Acupressure desensitization in psychotherapy. *Energy Psychology: Theory, Research, & Treatment, 1*, 31–44. Retrieved from http://www.eftuniverse.com/index.php?option=com_content&view=article&id=10579:

o-chemistry-of-counterconditioning-acupressure-desensitization-in-psychotherapy&catid=39:research-studies&Itemid=3213

Lipton, B. (2009). *The biology of belief: Unleashing the power of consciousness, matter and miracles.* Carlsbad, CA: Hay House.

Lipton, B. & Bhaerman, S. (2009). *Spontaneous evolution: Our positive future (and a way to get there from here).* Carlsbad, CA: Hay House.

Look, C. (n.d.). Sharing my experiences using EFT. Retrieved from http://www.eftuniverse.com/index.php?option=com_content&view=article&id=8846

McNeil, C. B., Eyberg, S., Hembree Eisenstadt, T., Newcomb, K., & Funderburk, B. (1991). Parent-child interaction therapy with behavior problem children: Generalization of treatment effects to the school setting. *Journal of Clinical Child Psychology, 20,* 140–151. Retrieved from http://pcit.phhp.ufl.edu/Literature/Funderburk%20et%20al%201998.pdf

Ortner, N. (2013). *The tapping solution: A revolutionary system for stress-free living.* Carlsbad, CA: Hay House.

Yates, B. (n.d.). EFT Hub Members download: Audio: Being specific, aspects and being persistent. Retrieved from http://eft-universe.com/index.php?page=shop.product_details&flypage=flypage.tpl&product_id=3&category_id=1&option=com_virtuemart&Itemid=26

Chapter 26
Tabletops and Table Legs
Annie O'Grady

Abstract

Emotional Freedom Techniques (EFT) employs a metaphor called Tabletops and Table Legs to explore and organize the contributing causes of a presenting personal problem. A tabletop represents a client's overriding issue such as "self-esteem" or "procrastination." These issues are viewed as the aggregation of the lessons the client learned from a series of specific events. Events are the table legs. From the practitioner's perspective, both tabletop and table legs are identified by the client, who also provides a subjective units of distress (SUD) rating for each table leg. Many presenting problems contain multiple tabletops. As the practitioner traces a sequence of tabletops and related events, a crucial core issue or a core belief underlying the particular problem can be revealed, and layers of emotional trauma released. When applied, this table metaphor facilitates EFT's often-startling speed in resolving even long-standing emotional or physical pain. The table metaphor not only aids the practitioner, but can also clarify for clients the inner processes that led to their presenting problem, as well as a potential solution through neutralizing specific painful events from the past and/or present that contributed to the formation of the issue.

Keywords: energy, EFT, tapping, acupoints, trauma treatment, healing

Annie O'Grady, EFT INT-1 practitioner, AAMET advanced practitioner, Matrix Reimprinting practitioner, and author of *Tapping Your Troubles Away with EFT,* has 30 years of alternative therapist experience in personal and transpersonal psychodynamics. She works with individuals and groups in person and on Skype. Send correspondence to Annie O'Grady, 310 South Terrace, Adelaide, South Australia 5000, or annie@EFTemotionalhealing.com.

When you set out to facilitate a new measure of peace for a troubled individual—whether client, friend, or yourself—the task of trying to navigate through the myriad memories, thoughts, and feelings that comprise a life experience can seem overwhelming. Fortunately, in keeping with the EFT directive to "Be specific," there is a simple strategy that:

- finds order immediately;
- highlights the *patterns* of suffering or limitation; and
- illuminates possible solutions.

This technique is called Tabletops and Table Legs. It provides a quick way of separating a problem into its parts, whether that problem is emotional, physical, or a performance difficulty. The Tabletops and Table Legs concept is central to EFT.

To apply the table metaphor, you designate a presenting issue as a tabletop. Clients will give you the words, stating what seems true to them, such as "I can't speak out," "I'm a misfit," or "I'm afraid of relationships." Tabletops are usually too global to achieve change by tapping on them directly, unless you are sneaking up on associated trauma.

With proper guidance, the client will also name the legs of the table. After labeling the issue, you look for what is holding up this particular tabletop, that is, specific events that have contributed to this problem. Each table leg represents *an actual event* whose impact contributes to the issue. If there were no related events, the issue would not exist.

To find relevant table legs, you might ask clients, "How do you know you're a misfit?" Clients will answer by listing events that have signaled that conclusion to them, such as "Because whenever I am in a group, I feel I don't belong." To elicit an event, you then ask, "Tell me about a time when that happened." Thus table legs will be events that typically still feel uncomfortable, and some could be traumatic.

You then apply EFT techniques to each important leg until the upset or physical stress fades away. That table leg collapses. You then move on to the next leg. When you have collapsed enough legs, the whole table falls.

A table formed from disturbing events may defy structural logic: There may be only two legs holding it up, or more than 100 legs. Legs also range in size; a table leg may be thick and strong (meaning the issue has a big emotional impact), or it may be emotionally spindly ("It was so long ago") while contributing negativity on the mental level.

Many people ask: Is it necessary to collapse every table leg? The answer is no. Typically, a tabletop supported by even 100 or more legs is likely to collapse after you have neutralized only 10 or 20 of the legs. This is because of the domino action of the generalization effect (see Chapter 25). Because many of these disparate events have underlying similarities and connections obvious to the subconscious mind, or neural network, clearing stress from a number of those events resonates the clearing effects through to related others, even though the conscious mind may not recognize the connections.

Major Table Legs

Clearly, traumas at any age are major among the table legs. Early life events that, to your EFT eyes, seem foundational (especially those occurring before the age of 6) may not seem as important to a client viewing them simply from an adult perspective. Here is where your trained perspective comes into play.

A client may casually describe one table leg as a young child's upset from the accidental, or purposeful, destruction of a particular chewed, battered, and be loved toy. To the adult mind, another toy would soon take the child's attention—no harm done—and there is a common assumption that the child won't remember, much less still feel the devastation of that loss years later. Even if a client has no immediate intensity on such a memory (e.g., saying, "That wasn't important, I don't know why I brought it up"), a little "just-in-case" tapping often uncovers emotional pain that has been hidden for years or decades yet is still contributing to some unwanted result in the present.

Collapsing this particular table leg may prove powerful enough to start unlocking, say, years of extended and debilitating grief over the loss of a family member, because present trauma is fueled by unprocessed past trauma.

Common sense and a little experience will build your confidence in recognizing such table leg opportunities for positive change. Note, however, that some complex issues will not fit neatly into the table model, though many issues will.

Working with the Table Model
How Long Will It Take to Collapse the Table?

Working with your table model by asking questions, paying attention to table leg memories that have a high SUD (subjective units of distress) level, resolving emotions, improving negative mind-sets by reframing, and other strategies may result in quick progress. Sometimes, however, collapsing only one or two legs by neutralizing those uncomfortable events and all their distinct parts takes a whole session. In that case, you can encourage the client by pointing out, "You have made a really good start toward your goal of being free of this problem." You can alert the client to begin noticing any encouraging changes in his or her reactions, opinions, and behavior. Even though the issue is not yet fully dealt with, early feedback may be "I'm not nearly so sad," "I don't buy into my coworkers' emotional stuff anymore," or "I was finally able to make that phone call."

How Do You Collapse a Table and All Its Legs?

Collapsing a table and all its legs means removing a troublesome issue, or pattern, from an individual's life in both the present and the future, facilitating both happier day-to-day living and progress toward the client's life aims. The collapse also removes emotional pain from old or recent related memories.

Core Issue and Core Belief

To collapse a presenting problem fully means that you need to use your detective skills to uncover and deal with a core issue or a core belief that will be hiding in its layers. What is the bottom line of the difficulty? For example, beneath a tabletop of "I'm afraid of relationships" may ultimately be a secret core belief of "I'm unlovable."

When you reach an underlying core, you see that the tabletop was merely a symptom of the problem. Once you have an overall view of the ramifications of the presenting problem, it is important to focus on the often hidden core tabletop, which usually came into being in childhood, because toppling this can facilitate de-stressing the rest. Yet, although stress from some later events may not easily give way completely until earlier events have been neutralized, chronology does not determine the intensity of the problem's cause.

- A core *issue* is likely to involve one or more traumas.
- A core *belief* can be formed either in childhood (e.g., "I'm wrong") or in a catastrophic experience as a teenager or adult (e.g., "I'm not safe"). A core belief is a negative emotional learning, often imprinted early in life, which then operates as self-fulfilling, to a greater or lesser extent. It is usually the result of conditioning but may also involve trauma.

Core beliefs I have heard people express in session include:

People hurt me.
I can't trust men/women/anyone.
I don't belong/I'm a misfit.
Nobody wants me/I'm unlovable.
I have to get out of here.
I have to be angry/ill/in pain to survive.
I have to fight to survive/life's a struggle.
I'm not good enough/not enough/worthless.
I'm bad/ugly/dirty.
There's something wrong with me/I'm not right.
I'm a disappointment/mistake/accident.
I can't do it/I'm weak/I'm helpless.
I have to do everything alone.
I can't get started/finish anything by myself.
I can't get enough.
Nobody notices/listens to me.
My love hurts others/I'm too much.
I'm a nuisance/a burden/in the way.
I'm misunderstood.
I'm cut off/separated.
I'm different.
I'm not safe.
Nothing works for me.

In the following cases that illustrate how to use the table metaphor, the practitioner's questioning unravels the problem down to an ultimate cause. Events labeled on such a mind map are dealt with according to their current conscious impact on the client, and/or to the practitioner's specialized understanding of what is likely to be most important. (I often hear clients say, "I had no idea I still felt that way!").

The order in which a practitioner chooses to deal with the chain of events and their emotional, mental, and/or physical consequences depends on several factors, such as the client's emotional or physical state and wishes, how the practitioner perceives the urgency of resolving each event, possible connections among events, the time available for processing, and other factors.

Although EFT has definite guiding principles and concrete techniques, there is no one-way-fits-all application, no healing by rote. The flexibility of mix-and-match tools built into EFT's collection of 48 techniques aids EFT's high success rate among a huge range of individual practitioners in different cultures and countries, and among a huge range of individual clients.

Here are two cases to illustrate the table metaphor and how I applied it.

Case 1: "I can't go in Elevators"
Tabletop with One Table Leg

Arnold, a farmer, agreed to try a one-hour tapping session with me at the suggestion of his mother while I was visiting her on their property. He had been trying for weeks to make an online booking for himself, his wife, and their teenage children to holiday in a foreign city. But he could not bring himself to make the commitment because of the terror he felt while looking at photos of high-rise hotels.

Arnold was mortally afraid of riding in elevators. He kept imagining having to deal with his overwhelming panic perhaps several times a day. This fear of elevators had haunted him from childhood, and its cause was well known in his family. When he was 8 years old, a playmate had locked him in the trunk of a car and had left him to cry in terror for hours.

Although Arnold had no interest in tapping, he was desperate. After introducing the method and showing him how to tap on EFT's acupoints, I suggested he simply follow what I was doing. As he tentatively told me what he was feeling, we tapped the edge off the problem: his embarrassment about not yet having made the holiday booking, although his whole family was awaiting the information.

When I asked him when his elevator phobia had begun, he easily offered the car trunk event as family history, and said he was willing to look at it. As this seemed a likely foundational event, I invited him to briefly contact his memory of the terrified little boy trapped for long hours in the small metal prison, dreading that he would die in there. I guided him to tap down that original terror via the Tearless Trauma Technique (see Chapter 28), followed by the Tell the Story Technique (see Chapter 20). To his amazement, collapsing this table leg over several minutes reduced his tabletop to a 0 on the SUD scale.

Next I invited Arnold to imagine a future ride in an elevator, and we tapped away some minor panic reactions to the imagery.

At the end of the hour Arnold went straight to his computer and booked the holiday. (Lacking access to an elevator at the time, this was the best way of testing our work.)

A year later he told me he had enjoyed the holiday despite the elevators it involved, and he was still delighting in being free of the phobia. He said, "I feel quite clever being able to talk to people now when I'm in an elevator, and I'm less anxious if it does something strange."

Tabletop: "I can't go in elevators."
Table leg: A childhood trauma.

Case 2: "I can't Start my Own Business"
Tabletop with Multiple Legs

Astrid, an attractive married woman in her late 20s, who described herself as having been stuck for 2 years in a state of anxiety and shame. She was ashamed that she had not been able to earn money in that time by starting her own training business and so was dependent on her husband's income, as well as leaving him with the full burden of their mortgage. She was ashamed that, although she knew how to teach other people to be leaders, she herself was too paralyzed with fear to start her business. She had left employment to do this, but had unaccountably "fallen in a heap."

She had spent 2 years trying to surmount her fears. Ultrasensitive to enquiries about how her new business was going, she had withdrawn from social events in the country town where she lives. She despised herself for "living a lie"—putting up a fraudulent front when she did see friends, by pretending she was fine. She was in despair about not being able to move forward into the entrepreneurial career that inspired her and for which she was well qualified. Now she suspected that her depressed state was threatening her marriage.

Astrid felt confused and helpless. Why was this happening to her? She had graduated with high marks from a prestigious business training course, had previously managed an office, led committees, and won awards.

In her first hour-long EFT session on Skype, I taught Astrid basic mechanical EFT and tapped with her as she began to tap down the fear and shame that were paralyzing her. I applied the table metaphor.

Tabletop: "I can't start my own business (because…)"

Table legs:

1. Astrid and her husband were still traumatized by having been the victims of a businessman they'd trusted, who had caused them, and their friends, to lose hundreds of thousands of dollars. They were still in debt.
2. A talented artist, she had started a child portrait business, which soon failed.
3. Former workmates had ridiculed her entrepreneurial ideas. She kept thinking, "What if they're right?"

Multiple Tabletops

Astrid later reported making some positive new moves, such as starting yoga classes and enjoying a day kayaking with her husband. She also began daily self-help tapping on her anxieties, shame, and fears.

Although Astrid would obviously have benefited to some extent if we had immediately neutralized each of the three table legs of this identified tabletop, I wanted to find the quickest way through to the main cause, especially because there was no certainty that she would return for more sessions. I asked, "Your portrait business failed because…?" Surprisingly, she said, "I can't accept money for my work. I don't deserve to be paid."

Astrid had previously been comfortable accepting payment as an employee. She'd had enough confidence to leave her last job because it paid too little for the work required. Then, faced with being paid cash for her own work, she was shocked to mysteriously "fall to pieces."

Here was a second tabletop, underneath the first: "I don't deserve money for my work."

After her first child portrait commission, Astrid was too nervous to ask for money but accepted a hardware store voucher as payment and, for another commission, a software package. She did not know how much money to charge, felt uncharacteristically helpless to decide, and thought she could never understand the necessary tax software—all solvable problems, but by now she felt unable to take any action and fell deeper into despair.

Astrid knew that, unrealistically, she felt compelled to be perfect, even as a beginner business owner, but she could not reason herself out of it. For 2 years now, escalating fears of possible client complaints had terrorized her, as she visualized people criticizing her behind her back to others in their country town. She thought this would somehow be worse if she had received cash.

After she recalled enjoying being unexpectedly paid $200 cash for winning a portrait award, we tackled her statement:

Even though I can't accept cash for my own work and I don't know why, I love and accept myself anyway, deeply and completely.

From a SUD rating of 10, we switched from tapping on that statement to tapping on its accompanying body sensation: "a black lump in my stomach." Astrid reached 0 in a few minutes, free of both "the black lump" and her belief that she couldn't accept cash payment. She was all smiles and could hardly believe the change, could hardly believe that she had not been able to charge money for her products or services. I asked her to test the result with cash before the next session.

Later she was able to advertise some of her artwork on eBay for the first time. She also happily attended a social function with her husband for the first time in 2 years, and confidently fielded the question she'd dreaded, "And what do *you* do?" For her whole situation to clear, however, we were just starting the work.

Tabletop 2: "I don't deserve money for my work."

Table legs:

1. Astrid felt responsible for the loss of hundreds of thousands of dollars in the business scam because she had recommended that business owner to her husband, and to their friends. She connected this huge money loss with her loss of faith in her own judgment.
2. Going back to childhood: For years her parents had paid her less pocket money than they gave to her elder sister, saying, "You don't need it."
3. At age 12 she had done a gardening job for a neighbor, who had screamed at her that she'd messed it up and wouldn't pay her.

Astrid had not told anyone, had hugged her shame.

4. At age 9 she had been sent to the shops for groceries but had lost the money. The ensuing family scene had imprinted the "knowledge" that she wasn't safe handling money.

But we were not quite at the core of the problem. Clearly, these and other events were pointing to a core belief that Astrid had carried from a young age, and which seemed to her to keep proving itself. Soon she voiced this herself: "Deep down, I feel I'm not worth it." Unless we reduced or eliminated the power of this belief, Astrid was likely to continue finding herself facing similar problems.

Tabletop 3: "I'm not worth it."
Table legs:

1. After the business loss she and her husband suffered, money was scarce in their household for months. Being in debt and having to scrimp and save daily made her feel worthless and useless.
2. Astrid shuddered while telling of 2 years at high school with an English teacher who continually red-inked her written assignments with negative comments, and never once affirmed her. In relation to her own work, the girl's vulnerable self-image went down and down, particularly in relation to her creativity.
3. Astrid's parents had been supportive but demanding. If she reported coming second in her school class, they would ask, "What went wrong, that you weren't first?"
4. She was never chosen for a sports team, which displeased her parents.
5. Her mother often reprimanded her for "wasting time daydreaming."
6. Parental comments repeatedly gave her the message that she was not as clever/pretty/valuable as her sister, who was now a doctor.
7. At age 7, on a school bus carrying students of various ages, she had been devastated when a teenage boy she admired said angrily to her, "You're stupid!" She took it to heart.

Clearly, Astrid had sunk into her depressed state under the weight of unresolved emotional situations from the past, stresses that had been building up for years. Now her improving outlook gave her confidence in EFT's effectiveness, and she seemed eager to continue. In order for her to start changing her belief "I'm not worth it," I asked, "How true is that statement?" and we tapped its current "truth" down from 10 to 0. Astrid was ecstatic. She e-mailed later: "I've been taking action! OMG, there must be heaps of other coaches, consultants, trainers out there who have a dream but somehow believe they are not worthy." That process took more edge off her inability to move forward.

For our aim that her new state would last, however, our table model showed we had other energy blocks to dissolve as well.

Personal Peace list. To take full advantage of uncovering these contributing causes, the remaining table legs now formed the start of Astrid's Personal Peace Procedure list (see Chapter 38). I explained that we would continue tapping through memories, and through other important memories that might be triggered, mostly using the Tell the Story Technique. To speed her progress she could also use that technique on this beginning life-clearing list herself. She would find that some items would have no emotional charge left, because of the generalization effect, so her list might shrink faster than she expected.

Trauma treatment. We moved now to begin neutralizing Astrid's trauma over the huge money loss and its emotional, mental, and physical consequences, not only for Astrid and her husband, but also for their friends, for which Astrid felt guilty. We began with the Tearless Trauma Technique, and continued into the Tell the Story Technique.

Even before we started this processing, test results were showing up in Astrid's life. She was now thinking about conducting her first business leadership course as a pilot program. A local firm had requested that she do this, to pay off a debt, and suddenly she felt able to at least consider it. The prospect loomed huge for her, because her embarrassment about owing money to people she knew was still excruciating, but she was learning to tap this down, sometimes with help. Her depression was on the way out—and a new project to inspire and help other people was being born.

Two months after our five sessions, Astrid reported that she had for the first time sold two of her hand made necklaces on eBay, had also won two drawing competitions, "almost completed my tax return, which was a horrible, horrible subject that caused me shame, but I cleared that blockage to make way for the new," and was a third of the way through writing a book while even sounding out publishers! Best of all, she said, "I have 90% finished designing and putting together my leadership course, and I have identified six local businesses that could use my services. I am going ahead in leaps and bounds."

The table metaphor had charted Astrid's tapping path from being frozen with fear and despair into new freedom.

Our Childhood "Truths"

We've seen how Astrid's core belief from childhood, "I'm not worth it," still affected her acutely as an adult. The belief had felt like such a deep truth for her that she had never questioned it, until we tapped it from 10 to 0 on the topic of receiving money for her creativity.

When we are children, our memories are laid down as specific events, such as: "Mom slapped my hand when I reached for another cookie at my sister's fourth birthday party and said 'Don't be greedy.'" Our reaction to "I'm greedy" may eventually surface as a big self-esteem issue of "I don't deserve" (tabletop and core belief), which plays out by undermining our choices in various parts of our lives, not just with food treats. We may feel that we don't really deserve an excellent partner, or plenty of money, or even to have anything at all that we desire. Therefore, if we do manage to get it, we are likely to sabotage it, so that we can be *right:* "See, I told you, you don't deserve it, and this proves it." Understandably, we seem to need the safety of believing what we think, however misguided our thought, or belief, might be. Such destructive programs (of which we are largely unaware) make life miserable.

Jill, 53 years old, came to me, saying, "I really lack self-confidence [tabletop]. I have all my life, although I had a good upbringing." She couldn't remember much about her childhood, however. Jill reported lacking confidence even at home. For instance, if her husband complained at a meal that the butter was hard, she would apologize: "It's my fault, I should have taken it out of the fridge earlier, sorry, dear." She told me, "I know it's pathetic, but I can't help it." Jill then confided a second tabletop: "I can't speak in a group." She said she would never say anything in a group of more than three people, "in case I said the wrong thing." Consequently, she had always limited her social life and her educational choices, out of fear. (Was the number three perhaps a signal that this mind-set had originated when she was very young in the presence of *four or more* people?)

At a recent barbecue party when new acquaintances (whom she hadn't spoken to) were all singing to a guest's guitar music, Jill joined in the singing but only by miming—"in case I did it wrong." We tapped down her fear and tapped as we reframed that memory, so that she could picture herself, wonderfully supported, singing so gloriously that everyone turned to listen in admiration. Now she couldn't stop smiling and giggling, as she absorbed the surprising feeling that something big was changing for the better. In fact, singing was a new joy to Jill, since she had discovered at age 50 that she had a beautiful voice, and had started lessons. At her first public performance, she had been shaking so much from nervousness (fear that she might "do it wrong") that she almost dropped the microphone. Through will power, she had managed to triumph at her 50th birthday party by performing a song for all the guests, in spite of her terror, yet the shaking had been almost as bad.

Now, having agreed to sing for a nursing home audience, she still worried about her stage fright. We tapped down her nervous symptoms both in memory and in mentally rehearsing the future performance. She later reported that she had sung confidently and well; both she and the audience had enjoyed the event, so she'd been surprised that her hand holding the microphone still shook a little. Clearly, although her fear of public performance was fading, some buried stress remained.

This big success had not, however, improved her daily self-judgments that whatever she did wasn't good enough and was probably wrong. We turned our attention to deeper causes. I asked, "What happens in your body when you think you might do it wrong?" At first, surprised, she said, "Nothing." Soon, though, she was able to recognize "a trembling in my stomach." We tapped on: *Even though my stomach trembles when I might do it wrong, I love and accept myself deeply and completely.*

Tapping frequently uncovers forgotten memories, spontaneously. This illustrates EFT's needle-sharp ability to show us ultimate causes, rather than our having to cast about among various possibilities, as traditional therapies have had to do for so long. During our third tapping round on "My stomach is trembling," Jill remembered crying on her first day at school. Then: "Oh, no, now I'm 6 years old, sitting at a desk at school. The teacher suddenly hits my hand hard with a ruler."

This memory of a single event was a large table leg. The teacher's attack shocked, hurt, and frightened her, and was never explained. Her SUD rating was 9, even now. Whatever we say to ourselves in a state of high emotion is like an order delivered to our subconscious. Jill agreed that her reaction at age 6 was probably something like: "I must have done something wrong. I don't know what I did wrong. I don't want that ever to happen again. So if I don't do anything, I can't be wrong, and I'll be safe."

From an EFT point of view, Jill had discovered a gem. So we began tapping to neutralize, within minutes, this imprinted memory table leg that had stressed her system, undiscovered, for 47 years.

Though Jill is a warm-hearted, humorous, and giving person, having a life motto of "Don't do anything in case you're wrong" resulted in a quiet life, a depressing view of herself, largely unexplored personal potential, and a less than satisfying marital relationship. She is currently excited about an expected move from the city to live with her husband in a beautiful environment on an isolated bush property, where, incidentally, social challenges as well as opportunities will be scarce. At 53, however, she is waking up to new possibilities, at a time when this highly effective technique for helping herself has unexpectedly become available. We are still working on her table issues.

Conclusion

The tabletop process gives you, as the practitioner, a shortcut to identifying a healing path for the client. You don't have to settle for facilitating only superficial emotional improvement, nor do you need to get lost in a massive jumble of information from the client. This process is an elegant mind map, which by reading this chapter you have now learned how to use.

Chapter 27
Tail-enders
Jenny Johnston

Abstract

This chapter describes what a tail-ender is and why it is so important to address in EFT. A concept that derives from neuro-linguistic programming, the "tail-ender" is an often quiet statement that contains objection or resistance to a positive affirmation or statement such as "Money comes easily to me." The tail-ender, or resistance to "easily," often flies under the radar of our conscious mind, subconsciously and energetically determining our patterns and behaviour. The chapter explores the importance of uncovering tail-enders, what to do when you find them, and how working with them can often reveal limiting core beliefs and memories. When tail-enders are tapped on and limiting beliefs cleared, positive patterns and affirmations are no longer hampered by them. The chapter gives a detailed example of how one woman's positive affirmation of "Money comes easily to me" was transformed after identifying her tail-ender and tapping through a childhood memory and the limiting beliefs that arose from it, which allowed her to feel congruent with that affirmation. Pat Carrington's Choices Method is also discussed, including one of the ways of dealing with self-sabotaging tail-enders: finding its antidote and using it to create a choice statement with a positive affirmation. The chapter concludes with the understanding that finding and tapping on tail-enders and the subsequent memories and limiting beliefs to which they lead is as important as doing the Personal Peace Procedure.

Keywords: self-sabotage, limiting beliefs, tail-enders, resistance, positive affirmations, core issues, inner critic, law of attraction

Jenny Johnston is an occupational therapist, clinical hypnotherapist, EFT Universe trainer, Matrix Reimprinting practitioner, and founder of Quantum EFT. She has worked with many veterans who suffer from PTSD and her commitment is for EFT to be recognized by Veterans Affairs authorities and used in mainstream programs. Send correspondence to Jenny Johnston, 4 Apollo Court, Frankston 3199, Victoria, Australia, or jenny@jennyjohnston.com.au.

We are taught that we can become more powerful and congruent with our energy by saying positive affirmations, seeing them vividly and feeling them with emotion, and thereby manifest our goals. The more positive and congruent we become, the higher our vibration and the more we attract similar vibrations into our lives. This is known as the Law of Attraction: like attracts like. As a result, many of us practice the art of being positive using positive affirmations, especially around New Year's. Many affirmations don't come to fruition, however, and most New Year's resolutions are forgotten by February. Why is that?

What Is a Tail-ender?

Imagine a beautiful red hot-air balloon. Inside, it is filled with positive affirmations that you want to release into the atmosphere, affirmations such as "My soul mate is with me now," "I am fit and healthy," "It's easy to maintain my ideal weight," and "I have an abundant life."

But these affirmations just aren't flying, as this beautiful red hot-air balloon is not moving off the ground. It's tied down with thick ropes to stakes in the ground—by "tail-enders." Tail-enders for this example might include "I'm never going to find my soul mate and I don't even know if he exists," I feel so tired and unfit," "I'll never lose this weight," or "How come I still have so many debts?"

A concept derived from neuro-linguistic programming, a tail-ender is often described as "the inner critic," the quiet voice in the background that we don't notice until we go looking for it. Undetected, under the radar, a tail-ender continually sabotages our positive affirmation, creating resistance, and is actually the source of our true energy and vibration. These "yes, but" statements represent negative self-talk and limiting beliefs.

Discovering tail-enders is like discovering gold! They represent tappable issues. When you identify a tail-ender, tap on it, and follow the energetic, physical, and emotional pathway, you are led to core issues, limiting beliefs, and the memories of events in which they were created. When you tap on these original core memories (cut the ropes), you allow your positive affirmations (the balloon) to be realized (to fly).

Tail-enders can also feel like self-sabotage or like the little devil on your shoulder that you hear in your mind when you say something positive. It may sound very sarcastic or remind you of someone saying something sarcastic to you, such as "As if *you* can do that," "Who do you think you are?" "You're kidding yourself," or "When pigs fly."

Tapping on tail-enders is like cleaning debris out of a wound before applying antiseptic and bandages (positive affirmations). By cleaning the wound first (tapping on tail-enders), you're able to apply the bandaging (positive affirmations) and easily and naturally heal. By not cleaning the wound first (allowing tail-enders to remain in place), you're inviting infection, and the healing (positive affirmations) will take longer and may be compromised.

Another helpful metaphor for tail-enders is: If you want to plant some sunflower seeds (positive affirmations), but your garden bed is filled with weeds (negative and limiting beliefs—tail-enders), the seeds will have difficulty germinating and taking root. In order to give the beautiful sunflowers the best chance of growing and blossoming, you need to till the soil and pull out the weeds (the tail-enders), one at a time, until they have all been removed. Now you have a fertile garden bed with plenty of room for the seeds (positive affirmations) to take root, develop, and blossom into sunflowers.

How to Find and What to Do with a Tail-ender

1. Begin by saying out loud a positive statement or goal, such as "I'm really going to travel to Paris this year." Tap on your EFT meridian points while you say it, and notice how you feel or how it "sits" for you in your body. Do you feel resistance? How congruent do you feel with it?
2. Score it on the validity of cognition (VOC) scale, with 0 being you don't believe that statement to be true, and 10 being you really feel it to be true. If your score is quite low, then you will certainly have a tail-ender, or resistance to the statement, and it won't feel believable. Keep tapping on the statement and notice what you feel in your body and what emotions, senses, and memories come up as you tap.
3. Notice what tail-ender comes up. Example: "But I never have enough money to

travel." Give the tail-ender a VOC score. Then begin tapping, using the statement of the tail-ender. Notice the first time you felt this way. Who does it remind you of?

4. Notice what memory or event comes up. Give the specific memory a SUD (subjective units of discomfort/distress) score, with 0 being no discomfort or distress, and 10 being maximum discomfort or distress. Tap on all the specific aspects as they come up, following the trail right back to the limiting beliefs, core issues, and memories.

5. When the SUD scores for your specific memories drop to a low number, you may then tap and choose your positive statement. Example: "I choose to have enough money to travel to Paris this year." See if you feel any other resistance or tail-enders come up. If so, find new specific events from the new tail-ender and tap as before until the SUD score is low.

6. When you can say your positive affirmation out loud with no resistance and you feel congruent with it, your VOC for the positive statement should also be high.

7. Now your energy is aligned with your positive statement and no longer compromised by a tail-ender. (Your balloon is ready to fly!)

Case Example of a Tail-ender

A participant at an EFT Level 2 workshop I led recorded a video testimony after having a wonderful shift when doing the tail-enders exercise. She has given me permission to talk about it. (See her testimony on my YouTube channel, EFT Australia, http://www.youtube.com/watch?v=NpbksSL3iuE.)

We will call her Nicki. The affirmation Nicki was working on was "Money comes easily to me." This statement had a low VOC for her. It was the "easily" part that held resistance for Nicki, as she felt that there was some sort of forbidden information that she wasn't allowed to have. Her tail-ender was "I'm fumbling around in the dark and I don't have the secret." The SUD score for this statement was high. Upon exploring the energetic body and emotional feelings while tapping, Nicki expanded the tail-ender until it became "I'm not allowed the key to go into the light-filled space; the authorities won't let me."

All of a sudden, a forgotten memory came into her awareness of when she began school at around 6 years of age. She already knew how to read and had been placed in grade 1, which was a beautiful, light-filled place with order and books and learning and she loved it. Then Nicki had her tonsils out and was away from school for a while. Returning to school, Nicki was sitting outside by herself at playtime, reading, and "the authorities" decided that she was not socially ready for grade 1 and so she was sent into the adjoining classroom, which was for the kindergarteners. This classroom was dark and chaotic and filled with sandboxes and finger painting. She could see the light-filled classroom next door but wasn't allowed in. It was then that she formed the limiting belief that the authorities have the key to the light-filled space of order and learning and she is not allowed in. Nicki was surprised that this memory came up, as she hadn't thought about kindergarten for many years. Yet she'd always had this sense that there was a mysterious conspiracy against her that kept her from being in the light-filled space of ease and learning.

After tapping on all of the specific aspects of that memory and the belief she had formed from it until the SUD went down to 0, Nicki felt empowered and the mystery was no more. This childhood memory and the limiting belief that arose from it had been running her life, without her realizing it. She had looked for the reason behind the mysterious feeling before but had never been able to get to its source. Now, having cleared the source of the tail-ender, Nicki was able to feel congruent (high VOC) with the affirmation "Money comes easily to me," and she was able to feel that she had finally been handed the keys.

Since then, Nicki has gone on to create a flourishing EFT business with ease and delight, she has even created two wonderful iTunes apps, and money is indeed flowing to her easily.

Another example of a positive affirmation, "I effortlessly maintain my ideal weight," may have a tail-ender such as "except that it takes hard work for me" or "then how come I'm still overweight?" or simply "in my dreams."

When you are tapping on the positive affirmation, the tail-ender appears when you go looking for it. Following the feeling of that tail-ender in the body, tap through all of the points until you notice a memory, feeling, or core belief come up. Treat the tail-ender as a tappable issue and see where it leads. When the energetic charge of the tail-ender has dropped to a low SUD rating, retest the positive affirmation and it should be much more congruent. If it isn't, perhaps you didn't get specific enough or get to core beliefs and memories.

There may be other specific memories (table legs; see Chapter 26) supporting this belief, to be tapped on. Be persistent and keep retesting the positive affirmation until the tail-ender has little or no energy. Then your energy will be consistent with the positive affirmation, unless another tail-ender arises to replace it. If another tail-ender arises, then go ahead and tap on that one, finding the memories and core beliefs related to that particular tail-ender. When all tail-ender energy is low, that positive affirmation should now feel positive.

Self-sabotage and Tail-enders

In her article on the EFT Universe website (www.eftuniverse.com), "How to Handle Self Sabotage using EFT," Patricia Carrington, PhD, EFT Master and the developer of the Choices Method, details two ways of dealing with tail-enders.

The first way is how I have just described, using EFT to identify the often unconscious hidden objection, self-sabotaging pattern, or limiting belief that is creating a negative outcome. We tap on the tail-ender and where it leads because this is actually what is being affirmed, as it carries the greatest vibrational charge. Dissolving the emotional charge of the "objection" and all the specific memories, aspects, and limiting beliefs then allows the charge to be assigned to the positive affirmation, goal, or choice and allows us to manifest what we truly desire in life instead of the opposite.

The second way is by using Dr. Carrington's Choices Method, in which you can include an antidote to the tail-ender in a choice statement while tapping. Here is an example:

Positive affirmation: *I have a successful business.*

Choice statement: *I choose to have a successful business.*

Tail-ender: *But I'll be a slave to my work and have no freedom or balance.*

Antidote to tail-ender: *To enjoy the balance and freedom within my successful business.*

New choice statement: *I choose to enjoy the balance and freedom that my successful business provides me with.*

In my opinion, it's best to use both of these methods together. That way you cover all bases. By dealing first with the origins of the tail-enders and all the specific memories, limiting beliefs, and core issues, the path becomes clear for the subconscious mind to fully accept a new affirmation or choice with the antidote to the tail-ender included.

Celebrate Your Tail-enders

The energy around our affirmations, choices, and goals shapes our lives, so we want to make sure that our energetic charge is with the positive rather than with the negative, objecting, resisting, or shadow side that is the tail-ender.

Another great way to find as many tail-enders as possible is to say, "I *want* to have a successful business *but* …" and make a list of all the statements that come up for you.

Tap on the tail-enders, one at a time, processing the emotions and memories associated with them, creating a clear passage for positive affirmations and higher vibrations to emerge. I believe this is as important as doing the Personal Peace Procedure. Clean out your energetic system so that you can vibrate higher and attract what you want into your life, allowing your positive affirmations, goals, and choices to create miracles.

Chapter 28
The Gentle Techniques
Jan L. Watkins

Abstract

Energy healing practitioners find that the emotional reactions of their clients can interfere with healing work. Emotional reactions may disrupt sessions and clients may avoid discussing distressing events when they fear uncomfortable emotional reactions. This paper describes three specific techniques in the Emotional Freedom Techniques (EFT) collection, called "the gentle techniques," which a practitioner can incorporate into sessions to minimize a client's emotional upset during a session. The efficacy and usefulness of the techniques are explored with references to the mind-body connection, memory storage, and the lingering impact of traumatic memories on the mind and body. The gentle techniques include three specifically entitled techniques: Sneaking Up, Tearless Trauma, and Chasing the Pain.

Keywords: gentle techniques, trauma, chasing the pain, pain, sneaking up, sneaking up on the problem, tearless trauma

Jan L. Watkins, JD, MSW, LCSW, EFT Expert practitioner and trainer, is in private practice in the Washington, DC area. She offers trainings and workshops in energy psychology, including EFT Universe certification training, to individuals and corporations. Send correspondence to Jan Watkins, 1313 Vincent Place, McLean, VA, 22101, or JanLWatkins@gmail.com. www.janwatkins.com.

Introduction to the Gentle Techniques

In the process of working through emotional issues, a client may become emotionally reactive and may even uncover unresolved trauma. By using EFT and the gentle techniques to target emotional distress as it arises during the session, a practitioner may be able to prevent emotional reactions from inhibiting the client's progress. The gentle techniques recognize that a client can only process emotional issues at his or her own pace, and they are carefully structured so that the client's emotional and physical reactions guide the work.

Clients may become uncomfortable when discussing events that they perceive as traumatic. For the purposes of discussing the gentle techniques, the word *trauma* is used in a general sense to mean any situation or problem that overwhelms the body-mind system. Trauma may result when an individual experiences an extreme event, such as a natural disaster or a violent situation. Trauma may also result when an individual encounters an ordinary, everyday situation that is subjectively overwhelming, possibly because of the individual's particular biology or background. For example, one child might experience an encounter with an angry authority figure as a traumatic experience, while another might be unaffected by the confrontation.

The brain processes normal, uncharged memories through channels that provide context and meaning, and an individual will generally be able to recall details of the event without experiencing distress. On the other hand, when a traumatic event occurs, the brain does not process the memory of the event in the way that it processes the memory of an everyday event, and an individual may experience discomfort when recalling the memory (Ecker, Ticic, & Hulley, 2012; Rothschild, 2000; Shapiro, 2001; Siegel, 2012). The brain may hold aspects of a traumatic experience in implicit, or unconscious, memory storage. Ecker et al. explain that when an individual encounters a stimulus that the brain associates with the event, he or she may experience unpleasant physical, mental, or emotional symptoms. The individual may feel like he or she is reliving the event rather than remembering something that happened.

Siegel (2012) explains that a memory is stored with aspects of cognition, physical sensation, and emotion. Any association with the memory can act as a cue or stimulus that triggers the body to feel like it reexperiences the event. There may be endless triggers that are capable of causing mental or physical reactions to unprocessed traumatic events (Rothschild, 2000). In addition to triggers formed immediately around an overwhelming or traumatic event, triggers may generalize and a client may come to associate a trauma with new or additional events, sounds, or other stimuli. "Classical conditioning can create chains of conditioned stimuli such that an individual trigger . . . may be several generations away from the original stimulus response scenario" (Rothschild, p. 32). For example, a client bitten by a large dog may become afraid of all dogs and then all four-legged creatures. Eventually, the client may avoid leaving his or her home to minimize the risk of encountering other four-legged creatures.

Trauma therapists are aware that a client with a history of trauma can be triggered unexpectedly, and that emotional reactions can quickly escalate, with the client becoming overwhelmed, retraumatized, or dissociated (Rothschild, 2000). A client without a known history of trauma may also be triggered unexpectedly. To avoid the possibility of retraumatization or abreaction, it is important that practitioners notice when the client becomes evenly mildly distressed, physically or emotionally, because the distress may indicate the presence of new triggers. EFT and the gentle techniques are effective tools for addressing the distress. Clients and practitioners find that abreactions are uncommon when energy psychology tools like EFT are used in conjunction with good clinical skills (Mollon, 2008; Schulz, 2009). Some clinicians have reported a preference for using EFT in highly charged situations or for using EFT in conjunction with other methods, such as Eye Movement Desensitization and Reprocessing (EMDR) when distress levels begin to threaten overwhelming the client (Hartung & Galvin, 2002).

The EFT gentle techniques address trauma and layers of new conditioning that have been created around the original trauma by approaching the client's system slowly, cautiously, and respectfully, from a distance, dealing with all layers of triggering sounds, sights, feelings, or thoughts, separately and thoroughly, before addressing the core event. The gentle techniques include three specifically entitled techniques—Sneaking Up, Tearless Trauma, and Chasing the Pain—and several other related approaches.

Sneaking Up

Sneaking Up: Background

There are often several layers of trauma surrounding a traumatic event, including a layer of trauma related to thinking about or discussing the event. A practitioner may use the Sneaking Up Technique to target the client's reluctance to discussing the traumatic event by carefully working specifically on the outermost layer of the trauma, the fear of discussing the traumatic event. The practitioner distances the client from the troubling event by identifying the distress associated with the experience of merely discussing the event.

In contrast to general EFT principles, which indicate a preference for specificity when tapping, the Sneaking Up Technique recognizes the importance of initially framing the issue or event from a distant and global perspective. When using the sneaking up approach, the practitioner starts as far away from the client actually tuning in to the trauma as possible, and has the client tap on the EFT meridian endpoints until the client is able to discuss specific aspects of the original core event. The sneaking up process deconditions the body's stressful response to the event. A possible Setup Statement might be "Even though I am terrified when I think of talking about that day, I deeply and completely love and accept myself." The Reminder Phrase might be "this terror."

The practitioner can also use sneaking up when a client expresses hopeless and catastrophic cognitions that inhibit progress. For example, a client might say, "I can't lose weight. I've always been this way" or "I'll never heal because this is genetic." Another might say, "I'll never find love." One 25-year-old who was no longer inspired by her policy work reported that she was "too old to start over." Job seekers frequently report, "No one is hiring" or "I can't get a job without experience and I can't get experience without a job." Another client reported, "This problem is too big for me." When the client expresses the cognition, the practitioner simply creates a setup with the belief and begins the EFT rounds. A Setup Statement to target cognitions might be "Even though I'll never heal, I deeply and completely love and accept myself, " with a Reminder Phrase of "never heal."

Sneaking Up: Guidelines

A practitioner tailors the sneaking up process to the client's specific situation within the framework of the following general guidelines.

After identifying the event, problem, or situation clients wish to address, the practitioner asks clients to select a word that is specific enough to remind them of the event they are discussing, but neutral enough that it does not act as a trigger for them to reexperience aspects of the trauma. A description such as "that day" might be sufficient. The practitioner might then ask them to identify the physical sensation or emotion that arises when they think about addressing the traumatic event and to assign a SUD (subjective units of distress) rating to that emotion or sensation. EFT is used until the SUD rating on the fear of discussing the event is 0. Once the client can comfortably refer to the issue without distress, the practitioner can continue the session by using EFT to target specific aspects of the issue directly.

When the Sneaking Up Technique is used for overwhelming cognitions, the practitioner simply incorporates the client's words into a Setup Statement by adding "Even though" at the beginning, and a positive affirmation such as "I deeply and completely love and accept myself" at the end. A Setup Statement might be "Even though this problem is too big for me, I deeply and completely love and accept myself," with the Reminder Phrase "this problem" or "too big." The practitioner continues to follow the client's cognitions and adjusts the Setup Statements as needed, reminding the client to report thoughts, memories, and feelings that surface during the tapping. The practitioner uses the client's language and resists adding positive language, reframing, or attempting to convince the client that the beliefs are not true. Cognitions may shift, emotions may surface, or physical sensations may result, giving the practitioner numerous options to proceed.

A related technique is called "Sneaking Away." If the client's emotional reaction appears to be escalating and it is undesirable to proceed with processing, or if the session is nearing an end, the practitioner might choose to distance the client from the topic by leading the client away from focusing on the issue. The practitioner may begin to refer to the problem in a more general way, reframe the problem in a more positive manner, or note the progress that the client has made and state a positive intention around ultimately successful processing. The practitioner may utilize other distancing techniques. The EFT practitioner might invite the client to "contain" the unresolved issue by envisioning, while tapping, the issue being put into a container that is then sealed. EMDR practitioners use containers to store charged memories between sessions (Shapiro, 2001). Setup Statements for sneaking away might include "Even though there is still some emotional charge left, I choose to put it aside for later and I accept myself."

Both the Sneaking Up and Sneaking Away Techniques recognize the importance of maintaining a client's comfort throughout a session. In her book *Creating Healing Relationships*, Hover-Kramer notes that because energy work can involve "deep intimacy of energy field interactions with clients," it is necessary to proceed with caution, curiosity, and profound respect for the client's mind-body system (2011, p. 29).

Sneaking Up: Case Studies

The Sneaking Up Technique was used with "Ross," a young teen client who was experiencing posttraumatic stress symptoms. Five years earlier, he had witnessed a violent event involving a family member. Ross was desperate for relief as nightmares and flashbacks continued. An increasing number of triggers caused panic reactions. He was no longer able to attend school. He was willing to try EFT, but terrified at the thought of starting the process, for fear of being overwhelmed while recalling the events. The practitioner assured him that sessions would progress according to his comfort, framed a successful outcome by asking how his life would change when the work was complete, and began sessions by "tapping in" resources, such as confidence and strength.

The sneaking up process began with Ross identifying a SUD level of 10 related to the *fear* of discussing the event. The practitioner used Setup Statements such as "Even though I'm afraid to talk about that night, I'm a good kid," with a Reminder Phrase of "fear," and "Even though I am terrified to even think about talking about it, I'm a good kid," with a Reminder Phrase of "terrified." Continuing the sneaking up approach with setups that addressed fear, terror, and unwillingness to address the event, Ross slowly began to reveal details of the event.

He reported three separate and distinct parts to the overall experience. The practitioner then used the sneaking up approach for each part separately, in this case choosing to start with the one Ross identified as the most troublesome. The EFT rounds included similar Setup Statements as those used for the overall event, such as "Even though I'm afraid to imagine the worst part, I'm a good kid," along with a Reminder Phrase of "I'm afraid," and "Even though I'm afraid that I'll have a panic attack if I remember it, I'm okay," with a Reminder Phrase of "panic attack."

The practitioner continued to use the sneaking up language, incorporating new information that Ross provided. Whenever a detail was revealed, such as "her face looked lifeless," a Reminder Phrase was added using Ross's words. Eventually, the practitioner began to elicit more details by asking questions during the sneaking up rounds and by modifying the Setup Statements and Reminder Phrases to include these details. Setup language continued to reflect the fear and terror of talking about the event, even though Ross was already discussing the details comfortably. One Setup was "Even though I'm afraid to talk about her face, I'm alright now." Eventually, Ross could verbalize all of the details of the event and all three parts had been processed.

The practitioner introduced the Tell the Story Technique and Ross was able to tell the entire story several times. Remaining triggers were desensitized as soon as they were identified. The sneaking up language was maintained throughout the EFT process and Ross experienced minimal emotional distress. Sneaking up was so effective that the entire event was desensitized while Ross continued to report, "I'm afraid to use any technique to address the trauma." Starting after the first session, his parents and primary therapist reported that trauma symptoms slowly but surely disappeared. The cautious teen eventually realized that no emotional charge remained. Two years later Ross reported that he had not experienced the symptoms again.

EFT practitioners can use sneaking up to target cognitions. One client expressed his belief that "The universe does not support me." After tapping on "Even though the universe does not support me, I deeply and completely love and accept myself," this client began to recount the many ways that things had worked in his favor. Another client shifted quickly from "There is nothing good about me" to "Well, I am a kind person." Another reported having absolutely no option other than staying in a dysfunctional relationship. After a few EFT rounds starting with the Setup Statement "I have no options" and "I accept myself," she reported, "I have plenty of options; I just don't like any of them."

Another client, "Bob," was trapped in an internal conflict. Bob and his wife had justified purchasing a very large home for the investment potential but also because family members needing care could move in. Bob's sister-in-law, still vital and working, was interested in moving into the extra space. Bob was conflicted about objecting and confused about his own position. He was not tuned in to emotions around the conflict but was engaged in a mental exercise that left him exhausted and trapped, without the ability to resolve the conflict. He wanted to be a supportive family member and reported, "I agreed to do it; I should want to do it; I can't say no."

The practitioner incorporated his cognitions into setups. The initial EFT Setup Statement was "Even though I have to decide now, I deeply and completely love and accept myself." After several rounds, the cognition switched to "I have no choice," and then "This isn't really what I agreed to." Eventually, after repeated rounds, the cognitions switched, reflecting Bob's clearer perspective. Bob realized that his spouse was not supporting his desire to delay the move and he felt coerced and cornered in the situation. Emotions began to surface while practitioner and client continued tapping, revealing Bob's resentment and anger.

The session began with Bob expressing limiting beliefs that kept him stuck. Addressing these limiting beliefs with the Sneaking Up Technique allowed underlying emotions and an earlier unresolved experience to surface. A family member had suffered in the past when no one was available to provide caretaking support. Once he tapped through the emotions and the unresolved event, cognitive shifts occurred. Bob reported, " I do have a choice and I can say no!"

Tearless Trauma
Tearless Trauma: Background

Like sneaking up, the Tearless Trauma Technique is based on the awareness that we have the ability to process unresolved, or improperly stored, memories while holding them in our awareness, but without fully tuning in to the memories using all of our senses. Both techniques involve distancing the client from the actual trauma to avoid emotional flooding. Whereas sneaking up distances the client by focusing on the fear of talking about the issue, tearless trauma allows the client to tune in to the trauma by distancing in a slightly different way. When using the Tearless Trauma Technique, the practitioner asks the client to *guess*, without tuning in to the event, what SUD level would result if the client were to tune in to the event.

EFT practitioners have found the Tearless Trauma Technique to be a valuable approach when training and working with groups because participants can process traumas with minimal distress and without revealing details to the group (Adams & Davidson, 2011). The Tearless Trauma Technique can be used with both groups and individuals, and is especially helpful for those who fear the emotional intensity they experience when speaking or thinking about traumatic incidents from their past.

Tearless Trauma: Guidelines

The steps for doing the Tearless Trauma Technique are as follows (EFTUniverse, n.d.):

1. Ask your client to choose a specific traumatic incident from the past to work on in this session. Request that it be one that occurred at least 3 years ago; this reduces the likelihood of a present event complicating the issue. For example, the client might say, "The time my grandfather slapped me when I was 10." Ask the client to be specific. The phrase "My grandfather abused me" is too general because the abuse may have occurred in numerous incidents. Be aware that during the session you might have to ask the client to stay with the original issue because it is natural as the original issue resolves to move on to other issues.

2. Ask your client to estimate (on a scale of 0 to 10, with 10 being the most intense) what the emotional intensity would be if he or she were to imagine the incident. Instruct the client *not* to imagine it, but simply to guess what the intensity would be if he or she did imagine it. (Despite this instruction, some close their eyes and imagine it anyway.) This estimate is useful, while allowing the client to avoid great emotional pain. Write down the client's estimate.

3. Work with the client to develop a phrase to use in the EFT process, such as "this grandfather-slap emotion." Then do a tapping round.
4. After the round, ask the client to estimate again what the intensity would be if the client were to imagine the incident. Compare that rating to the original one. It is usually a significantly lower number.
5. Do more rounds of EFT, with new intensity estimates between each one. Three or four rounds bring nearly everybody's estimate down to 0 to 3.
6. When the client's guess has dropped to an acceptably low rating, do another round of tapping. Then ask the client to imagine the incident. Note that this is the first time you have made this request (prior to this you only asked the client to guess at the emotional intensity he or she would experience *if* imagining the incident). Now ask the client to rate the emotional intensity of the incident. Most people go to 0, but if your client does not, address the remaining aspects of the incident with the Watch the Movie Technique or Tell the Story Technique.

Tearless Trauma: Case Studies

"Brenda" came for EFT on her physician's recommendation because she was continuing to experience symptoms from unresolved trauma related to having a newborn child in the neonatal intensive care unit (NICU) for 4 weeks after a premature birth. Very emotional, she was having difficulty functioning as a single working mother. She was unable to discuss the hospital experience without significant distress and was generally very tearful. Before using EFT for the hospital experience, the practitioner had Brenda tap continuously while sharing some of her history. She identified experiences in her childhood that made her feel out of control and disrespected, reactions she had felt during the hospital experience. Before addressing the highly charged hospital experience, Brenda and the practitioner used EFT on several key childhood events and used surrogate tapping for her child by imagining what the NICU experience might have been like for the newborn.

Tearless Trauma was then used for Brenda's hospital experience. The practitioner instructed her not to tune in, but to guess what the SUD rating would be if she did tune in to the NICU trauma. Brenda guessed a 10. The practitioner guided her through EFT rounds, with the Setup Statement "Even though the NICU happened, I deeply and completely love and accept myself," and a Reminder Phrase of "NICU." They used EFT's Basic Recipe, including the 9 Gamut Procedure. After several rounds, Brenda was puzzled, reporting, "I'm getting a 6. I don't know why." Her SUD level continued to drop quickly. Eventually, she guessed that she could tune in to the NICU experience without a physical or emotional reaction and reported a SUD score of 0. The practitioner guided Brenda through the Tell the Story Technique until all remaining aspects were cleared. Next they used Tearless Trauma for the emergency birth, clearing that as well. Months later, Brenda reported that she still had no negative emotional reaction to the experience and had even become a hospital volunteer, visiting with mothers of babies in the NICU.

Chasing the Pain

Chasing the Pain: Background

Chasing the Pain is a gentle technique that recognizes and takes advantage of the mind-body connection. EFT practitioners observe that emotional issues often manifest in physical form as noticeable sensations in the body, and that these body sensations "move" throughout the body when they are addressed with EFT. Emotional issues that underlie body sensations can be processed using EFT, without clients needing to identify underlying emotional issues or experience related emotional pain. Consistent with the EFT "Discovery Statement," that "the cause of all negative emotions is a disruption in the body's energy system" (Craig, 2011, p. 71), practitioners regularly observe that working on physical issues alleviates emotional issues and working on emotional issues reduces physical pain.

By focusing on physical pain rather than emotional issues, and using EFT to alleviate the pain while following or chasing it as it moves around the body, it is possible to work through issues with minimal emotional distress and discomfort. Chasing the Pain supports the possibility of long-term permanent positive trauma resolution. Because the client does not have to focus on the emotional issue, the client may feel increased confidence in continuing with emotional work, and the risk of abreactions, retraumatization, and dissociation may be decreased.

The *Diagnostic and Statistical Manual of Mental Disorders, 4th Edition (DSM-IV)* of the American Psychiatric Association recognizes the overlap of physical and psychological symptoms in various diagnoses. Body workers and mental health practitioners have incorporated knowledge of the mind-body connection successfully into their practices (Eden, 2008; Hay, 1999; Levine & Phillips, 2012; Sarno, 1991; Shapiro, 2001). Francine Shapiro, founder of Eye Movement Desensitization and Reprocessing (EMDR), refers to the concept of somatic or pain memories, where physical symptoms linger in the body because of unprocessed emotional memories (Shapiro, 2012).

Scientific research supports the existence of a "rich and intricate multidirectional communication system linking the brain, the mind, the immune system, and potentially all other systems of the body, from the heart, to the lungs, to the skin" (Borysenko, 2007, p. 14). Scientists believe that the mind-body connection is integral to memory storage. According to psychiatrist Daniel Siegel (2012), the brain forms some memories with multiple sensory representations, so that activation of one sensory aspect might cause activation of a related aspect (p. 49). For example, Siegel explains, if a person was hungry during a visit to the Eiffel Tower, it is possible that he or she might feel hungry when thinking about the Eiffel Tower. The brain may store various aspects of the visit to the Eiffel Tower together, so that the individual might also associate thoughts about the Eiffel tower with other aspects of the visit such as body sensations, sights, smells, emotional states, and body movement (p. 50).

Stephen Levine, founder of Somatic Experiencing, suggests that emotional processing can take place without conscious memory, since the information is accessible through the body. "In order to resolve any pain condition successfully, it is necessary to work always with the emotional pain aspects, as well as with the physical sensations and the thinking mind's limiting beliefs" (Levine & Phillips, 2012, p. 24). Levine supports his conclusion with reference to brain scan research indicating that when the brain receives pain signals, "three specific areas light up simultaneously; the limbic system (the emotional center), the sensory cortex (which governs sensation), and the cerebral cortex (which organizes thoughts and beliefs)" (Melzack & Wall, 1996, cited in Levine & Phillips, 2012, p. 24).

Clinical studies show that when EFT is used for psychological symptoms, physical pain improves, and when EFT is used for physical pain, psychological symptoms improve (Church, 2013). In one study, 86% of veterans with clinical levels of PTSD were subclinical after six sessions of EFT. Further analysis of the data from this study indicated that after tapping for traumatic memories, symptoms of anxiety and depression improved and pain ratings decreased (Church, 2013). In another study, participants reported a reduction in fibromyalgia pain after using EFT for emotional issues (Brattberg, 2008). Other research also documents physical improvements after the use of EFT, including cortisol reduction, pain relief, and reduction in brain frequencies associated with fear (Church, 2013).

A practitioner may find that focusing on physical pain is more effective than focusing on emotional pain in a number of situations, and may choose to use the Chasing the Pain Technique. The client might report that thinking about an issue generally produces a physical response, or the client may exhibit discomfort when addressing emotional aspects of problems. The practitioner might ask the client, "Where do you feel that in your body?" Additionally, the practitioner might notice that the client is experiencing body discomfort while discussing an emotional issue, or the client may have mentioned the presence of physical symptoms during the general information-gathering portion of the session. The client might report, "I have had a headache all day thinking about it," or "I get sick to my stomach every time I think of it," or "I have had back problems since 1999 when I got fired." Chasing the pain can also be used to minimize distress whenever a client becomes suddenly distressed during a session.

Additionally, this technique is useful for clients who are uncomfortable processing emotions. This can include veterans, others who are trained to be in control of their emotions, or those from cultures that discourage emotional expression or see it as a sign of weakness. Although these individuals may not share feelings with a therapist, they may be willing to talk about physical symptoms and pain.

The Chasing the Pain Technique, like the other gentle techniques, reduces the likelihood of abreaction and dissociation, because overwhelm is less likely when the client does not directly address aspects of an overwhelming memory. With the client's body sensations setting the pace, the likelihood of emotional comfort and safety is increased. The technique also has an added advantage of teaching the client about the mind-body connection and encouraging him or her to stay grounded and in the present moment, focusing on sensations in the body, rather than the story surrounding the distress.

Chasing the Pain: Guidelines

When using the Chasing the Pain Technique, the EFT practitioner directs the client to carefully notice the unique quality of the body's sensations and then applies EFT to address the sensation. The practitioner encourages the client to give careful attention to the qualities of the pain, using the EFT technique of specificity to describe the pain in detail. An example of a Setup Statement is: "Even though I have this sharp, pulsing, dime-size pain behind my right knee, I deeply and completely love and accept myself." As the practitioner elicits detail about the location of the pain, the client stays tuned in to the body. As the practitioner and client chase the pain as it moves around in the body, the practitioner assists the client in modifying Setup Statements and Reminder Phrases.

General guidelines are:

1. Identify a physical pain, sensation, or discomfort.
2. Assign a SUD rating to the physical experience.
3. Ask the client to articulate any features of the problem he or she can identify, including the location, color, shape, size, texture, and density of the problem.
4. Create a specific Setup Statement that uses the client's precise description of the problem and apply EFT to address the physical pain.
5. Continue with EFT rounds, refining the Setup Statement and Reminder Phrases, creatively identifying characteristics of the body pain. For example, the client might give the pain a "voice" and allow the pain to express itself.
6. Chase the pain and tap on newly identified pains until the SUD rating for each pain or issue is 0.
7. Address any emotions or core events that arise during the session.

Chasing the Pain: Case Studies

When the predominant symptom presented by a client is physical pain or sensations that occur when the client thinks about an issue, the practitioner may choose to begin by tapping on physical symptoms. One workshop volunteer, "Susan," agreed to work on stomach pain and nausea that surfaced after the previous day's workshop. She intuited that the pain might relate to an emotional issue, but the issue was unknown to her. The EFT Setup Statement and Reminder Phrase focused on "this nausea." Subsequent setups addressed the physical sensations as they moved to her shoulders, legs, and feet. The setups targeted "dull right shoulder pain," "pain shooting down my right leg," and "energy stuck in my feet."

The tapping resulted in an unexpected emotional release. Susan began to report her experience of not being supported, always having to work hard, feeling unworthy, and being discouraged from expressing emotions as a child. She discovered a deeply held belief that she was unworthy unless she worked hard. The practitioner invited Susan to continue tapping as she remained aware of her body and reported her thoughts and feelings. She eventually reported that all nausea and physical symptoms had disappeared. She reported that two significant aspects, possibly related to specific events, had cleared, but that she was unsure of exactly what they were. A month after the workshop, she reported, "I feel absolutely freer and other breakthroughs have come that go to the core of who I am."

Physical symptoms can sometimes disappear without any emotional processing. In an introductory EFT workshop, participants selected a personal issue and tapped along as the instructor worked with one individual. One participant's vertigo vanished after three EFT rounds. Another reported that she was puzzled when her persistent tennis elbow vanished after a few rounds of tapping.

Other Gentle Approaches

A practitioner may incorporate other gentle approaches into the session to minimize a client's emotional distress. Practitioners can use intuition, creativity, and other areas of expertise along with the many Clinical EFT techniques to ensure gentle processing of emotions. Experienced EFT practitioners always apply the most basic EFT rule: Once the client is tuned in, simply "keep tapping."

Continuous tapping. The practitioner invites the client to tap on EFT points while talking, without interrupting the flow of the session. The practitioner can suggest continuous tapping at any time to minimize stress. For example, this is useful when the client begins to describe a problem and the practitioner has not yet created an appropriate Setup Statement.

Global tapping. A practitioner uses a global approach to target emotions by combining and naming traumas in a general way. For example, all bullying instances might initially be grouped and processed globally.

Tapping in resources. The practitioner asks the client to identify desired resources, such as strength, confidence, and courage that will be useful during emotional processing. Using this approach, adapted from EMDR (Shapiro, 2000), the client taps while tuning in to memories of feeling the desired trait or while imagining what it would feel like to have these traits.

Dissociation and distancing. EFT practitioners use distancing and dissociation in combination with EFT techniques. Dissociation occurs when the client experiences some level of detachment from his or her emotions, cognitions, actions, or surroundings. This is generally considered an undesirable side effect of trauma and retraumatization. However, the EFT practitioner may induce simple forms of dissociation where appropriate. For example, a practitioner may suggest during the Movie Technique that the client imagine watching himself or herself watching the movie of the upsetting event. The client may also be guided to interact with "parts" to gain insight and process trauma. For example, a client may identify a "part" that is resistant to change and tap on "Even though a part of me does not want to let this go, I deeply and completely love and accept myself." Or the client may interact with child parts during emotional processing rather than experience the event directly.

A practitioner uses distancing techniques by having the client tune in to the event in a restricted way. The Tearless Trauma and Sneaking Up Techniques incorporate distancing to maintain client comfort and reduce distress. The practitioner can also use distancing during the Movie Technique by guiding the client to watch a movie of the event from behind a curtain or screen, rather than watching the movie directly. Occasionally, a client will need multiple levels of distancing. Adding a guide or resource that supports the client while she or he watches the movie creates a second level of distance. For example, the client can imagine viewing the movie with a trusted person or from a safe place. Having the client envision watching the movie from outside the building where it is playing creates a third level of distance. Having the client remove the movie to another planet creates a fourth level of distance. Clinical psychologist Fred Gallo (2007) describes additional distancing techniques: visualizing the movie dimly, upside down, in fast forward or slow motion, in black and white, or with muffled sound.

Conclusion

EFT and the gentle techniques can be used as stand-alone modalities or easily incorporated into other practices. These techniques focus on the uniqueness of a client's reaction to life experiences. When a practitioner utilizes the gentle techniques to manage a client's distress during a session, the likelihood of successful trauma resolution increases. Additionally, when clients discover that they can process emotional issues without pain, they are likely to be empowered to continue emotional work.

References

Adams, A. & Davidson, K. (2011). *EFT comprehensive training resource*. Santa Rosa, CA: Energy Psychology Press.

Borysenko, J. (2007). *Minding the body, mending the mind*. Cambridge, MA: De Capo.

Brattberg, G. (2008, August–September). Self-administered EFT (Emotional Freedom Techniques) in individuals with fibromyalgia: A randomized trial. *Integrative Medicine: A Clinician's Journal, 7*(4), 30–35.

Church, D. (2013). Reductions in pain, depression, and anxiety symptoms after PTSD remediation in veterans. *Explore: The Journal of Science and Healing* (in press).

Craig, G. (2011). *The EFT manual* (2nd ed.). Santa Rosa, CA: Energy Psychology Press.

Ecker, B., Ticic, R., & Hulley, L. (2012). *Unlocking the emotional brain: Eliminating symptoms at their roots using memory reconsolidation*. New York: Routledge.

Eden, D. (2008). *Energy medicine* (2nd ed.). New York, NY: Tarcher/Penguin.

EFT Universe. (n.d.). *EFT tutorial center: The Tearless Trauma Technique*. Retrieved from http://www.eftuniverse.com/index.php?option=com_content&view=article&id=9213

Gallo, F. (2007). *Energy tapping for trauma: Rapid relief from post-traumatic stress using energy psychology*. Oakland, CA: New Harbinger.

Hartung, J. G. & Galvin, M. D. (2002). Combining Eye Movement Desensitization and Reprocessing (EMDR) and energy therapies. In F. P. Gallo (Ed.), *Energy psychology in psychotherapy: A comprehensive sourcebook* (pp. 179–197). New York, NY: W. W. Norton.

Hay, L. (1999). *You can heal your life*. Carlsbad, CA: Hay House.

Hover-Kramer, D. (2011). *Creating Healing Relationships: Professional standards for energy therapy practitioners*. Santa Rosa, CA: Energy Psychology Press.

Levine, P. A. & Phillips, M. (2012). *Freedom from pain: Discover your body's power to overcome physical pain*. Boulder, CO: Sounds True.

Melzack, R. & Wall, P. D. (1996). *The challenge of pain*. New York, NY: Penguin.

Mollon, P. (2008). *Psychoanalytic energy psychotherapy*. London: Karnac.

Rothschild, B. (2000). *The body remembers: The psychophysiology of trauma and trauma treatment*. New York, NY: Norton.

Sarno, J. E. (1991). *Healing back pain: The mind-body connection*. New York, NY: Warner.

Schulz, K. (2009). Integrating energy psychology into treatment for adult survivors of childhood sexual abuse. *Energy Psychology: Theory, Research, & Treatment, 1*(1), 15–22.

Shapiro, F. (2001). *Eye Movement Desensitization and Reprocessing (EMDR): Basic principles, protocols, and procedures* (2nd ed.). New York, NY: Guilford.

Shapiro, F. (2012). *Getting past your past: Take control of your life with self-help techniques from EMDR therapy*. New York, NY: Rodale.

Siegel, D. J. (2012). *The developing mind: How relationships and the brain interact to shape who we are* (2nd ed.). New York, NY: Guilford.

Chapter 29
The 9 Gamut Procedure: Procedure, Evidence, Case Histories, Indications, and Clinical Refinements

Dawson Church

Abstract

Clinical EFT includes a technique derived from Thought Field Therapy called the 9 Gamut Procedure. The procedure specifies a series of eye movements, as well as exercises intended to stimulate both hemispheres of the brain. Research demonstrates that the recall of traumatic memories by clients produces anomalies in peripheral vision in the majority of psychiatric patients; these are resolved after the emotional intensity of the triggering memories has been successfully treated. Eye movements appear to assist in the reprocessing of traumatic memories, and evidence suggests that rather than placebo they are an active ingredient in therapies such as EMDR (Eye Movement Desensitization and Reprocessing) and ART (Accelerated Resolution Therapy). The 9 Gamut Procedure is used with EFT's Full Basic Recipe, between two sequences of EFT tapping. Three case studies, as well as a description of the procedure, are presented here. Indications for the use of the 9 Gamut Procedure include: disturbing emotions that can't be linked to a specific event, womb trauma, birth trauma, traumatic incidents that occurred very early in a person's life before memory formation began, many similar traumatic events, core beliefs not linked to a specific event, persistent behaviors for which a basis in actual events cannot be found, when the available time frame for a session is limited, and when a client's distress does not diminish using the short version of EFT's Basic Recipe. Further clinical refinements to maximize the impact of the procedure, as well as hypotheses for future research on the 9 Gamut, are presented.

Keywords: 9 gamut point, 9 gamut procedure, nine gamut, eye movements, humming, trauma, resistance, peripheral vision, traumatic events, memory reprocessing

Dawson Church is a health writer and researcher in the field of energy medicine. He is author of the award-winning best-seller *The Genie in Your Genes*, editor of the peer-reviewed professional journal *Energy Psychology*, executive director of the National Institute for Integrative Healthcare (niih.org), and CEO of Energy Psychology Group (EFTuniverse.com). Send correspondence to Dawson Church, 334 Fulton Road, #442, Fulton, CA 95439, or dawsonchurch@gmail.com. The author receives income from books and speaking engagements on the approach described in this chapter.

The 9 Gamut Procedure (Callahan, 1985) is believed to engage parts of the brain involved in the nonverbal resolution of trauma. It involves eye movements, humming, and counting. It includes behaviors designed to engage both the left and right hemispheres of the brain, as well as eye movements. The 9 Gamut Procedure is part of EFT's Full Basic Recipe (Church, 2013). It involves nine actions performed while tapping a point called the "Gamut" point located on the Triple Warmer acupuncture meridian on the back of the hand.

Location Within EFT Techniques

The Full Basic Recipe is an expanded version of the Basic Recipe used in Clinical EFT. The simpler Basic Recipe omits the 9 Gamut Procedure and also omits tapping on the hand points described in the Full Basic Recipe. In the Full Basic Recipe, the 9 Gamut Procedure is used immediately after the initial tapping sequence described in the Basic Recipe, that is: First Tapping Sequence, 9 Gamut, Second Tapping Sequence.

Because the Full Basic Recipe takes longer, around 2 minutes, while the Basic Recipe takes under a minute, the Full Basic Recipe isn't used unless a client is failing to make progress as measured by their subjective units of distress (SUD) score (Wolpe, 1973). The 9 Gamut stands alone and can be used in conjunction with, or independent of, EFT's Basic Recipe. Clinical experience has shown that the 9 Gamut is particularly useful with certain classes of psychological trauma (detailed later in this chapter).

The Evidence Base

Research shows that eye movements such as those prescribed in the 9 Gamut Procedure are instrumental in reprocessing old traumatic memories. The University of South Florida (USF) conducted a study of people with posttraumatic stress disorder (PTSD) and depression, using a novel psychotherapeutic method called ART or Accelerated Resolution Therapy (Kip et al., 2012). ART uses eye movements and has a client perform these while thinking about an emotionally triggering event. Researchers using ART found that the emotional charge held in such memories of traumatic events was rapidly reduced by eye movements. ART concludes by having clients pair the eye movements with the imagination of a desired outcome. According to the descriptions of the study, "the patient fluctuates between talking about a traumatic scene, and using the eye movements to help process that information to integrate the memories from traumatic events. The two major components of ART include minimizing or eliminating physiological response associated traumatic memories, and re-envisioning painful or disturbing experiences…" (Hudak, 2012). Participants in the study experienced dramatic drops in PTSD and depression symptoms, as well as improved sleep.

Other Clinical EFT Techniques such as the floor to ceiling eye roll (Feldenkrais, 1984) also use eye movements to reduce emotional distress. Bandler and Grinder (1979) believed that lateral eye movements correlate with aspects of experience such as internal dialogue, kinesthetic sensations, and imagery.

A study confirming the link between eye movements and PTSD involved a collaboration between a psychiatrist and an ophthalmologist (Tym, Beaumont, & Lioulios, 2009). They studied 100 patients, and found that those with PTSD had persistent difficulty maintaining the stability of their peripheral vision while contemplating a traumatic event. After successful psychiatric treatment, however, the eye fluttering disappeared, and they were able to recall the event without either emotional distress or visual impairment. According to another published report, 90% of psychiatric patients have these visual anomalies (Tym, Dyck, & McGrath, 2000). After World War II, an ophthalmologist described visual disturbances in soldiers with what we now call PTSD (Traquair, 1946, p. 282).

Neuroscientists don't know exactly why this association between traumatic memories and eye movements occurs. It may be linked to the ability of the brain to process a disturbing event. The midbrain or limbic system contains structures that are responsible for turning short-term memories into long-term ones. This memory processing function is impaired in patients suffering from PTSD. In discussing this theory, an article in *Scientific American* (Rodriguez, 2013) summarized how research into EMDR (Eye Movement Desensitization and Reprocessing; Shapiro, 1989), a therapy which is as effective as EFT for PTSD (Karatzias et al., 2011), demonstrates that the eye movements are an active ingredient of the therapy and not an inert placebo.

Following are three case histories from the story archives on EFT Universe (EFTuniverse.com) showing uses of the 9 Gamut technique.

Case History 1: Fast Pain Relief

By Pete Hawk

I've been introducing EFT to a few coworkers during slow periods (mainly during night shift). The other night one was in terrible pain since she had been doing lots of exercise to a workout video at home. She was walking around the room very slowly, saying it felt like she was learning to use her legs for the first time.

She was saying, "Man, I need a massage, like *now*!" Finally, after hearing this a few times, I said, "If you are open to it, I can help with a really neat experimental therapy that will just take a few minutes and will most likely work wonders for you." She said, "Yeah!" So after getting her pain intensity level of 8 out in the open, we started tapping.

I told her to "just do what I do."
"Even though my legs are in so much pain right now…" (x2)
"Even though I may have pushed myself too hard while exercising…"

We did three complete rounds including the 9 Gamut, and I then asked her to stand up and walk. Here are her exact words:
"No f'ing way! Oh my God! Oh my God! That's amazing! It's like a 2 now! I can't believe it!"

I asked if she wanted to keep going to get it down to a 0, but she was so happy that a 2 was good enough and easy to live with. I told her it didn't matter if she believed in it or not, it "just works." Even while doing the tapping she was so doubtful and skeptical that it wouldn't work "for her." The whole thing was over in less than 10 minutes. She didn't need a massage anymore.

Case History 2: Excessive Emotionality in a Brain-Damaged Child

By Tana Clark

I am an EFT practitioner and have a daughter who is brain damaged from birth. She did not get enough oxygen due to the cord around her neck for a lengthy time. I work with her almost on a daily basis with EFT. She can become very emotional at times, and it seems to take her hours to get over it. I have tapped with her on many occasions for this problem. I noticed that if I did not do the Gamut point, she didn't seem to settle down.

Finally, I just started doing the Gamut point when she "got stuck in the right brain." Now when she gets stuck, we immediately do a sequence and the 9 Gamut Procedure, and have 100% success rate to evaporate her emotion. When people get extremely emotional and can't seem to find a way out, they are stuck in the right brain.

Many people have problems being stuck in the right brain, and many of us have had the experience where we just can't stop crying. Doing the eye movements keeps our brain moving from right brain to left brain to right brain. It helps the brain work together instead of being stuck in one side.

Not too long ago I met a mother in the grocery store who had a 13-year-old boy with her. He was crying and carrying on much like my daughter does when she is "stuck." I waited until I could talk to her alone. By this time the boy had settled down, so I explained what I do, and gave her a quick lesson in EFT.

She said that her son has special needs, and the doctor says that when he acts that way, he is stuck in the right brain. I showed her what to do, and she was very excited to try it with him. I also used it for a teenager whose family was moving; she was very upset about it and kept crying and crying. No amount of setup and sequence helped her feel less emotional. We moved to the 9 Gamut Procedure and, like magic, the tears dried up.

Using the shortcut, we often leave out the 9 Gamut Procedure. But if there is a large amount of emotion, it is extremely helpful. I couldn't do without it.

Case History 3: Resolution of Vertigo and a Car Crash Memory in a Phone Session

By Edward Miner

I am a hypnotherapist and am always looking for better ways to help people get over their problems. Last evening, I talked with my sister, who lives in another state, about a condition of severe vertigo. She was in a minor automobile accident 2 weeks ago, experienced whiplash, and several days later started experiencing the vertigo.

I just got off the phone with her and want to report that she was symptom free when I hung up.

In all it took about 15 minutes to explain EFT and run through it about four times, testing between each run. I initially started the set up with "Even though I have this vertigo and dizziness I completely love and accept myself," but didn't see much movement. I adjusted to "Even though I have this vertigo and dizziness, I completely forgive myself or anyone else who may have contributed to it." After a run-through and a 9 Gamut Procedure, she was experiencing no symptoms. I had her move around a lot more and she found that when she tipped her head back, she still had a dizzy feeling, but the rotation was slower. When I asked her if the feeling had an emotion, she said "annoyance," so we tapped on "the annoyance emotion." Subsequent SUD testing could find no more feelings of dizziness. She was amazed because she said that this was the worst time of day, just before she went to bed, and just prior to taking her medicine.

I told her that I didn't know if it would last, but that now she has a way to handle the symptoms in less than 5 minutes.

I've been sold since I started working on myself. However, this newcomer is elated because I was able to hear the healing happen more than 700 miles from where I was sitting as I talked her through the process.

Indications

Experience with tens of thousands of clients has shown the 9 Gamut Procedure to be effective even when the other parts of EFT's Basic Recipe are unable to provide resolution to a problem. The previous cases histories are typical. In the first one, the client has generalized leg pain without any obvious emotional component. In the second, a mother finds that her brain-damaged daughter's excessive emotionality is calmed by the 9 Gamut Procedure. In the third, vertigo that has affected a client since an auto accident is resolved in a phone session. It is likely that many different aspects of the car crash, and possibly the leg pain, were addressed at the same time by the 9 Gamut.

For these reasons, during Clinical EFT training and certification, the 9 Gamut is emphasized; slow eye movements covering every point in the field of peripheral vision are found to be particularly valuable. The following are particular indications to use the 9 Gamut Procedure:

- Disturbing emotions that can't be linked to a specific event.
- Traumatic incidents that occurred very early in a person's life, before memory formation began (age 5 and earlier).
- When there are a great many similar traumatic events, such as frequent childhood beatings, many battlefield memories.
- Womb trauma. Stress hormones such as cortisol and adrenaline cross the placental barrier; a child may be "learning" stress at the level of molecular conditioning even before birth.
- Core beliefs (such as "I'm not lovable" or "The world is not a safe place") that cannot easily be linked to specific events.
- Persistent behaviors for which a basis in actual events cannot be found, such as procrastination, lateness, irrational fear and irritation, disproportionate anger, and similar patterns.
- When the available time frame for a session is limited.
- Clients whose SUD level is not going down using EFT's shortcut Basic Recipe.

Procedure

To begin the 9 Gamut Procedure, you first locate the Gamut point. It is on the back of either hand a halfinch below the midpoint between the knuckles at the base of the ring finger and the little finger. If you draw an imaginary line between the knuckles at the base of the ring finger and little finger and consider that line to be the base of an equilateral triangle whose other sides converge to a point (apex) in the direction of the wrist, then the Gamut point would be located at the apex of the triangle. With the index finger of your tapping hand, feel for a small indentation on the back of your tapped hand near the base of the little finger and ring finger. There is just enough room there to tap with the tips of your index and middle fingers.

Next, you perform nine different steps while tapping the Gamut point continuously. These nine steps are:

1. Eyes closed.
2. Eyes open.
3. Eyes down hard right while holding the head steady.

4. Eyes down hard left while holding the head steady.
5. Roll the eyes in a circle as though your nose is at the center of a clock and you are trying to see all the numbers in order.
6. Roll the eyes in a circle in the reverse direction.
7. Hum 2 seconds of a song (such as "God Save the Queen" or "Happy Birthday").
8. Count rapidly from 1 to 5.
9. Hum 2 seconds of a song again.

The nine actions can be performed in any order, except that the last three, humming, counting, and humming again, should be performed in that sequence. It's easier for client and practitioner to perform them in the sequence described here since this avoids having to remember which ones have been performed. If a song arouses negative associations (for example, "Happy Birthday" may awaken memories of unhappy birthdays), an emotionally neutral song should be chosen.

Clinical Refinements

I have found that when administering the 9 Gamut as a practitioner, it is extremely important to observe the client's eye rotation. Clients can persistently jump over some portion of the visual field. For instance, I worked with a client with a close relationship with her father and a distant relationship with her mother. Her father had died recently, and her core belief, compounded by a recent divorce, was "I'm all alone." The strength of her cognition around this belief was a 10. Though she had begun the session presenting with a minor issue having to do with a coworker, her more fundamental layers of grief began to surface involuntarily.

When doing the 9 Gamut, this particular client's eyes persistently skipped over the lower right quadrant of her peripheral vision. She was also crying uncontrollably and unable to tap or follow directions as she began to feel her grief deeply in the safe environment of the EFT session. Complicating matters, we only had 15 minutes in which to complete the session, which is why I emphasized the 9 Gamut in this case.

Observing her inability to view one quadrant, I used my hand to guide her. I asked her to follow my hand with her eyes while I slowly described a large circle with my fingertips. She still skipped over the same quadrant. I slowed down further, and moved my fingers through the part of the arc she had trouble viewing until she was able to complete the entire circle. I had her say, "I'm all alone," periodically as a Reminder Phrase. I then reversed direction, and spent a minute or two working on only the problematic quadrant, going in both directions. Eventually, she exhibited many physiological signs of stress relief, such as sighing, a relaxation of the trapezius muscles in her shoulders, yawning, and deeper breathing. Her SUD numbers dropped slowly and steadily.

Out of time, I tested her level of intensity on the cognition "I'm all alone." She smiled and told me she has a great group of friends and two sisters with whom she's close, and that she feels stronger for having survived divorce.

Some clients are unable to perform the 9 Gamut Procedure without such a visual reference from a practitioner's fingertips. Because EFT is primarily a self-help technique in which the power of transformation should rest in the client and not the practitioner, my preference is to encourage clients to perform the 9 Gamut on their own as soon as possible. However, clients typically have difficulty in perceiving when their eyes are skipping over a particular area of their peripheral vision. Even when asked to notice and correct for this, many clients are unable to do so.

For this reason, clients usually find the 9 Gamut easier when a practitioner leads them through the procedure. This can be successful even if the session is being conducted over the phone, as in Case History 3. The procedure is straightforward enough that a verbal description by a practitioner is sufficient for a geographically distant client to perform it. Distant sessions with visual contact such as delivered by Skype, Google Plus, or Facetime are easier since the client can follow the practitioner's eye movements, and the practitioner can see whether the client is following the procedure.

The old model of memory believed that memory was static, like taking a picture out of a photo album, looking at it, and putting it back in the album unchanged. New models of brain function, however, show that when we recall a memory, we might associate the memory with cues from the present. For example, the memory of a rape might be terrifying for a client to remember alone. When told to a sympathetic therapist in a safe setting, elements of the current setting may be incorporated into the emotional content of a memory.

This phenomenon, called memory reconsolidation, is well understood (Arden, 2013).

I believe that subsequent research will show that something similar is happening when clients perform the 9 Gamut Procedure. Research tools such as fMRI and magnetoencephalograph, which identify the areas of the brain that are active during recall of a memory, show activation of the fear centers of the midbrain during the recollection of a traumatic event. It's likely that these areas will show a reduction or even complete extinction of these neurological patterns after the 9 Gamut.

For these many clinical reasons, backed by the emerging science linking eye movements to memory reconsolidation, the 9 Gamut is an essential part of every Clinical EFT practitioner's toolkit.

References

Arden, J. (2013). PTSD, neurodynamics and memory. In D. Church & S. Marohn (Eds.), *The clinical EFT handbook*, Vol 1. Santa Rosa, CA: Energy Psychology Press.

Bandler, R. & Grinder, J. (1979). *Frogs into princes: Neuro linguistic programming.* Moab, UT: Real People.

Callahan, R. (1985). *Five minute phobia cure: Dr. Callahan's treatment for fears, phobias, and self-sabotage.* Blair, NE: Enterprise.

Church, D. (2013). The EFT manual (3rd ed.). Santa Rosa, CA: Energy Psychology.

Feldenkrais, M. (1984). *The master moves.* Cupertino, CA: Meta Publications.

Hudak, A. (2012). Accelerated Resolution Therapy shows dramatic reductions in PTSD symptoms, USF Nursing study reports. *USF Health.* Retrieved from http://hscweb3.hsc.usf.edu/blog/2012/07/26/accelerated-resolution-therapy-shows-dramatic-reductions-in-ptsd-symptoms-usf-nursing-study-reports

Karatzias, T., Power, K., Brown, K., McGoldrick, T., Begum, M., Young, J., ... Adams, S. (2011). A controlled comparison of the effectiveness and efficiency of two psychological therapies for posttraumatic stress disorder: Eye Movement Desensitization and Reprocessing vs. Emotional Freedom Techniques. *Journal of Nervous and Mental Disease, 199*(6), 372–378. doi:10.1097/NMD.0b013e31821cd262

Kip, K. E., Elk, C. A., Sullivan, K. L., Kadel, R., Lengacher, C. A., Long, C. J., ... & Diamond, D. M. (2012). Brief treatment of symptoms of post-traumatic stress disorder (PTSD) by use of Accelerated Resolution Therapy (ART). *Behavioral Sciences, 2*(2), 115–134. doi:10.3390/bs2020115

Rodriguez, T. (2013, January 18). Can eye movements treat trauma? Recent research supports the effectiveness of eye movement desensitization and reprocessing. *Scientific American.* Retrieved from http://www.scientificamerican.com/article.cfm?id=can-eye-movements-treat-trauma

Shapiro, F. (1989) Eye movement desensitization and reprocessing: A new treatment for posttraumatic stress disorder. *Journal of Behaviour Therapy and Experimental Psychiatry, 20,* 211–217.

Traquair, H. M. (1946). *An introduction to clinical perimetry* (5th ed.). London, UK: Henry Kimpton.

Tym, R., Beaumont, P., & Lioulios, T. (2009). Two persisting pathophysiological visual phenomena following psychological trauma and their elimination with rapid eye movements: a possible refinement of construct PTSD and its visual state marker. *Traumatology, 15*(3), 23–33.

Tym, R., Dyck, M. J., & McGrath, G. (2000). Does a visual perceptual disturbance characterize trauma-related anxiety syndromes? *Journal of Anxiety Disorders, 14*(4), 377–394.

Wolpe, J. (1973). *The practice of behavior therapy* (2nd ed.). New York, NY: Pergamon Press.

Chapter 30
Reframing the Problem
Ann Adams

Abstract

Reframing can be an effective tool when used with Emotional Freedom Techniques (EFT) to modify cognitions around an event. The concept of reframing comes from neuro-linguistic programing (NLP) and cognitive behavior therapy (CBT). Reframing is the process of changing the perception of a situation so that it is neutralized or viewed as positive rather than negative. Reframing changes the meaning of an event, person, or relationship. The process of reframing in EFT is often misunderstood and misused, by both experienced and inexperienced practitioners. Reframes are not critical to the successful use of EFT, but the ability to fully integrate reframing can increase EFT's speed and effectiveness. Appropriate reframes can be used at the beginning of a session to reinforce currently unacknowledged positive attributes and strengths and at the end of a session when the emotional intensity is low and acceptance of a different perspective is more likely. Reframes can be divided into conservative and bold categories. This chapter clarifies reframing, gives the steps for the effective use of reframing, defines the most common reframes, and offers examples for each type. The chapter also provides questions for checking the accuracy of the reframe as well as simplified approaches for presenting reframes successfully.

Keywords: EFT, reframing, types of reframes

There is no torment that cannot be solved by simply reframing the problem.
—Kaja Perina (2012)

Ann Adams, LCSW, teaches EFT and mentors practitioners internationally. She created EFT4PowerPoint.com, a comprehensive training program used by EFT trainers all over the world, coauthored *EFT Comprehensive Training Resource: Level 1 (& 2)*, and codirected the EFT Masters Program. Send correspondence to: Ann Adams, 46 Ridgeview Drive, Silver Creek, GA 30173, or master@eft4powerpoint.com.

Early in life we begin to make decisions about the world and ourselves. These decisions help us make sense of the world and constitute the "frame" through which we observe the world. We often use only a portion of the total available facts in any situation to make assumptions and presuppositions about the total meaning. This can be a useful coping mechanism, as it helps us make decisions quickly about a situation and move on without having to reevaluate everything that happens. Our frame influences how we react to and think about occurrences in our lives. The frame can be positive or negative, accurate or inaccurate.

EFT takes the concept of reframing from neuro-linguistic programing (NLP) and cognitive behavior therapy (CBT). Developed in the 1970s, NLP was the culmination of studying what highly effective therapists actually did to foster change in clients' behavior and beliefs. One of the noted effective similarities among these experts was reframing. Reframing is a very old concept; it's been around for at least as long as fairy tales. The story of the Ugly Duckling provides a classic example of reframing. When the young bird looked at himself through a different "frame," he was a beautiful swan instead of an ugly duckling.

Reframing is based on the idea that the meaning of anything depends on the point of view. When we view an event from a different setting, context, or frame, its meaning changes. When we change the meaning, our response to the event, our behaviors, and even our thinking and beliefs around the event can change as well.

What we feel, think, and do is the result of what we believe about ourselves and the world around us. Our beliefs shape how we assess what is happening to us and around us. Our assessments are often efficient, as our interpretations guide us, without much conscious thought, as to how we should respond, thereby saving time and energy in evaluating or reevaluating everything that happens. Sometimes, however, these interpretations or evaluations create emotional or behavioral responses that are harmful or painful to us; that is, we suffer when we don't need to suffer. This concept is foundational in EFT and several traditional therapies, including cognitive behavior therapy (CBT), which, like NLP, was developed in the 1970s.

CBT employs a technique called cognitive restructuring (Binggeli, 2010), which uses reason, logic, and evidence to help clients become curious about and more aware of their cognitions (i.e., what they are telling themselves). As they are aware of a feeling or belief, they ask themselves reality-based questions such as: "What am I saying to myself as I am feeling this emotion? What facts do I have to support this thought?" The goal of CBT is to replace distorted thinking with more accurate, believable, and useful thinking, in essence, reframing it. One challenge to this process is that people often already know their thinking is distorted and that their reactions to an event are not reasonable to the situation, but they seem unable to change it.

Though EFT does not ignore cognitions, it focuses instead on balancing the energy of the emotion involved with the belief, cognition, and behavior. When this energy balance occurs, the emotion is neutralized and cognitions change to more adaptive thoughts, which leads to more adaptive behaviors.

A key goal of most therapists regardless of the modality used is to assist clients in gaining a healthier, more positive perception of their problems and, in so doing, work toward more adaptive coping skills. It is not what happens to us that upsets us; it is how we *perceive* that event that is the source of the upset. The goal of reframing is to shift how we look at or feel about a situation with the purpose of having a more useful response to it. An appropriate reframe delivered at the appropriate time while tapping often creates a new way of evaluating the situation that fits the actual events of the situation, as well as or even better than the earlier perception, or frame. An effective reframe changes the meaning of an event or situation, while the actual facts of the situation remain the same.

Skillful reframes, plus good timing, make it possible to impact and change what we previously thought was reality. We are able to use additional facts to reassess the situation. We use this concept when talking with our friends. Isn't part of the empathy we share with our friends a way to help them see their upset from a different perspective, more positive and focused toward problem solving? On the downside, we also may attempt to reframe someone's point of view in an attempt to persuade that person to our viewpoint. This is a risk to watch for as you work with a client, a risk that decreases as you tap away your own issues and misperceptions.

How do we keep our suggested reframes in the client's best interest and, in addition, keep from imposing our own views, values, perceptions, and prejudices? After all, each of us has our own frames for making meaning out of the world. The answer is that EFT is client centered; we focus on using the client's words and stories as we tap. Skilled reframers who have consistently worked on their own issues are able to grasp quickly a client's existing "frame" and use that information to help change the client's perception with additional information not previously observed. Timely reframes that "land" with clients can quickly change their view of the situation and of themselves. The reframing of an event, incident, or issue by the person who experienced the event may be critical to resolving it. But is the practitioner sharing the right reframe, at the right moment, critical to clients' ability to reframe their issues? The answer is no. EFT conducted thoroughly can resolve all of the aspects of the issue and create the internal peace and calm that allows clients to form a reframe—by themselves. Certainly, "the right reframe offered at the right time encourages the shift and speeds the process" (Adams & Davidson, 2011), but it is the client that makes the shift.

An accurate reframe made by a practitioner can be helpful and speed the healing process, but reframes by the practitioner are by no means critical. Further, when it comes to reframing, it pays to be cautious. Poorly timed reframes, or reframes that follow the practitioner's agenda versus the client's agenda, can slow the healing process. Rapport may be lost. Clients may feel they did not live up to the practitioner's expectations or, worse, may feel so misunderstood or manipulated that they leave and don't come back, generally without telling the practitioner why.

Before You Reframe

The actual reframing of any situation is up to the client, not the practitioner. When someone has cleared all the aspects around an issue, a new perspective or a reframing of that issue occurs, generally very naturally. The critical part for the practitioner is to help the client identify and resolve all the aspects around the issue, including the emotions.

This approach should be reassuring to both persons new to the EFT field and experienced practitioners. Indeed, it may reframe how you look at reframing! After all, it is a little grandiose of us to entertain the idea that another's perception of an issue can only be changed by a brilliant reframe from the EFT practitioner.

The key task for the practitioner is making sure that the client clears all the aspects, parts, and pieces of an issue. Realizing that reframing in EFT can happen naturally and is not essential may help remove the pressure from you of feeling that you *must* create a reframe. The EFT basics work very well without any reframes.

When learning any new skill, it helps to become very comfortable with the basics before moving on to more advanced concepts or attempting to modify the "rules" of the skill.

What this means in EFT is:

- Become very good at the basics before beginning to use reframes.
- Get comfortable using the client's language and story in your Setups and Reminder Phrases.
- Learn to identify the "frame" the client has of the world.

For those of you who would like to become better at reframing, the approaches detailed in the following sections will help you create reframes that fit your clients. Keep in mind that your job is to discover how each client's specific issue is currently "framed" and to decrease its intensity—to a minimum of 3 on the SUD scale—before you even think about offering a reframe. Both timing and accuracy are important for a reframe to be fully accepted.

Using Reframes at the Beginning of a Session

Although reframes are most often used toward the end of resolving a specific event, they may also be used at the beginning of a session to reinforce clients' willingness to work on their issues. Reframing the acceptance part of the Setup begins to reframe their self-view and show a more solid reason for accepting themselves and their issues. Some clients come with such a lack of self-acceptance that they have difficulty saying the standard Setup, *"I deeply and completely accept myself."* The following gentle reframes used where appropriate at the beginning of a session sidestep their resistance:

> *Even though I have all these problems and I'm not sure where to start, I recognize that I have the courage to begin the process of looking for solutions to these problems.*

> *Even though I have so many negative feelings that they overwhelm me, I can at least give myself credit for taking the first step.*
>
> *Even though I am very afraid to look at this event, I can take my time and realize I control how much and how fast to go.*
>
> *Even though my life is a mess and I don't even know where to begin, I can appreciate that I am sitting here with this EFT person and am willing to try something new to increase peace in my life.*

In these examples, we are using the more general presenting problem, for example, that their life is not going well or is overwhelming, and we are still working on establishing rapport and a place of safety. This is a variation on the "rules" for reframes, as you are not yet working on a specific event.

The "Rules" for Reframing

First, you gather enough information about the client's issue to get to a specific event related to the presenting problem.

Second, you use words and phrases from the client's story to create a meaningful Setup and include an acceptance phrase that the client will actually accept.

The default acceptance phrase is *"I deeply and completely accept myself."* Some practitioners add even more to this, for example, *"and I love and respect myself."* If, however, our clients actually deeply and completely accepted, loved, and respected themselves, I doubt they'd be sitting in our offices. Can you tell them, "Just say it anyway"? You can, but I'm of the persuasion that, saying it does not make it so—even with tapping. A key goal in working with people is to respect where they are now.

It deepens rapport and trust to work on an acceptance statement clients feel is true for them in the moment. I often remind my clients that we are only *asking for acceptance for this one moment in time*. We are not asking them to accept everything about themselves forever. Initially, you can use a variation of *"Even though I have such a hard time getting through life and feel like such a failure, I can accept for one moment right this very second that I could be okay."* Or *"I can accept that at least x% of me could possibly be okay."*

Using these types of acceptance reframes gives you great practice in reframing the problem after the client's intensity is down to 3 or lower on the SUD scale.

Third, reframes are most effective when clients have decreased their intensity to a 3 or below. As long as the intensity remains above a 3, concentrate on using words from their story and checking to ensure you have covered all the aspects involved. Sometimes this happens with amazing speed; other times, significant detective work is necessary to uncover the issues that are keeping the intensity high.

Fourth, the last "rule" for sharing reframes is to develop a Setup phrase that begins just like any other Setup—acknowledging the issue—then add a reframe in place of the acceptance statement. Good reframes that land are built from listening closely to how the client frames the issue and offering a timely alternative that makes sense to the client. We use lots of Setups and Reminder Phrases that are exactly the client's words or a paraphrase of the client's words. Reframes, in contrast, are most often your own words, your gift of a different way for the client to look at, or frame, the issue.

Conservative Reframes

A conservative reframe is a statement that will likely be easy for a client to accept, a generic statement that addresses the obvious in a way not yet considered. Generic statements such as these could explain many situations:

> *I was doing the best I could.*
> *Maybe they were doing the best they could.*
> *I was just a child. That strategy worked great when I was 3, but I have better strategies to pick from now.*
> *She had a lot of problems. He was a wounded soul.*
> *The accident wasn't my fault. I was just there.*
> *Of course, I make mistakes—like the rest of the human race.*
> *I can begin to understand what may have caused this.*
> *That happened a long time ago and I survived.*
> *That was then; this is now.*
> *Even though I am terrified there will be a fire in the house, I can be cautious instead of fearful.*

Always, always check with the client about the appropriateness and correctness of any reframe, whenever it may be used, as to its meaning for the client. For example, you could ask:

- Does that fit?
- Is that right?
- Is that how you see this now?
- What would be more accurate?

As a practitioner, you will want to know if your reframe "landed," meaning that the client accepted the reframe. Sometimes you can tell immediately by watching the body language. Did they recoil, lean back, roll their eyes, shake their head, smile, nod, or exhibit any other physical response—pro or con. Some will tell you outright whether the reframe fit or not. Keep in mind that clients will not always tell you. This is particularly true of clients who have never felt they lived up to others' expectations. They may even agree when they really don't agree. To quote John Morley, "You have not converted a man because you have silenced him." These are key reasons to keep rapport, go at a client's pace and always check for appropriateness. Just because EFT can resolve things quickly does not mean we should go as fast as EFT can go.

It is more conservative, and therefore easier for a client to accept, to use conditional words such as: *maybe, I'll consider, someday I might, it might be possible to, I'll think about, but not yet.* Such languaging makes it easier for the client to feel comfortable in either accepting or rejecting the reframe. A reframe offered with respect and rapport, whether accepted or rejected, can simply give you and your client more information with which to continue your session.

Bold Reframes

Bold reframes ask for a bigger change in perception, making them more of a challenge for the client to accept. Some categories of reframes, which often overlap, are:

- **Pointing out patterns.** This reframing approach gives insight into similarities between the current event and other times the client experienced the same emotion or behavior. Memories are often connected to other events that brought up similar emotions. Pointing out patterns may also be used when someone is not fully ready to let something go. Here are some examples of this type of reframe:
  - *Even though it makes me crazy when my boyfriend tries to solve all my problems, I realize he is pushing all the same buttons as my father.*
  - *Even though I do a slow burn in meetings when my coworkers interrupt me, it reminds me of how I felt when my teacher allowed my classmates to interrupt me.*
  - *Even though I still want to blame the government for all my money problems, I can let go of just this one part of the story.*
  - *Even though my mother never accepted me for who I am and constantly kept correcting me, maybe it was her misguided attempt to protect me from the world.*
  - *Even though I'm still holding onto the anger because he robbed me of everything important to me, now it's me that is robbing myself of peace in my life.*
- **Good-natured humor.** Taking a belief or perception and pointing out the humor or ridiculous nature of it can bring healing to it. Laughter is indeed good medicine. Sometimes reducing the situation to the ridiculous can enable a rapid cognitive shift. Once again, be cautious; humorous reframes can backfire. Be sure of strong rapport and client readiness before you introduce reframes like these:
  - *Even though I react to this the same way I did in first grade, I realize I am taking the problem-solving advice of a 6-year-old.*
  - *Even though I'm responsible whenever anything bad happens—I'm so powerful I can even cause earthquakes and tornados…*
- **Understanding and readiness to forgive.** Understanding where the other person, or yourself, was coming from when the event occurred is important in releasing the negative energy and emotions around the event. When the emotions are down to a 0, understanding, and even forgiveness, often happens naturally. Forgiveness means different things to different people. Before you use the word forgiveness

in a reframe, it is helpful to know what forgiveness means to the client. Forcing forgiveness before the client is ready is a sure way to lose that client, temporarily if not permanently. Here are some examples of this type of reframe:

- *Even though she wrote that nasty e-mail, I realize she has her own problems.*
- *Even though my dad beat me, and that will never be okay, I realize he was operating on his own experiences and internal demons.*
- *Even though the old man died in the fire, I realize I am not responsible, I was just there.*
- *Even though my mother won't speak to me now, I realize she has mental problems and is acting in ways to protect herself, given what she thinks and believes.*
- *Even though my brother beat me up for no reason, I can forgive him now because he was reacting to the beatings my father gave him.*

• **Addressing the client's role.** Using conditional words such as *"I can think about forgiving him," "I can entertain the possibility that..."* and *"I can accept that she had her own reasons that had nothing to do with me"* make it even easier for the client to accept the reframe. At times, accepting responsibility for our own response to a situation is necessary before we can move on. Reframes such as the following can help clients acknowledge their role:

- *Even though my sister embarrassed me on prom night, it is my reaction to her words that hurts.*
- *I am not upset about what happened, after all it's not happening anymore; I'm upset by my memory of it.*
- *Even though I've been grieving for over 40 years and I know that he would not want me to do that, I am using my feelings to protect me from getting hurt again.*

After listening carefully to the client's story and gaining perspective on the frame he or she uses in the world, the best reframes seem to come from the practitioner's intuition. Some of my very best, perfectly timed and totally accurate, reframes were a surprise. Coming up with such reframes is amazing to me because I have no idea where such intuitive reframes originate; they are not conscious thought. Intuition is the ability to "get out of our own way" so that we can hear that quiet little voice in our heads—our intuitive guidance. Intuition is best developed by doing our own work to deal with our issues, paying close attention to the client, and gaining experience in listening and trusting our internal guidance. Hearing and trusting our intuition is easier the less interference we have from our own issues. The best EFT practitioners make a daily practice of using EFT for themselves to decrease or eliminate the chance they could be pushing their own agenda.

Conclusion

Reframes are not critical to successful use of EFT; however, reframes can be both a challenging and highly rewarding part of using EFT. The type of reframe you use depends on the situation, the client, the context, and the story. Pay close attention to your client, develop and deepen rapport, learn to ask good questions, don't be in a hurry, use EFT daily for your own issues, and become skilled at using EFT before you add reframes.

References

Adams, A., & Davidson, K. (2011). *EFT comprehensive training resource: Level 2.* Fulton, CA: Energy Psychology Press.

Binggeli, N. (2010, February 5). CBT techniques, part 1: Cognitive restructuring. Retrieved from http://www.nelson-binggeli.net/NB/CBT-CR.html

Perina, K. (2012, September–October). Life lessons from PT gurus and those who've taught us well. *Psychology Today, 45*(5), 3.

Chapter 31
Daisy Chaining
Valerie Lis

Abstract

An EFT session will often unfold into a series of memories and events (metaphorically, each memory or event is the center of a daisy), each with related aspects (the petals around each daisy center). The series or string of "daisies" emerging one after another in an EFT session is termed "daisy chaining." Daisy chaining occurs naturally, as when the client experiences a reduction in the subjective units of distress (SUD) level of the initial issue and spontaneously moves on to another event. If savvy practitioners and clients recognize and monitor this process, however, more dramatic and powerful shifts will occur. The exchange between practitioner and client should be interactive, with the practitioner watching carefully for cues from the client. It may be helpful to use the following procedure: (1) Identify stress in the client and tap; (2) during the moment of silence after tapping, evaluate the client's verbal and physical cues and look for new memories and cognitions; (3) from this information, determine what to focus on next; and (4) continue to follow the process, allowing the session to flow spontaneously. Mastering the concept of daisy chaining empowers a practitioner to obtain deeper, more profound results with every tapping session.

Keywords: daisy chaining, chains, follow the process, aspects

Valerie Lis, MA, EFT-EXP, offers certification workshops through EFTuniverse.com, customized group training, and individual sessions. She teaches and trains corporate, business, and sales leaders, health professionals, and college students. Send correspondence to Valerie Lis, 33 Fourth Street NW, Osseo, MN 55369, or valerie@valerielis.com.

An EFT session will often unfold into a series of memories and events, each with related aspects. As soon as one issue is resolved, another one appears. Resolving that issue brings a new one, and so on. This provides a healing opportunity that some practitioners compare to peeling layers of an onion. It can also be viewed as a string of circles or daisy centers (memories and events), each surrounded by petals (aspects). The process of one circle or daisy following another is called daisy chaining.

As this sequence of memories evolves, it may take on a life of its own. Surprises are often revealed. Long-forgotten memories may reappear. The client may have a sudden spark of inspiration or insight. Or in a synchronistic way, a session may come full circle, with new revelations about an issue from the beginning of the session.

Daisy chaining is common and most EFT practitioners recognize it easily. It is a natural process. As the subjective units of distress (SUD) rating for the first event drops, the next event seems more urgent, so that the client spontaneously goes to it. A succession of events can evolve around a topic, as shown in the following example. Mary (name changed) described herself as having the continuing problem of being unable to rest. In this session, a series of events began to unfold. After tapping on related aspects for each event, the next event was revealed. Each incident is associated with Mary's primary issue of an inability to "rest."

- Mary felt that resting was a sign of laziness. She was ashamed of her cultural background (Native American). She perceived Native Americans as traditionally lazy.
- She recalled a relative who spent a great deal of time sleeping. Mary had not wanted to be "lazy" like this person.
- Mary remembered a hospital stay. She had been afraid that spending too much time in bed would cause her to go crazy.
- According to Mary's religious beliefs, Sunday was considered a "day of rest;" it was considered a sin to work. She disobeyed this commandment and consistently worked on Sunday. As a result, she felt guilty.
- She remembered a road trip with a group of people. She had a bladder infection and needed to stop at a rest area many times during the trip. The driver had been angry each time he had to stop, and Mary had been embarrassed.
- Mary remembered a story from childhood in which two teenagers were attacked when parked in a rest area.
- She remembered another event where three of her friends had been badly beaten at a rest area.
- Suddenly, Mary recalled a memory from when she had rheumatic fever as a child. There was a great deal of fear over her "weak heart." A caregiver yelled for her to go to bed saying, "You need your rest or you will die!" Mary had screamed back, "And if I stay one more minute in bed, that will kill me too!" This memory had been quite traumatic for her.

The daisy chain process often follows the progression shown in this example. As each event was cleared, Mary recalled a new event. Near the end of the session, an intense incident from childhood came to mind, representing the origin or core. Resolving the emotional stress associated with each of these memories produced a profound clearing for her.

The next example of daisy chaining involves a woman who was suffering from depression. Her session evolved as follows: She began by mourning the loss of a loved one, then moved on to mourning the loss of her job, then to mourning the loss of her youth, and then to mourning the loss of herself. In her final round of tapping, she realized that her worst states of depression usually occurred *in the morning!*

Daisy chaining occurs naturally. Recognizing and harnessing its power, however, leads to more effective and efficient EFT sessions. To receive the greatest benefit, the exchange between practitioner and client should be interactive, with the practitioner watching carefully for cues from the client. The cue could be a physical change such as the blinking of an eye, a twitch, or a quivering voice. Or it could be more recognizable, such as when a client recalls a memory or an event. To follow the daisy chaining process, the session should be based on cues derived from the client.

To achieve beneficial results, it may be helpful to use the following procedure:

1. Identify stress in the client and tap.
2. Immediately after tapping, watch for a moment of silence. This is a good time to

evaluate the client's verbal and physical cues and identify new memories and cognitions.
3. From this information, determine what to focus on next and tap again.
4. Continue to follow the process throughout the session. Especially during moments of silence, practitioners should also watch for their own sparks of insight, ideas, and memories.

To obtain the greatest benefit from daisy chaining, keep in mind the following points:

- Remember that every client is an individual with his or her own personal issues and thoughts.
- Maintain focus on the client throughout the entire session. Nervous twitches and changes in the voice may signify that more tapping needs to be done.
- Notice memories that come up during a session. Ask the client to share memories when they occur.
- Pay special attention to the client's cues during the quiet time that immediately follows a round of tapping. Practitioners may experience sparks of insight during this time as well.
- The practitioner should not ignore client feedback in an attempt to control the session. Since the clients are experts on themselves, they can provide valuable clues to their own self-healing process.
- Asking questions such as "How do you feel now?" or "Has anything changed?" or "What does that remind you of?" can help the client recall originating memories and core issues.
- Tapping scripts should be avoided, except as a source for ideas.
- EFT appears to tap into the body's natural rhythm for healing. To gain the greatest benefit, allow the session to flow spontaneously based on the client's cues, memories, and cognitions.

As a caution, following the events as they unfold does not mean jumping erratically from issue to issue. Some clients, especially those who are overwhelmed, may have fleeting thoughts and want to move too quickly. In these cases, it may be necessary for the practitioner to take the lead to provide more focus for the client. Not only is it confusing to track multiple issues, it can also lead to poor outcomes.

In summary, daisy chaining is a natural process that can also be facilitated. It is recognized when a client who experiences a reduction in the SUD level of the initial issue immediately moves on to another event. To obtain the greatest benefit from daisy chaining, the practitioner should watch for cues from the client, especially during the quiet moments that follow a round of tapping. The practitioner should also allow the session to flow spontaneously, watching for cues from the client and requesting that the client share memories when they occur. Daisy chaining is an important concept. Practitioners who understand and work with it will often produce deep, profound results in their EFT sessions.

Chapter 32
When Physical Symptoms Persist (Persistence)
Alina Frank

Abstract

The importance of being persistent when applying Emotional Freedom Techniques (EFT) cannot be stressed enough. It is also necessary to understand the nature of why symptoms may persist and become chronic. Numerous case studies and accounts of miraculous EFT healings may give the newcomer the impression that all problems, whether physical or emotional, can be cured in a matter of minutes. These stories can be found on the Internet and in mass media. Though EFT can indeed lead to "one-minute wonders," that is not a universal truth. Some issues are complicated and have many different aspects or components. Other issues simply take longer because the root of the problem may be buried in the subconscious mind. In these cases, the assistance of a skilled EFT coach can help the individuals gain the transformation they seek, but letting go of the expectation that it can occur in quick order is essential.

Keywords: persistence, one-minute wonders, complicated issues and EFT, chronic pain, physical symptoms

Alina Frank is a master life coach and international EFT and Matrix Reimprinting trainer with a private practice specializing in romantic relationships and sexuality. Since 2005 she has trained and mentored thousands of EFT practitioners and health care professionals. Send correspondence to Alina Frank, 1093 Village Loop, Langley, WA 98260, or alina@tapyourpower.net. www.EFTTappingTraining.com.

When a new client comes to me with any physical symptoms, I always ask, "Have you seen a doctor for this?" This becomes an even more critical question when individuals have been suffering with persistent complaints for at least three months. At that point their condition has become, by medical standards, chronic and has a greater likelihood of resulting from a more serious medical cause. Remember, EFT works on the energetic disruption and does not directly treat physical conditions or diseases, so it is important that clients' physical concerns have been appropriately and correctly identified. In a best-case scenario, clients are being well served by their physician or mental health care provider while simultaneously working with their EFT practitioner.

Sometimes an EFT client is receiving simultaneous medical care but has not gotten a correct diagnosis. In working with a client, when I have systematically worked through all the energetic and emotional components of the case and the individual's physical problems have still not resolved, I suspect that there may be something happening on the physiological level that has not been identified and I encourage that person to get another medical opinion.

I once had a client who could not lose weight. He came to see me after trying many programs, diets, and treatments with a variety of health care professionals. We tapped on all his emotional issues, secondary gains, and frustration at not seeing results no matter what he tried. After about six sessions, I felt our work together was complete, but he was still not able to see a difference on the scale. I encouraged him to keep seeking medical attention to determine if there was something underlying his weight problem. He thanked me a few months later when his medical team discovered a tumor that was at the root of his inability to shed pounds. Let this serve as a cautionary tale. If you work with physical issues, you need to make certain that allopathic routes are taken in conjunction with tapping. That said, there are certain concepts to explore in using EFT with persistent or chronic physical issues.

The desire to experience a one-minute miracle cure on a long-standing physical condition is seductive. Some people arrive for their session having suffered headaches since they were children; others report chronic fatigue or fibromyalgia syndromes, autoimmune conditions, food allergies, long-standing back pain, or other conditions that have been a source of life restrictions for months to decades. EFT has been touted as one of the modalities capable of quick results. There are thousands of cases studies and anecdotal stories about instant cures. These accounts lead people to have high expectations. When instantaneous resolution doesn't happen for you or your clients, it can be frustrating and disappointing. If you are working unsuccessfully on your own issue, the temptation to quit can be quite strong. If you are assisting clients with such hopes, they may become so discouraged that they discontinue sessions. Fortunately, there are some concepts to remember and steps to take that will increase the likelihood that your clients and you will achieve positive results.

The Role of Physical Conditions

When illness or pain is present, standard EFT questions are: What was happening that was stressful before the onset of the symptoms? Is the pain (or other symptom) acting as a metaphor for an aspect of your life that is not working, for example, who or what is a pain in your neck? When conditions continue for long periods of time the questioning may go deeper to assist clients in looking more specifically at what they are not paying sufficient attention to in their lives, at what is still not working.

A client whom I'll call Jessica complained of foot pain. When asked when the foot pain developed, she responded that it began when she was working as an administrative assistant at a computer software company. During the inquiry exploring the timing of the onset of her foot pain, she revealed that the pain had begun after a series of confrontations with her boss. We tapped on each of those confrontations that had led to her leaving her job and the company. After the session she rated her pain as 0 on the SUD (subjective units of distress) scale. I always make it clear to my clients that if symptoms return, it is not that EFT did not work, but that we have other aspects of the problems to uncover and resolve. One month later, Jessica returned with a flare-up of foot pain, though less intense than her initial complaint. When asked further not only about the work confrontations, but also specifically about her boss and whether he reminded her of anyone, she made the connection that her boss acted just like her father. The two men even shared the same nationality. This began a deeper exploration into unresolved issues that she still held with her father. Upon successful completion of several more sessions, Jessica's foot pain resolved and has not returned.

Stress is something that may seem amorphous but can actually be measured. One way to examine how stress exists in the body is by measuring changes in cortisol levels in the saliva. When a body is under stress for long periods of time, we can see resulting physiological and even pathological changes in a person's cardiovascular (Raab, 1966), gastrointestinal (Hislop, 1971), and immune systems (Segerstrom & Miller, 2004). Emotional stress can result in poorer outcomes for people that have been diagnosed with a wide variety of such conditions. If you have ever had a serious illness, been a caregiver to someone with a serious illness, had to go through a hospital waiting room, or have had to wait for potentially horrible news from a lab test, you know that many health care–related situations are huge stressors. These stresses can be greatly alleviated with EFT. Taking the time to recognize what is not working in our lives, recognizing the crucial need for self-care, and developing the skill of deep listening that can occur from having physical challenges are some of the gifts to glean from disharmony in the body.

Why a Physical Issue Might Be Persisting

If an undiagnosed medical problem is not the reason a physical issue is persisting during EFT work, there may be some concrete ways that you are not applying EFT as effectively as you could. On any given day an EFT enthusiast will call me looking for answers as to why the process hasn't worked for them personally. A student may e-mail me wondering why a client isn't getting great results. I have found that going through this short checklist involving the top reasons this happens is always helpful:

- The statements being used are too global.
- Check for missing aspects of the problem.
- Identify secondary gains.
- Persistence, persistence, persistence.

The statements being used are too global. The preponderance of EFT resources online and through other media has been useful for promoting awareness of tapping, but they have also sent mixed messages about how to apply EFT effectively. Though some people get relief from symptoms by using generic tapping scripts and videos, this is not true for the majority. Remember the EFT mantra, "For results to be terrific, it helps to be specific!" (coined by Ann Adams; see Chapter 21). Being specific with EFT means finding any and all related aspects to an issue, including those specific events and traumas that led to the disease or dysfunction. A little trick is to ask yourself if you can answer the questions who, when, and where with your Setup Statement. For example, "Even though I'm angry at Larry for the way he talks to me" answers the question of who (Larry) but doesn't answer when and where. A more complete statement would be "Even though I'm angry at Larry for the way he talked to me at dinner last night" (answers when), but an even better statement would be "Even though I'm angry with Larry for calling me an idiot last night at dinner."

Our brains continuously generalize and categorize events. Rarely will your clients begin a session by offering, "I feel like I'm never good enough and I have a great example of this, like last night at dinner my husband, Larry…" Your job is to continue to ask for evidence and examples of why they feel they aren't good enough, feel alone, feel that other people aren't safe to be around, and so on. New practitioners especially may feel apprehensive about asking for more clarity and information before they begin to tap. If this is something you find yourself doing, then ask yourself why and tap on those answers! One of the best qualities of a good EFT coach is the ability to be insatiably curious about why clients feel or perceive a situation the way they do.

Check for missing aspects of the problem. The wish to witness healing in your clients (or yourself if you're working on you) could be preventing you from looking at all the contributing factors. You might look at some pieces, explore them, tap through them, and then when your client says, "That feels okay now," you want so badly for it to be true that you omit thorough testing. I encountered this in a session with an EFT coach who came to me as a client. He said he had worked on an event, but when I recreated the scene by role-playing the part of his mother, we soon discovered that there were other aspects that were still in need of attention. When we addressed the tone of voice his mother used, the look on her face, and the beliefs that he formed as a result (all the aspects he had missed on his own), his chronic skin issues vanished. The more traumatic an event, the more likely there will be hidden aspects trapped in the trauma capsule. These aspects often show themselves with more comprehensive testing beyond just asking a client for the SUD level and a simple "How do you feel now?"

When we test our work in the real world, role-playing, asking pointed questions, and/or vividly imagining scenarios, our clients feel more confident about the work we do with them. Also note that this is a benefit of working on your own issues with another person, as you aren't as likely to test yourself as thoroughly. You also may not explore all the relevant aspects when self-applying EFT. It's critical to always tell your clients (and know this yourself for your personal work) that if they still haven't resolved the issue, then it is likely that another aspect of the problem will need to be worked on. Knowing this will help ensure that the work continues and that they don't think EFT was a waste of time and effort.

Aspects to examine closely when working on physical issues include the trauma of the diagnosis given (when and how they heard the news), trauma created around treatments and failure of treatments, what negative situation(s) were occurring in their lives six months to a year leading up to the condition, the losses associated with having this condition, and the stressors created by having these limitations.

Identify secondary gains. Any physical condition that has not responded to persistent EFT, that hasn't responded to any approach for that matter, and that has been lingering for more than a few months likely has accompanying secondary gains. The unconscious reasons why any person would want to hold onto a condition or illness are critical to understand in your search for solutions. This is also an area of discussion that must be treated with gentle care and compassion. (I've had to tap with clients who have had practitioners tell them that they were to blame for their own illness and not healing.) Please enter into this conversation with yourselves or with your clients gently by sharing with them that this happens below the level of conscious awareness. I often don't enter into this topic at all in a first session unless it is with a practitioner who understands the concept.

Some of the secondary gains that are most common with long-standing physical issues include the fear of change in relationships if one were to heal, the fear of losing assistance (financial or otherwise), and the realization that other fears will need to be faced (such as the social anxiety that may arise when one is no longer bedridden and housebound).

Persistence, persistence, persistence. There was a short video in the EFT community that showed a man gushing over the fact that he no longer needed a wheelchair and that doctors couldn't find traces of his multiple sclerosis anywhere in his body. He attributed his miraculous healing to EFT. What he didn't say was is that he worked on himself and used a practitioner for over a year to achieve that goal! Layers and layers of our problems and issues reveal themselves as we do this work. Some people might need to go through the experience of learning from their illness in order to evolve and grow. That is exactly what happened with me in the 12-year healing journey I was on that eventually led me to EFT. Through tapping I gained valuable insights as to why I needed to go through that lengthy exploration and, as a result, I have gained immeasurable understanding of what my clients go through.

As practitioners, we can never really know what's best for our clients, but even if the process is slow, EFT can be a remarkable tool through which to gain inner strength and determination.

References

Hislop, I. G. (1971). Psychological significance of the irritable colon syndrome. *Gut, 12,* 452–457. doi:10.1136/gut.12.6.452

Raab, W. (1966). Emotional and sensory stress factors in myocardial pathology: Neurogenic and hormonal mechanisms in pathogenesis, therapy, and prevention. *American Heart Journal, 72,* 538–564. Retrieved from http://www.sciencedirect.com/science/article/pii/0002870366901128

Segerstrom, S. C. & Miller, G. E. (2004). Psychological stress and the human immune system: A meta-analytic study of 30 years of inquiry. *Psychological Bulletin, 130,* 601–630. Retrieved from http://psycnet.apa.org/?fa=main.doiLanding&doi=10.1037/0033-2909.130.4.601

Chapter 33
EFT Through Phone, Videoconferencing, and Other Online Modalities
Carol Crenshaw

Abstract

EFT is a powerful tool and, as practitioners, we want it to be available to as many people as possible. Phone, Skype, and other online options make it possible to work with clients all over the world. Phone sessions allow you to work with people who live far away from you, with those who prefer to do sessions by phone instead of traveling for a session, and with people who live close by but have busy schedules. In addition, people looking for a specialty rather than a geographic location will contact the practitioner who offers that specialty, regardless of where he or she lives. Phone is a convenient option for people who travel a lot, have young children at home, work long and/or erratic hours, or don't want to spend time traveling. Phone work also gives you the option of taking notes without having to look at the client. Other pluses include not having to be concerned with your appearance or the appearance of your office, and saving travel time. Phone sessions do include some challenges, such as needing to pay attention to nonvisual cues (e.g., voice tone and rate of speech) to compensate for not seeing the client, and the need to ensure that the client knows the tapping points in advance. Phone work also offers teleconferencing options. Practitioners can reach a large number of people at once, and some clients feel more comfortable with this more anonymous method. When working with groups of people in your locality, you can alternate in-person and teleconference sessions. Online options such as videoconferencing allow you some of the same advantages as phone but require that you pay attention to your appearance and the appearance of your office. There can be technical challenges with Skype and other videoconferencing technology, such as having trouble getting connected or sound interference. Other online modalities that are helpful when doing group work are webinars, blogs, chat rooms, and social media. Here people with similar interests can form an online community for support and to share ideas and experiences.

Keywords: Skype, videoconferencing, EFT phone sessions, teleconferencing, group EFT sessions, EFT in groups, webinars, blogs, Facebook, Twitter, tapping points

Carol Crenshaw, EdM, MS, is a meditation instructor, yoga teacher trainer, dietary consultant, University of Phoenix faculty member, and certified EFT practitioner who specializes in weight loss. Send correspondence to Carol Crenshaw, 8238 Ames Street, Indianapolis, IN 46216, or carol@MakingWeightLossEasy.com.

Working in person has its definite advantages. There is a certain intimacy being face-to-face with clients. If they break down emotionally and are unable to tap on themselves, you can tap on them (with permission and if touch is allowed in your jurisdiction). You are right there with them and the therapeutic presence can be comforting. In addition, you can monitor nonverbal cues such as posture, facial expression, breathing patterns, and movements. Why then would anyone choose alternatives? What benefits do they provide?

Because EFT is such a powerful tool, we want to make it available to as many people as possible. Imagine being able to work with anyone on the planet! The possibilities are unlimited when we expand beyond face-to-face sessions and include the tools of phone and online resources.

EFT Phone Sessions

Working on the phone obviously allows you to work with people who live far from you. Clients sometimes do an Internet search for a certified EFT practitioner near them. If they don't find someone in their city, they will look in a nearby city and plan to do a little traveling. They may not know that phone or Skype are possibilities and may be glad when you present easier options to them.

Clients looking for a practitioner who specializes in their particular challenge, such as pain, smoking addiction, or posttraumatic stress disorder (PTSD), may do an Internet search by specialty and discover practitioners outside their area. Using phone or Skype makes it possible for you to extend the reach of your expertise to many more that need the kind of help you offer. Practitioners should mention in their promotions that they do phone and Skype sessions.

Some people choose the phone option even when they live near your office or in the same city. If clients have a busy schedule or travel a lot, you can arrange a time when they can conveniently take a break from work to fit in a session. If they have children at home, phone sessions can be easier to manage than getting a babysitter in order to come to in-person appointments. Some people just don't like to spend extra time traveling. They save time having sessions from home, and so do you. On the phone, neither of you has to be concerned about your appearance. Nor you do have to be concerned about your office being in presentable order.

It can also be easier to take notes when working via phone. In person, you are devoting part of your focus to making eye contact with the person. It takes some skill to do this and, at the same time, take notes about what they're saying. On the phone this factor is eliminated, although other challenges take its place. On the phone you need to listen to nonvisual cues to get the information you need. These include changes in tone of voice, rate of speech, pauses, sounds in the breath, sighs, and so on. I once worked with a woman who went totally silent when something intense came up for her. This was rather disconcerting. I did not know what was happening with her and sometimes a minute would pass before she said anything again, even though I called her name a few times. When she did speak, she was fine and seemed to be using the time to process something. From my end, however, it was hard to know this.

Use of the phone also gives you the option of teleconferencing. With a teleconference, you can reach a large number of people at once, from close or far away. For people who live in remote areas and don't have access to a practitioner, the phone option can be a life saver. I.e., in the case of traumatized clients who really need help. It is also a viable option for those with financial restrictions.

Other people enjoy the anonymity of the phone—no one knows who they are and what they are doing. For some people it feels safer to do an EFT session in this manner. An example would be veterans who fear the stigma of treatment by a mental health professional. In a study by Hartung and Stein (2012), 49 veterans with clinical PTSD symptoms were treated with either six in-person office EFT sessions or six EFT phone sessions. Significant improvement was found in the subjects treated in the office after three sessions, while the subjects treated on the phone showed significant improvement after six sessions. A 6-month posttreatment assessment showed that 91% of subjects treated in the office and 67% of those treated by phone no longer met PTSD diagnostic criteria ($p < .05$). While not as efficacious as office visits, phone visits were still quite effective in remediating PTSD symptoms in about two thirds of the cases.

If you are working with someone on the phone for the first time, you need to make sure in advance that they have access to a diagram or video of the tapping points. This is definitely a scenario in which "one picture is worth a thousand words."

You can also personalize the phone experience by exchanging pictures beforehand so you each have a face to connect with the voice.

In my EFT groups, I use an alternate week system. The first week we meet in person. The second week we meet through teleconference. For the remainder of the weeks we alternate. Because they have met in person the first week, participants have a face to go with each name and feel that they have gotten to know each other a little bit. They also enjoy the savings in travel time each teleconferencing week offers, allowing them to get home earlier or take a break from work and then still be there to finish up before they leave for the day. I also enjoy being home and getting a few personal things done before and after the session, rather than using the time for travel. As a further advantage, many teleconference companies will record your sessions. This is especially useful for clients who have to miss the session and want to listen to it later.

There are some disadvantages to working on the phone. For one, if you are using a cell phone, you will need to make sure that it is sufficiently charged to get through the session. Second, many clients put their phone on speakerphone mode, which leaves their hands free for tapping, but makes it hard for the practitioner to hear clearly. Using good headphones or a headset with wireless Bluetooth connectivity can be a way around this problem.

EFT via Video Calls or Videoconferencing

Doing EFT sessions via video calls (e.g., with Skype) or videoconferencing is another option, one that offers the same benefits as working on the phone. To recap, these include: working in the comfort of your own home, savings in travel time, and access to people who live far away. In addition to Skype, there are now other options for working "face-to-face" on the Internet. These include Apple's FaceTime videoconferencing service and Google Hangouts.

There are other advantages to Skype or videoconferencing versus phone work. For practitioners and clients who prefer to work face-to-face, Skype sessions can be a more comfortable and personable option. As a practitioner, you have more feedback about what clients are experiencing than that revealed by voice alone, including clues from posture, breathing, and facial expressions. You can also see whether clients are tapping on the right points, and can easily teach the points if it is their first session with you and they are new to EFT. Some Skype/videoconference practitioners experience being able to see "the whole picture" with more clarity than in an in-person session. They notice details that they might otherwise miss when the client is physically in the same room with them. Distance appears to create detachment, somewhat like watching a movie. This provides a way to catch nuances in the client's body language that might be lost when physically present with the client.

One disadvantage of Skype/videoconferencing is you have to pay more attention to your appearance and the appearance of your office—nothing will remain hidden like it is on the phone! Another factor to keep in mind is that you may sometimes experience technical difficulties with the system. It can be hard to get connected and sounds in the background can create interference. Sometimes there will be a period during which the audio or video connection freezes, after which the system returns to normal. Sometimes you can see your client moving but not hear what he or she is saying. It can take ingenuity to get the system working smoothly, but you can always use the phone as backup. In one of my Skype sessions, we were able to see but not hear each other. I called my client on the phone to suggest we hang up and she call me back on Skype (since my calling her was not working). When I called, however, we discovered that we could do the session using phone and Skype; we saw each other on Skype and heard each other on the phone. A good strategy in such situations is "whatever works."

Other Online Modalities

For those who like to work with people in groups, webinars are another option. Here you can reach a large number of people and disseminate information and techniques in a relatively short time. If your webinar is available for a set amount of time, such as 24 hours per session for the Tapping World Summit, then people have the convenient option of listening according to their schedules. Webinars also give you the opportunity to present other programs you offer, such as individual sessions, packages, CD/workbook sets, and other programs. The webinar can potentially lead to further work with participants who resonated with what you said. They might contact you with additional questions they'd like answered, will want to work with you on an individual basis, or will want to purchase your materials.

Blogs are another online modality through which you can introduce people to your ideas and style of working, and allow them to share ideas with each other. When this happens, you are creating an online community that shares a common interest and goal. When someone benefits from your blog, they will feel they are getting to know and trust you and will be more receptive to doing EFT sessions with you.

Chat rooms and social media such as Facebook and Twitter present other options for people in groups to communicate with each other. When working with groups, these online resources offer opportunities for people to stay connected with each other between sessions. If people are tapping by themselves and do not have any group or other support system in place, an online resource such as a chat room gives them the opportunity to share with others and feel connected to others with like goals. They can share ideas, successes, and frustrations, and get feedback from others on ideas and experiences they have had with EFT. These modalities also expose you the practitioner to additional people who might not otherwise find you.

Case Examples

I did a series of EFT phone sessions with a client who lived about an hour away from my office. This client had a young baby and traveling was very difficult. She arranged the time so she was able to put the baby down for a nap right before our sessions. The baby would generally sleep for about an hour—perfect timing. Once in a while the baby would wake up during the session and be fussy. I suggested that she tap on the baby and it worked like a charm. She found that tapping on top of the baby's head solved the problem. Once or twice during this series of sessions someone rang the doorbell or otherwise interrupted her. At these times she would call me back when she was done. In the meantime I would work on my computer. Since I allotted extra time for these sessions, I was fine with it because my time was not being wasted in the interim.

Another advantage of working this way was that it allowed her to focus on herself when her husband and other children were out of the house. In addition, her husband was not a big fan of alternative methods, so it was better that he was not around to see what she was doing. She was able to release a lot of memories from her traumatic childhood and resolve some present challenges that stemmed from her past. As the weeks went on, she relaxed more and more. I'm sure that these changes impacted her whole family—something that would not have been possible without phone sessions.

On the EFTUniverse website, there is the case study of Donna Kusz who suffered year of physical and emotional abuse from her angry father. This resulted in her suffering from depression and panic attacks as an adult. After one phone session with Dr. Alexander Lees, she experienced great relief. He began by helping her clear some of her depression, so she was in a happier state of mind to work on her goal, which was to write a book on panic disorders. He then jokingly (or not) suggested that she also write a book on depression! According to Donna's account, she cried as well as laughed during the session. This 1-hour session brought her amazing relief. In her words, "With the help of EFT and Dr. Lees, I feel overwhelmed with relief. I have recovered a part of what I consider to be my great loss, the loss of my self-worth."

Another touching case on the EFTUniverse site is related by Connie Kvilhaug. I'm sure every mother can relate to this one. What can you do when your daughter is in great distress and you are nowhere close to comfort and help her? Connie received a call from her daughter who was away at college and suffering from her first broken heart when her boyfriend broke up with her. Connie knew that, even though her daughter called her for help, she was not one to take advice from her mother or even appreciate what she had to say. Connie felt that she was getting nowhere fast talking to her, so she proposed tapping with her distressed daughter. After about a half hour of tapping, her daughter stopped crying and had calmed down considerably. Connie told her now-exhausted daughter to drink a few glasses of water, relax, and go to bed. The next day her daughter felt fine. Even though she still felt bad about what had happened, her deep feelings of hurt were gone and she was ready to move on and meet someone new. All those anticipated weeks or months of feeling badly were wiped out with that simple phone tapping session.

One of my current Skype clients has experienced some major changes in her life since she began tapping. Linda wanted to work with me because of my expertise in using EFT for weight-loss issues. As she lives in another city and traveling would be too time-consuming, she was grateful that I could offer her the option to work via Skype. Linda is a good example of how perseverance pays. Her presenting challenge was weight loss, and it is taking her some time to achieve her weight-loss goal. In the process, however, her whole life is changing.

After many years of being alone post-divorce, one of her goals was to have a male companion. We had several sessions together and she experienced a significant shift. She announced that a man in one of her meet-up groups was interested in seeing her outside the group. Why was this a big shift for Linda? First, because she had said numerous times, with obvious pain in her expression (which I could observe because we were conducting the session via Skype), that she was passed over by men because of her size. The second reason this was a big shift for her was because the meet-up group was mostly women and the man had singled her out.

After starting to lose weight initially and then getting stuck, with several weeks of no further loss, Linda is now steadily losing weight. She is more motivated to exercise and is exercising regularly, which she wasn't doing at all when we started working together. She is also now strategizing on how she can fit healthy eating and exercise into her busy schedule. Linda has bought some new clothes and is about to change her hairstyle—all indicators of how she is feeling about the new Linda. Each week I look forward to hearing about what has happened since our last meeting. At this point in our work together, she always has something fun and positive to report.

Conclusion

The array of options detailed in this chapter may seem overwhelming. It is best to start with the one with which you are most familiar and comfortable. From there, if you choose, you can slowly expand the modalities you employ, as you are ready to try the next one. Whichever way or ways you choose to go, you can't go wrong using the magic of EFT! Having these extra options will give you ways to help many more people, who will in turn impact the lives of all those around them. Plus you will have the opportunity to facilitate more sessions, getting more practice and further honing your skills.

Reference

Hartung, J., & Stein, P. (2012). Telephone delivery of EFT (Emotional Freedom Techniques) remediates PTSD symptoms in veterans: A randomized controlled trial. *Energy Psychology: Theory, Research, and Treatment, 4*(1), 33–42.

Chapter 34
The Constricted Breathing Technique
Claudia Schecter

Abstract

This paper explores and teaches the Constricted Breathing Technique, a unique exercise for taking control over the autonomic nervous system. The first section explains the connections between respiration and emotions, how emotional states such as fear, anxiety, and sadness create a chain reaction of chemical releases in the body, causing tension in the breathing. The next section lists different applications of the Constricted Breathing Technique and teaches how to use it. The chapter concludes with two case studies in which the Constricted Breathing Technique was applied with exceptional results.

Keywords: constricted breath, constricted breathing technique, breath and emotions, respiratory distress, regulate breath, EFT, Emotional Freedom Techniques

> *Holding on to anything is like holding on to your breath. You will suffocate. The only way to get anything in the physical universe is by letting go of it. Let go and it will be yours forever.*
> —Deepak Chopra

Claudia Schecter, NHC, EFT Expert practitioner, has more than 20 years of experience as a naturopath and coach, specializing in energy psychology, energy medicine, and spiritual psychotherapy. She is an EFT and Matrix Reimprinting trainer and coach, and teaches and coaches internationally in English and in German. Send to Claudia Schecter, 4364 Earnscliffe, Montreal QC, Canada H4A 3E8, or claudia@quantumbalance.ca.

Have you ever noticed that when people experience a shock or trauma of any sort, they stop breathing, catch their breath, or hold their breath? The association between breath and emotions is readily acknowledged and seen in familiar phrases such as "Give me some breathing space," "It took my breath away," or "huffing and puffing" in anger.

When under stress, we tend to change our breathing in response to changes in emotional states, such as fear, anxiety, or sadness. These changes are automatic, regulated by the autonomic nervous system, causing a chain reaction of chemical releases in the body, creating tension in our breathing and much more.

Researchers have documented the relationship between breathing and emotions in subjects listening to natural noises or unpleasant sounds (Masaoka & Homma, 1997; Gomez & Danuser, 2004) and also looking at photographs or movies that hold an emotional charge and intensity (Masaoka & Homma, 2008).

Restrictive breathing patterns can be a result of a subconscious coping mechanism of suppressing emotion. When under emotional distress, people often respond by holding their breath and thus stifling the flow of their emotions, holding everything in and suppressing feelings felt during traumatic physical and emotional events that can date back as far as early childhood, birth, and even gestation. Our unexpressed emotions and feelings affect the intensity of our emotional responses to what is happening around us, which in turn often has a negative impact on our quality of life.

Many people have some degree of constriction in their breathing, which is frequently caused by underlying emotional issues. By focusing on the breath while doing EFT, it is often possible to clear or greatly reduce the emotional contributor that is stopping the person from having a full and smooth respiration.

Uses for the Constricted Breathing Technique

The Constricted Breathing Technique is a simple, yet very useful technique:

- It can demonstrate the effectiveness of EFT to newcomers and skeptics in minutes, by allowing them to breathe more freely. Often their stress is reduced greatly in the process as well.
- It can be used as one of EFT's "Gentle Techniques" to release high emotional intensity during a session without focusing on the details of the underlying traumatic event.
- It can bring clarity to disturbing events and let emotional issues surface.

How to Do the Constricted Breathing Technique

1. Take two or three full inhalations to stretch out your lungs. That way any improvement in the breathing capacity after the tapping can clearly be attributed to EFT. (Be careful not to hyperventilate…take your time.)
2. On your next full inhalation, assess the depth of your breath on a percentage basis (a full deep inhalation being 100%) and make a note of the percentage you assigned. It is great if you feel you are at 100%, but do the exercise anyway…as many people experience improvement, even though they thought they were at 100%.
3. Now do a round of basic EFT Setups on the Karate Chop point such as: "Even though I am not breathing to my full capacity, I accept myself," "Even though I can only fill my lungs 70%, I accept myself."
4. Next go through the tapping points with the Reminder Phrase "I can't breathe to my full capacity" or "I can only fill my lungs 70%."
5. Take a slow deep breath and assess your percentage again.
6. Continue with subsequent rounds of EFT until you have reached your maximum breathing capacity of 100%.

Under rare circumstances the breathing capacity does not change or even gets worse. This is usually an indication that there is an underlying emotional issue that needs to be addressed. Often these emotions are related to specific events experienced as far back as early childhood that have surfaced while doing this exercise. If this happens to someone you are working with, you may want to find specifics by asking questions such as:

- "What does this breathing constriction remind you of?"
- "Is there any area in your life where you feel blocked or constricted?"

- "If this constriction had a voice, what would it say?"
- "If there was an emotion contributing to this constriction, what would it be?"

Case 1

I once taught the Constricted Breathing Technique during an EFT demonstration. It was a mixed crowd of attendees; some already knew a little EFT or had at least heard about it, but most were complete newcomers and many of them very skeptical.

I briefly explained the technique and asked the attendees to stretch out their chests by taking a few deep breaths so they could be sure that the change in their breathing capacity could be attributed to EFT. I then guided the group through a few rounds of tapping and had them evaluate their breathing again. Some felt a tremendous expansion in their breathing capacity, but as others still had some constriction left, I led them through a few more rounds of EFT. After the second evaluation through a deep inhalation, a woman with a 35-year history of respiratory distress approached me in complete disbelief. Her breathing constriction had gone down from an 8.5 to a 0.5–1. She said that she did not remember ever having such a full breath and, being a nurse, she thought this could never be possible given her health condition.

I cautioned her that the breath constriction might come back as other deep-seated emotions that could be the subconscious contributors to her breath constriction surfaced. I explained to her that this did not mean that EFT did not work; it only meant that there was more to do. I also pointed out that she now had a powerful tool to regulate her breath as part of a daily energy hygiene protocol and to do this 3 to 5 minute routine several times a day.

She called me back 8½ weeks later to tell me that she had done the technique daily and that her prescribing physician had just taken her off her respiratory medication.

Case 2

Matthew came to my office when he was 5 years old. He had severe asthma and was on two medications. He had to miss a lot of school during cold season because simple colds affected him so much that they would send him to the emergency room.

Matthew was too young to give me a SUD in numbers, but he was able to show me with outstretched arms how difficult it was for him to breathe. He stretched both arms out as far as he could—his breath was that labored.

We did a few rounds of EFT, tailored to a 5-year-old child.

"Even though it is so hard to breathe, Mommy loves me anyway."

"Even though it feels tight when I breathe, I am a good boy."

After three rounds of tapping, his little face lit up and he said, "I can breathe now."

The change in his breathing capacity was so profound for the little boy that he continued tapping with his mother and also alone.

Matthew is now 14 years old. His asthma is gone, but he still uses EFT regularly. He now taps when he feels nervous about an upcoming exam. With the asthma gone, Matthew was able to join the school soccer team and is now teaching EFT to his teammates to enhance his team's sport performance.

Caution: Although the Constrictive Breathing Technique can be very effective for respiratory disorders, always consult with a medical professional and never stop any medication without the advice of your prescribing physician.

Conclusion

The breath is a window to the mind, body, spirit, and emotions. It is also an essential tool in taking control of your emotions. The constrictive breathing technique can be used as a powerful addition to a daily energy routine. You now have a tool to address emotions, anxiety, and physical issues and also to control excessive stress. By doing so you are able to positively balance the autonomic nervous system, which is responsible for controlling varied aspects of our health.

References

Gomez, P. & Danuser, B. (2004). Affective and physiological responses to environmental noise and music. *International Journal of Psychophysiology, 53,* 91–103.

Masaoka, Y. & Homma, I. (1997). Anxiety and respiratory pattern: Their relationship during mental stress and physical load. *International Journal of Psychophysiology, 27,* 153–159.

Masaoka, Y. & Homma, I. (2008). Breathing rhythms and emotions. *Experimental Physiology, 93,* 1011–1021.

Chapter 35
Dissociation
Valerie J. Burke

Abstract

A dissociative client can be challenging for even the most skilled therapist and may take the inexperienced EFT practitioner by surprise. Dissociative states are often experienced by individuals with a history of trauma, especially childhood trauma. Dissociation serves to protect the individual from experiencing and reexperiencing unbearable emotional stress. Symptoms may include depersonalization (feeling detached from one's body), derealization (feeling disconnected from one's surroundings), memory loss, and identity confusion, among others. Dissociative symptoms can significantly hamper therapeutic progress because they impair your client's ability to be present, so it is important to know how to recognize them. Dissociation should be normalized and its purpose explained to your client in a supportive, neutral manner. Treatment goals include increased awareness of somatic sensations, nervous system stabilization, increased dialogue between fragmented parts of the self, increased compassion and empathy between parts, and integration of the different parts of your client's personality into a cohesive whole. Distancing techniques are very important when treating individuals with dissociative tendencies, as deeply buried feelings can overwhelm the client if unearthed too quickly. Grounding is critical.

Keywords: dissociation, dissociative states, derealization, depersonalization, trauma, capsule

Valerie J. Burke, MSN, is a certified EFT practitioner. As a registered nurse for more than 20 years, she has extensive mental health experience, including a private practice treating traumatized children and assisting law enforcement with mental health emergencies. Besides her EFT practice, she is currently a content writer for www.Mercola.com. Send correspondence to Valerie Burke, 924 7th Avenue SE, Olympia, WA 98501, or val@panthertap.com; www.panthertap.com.

Dissociation is one of the most fascinating phenomena you'll see in your practice. Mild dissociative states are so ordinary that you probably experience them yourself on a daily basis without even realizing it. Dissociation varies along a continuum of mild to severe; only when symptoms are on the severe end of the spectrum are they considered pathological.

Dissociative identity disorder or DID (formerly called multiple personality disorder or MPD) is marked by *extreme* dissociative states, as notably depicted in the book *Sybil* (Schreiber, 1973). In DID, the psyche fragments itself into multiple distinct "identities" or parts—sometimes *hundreds* of them. These parts are all actually competing aspects of one personality, as opposed to "multiple personalities." This degree of dissociation is rare, but lesser instances are quite common and important for EFT practitioners to learn to recognize. Dissociation can bring your client's progress to a screeching halt, so it's important to know why it occurs and what it looks like. This chapter addresses those issues, as well as providing you with some practical tools for helping a dissociative client.

Dissociation is a key feature in a number of psychological disorders, including amnesia and fugue states, schizophrenia, conversion disorders, mood disorders, acute stress disorder (ASD) and posttraumatic stress disorder (PTSD), eating disorders, and addictions. Diagnosing psychiatric disorders is beyond the scope of this chapter, but, fortunately, diagnostics are not necessary in order to treat dissociative symptoms with EFT.

Treating highly dissociated individuals requires a great deal of skill and expertise. These clients may present with horrendous histories of trauma and abuse and may be better served by a trauma specialist. As an EFT practitioner, you must take care to practice within your professional limits and comfort zone. Overlooking this could have disastrous effects on your client, potentially retraumatizing her and causing a serious therapeutic setback, or worse. As the adage goes, "Don't go where you don't belong." Yet, even the best-intentioned therapists occasionally walk into a minefield when a client unexpectedly exhibits dissociative symptoms, so it's wise to be prepared for this possibility.

Dissociation Can Be a Serious Stumbling Block in Treatment

Dissociation can seriously hamper therapeutic progress because it interferes with your client's capacity to be present. Dissociation is that state of detachment and inaccessibility that ultimately prevents any progress or healing. It is often difficult for the practitioner to monitor a client's level of activation and distress because dissociation masks their true psychological state, often making them quite difficult to read.

Dissociation may cause your client to leave the room suddenly mid-session when you've barely touched on the issues. Or the individual may enter a state of inconsolable panic that you didn't see coming. The difficulty is that dissociation has the greatest impact on the part of the client *that needs healing the most*—the part that is most vulnerable and injured. This is the part that dissociation serves to "protect," the part that tends to "disappear" during your session.

As a first step in learning how to handle this potential problem, let's explore further what dissociation is.

Definitions of Dissociation

Dissociation has many descriptions but no unifying definition in the scientific literature, reflecting the persistent academic controversy around the concept (Spitzer et al., 2006). The mechanism of dissociation was first introduced by Pierre Janet in the late 1800s. The DSM-IV describes dissociation as a "disruption in the usually integrated functions of consciousness, memory, identity, or perception of the environment." But the ICD-10 defines it as "partial or complete loss of the normal integration between memories of the past, awareness of identity and immediate sensations, and control of bodily movements."

In his book *EFT for PTSD* (Craig, 2008, p. 243), Gary Craig defines dissociation as: "A state of acute mental decompensation in which thoughts, emotions, sensations, and memories are compartmentalized such that there is a lack of connection between things that are normally associated with each other." He goes on to say that the person's emotional response to past events prevents those events from being integrated into the person's awareness, producing gaps or discontinuities. Robert Scaer, author of *The Body Bears the Burden: Trauma, Dissociation, and Disease* (2007), defines dissociation as "corruption of the present moment by past memory."

There are almost as many definitions of dissociation as there are people to ask. Regardless of which definition you choose, dissociation is marked by a "disconnect" from perception of one's body or surroundings, thoughts, emotions, memories, and/or identity. Symptoms may include:

- **Depersonalization:** Feeling detached or disconnected from one's body; the client may say, "I feel strange. I feel like I'm floating away. I feel far from myself. I feel like a puppet," and/or describe "out of body" experiences.
- **Derealization:** Feeling disconnected from one's surroundings; the world seems unreal or distant, as if it's a movie; feeling "spaced out"; looking at the world through a veil; in a trance like state; objects seem diminished in size, unsolid, artificial, or dreamlike.
- **Dissociative amnesia:** Episodes of memory loss, missing time, or blackouts; inability to recall places, people, or events.
- **Identity confusion or alteration:** Shifting into alternate identities or personalities.

Normal Versus Pathological Dissociation

"Normal" dissociation comes in many familiar forms. Day dreaming, losing track of time while immersed in a novel or movie (or you can't remember what you just read), and "highway hypnosis" (not remembering your drive home from work) are examples of benign dissociative states. These can be triggered by fatigue, sleep deprivation, illness, stress, or physical disorders, such as migraines and epilepsy (Stone, 2006).

You might be surprised that dissociation can actually offer you an advantage in certain situations by allowing you to filter out distracting stimuli (compartmentalization) that would interfere with the task at hand. For example, being "in the zone" is a form of dissociation familiar to athletes, performers, artists, and others who willfully harness this tool as a means of achieving excellence. People actually seek out dissociative states, both constructively and destructively, through meditation, exercise, dance, music, drugs, and risk taking. Dissociation can be adaptive professionally as well. For example, if you are having surgery and your surgeon is unable to compartmentalize the argument he had with his wife over dinner the night before, you might be in trouble! Being able to utilize dissociation is also central to a therapist's ability to sit with a client without becoming overcome with emotion.

When dissociation becomes chronic and an individual is unable to remain present or live an integrated life, then it is no longer adaptive. The remainder of this chapter deals with maladaptive, or pathological, dissociation.

Understanding the Evolutionary Brain

A basic understanding of the human brain is helpful in understanding the dissociative process. Dissociation is the mind's natural response to shock and extreme stress, enabling us to "bear the unbearable" and sparing us excruciating pain. Some view dissociation as a mechanism humans adapted in order to survive immensely stressful situations. For example, when Paleolithic man was being charged by amammoth, he needed to blunt the terror long enough to escape. Dissociation itself can be viewed as a type of escape.

The evolutionary (triune) brain can be divided into three parts:

1. **Reptilian brain (brainstem and cerebellum):** Most primitive and instinctual part, regulates heart rate, breathing, body temperature, balance etc.; often "communicates" in somatic sensations
2. **Limbic brain (amygdala, hypothalamus, hippocampus):** Emotional responses, memories, and reflexive judgments
3. **Neocortex (cerebrum):** Unique to mammals; cognitive processes including abstract thought, language, and imagination.

During trauma, the more primitive parts of the brain (mostly reptilian) are activated. Other parts of the brain shut down, including thinking, talking, and feeling emotion. This is why trauma survivors often experience physical symptoms—the "reptilian brain" is largely responsible for processing both trauma and somatic sensation.

Fight, Flight, or Freeze: How Wild Animals Process Trauma

Why is it that wild prey animals quickly return to normal after life-threatening encounters, whereas humans become "traumatized" and develop compensatory mechanisms such as dissociation? Peter A. Levine (1997) explored this issue in depth and developed a theoretical model called Somatic Experiencing (SE). According to Levine, animals in the wild have innate mechanisms that regulate and discharge the high level of energy associated with defensive survival behaviors, giving the animals a type of "trauma immunity."

The initial response to life-threatening situations is essentially the same across the animal kingdom. Animals normally respond to an attack with a large burst of energy (in either fight or flight), and then quickly return to their status quo. If escape is not an option, then instead of fighting or fleeing, the animal freezes or plays dead. Once the danger has passed, the immobilized animal *releases the energy* from its heightened state of arousal by shaking or quivering for a short while. If the animal was running when attacked, its legs may thrash about in a running pattern as it unfreezes. According to Levine, this discharge of energy, controlled by the most primitive part of the brain, acts to prevent trauma. After all, no animal could survive for long in the wild if paralyzed with fear.

When Humans Can't Escape, We Freeze

Like wild animals, humans freeze when faced with a life-threatening situation in which escape is deemed impossible. But, *unlike wild animals,* humans lack an innate mechanism to discharge the unspent survival energy, which ends up getting "stuck" in the body's energy system. Unlike wild animals, we use our higher brain functions (neocortex) to analyze and try to make sense of the experience... to a fault.

When a human experiences physical assault, sexual abuse, or another highly stressful event, the trauma is reexperienced as intrusive memories, flashbacks, anxiety, nightmares, and physical sensations. The individual may get caught in a vortex of painful images and feelings that Scaer calls "the dissociation capsule" (Scaer, 2007). The dissociation capsule contains procedural memories for the autonomic, somatosensory, and emotional experience of the trauma.

Dissociation protects us from the stress of retraumatization, from reliving the awful event over and over again. Dissociation is under the control of the parasympathetic nervous system, which causes endorphins to be released that blunt our perceptions and create a calmer, but surreal, perceptual state. This "perceptual analgesia" serves to protect a child from terrible pain, but it can also cause a total disconnect from one's emotions, robbing the individual of all joy and happiness. If you have a client who recounts a horrific experience but shows no emotion, he may be dissociated. In cases like this, an *increase* in emotional distress may actually be a sign of healing. Consider the following example.

Case Example: Detachment from Deeply Buried Trauma

My first experience with a severely dissociative client came as quite a surprise while conducting an "EFT practice session" as part of my EFT certification process. A friend's seemingly healthy husband volunteered for a tapping session "just for fun," stating he really had no emotional issues to work on. I graciously accepted his offer and suggested we "just do some tapping and see what comes up."

He shared that he was quite unhappy living in this country, which in his mind was going down the tubes, and he provided me with a verbal laundry list of political corruptions to make his point. There was a clear undercurrent of rage in his words, but *not in his affect.* He shared that he had spent his younger years in the military, stationed in the Middle East. But what came next was truly shocking.

He began describing in great detail a string of horrific experiences during this period of his life, including torture. He described being held down by two large nurses and having his "sinuses drilled," being electrically shocked, plus some other equally nightmarish experiences. As he recounted these stories, his affect remained unchanged, even matter-of-fact, and at times inappropriately jovial. He reported a SUD (subjective units of distress) level of 1 to 2 throughout the session. I believe he was dissociative. I had him tap as he told these stories, anticipating some eventual bubbling up of emotion, but none came. All of the feelings connected to these horrendous events were deeply locked away, probably as a means of preserving his ability to function. I invited him to come back for another session, which he declined. But it was a stark example for me about how powerful dissociation is and how it can hide itself from view.

If we remember that dissociation is maintained when energy is stuck in the body, then it makes sense that unblocking this energy in a gentle, controlled fashion will decrease the need for dissociative states, as the client no longer requires their protection. But the energy must be released in *tiny pieces* so as not to flood the client. Fortunately, EFT is masterful at gently clearing these energy blocks. I regret that my dissociative volunteer did not return for more tapping. A few months later, I learned he had fallen into a significant depression, which is common among trauma survivors.

Signs Your Client May Be Dissociative

Recognizing dissociative symptoms begins with identifying risk factors. One of the best ways to do this is by collecting a good history, right at the start. The following are indicators that your client may be experiencing dissociative states (Fisher, 2001; Steinberg, 2008):

- Somatic symptoms, such as unexplained pains, sudden mid-session headaches, scanning or blinking eye movements
- Childlike mannerisms or behaviors that seem unusual for the client's age, cognitive ability, profession, or social position
- Abruptly leaving the treatment session, inability to make eye contact, or becoming mute
- Significant memory problems, difficulty maintaining continuity between sessions; trouble "tracking"; missing time or experiencing blackouts
- Internal conflicts over identity (for example, client who ordinarily trusts you may suddenly fear you're going to hurt her)
- Lack of integration of behavior, affect, perception, or experience; aspects of presentation just don't seem to add up (as in my case example)
- Unable to move forward with life; ambivalent and extremely indecisive despite cognitive ability, education, and support
- History of trauma (especially in childhood); physical, emotional, or sexual abuse or mistreatment; victim of natural disaster, car accident, terrorist attack, etc.
- History of seeing multiple mental health-care practitioners with little progress; non-responsiveness to psychiatric medications
- History of short, chaotic, dysfunctional relationships.

Psychological reversal. Psychological reversal can be regarded as a type of dissociation. Reversals signify inner conflict between different parts of the self with competing agendas. These personality parts want to fight among themselves, and this manifests in the client's life as conflict and self-sabotage. Tapping on the Karate Chop point while saying the Setup Statement gives voice to these competing parts and helps pave the way for their integration. Integration is one of the most basic treatment goals for a dissociative client.

Approaches to Treatment

Proceed with caution: Slow and steady wins the race.

Normalizing. Dissociative symptoms are underreported to healthcare providers for a couple of reasons. Clients have a difficult time putting their dissociative symptoms into words, and they often fear they are losing their minds. Therefore, it is important to normalize these symptoms and help your client understand that dissociation does not equate to madness. Help your client understand that her mind has been trying to protect her, but now you are going to help her integrate these different parts of herself.

Distancing. Care must be taken not to overwhelm dissociative clients by digging out buried feelings too quickly, so proceed with caution. Going at core issues full-borehead-on may retraumatize your client or trigger an abreaction. Keep traumatic memories at a safe distance until your client is able to handle them. Approaches like the Tearless Trauma and Watch the Movie Techniques are helpful here. If your client's distress level is high, have her describe the events in past tense, moving back to present tense only when her SUD level comes down. If your client is highly triggered, tapping without words may help bring down her intensity. It's generally best to tap *with* dissociative clients rather than *on* them, as many are anxious about being touched.

Container technique. The Container Technique can provide distance from a stressful memory, similar to tapping on a movie title instead of viewing the movie itself. The Container Technique involves helping your client imagine a vessel of some kind (could be a box, chest, or bag) in which she can lock up the disturbing memory or feeling until she is ready to deal with it at a later time. This is especially helpful if the session is coming to an end and there is not enough time to achieve full relief.

Creating a safe place. A tool that can be quite helpful for a dissociative client is the creation of a safe place. A safe place provides an always-accessible mental refuge for any time she feels anxious, overwhelmed, or unsafe. The place could be real or imaginary, like a garden, beach, or riverbank, and should be chosen by the client, not the practitioner.

Memory recovery. Many individuals with dissociative symptoms are unable to remember events, people, or places, or their memories are hazy and chaotic. Inability to remember events clearly is often a source of distress for clients. It is important to help your client understand that remembering a trauma is not the answer to resolving it. There should be no attempts to persuade clients to venture into therapeutic waters for which they are not ready. The memories might or might not return but should never be forced.

Facilitating internal communication, trust, and empathy. Dissociation is marked by competing parts of the psyche. You can count on the fact that not all of these parts will love the idea of "being in therapy." The client may consciously believe she wants to get better, but an unconscious part may be fearful, mistrusting, and try to sabotage her efforts. It's important to remember there is nearly always a part that takes the "opposite position" to the one you're seeing. It is also useful to remember that, no matter how regressed, helpless, or confused a client is at a given moment, there are other parts that are competent, optimistic, resourceful, and determined to survive.

One of the most challenging tasks with dissociative clients is fostering internal communication, compassion, and cooperation between the various personality parts, and helping your client learn how to differentiate her "adult self" from her "traumatized self" (or selves). Resolving ambivalence requires integrating these various perspectives. It is especially difficult for a client to believe there is an untraumatized person within her, especially when she is feeling desperately hopeless and fearful. It may help to ask questions such as, "Who is in distress" "How old is that part?" "Is there a part who feels empowered and can help?" "What might that part be trying to tell you?" The use of tail-enders may be helpful in determining what the hidden parts may be trying to say. They may try to communicate through images, memory fragments, or body sensations. Each time the client makes a connection with a part of herself, she is increasing her level of integration, thereby decreasing her need for dissociation.

Remember, you are the therapist for *all* the parts of your client, not just some. If you're going to help the client to integrate them, then you can't take sides. Once these parts are identified, every one of them must be given a voice. Tap on all viewpoints, as if several people are having a debate. Perhaps the client's "adult self" can take on the role of "compassionate mediator." Focus on helping your client develop empathy for the different voices within her.

Working with somatic sensations. Somatic sensations are quite common among dissociative individuals. In order to resolve trauma, you don't necessarily have to work with emotions directly; working with somatic sensations may be enough. Helping your client become more attuned to subtle body sensations will help her stay grounded in the present and will facilitate integration. Somatic sensations are emotions expressed in the body and are often a direct link to the reptilian brain, so working with them can help restore balance to your client's nervous system. Examples of somatic sensations include temperature changes, tightness or pressure, goose bumps, trembling, yawning, breath release, posture changes, or a sense of expansion versus restriction.

Somatic sensations may also give you clues that your client is moving too fast. Pay attention to things like rapid speech or vocal restriction, a startled expression, increased anxiety, increased heart rate and breathing, or appearing as if she's "checking out."

Pendulation. A technique used in Somatic Experiencing as well as in EMDR, pendulation can be helpful for improving nervous system regulation. It involves alternating the focus of attention between uncomfortable body sensations and comfortable ones. This back-and-forth motion helps discharge the activation of the nervous system, gradually moving your client in and out of the trauma so it can be worked through in a gentle, supported manner.

First, the client is asked to think of something that creates a positive sensation—the song of a bird, a loved one, a pet, a peaceful memory, a color, or a sensation in the body. This is called "resourcing." Then the client is guided to alternate between the negative trauma-associated sensation and the positive resource sensation (i.e., between the "trauma vortex" and the "healing vortex"). Pendulation can be adapted for EFT by alternating statements between trauma and resource with each tapping point. Take care to evaluate your client's SUD level frequently so you can monitor her progress and adjust your technique accordingly. If the client becomes overwhelmed, stay with the resource and just tap through the points. If the client shows signs of increased dissociation, have her go to her safe place or try some grounding.

Grounding

In order for EFT to be most beneficial, your client needs to remain present. Grounding is essential to help your client reconnect to her body and surroundings. Grounding is also helpful when a client becomes overwhelmed, has an abreaction, or just "goes away." Grounding is an excellent way to end a session so that your client is firmly anchored in the present before departing your office.

Basically, our five senses ground us to the physical world, so you can use your client's senses to refocusher awareness from internal to external. EFT itself is not necessarily grounding, especially when tapping on the head and upper body. There are many common grounding techniques, but not all of them work in every situation, so it is helpful to have a variety in your tool kit. Donna Eden and David Feinstein provide some great grounding exercises in their book *Energy Medicine: Balancing Your Body's Energies for Optimal Health, Joy, and Vitality* (Eden & Feinstein, 2008). The following are examples of some basic grounding techniques:

- **Auditory:** Verbally orient client to time, place and person; "This is not happening to you now. You're just remembering how afraid you were." Reassure her she is safe here with you. If she doesn't respond, try speaking her name.
- **Visual:** Have her open her eyes, look around, and describe what she sees; "What color is your chair?" "How many books do you see on the table?"
- **Eye movements:** Opening the eyes helps a person return to the present; closing the eyes increases emotional intensity and can make a client to go deeper into the trauma; use the 9 Gamut sequence, or just have your client move her eyes gently from side to side while following your hand.
- **Tactile:** Have her feel the weight of her feet on the floor; stomp her feet; rub the inside of her wrists or ankles; place a familiar object into her hands, such as her purse or a tapping bear
- **Olfactory:** Hold a strongly scented tea bag (peppermint or ginger) or a cinnamon stick under your client's nose
- **Other:** Have her focus on her breathing. Use visualization: "Visualize roots growing from the soles of your feet deep into the Earth, firmly anchoring you to the ground."

Summary

A dissociated client can be challenging for even the most skilled therapist and may take the inexperienced practitioner by surprise. If you plan to work with victims of trauma, it would be wise to familiarize yourself with dissociation, as this is a common reaction to traumatic events. Dissociative symptoms have a multitude of presentations, from internal conflict and ambivalence to memory loss, feeling detached from one's body, or a comment like "I just can't feel anything anymore."

Dissociative symptoms should be normalized and their purpose explained to your client in a supportive, neutral manner. Resolving dissociative symptoms requires helping your client discharge the survival energy that became "frozen" in the body when she was unable to escape from an intensely stressful circumstance. Treatment goals include increased awareness of somatic sensations, nervous system stabilization, increased dialogue between fragmented parts of the self, increased compassion and empathy between parts, and integration of the different parts of her personality into a cohesive whole. Distancing techniques are very important when treating individuals with dissociative tendencies, as deeply buried feelings can overwhelm the client if unearthed too quickly. Grounding is critical.

References

Craig, G. (2009). *EFT for PTSD*. Santa Rosa, CA: Energy Psychology Press.

Eden, D. (2008). *Energy medicine* (2nd ed.). New York, NY: Tarcher/Penguin.

Fisher, J. (2001). Dissociative phenomena in the everyday lives of trauma survivors. Paper presented at the Boston University Medical School Psychological Trauma Conference. Retrieved from http://janinafisher.com/pdfs/dissociation.pdf

Levine, P. (1997). *Waking the tiger: Healingtrauma: The innate capacity to transform overwhelming experiences*. Berkeley, CA: North Atlantic Books.

Scaer, R. (2007). *The body bears the burden: Trauma, dissociation, and disease* (2nd ed.). New York, NY: Haworth Medical Press.

Schreiber, F. R. (1973). *Sybil*. Chicago, IL: Regnery.

Spitzer, C., Barnow, H., Freyberger, H., & Grabe, H.J. (2006). Recent developments in the theory of dissociation. *World Psychiatry, 5*(2):82–86. PMid:16946940 PMCid:1525127

Steinberg, M. (2008). In Depth: Understanding dissociative disorders. *Psych Central*. Retrieved from http://psychcentral.com/lib/2008/in-depth-understanding-dissociative-disorders/all/1/

Stone, J. (2006). Dissociation: What is it and why is it important? *Practical Neurology, 6,* 308–313. doi:10.1136/jnnp.2006.101287

Chapter 36
Borrowing Benefits
Karin Davidson

Abstract

Borrowing Benefits, a psychotherapeutic method developed by Gary Craig through the use of Emotional Freedom Techniques (EFT), refers to the process by which an individual can experience relief from his or her own issues by tapping along with an observed session or demonstration. This technique has gained merit through a study by Jack E. Rowe, PhD, in 2005 as well as countless case studies and individual accounts. This chapter details Rowe's research, describes the technique and its applications, and briefly explores the concepts of associated memory and empathic parallel, two psychological concepts that play significant roles in understanding how Borrowing Benefits works and why an individual can experience relief from his or her own issue even when the work of EFT is only being observed.

Keywords: Borrowing Benefits, tapping along, demonstrations, observation, Patricia Carrington, Rowe study, group work

Karin Davidson, CHT, international trainer and speaker for EFT and other energy psychology modalities, maintains a private EFT practice and coauthored the *EFT Comprehensive Training Resource Level 1 (& 2)*. An award-winning producer, she has produced over 500 television and DVD training programs in a wide range of educational subjects. Correspondence should be sent to Karin Davidson, 303 North Providence Road, Media, PA, 19063, or info@howtotap.com.

Borrowing Benefits is a term used for the process in which an individual decreases the intensity of his or her own issue(s) by tapping along with an observed, heard, or read EFT session or demonstration. This phenomenon has been observed in individuals as well as groups, and has been measured using the SCL-90-R (Symptom Checklist 90 Revised). Developed by Gary Craig, founder of EFT (Emotional Freedom Techniques), Borrowing Benefits can be applied across the spectrum of energy-related methods and interventions. Whether the observed session or demonstrations occurs in a classroom, workshop, or online setting, the positive results of this technique are consistent.

The process of Borrowing Benefits is notable because it does not require the observer to have an understanding or experience in EFT. As long as the observer is able to choose an issue and has a basic knowledge of the appropriate points, he or she can borrow benefits. This works for several reasons. Patricia Carrington, psychologist and renowned EFT practitioner, explains:

> First, an identification with the other person takes place on a profound level when we are tapping along with that person and repeating the words used by him or her. It seems that stimulating the meridian points while we are observing the tapping person makes the process more powerful than our usual identification with or empathy with another person. (Carrington, n.d., p. 1)

In all of its complexities, the brain is able to create empathic parallels between what is observed and the issue or issues chosen. The reason that observers are asked to "set the issue aside" is this allows the subconscious mind to draw these parallels on levels at which the observer may not be consciously aware. Put simply, common emotions and reactions can be generalized across experiences. For example, anger is anger, regardless of in which context it may occur and despite the intensity or subjective definition of their anger. If a demonstration subject chooses an event in which she is angry with an uncle for making a joke at her expense in front of the entire family, that sense of anger can be generalized to the audience member who is angry with his mother for divorcing his father, without the audience member being aware. The subconscious mind is able to make these empathic parallels and generalizations on a level that is much more efficient than the conscious mind, and one may not even be aware of the parallels that can potentially be drawn.

In the same way, associative memory plays a significant role in the efficacy of Borrowing Benefits. Put simply, associative memory refers to one's ability to recall a previously experienced item by thinking of something it is linked with. However, the concept of Borrowing Benefits utilizes a broader understanding of the term, that is, that human perception is, in large part, learned. In other words, everything from the interpretation of basic sensory inputs (e.g., how one understands not to touch a hot stove) to the often complex truths of the subconscious mind (e.g., a belief that work comes before play) is based in learned perception. When one looks through a window and sees rain, the understanding of this image happens in the brain, not the eye. "Information from the eye, like the piece of a puzzle, is analyzed in the brain and fitted into meaningful forms" (*Art technologies 1201*, 1997, p. 5). In the same way, most individuals have learned to interpret this perception of rain and associate it with the necessity of an umbrella. No one was born with the understanding of the correlation between rain and an umbrella; rather, it was learned through relationships and experience. In order to produce appropriate responses to the stimuli one encounters on a day-to-day basis, one's system "must create and enrich context-dependent memory representations, which are adapted to different environments" (Chartier, Giguere, & Langlois, 2009, p. 568).

These processes of perceptual learning and associative memory allow the subconscious mind to create, evaluate, and regroup perceptual patterns, including those based on negative experiences, memories, and events. Along with the creation of empathic parallels, they also allow the process of Borrowing Benefits to be one that is effective in beginning to address the respective issues of those who employ it as a method within EFT. Researcher Jack E. Rowe, PhD, of Texas A&M University observed and measured this process. Dr. Rowe recruited 102 participants from a list of those registered to attend an advanced EFT workshop in 2003. Participants were asked to employ the Borrowing Benefits method and were tested at five intervals: two pretests (30 days before the workshop and at its beginning), and three posttests (at the end of the workshop, 30 days after the end of the workshop, and 6 months after the end of the workshop). Symptoms were measured using the Symptom Assessment-45 (SA-45), a self-report inventory, and a shortened version of the Symptom Checklist-90-Revised (SCL-90-R). The changes in all scales between the pre and posttests were significant, and showed highly significant reductions in symptoms of psychological distress, from anxiety to psychoticism, demonstrating the immediate efficacy of the Borrowing Benefits process. Notably, the 1- and 6-month posttests also demonstrated a sustainable reduction in symptoms, although the reductions subsided somewhat. Dr. Rowe concluded that "while these reductions subsided somewhat after 6 months, they remained highly significant suggesting long-term beneficial effects of group EFT treatments" (Rowe, 2005, p. 7).

A good metaphor for understanding how perceptual learning and associative memory work in the brain and are applied to a process like Borrowing Benefits comes from modern-day Internet search engines, such as Google. During Borrowing Benefits, the subconscious mind is working on drawing parallels and creating appropriate associations between the issue that has been "set aside" and that being addressed by the observed session, much like Google works to find appropriate results when you use it to search for a word or phrase. For example, if someone were to say to you the phrase "bird on a fence," your mind would essentially "Google" the phrase, recalling potentially hundreds of images and instances in which it has experienced "bird on a fence." The mind then chooses the image or instance that applied itself most effectively to the context of the current experience—immediately and without conscious realization. In this example, the process of "Googling" and "choosing" is actually the processes of perceptual learning and associative memory at work. During the process of Borrowing Benefits, the subconscious mind is constantly working behind the scenes in the fashion of an Internet search engine to find, choose, and apply the most effective applications of the observed session, even if the relation is not cognitively apparent.

Along with a body of anecdotal evidence provided by individuals who have experienced Borrowing Benefits with remarkable success, there search by Dr. Rowe and the ever-growing understanding of perception, associative memory, and other complexities of the brain have marked the Borrowing Benefits process as one that is significant as an effective tool among EFT treatments.

How to Conduct Borrowing Benefits

The steps to the Borrowing Benefits process are as follows:

1. Choose a specific issue and label its intensity on the SUD (Subjective Units of Distress) scale of 0 to 10, 0 representing no intensity at all, and 10 representing the highest intensity.
2. Write down both the identified issue and its individual intensity.
3. Set the issue aside, that is, do not focus on that issue, instead, focus attention on the demonstration or video.
4. Tap along with the demonstration or video, repeating the same words as the demonstration client.
5. At the end of the demonstration, again test the personal specific issue's intensity.

Normally, a leader or practitioner will introduce the Borrowing Benefits process before focusing on an individual in front of an audience, actual or virtual. The practitioner instructs observers to choose a specific, measurable issue that is relevant to them, title it for the sake of reference, and label its intensity. The observers then set aside their own issues and focus on tapping along with the session at hand, or the demonstration. In a group setting such as this, the practitioner can instruct the audience to test and make note of the intensity of their original issue whenever the practitioner would normally allow time for this in the demonstration. According to Gary Craig, the practitioner's role in a Borrowing Benefits session is two fold: "Conduct the best session you can on one individual with all of the skills you have developed, and stop at appropriate intervals to be sure the group is following the instruction" (Craig, 2008). It should be noted, however, that many EFT users have reported that Borrowing Benefits worked for them even though they didn't follow the rules and just tapped along. Vicki, a licensed clinical social worker with more than 15 years of experience in both inpatient and outpatient settings, primarily in addiction counseling, says, "I find I am much more peaceful week in and week out simply because I am tapping all day with my clients." The effects of Borrowing Benefits can be observed in formal group settings or an individual can follow the same steps with any demonstration, video, or session.

Applications of Borrowing Benefits

I often have new clients bring in friends or family members with them for the first 5 minutes of their first appointment. As a demonstration, we choose an emotion about a scene in a movie. Using a strong reaction to a movie scene allows demonstration with less possibility of attendees becoming overly emotional while still experiencing the benefits of EFT. Each chooses their own movie scene, labels their emotion, and rates the intensity of that emotion. They each write their emotion and intensity level from 0 to 10 on a piece of paper. We then use EFT with the new client on that individual's emotion only. The other attendees repeat along with the new client using only the label the client ascribed to his or her emotion for that movie scene. After tapping along for 2 or 3 rounds (rounds are tapping a specific set of EFT points), all attendees are asked to reassess their own intensity on their original emotion. In my experience, the intensity for the vast majority of attendees lowers. In the rare case in which the intensity raises or remains the same, that person's emotion becomes the new focus. This raising or unchanging of intensity can then be used to demonstrate the concept of related issues or aspects.

I have produced over 80 EFT training DVDs. The last step before DVD replication is to watch the DVD master and make sure there are no dropouts, errors, skips, and so on. I have always used Borrowing Benefits during these final checks. I identify an issue and its aspects and rate their intensity SUD levels. I write these down and then put all my focus on the training DVD and demonstrations. I simply tap along with the demonstrations, repeating whatever words they are using. My focus is on the DVD master and not on my own issue. When the DVD is over, I check my written intensities, and they are always lower and very often down to 0 intensity. Some of the issues I have tapped on in this way over the years are:

- Overwhelm from having too much to do and not enough time.
- Fear of not making enough money.
- Fear of various health issues with myself and loved ones.
- Overwhelm for having to complete taxes.
- Various pains.
- Feeling low/depressed/unmotivated.
- Fatigue.
- Grief over various events.
- Pressures of changing rules and regulations.
- Fear of overeating at an all-you-can-eat brunch.
- Anxiety about teaching a workshop with an unfamiliar PowerPoint presentation.
- Stress about a new very skeptical client who made it very clear this is her last hope; she believes that nothing works; but if it does, she would like to introduce it to her extended family.
- Reaction to something someone said to me or others.
- Fear I'm taking on too much.
- Death of my father, relatives, and pets. (Note: This is a very gentle way to begin to deal with death and grief. If doing this on your own, be careful not to go too deep into writing down the aspects and numbering them; keep yourself safe. Quickly write a single aspect and the intensity level and turn the paper over and focus on the content of the session you are watching. And, obviously, don't watch a session regarding grief or death.)
- Self-doubt in specific areas.
- Various annoyances regarding my husband.
- Particular injustices in the world.
- Body image.
- Health issues as they arose.
- Various household issues as they arose (technology problems, car issues, yard problems, appliance breakdowns, unit malfunctions, etc.).
- Uncertainty regarding specific important decisions.
- Test anxiety.
- Procrastination in specific projects.

Conclusion

Borrowing Benefits is a simple and gentle method for using EFT. It can be accomplished without divulging details to anyone else. The only skills needed are to identify your issue and its aspects, measure intensities, and tap along; in-depth knowledge of EFT is unnecessary. Using Borrowing Benefits is a powerful tool in introducing EFT because it can be profoundly individual even in a group setting. It has the remarkable impact of personal clearing using EFT without focusing on one's own issues and aspects, and simply tapping while repeating another client's words.

References

Art technologies 1201: Perception, art, and technology. (1997). St. John's: Government of New found land and Labrador. Retrieved from http://www.ed.gov.nl.ca/edu/k12/curriculum/guides/art/art1201/sectn2.pdf

Carrington, P. (n.d.). Solving the mystery of Borrowing Benefits in EFT [Web log post]. Retrieved December 17, 2012, from http://masteringeft.com/masteringblog/solving-the-mystery-of-borrowing-benefits-in-eft-article

Chartier, S., Giguere, G., & Langlois, D. (2009). A new bidirectional heteroassociative memory encompassing correlational, competitive and topological properties. *Neural Networks, 22*, 568–578.

Craig, G. (2008). *Tutorial #10: Conducting a Borrowing Benefits Group*. EFT Intermediate Library.

Rowe, J. (2005). The effects of EFT on long-term psychological symptoms. *Counseling and Clinical Psychology Journal, 2*(3), 104.

Chapter 37
The Floor to Ceiling Eye Roll
Claudia Schecter

Abstract

This paper describes the "floor to ceiling eye roll" technique, a unique eye exercise first discovered by Roger Callahan that can rapidly bring a remaining low level of emotional or physical discomfort from a SUD (subjective units of distress) level of 1 or 2 down to a 0. The chapter explains how an EFT practitioner can guide his or her client through the exercise and also how an individual can easily apply this technique without outside help. It describes the location and energetic effect of the "Gamut point," which is an essential component for the execution of the floor to ceiling eye roll.

Keywords: floor to ceiling eye roll, EFT eye exercise, Gamut point, EFT, Emotional Freedom Techniques

Claudia Schecter, NHC, EFT Expert practitioner, has more than 20 years of experience as a naturopath and coach, specializing in energy psychology, energy medicine, and spiritual psychotherapy. She is an EFT and Matrix Reimprinting trainer and coach, and teaches and coaches internationally in English and in German. Send correspondence to Claudia Schecter, 4364 Earnscliffe, Montreal QC, Canada H4A 3E8, or claudia@quantumbalance.ca.

The floor to ceiling eye roll technique was discovered by Dr. Roger Callahan, the founder of Thought Field Therapy. It is a highly effective stress-relieving technique that can be used as a stand-alone modality, that is, as a useful shortcut during an EFT session to bring a low level of intensity (subjective units of distress, or SUD, level of no more than 2 out of 10) quickly down to a 0 without having to apply the full EFT Basic Recipe. The floor to ceiling eye roll is also very discreet and can be easily applied when circumstances may not allow tapping the body points.

How to Do the Floor to Ceiling Eye Roll

To perform the floor to ceiling eye roll, repeat the Reminder Phrase (or the issue that is presenting itself) while continuously tapping the Gamut point and, without moving your head, take 6 or 7 seconds to slowly move your eyes looking from hard down to the floor to looking hard up to the ceiling, still repeating the Reminder Phrase.

Some clients may need a visual aid to help them perform this eye exercise smoothly. In that case, guide your client using your hand as a focus aid. If you are working on yourself, you can begin tapping the Gamut point while holding both hands down in front of you. Keeping your head straight, gaze down to the floor and slowly raise your hands with straight arms. Once your hands come into your field of vision, follow them with your eyes till you are looking straight up to the ceiling.

The Gamut Point

The Gamut point is the third point on the Triple Warmer acupuncture meridian, which is believed to be related to the "fight or flight" response. According to Donna Eden, the Triple Warmer has a strong relationship with all the other meridians and usually dominates over them in times of threat or perceived threat. Tapping on or massaging the Gamut point when your body goes into stress calms the Triple Warmer and can bring an overall feeling of relaxation and well-being.

To find the Gamut point, make a fist with either hand and you will find a small depression between the knuckles of the ring finger and the little finger on the back of the hand. Use two or three fingers of your other hand to tap on that indentation. It does not matter which hand you are tapping on.

How the Floor to Ceiling Eye Roll Helped at a Business Meeting

Chelsea came to me because she had a severe phobia of public speaking. She was a very likable, brilliant young woman with a promising career in a job she loved. Her fear of public speaking, however, was holding her back in many areas of her life, especially professionally. Chelsea had just received a promotion that required her to give presentations to groups of all sizes. The thought of an upcoming convention at which she was scheduled to be one of the presenters sent her into complete terror. That was when she realized something needed to change and she scheduled an appointment with me.

I saw Chelsea several times over the course of a few weeks and we discovered past events in which she had felt uncomfortable and at times even traumatized. There were incidents at school when she had to give an oral presentation, at college, and also at family reunions. We addressed each event with clinical EFT and collapsed the energetic charges she was still holding when she tuned into these memories. We tested thoroughly after each event using a variety of the testing methods.

Chelsea then tested the upcoming event by vividly imagining herself on the podium addressing the assembly and it no longer held any emotional intensity. All her physical symptoms of the anxiety were gone! We both knew that she was ready to give the presentation. After all, what testing method is better than being exposed to the actual situation?

I prepared Chelsea for the possibility that some remaining intensity might surface once she was at the event. I then taught her the floor to ceiling eye roll, which she could do easily and discreetly should the need arise. Not surprisingly, a small aspect did come up just before Chelsea had to step to the podium, but she had a powerful new tool at her disposal. She tapped away her discomfort quickly and discreetly and was able to deliver her presentation with a calm and focused composure.

Conclusion

It is not necessary to do full rounds of EFT when you have low emotional intensity (SUD level of 2 or below). A few seconds of tapping on the Gamut point while doing the eye roll is often all that needs to be done to release the stress.

Chapter 38
Personal Peace Procedure
Angela Amias

Abstract

In the course of life, every individual inevitably encounters challenging experiences, ranging from minor upsets to the truly traumatic. Often times, these experiences continue to impact our present lives negatively, even when years or decades have passed since the original event. Although EFT is most commonly used to treat key issues currently causing emotional distress or disruption in an individual's life, the Personal Peace Procedure is designed as a more comprehensive approach to healing, one that enhances emotional, mental, and physical well-being by systematically clearing the emotional debris that otherwise accumulates over a lifetime. Frequently, the roots of current issues are found in the cumulative effect of early events. Because our bodies store memories of these experiences at a physiological level and respond to reminders of these events by activating the stress response system, neutralizing the emotional reaction to these memories reduces the likelihood of being triggered by old issues and leads to a greater sense of peace and well-being. Benefits of the Personal Peace Procedure include feeling calmer and happier, better relationships, improvement in an array of health conditions, and enhanced self-esteem.

Keywords: EFT, Emotional Freedom Techniques, Personal Peace Procedure, stress, trauma

Angela Amias, LISW, is a psychotherapist in private practice and cofounder of Creative Transformations: Integrated Approaches to Healing. She specializes in using a holistic approach to assist individuals in living life with purpose and joy. Send correspondence to Angela Amias, 221 East College Street, Suite 211, Iowa City, IA 52240, or angela@create-transformations.com.

In the course of a lifetime, each of us inevitably encounters an array of experiences ranging from seemingly inconsequential to profound that combine to create the unique individuals we are today. Although many of these events are positive, there are also experiences that create stress, discomfort, and difficulty in our lives. Even when we are unaware of how these past experiences continue to affect our current lives, we are often painfully aware of our tendency to overreact to certain events or situations in our daily lives, without understanding why we respond the way we do. The Personal Peace Procedure is a technique designed to create comprehensive healing in our lives by addressing these experiences in a systematic manner, in order to neutralize the roots of current issues.

Let's consider the phrase "emotional baggage" in this context. Imagine for a moment that each of us has a box containing all our unpleasant life experiences, large and small, all jumbled together. If you were to take a peek inside your box right now, you'd probably notice that a lot of the experiences in there are ones you've been carrying around since childhood. Many of these experiences might seem insignificant, especially when viewed through the eyes of an adult. Yet those same events, when we experienced them as impressionable, vulnerable, and trusting children, affected us on a deep level. And it is at that deep level that the memories are stored in our bodies.

When viewed in this context, it is easier to understand how the roots of our current issues can often be found in these early events, even when these events appear minor in relation to the whole of our lived experience. For example, a hypersensitivity to criticism from a supervisor at work could be related to an early experience of being criticized or humiliated by a third-grade teacher. It is often difficult to recognize these connections on a cognitive level, but when you tune in to the emotions underlying the experiences, especially while tapping, the connection frequently becomes apparent. The purpose of the Personal Peace Procedure is to reduce the likelihood of being triggered by these old issues, to let go of our emotional baggage and thereby create more peace within ourselves and our lives.

The Procedure

To begin the process, start by making a list of every negative past experience or event you can recall. You can organize these by themes or categories, such as embarrassment, abandonment, failure, and so on, or you can simply list events as they come to mind and organize them into categories when you're finished. It's generally recommended that you purchase a journal or notebook to use for this process. This makes it easier to track your progress with the procedure. If privacy is a concern, creating a password-protected computer document is also an option.

As always with EFT, be specific when making your list. Give each event a title, as though it were a mini-movie, for example, "Mom yelled at me in front of all my friends," "I lied about breaking the window," or "the car wreck." If you are thorough with the list-making process, you should come up with 100 or more discrete events to include on your list. If an event comes to mind that doesn't seem to bother you anymore, trust that it came to mind for a reason and add it to the list.

If you're feeling inspired and energized, you can make this list in one sitting. Depending on your life experiences, however, this process may take some time and the act of listing every negative event in your life can be very stressful in itself. If you feel overwhelmed by this process, you can break it up over a period of days, rather than doing it all at once. Whether you choose to do it all at once or over a few days, be sure to take good care of yourself during this process. If you notice a lot of emotions coming up as you are making the list, tap on the feelings as they arise. It is not uncommon for individuals with a history of childhood abuse or trauma to experience feelings of anger or revictimization about having to work through these experiences in which they had no control or choice. This reaction is absolutely understandable and can make the process seem daunting. In cases such as these, my recommendation is to take it slowly, be gentle with yourself, and get support from a trusted friend, therapist, or EFT practitioner as you begin the process of healing the emotions connected to these experiences.

For each event you include on the list, rate the intensity of your emotional response on the 0–10 SUD (subjective units of distress) scale, with 10 being the most distressing. You can do this for each event as you add it to the list, or you can wait until you finish your list and then give each event a SUD rating. This step is important because it will help you monitor your progress with tapping and it also provides a way to organize your approach to the Personal Peace Procedure. It is often recommended that you begin by tapping on the most intense experiences first. There is good reason for this recommendation: Most people find that neutralizing the emotional charge attached to the "big ones" also reduces the emotional intensity of similar experiences. For certain individuals, however, especially those with traumatic childhoods, the act of facing the big issues right away can feel overwhelming and can cause them to avoid the Personal Peace Procedure altogether. In these cases, I generally recommend beginning with events with moderate to moderately high SUD ratings. It is a good idea to check in with yourself during this process. If you find that you dread tapping or are consistently finding excuses to avoid working on the Personal Peace Procedure, start working with some of the easier issues on the list. They are typically easier to clear and can give you a sense of success that will help sustain you while working on the more difficult experiences.

Tap on at least one issue per day. Make the Personal Peace Procedure part of your daily routine of self-care by setting aside 15 minutes per day to tap. Begin by selecting the issue you'd like to address, making a note of any aspects of the issue that come to mind so you can make sure to address those during tapping. Other aspects you haven't yet identified may come to the forefront while tapping. Tap until the intensity around the incident is at a 0 or is as close to 0 as possible. Some events may not initially drop to a 0 because they are connected with other events on your list; however, when those additional experiences are addressed, the remaining emotional charge around the initial issue will usually dissipate as well. Some issues take more time and more persistence than others. You may find yourself working on the same experience for a few days, whereas on other days you are able to clear more than one issue in the time you set aside for tapping.

When I explain the Personal Peace Procedure to clients, the response typically falls somewhere between overwhelm and disbelief or dismay. Certainly, the prospect of addressing 100 or more separate events can feel very intimidating. Fortunately, the generalization effect works just as well in the Personal Peace Procedure as it does in other EFT work. In fact, by giving SUD ratings to each event before you begin tapping on any event, you can measure the generalization effect as you move through the process. For example, let's say you begin with 15 events in the category of "jealousy."

After neutralizing the emotional charge around seven of them, you may review your list again and realize that none of the other events holds any remaining emotional charge.

One of the wonderful benefits of EFT is that after we've neutralized an issue, we often forget how much it used to bother us. Once an experience loses its emotional charge and we have no reaction to thinking about it, it can be hard to recall how we used to feel. This also means, however, that it can be difficult to recognize the progress we've made. So pay careful attention to how things are changing as you work through this process. Set an intention to notice subtle, and not so subtle, changes in your overall sense of well-being, your physical health, and your relationships. Pay particular attention to how you respond in situations that used to trigger an outsized reaction from you. Stress has a measurable effect on physical and emotional health. Our bodies carry memories of past events, and reminders of these events can activate the stress response in our bodies. Therefore, it makes sense that clearing the emotional responses tied to these old events can lead to a renewed sense of health, both physical and emotional. Better health, improved relationships, a more positive sense of self, feeling calmer and happier—these are all benefits of the Personal Peace Procedure.

For EFT practitioners, there is an additional benefit gained through this process, one that increases professional effectiveness as well as personal peace. Just as therapists are strongly encouraged to attend therapy themselves, working on our own issues systematically with EFT decreases the likelihood that our unhealed personal issues will unintentionally impact our work with clients. Otherwise, when clients present with issues similar to ours, the resonance between the two can trigger our own emotional reactions. Working through our personal issues allows us to be fully present with our clients and their unique experiences.

Though the Personal Peace Procedure can be done completely on your own, you might consider working through the process with a tapping partner, an EFT practitioner, or a therapist. There are several benefits to this. Working with a tapping partner can be useful for providing support and a measure of accountability. Sometimes making a commitment to another person can help us follow through with commitments we've made to ourselves. If you find that you are having trouble neutralizing the emotional charge around specific events, or if you have a history of childhood abuse or a history of trauma of any kind, the support of a professional skilled in working with EFT and trauma can be immensely beneficial to your healing process.

Let's return to that box I mentioned earlier, the one containing all the unpleasant life experiences we'd rather ignore or forget. Thus far in our lives, all those experiences that ended up in that box have been rattling around, causing us stress and discomfort, even when we've tried to keep the lid on them. Now you have the opportunity to open that box and take each one out, to consider it, heal it, and see it in a new light, as something from the past that no longer has the power to impose upon your present-moment experience. It takes a certain amount of courage to undertake this process, but, with time and dedication, the box will be emptied and what you'll be left with instead is emotional freedom.